GREAT LIVES
FROM
HISTORY

GREAT LIVES FROM HISTORY

Twentieth
Century
Series

Volume 4
Mas-Ror

Edited by

FRANK N. MAGILL

SALEM PRESS

Pasadena, California   Englewood Cliffs, New Jersey

Library of Congress Cataloging-in-Publication Data
Great lives from history. Twentieth century series / ed-
ited by Frank N. Magill.
    p.   cm.
Includes bibliographical references.
Includes index.
    1. Biography—20th century. 2. Community leader-
ship. 3. World history. I. Magill, Frank Northen,
1907-   .
CT120.G69   1990
920'.009'04—dc20
[B]
[920]   90-8613
ISBN 0-89356-565-2 (set)   CIP
ISBN 0-89356-569-5 (volume 4)   AC

LIST OF BIOGRAPHIES IN VOLUME FOUR

LIST OF BIOGRAPHIES IN VOLUME FOUR

TOMÁŠ MASARYK

Born: March 7, 1850; near Göding, Moravia, Austrian Empire (now Hodonín, Czechoslovakia)
Died: September 14, 1937; Lány, Czechoslovakia
Areas of Achievement: Government, politics, and philosophy
Contribution: Masaryk was a professor of philosophy, an author, and a statesman who was the principal founder and first president of Czechoslovakia. He secured the support of the Western liberal powers during World War I for the Czechoslovakian cause and was awarded numerous honors including a D.C.L. from the University of Oxford in 1928.

Early Life

Tomáš Garrigue Masaryk was born in Moravia in 1850 to a Slovak father and a German-speaking Czech mother. His homeland was part of Austria-Hungary and his father was employed as a coachman on an imperial estate. Because of the low social position of his parents, it was difficult for him to receive an education. His father encouraged him to enter a trade and for a while he worked as a blacksmith. He was finally able to attend school in Brno and completed his secondary education in Vienna in 1872. He supported himself by tutoring wealthy students, and in appreciation their parents helped him to further his education. He entered the University of Vienna and completed his doctorate in 1876. Following his graduation, he spent a year studying at the University of Leipzig, where he met an American student of music, Charlotte Garrigue. They were married in New York in 1878. She was a major influence in his life, causing him to have a greater understanding of international affairs than most Czech leaders of his day. In order to symbolize the closeness of this relationship, Masaryk adopted his wife's maiden name and thus became known to the world as Thomas Garrigue Masaryk. Charlotte also influenced his religious views. He had already left the Roman Catholic faith in which he was reared, and now he adopted many of the Unitarian views of his wife. Not only did his marriage change his religious outlook, but also it led him to adopt English as his third language after Czech and German.

In 1879, Masaryk became a lecturer at the University of Vienna, and in 1882 he was appointed professor of philosophy at the Czech university in Prague. His position gave him the opportunity to become one of the leaders of the rising nationalist movement among his people. Masaryk's mind had a practical bent, causing him to use his philosophic training to try to solve the problems of life and to work toward a more just society. He had little interest in problems of epistemology or cosmology. In the early stages of his career, he reacted against German philosophy, accepting British empiricism and logical positivism. His philosophical position can be described as realism, an outlook that accepts not only reason but also the will, the emotions, and the senses. His main interest, however, began to concentrate on sociology and the philosophy of history. These preoccupations were reflected in his book *Der Selbstmord als sociale Massenerscheinung der modernen Civilisation* (1881; *Suicide and the Meaning of Civilization*, 1970) and several other works on the Czech Reformation and the early nineteenth century Czech nationalist revival.

Life's Work

Masaryk became one of the most popular teachers in the university at Prague, and he used his academic role to attack political and social injustices. As he elaborated his views they came to include a search for scientific truth, a pragmatic approach to life, a rejection of force and extremism in human affairs, and an emphasis on morality. As the author of numerous books and as a muckraking journalist, he entered into debates on the important social issues of the day.

Masaryk demonstrated his devotion to his ideals by exposing two ostensibly early Czech poems that were regarded as the Slavic counterparts to the *Nibelungenlied* but were in reality early nineteenth century forgeries. He also challenged the anti-Semitism of his homeland by proving the innocence of Leopold Hilsner, a Jew accused of the ritual murder of a Christian in 1899. Despite his involvement in these practical issues, Masaryk found time to publish several volumes including *Česká otázka; Snahy a tužby národního obrození* (1895; the Czech question), *Die philosophischen und sociologischen Grundlagen des Marxismus* (1899; the philosophical and sociological foundation of Marxism), and *Russland und Europa* (1913; *The Spirit of Russia*, 1919). These works assigned a key role in the improvement of the human condition to the Czech nation through the transmission of its ancient ideals as embodied in the Hussites and the Bohemian Brethren. Such an outlook, Masaryk believed, could be an effective antidote to the materialism, selfishness, and alienation of modern society. His writings and teachings were meant to educate the Czech people in their own tradition. As he interpreted their history, it was an enduring defense of democracy in church and state.

Masaryk believed that Hussite ideals would give his people an orientation toward the ethical and democratic outlook of Western civilization, and he was suspicious of the Pan-Slavism and communist ideology emanating from Russia. His book on Russia dealt with the philosophy, religion, and literature of his great Eastern neighbor. He was extremely critical of Russia, characterizing the land as preserving the childhood of Europe through the mass of ignorant peasants. Russian nobles were no better, he stated, because they were half-educated, immoral, boorish, cruel, and reactionary. Their example had set the pattern for the entire society. Those such as the Marxists who wanted revolution were suggesting a cure little better than the illness. On occasion he would refer to the Bolsheviks as the "new Jesuits" because of their opposition to religion and accepted standards of Christian morality.

In 1890, Masaryk entered politics as a member of the young Czech Party, and in 1891 he was elected to the Austrian Reichsrat (parliament). His disagreements with some of the emotional outbursts of his fellow party members led him to resign in 1893. In March, 1900, he started the Realist Party, which more accurately expressed his aim for reform within the imperial framework. He was returned to the Reichsrat in 1907 and served until 1914. As a member of the Reichsrat, he represented the leftist position among the Slavs and tried to achieve greater autonomy for them within the empire. He also wished to end the alliance between Germany and Austria-Hungary and to stop the imperialistic policies of Austria in the Balkans. The tension between the empire and the Slavs in the Balkans led to the Agram (now Zagreb) Treason Trials in 1908, during which Masaryk exposed the weak case of the Austrians against a group of Serbs. He proved that the government's charges rested upon forged documents. As a result, the Viennese historian, Heinrich Friedjung, was sued for libel. Masaryk demonstrated that Friedjung had accepted documents in good faith that were fabricated in the office of the Austrian foreign ministry. His fearless stand for the truth in this case further enhanced his worldwide reputation.

The outbreak of World War I was a decisive event in Masaryk's life. Austrian involvement in the conflict led him to believe that the time had come to work for an independent Czech nation. He left Austria in December, 1914, and lived for the next few years in various places in Western Europe and the United States including Geneva, Paris, London, Chicago, and Washington. In 1915, he founded the Czechoslovak Council with Edvard Beneš and Milan Stefanik. The council had two aims: first, to bring together various groups of Czech and Slovak émigrés and, second, to secure Allied recognition of the council as the representative of the Czechoslovakian people. More than 120,000 Czech troops fighting on various fronts for the Allied cause recognized the council as their government.

Relying on his reputation and the aid of such eminent authorities on Eastern Europe as Ernest Dennis, Wickham Steed, and R. W. Seton-Watson, Masaryk began a propaganda campaign to convince the Allies of the necessity of breaking up Austria-Hungary so that the various people of that polyglot empire would be able to control their own destinies. As part of this program of self-determination, Masaryk wanted to establish a democratic Czech and Slovak confederation along with a number of new Eastern European states founded on ethnic principles which would act as a bulwark against German imperialism. He also tried to focus Western attention on the courageous activities of the Czech legion fighting on the crumbling Eastern Front. Between May, 1917, and March, 1918, he was in Russia trying to work out an alliance with the provincial government that had come to power following the overthrow of the czarist regime. After the Bolshevik Revolution, he left Russia and went to the United States. The large Czech and Slovak population greeted him warmly. These immigrants were an important factor in his success because of their political and economic support for his organization. Also, Masaryk met with President Woodrow Wilson and with Secretary Robert Lansing and succeeded in securing the Lansing Declaration of May, 1918, which recognized the independence of Czechoslovakia. In addition, the new nation's existence was made one of Wilson's Fourteen Points, an important document on which the peace settlement was based. After receiving the firm support of the American government, Masaryk came to terms with the Slovak immigrants in the United States though the Pittsburgh Pact of May 30, 1918. This document promised a large measure of home rule to the Slovak element of Czechoslovakia and was to lead to considerable tension in the future.

The new republic was proclaimed in October, 1918, and Masaryk returned to Prague as president on December 21, 1918. He was reelected to the presidency in 1920, 1927, and 1934. The country had problems not only with relations between the Czechs and the Slovaks but also with the large German and Hungarian population. Masaryk did his best to respect the rights of the minorities under Czech control, but he was forced to deal with economic problems caused by the Great Depression and with a growing Nazi movement among the German citizens. After a prolonged illness, he resigned in 1935 and died at his residence near Lány in 1937.

Summary

The life and ideals of Tomáš Masaryk were shaped by the age in which he lived. The nineteenth and early twentieth centuries were a period when liberalism and nationalism triumphed. Consequently Masaryk's desire for political freedom and national independence reflect this background. Not only was Masaryk a scholar and theorist but also he was a man able to apply his ideas to practical politics. During the years in which he served as President of Czechoslovakia, although his position was constitutionally weak he brought peace and stability to the land and guided it in a democratic direction. He also established friendly relations with Austria and Germany and to a certain extent even with Poland and Hungary. His humanitarian outlook on social and political problems, combined with his humble yet dignified manner, endeared him to his fellow countrymen and to many people in the Western liberal democracies. Of all the new nations created by the Peace of Versailles, Czechoslovakia came closest to reflecting the hope of a just world envisioned by Woodrow Wilson. Much of the credit for this achievement belongs to Masaryk.

During the closing years of his life, however, Masaryk was troubled about the future of his country. His philosophic training and democratic outlook led him to realize the danger to Central Europe because of the rise of the Nazi movement in Germany. The heir to his political legacy, Beneš and Masaryk's son Jan were to be confronted with the ravages of their homeland brought on by World War II and the subsequent Soviet domination of Eastern Europe.

Bibliography

Čapek, Karel. *Masaryk on Life and Thought*. Translated by M. Weatherall and R. Weatherall. London: Allen & Unwin, 1938. Another volume of Čapek's interviews with Masaryk. This one is concerned with his thoughts rather than his actions and includes chapters on epistemology, metaphysics, religion, the problems of culture in the modern world, politics, and nationalism. As with the volume on Masaryk's life, this one is scrupulously careful in presenting an accurate presentation of the material.

_____. *President Masaryk Tells His Story*. New York: G. P. Putnam's Sons, 1935. Masaryk spent several weeks with Čapek over the period of many years while the president recounted his life. He reminisced about his childhood, education, and the tumultuous events involved in the creation of Czechoslovakia.

Selver, Paul. *Masaryk: A Biography*. London: Michael Joseph, 1940. A general study of Masaryk's life based upon excellent sources. Contains material that had never been available in English before. Selver has written an excellent book that is notable for the frequent quotations from Masaryk.

Seton-Watson, R. W. *A History of the Czechs and Slovaks*. London: Hutchinson, 1943. This general history of the Czechoslovakian people is a thoughtful introduction in English to many of the problems with which Masaryk was forced to deal. Written by one of the first professors of Czechoslovak studies at the University of London and an acquaintance of Masaryk.

Thomson, S. Harrison. *Czechoslovakia in European History*. Reprint. Hamden, Conn.: Archon Books, 1965. A scholarly, readable volume that makes the story of Masaryk's nation accessible to English students. Thomson has provided his readers with the main themes of Czech history in a sympathetic yet fair manner. Probably the finest one-volume introduction to the land of Masaryk.

Zeman, Zbynek. *The Masaryks: The Making of Czechoslovakia*. London: Weidenfeld & Nicolson, 1976. This dual biography of Tomáš and Jan Masaryk gives a variety of interpretations of the legacy of these two individuals. Some looked on Tomáš Masaryk as a "philosopher-king," while others regarded him as a "scholar-saint," but in reality his legacy was more ambiguous. Zbynek discusses some of the Marxist criticisms of Masaryk, among them that he plotted against Vladimir Ilich Lenin and Joseph

Stalin, was supported by international bankers, and that his presidency was a very expensive affair.

Robert G. Clouse

LÉONIDE MASSINE
Leonid Fyodorovich Miassin

Born: August 8, 1895; Moscow, Russia
Died: March 16, 1979; Cologne, West Germany
Area of Achievement: Dance
Contribution: Massine's career as a performer and creator of dance changed
the nature of the art. His stage presence and dance style made a powerful
impression in Europe and the United States and helped to establish the
companies with which he worked as the leading forces in the renewal of
ballet. His choreography was especially innovative in its collaboration
with music and depth of characterization.

Early Life

Leonid Fyodorovich Miassin (his name was changed to Léonide Massine
by Sergei Diaghilev when he joined the Ballet Russe company) was born in
Moscow in 1895. He was the youngest of five children, four boys and one
girl, in a closely knit, warm family. His father played French horn in the
Bolshoi Theater orchestra, and his mother was a soprano in the Bolshoi
Theater chorus. Although his parents were both artists, they never assumed
that Massine would have a career in the arts. His elder brothers studied
mathematics and engineering. The eldest, Mikhail, became a professional
soldier; Gregori became an engineer; and Konstantin died after a hunting
accident when he was twenty-one. Raissa, the only sister, was closest to
Massine in age and was his frequent playmate. They especially enjoyed
dancing folk dances and playing games with the children of a family that
worked as household servants for their parents. Often Massine would amuse
himself on the mouth organ. As an adult, he recalled the happiness of this
time and commemorated it by incorporating his childhood games and dances
in his ballets.

A friend of his mother observed Massine dancing alone and suggested that
his parents enroll him in the Moscow Theater School to be trained as a
dancer. He underwent the entrance examination, which included a physical
examination to judge if he could develop into a dancer. He was admitted on
a one-year trial basis and, after the year, he was accepted as a permanent
student.

Massine fell in love with the world of the theater. His slight build, dark
coloring, and skill awarded him his first role. He portrayed the dwarf, Cher-
nomor, in *Russlan and Ludmilla*, by the Russian composer Mikhail Glinka.
Although wearing an exotic costume and an immense beard was the most
required of him, it was his first character role and the beginning of a series
of professional appearances as a child actor. He made hundreds of performances at the Maly and the Bolshoi theaters in Moscow. He also appeared in

ballets at the Bolshoi, but, by age fifteen, Massine began to think he would be happier in the theater than in ballet. He found the plays more interesting, the actors more intelligent, and, except for that of Peter Ilich Tchaikovsky, the ballet music second rate. Typical of his lifelong dedication to broadening his education, he began to study the violin and painting while a teenager. His parents retired to a country home, and Massine moved into a room near the theater school. He delved into reading works by Fyodor Dostoevski, an exceptional pursuit for a dancer.

At this time, the leading choreographer for the theater was Alexander Gorsky. Massine admired his personality but believed that he could not transmit his ideas to his dancers, move big groups across the stage, or choreograph dances in authentic foreign styles. These were all to become central concerns of Massine's mature work. Massine was graduated from the Moscow Theater School in 1912 and joined the Bolshoi company.

In 1913, Massine danced the Tarantella in *Swan Lake*. Diaghilev, director of the Ballet Russe company, was in the audience. Michel Fokine, the leading choreographer of Diaghilev's company, was to create a ballet, *La Legende de Joseph*, based on the biblical story; Diaghilev selected Massine as Joseph. After an interview with Fokine, Massine was offered the role and a position in the company, but he would have to leave Moscow in two days. His friends advised him not to go, as it would abruptly end his blossoming theater career. Massine himself decided to reject the offer. When he met Diaghilev again, however, he suddenly said yes and thus created an entirely new life for himself.

Life's Work

As a choreographer and dancer, Massine always sought the most encompassing expression by including the finest work not only in dance but also in music, painting and design, and literary and philosophical thought. A fusion of the arts was the ideal of Diaghilev's ballet. By taking an immediate interest in the education of Massine, Diaghilev helped to develop Massine's already broad curiosity and learning. Even as a young man, Massine was never content to be only the instrument of his mentors. His artistic contributions went beyond the strictures laid out by Diaghilev to different areas of art, especially in his use of major symphonic works, as Diaghilev had a preference for obscure music. Massine also developed his work further by his precise use of traditional dance from various cultures. Scholarly in his preparation, Massine differed from other choreographers by his interest in and knowledge of arts other than dance and his willingness to study.

Massine's role as Joseph had been a success though the ballet was not. Performed in Paris in 1914, it elevated Massine to sudden stardom. He still wanted to improve his technique, however, and studied with ballet master Enrico Cecchetti. He found that the academic ballet he had learned in the

Moscow Theater School was not enough to meet the demands of Fokine's style, inspired by the freer movement of Isadora Duncan.

When World War I broke out in Europe, in 1914, Diaghilev's leading male dancer, Vaslav Nijinsky, and much of the company was in the United States. This gave Massine the opportunity to work with composer Igor Stravinsky and designer Mikhail Larioniov and to experiment in new work with Diaghilev. In 1915, Massine created his first ballet, *Soleil de nuit* (midnight sun), in which the Russian dances and games of his childhood appear as the basis of the choreography. The music was by Nikolay Rimsky-Korsakov.

In only four years, Massine produced masterpieces of ballet. In each one, he pushed the art form into new areas. In 1917, he premiered *Les Femmes de bonne humeur* (the good-humored ladies), with music by Giuseppe Scarlatti, and *Parade*, a collaborative work with costumes and sets by Pablo Picasso and Jean Cocteau and music by Erik Satie. *Les Femmes de bonne humeur* incorporated the Italian *commedia dell'arte* style of masked characters representing personality types. Massine created the first of many parts no one has adequately been able to fill after him because of his stage presence and precisely choreographed characterization.

La Boutique fantasque (1919), Massine's next work, is the story of a shop whose toys come to life. The characterization of the shopkeeper, assistant, Russians, Americans, dolls, and even poodles is presented in careful detail. Massine appeared with Lydia Sokolova in a can-can, which became one of the celebrated dances in ballet history. *Le Tricorne* (the three-cornered hat) premiered in 1919 in London. It was the result of Massine's wartime studies in Seville of Spanish classical and folk dance. Massine's accomplishment was to take the true movement and rhythm of the dances and put them into ballet without giving them a false prettiness.

Massine's last work for Diaghilev's company at this time was a reproduction of *The Rite of Spring*. The ballet for Stravinsky's music had been originally choreographed by Nijinsky. When Diaghilev was angered by Nijinsky's marriage, Nijinsky left the Ballet Russe. Massine rechoreographed the controversial piece. The primitive-sounding music with its complicated and jagged rhythms supported the creation of modern movements to express an ancient story of a community sacrificing a young woman. Latter-day dance enthusiasts have engaged in pointless debate over which was the superior version of the dance. Massine's was not adequately recorded, and Massine himself would not involve himself in such a debate. His version was a great success when performed. The chief choreographic element was the use of the dancers' weight to create an earth-bound look and shape to the movement. This was the opposite of the ethereal look of classical ballet and its appearance of airborne lightness. The use of weighted movement was a basic element of modern dance, and Massine understood its usefulness in creating dramatic tension and expression.

A personal dispute with Diaghilev led Massine to quit the company in 1921. In only six years, he had created a body of work that made major changes in ballet. He formed his own company and produced several works for the "Soirées de Paris" organized by Le Comte Étienne de Beaumont. These included *Salade*, music by Darius Milhaud, *Mercure*, music by Satie and decor by Picasso, and *Le Beau Danube*, music by Johann Strauss; all appeared in 1924. Diaghilev convinced Massine to rejoin his company after these successes; the second engagement with Diaghilev lasted from 1925 to 1928.

Massine's second time with the Ballet Russe produced still more experiments with movement, themes, and the adventurous use of music. *Zéphere et Flore* (1925) had costumes and decor by the cubist artist Georges Braque and music by Dukelsky. *Les Matelots* (1925) was the first of an ongoing tradition of lighthearted dances about three sailors on the town. *Les Pas d'acier* (1927), with music by Sergei Prokofiev, started another tradition in dance—that of the dancers taking on the angular, abrupt movement style of machinery, expressing fear of automation and the encroaching "steps of steel" of the title. During this same period, Massine worked as dancer-choreographer for the London Cochrane Revues and as solo dancer and ballet master of the Roxy Theater of New York. In 1930, he revived *The Rite of Spring* for Martha Graham. He also choreographed for the Rubinstein company from 1929 to 1931.

In 1932, Colonel de Basil began his own Ballet Russe de Monte Carlo, and Massine joined the company as ballet master in 1933. In this period, Massine choreographed three of his symphonic ballets: *Les Présages* (1934), for Tchaikovsky's fifth symphony; *Choréartium* (1934), for Johannes Brahms's fourth symphony; and *Symphonie fantastique* (1936), for music by Hector Berlioz. Although these works are among Massine's greatest achievements, they are also perhaps the least appreciated. They demonstrated his mastery of music of the greatest scope and complexity and his interest in themes of the broadest human concerns. It is rare for ballet reviewers to know music well or for music reviewers to know ballet. Massine's fusion of art forms reached for a unity of art and understanding on a scale as grand as human aspirations.

Massine choreographed more than one hundred ballets. He worked with other companies including New York's Ballet Theater in 1942-1943. In 1945-1946, he toured his own company, Ballet Russe Highlights. His work continued to grow by using the best of music and the widest variety of human concerns and expressions from the frivolity of *Gaîté parisienne* (1938) to the religious inspiration of *Laudes Evangelii* (1952). In keeping with his interest in innovations, he made three notable films: *The Red Shoes* (1948), *Tales of Hoffman* (1951), and *Carosello Napoletano* (1953; *Neapolitan Carousel*). He continued his dedication to the study and presentation of dances of specific cultures by studying the dances of American Indians and presented lecture-demonstrations on the subject throughout the world. He devoted much of his later life to the study of the theoretical essentials of choreography and wrote a book on the subject while a teacher at the Royal Ballet School in London.

Summary

As a dancer, Léonide Massine's greatest accomplishments were his own performances, celebrated for not only his technique but also the delicate and precise characterizations that no one has been able to duplicate. As a great performer, it will be possible to memorialize him only through the accounts of his audience. He was best known for his character roles in lighthearted ballets, and he captured the imaginations of all who saw him. His greatest contributions, however, were in his unification of the arts of the actor, dancer, and musician. His reputation suffered sometimes in commentary by those who preferred the discrete categorization of the arts or those who were displeased when he left Diaghilev, but his curiosity, energy, and restless self-education made him a great artist. His gifts of understanding several art forms and his willingness to study outside his own cultural sphere allowed his work to transcend more narrow outlooks and encompass the broadest sense of the human comedy.

Bibliography

Antony, Gordon. *Massine: Camera Studies by Gordon Antony, with an Appreciation by Sacheverell Sitwell*. London: George Routledge & Sons, 1939. Excellent black-and-white photographs of Massine in his most famous roles. Sitwell's commentary credits Massine for a unique greatness combining the skills of both dancer and choreographer, and for his unusually fine intelligence, especially in identifying great artists in other fields and bringing them to the public.

Grigoriev, S. L. *The Diaghilev Ballet, 1909-1929*. Edited and translated by Vera Bowen. London: Constable, 1953. The memoirs of one of Diaghilev's company who was with the company from beginning to end. There is much discussion of Massine.

Gruen, John. *The Private World of Ballet*. New York: Viking Press, 1970. A collection of descriptions and interviews. Gruen interviewed Massine while he was in New York working with the Joffrey Ballet. He includes information from an interview with Eugenia Delarova Doll, a ballerina who had been married to Massine.

Haskell, Arnold. *Diaghilev: His Artistic and Private Life*. New York: Simon & Schuster, 1935. Places Massine at the center of the rebuilding of Diaghilev's company and portrays him as a key figure of the renaissance of ballet; this is a thorough history of the Ballet Russe and its founder.

Kochno, Boris. *Diaghilev and the Ballet Russe*. Translated by Adrienne Foulke. New York: Harper & Row, 1970. Kochno became Diaghilev's private secretary in 1921, edited programs, and composed ballet librettos. His is an insider's look at the company, dancers, and ballets. This is a large-format book with illustrations and photographs.

Massine, Leonide. *Massine on Choreography: Theory and Exercises in Composition*. London: Faber, 1976. Massine considered this study the crowning achievement of his life's work and a way to transmit what he had learned through experience to successive generations.

_____. *My Life in Ballet*. London: Macmillan, 1968. An autobiography that narrates family life as well as artistic accomplishment. Massine reflects on the relationships within the ballet world and the vagaries of his personal fortune and maintains a generous attitude toward all of his colleagues and a consistent modesty about himself.

Leslie Friedman

HENRI MATISSE

Born: December 31, 1869; Le Cateau-Cambrésis, France
Died: November 3, 1954; Nice, France
Area of Achievement: Art
Contribution: Matisse became the leader of the French expressionists called Les Fauves, or wild beasts. When the artists of that unofficial movement dispersed, he steadfastly and daringly simplified painting to the point of abstract decoration.

Early Life

Henri-Émile-Benoît Matisse was born in extreme northern France at Le Cateau-Cambrésis, the town of his grandparents, but spent his youth in nearby Bohain-en-Vermandois, where his father Émile had financial interests in a drugstore and a grain elevator. Little is known of the boy's early youth, but not long after the age of ten Matisse was sent to Saint-Quentin, some distance to the south, to study Latin and Greek. Up to age eighteen, Matisse moved dutifully from one school to the next without exhibiting an inclination toward any particular profession. In 1887, however, he went to Paris to study law and did so with his father's blessing. In three years he completed legal coursework, passed the required examinations, and returned to Saint-Quentin, where he began a monotonous existence as a clerk in a lawyer's office.

That type of life might have continued for many years had Matisse not attended morning classes in 1889 at the École Quentin Latour, where he drew from sculpture casts, and had he not had appendicitis, necessitating a long convalescence that was alleviated by his mother's gift of a box of paints, brushes, and an instruction manual. The latter changed Matisse's life. Within two years, he abandoned law and traveled to Paris to prepare for entrance exams to the École des Beaux-Arts, the official, state-supported school for the arts in France. His preparation took place at the respectable Académie Julian under the well-established painter Adolphe William Bouguereau. Disagreeing with Bouguereau's insistence upon conservative modes of painting, Matisse became disillusioned, left the school, and failed his first entrance examination to the École des Beaux-Arts.

Frustrated, but not defeated, Matisse fortunately met Gustave Moreau, a symbolist painter and a new instructor at the École des Beaux-Arts, who allowed him to enter his class unofficially upon seeing some of his drawings. In addition to Moreau's instruction, the teacher encouraged Matisse to copy artworks in the Louvre, which he did diligently during 1893 and 1894. By the winter of 1894, he passed the entrance exam into the École des Beaux-Arts and then officially entered Moreau's painting class. Moreau was an important key to Matisse's development. He inspired Matisse through his enthusiastic teaching, lavish attention, and his encouragement to grow independently, free of dogma or pressure for stylistic conformity. Moreau also encouraged Matisse and other students to go into the streets to study actual life and to seek out new works by painters at the galleries.

In 1895, Matisse began to paint outdoors, first in Paris and over the next few years in Brittany as well. There he met the Australian Impressionist painter John Russell, who as a friend of Claude Monet and the late Vincent van Gogh, passed on their emphasis on remaining independent in one's development. Coinciding with his new interest in plein air painting, Matisse became aware of Impressionism on a grand scale when the Gutave Caillebotte Bequest Collection was exhibited at the Musée Luxemburg, Paris.

A modicum of success came to Matisse in 1897 when he exhibited the painting *La Desserte* at the Salon de la Nationale after having been elected an associate member of the Société Nationale the previous year. Encouraged, his next several years were marked by intense drawing, painting, more study at the École des Beaux-Arts, the Académie F. Carrière, the studio of La Grande Chaumière, plus much travel. Those same years up through 1903 were also marked by financial hardships, yet bright spots too, such as viewing the van Gogh retrospective show at the Galérie Bernheim-Jeune. The faith that Matisse had in his independent stance, his receptivity to new currents, his great capacity for work, and his affinity for color as structure coalesced, and Matisse's name and work were soon known with thunder.

Life's Work

By the first years of the twentieth century, Matisse's explorations in color and painting structure gained momentum. His canvas *Luxe, Calm, et Volupté* of 1904-1905 was executed almost entirely in the Neo-Impressionist manner of dots and small bars of bold colors. Its imagery alluded to an arcadian existence, its setting to the Mediterranean coast, and its title to Charles Baudelaire's "L'Invitation au voyage."

Matisse understood Neo-Impressionism with its near-scientific approach to optics and perception, but with this painting he mostly derived a mosaic effect which definitely pointed him closer to abstraction. By 1905, when Matisse was in his mid-thirties, his work was still not unequivocally his in style or content. Yet, a trip the same year with painter and friend André Derain to the Mediterranean fishing village of Collioure changed his art forever.

From his collaboration with Derain and his immersion into the sun-drenched vibrant colors of southern France, Matisse reworked older paintings of Collioure and the immediate environs. In these paintings, tree trunks were painted with bold strokes and equally bold, arbitrary shots of color. Actual or descriptive colors were sacrificed for an intuitive, spontaneous approach in which each color stroke was related to all other color marks in the composition. When Matisse returned to Paris that fall, he used his new Collioure approach in a portrait of his wife entitled *Woman with the Hat.* Utilizing the standard society portrait mode, Matisse again disregarded actual colors and applied those reflecting his feelings of the moment.

The French public first viewed *Woman with the Hat* and four other Matisse paintings in the same manner at the Salon d'Automne that same year. These were joined by a number of other vigorous color experiments by his academy friends Derain, Henri Manquin, Charles Camoin, and Albert Marquet. Salon organizers assumed a new movement was forming and hung all paintings by the above men in the same room. Art critic Louis Vauxcelles, noticing that the paintings surrounded a statue in the conventional academic style, lamented that the scene reminded him of Donatello, a Renaissance sculptor, surrounded by *les fauves*, or wild beasts. Upon appearing in a printed review, the name stuck to a movement that was not intended, had no agreed upon theories, no manifesto, and no regular meetings or organization.

Vauxcelles' reaction of shock was equaled by that of the general public, which was not impressed by unrepressed colors and did not comprehend such color as a direct expression of the joy of life. Instead most viewers were bewildered, aghast, and believed that the Fauve paintings were insulting and a hoax. By contrast, the intended messages of color for color's sake and painting as a physical act of exhilaration were not lost on young European painters. Color became synonymous with expressionism—Fauvism in France and Die Brücke and Der Blaue Reiter in Germany.

The Salon d'Automne of 1905 brought Matisse to the attention of wealthy collectors of modern art and patrons including Leo and Gertrude Stein, Michael and Sarah Stein, the Cone sisters Etta and Claribel, as well as Sergei Shehukin. Soon Matisse was pursuing even bolder color schemes and more radically simplified structure resulting in the landmark paintings *Harmony in Red* (1908-1909) and the monumental diptych *Dance and Music* of 1910. This pair explored music and athletic rhythmic responses to it in a universal, timeless distillation. *The Red Studio* of 1911 was even more advanced in its reductive color space, yet it is touched with whimsy—viewers are invited symbolically to pick up one of the painted crayons on a foreground table and participate in the picture.

Matisse's appreciation of Muslim culture resulted in working voyages to North Africa in 1911-1913. In Tangier, Morocco, he conceived and developed a triptych involving a local model named Zorah, Muslim architecture and the tropical sun reflecting on both. This immersion into a non-Western environment had a long-standing impact on Matisse, for, during the war years 1914-1918 and throughout the 1920's, he was increasingly engrossed in an exotic visual dialogue with models in his studios whether in Paris or southern France at Nice. Typical of his oriental themes is *Decorative Figure* (1927), which exudes relaxed detachment and indolent luxury.

Noteworthy activity later in life included his decoration of the Dominican Chapel of the Rosary at Vence and his extraordinary cut paper collages. The clinically white spartan interior of the Vence Chapel is barely relieved by Matisse's calligraphic murals of the *Stations of the Cross* on one wall near the altar and equally large *Madonna and Child* and *St. Dominic* compositions on the adjacent walls. The compositions were rendered in black outlines only.

Matisse's collage work was composed of prepainted sheets of paper cut with scissors and glued to a support, often a white wall. When declining health in the 1940's forced the artist to work in bed, paper cut-outs did not represent a withdrawal from art. Through this medium, Matisse masterfully summed up themes and experiments covering a sixty-year career. Yet his compositions were anything but redundant, especially not those devoted to jazz and Caribbean rhythms. The cut-outs blaze with color, energy, and a celebration of life understandable by connoisseurs and children alike. Matisse's celebration of life came to a close at his death on November 3, 1954, in Nice, after which he was buried at Cimiez.

Summary

Coming late to art, Henri Matisse was nevertheless blessed by two factors: a tremendous capacity for work and a long life to see that energy mature. He came to painting from a preparation in law but seemed to possess an independent nature wary of influences and a willingness to explore directions even though the way was paved with doubt and disappointment.

Matisse's innate gifts in painting revolved around color and design. He was quite content to produce near abstractions with a cross-referential color structure. His imagery was always approximately representational, and his spaces were never overly rational or splintered like those of Cézanne. His art reflected the attitude that painting is a superior distraction. It was his diary, his mistress, his labor, and his intellectual stimulation. Matisse's worlds of the studio, indolent models, Mediterranean environments, and chromatic geometry were part of an aloof existence.

Basically apolitical, Matisse worked with almost total indifference through two world wars while maintaining his own world of balanced opposites, security, and comfort. Matisse believed that the audience for fine art is relatively small and comes from the educated bourgeoisie. Thus, for that audience, he strove to produce art that would have the same soothing effect as a good armchair for tired business professionals.

Bibliography

Barr, Alfred H., Jr. *Matisse: His Art and His Public*. New York: Museum of Modern Art, 1951. Considered the standard work on Matisse for decades, though it is seriously challenged now by Pierre Schneider's monograph of

1984. Terrific organization of data is matched by an uncomplicated writing style and indulgent notes on the text, and thoughtful appendices far outweigh the value of the eight color plates and too many poor quality black-and-white illustrations.

Elderfield, John. *The Drawings of Henri Matisse*. New York: Thames and Hudson, 1985. A long overdue examination of the role played by drawing for an artist known as one of the major colorists of the twentieth century. The text was sensitively researched, bringing to readers rarely explored ideas and frames of reference by Matisse. Contains notes and a catalog of 159 drawings.

Escholier, Raymond. *Matisse: A Portrait of the Artist and the Man*. Translated by Geraldine and H. M. Colvile. New York: Frederick A. Praeger, 1960. A good biography that contains a small, selected bibliography and several reproductions.

Jacobus, John. *Henri Matisse*. New York: Harry N. Abrams, 1983. A monograph from a series on major twentieth century European modernists. The too-brief biographical overview is, however, punctuated with well-chosen drawings and well-known paintings. The main section comprises forty color plates of key paintings, each preceded by a page of interpretation.

Matisse, Henri. *Henri Matisse: Drawings and Paper Cut-outs*. Introduction by Raoul Jean Moulin. Translated by Michael Ross. New York: McGraw-Hill, 1969. Moulin's thesis is that Matisse drew with scissors and pre-painted cut paper as well as he did with a lithographic crayon.

_____. *Matisse: Fifty Years of His Graphic Art*. Text by William S. Lieberman. New York: George Braziller, 1957. A survey of Matisse's prints that reveals his lifelong fascination with the female image mystique.

Russell, John. *The World of Henri Matisse, 1869-1954*. New York: Time-Life Books, 1969. A cultural-historical approach to art, this is a frank, entertaining, and well-illustrated work. Russell brings to light valuable data regarding the artist's friendships with other Fauve painters. The chapter on the early collectors and patrons is admirable in its depth.

Schneider, Pierre. *Matisse*. Translated by Michael Taylor and Bridget Strevens Romer. New York: Rizzoli, 1984. Herein Matisse is documented in a sumptuous and exhaustive fashion. Schneider covers every aspect of Matisse's life and career and illustrates brilliantly the importance of drawing for an artist revered as a colorist. Stresses the importance of women in Matisse's painting. Contains a biographical appendix and several photographs.

Tom Dewey II

KONOSUKE MATSUSHITA

Born: November 27, 1894; Wasa, Wakayama Prefecture, Japan
Died: April 27, 1989; Osaka, Japan
Areas of Achievement: Business and industry
Contribution: Matsushita was an energetic manufacturing and marketing genius who built the world's biggest multinational electric home appliance industry—Matsushita Electric Company. In the process, he developed a revolutionary management system that has influenced industry worldwide.

Early Life

Konosuke Matsushita was born in Wasa, Wakayama Prefecture, south of Osaka, on November 27, 1894. The youngest of eight children, he had two brothers and five sisters. His father, Masakusu, was a well-to-do farmer but became impoverished because of his loss in speculative investments in the rice market. Losing all fortunes, including house and land, Matsushita's parents were forced to leave the village and move to Wakayama City, where they started a small shop selling wooden clogs (*geta*). Matsushita was then four years old. The clog business did not go well and worse, Matsushita's two brothers and a sister died of influenza. In desperation, Matsushita's father left home for Osaka looking for a job and eventually found one. When Matsushita was ten, his father found him an apprentice job in a *hibachi* (charcoal brazier) shop in Osaka. Matsushita was then in his fourth year at the local elementary school, but his formal education had to be terminated, and he had to start practical training as an apprentice, learning about careful work and sound business practices. Three months afterward, Matsushita moved on to a bicycle shop, where he worked as an apprentice. Repair work was not a matter of simply replacing parts but producing new parts. Matsushita worked for the shop for five years, acquiring needed skills that would later prove to be most essential for producing the electrical devices that would make him Japan's richest man. In 1910, foreseeing the potential opportunity in growing electric power and technology, fifteen-year-old Matsushita left the bicycle shop to join the Osaka Electric Light Company as an assistant wiring technician. After one year of hard work, he was promoted to foreman of the installation technicians—the youngest foreman on the payroll. For the next few years, he would gain the invaluable experience of managing people and making decisions, which would later prove to be most indispensable in his managerial career in one of the top corporations in the world.

In September, 1915, Konosuke married Mumeno Iue, who would play a vital role in establishing Matsushita Electric Company as cofounder and faithful supporter throughout their seventy-four years of marriage. In 1917, Matsushita left Osaka Electric Company to manufacture an electrical light socket that he had designed. His entire capital for the venture was about one hundred dollars. The first experiment was a failure. After persistent efforts, Matsushita succeeded in making an electric attachment plug that brought him a profit of about forty dollars. Encouraged by this success, Matsushita decided to establish Matsushita Electric Company with his wife and her brother. The company was established on March 7, 1918, in the Matsushita's small tenement house in Osaka, which would afterward be developed into Japan's largest electric and home appliance industry.

Life's Work

The three hardworking members of the Matsushita Electric Company gave everything to improve the quality of attachment plugs and two-way sockets, which Matsushita designed. The sales of the plugs escalated quickly, because the products were attractive and of high quality. Moreover, Matsushita's plugs were considerably lower in price than others on the market. Toward the end of 1918, the sales of the plugs increased sharply, and, consequently, Matsushita had to increase the number of his employees to twenty. The company was now producing five thousand plugs a month. By this time, Matsushita had learned many lessons in business and management. He was firmly convinced that the major ingredients for success in business were establishing a solid plan, making steady and consistent effort, winning complete loyalty of employees, giving careful training to employees, manufacturing a product one believes in, and winning the trust and confidence of customers and suppliers. These elements would later be incorporated into the governing principles of management in the Matsushita Electric Company.

In 1923, Matsushita's company took a major step by designing and manufacturing a battery-powered lamp for bicycles, the major mode of transportation for commuting workers, who were forced to travel on risky roads after dark. Matsushita was confident that the new product would sell well because it would replace the troublesome, old-fashioned candle-lit lanterns. Moreover, the battery lamp was more economical than candles and was much easier to operate. To Matsushita's surprise, sales of the lamp did not go well at all, because retailers were distrustful of dry-cell batteries. Matsushita, therefore, adopted a revolutionary sales campaign. He decided to convince the retailers that his lamp would shine for thirty hours by placing a battery lamp in each one of the skeptic retailers' stores and turning on the switch. The plan worked, and soon the orders for the lamp poured in. His bold salesmanship successfully gained the great confidence and trust of his retailers and customers. By 1929, the Matsushita Electric Company had three hundred employees and produced electric irons and heaters, in addition to the plugs and battery lamps. In 1929, the Matsushita Electric Company's sale of lamps hit 1.8 million a year.

In December, 1929, the Matsushita Electric Company, like all other companies in Japan, was critically affected by the worldwide depression. The Japanese newspapers were filled with reports of factory closings and labor disputes resulting from wage cuts and layoffs. At this critical time, Matsushita made a significant decision that would become his company's governing policy—the policy was that of lifetime job security. The company would not dismiss or lay off any worker. This policy of giving complete job security to his employees brought about very positive and beneficial results. The employees were more loyal to the company and worked harder, and the company's operations quickly revived. By February, 1930, the company thrived despite the fact that the depression dragged on. The company business went so well that Matsushita had to build two new factories during the first half of that year.

The year of 1932 was an important landmark for Matsushita. In this year, his philosophy of life was clearly defined and firmly crystallized. One day, he visited a temple, where he witnessed a large number of the Buddhist congregation building their temple diligently and with profound devotion. Matsushita vividly realized that religious groups had a well-defined purpose in life, a fact which makes them different from others. This realization prompted him to define his own mission: As an industrialist he was to serve society, and his duty was to produce and supply useful goods to improve living conditions of people in the society. He believed that material abundance was an important precondition for creating a prosperous, happy, and peaceful society.

In the same year, the Employee Training Institute was established to educate young employees to become core members of the company. The institute offered them a three-year course of electrical engineering and business curriculums. The students would study four hours and receive four hours of practical training. This program was established based on Matsushita's firm belief that the success or failure of the company depended entirely on its employees, and the high standards of the company must be maintained by the high caliber of employees.

In 1933, Matsushita established the divisional management system, dividing the company operations into three main product groups—radios, storage batteries and lamps, and electric fixtures. The major aim of the system was clearly to evaluate performance and achievement of each division and to develop capable managers who would be able to manage their own division by themselves. By the end of 1936, the Matsushita Electric Company was producing more products, including radio sets, electric heating appliances, phonographs, batteries, fans, stoves, and other electric appliances. The company's sales volume was estimated at about 4.7 million dollars. The scope of the company's business grew, and it expanded further. By 1940, it had thirty plants with ten thousand employees.

During World War II, the Matsushita Electric Company, like all other major companies, was drafted for military production. It produced two-hundred-ton wooden transport ships and airplanes. Immediately following the war, the Matsushita Electric Company quickly resumed the manufacturing of home appliances with a work force of fifteen thousand. Its operations were abruptly suspended, however, by the American Occupation authorities. The Occupation authorities designated Matsushita a *zaibatsu* (financial clique) and froze all of his assets. The Occupation authorities saw that the *zaibatsu* system, made up of a dozen giant families, had controlled 80 percent of the country's industrial and financial enterprises and such excessive concentration of economic power was a serious obstruction to the democratization of Japan. In fact, the Matsushita Electric Company was not a *zaibatsu*, although it had grown to a giant size and had the look of a powerful combine, and that led to the misconception of the Occupation authorities. In October, 1950, after four years of appeals, Matsushita's people, including the company labor union, managed to convince the Occupation authorities that the Matsushita Electric Company was not a *zaibatsu*, and Matsushita's name was finally lifted from the purge list.

In the beginning of 1951, the Matsushita Electric Company resumed its production operations with its work force of thirty-eight hundred employees. With Japan's speedy economic recovery, partly the result of the Korean War, the Matsushita Electric Company enjoyed a rapid growth. Now the Japanese could afford Matsushita's newly manufactured washing machines, refrigerators, and televisions. The sales of the company rose from 17 million dollars in 1951 to 186 million dollars in 1961. In that year, the company's empire swelled to eighty-nine plants, employing forty-nine thousand workers. The company added a startling array of products, including television sets, tape recorders, electric pencil sharpeners, freezers, and computers. Matsushita's products would rapidly change the Japanese life-style. In January, 1961, Matsushita, with gratifying conviction that the company was soundly established with his management philosophy, resigned as its president, assuming the role of chairman of the board. He was succeeded by his son-in-law and adopted son, Masaharu. (Matsushita's only son died when he was two years old.) Matsushita remained as chairman until 1977. Thereafter, he served the company as executive adviser until his death on April 27, 1989. At the age of ninety-four, he died of pneumonia in a hospital that he had founded.

Summary

Konosuke Matsushita indeed was one of the most successful industrial and managerial tycoons of the twentieth century. He rose from near-poverty to establish the world's largest manufacturing empire of home appliances. In 1986, the Matsushita empire had a work force of 165,000 and had 101 overseas subsidiary companies and plants engaging in productions in thirty-eight countries. In the same year, the total annual sales of the sixty-five

Matsushita Group companies in Japan were estimated at 40 billion dollars. The Matsushita employees were producing more than fourteen thousand varieties of products to be distributed to every corner of the world.

The impact of Matsushita products upon the social life of people during the second half of the twentieth century was great. An abundance of Matsushita's products not only raised the standard of living for millions but also radically changed their life-styles. Matsushita's products also considerably liberated millions of women from long days of household drudgery and gave them more leisure time to engage in creative activities. In the early 1960's, when Anastas Mikoyan, then the Soviet Union's vice premier, was boastfully explaining to Matsushita how the Bolsheviks had liberated the Russians from exploitation, Matsushita braggingly declared that he was instrumental in liberating Japanese women from the heavy burden of labor in their households.

Matsushita made many significant contributions in the business and managerial sectors. He was the first employer in the modern business world to implement the policy of lifetime employment and to found a welfare system that provided workers with housing, gymnasiums, hospital care, and wedding halls. He was the first Japanese employer to institute the five-day work week and was also the first one to establish an employee training institute to train young workers. He was also the first man to establish the divisional management system in order to facilitate efficient performance of company operations. It is not surprising to find that some of the best-managed corporations in the United States, including International Business Machines (IBM) and Delta Air Lines, have already adopted the Japanese model of management instituted by Matsushita.

Bibliography

"Background to PHP—30 Years." *PHP Intersect*, September, 1976: 75-80. An invaluable interview article by the staff of the Peace, Happiness, and Prosperity (PHP) Institute for *PHP Intersect*, its monthly magazine. Gives an excellent background account of PHP Institute told by Matsushita, the founder of the institute. The article discusses the founding of the institute in 1946, the goals of the institute, and how those goals are to be achieved.

"Following Henry Ford." *Time* 79 (February 23, 1962): 93-97. This article covers Matsushita's success story. Shows how the Matsushita Electric Company was established and how it expanded to become the biggest home appliance industry in the world.

"Konosuke Matsushita of Matsushita Electric, Interview." *Nation's Business* 59 (January, 1971): 32-37. Matsushita responds to many questions about his early apprentice years, the founding of his company in 1918, the establishment of his division system, the post-World War II period, and his success. A brief but valuable account of Matsushita's life.

"Matsushita." *Harvard Business School Bulletin*, February, 1983: 8-9, 49-116. This work, a very informative account of Matsushita's life, philosophy, and contributions, consists of four parts: Part 1 traces the historical development of Matsushita's industrial complex in Osaka from 1918 to the early 1980's; part 2 describes the success story of Matsushita Industrial Canada; part 3 provides comprehensive details of the founding of the Matsushita School of Government and Management in 1979; and part 4 recounts the personal story of the lifelong friendship between Matsushita and Shozo Hotta, an honorary chairman of the Sumitomo Bank. Matsushita is depicted as an idealist and a great achiever.

Matsushita, Konosuke. *Quest for Prosperity: The Life of a Japanese Industrialist*. Tokyo: PHP Institute, 1988. An excellent autobiography—the last of Matsushita's major works—written in 1988, one year prior to his death. The author relates many interesting and invaluable anecdotes of his many years of experience. Contains a good chronology and a bibliography.

Pascale, Richard Tanner, and Anthony G. Athos. *The Art of Japanese Management: Applications for American Executives*. New York: Simon & Schuster, 1981. This book is well worth reading for those who wish to study and learn about the ways in which many Japanese industries are more successful than American industries. The authors use the Matsushita Electric Company as a Japanese example.

Won Z. Yoon

VLADIMIR MAYAKOVSKY

Born: July 19, 1893; Bagdadi (now Mayakovsky), Georgia, Russian Empire
Died: April 14, 1930; Moscow, U.S.S.R.
Area of Achievement: Literature
Contribution: Mayakovsky was the poet laureate of the Russian Revolution. Celebrating the modern technological age, he became the voice of the masses. Combining propaganda and innovative poetic techniques, he created sweeping epics, mass spectacles, and dramatic slogans that brought a vibrant literature to the people in the streets.

Early Life

Vladimir Vladimirovich Mayakovsky, born in Bagdadi, Georgia, was an unpromising student who became involved in revolutionary activities early in his life. When his family moved to Moscow, the young Mayakovsky became fascinated with the spectacle of the 1905 Revolution. At the age of fourteen, he joined the Bolshevik Party and was arrested for revolutionary activities. In prison, he started to write poetry and to learn the power of literature. Mayakovsky eventually rechanneled his revolutionary zeal in the direction of creating socialist art and enrolled in the Moscow Institute of Painting, Sculpture, and Art, where he was introduced to modern art by David Burlyuk, an expressionist turned cubist. He also joined the Futurist movement, whose principles he was to embrace for the rest of his life. Mayakovsky supported the Futurists in their call for a dynamic art that would separate itself from the literature of the romantic past and celebrate the urban landscape. Dressed in conspicuous outfits, Mayakovsky went on tour reciting his poetry and giving lectures on art. These performances provided excellent training for his future role as an artistic ambassador for the Soviet Union. In his early poetry, he experimented with unmelodious sounds, distorted syntax, unusual words, bizarre figures of speech, and hyperbolic images. In 1913, he wrote, directed, and acted in his first drama, *Vladimir Mayakovsky* (1913; English translation, 1968). The play is a monodrama in which there is essentially only one character—Mayakovsky, the suffering poet; all the other characters are dreamlike reflections of various elements of his ego. A plotless series of long interior monologues written in fractured verse, this early drama introduced some of the themes and techniques that he would develop in his later works. It calls for the destruction of past cultures, concentrates on images of urban technology, presents a future-oriented vision, introduces the themes of martyrdom and suicide, and hints at a revolution to come.

In 1913, Mayakovsky also became associated with the literary theorist Osip Brik and fell in love with Osip's wife Lili. The Briks aided him in his career as a Futurist poet, and his love for Lili inspired many of his poems. In fact, she inspired his first epic poem, *Oblako v shtanakh* (1915; *A Cloud in*

Pants). In this poem, the poet starts with an incident of rejected love and builds to scenes of crucifixion and martyrdom. In "Chelovek" ("Man"), published in 1916, Mayakovsky explores cosmic themes in the form of a parody of the life of an orthodox saint. This poem paved the way for the cosmic sweep of his later poetry. Mayakovsky was already a poet with a mission, and the Russian Revolution gave him a platform from which to convey his message.

Life's Work

Mayakovsky was a poet of the Revolution. From propaganda slogans to epic poems, from poetry readings to mass spectacles, Mayakovsky was imbued with the ideas of the Revolution. He even called it "my Revolution." During the Revolution, he joined in the Futurists' program to take art into the streets and to bring it directly to the masses. Between 1918 and 1921, he created poster art with poetic captions.

In order to reach the people more effectively, he turned to theater. On November 7, 1918, in collaboration with the avant-garde director Vsevolod Meyerhold, Mayakovsky commemorated the first anniversary of the Revolution with his second play *Misteriya-buff* (1918; *Mystery-Bouffe*, 1933). In this play, he parodies a medieval mystery cycle. In true propaganda style, Mayakovsky caricatures the enemies of Communism: the greedy capitalist, the compromising Mensheviks, the inactive intellectuals, and the Soviet merchants. Along with Meyerhold, Mayakovsky helped to transform the stage from a two-dimensional, photographic representation of reality into a constructivist circus.

During this period, Mayakovsky continued to create moving epic poetry. In *150,000,000* (1920; English translation, 1949), Mayakovsky pits the giant Ivan, a symbol for 150,000,000 cold, hungry, desperate Russians, against the grotesque capitalist warrior, Woodrow Wilson, who sinks to the bottom of the sea. In *Pro eto* (1923; *About That*, 1965), he transforms a story of rejected love into an agon on his martyrdom and his resurrection in a futuristic world. This love poem shows his ability to elevate personal tragedy to the level of the messianic. In his greatest epic, *Vladimir Illich Lenin* (1924; English translation, 1939), he mixes comic and epic styles to celebrate the sweep of history. The use of cosmic imagery, the archetypal pattern of death and resurrection, the visions of futuristic worlds, and the interweaving of hard-hitting polemics with intricate poetry won for Mayakovsky national fame as an epic poet.

Mayakovsky soon became the artistic ambassador for the Soviet Union. In this capacity, he traveled throughout Germany, France, Eastern Europe, and the United States promoting Communism, speaking out for his brand of Soviet art, and writing travelogues and poems. He also established several journals and organizations to promote his own artistic programs. In his journal *Lef*, he proclaimed the need to slough off the decadent bourgeois culture and to create a proletarian art. His line "Time Forward March!" became the battle cry for the revolutionary art that would lead humanity into a new age of technology. When *Lef* went out of circulation, Mayakovsky created *New Lef* to restate his position. Again, he called for an art that was utilitarian but still avant-garde, attacking Maxim Gorky and other noted Soviet authors for their return to heroic and realistic depictions of Soviet life.

Mayakovsky also tried to move theater away from psychological realism. By 1927, however, the tide of Soviet politics was changing. Soviet society was searching for stability, and revolutionary art was giving way to Socialist Realism. Critics attacked Mayakovsky's art as bombastic and bohemian and accused him of lacking sincerity and concern for individual human problems. He met his critics head on with the production of *Klop* (1929; *The Bedbug*, 1931), a play in which the enemies of socialism are depicted as grotesque caricatures. In the character Oleg Bayan, Mayakovsky lampooned Vladimir Sidorov and other reactionary poets of his time, who not only saw their doubles on stage but also demanded an apology. He also satirized the Soviet program of modified capitalism (the so-called New Economic Policy) in his depiction of a beauty parlor and in his caricatures of hawking merchants peddling everything from lampshades to sausage balloons. In *The Bedbug*, Mayakovsky emphasized overt theatricalism over realism. In the Meyerhold production, actors marched through the audience hawking bras while the set consisted of everything from kitsch art to multimedia scenery. Mayakovsky had created a theater of public spectacle that included everything from temperance propaganda to clown acts. *Banya* (1930; *The Bathhouse*, 1963), Mayakovsky's last play produced within his lifetime, was his most vicious attack on his contemporaries, especially those in the Soviet bureaucracy. Everywhere in the play there were official bureaus with lengthy acronyms, but nothing ever got done. In the third act, he used the play-within-a play device to satirize the realistic school of the Moscow Art Theater as well as the poetic style of the Russian ballet theater. Mayakovsky reduced the objects of his satire to grotesque types, broke with fourth-wall realism, and tried to jar his audience into the action. Again Mayakovsky tried to create a theater of spectacle that would magnify, not mirror reality. The play angered many in the literary establishment and closed after three performances.

In his last great poem, *Vo ves golos* (1930; *At the Top of My Voice*, 1940), Mayakovsky depicted himself as he had always depicted himself: as a poet of the future, a poet of the people, and a poet of the Communist Party, loyal to the cause. Having been refused an exit visa, despondent over the boycott of a retrospective exhibition of his work, and disillusioned over the failure of *The Bathhouse*, Mayakovsky shot himself on April 14, 1930. In his suicide note, he wrote that he did not want to list his grievances; instead, he proclaimed: "Night has imposed a starry tribute on the sky/ It is in such hours that one rises and speaks to/ the ages, history, and the universe." To the end, Mayakovsky was a poet with a revolutionary vision.

Summary

Vladimir Mayakovsky was indeed the poet of the Revolution. As a member of the Futurist movement, he broke with the heroic literature of the past and the sentimentality of bourgeois realism to fight for a democratic art that would allow the free word of the creative personality to be "written on the walls, fences, and streets of the cities." He wanted a new form of poetry that would cry out to the people, abandon traditional imagery, praise the urban landscape, and hail the coming of the utopian commune. To accomplish this artistic revolution, Mayakovsky created a literature that eschewed the notion of absolute value and eternal beauty and spoke directly to the masses—a literature that produced poetic devices that were based more on their ability to propagandize than on their ability to create aesthetic embellishments.

As a dramatist, Mayakovsky, with the aid of the director Vsevolod Meyerhold, revolutionized modern theater. He brought the action of the drama into the audience, breaking the bonds of keyhole realism. He also replaced realistic characters with grotesque figures—slapstick clowns bouncing across constructivist three-dimensional sets composed of ropes, grids, and platforms. In essence, he created a theater of spectacle.

Upon his death, Mayakovsky was accorded a state funeral; he was widely mourned. In 1938, Joseph Stalin proclaimed him one of the most important socialist poets. In the Soviet Union, both a town and a square were named for him. Today, he is one of the most highly acclaimed Soviet poets, and his influence has reached beyond the Soviet Union.

Bibliography

Brown, Edward J. *Mayakovsky: A Poet in the Revolution*. Princeton, N.J.: Princeton University Press, 1973. The first major critical biography of Mayakovsky in English. The book shows a close connection between Mayakovsky's life and his works. It provides close readings of Mayakovsky's major and minor works and even focuses on his didactic verse. Most important, it examines Mayakovsky's work in context with the social, political, and artistic revolutions that helped to structure his artistic vision. Contains an annotated bibliography of works by and on Mayakovsky.

Shklovsky, Viktor. *Mayakovsky and His Circle*. Edited and translated by Lily Feiler. New York: Dodd, Mead, 1972. A tribute to Mayakovsky by a close associate and intimate friend. The book not only covers the relationship between Shklovsky and Mayakovsky but also focuses on the other figures in the Futurist movement in Russia. Although it promotes Shklovsky's Formalist bias, it is a good firsthand account of Mayakovsky's development as a poet as well as a history of the artistic revolutions in Russia from 1910 to 1930.

Stapanian, Juliette R. *Mayakovsky's Cubo-Futurist Vision.* Houston: Rice University Press, 1986. An analysis of Mayakovsky's poetry in the light of developments in the fine arts during the early part of the twentieth century. Stapanian shows a correlation between Mayakovsky's poetic techniques and the artistic styles of the cubist and the Futurist painters. She demonstrates how the images in his poems mirror the fractured and multidimensional images in Cubo-Futurist art.

Terras, Victor. *Vladimir Mayakovsky.* Boston: Twayne, 1983. An excellent critical introduction to Mayakovsky. The book provides a clear, well-organized biographical sketch of Mayakovsky's life followed by a close analysis of his major works. Terras defines critical terms, traces the history of artistic movements, and provides a clear critical assessment of Mayakovsky's works. The book also contains a comprehensive checklist of Mayakovsky's work and an annotated bibliography of secondary sources.

Woroszylski, Wiktor. *The Life of Mayakovsky.* Translated by Boleslaw Taborski. New York: Orion Press, 1970. A translation of a 1966 work by a Polish poet. The book is an encyclopedic compendium of documentary sources on Mayakovsky's life and work, including police reports, personal letters, impressions of close associates, and interviews with intimate friends—all interspersed with samples of Mayakovsky's poetry. It is a good reference work for someone looking for primary source material, but it does not present a clear perspective for the reader who is unfamiliar with Mayakovsky's work.

Paul Rosefeldt

GOLDA MEIR

Born: May 3, 1898; Kiev, Ukraine, Russian Empire
Died: December 8, 1978; Jerusalem, Israel
Areas of Achievement: Government and politics
Contribution: Meir was a leading Zionist and inspirational figure for world Jewry who rejected life in the United States to immigrate to Palestine in 1920. She became a major role player in Zionist organizations there, eventually rising to become Israel's first ambassador to the Soviet Union (1948), minister of labor (1949), foreign minister (1956), and prime minister (1969).

Early Life

Golda Meir was born in Kiev, Russian Empire, on May 3, 1898. Her father was Moshe Yitzhak Mabovitch, who was a carpenter by training. Moshe and his wife had three children: Sheyna, Golda, and Zipke. The family moved from Kiev to their ancestral town of Pinsk after Golda's birth but ultimately sought to leave Russia because of the violent attacks that threatened Jewish life there. In 1906, the family immigrated to Milwaukee, Wisconsin. Golda worked with her sisters in the family's grocery store. Sheyna became involved in 1915 in the Poale Zion movement, a labor- and socialist-oriented branch of the Zionist movement, which in turn became an inspiration for Golda. Poale Zion aspired to national and social equality of the Jewish people in their own homeland through labor.

Golda fled home in 1912 at age fourteen and moved to Denver to live with Sheyna, who had gone there earlier for treatment of tuberculosis. Four years later (1916), she returned to Milwaukee under extreme parental pressure. While in Denver, she met Morris Meyerson (the name was Hebraized to "Meir" in 1956), whom she married in 1917. For a short time after her return to Wisconsin, Golda was enrolled in Milwaukee Normal School for Teachers. The idea of living and working in the United States did not have much appeal for Golda, who was more attracted to the Poale Zion leaders A. D. Gorden, Nachman Syrkin, and Shmaryahu Levin. She was instrumental in organizing the first Midwest marches in Milwaukee to protest the 1919 pogroms against the Jews in the Ukraine. On May 23, 1921, the Meyersons departed for Palestine on the SS *Pocahontas*. They arrived in Egypt and then transferred by train to Tel Aviv. During the fall of 1921, the Meyersons joined Kibbutz Merhavia (a collective farm based on egalitarian principles). The kibbutz placed Golda face-to-face with issues relating to feminism and female emancipation. Golda, however, never considered herself a feminist. She worked in the fields picking almonds, planting trees, and taking care of chickens. On kitchen duty, she became famous for introducing oatmeal and glasses in an otherwise Spartan environment.

In 1922, the Meyersons left Merhavia because of Morris' health and because of his unwillingness to have a child reared by the collective methods of the kibbutz. Their first child, Menachem, was born in November, 1923. The Meyersons moved to Jerusalem to work for Solel Boneh, a government-owned company that was at that time in poor financial standing. A second child, Sarah, was born during the spring of 1926. Meir later lamented that if she could do things over again, she would have remained on the kibbutz. In this period, Meir believed that the application of Jewish labor to Palestine would also improve the quality of life for the Arabs. She always believed that had been the case, justified by the rise in the Arab population during the period of the British mandate over Palestine.

Life's Work

During 1928, Meir became secretary of Moezet ha-Poalot, the Women's Labor Council of the Histadrut (Jewish labor union of Palestine/Israel) and supervised training of immigrant girls. In 1932, she was sent back to the United States as a representative to the Pioneer Women's Organization, where she would remain until 1934. Around this time her marriage broke up, but there was never a divorce. Morris continued to live in Israel and died there in 1951.

In 1934, Meir became a member of the executive committee of the Histadrut and head of the political department, which allowed her advancement into higher circles. In 1938, she was a Jewish observer to the Evian Conference, which failed to solve the problem of Jewish emigration from Europe in the face of Nazi brutality. During World War II, Meir was a member of the War Economic Advisory Council set up by the mandatory government in Palestine. In 1946, Meir was made acting head of the Jewish agency after the British mandatory authorities arrested the leaders of the Jewish community following outbreaks of violence in the country. She later commented that her failure to be arrested was a minor insult of sorts because the British apparently believed she was unimportant. In fact, she was one of the most important negotiators for the Jewish community of Palestine during the last two years of the mandate. Meir remained as head of the Political Department until statehood.

During the last years of the mandate, Meir was an active opponent of Ernst Bevin, British foreign secretary, who favored the position of the Palestinian Arabs. Meir was indignant over powerlessness imposed on Jews by the white paper of 1939. She also expressed regret with the boundaries for a Jewish state proposed by the United Nations Special Committee on Palestine (UNSCOP) in 1947, which excluded Jerusalem and parts of Galilee from the Jewish zone. In November, 1947, the United Nations proclaimed the partition of Palestine. In January, 1948, Meir visited the United States in the hope of raising between $25 and $30 million from American Jews for the

State of Israel's survival. In fact, she raised more than $50 million.

Meir visited King Abdullah of Transjordan twice in an attempt to avert war between Jews and Arabs. The first time was November, 1947, when Meir, acting as head of the political department of the Jewish Agency, met the king in a house at Naharayim, near the Jordan River. At this meeting, Abdullah indicated his desire for peace and that the two shared a common enemy, Hajj-Amin al Husseini, the Mufti of Jerusalem and leader of the Palestinian community. On May 10, 1948, the two again met in Amman after Meir crossed into Transjordan in disguise, hoping to avert a Jordanian invasion of Palestine. Abdullah asked her not to hurry in proclaiming a state. She responded that Jews had been waiting for two thousand years. Abdullah requested that the Jews drop their plans for free immigration. Later, rumor had it that Abdullah blamed the war on Meir, as she was perceived as being too proud to accept his offer.

Meir was one of the twenty-five signators of the Declaration of Independence on May 14, 1948. Shortly thereafter, she was again dispatched to the United States for additional fund-raising. She again raised millions of dollars which helped the state survive. Meir, however, did not have time to savor the fruits of statehood and was immediately dispatched to Moscow in 1948 as Israel's first ambassador to the Soviet Union. She arrived in Moscow on September 3, 1948, and established the Israeli mission there. She became the center of a famous demonstration outside the Moscow synagogue on Rosh Hashanah, 1948, which was one of the first indications that Zionist aspirations still existed among Soviet Jews. More than fifty thousand Soviet Jews came to see the first Israeli delegation in Moscow, which provided the first hint of the potential of a large exodus of Jews to Israel and the West.

After departing Moscow in 1949, Meir served in the Israeli Knesset (parliament) until 1974 and rose to many top governmental positions. As a member of the Mapai (labor) Party, she was elected to the First Knesset in 1949 and was appointed minister of labor. In charge of the large-scale immigration of Jews from Arab lands, particularly Iraq and Morocco, she was responsible for settling newcomers in tents and later in permanent housing. More than 680,000 Jews from Arab lands arrived in Israel during the period of her ministry. She had running battles with Minister of Finance Levi Eshkol about financial allocation for housing. All newcomers, however, were placed under shelter when they arrived in Israel, although conditions were very poor from 1950 to 1952. Meir's theory was that all new immigrants had to be employed and get paid for their work. This employment came through huge public works projects, focusing on road building.

Meir herself believed that the most significant thing she did in politics was the work connected with the Ministry of Labor, because it symbolized social equality and justice. She was instrumental in the presentation of Israel's first National Insurance Bill in 1952 which came into effect in 1954; the establishment of vocational training for adults and youngsters by allying the Ministry of Labor with older voluntary Jewish organizations such as the Histadrut (labor union), Organization for Rehabilitation Through Training (ORT), Hadassah (women's organization), and Women's International Zionist Organization (WIZO); and the development town projects, which were of only modest success.

In 1955, Meir attempted to become mayor of Tel Aviv but was defeated when the religious bloc in the Israeli Knesset refused to vote for a woman. In 1956, Meir became foreign minister, succeeding Moshe Sharett. She flew to France in 1956 with Shimon Peres and Moshe Dayan to plan a joint attack on Egypt as an ally of Great Britain and France. She gave a speech at the United Nations General Assembly in March, 1957, in which she announced the Israeli military withdrawal from the Sinai Peninsula and Sharm-el-Sheik, which had been occupied by Israel in October, 1956, as a response to Gamal Abdel Nasser's blockade of the Gulf of Aqaba, and in which she called for all states of the Middle East to join in peaceful endeavors.

As foreign minister, Meir developed an energetic development program with emerging African nations. Part of this strategy was to obtain votes at the United Nations, but the bottom line on Israeli-African policy was the common history of suffering. Oppression against the Jews, in Meir's mind, was similar to African slavery and European imperialism. During the late 1950's, Meir traveled to Ghana, Cameroon, Togo, Liberia, Sierre Leone, Gambia, Guinea, the Ivory Coast, and other states. African leaders often found her honest in her appraisals of the possibilities of development and the problems of instant solutions. The African policy, however, collapsed during and after the 1973 War, when most African states bowed to Arab oil pressure and severed relations.

In 1965, Meir retired as foreign minister and became secretary-general of the Labor Party (Mapai). This was a critical period in the development of the center-left Israeli political parties, as part of the Labor Party had split with David Ben Gurion to establish Rafi, while Achdut Ha Avodah represented another position of labor. Meir believed that unification was necessary to ensure the future of the Labor Party. During the crisis before the Six-Day War, Meir was brought into the government and supported a hesitant Eshkol. After the war, she participated in the unification of the three labor parties into the new Israel Labor Party.

When Prime Minister Eshkol died on February 16, 1969, Meir was chosen as prime minister (March 7, 1969) as a means to avoid an open struggle between Moshe Dayan and Yigal Allon. On matters involving peace with the Arabs, Meir was often said to possess hard-line bargaining positions. She believed that the only alternative to war was peace and the only way to peace was negotiations. She indicated her willingness to go anywhere to talk peace and to negotiate anything except national suicide. She was never willing to talk with the Palestine Liberation Organization (PLO), however, which she viewed as a terrorist organization.

Late in 1969, Meir went to the United States to meet with President Richard Nixon, as well as to fill a shopping list for weapons, especially a specific request for twenty-five Phantom and eighty Skyhawk jet aircraft. It was a warm meeting with the American president, and Meir stayed on for an extended speaking tour. In January, 1973, Meir met with Pope Paul VI, the first Jewish head of state to do so.

The October, 1973, Yom Kippur War was a watershed in Israeli history and a horrible period in Meir's life. She became aware of plans for an Egyptian and Syrian attack against Israel but held off mobilization of re-serves. Israel won the war but with substantial casualties. Meir also had a rift with General Ariel Sharon over disposition of the Egyptian Third Army, which had been surrounded by Israeli forces in Sinai. Meir, in order to save Sadat's position as possible negotiator, ordered Sharon not to move against the Third Army. Meir also had ambivalent feelings about United States Secretary of State Henry Kissinger, who threatened economic retaliation against Israel during cease-fire and disengagement negotiations. In the end, Meir believed that she had been correct in rejecting a preemptive strike against the Arab states, as the Arab attack ensured American aid, which, she believed, saved lives.

The Labor Party again prevailed in elections held on December 31, 1973, but Meir resigned less than four months later, on April 11, 1974. She be-came a casualty of the Yom Kippur War, so to speak, after the Agranat Commission's report indicted the general staff, the military intelligence, the Sinai field commanders, and David Eleazar, who was the commander in chief, but not the minister of defense, Moshe Dayan. Meir left office June 4, 1974, at age seventy-six. She continued as a spokesperson for Israel in academic and public circles.

Summary

Golda Meir was one of the most beloved of Israel's leaders but unfor-tunately left office after what became a national disaster—the Yom Kippur War. Still, she was highly regarded, even by her former enemies. In Novem-ber, 1977, when President Anwar el-Sadat of Egypt went on a peace mission to Israel, Meir was at the airport to greet him; Sadat regarded her as "the tough old lady." Meir was generally considered a tough and often stubborn politician, holding onto views that had a foundation deep in her Zionist ideology, which was influenced by memories of atrocities against the Jews in Eastern Europe during her childhood and the Holocaust of World War II. This quality was useful for Israel as an embattled people but became prob-lematic once peace initiatives appeared, for Meir often believed such initia-tives were insincere.

Meir helped create certain problems in the peace process that continued beyond her tenure as prime minister. She failed to establish any specific position about the occupied territories—the West Bank and Gaza Strip. She insisted upon direct negotiations with the enemy and opposed any form of mediation by outsiders. She refused, perhaps correctly, any interim withdrawal before a peace treaty was signed. Her most serious misjudgment was probably the failure to take up Sadat's explorations for peace in 1971. Yet she was an exponent of peace and held a consistent view. Meir died in Jerusalem on December 8, 1978, of leukemia, which she had known about since the early 1970's but managed to hide from public view.

Bibliography
Martin, Ralph. *Golda Meir: The Romantic Years*. New York: Charles Scribner's Sons, 1988. An examination of Meir's personal life, with less emphasis on the politics of the Middle East.
Meir, Golda. *My Life*. New York: G. P. Putnam's Sons, 1975. The most valuable work for understanding the life and accomplishments of Meir. This is not a diary but rather an exposition of what Meir believed were her most important accomplishments. Includes some texts of her more important speeches.
Rafael, Gideon. *Destination Peace: Three Decades of Israeli Foreign Policy*. New York: Stein & Day, 1981. An examination of Israeli foreign policy from the perspective of an individual who served as Israeli ambassador to London, permanent representative to the United Nations, and director-general of the Israeli Foreign Ministry. Contains many insightful references to the career of Golda Meir.
Sachar, Howard M. *A History of Israel*. 2 vols. New York: Oxford University Press, 1974. A comprehensive history of Zionism and the state of history, with particular references to Meir's prime ministry.
Shenker, Israel. "Golda Meir: Peace and Arab Acceptance Were Goals of Her Years as Premier." *The New York Times*, December 9, 1978: 7. This is an article that appeared as part of an extensive obituary of Meir, summarizing her main approaches to the peace process.
Syrkin, Marie. *Golda Meir: Israel's Leader*. New York: Putnam, 1969.
_____. *Golda Meir: Woman with a Cause*. New York: Putnam, 1963. Two early and sympathetic portraits by a fellow American Zionist. Syrkin's father, Nachman Syrkin, was a leading labor Zionist and strong influence on Meir during the 1930's. These portraits are, therefore, based on a very close friendship between two women Zionist leaders. Neither of the works, however, gives a full picture of Meir's life, as they were completed before her tenure as prime minister was completed.

Stephen C. Feinstein

LISE MEITNER

Born: November 7, 1878; Vienna, Austro-Hungarian Empire
Died: October 27, 1968; Cambridge, England
Area of Achievement: Physics
Contribution: Working as a pioneer in a field to which few women were drawn—nuclear physics—Meitner's joint research with chemist Otto Hahn (and later Fritz Strassmann) yielded the discovery of new radioactive elements and their properties and paved the way for the discovery of uranium fission.

Early Life

Lise Meitner was the third of eight children born to Hedwig Skovran and Philipp Meitner, a Viennese lawyer. Meitner had a very marked bent for mathematics and physics from a young age but did not begin her schooling immediately. This was partly because of prevailing attitudes in Vienna regarding the education of women. In order to regain the several years she had lost, she was tutored privately. After receiving a matriculation certificate from the Academic *Gymnasium* (high school) in Vienna, Meitner went on to the University of Vienna where, from 1901 until the end of 1905, she studied mathematics, physics, and philosophy. She decided early to concentrate on physics, realizing that she did not want to be a mathematician. During this time, she met with some rudeness from her fellows, since a female student was then regarded as something of a freak. In 1902, however, she had the good fortune to begin her study of theoretical physics under the stimulating and inspiring tutelage of Ludwig Boltzmann, who was a zealous advocate of atomic theory (the idea that all matter is composed of tiny, invisible, and, at that time at least, indivisible components). This was by no means generally accepted by physicists of the day, but in Boltzmann's view the discovery of radioactivity supplied the experimental proof that tiny particles, or atoms, formed the building blocks of all things.

In 1905, Meitner finished her doctoral thesis on heat conduction in nonhomogeneous bodies and became the second woman to receive a doctorate in science from the University of Vienna. She soon became familiar with the new field of radioactivity and was ready to enter the realm of atomic physics at the beginning of a promising new period in that branch of science.

Life's Work

Though Meitner had no intention of making the study of radioactivity her specialty, this would become her life's work. After graduation, she persuaded her parents to allow her to go to Berlin to study with the theoretical physicist Max Planck for a few terms, but the intended short stay became a thirty-one-year period of research pushing back the frontiers of atomic physics and radioactivity.

Meitner arrived in Berlin in 1907 and enrolled in Planck's lectures. He was one of the world's most notable scientists, having developed the theory of thermal radiation (or quantum theory) in 1900 and having been one of the first to recognize and stress the importance of Albert Einstein's special theory of relativity. Meitner spoke of him not only with respect and admiration but also with much affection. Yet as important as Meitner's association with Planck was, it was her friendship and her long and productive collaboration with Otto Hahn that would change the course of atomic science.

Meitner and Hahn also met in 1907, and, finding that she had the opportunity for experimentation, Meitner decided she wanted to work with Hahn and keep to the study of radioactivity. After some persuasion, they finally received permission from Emil Fischer, the director of the Chemical Institute of Berlin where Hahn was working, to become a research team with the provision that Meitner promise not to go into the chemistry department, where the male students did their research and where Hahn conducted his chemical experiments. For the first few years, their joint research was confined to a small room originally planned as a carpenter's shop. When women's education was officially sanctioned and regulated in Germany in 1909, Fischer gave permission at once for Meitner to enter the chemistry department. In later years, he was most kind to and supportive of Meitner, eventually helping her to establish and become head of the new department of radiation physics in the Kaiser Wilhelm Institute for Chemistry in 1917.

In 1912, the Kaiser Wilhelm Institute for Chemistry was opened as a part of the University of Berlin, and Hahn became a member. Meitner became an assistant to Max Planck at the university's Institute for Theoretical Physics. Far from ending their cooperative effects, this development meant that the Meitner-Hahn partnership could continue with greater facilities and an enlarged staff. Their collaboration was a fruitful one for both of them. Hahn, a future Nobel laureate, brought to the team a splendid knowledge of organic chemistry; Meitner brought an expertise in theoretical physics and mathematics. Together they would be responsible for some important advances, including their 1917 discovery of the rare radioactive element 91, protactinium.

Though World War I did not dramatically affect her in a personal way, Meitner maintained that physics during World War I changed decisively because of Niels Bohr's work on the structure of the atom. In her opinion, his research on the atomic nucleus gave an extraordinary impetus to the development of nuclear physics itself, finally leading to the fission of uranium. She first met Bohr in 1920 and got to know him personally a year later. Her respect and gratitude stemmed not only from her opinion that no one—not even the great Ernest Rutherford—had such a worldwide influence on physicists as Bohr but also from the great efforts extended by him to regain for Germans admittance to scientific conferences, from which they had been strictly excluded in the postwar years. In the years following their first meetings, Meitner took part in many of Bohr's famous conferences, which were held at almost annual intervals in Copenhagen and at which were discussed new advances in physics and neighboring fields.

From 1917 to 1926, Meitner continued to conduct her own research on the nature of beta rays. The interpretation of the physical properties of radioactive substances continued to be an area of personal interest. She was the first to maintain that, in the process of disintegration of radioactive materials, the emission of radiation follows rather than precedes the emission of the particles. During this time, she won considerable acclaim for herself and in 1926 was named professor extraordinary at the University of Berlin. This was a position she would be able to retain only until Adolf Hitler's anti-Semitic decrees forced her to leave the post. Although all the children in Meitner's family had been baptized, and Lise herself had been reared as a Protestant, both of her parents were of Jewish background and this brought upon her the condemnation of the Nazis. For a few years after Hitler came to power in 1933, however, the change in government did not affect Meitner's collaboration with Hahn.

Meitner never invented a laboratory instrument or experimental technique of her own, but she rapidly adopted any new methods to her research and used them in innovative ways. From 1926 to 1933, Meitner became a pioneer in the use of a device called the Wilson cloud chamber for Charles Thomson Rees Wilson. In 1926, she was able to use it to measure the track length of slow electrons. In 1933, she was also one of the first to photograph in a chamber and to report on the tracks of positrons formed from gamma radiation.

In the early 1930's, nuclear physics made profound and dramatic advances when the neutron was discovered by Sir James Chadwick and artificial radioactivity was discovered by Frédéric Joliot and Irène Joliot-Curie. New techniques in experimentation were now possible, and in 1934 Meitner and Hahn began to follow up the work of a group of scientists in Italy headed by Enrico Fermi, who had bombarded uranium with neutrons and found several radioactive products thought to be transuranic elements (elements with an atomic number higher than 92, or uranium). Meitner and Hahn soon found a new group of radioactive substances that could not be identified with any of the elements just below uranium in the periodic table. Only one assumption was possible—that they were higher. Still, unanswered questions and puzzling results remained, even though another scientist, Fritz Strassmann, had joined Meitner and Hahn.

As the spring of 1938 arrived and Austria was occupied by the Nazis, Meitner was forced to leave Germany. Robbed now of protection owing to her foreign (Austrian) nationality and with the enforcement of Nazi policies regarding individuals of Jewish origin, Meitner knew that it was only a matter of time before she would face even graver choices. She went first to The Netherlands, then to Copenhagen as a guest of Niels Bohr and his wife, and finally to Stockholm to work in the new Nobel Institute, where a cyclotron was being constructed.

Meitner was sixty years old when she went to Sweden. Nevertheless, she continued her hard work, built up a small research group, and did experiments on the properties of radioactive elements formed with the cyclotron. Yet her most famous contribution to physics came shortly after she arrived in Stockholm.

In Berlin, Hahn and Strassmann had continued their work after Meitner left. She wrote to Hahn for data on the properties of the substances produced by their experiments. Hahn and Strassmann conducted more tests to prove the existence of radium but could only identify products resembling barium isotopes. Meitner discussed this new information with her nephew, the physicist Otto Frisch, who was working in the laboratory of her friend Bohr. Meitner and Frisch concluded that the uranium nuclei had split into two fragments and that a large amount of energy had been released. Meitner actually used Einstein's mass-energy equivalence equations to do the calculations. Immediately, Meitner and Frisch prepared a communication for the British science journal *Nature*, in which they introduced the term "nuclear fission" to elucidate scientific principles previously thought to be impossible. For a short time after 1939, Meitner continued to investigate the nature of fission. In 1950, independently of others doing similar research, Meitner advanced accepted ideas concerning the asymmetry of fission fragments and worked on various aspects of the shell model of the nucleus.

Meitner's residence in Stockholm eventually became permanent. In 1947, after having spent half a year as a visiting professor at Catholic University in the United States, she became a citizen of Sweden, retired from the Nobel Institute, and went to work in a small laboratory that the Swedish Atomic Energy Commission had established for her at the Royal Institute of Technology. In 1960, Meitner left Sweden and retired to Cambridge, England, to travel, lecture, and enjoy her lifelong love of music. She had lived a full life, but her strength gradually deteriorated and she died a few days prior to her ninetieth birthday.

Summary

Lise Meitner was a true pioneer. She helped revolutionize the science of physics and its concepts. Her active participation in nuclear research resulted in the discovery of new elements and paved the way for the discovery of atomic fission, a term she helped coin and a process she helped interpret correctly. She entered her field at a time when women in science were not only a rarity but also an oddity. This is nowhere better demonstrated than at the first meeting between Meitner and Rutherford, who stopped in Berlin in 1908 to see his pupil Hahn on his way home from Stockholm after receiving the Nobel Prize in Chemistry. When he saw Meitner he said in great astonishment: "Oh, I thought you were a man!" It was no mean task to overcome some of the prejudices and preconceptions that were far less harmless than Rutherford's mistake. Yet she overcame these attitudes, and Meitner's contributions to nuclear physics are acknowledged to be of the highest rank.

Honors came to Meitner from all quarters throughout her long life. She earned a distinguished reputation in the 1920's, receiving, in 1924, the Liebnitz Medal of the Berlin Academy of Sciences and, in 1925, the Lieber Prize of the Austrian Academy of Sciences. In 1947, she was awarded the Prize of the City of Vienna and in 1949 the Max Planck Medal. Meitner was elected a foreign member of the Royal Society of London in 1955 and of the American Academy of Arts and Sciences in 1960. In 1966, she shared the United States Atomic Energy Commission's Fermi Award with Hahn and Strassmann. In addition, four American educational institutions (Syracuse, Rutgers, Smith, and Adelphi) bestowed upon her honorary doctorates in science. The list of awards is impressive, but they are simply a by-product of Meitner's love of science. Perhaps, that is why she continued her work well beyond the years when most others have stopped.

Bibliography
Frisch, O. R. "Lise Meitner." In *Dictionary of Scientific Biography*, edited by Charles C. Gillispie, vol. 9. New York: Charles Scribner's Sons, 1972. This compact but thorough article was authored by Meitner's colleague and nephew, who participated in the events surrounding the discovery and naming of the fission process. Contains a detailed bibliography. Very accurate scientifically but not for the layperson.
Graetzer, Hans G., and David L. Anderson. *The Discovery of Nuclear Fission: A Documentary History.* New York: Van Nostrand Reinhold, 1970. This short volume is an invaluable source. Provides reprints of the original papers and reports by scientists who first uncovered the problem and meaning of nuclear fission. Includes several of the original papers that provided a basis for the application of nuclear fission to military or peaceful purposes.
Hahn, Otto. *My Life: The Autobiography of a Scientist.* Translated by Ernest Kaiser and Eithne Wilkins. New York: Herder and Herder, 1970. Because this volume presents the life of Meitner's collaborator in great detail, much information is contained about Meitner throughout. Engaging reading that presents a detailed background of the long partnership as well as an account of the discovery of fission and its interpretation by Meitner.
Meitner, Lise. "Looking Back." *Bulletin of the Atomic Scientists* 20 (November, 1964): 2-7. The most complete autobiographical account of Meit-

ner's life that is available in the English language. With clarity and charm, Meitner discusses her life from her youth through the discovery of atomic fission.

Sparberg, Esther B. "A Study of the Discovery of Fission." *American Journal of Physics* 32 (1964): 2-8. Reviews the history of the discovery of fission and succinctly discusses Meitner's place in that history. Contains some interesting statements made by Meitner.

Yost, Edna. "Lise Meitner: Physicist." In *Women of Modern Science*. New York: Dodd, Mead, 1959. Written before Meitner's death, this chapter is one of the most readable accounts of her life yet published. Particularly good at discussing the professional associations made by Meitner during her life. Relates her work to that of other famous scientists and emphasizes the honors that came to her.

Andrew C. Skinner

ERICH MENDELSOHN

Born: March 21, 1887; Allenstein, Germany
Died: September 15, 1953; San Francisco, California
Area of Achievement: Architecture
Contribution: Mendelsohn did at least as much as such better-known contemporaries as Le Corbusier, Walter Gropius, and Ludwig Mies van der
Rohe to develop and popularize modern architecture. Even more fully
than the other founders of the so-called International Style, Mendelsohn
was the representative architect of modern world industrialism—of machine, steel, concrete, and glass.

Early Life
Erich Mendelsohn was born March 21, 1887, in the town of Allenstein in
East Prussia, Germany (now Olsztyn, Poland). His father was a well-to-do
Jewish businessman of Russian-Polish background. His mother was a talented musician, and Mendelsohn's lifelong interest in musical rhythms and
forms (with Johann Sebastian Bach his favorite composer) had a major impact on his architecture. As early as the age of five, Mendelsohn appears to
have resolved to be an architect. After a year at the University of Munich
studying economics, he switched in 1908 to the Berlin Technische
Hochschule to begin work in architecture. Two years later, he transferred to
the Technische Hochschule at Munich, where he obtained his degree in
architecture in 1912. Shortly after the outbreak of World War I, he enlisted
for military service in the engineers. He served on the Eastern (Russian)
Front until late 1917; then he was transferred to the Western Front, where he
remained until the war's end. In 1915, he married Luise Maas, a talented
cellist; they had one daughter. The surviving Mendelsohn letters show a
young man filled with restless energy and a strong creative drive. "Everywhere," he wrote in 1913, "new ideas, new achievements. How can one
possibly look on idly, and not, with every fibre of one's being, desire to take
a part?" As it was for so many others of his generation, the experience of
World War I was an emotional and cultural watershed. "As few before us,"
he would recall, "we felt the meaning of living and dying, of end and
beginning—its creative meaning in the midst of the silent terror of no-man's
land and the terrifying din of rapid fire."
Mendelsohn had a lifelong interest in, and enthusiasm for, Greek art, the
classical simplicity of which would inspire him. Yet the most important
influence shaping his early architecture was his association with the Blaue
Reiter (Blue Rider) group of expressionist painters led by Wassily Kan-
dinsky. The keynote of the application of the expressionist aesthetic to architecture was that the character of a building should be determined by its
purpose. The sketches that Mendelsohn did between 1914 and 1918 (many

done while he was serving in the trenches) show his fascination with themes that would characterize his mature work: his attraction to steel, concrete, and glass; his fascination with the horizontal and broad plain surfaces; his juxtaposition of curved forms with straight lines; and his conception of a building as not simply a machine fulfilling its purpose but an organic unit, with each part belonging to the whole and each form growing out of another.

Life's Work

Immediately after his demobilization, Mendelsohn started his own architectural practice. An exhibition of his sketches entitled "Architecture in Steel and Concrete" at the famous avant-garde art gallery of Paul Cassirer in Berlin created a sensation. What catapulted him into sudden fame was his design of the Einstein Tower (1919-1924) at Potsdam, a suburb of Berlin; it was a combination of cupola observatory and astrophysical laboratory for further research into Albert Einstein's theory of relativity. Although conceived in reinforced concrete, the main body was built in brick with a cement façade because of the postwar shortage of cement. The rounded shapes that compose the building, both in general mass and details, coupled with the deep window recesses are expressive of optical instruments while simultaneously conveying an aura of the mysteries of the universe. Further evidence of Mendelsohn's virtuosity was furnished by his next two major projects. The first was a hat factory at Luckenwalde (1919-1921) consisting of four long sheds made up of a series of triangular concrete arches curved at the springing with brick walls and rubberoid roofing. The second was his addition to the *Berliner Tageblatt* newspaper building (1921-1923), done in collaboration with Richard Neutra. The structure consisted of a steel frame encased in concrete, with its long horizontal lines and horizontal windows in contrast to the vertical emphasis of the nineteenth century main building.

A major turning point in Mendelsohn's development was his contact with the Dutch painters and architects of the De Stilj school, most importantly J. J. P. Oud. Mendelsohn took as his goal the fusion of the romantic free-form impulses of expressionism with the geometrically inspired rationalism of the De Stilj group. Perhaps even more influential was his visit to the United States in 1924, during which he met Frank Lloyd Wright and was deeply impressed by Wright's call for an architecture reflecting the organic structure of natural forms. After his return, he published *Amerika: Bilderbuch eines Architekten* (1926; America: picturebook of an architect), containing seventy-seven photographs of the more important buildings he had seen, accompanied by his personal commentaries. Trips in 1925 and 1926 to the Soviet Union to oversee construction of his design for a factory for the Leningrad Textile Trust resulted in the publishing in 1929 of *Russland, Europa, Amerika: Ein Architektonischer Querschnitt*, a comparative appraisal of new developments in architecture in the three places. The finest expressions of Mendelsohn's mid- and latter-1920's architectural work were his department store designs: the Herpich Fur Store in Berlin (1924); the Schocken stores in Nürnberg (1926-1927), Stuttgart (1926-1928), and Chemnitz (1928-1929); and the Petersdorff store in Breslau (1926-1927). The distinguishing features of those stores was his making the front outer wall a screen of chiefly glass to maximize the natural light during daytime plus his typical emphasis on long horizontal lines.

Mendelsohn's last five years in Germany, 1928-1933, were ones of intense activity, during which he had as many as forty assistants and draftsmen working for him. Many of his projects remained unbuilt, but the completed work included three outstanding designs. One was Berlin's Universum motion picture theater (1927-1928), with an elongated horseshoe interior and curved balcony front that maximized the number of seats with an undistorted view of the screen. The second was his own home on a slope overlooking Havel Lake on the outskirts of Berlin (1929-1930); it is a masterful arrangement externally and internally of plain rectangular forms that succeeded in blending harmoniously with its site. The third was Columbushaus (1929-1931), a twelve-story office building at Postdamerplatz, Berlin, featuring a technically innovative steel skeleton with a façade of horizontal bands of glass and polished cream travertine.

In 1932, Mendelsohn was elected a member of the Prussian Academy of Arts, but in March, 1933, following Adolf Hitler's takeover of power, he left Germany and settled in Great Britain. He first entered into a partnership in London with Serge Chermayeff; in 1936 he set up an independent practice. He became a naturalized British subject in 1938, and, in February, 1939, he was elected a fellow of the Royal Institute of British Architects. The most distinguished of his British buildings is the De la Warr Pavilion at Bexhill-on-the Sea (1933-1935). A longish, low horizontal steel-and-glass building, the pavilion admirably fits in with the adjacent sea. Another typical Mendelsohn touch was his breaking of the long horizontal movement of the building by two semicircular glass projections enclosing staircases at either end of the central block.

After 1937, Mendelsohn's principal work was done in Palestine. In February, 1939, he left Great Britain to make Palestine his home. Architecture in Palestine presented new problems for the northern Europe architect, such as keeping out rather than letting in the sunlight and handling the extremely wide variations in temperature between day and night. Mendelsohn's success in adapting European modern architecture to this new environment is shown by the Chaim Weizmann house in Rehovot, near Tel Aviv (1935-1936); the Salman Schocken house and office/library in Jerusalem (1935-1936); the Government Hospital in Haifa overlooking the Bay of Acre (1936-1938); and the Anglo-Palestine Bank in Jerusalem (1937-1939). His most important work was the Hadassah University Medical Center (1936-1938) on Jerusalem's Mount Scopus, a complex of three reinforced concrete buildings faced with cream Jerusalem limestone arranged in narrow panels and narrow vertical windows. Perhaps the most striking features of his Palestine work were the orientation of the buildings to take advantage of the prevailing breezes coupled with the painstaking design of the surrounding gardens to complement the building masses.

The outbreak of war led to a halt in further building in Palestine. After unsuccessful efforts first to join the British army and then to obtain a war job, he left for the United States in March, 1941. Shortly after his arrival, New York City's Museum of Modern Art presented an exhibition of his work, and he received invitations to lecture at universities across the country. Lectures that he delivered at the University of California-Berkeley in April, 1942, were published two years later as *Three Lectures on Architecture*. With America's entry into the war, new building came to a standstill. Fortunately, Mendelsohn was awarded in 1943 a Guggenheim Fellowship for two years. From May, 1943, to October, 1945, he lived at Croton, thirty miles north of New York City in a house overlooking the Hudson River; then he moved to San Francisco, where he resumed the practice of architecture. The first of his American buildings to be completed was the Maimonides Hospital in San Francisco (1946-1950). Its outstanding feature was the balconies with white balustrades that swung out in rhythmic curves to give the effect of lacy ribbons. Most of his American work consisted of designs for Jewish synagogues or temples combined with community centers. Four of these designs were built—one in St. Louis (1946-1950), one in Cleveland (1946-1952), one in Grand Rapids, Michigan (1948-1952), and one in St. Paul, Minnesota (1950-1954), which was completed after Mendelsohn's death to a partially altered plan. Mendelsohn died September 15, 1953, from cancer in a San Francisco hospital. He was cremated and, according to his wishes, his ashes were scattered in an unrecorded place.

Summary

Erich Mendelsohn was given to philosophizing in rather ponderous Germanic fashion upon the nature of architecture. In his 1942 lectures at the University of California, he took as his major target architecture that, "instead of being in plan and appearance the true expression of a building's utility, material, and structure, tried to hide its own life behind the lifeless ornamental features of a bygone society." He identified as "the main issue of building: to simplify life in accordance with and in consequence of the technical inventions and scientific discoveries of our age." The hallmark of that simplification was the quest for an organic unity.

Mendelsohn's achievements were the more remarkable given that he lost one eye in 1921 because of cancer and the remaining one was weak. He was one of the fathers of the International Style, but he avoided the boxlike monotony that became associated with that school. A major reason for his success in doing so was his juxtaposition of curvilinear forms to temper his use of long horizontal and rectangular spaces. One example was his repeated use of the semicircular projection to break the horizontal movement of his buildings; another was his fondness for the spiral staircase. A second recurring theme is his adaptation of the structure not simply to the building's purpose but to the natural environment of its site—including the climate as well as the physical terrain. The most distinctive feature of his work, however, is genius for achieving an organic unity in which there is a oneness of exterior and interior, in which each part has a definite function in relation to the other parts, and in which there is the rhythmic continuity of the different parts appearing to flow into one other as an integrated whole.

Mendelsohn is less well known than most of the other founders of modern architecture. One reason is that his inflexible and uncompromising attitude toward his designs antagonized would-be clients. Yet the major reason appears to be, simply, bad luck. Many of his most imaginative designs never got beyond the paper stage, and many of his most outstanding completed buildings were done in the backwater of Palestine. He also died at a relatively young age compared to such contemporaries as Le Corbusier, Gropius, and Mies van der Rohe.

Bibliography
Mendelsohn, Erich. *The Drawings of Eric Mendelsohn.* Edited by Susan King. San Francisco: California Print Co., 1969. This catalog of an exhibition of 133 of Mendelsohn's drawings is invaluable for understanding his work methods and tracing the evolution of his architectural style. King's introduction provides useful background. Included is a listing of Mendelsohn's own published writings and unpublished lectures, writings about him, and exhibitions on him.
_____. *Eric Mendelsohn: Letters of an Architect.* Edited by Oskar Beyer. Translated by Geoffrey Strachan. London: Abelard-Schuman, 1967. These letters—mostly to Mendelsohn's wife before and after their marriage—span the years 1910 to 1953 and constitute an invaluable source, illuminating Mendelsohn's intellectual, emotional, and aesthetic development. An introduction by the distinguished architectural historian Nikolaus Pevsner briefly but judiciously appraises Mendelsohn's contribution to modern architecture.
_____. *Three Lectures on Architecture.* Berkeley: University of California Press, 1944. These lectures—presented at the University of California-Berkeley in April, 1942—constitute the fullest expression of Mendelsohn's philosophical reflection on the nature of architecture. Required reading for students wishing insight into the intellectual presuppositions shaping and undergirding Mendelsohn's work.

Pehnt, Wolfgang. *Expressionist Architecture*. Translated by J. A. Under-wood and Edith Küstner. New York: Praeger, 1973. The volume has only a brief chapter directly on Mendelsohn, but it is the fullest available account of the expressionist impulse/movement in European architecture and, thus, important for placing Mendelsohn's early work in context.

Von Eckardt, Wolf. *Eric Mendelsohn*. New York: George Braziller, 1960. Von Eckardt's brief text for this volume in the Braziller Masters of World Architecture series is on the superficial side but provides a helpful introduction for the beginning student. The volume includes approximately eighty pages of illustrations, half of which are reproductions of sketches and models that were never built. Includes a chronological listing of Mendelsohn's buildings and projects plus a bibliography.

Whittick, Arnold. *Eric Mendelsohn*. 2d ed. New York: F. W. Dodge, 1956. Whittick is an enthusiastic Mendelsohn booster and had access to Mendelsohn's still unpublished letters, sketches, and plans. The text is written for the nonspecialist. There are 75 black-and-white photographs and 109 reproductions of drawings, sketches, plans, elevations, and sections.

Zevi, Bruno. *Erich Mendelsohn*. New York: Rizzoli, 1985. One of the leading architects of the present day, Zevi is a strong admirer of Mendelsohn. The volume consists of a brief overall appraisal, "Mendelsohn and the Path from Expressionism to the Organic," followed by brief descriptions/analyses of his more important designs. Contains excellent accompanying illustrations.

John Braeman

PIERRE MENDÈS-FRANCE

Born: January 11, 1907; Paris, France
Died: October 18, 1982; Paris, France
Areas of Achievement: Economics, government, and politics
Contribution: Mendès-France was a Left-leaning French politician of the
Radical Party who is best remembered for negotiating an armistice with
the Vietminh in 1954, which ended the French Indochina War, and for
opening the negotiations which led to Tunisian independence. More generally, he acted as the conscience of the democratic non-Communist Left
in France during the Fourth and early Fifth republics.

Early Life

Born into an assimilated Jewish family in Paris in January, 1907, Pierre
Mendès-France received a secular republican education at the Lycée Turgot
and the Lycée Louis-le-Grand, followed by studies at the Faculty of Law and
the École Libre des Sciences Politiques. In 1924, he helped found the Ligue
d'Action Universitaire Républicaine et Socialistes (LAURS), an anti-Fascist
student organization.

The early renown of Mendès-France was a result of his expertise in economics and finance. His thesis for the doctor of law degree, submitted in
1928, was entitled "La Politique financière du gouvernement Poincaré." A
1929 article, "Les Finances de l'état démocratique," and a 1930 book, *La
Banque internationale*, focused on the central role of economics in the modern world and argued that the effective solution to practical difficulties required international solutions and, therefore, international organizations.
These early publications, boldly critical of individualist law, were very well
received and made Mendès-France a well-known figure, though in 1930 he
was only twenty-three years old.

Life's Work

The active political career of Mendès-France lasted for forty years. In
1932, he was elected deputy for the city of Louviers (Eure département); at
twenty-five, he was the youngest deputy in the National Assembly. Though a
member of a Radical Party, he was considered a "Young Turk," along with
Jacques Kayser, Pierre Cot, Gaston Bergery, Jean Zay, and Gaston Manner-
ville. In May, 1935, he was elected mayor of Louviers, a position he held,
except for the interruption of the war, until 1958. He devoted himself to
financial and economic matters: In the National Assembly, he spoke in favor
of government loans to farmers and was a member, then chair, of the
Customs Committee; as a lawyer, he defended peasants; as mayor in
Louviers, he oversaw the installation of public utilities and the provision of
social welfare.

A strong proponent of the Popular Front strategy, Mendès-France was reelected to the National Assembly in 1936. He was critical of the delayed devaluation of the franc by the Blum government, favoring instead immediate devaluation, and he opposed the policy of nonintervention in the Spanish Civil War. He nevertheless remained a vocal supporter of the government's record of reform, and in 1938 entered Léon Blum's second government as under-secretary of the Treasury. With Georges Boris, he authored the first French planning program, but in less than a month, and before implementation could proceed, the government fell.

With the outbreak of World War II, Mendès-France joined the air force. He was first assigned to the Levant but was on leave in Paris when the invasion of France began. He traveled to Louviers (he was still the elected mayor), witnessed the flight of French refugees fleeing the German army, and himself returned to Paris after receiving a shrapnel wound in the shoulder on June 9. He traveled southward as the Germans advanced and gained passage to Casablanca on the ship *Massilia*.

This "flight" became one portion of the charge of desertion trumped up by the Vichy government. Arrested on August 31, 1940, Mendès-France was transferred to Clermont-Ferrand where he was tried, convicted, and sentenced to six years in prison. After a failed appeal, Mendès-France escaped from prison (on June 21, 1941). He lived underground for several months, mostly in Grenoble, and then escaped, via Geneva and Lisbon, to London on March 1, 1942, to join Charles de Gaulle and the Free French. Between October, 1942, and November, 1943, he rejoined his squadron at Hartfordbridge, England, and flew about a dozen bombing operations.

In November, 1943, Mendès-France moved to Algiers and became the Commissioner of Finance in the French National Liberation Committee (CFLN). In this capacity, he prepared for reconstruction and represented Free France at the international meeting at Bretton Woods (June, 1944) that established the World Bank and the International Monetary Fund (IMF). Following liberation, he was appointed minister of national economy in Charles de Gaulle's first government. He urged a policy of austerity, including the reduction of the volume of inflated currency in circulation; the restriction of consumption; wage and price controls; the freezing of bank accounts; a tax on capital gains; and state-imposed discipline on some production and exchange. De Gaulle rejected his advice in favor of the more laissez-faire policy advocated by minister of finance René Pleven, and as a result Mendès-France resigned in April, 1945.

Mendès-France returned to his duties as mayor of Louviers and was elected deputy, first to the Constituent Assembly in 1946, and then to the National Assembly in 1951. His various roles in formulating economic policy were arguably even more important: He taught courses at the École Nationale d'Administration on the fiscal and budgetary problems posed by planning and reconstruction, was a member of the Executive Committee of the IMF and World Bank, and became France's representative, from 1947 to 1951, to the Economic and Social Council of the United Nations.

The issue that catapulted Mendès-France to the center of French politics was not economic policy, however, but colonial policy. After 1950, he became a vocal public advocate of a negotiated settlement in Indochina that would entail the gradual evacuation of French troops and called for free elections and national independence for Vietnam. This campaign, coupled with his calls for dialogue with North Africa and his program for fiscal and economic reform, made Mendès-France the statesman of choice for many young technocrats and intellectuals.

His brief tenure as premier began on June 18, 1954, in the midst of the debacle of Dien Bien Phu. Mendès-France moved quickly to open direct negotiations with the Vietminh in Geneva, and he succeeded in arranging the armistice that halted the fighting. Simultaneously, he traveled to Carthage to set in motion the negotiations that led to the internal autonomy of Tunisia. Finally, Mendès-France oversaw, after the French rejection of the European Defense Community, the London Agreements that led to German rearmament and English attachment to continental security. While Mendès-France was occupied with foreign policy issues, economic policy was left in the hands of the more moderate Edgar Faure, and by the time Mendès-France himself took over control of the Finance Ministry, on January 20, 1955, opponents were preparing to bring down the government.

The government fell on February 2, 1955, during a debate on the Maghreb. Many analysts believe that the underlying cause was too much success: Mendès-France had succeeded in the politically delicate tasks for which he had been given political power—of extricating France from Vietnam and establishing a Western European union. Once achieved, Mendès-France was viewed as expendable by more traditional politicians of the Fourth Republic.

Mendès-France turned his attention to a consolidation of power for his progressive faction within the Radical Party. He was instrumental in forming the Republican Front, which brought together the parties of the non-Communist Left. The coalition won the elections of December, 1956, and Mendès-France served briefly as minister without portfolio in the government of Guy Mollet. He resigned in May, 1957, because of his opposition to the hard-line Algerian policy of the Socialist Party leader. Mendès-France became spokesman for the democratic opposition on the Left: He was critical of government policy in North Africa; he almost alone warned against the consequences of the Suez adventure; he voted against the Treaty of Rome establishing the Common Market; and he opposed de Gaulle's return to power in 1958. He was so out of step with national opinion that he lost the support of his constituency in Louviers in the elections of November, 1958.

The following year, Mendès-France, now fifty-two years old, broke with the Radical Party, declared himself a socialist, and adhered to a splinter party of the Socialist party that was attempting to distance itself from the policies of Mollet.

His brief return to the center of national politics occurred in 1967-1969. In March, 1967, he was elected deputy for Grenoble. During the crisis of 1968, he sympathized with the striking workers and students, attended the demonstration in Charléty, and even suggested (during de Gaulle's dramatic disappearance) that he might lead a provisional government. In the Gaullist landslide that followed, he lost his assembly seat (by 132 votes). In 1969, he and Gaston Defferre ran a campaign against Georges Pompidou and the Gaullist system. They were badly beaten, and for all practical purposes Mendès-France passed from active political life. He died on October 18, 1982.

Summary

Pierre Mendès-France was probably the most influential figure in postwar French political life after Charles de Gaulle, despite the fact that he headed a government for only 245 days. His early renown came in the field for which his academic work best prepared him—economics. At the age of twenty-one, he published a refutation of Henri Poincaré's stabilization program, which made him famous. At thirty-one, he coauthored the first French planning program with a member of Léon Blum's Popular Front cabinet. At thirty-seven, he was the interlocutor of John Maynard Keynes at Bretton Woods. At thirty-eight, he called on de Gaulle to stabilize the economy in liberated France. Known for his rigor and his scrupulous attention to economic facts, he was the hardheaded conscience of a French Left which, too often in Mendès-France's opinion, allowed flights of utopian fancy to obscure reality.

The event for which Mendès-France will be best remembered is the ending of French involvement in Indochina during his premiership between June, 1954, and February, 1955. Perhaps no European colonial power has withdrawn from its colonial possessions with greater human costs. It was Mendès-France who began the painful process of extricating France from its colonial past. Not only did he end the French war in Vietnam but also he began the negotiations in relatively friendly circumstances that led to the independence of Morocco and Tunisia.

For many in France, Mendès-France restored hope that reason and politics did not necessarily exclude each other; he represented a politics that was neither useless nor corrupt. In the words of François Mitterrand, "Pierre Mendès-France awakened our consciences."

Bibliography
Lacouture, Jean. *Pierre Mendès France*. Translated by George Holoch. New

York: Holmes & Meier, 1984. This political biography is the best available book on Mendès-France. It describes with a sure hand the French political world to which Mendès-France not only reacted but also helped to shape.

Mendès France, Pierre, and Gabriel Ardant. *Economics and Action*. New York: Columbia University Press, 1955. The essential book on Mendès-France's economic thought.

Rioux, Jean-Pierre. *The Fourth Republic, 1944-1958*. Translated by Godfrey Rogers. New York: Cambridge University Press, 1987. The history of the French Fourth Republic, written by a French expert.

Werth, Alexander. *The Strange History of Mendès-France and the Great Conflict Over French North Africa*. London: Barrie Books, 1957. Published during the final crisis of the French Fourth Republic, this book provides a sense of the drama of this period by a close observer. The greatest part of the book deals, as the title indicates, with the crisis of the French North African Empire.

Williams, Philip M. *Crisis and Compromise: Politics in the Fourth Republic*. London: Longmans, 1964. A standard history of the Fourth Republic by a British expert.

K. Steven Vincent

GIAN CARLO MENOTTI

Born: July 7, 1911; Cadegliano, Italy

Area of Achievement: Music

Contribution: Menotti is known primarily for his opera compositions, for which he composed the music and wrote the libretti. He is also a composer of ballets, concerti, and orchestral music.

Early Life

Gian Carlo Menotti was born in Cadegliano, Italy, on July 7, 1911, to wealthy parents who were able by their financial and cultural backgrounds to nurse his immense musical interests. At the early age of four, Menotti began studying piano, and, by the age of six, he had progressed to the point of composing his own melodies and simple accompaniments. On his ninth birthday, Menotti was given a puppet theater by his parents. This was a source of great fun and learning for Menotti, as he not only wrote and directed his own plays but also composed his own music for the productions. His first full-length opera was written in 1922, when he was eleven years old.

In 1923, the Menotti family moved to Milan, where Gian Carlo was enrolled in academic school, in which he displayed very little interest. At this same time, however, he also began studying at the Milan Conservatory of Music, where he was a regular student from 1923 to 1928. During this time, he composed a second full-length opera entitled *The Death of Pierrot*, the last act of which sees all the characters kill themselves. While studying at the conservatory, Menotti was also in demand as a pianist. Handsome, intelligent, and musically gifted, he was proudly exhibited in the most fashionable Milanese salons and was so spoiled that he refused to practice as he should have.

His mother was wise enough to realize that the musical growth of her son was somewhat stunted in Milan. Compelled to travel to South America to untangle some of her husband's interests following his death, she took her son with her in hopes of stopping off in New York City on the return trip. Menotti was seventeen at the time and enjoyed visiting the different cultures of the Western world. On the return trip to Italy, they did stop in New York to visit an old friend of the family, Tullio Serafin, then conductor at the Metropolitan Opera House. Serafin introduced the Menottis to Rosario Scalero, an eminent composition teacher at the Curtis Institute of Music in Philadelphia. To Scalero, Menotti seemed to be only an undisciplined boy, in spite of his talents, but through a solemn promise by Menotti, Scalero consented to teach him the fine points of composition. Menotti's mother returned to Italy, leaving the young man in a strange new country, where he not only had to work hard and practice but also had to learn a new language—English. This he did by attending the motion picture show four times a week.

Life's Work

By the time he reached the age of twenty-two, Menotti was able to graduate from writing contrapuntal class exercises and began working on his first mature opera, *Amelia Goes to the Ball*. This one-act comic opera was produced in Philadelphia and New York by students and faculty of the Curtis Institute and was conducted by Fritz Reiner in 1937. Menotti's operas are important as theatrical spectacles. Their greatest significance does not lie in the musical score, as it does with most operas. His music is sometimes more functional than inspired. Menotti draws from every available style and idiom to cater to his dramatic needs: from the popular to the esoteric, from the lyrical to the dissonant, from the romantic to the realistic. For the operas of Menotti, music is never an end but a means, and the end is realized in projection of effective theater.

Because of the necessary flow of the music to provide the listener with something substantial, portions of Menotti's operas are seldom heard in the concert setting. The music loses its appeal when not heard in sequence of the story. Within the theater, however, his music carries tremendous impact and serves to tie the production together, provide a continual flow, and enhance the other artistic qualities of the productions.

Menotti had written his first libretto in Italian, but henceforth he would write all his opera libretti in English. The musical format for *Amelia Goes to the Ball* is in traditional style, with solo arias, duets, trios, and recitatives. The style is happy and tuneful, although at times spiced with a touch of discord or polytonality. The impressive nature of this work led to a commission by the National Broadcasting Company (NBC) to write an opera exclusively for radio production. On April 27, 1939, NBC introduced the work *The Old Man and the Thief*, also written in a comic vein.

Meanwhile, in 1938 Menotti received word that his opera *Amelia Goes to the Ball* had been accepted by the Metropolitan Opera Company for its 1938 season. It was played seven times during that and the following season. Several years later, in 1942, the Metropolitan Opera commissioned an opera by Menotti, entitled *The Island God*. This opera, unfortunately, was not well received by the public.

Menotti became determined to compose a successful serious opera, as he had thus far only seen success with his comic operas. *The Medium*, first heard in New York City in May of 1946, proved to be the work that opened to public view Menotti's far-reaching dramatic powers. Since the first performance of *The Medium*, it has become one of the most famous American operas. It has been given more than one thousand performances in the United

States, London, Paris, and Italy, and has also been made into a stirring motion picture.

Between 1948 and 1958, Menotti continued to compose, write, produce, and direct operas, sometimes as commissioned works, sometimes at his own pleasure, but always intelligent, quality productions. In 1958, Menotti founded the Festival of the Two Worlds in Spoleto, Italy. As founder and president, he has been responsible for the presentation of several provocative contemporary operas.

On Christmas Eve, 1951, the production of *Amahl and the Night Visitors* was seen for the first time. This very popular work of Menotti is unique in that it is the first opera produced expressly for television transmission. The broadcast was repeated the following Easter and Christmas by NBC and has since been staged by many opera companies, including the New York City Opera.

Like Richard Wagner, Menotti is a one-man theater. He not only writes his own text and music but also is his own stage director and casting director and has a general command of every other aspect of the production, much like he did at age nine with his puppet theater, only on a much grander scale. Menotti seems to have an extraordinary sixth sense for finding small details that may enhance good drama. His ability to see clearly all details of the production even before rehearsals have begun, combined with his sense for what he desires to see in his opera in spite of popular opinion, has led him often to select many comparatively inexperienced and unknown singers and performers for his works.

Menotti is known first and foremost as an opera composer, and though Italian born and reared (retaining his Italian citizenship), he is considered to be America's greatest composer of opera, because of his training in Philadelphia and his residency in New York City. He has also written a concerto for piano and orchestra, another concerto for violin and orchestra, some pieces for orchestra, and some ballet music. These pieces, however, have not seen the publicity or the public acceptance of his operas.

His orchestration usually requires small groups of instruments in balance with small casts. His operas very seldom use the chorus so popular with other composers, and he relies on his solo singers to carry the work. This combination of relatively small performing forces has made his operas approachable by small opera companies and even school production groups. Especially popular with school-age students is *Amahl and the Night Visitors* because of its familiar message of Christmas and because the lead character is a young boy.

Menotti uses the standard orchestral instruments for the most part. Very seldom does he venture into the lures of uncommon instrumental techniques for the sake of effect. He prefers, instead, when special effects are called for, to create them on the stage rather than in the orchestra pit. Although his music is spiced with twentieth century composition techniques such as polytonality and discords, the audience generally feels at ease as the music begins near and never strays very far from the tonal center. His melodic structure may not always be singable to the average listener, but it is always listenable and pleasant to the ear.

Amahl and the Night Visitors is probably Menotti's most popular opera. The music ranges from tender to exciting as the story of the three wise men following the star of the Christ child unfolds. During their travels, they come upon the poor home of Amahl, a crippled beggar boy, and his mother. When Amahl learns of the wise men's purpose, he gives his set of small crutches to the Magi as a present to the Holy Child. As Amahl goes forth to present his gift to the kings, he discovers that a miracle has taken place and that he is able to walk. This work thrives on beautifully flowing arias and angelic choruses. The emotion of the opera can only be felt when the entire production is presented. Therefore, it does not break down into concert sections well. Although *Amahl and the Night Visitors* was written for and introduced by the television screen, it has also been presented with immense success on stage.

Summary

Gian Carlo Menotti's eclecticism carries him from a Puccini-like lyricism to the most advanced composition idioms. He can be romantic or dissonant, lyrical or mystic. Yet he never seems to sacrifice unity of concept or coherence of viewpoint. Menotti is above all else a man of the theater. He writes his own libretti and music and commands full control of the production of his operas. His operas are not only a vehicle for musical expression but also a vibrant and pulsating stage experience. Perhaps for this reason Menotti has commanded a larger and more varied audience than any other composer in the twentieth century.

Bibliography

Austin, William W. *Music in the Twentieth Century: From Debussy Through Stravinsky.* New York: W. W. Norton, 1966. This book discusses the student/teacher relationships of twentieth century composers such as Menotti. It also discusses Menotti's works in relationship to music of other composers.

Drummond, Andrew H. *American Opera Librettos.* Metuchen, N.J.: Scarecrow Press, 1973. Drummond lists all Menotti's operas and quotes the poetic text of each. This book allows the reader the opportunity to see Menotti's creative literary work.

Ewen, David. *David Ewen Introduces Modern Music.* Philadelphia: Chilton, 1962. Ewen, a highly respected music historian, offers an in-depth discussion of Menotti's life, works, and contributions to music and opera as well as brings to the light his ability as a theater director and his staging genius.

Howard, John Tasker, and Arthur Mendel. *Our Contemporary Composers.* New York: Thomas Y. Crowell, 1946. This source quotes music critics in discussing Menotti's operas. There is also a list of the few works by Menotti that were not written for the opera stage but for concert settings.

Myers, Rollo H., ed. *Twentieth Century Music.* New York: Orion Press, 1968. This book gives a brief description of the performing elements that make up Menotti's operas and lists each of his operas in chronological order. A good description of Menotti's work without in-depth details.

Reis, Claire R. *Composers in America.* Rev. ed. New York: Macmillan, 1947. Following a brief synopsis of Menotti's career, Reis offers a complete list of works, dates, and publishers of Menotti's works.

Salzman, Eric. *Twentieth Centry Music: An Introduction.* Englewood Cliffs, N.J.: Prentice-Hall, 1967. Salzman compares Menotti's theater talent to that of Puccini, describing how it goes beyond music and enters the areas of drama, stage usage, and function of characters among other things.

Robert Briggs

MAURICE MERLEAU-PONTY

Born: March 14, 1908; Rochefort, France
Died: May 4, 1961; Paris, France
Area of Achievement: Philosophy
Contribution: Merleau-Ponty, French philosopher and man of letters, was one of the most original and profound thinkers of the postwar French movement of existential phenomenology.

Early Life

Maurice Merleau-Ponty's father died before his son was seven years old, and Maurice, his brother, and his sister were reared in Paris by their mother, a devout Catholic who gave her children a strongly religious upbringing. It was not until the 1930's that Merleau-Ponty eventually became discontented with the established Church and ceased to practice his faith. At one point in his life, he even admitted to being an atheist but then altered his position to one of agnosticism. His final position with regard to religion is not known; what is clear, however, is that some degree of reconciliation with the Church of his early years must have occurred prior to his sudden death in May of 1961, since a Catholic Mass was said at his funeral.

According to the testimony of his own writings, Merleau-Ponty's childhood was happy, so happy that his adult years never quite provided him with the same sense of complete fulfillment. The death of his father while the boy was still very young is thought to have affected the boy immeasurably, and as a result he became extremely close to his mother and remained completely devoted to her until her death only a few years prior to his own.

Merleau-Ponty received his secondary education at the Lycée Louis-le-Grand, and then studied at the École Normale Supérieure in Paris. After taking his *agrégation* in philosophy in 1931, he taught in a *lycée* at Beauvais for the next five years. He then held a research grant from the Caisse de la Recherche Scientifique for a year and subsequently took up teaching again, this time at the *lycée* in Chartres. In 1935, he returned to Paris as a junior member of the faculty at the school he had attended, the École Normale.

Life's Work

In the winter of 1939, after the Nazi invasion of Poland, Merleau-Ponty entered the army and served as a lieutenant in the infantry. While in the army, he wrote his first major work, *La Structure du comportement* (1942; *The Structure of Behavior*, 1963). Although the work was completed in 1938, when he was thirty years old, because of the war, the book was not published until 1942. Perhaps the most important thesis of this work is Merleau-Ponty's reinterpretation of the distinctions between the physical, the biological (or vital), and the mental dimensions of existence. These dimensions were treated by him as different levels of conceptualization at which human behavior could be studied, and they were distinguished by the degree to which the concepts used were useful and meaningful. While Merleau-Ponty was very insistent upon the irreducibility of these distinctions, he also maintained that they were logically cumulative, such that biological concepts presuppose physical concepts, and mental concepts presuppose both. Yet, at the same time that he defended this thesis of the logical interdependence of the physical and the mental, Merleau-Ponty rejected in principle all attempts to explain this relationship in causal terms. Merleau-Ponty's first work, then, was both a sustained and powerful attack on behaviorism in psychology as well as a new philosophical interpretation of the experimental work of the Gestalt psychologists.

After the demobilization of France and during the German Occupation, Merleau-Ponty again returned to teaching and writing. Continuing his critique of traditional psychology, in 1945 he published what was to become his masterwork: *Phénoménologie de la perception* (1945; *Phenomenology of Perception*, 1962). This second book examined what he viewed as traditional prejudices regarding perception in order to advance a "return" to things themselves. According to Merleau-Ponty, understanding the body itself involves a theory of perception. One is able to know oneself only through relationships with the world, and the world is not what one thinks it is but what one lives through. Drawing heavily upon, but also modifying, the phenomenological techniques of Edmund Husserl as well as the existential threads in the thought of Gabriel Marcel and Martin Heidegger, Merleau-Ponty, in this work, begins to construct a personal synthesis, an original philosophical interpretation of human experience. For this reason he is considered to be one of the originators of contemporary existential philosophy and, in the opinion of one of his notable colleagues, Paul Ricoeur, "was the greatest of the French phenomenologists."

After the Occupation of France ended, Merleau-Ponty joined the faculty of the University of Lyon and at the same time (in 1945) became coeditor of the existentialist periodical *Les Temps modernes* with Jean-Paul Sartre, a former schoolmate and longtime friend. By 1950, Merleau-Ponty's reputation was established, and he took a position at the Sorbonne as professor of psychology and pedagogy. He was to remain in this post for only two years. Then, in 1952, he was appointed to a chair at the Collège de France. This was the chair that had been left vacant by the death of Louis Lavelle and that had previously been occupied by Henri Bergson and Édouard Le Roy. Merleau-Ponty, in fact, was the youngest philosopher ever to hold this position—one of the more prestigious in French academic life—and he retained it until his death in May, 1961. Merleau-Ponty was happily married to a woman prominent in her own right as a physician and psychiatrist in Paris, and they had one child, a daughter.

All Merleau-Ponty's work demonstrates a familiarity with both current scientific research and with the history of philosophy, a combination that gives his work a more balanced character than that of the other existentialists. Another of his major concerns was with political and social philosophy as well as the problems of everyday politics. Consequently he wrote numerous newspaper articles on contemporary events and problems. His more sustained essays on Marxist theory and leftist politics, however, were gathered in two collections: *Humanisme et terreur* (1947; humanism and terror) and *Les Aventures de la dialectique* (1955; the adventures of the dialectic).

In the former work, Merleau-Ponty leaned so far in the direction of Marxist historicism as to argue that historical undertakings are to be judged retroactively by their success or failure and that to act "historically" is inevitably to submit oneself to this "objective" judgment of events, in which personal intentions, good or bad, are irrelevant. Simultaneously, however, he rejected the orthodox Marxist view that a scientific theory of the logic of historical development is accessible as a basis for such action. The latter work, exhibiting a new direction in the philosopher's social thought, contains a powerful critique of the French Communist Party, with which he had earlier sympathized. Marxism, in his opinion, was a timely device for thinking about human needs and contingencies in modern industrial society; he, however, rejected its dogmatic rigidity, particularly its claims to predictive power and historical mission, and the nonliberating, totalitarian features that had become associated with it.

Well to the left of Sartre during the 1940's, Merleau-Ponty was close to the Communists from 1945 to 1950 and played a crucial role in linking existentialist and Marxist thought during that period; by 1955, however, he was no longer engaged in Marxist politics. From 1950 on, Sartre, on the other hand, was moving closer to Marxism. For some years after 1955, Sartre was occupied almost exclusively with the existentialism-Marxism debate, which since 1945 had continued to be an explosive issue in French intellectual and political life. The ideological split with Sartre led to an open break with him and to Merleau-Ponty's resignation from the editorship of *Les Temps modernes*. Nevertheless, Merleau-Ponty's political views remained decisive for Sartre, as the latter freely admitted in a memoir published after Merleau-Ponty's death.

Essays and articles on language, literature, the aesthetics of film, and painting were also undertaken by Merleau-Ponty in the busy final decade of his life. In these essays, published as collections entitled *Sens et non-sens* (1948; *Sense and NonSense*, 1964) and *Signs* (1960; English translation, 1964), he sought to work out some of the implications of his thesis on the primacy of perception using Husserl as his fundamental reference point for epistemological grounding and dialogue. Merleau-Ponty had hoped to conclude his analysis of the prereflective life of consciousness with a survey of the major modes of reflective thought in which he would seek to determine their criteria for validity and truth. At the time of his sudden death from a coronary thrombosis in 1961, he had written only incomplete fragments and sketches.

Summary

Maurice Merleau-Ponty's career included two principal aspects. He was, first, a professional philosopher and teacher of philosophy whose main body of work was done in the field of philosophical psychology and phenomenology. In addition, he was a man of letters who wrote extensively on political and aesthetic subjects and actively participated in the intellectual life of his time. Despite the fact that Merleau-Ponty is sometimes viewed as a kind of junior collaborator of Sartre, both his philosophical work and his more general writings reveal a mind and a mode of thought that developed in a fully independent manner and that are at once very different from Sartre's and, in terms of intellectual rigor and elegance, often demonstrably superior.

As in the case with other "existentialist" philosophers, there are no "disciples" of Merleau-Ponty in the strict sense of the word, since his method was his life. To adopt his method then, would be to begin to experience the world in a new way, with a new philosophy, and not with a continuation of Merleau-Ponty's life and thought. Thus it is not by virtue of his existentialism, Marxism, or phenomenology that he has made his greatest contribution, but rather by the extent to which, through each of these, he has been able to illuminate the lived human quality of existence. It is in and through his uniqueness that his impact will be felt most strongly.

Bibliography
Bannan, John F. *The Philosophy of Merleau-Ponty.* New York: Harcourt, Brace & World, 1967. The aim of Bannan's excellent and very thorough work is not to locate the thought of Merleau-Ponty among the classic positions in the history of philosophy but to focus upon his more immediate context—his relations with Husserl's work, with Sartre, and with Marxism. Contains a very brief biographical note on the philosopher.
Dillon, M. C. *Merleau-Ponty's Ontology.* Bloomington: Indiana University Press, 1988. This well-documented, scholarly work approaches Merleau-Ponty in the historical context out of which Merleau-Ponty's ontology, his alternative to Cartesian knowledge, arose. This lengthy work also contains an excellent bibliography and extensive notes.
Mallin, Samuel B. *Merleau-Ponty's Philosophy.* New Haven, Conn.: Yale University Press, 1979. In this lengthy and scholarly work, the author's purpose is to provide a unified and comprehensive interpretation of Merleau-Ponty's philosophy. His method is to analyze extensively the concepts that are central and original to Merleau-Ponty's philosophy and the

way in which they form an integrated whole. The work also contains a bibliography of primary and secondary sources and an appendix consisting of a table of contents of the philosophy of perception and its integration into the text.

Rabil, Albert, Jr. *Merleau-Ponty: Existentialist of the Social World.* New York: Columbia University Press, 1967. In this well-respected and lengthy work, Rabil suggests that in Merleau-Ponty more than any other philosopher a dialectical tension exists in his existentialist preoccupation with self-understanding and the social orientation of the politically minded and the reformer. The author analyzes the sources, the vision and the viability of this "social philosophy." Contains a bibliography and extensive notes.

Spurling, Laurie. *Phenomenology and the Social World: The Philosophy of Merleau-Ponty and Its Relation to the Social Sciences.* London: Routledge & Kegan Paul, 1977. Spurling argues that Merleau-Ponty's philosophy can be understood as a dialectic between a discipline and a transcendental impulse and that it is this overall dialectical relationship that offers a coherent perspective on being in the world, especially on those areas of thought often considered to be the exclusive domain of the social sciences. Contains a bibliography and extensive notes.

Whitford, Margaret. *Merleau-Ponty's Critique of Sartre's Philosophy.* Lexington, Ky.: French Forum, 1982. Rather than presenting a straightforward comparison of the two philosophers' thought, the author of this brief but illuminating book focuses upon the limits of Merleau-Ponty's critique of Sartre. Cogito, freedom, temporality, others, ontology, phenomenology, and dialectic are the categories discussed.

Genevieve Slomski

OLIVIER MESSIAEN

Born: December 10, 1908; Avignon, France

Area of Achievement: Music

Contribution: Messiaen is the most important French composer of the twentieth century's second half. His catalog of compositions (which numbers more than seventy works) includes pieces for solo keyboard, chamber ensemble, electronic media, orchestra, oratorio, art song, and opera. He is the most significant composer for the organ since Johann Sebastian Bach.

Early Life

Olivier-Eugène-Prosper-Charles Messiaen was born in Avignon, France, on December 10, 1908, the son of parents well known in French literary circles. His mother was the poetess Cécile Sauvage, and his father, Pierre, was an English teacher respected for his critical translations of Shakespeare. Recognizing the young Messiaen's musical gifts (by eight he had taught himself piano), Pierre encouraged him with gifts of scores to Hector Berlioz's *Damnation of Faust* and Wolfgang Amadeus Mozart's *Don Giovanni*. After a move to Nantes in 1918, Messiaen, now ten years old, began formal studies in harmony with the local teacher Jehan de Gibon. Soon after the boy began his studies, Gibon presented Messiaen with the score to Claude Debussy's opera *Pelléas et Mélisande*. Later, the mature composer described that gift as "a real bombshell . . . probably the most decisive influence of my life."

In 1919, the family moved to Grenoble. In the fall of that year, Messiaen was enrolled in the Paris Conservatoire, where he studied under France's leading musicians (Maurice Dupré taught him organ and Paul Dukas tutored him in composition). The student flourished. In 1926, Messiaen took first prize in fugue and in 1928 first prize in piano accompaniment. Firsts in music history and composition followed in 1929 and 1930. The year of his prize in fugue also saw the appearance of his first publication, the organ work *Le Banquet céleste* (the heavenly banquet). In 1929, Messiaen's final complete year at the Conservatoire, he published a set of eight preludes for piano. While the preludes particularly showed the influence of Debussy, in both of these early publications the characteristics of Messiaen's mature style were present. Both used chromatic scales (or "modes") of the composer's own invention (as opposed to culturally received scales, such as G minor or D major). Both used nontraditional rhythms, Messiaen stretching note values in *Le Banquet céleste* to the point at which meter was lost within the six minute (but only twenty-five measure) piece. In both works, much of their interest and significance lay in Messiaen's musical exploitation of instrumental color. Finally, and here the preludes were somewhat atypical, aspects of Christianity sparked Messiaen's imagination and served as programmatic titles.

Life's Work

Messiaen left the Conservatoire in 1930, having won twice as many "firsts" as Debussy and with two publications already before the public. He was appointed principal organist at the Church of La Trinité (one of Paris' most important liturgical positions) in 1931. Teaching responsibilities at the École Normale Supérieure and at the Schola Cantorum were added five years later. In 1936, he married the violinist Claire Delbos (the dedicatee of his first song cycle, *Poèmes pour Mi*). A year later their son Pascal was born. Through these years, Messiaen composed for organ as well as for chamber ensembles and even for a new electronic instrument, the ondes martenot.

All of this work was broken off by World War II. Although thirty-one (and therefore beyond the reach of general conscription), Messiaen volunteered for the army, serving as a hospital attendant. Overtaken by the Germans near Nancy in June, 1940, the composer was imprisoned in a prisoner of war camp near Görlitz in Silesia. There in the prison camp, Messiaen wrote what was universally to be regarded as one of the century's most remarkable works, the *Quatuor pour la fin du temps* (quartet for the end of time). Finding a clarinetist, violinist, and cellist among his fellow prisoners, Messiaen wrote the piece for himself and this ensemble, premiering it before the five-thousand-member camp on January 15, 1941.

The quartet began the fully mature period of Messiaen's work. A highly evocative series of meditations upon the Apocalypse (its title has a double meaning, referring both to Revelations 10:5-6 and to Messiaen's own new rhythmic character), Messiaen here made extensive use of bird calls for the first time (the quartet's first movement, "Liturgie de Cristal," opens with the calls of a black bird on the clarinet and the nightingale on the flute). Herein Messiaen first used "nonretrogradable" rhythms, or complex rhythmic patterns that whether read from left to right or right to left remain the same. This kind of rhythmic device (and others derived from his studies of Hindu ragam) continued Messiaen's movement toward completely nonmetric rhythm first seen in *Le Banquet céleste*.

Repatriated in 1942, Messiaen returned to Paris, where he was appointed professor of harmony at the Conservatoire. During the next decades, he began to be seen as a leader of the avant garde, some of the next generation's leading composers seeking out his teaching in Paris and elsewhere (both Pierre Boulez and Karlheinz Stockhausen were his students). He continued to compose in the manner established in the *Quatuor pour le fin du temps*.

Those characteristics, however, began to burden many of Messiaen's listeners. His works' lengths and almost hyper-baroque textures offended musicians increasingly influenced by Anton von Webern's terse severity. The Christian themes and unabashed emotionalism of Messiaen's works seemed both hopelessly naïve and out of step with postwar materialism. For the first time since the brouhaha that had greeted Igor Stravinsky's *Rite of Spring* in 1913, the Parisians rioted at the premiere of Messiaen's *Trois Petites Liturgies* on April 21, 1945. The press followed the performance with a sustained, critical barrage.

While surprised by the critics' ferocity (one writer later called it a "dance of glory and death around Messiaen"), the composer appeared undisturbed. He followed *Trois Petites Liturgies* with even more challenging works, between 1944 and 1948 completing major pieces for piano, voice, and orchestra. A symphony was commissioned by Serge Koussevitzky for the Boston Symphony and was premiered by Leonard Bernstein on December 2, 1949. In this symphony, entitled *Turangalîla*, Messiaen continued his interest in Hindu music, both constructing its title from two Hindi words ("Lîla," meaning game, and "Turanga," meaning time) and employing again Hindu and symmetric rhythms. Messiaen was at his most adventurous in his 1949 piano work *Mode de valeurs et d'intensités*. Here he systematically ordered thirty-six pitches, twenty-four note values, twelve kinds of articulation, and seven dynamic levels. This kind of "total serialization," while only experimental for Messiaen, was to have a profound impact upon younger composers.

In 1943, when Messiaen had been privately teaching a class in analysis and composition, he met Yvonne Loriod. Impressed by her virtuosity, Messiaen wrote his major piano works of the period—*Visions de l'amen* (1943), *Reveil des oiseaux* (1953), and *Catalogue des oiseaux* (1958)—for her. Loriod and Messiaen were married in 1962, his first wife Claire having died three years earlier after a ten-year illness.

Messiaen's energies in the years 1960 to 1980 were channeled primarily into the creation of six huge ensemble compositions: *Chronochromie* (1961), *Couleurs de la cité céleste* (1963), *Et exspecto resurrectionem* (1964), *La Transfiguration de Notre Seigneur Jesus-Christ* (1969), *Des canyons aux étoiles* (1974), and *Saint François d'Assie* (1983). *Chronochromie* (literally "time-color") was a sixty-minute, seven-movement work for full orchestra with a greatly enlarged percussion section. Its sixth movement ("Epôde") was remarkable for its evocation of bird song performed by solo strings in eighteen individual parts. *Couleurs de la cité céleste* was premiered by Boulez in 1963, three years after *Chronochromie's* completion. It was another hour-long work but for an ensemble reduced from the earlier piece's heroic dimensions (thirteen winds and seven percussionists).

In 1964, Messiaen fulfulled a commission from the French government for a work memorializing the two worlds wars' dead with *Et exspecto resurrectionem*. This composition for large woodwind, brass, and percussion ensemble (the composer even required three different sets of gongs) was premiered the following year in Paris' St. Chappelle, with repeated performances throughout France. *La Transfiguration de Notre Seigneur Jesus-Christ* was begun in 1965 and premiered in Lisbon four years later. For the first time since the 1945 *Trois Petites Liturgies*, Messiaen returned to writing for chorus and solo singers. For the fourteen-movement oratorio, he drew texts from the Bible, Saint Thomas Aquinas' *Summa*, and from the Roman rite for the Feast of the Transfiguration. After a visit to Utah in 1970, Messiaen completed a twelve-movement orchestral piece, *Des canyons aux étoiles* (premiered in New York on November 20, 1974).

François d'Assie is Messiaen's only dramatic work. Commissioned by the Paris Opéra in 1975, Messiaen himself composed both the libretto and the score in a labor that lasted eight uninterrupted years. The resulting opera, although not without its detractors, was perhaps his masterpiece. A synopsis of his entire creative life, requiring extraordinary forces (a two-hundred-member chorus, three antiphonal ondes martenots, a huge orchestra, and a length of four and a half hours), it has received repeated performances since its Paris premier in 1983.

Summary

Although his work itself is not at all traditional, Olivier Messiaen's view of himself as a Catholic artist places him firmly within the tradition of Christians whose art served primarily theological and propagandistic purposes. Thus the anonymous sculptors of Chartres, Michelangelo, Heinrich Schütz, Bach, and Dante, are all Messiaen's forebears. Indeed, of nineteenth century composers, the one Messiaen most closely resembles is Anton Bruckner, although without that Austrian's provincialisms.

As a youth Messiaen did not participate in the cynical witticisms of Francis Poulenc and Darius Milhaud. Interested in Indian music, he became neither an ethnomusicologist nor an Eastern mystic. Although his work was crucial to the development of totally serialized music, Messiaen's work was never an exercise in the cerebral. One of the era's most important teachers, he founded no "school," nor were his students united by any particular characteristic. Thus, while his aesthetic can be seen as a continuation of at least a fifteen-hundred-year-old tradition, within the twentieth century Messiaen is unique. Stylistically, his work stands apart from any of the movements that characterized (and polarized) modern music.

Bibliography

Griffiths, Paul. *Olivier Messiaen and the Music of Time*. Ithaca, N.Y.: Cornell University Press, 1985. A significant and highly detailed study of Messiaen largely intended for the specialist but useful also to the general reader.

Hold, Thomas. "Messiaen's Birds." *Music and Letters* 3 (1971): 113. An important essay on the composer's quotation and employment of bird calls.

Johnson, Robert Sherlaw. *Messiaen.* Berkeley: University of California Press, 1975. A thorough but dated study of Messiaen's work. Johnson includes charts that are helpful in untangling the relationships in some of Messiaen's larger compositions.

Machlis, Joseph. *Introduction to Contemporary Music.* 2d ed. New York: W. W. Norton, 1979. Machlis is one of his generation's best writers on music. A man of broad cultural understanding (he is the translator of at least sixteen operas), he is able to clearly draw this century's significant lines of musical changes. Helpful also is his concluding "dictionary," which presents brief biographies of several hundred contemporary composers, including Messiaen.

Messiaen, Olivier. *The Technique of My Musical Language.* Translated by John Satterfield. Reprint. New York: American Biographical Service, 1987. Any study of Messiaen should begin with this apologia for his musical style. Messiaen's frequently poetic descriptions of his ideas are of particular interest to the nonspecialist reader.

Nichols, Roger. *Messiaen.* 2d ed. New York: Oxford University Press, 1986. The best introduction to the composer in English. Highly readable and sympathetic to Messiaen's work, Nichols provides a vivid portrait of the artist and his art in his eighty-seven-page text.

Michael Linton

VSEVOLOD YEMILYEVICH MEYERHOLD
Karl Theodor Kasimir Meyergold

Born: February 9, 1874; Penza, Russia
Died: February 2, 1940; Moscow, U.S.S.R.
Areas of Achievement: Theater and acting
Contribution: Meyerhold departed from the powerful naturalistic influences of Constantin Stanislavsky and the Moscow Art Theatre to experiment with more abstract forms of theater. Representing the other side of the universal duality in theater—expressionistic versus naturalistic—he dared to experiment with an ingenious stage language of his own invention and devised the constructivist principles of set design and the bio-mechanical approach to actor training.

Early Life
Born Karl Theodor Kasimir Meyergold and of German parentage, Vsevolod Yemilyevich Meyerhold converted to the orthodox faith and adopted Russian nationality in 1895, thereby avoiding conscription into the Prussian army. In Moscow ostensibly to study law, he began to frequent the theater, where he was often disappointed by the mediocrity and pointlessness of the fare. In 1896, he joined the Moscow Philharmonic Society's drama school, auditioning for the well-known Vladimir Nemirovich-Danchenko with a speech imitated in gesture and style from Stanislavsky's Othello. On graduation, he was invited to become a member of the Moscow Art Theatre, which had been formed by Nemirovich-Danchenko and Stanislavsky in 1898.

From the outset, Meyerhold's work at the Moscow Art Theatre came in conflict with the central mission of Stanislavsky and Nemirovich-Danchenko. He believed that he had discovered the limitations of the realistic acting style and held strong opinions against the aesthetic value of naturalism in the production of such playwrights as Anton Chekhov and Henrik Ibsen. His leadership of the Theatre-Studio, a branch of the Moscow Art Theatre, was the beginning of his departure from the tradition (however young) of naturalism.

For four years, Meyerhold was a member of the Moscow Art Theatre's acting company, playing some eighteen roles in a wide range of characterizations. His gaunt, angular face prevented his complete metamorphosis into the more romantic fictive characters, although he did play Treplev in Chekhov's *Chayka* (1896; *The Sea Gull*, 1909). According to his notes during these four years, he was even then in search of new forms; his first attempts at a stylized approach to the stage came in 1905, with *La Mort de Tintagiles* (pb. 1894; *The Death of Tintagiles*, 1899), by Maurice Maeterlinck, a Belgian playwright writing what Meyerhold termed "The New Theatre," a passive, actor-oriented, nonhistrionic dramatization of a silent moment in the tragedy of quotidian life.

A brief association with Vera Komissarzhevskaya's Dramatic Theatre in St. Petersburg from 1906 to 1908 served as a transition for Meyerhold from the Moscow Art Theatre to the less protective environments of commercial theater. Meyerhold's apprenticeship ended in 1908, when he accepted a position at the St. Petersburg Imperial Theatres, where, from 1908 to the October Revolution of 1917, he was to explore the possibilities of his unique theatrical vision in the unlikely venues of commercial enterprise, working at a series of "official" St. Petersburg theaters.

Life's Work

"The essence of stage rhythm is the antithesis of real, everyday life," declared Meyerhold as early as 1909, referring to his production of Richard Wagner's opera *Tristan and Isolde* at the Mariinsky Theatre but stating at the same time one of the principles on which he built his theatrical style. Even during the years of his commercial acting successes, Meyerhold experimented in the private theaters of St. Petersburg, especially the intimate theater style of The Interlude House, run by a fellowship of actors and artists. In order to avoid contractual complications, he adopted the pseudonym Dr. Dapertutto, under which name he created many of his most imaginative stage pieces. His contribution to an evening of pieces in October, 1910, which he called *Columbine's Scarf*, was a haunting, chillingly grotesque pantomime based on Arthur Schnitzler's *Der Schleir der Pierrette* (1910; the veil of Pierrette) but turned the romantic story into a tragedy. It was typical of Meyerhold's attempts at this time to treat traditional stage literature with a new interpretation.

By 1912, Meyerhold was splitting his theater career between a hectic acting and directing schedule at the Mariinsky Opera in St. Petersburg and a company of actors and artists in Terioki, under his artistic leadership, living in a communal environment. He still had time to write and publish his theories on theater in 1913. The smaller theater gave him several opportunities to experiment with a minimalist stage set, almost devoid of realistic setting, more a platform and background for action than an integral part of the play itself. These attempts solidified his theories about the function of the stage set, not as a photographic reproduction of real space but as an environment for the machinery of the stage action to be magnified, moved from site to site, and explored.

While his experiments were being well received in the smaller theater community, his "extravagances" in the larger theater were beginning to be criticized by a more and more vocal "populist" political body. Meyerhold began to be characterized in the press as decadent and megalomaniacal. Scholars regard this production (*Masquerade*) as the culmination of Meyerhold's St. Petersburg career; it was to be revived repeatedly after the Revolution by Meyerhold himself as well as by his successors.

The 1917 Revolution transferred all artistic endeavors into state control. Theater, the most public art, saw many changes, but Meyerhold's own "reforms" continued to progress as a kind of parallel to the revolutionary changes around him. He started a theater school in what was now called Petrograd, under the Theater Department of the Commissariat of Enlightenment. The real question was how the repertory would change with the new political overview; after World War I, theater, according to the *Petrograd Pravda*, needed to be "born of that same Revolution, which we all look upon as our own great mother." Meyerhold's futurist ideas, in tandem with Italian theater developments around the same time, were received with mixed reaction from the press. It soon became clear that Meyerhold's theatrical activities would always be viewed as a political statement, interpreted by each side (the conservative reformists and the radicalists) according to its own lights.

Meyerhold enjoyed the strongest support for the juxtaposition of his art form and the Communist Party ideology when, in 1921, he was appointed director of the State Higher Theatre Workshops in Moscow. It was a theater school, complete with courses in history and theory. By now "Master," Meyerhold could formulate his acting theories into an actual course of study. A highly physical approach to acting, his "biomechanics" grew out of a series of physical fitness exercises, coupled with stage combat techniques. Awarded the title of "People's Artist" in 1923 for twenty years of service to the theater, Meyerhold was free to examine the productive results of long years of experimental uncertainty in a series of highly publicized productions matching his acting theories to his staging style in a theatre in Moscow named after himself.

In 1926, probably the height of Meyerhold's career, the play by Nikolai Gogol entitled *Revizor* (1836; *The Inspector General*, 1890) finally brought together all the potential of Meyerhold's theories in a highly successful stage production, seen today as a model of alternative theatrical presentation. Too controversial, however, was a play by Sergei Tretiakov whose thesis was contradictory to the Soviet "line" on the importance (or nonimportance) of family life; this and similar experiments eventually were to undermine Meyerhold's popularity with the bureaucracies under whose authority he worked. On the other hand, Meyerhold and the playwright Vladimir Mayakovsky were particularly productive partners during this period, working together in some ten works, including *Klop* (1929; *The Bed-bug*, 1931) and *Banya (1930; The Bathhouse*, 1963).

The Soviet government, entering the period of repressive measures that is now called the Stalin era, was not always happy with Meyerhold's view of the world as expressed on stage. Meyerhold himself, in what can only be seen as a heroic defiance of good sense, continued to insist on the autonomy of the artist over the wishes of the social system, refusing to acknowledge any demands of the state to use his stage as a propaganda platform and ignoring the growing tensions and the clear signs of his incipient disfavor. In 1939, the government-controlled press had damned Meyerhold's "decadent" work, primarily for failure to reduce his chaotic productions down to the Socialist Realism seen by the government as the proper sphere for theater. An anti-intellectual bias was working against him from 1930 to his death in 1940. Claims that he had ruined his theater were nothing more than excuses for closing it down in 1939. A victim of the paranoia of the Soviet government on the eve of World War II, Meyerhold was arrested shortly thereafter and shot in 1940.

Summary

Over a long career, Vsevolod Yemilyevich Meyerhold established a distinct ideology of theatrical presentation characterized by rapidly changing "loci" simply suggested by a montage of set alterations on a central "plateau," or general acting area (sometimes referred to as "cinefication"), a method of physical preparation for actors (called biomechanics) complementing or rivaling that of Stanislavsky, and a style of visual spectacle celebrating the rise of industrial and technological invention, called "constructivism," that today informs virtually all scenic design. His mature work, itself iconoclastic and irreverent, in so many ways the theatrical equivalent of the Bolshevik Revolution and its ideologies, and in other ways antithetical to the Socialist Realism embraced by its less imaginative political leaders, is responsible for the strength of the continuing combative dichotomy that still gives live performance its viability in an age of mass media: the dialectic between theater as hyperrealization of actual life and theater as an independent language whose vocabulary is larger than mere representational photographic replication and closer to the abstract spirit of theater handed down to Western civilization from the Greeks.

In the wide-ranging reexamination of aesthetic principles begun after World War II, modern theater practitioners found themselves more indebted to Meyerhold's vision and daring and more comfortable with the stage vocabulary that he had designed and implemented than his Soviet executioners could have imagined; Bertolt Brecht, the East German director of presentational, propagandistic, "alienation" theater, acknowledged a considerable debt to Meyerhold's innovations, as have such highly regarded modern experimental directors as Jerzy Grotowski and Peter Brook. In fact, every experimenter in theatrical forms from 1950 on owes a debt to Meyerhold, who turned his back on the invidious and ultimately self-defeating naturalism of his peers and tutors to discover theater's unique power to communicate directly.

Bibliography

Braun, Edward. *The Theatre of Meyerhold: Revolution on the Modern Stage.* New York: Drama Book Specialists, 1979. An important critical biography and a thorough examination of Meyerhold's entire career, taking advantage of Braun's thirteen years of study on the same figure. Deliberately avoids comparisons with contemporaries and successors, concentrating instead on the details of Meyerhold's own contributions. Includes many illustrations, strong notes, a bibliography, and an index.

Eaton, Katherine Bliss. *The Theater of Meyerhold and Brecht.* Contributions in Drama and Theatre Studies 19. Westport, Conn.: Greenwood Press, 1985. Defends the idea that the main source of inspiration was Meyerhold. The interchange of ideas between Germany and Russia, an exchange that went both ways, culminated in Brecht's visit to Russia in 1936, three years into his own exile and three years before Meyerhold's arrest and execution. A sturdy critical comparison, leaning slightly toward an overenthusiastic appraisal of Meyerhold. Includes a bibliography and an index.

Hoover, Marjorie L. *Meyerhold: The Art of Conscious Theater.* Amherst: University of Massachusetts Press, 1974. A full-length scholarly study coinciding with the one hundredth anniversary of his birth, and, excepting Braun's compilation of primary material, the first critical account in English of Meyerhold's work.

Meyerhold, V. E. *Meyerhold on Theatre.* Edited and translated by Edward Braun. New York: Hill & Wang, 1969. The first, and for years the only, study of Meyerhold in English, these excerpts from his theoretical writings are woven together with Braun's commentaries to present a unified documentary record that validates his respected reputation in Europe and the United States. Includes more than fifty illustrations.

Rudnitsky, Konstantin. *Meyerhold the Director.* Translated by George Petrov. Ann Arbor, Mich.: Ardis Press, 1981. Generated from archives hidden by the filmmaker Sergei Eisenstein, Meyerhold's former student, and used here for the first time, this authoritative study concentrates on the artist as a director who worked in many contradictory styles. The more than two hundred illustrations include heretofore unpublished production stills and diagrams of Meyerhold's stage blocking. Includes an index.

Sayler, Oliver M. *Inside the Moscow Art Theatre.* Reprint. Westport, Conn.: Greenwood Press, 1970. For years, since its original publication in 1925, the definitive study of the Moscow Art Theatre, this report is interesting for comparisons between the traditional realism of Stanislavsky and the "cubist," "Futurist," "theoretical" Meyerhold, who is mentioned only five times, always as a foil for Sayler's real subject. Index.

Schechner, Richard. *Environmental Theater.* New York: Hawthorne, 1973. As a highly visible successor of the experimental styles of previous "anti-illusion" stage directors, Schechner pays homage to Meyerhold's overwhelming influence by citing whole passages of his theories throughout this study of the Performance Group. A clear example of how Meyerhold's work broke ground for the next generations of presentational theater practitioners. Bibliography and index.

Thomas J. Taylor

ANDRÉ MICHELIN and ÉDOUARD MICHELIN

André Michelin

Born: January 16, 1853; Paris, France
Died: April 4, 1931; Paris, France

Édouard Michelin

Born: June 23, 1859; Clermont-Ferrand, France
Died: August 25, 1940; Orcines, Puy-de-Dôme, France
Areas of Achievement: Business, industry, invention, and technology
Contribution: The Michelin brothers pioneered the use of pneumatic tires on automobiles and were also leaders in the development of the radial-ply tire as well as steel-reinforced tire construction. They founded a motorist's travel guide company that produces handbooks for numerous tourist destinations throughout the world.

Early Life

André Jules Michelin was born in Paris in 1853. During childhood, he showed a talent for art and, on completion of elementary school near Clermont-Ferrand, entered the Académie des Beaux-Arts in Paris to study architecture. He left before obtaining his degree to learn the art of map-making at the French Ministry of the Interior. André subsequently opened several shops in Paris, where he produced and sold locks for wrought-iron gates and metal picture frames of his own design.

Édouard was born six years after his brother in Clermont-Ferrand and also went to Paris, where he pursued painting at the École des Beaux-Arts and opened a studio in the Montparnasse area of Paris. Édouard painted portraits, landscapes, and biblical and battle scenes for sale and began developing a talent for free-hand drawing.

Art was not to be the lifelong vocation of the Édouard brothers. Édouard returned to Clermont-Ferrand in 1888 to assist with a small rubber business. The enterprise had been started in the mid-nineteenth century by a maternal grandfather and a cousin who was related by marriage to Charles MacIntosh, the Scottish chemist who experimented with the rubberization of textiles and whose name became synonymous with raincoats. The shop had originally produced farm equipment, but later, as a result of the indirect association with MacIntosh, added rubber products such as balls, tubes, valves, and elastic bands. When the founders of the business died, it passed to the Michelin brothers, and their careers focused increasingly away from Paris toward Clermont-Ferrand.

Life's Work

The first pneumatic bicycle tires were produced by the English in 1888 and facilitated a considerably more agreeable ride than the earlier solid rubber and iron-clad types. Yet because the tire was glued to the rim, blow-outs were time-consuming to repair, severely inhibiting the widespread application of pneumatics to wheeled travel. The Michelins' first contact with pneumatic tires came with a cycling Englishman who brought his vehicle to the shop in Clermont-Ferrand for a puncture repair. The task took hours, largely because of the time required for the glue to dry. Édouard recognized the potential of pneumatics and began developing a removable bicycle tire that could be changed in minutes. By 1891, he had perfected such a system and entered the Paris-Brest-Paris 750-mile bicycle race to test and publicize the demountable pneumatic tire. The Michelins' tire was the only one of its type among the 211 participants, and their rider won the race by an eight-hour lead. In the following year, more than ten thousand bicycles were equipped with Michelin tires, and the company became the unquestioned leader in the bicycle tire business.

During the mid-1890's, France was a front-runner in the incipient world automotive industry. A major obstacle to the development of that industry lay in speeds. Automobile tires, which at that time were either ironclad or solid rubber, tended to come apart at speeds exceeding thirteen miles per hour. Even at lower velocities, the ride remained less than pleasant. André Michelin rode as a passenger in the 1894 motor car race from Paris to Rouen, an experience that persuaded him that the future of the automobile industry lay with the more comfortable and quiet pneumatic tire. The Michelin brothers pioneered the application of pneumatic tires to automobiles, testing and introducing them in the 745-mile Paris-Bordeaux-Paris race in June, 1895. Of the forty-six participants who entered the race, the Michelin car survived the race with nine others, demonstrating that the demountable pneumatic tire offered a viable option to its ironclad and solid rubber predecessors. By 1896, more than three hundred taxis in the city of Paris ran on air-filled Michelins.

André and Édouard continued improvements on tires, testing innovations in subsequent races. By 1901, an electrically driven car on Michelin tires had set a record of sixty-two miles per hour. Two years later, tires with anti-skid treads were introduced, and, in 1906, Michelin became one of the first companies in Europe to market an automobile tire with a detachable rim. During 1908, Michelin experimented with the principle of dual-pneumatic tire sets for trucks, and, after four years of experimentation, the first Michelin truck tires appeared on the market. In 1923, low-pressure balloon tires were introduced, providing a smoother ride, increased load capacity, higher speed capability, and longer tire life. The company began research in 1929 on the application of rubber tires to railroad travel. In order to support the increased weight associated with railcars, the Michelin Company augmented the tires with steel bands. Experience with rail tires gave the firm a considerable lead over other manufacturers in the application of steel reinforcements, and the Michelin Company eventually produced the first steel-belted radial tires for automobiles in 1948. Another by-product of the research into suitable pneumatic rail tires was the Micheline, a lightweight railcar produced in several models by the Michelin Company. The Micheline inaugurated service between Paris and Deauville in 1931, achieving an average speed of sixty-five miles per hour. By 1938, the Micheline averaged five million miles of service annually. Because of the heightened traction problems associated with the use of rubber on steel tracks, new research into tread designs was undertaken, resulting in enhanced wet traction tires.

Apart from tires, the Michelin brothers contributed most significantly to automobile travel by a series of guidebooks to assist motorists. In 1900, André added a road map department to the business, and later the company began publishing a travel guide that amplified the maps with listings of gas stations, repair shops, and Michelin tire dealers. Ultimately, hotels and restaurants were included with quality ratings, and Michelin Guides evolved into the most well-known and widely used handbooks of automobile touring. In 1908, André created a Car Traveler's Information Bureau in Paris, which furnished itineraries and road information, and further promoted automobile travel in France by embarking on a campaign to number routes and by donating road signs and posts. In 1927, the brothers financed the placement of concrete pillars along the Paris-Nice route featuring letters formed of enameled lava, which could be seen from a distance day or night. The French government subsequently approved these signs for use elsewhere in France.

The Michelin brothers also instituted progressive practices in employee relations. In 1901, they established a health center that provided medical care to Michelin employees at a fraction of the normal cost. The company later provided a maternity hospital, an anti-tuberculosis dispensary, a ninety-bed sanatorium, a sixty-bed hospital, and a dental clinic. The brothers began building settlements of low-rent housing for workers in 1909. Swimming pools, theaters, playing fields, gardens, and cinemas were added over the years, and eventually there were seventeen settlements totaling 865 buildings that contain 3,698 apartments available to employees of Michelin enterprises.

Édouard recognized early in the company's development that workers in the shop understood obstacles to tire improvement best. Employee participation in problem-solving and innovation was encouraged from the outset, and Édouard praised and rewarded workers who challenged his opinions and decisions for the betterment of the company.

The Michelin penchant for innovation extended to the nascent aviation industry as well. The brothers encouraged distance and speed achievements in French aircraft development by offering a 100,000 franc prize to the first pilot to set a speed record flying a predetermined route that circled the Arc de Triomphe. André was particularly interested in the potential military applications of aviation, working before World War I to persuade France that its military future lay in air power and, after the war, to motivate the French and their allies to deal with the threat of aerochemical attack by Germany.

Summary

André Michelin died on April 4, 1931, and was followed by his younger brother, Édouard, on August 25, 1940. The outstanding contribution of the Michelin brothers to modern transportation derived from their ability to anticipate the future of the automobile industry and to create the breakthroughs that would make travel safe, convenient, and accessible for the average person.

The company founded by André and Édouard continued under the direction of younger Michelin family members. In the early 1950's, the firm became a holding company, and by the 1970's the Michelin enterprise employed more than 100,000 workers in facilities throughout Europe, in Africa, and in the United States. Michelin is known for its tight family control, its secretive management and marketing practices, and its assiduous guarding of technical know-how. The company has always been and remains among the top world producers of tires.

Bibliography

Coates, Austin. *The Commerce in Rubber: The First 250 Years.* New York: Oxford University Press, 1987. Coates's chapter on the advent of rubber products in Europe includes a respectable treatment of the early years of the professional lives of the Michelin brothers, extending through their first application of pneumatic tires to the motor car.

Day, John. *The Bosch Book of the Motor Car.* New York: St. Martin's Press, 1976. Day's chapter entitled "Wheels, Tyres, and Brakes" offers a concise description of the development of plys, treads, and detachable pneumatic rims, and the Michelin contribution to these developments.

Levy-LeBoyer, Maurice. "Innovation and Business Strategies in Nineteenth and Twentieth Century France." In *Enterprise and Entrepreneurs in Nineteenth and Twentieth Century France*, edited by Edward C. Carter et al. Baltimore: Johns Hopkins University Press, 1976. LeBoyer provides a concise but quite sufficient description of the dynamics affecting the economic environment into which French entrepreneurs came during the early years of the Michelin tire business.

Norbye, Jan P. *The Michelin Magic.* Bridge Summit, Pa.: Tab Books, 1982. This volume provides an excellent history of the Michelin Company from its inception until the early 1980's. It includes considerable information on the lives of André and Édouard Michelin and their contributions to the tire industry. This is the outstanding resource for the story of Michelin research and development.

Setright, L. J. K. *Automobile Tyres*. London: Chapman and Hall, 1972. Setright discusses all aspects of tires, including the history of their development and the Michelin role in that process. The focus of this work is on the modern legacy of tire research.

Margaret B. Denning

DARIUS MILHAUD

Born: September 4, 1892; Aix-en-Provence, France
Died: June 22, 1974; Geneva, Switzerland
Area of Achievement: Music
Contribution: Perhaps the most famous composer of the mythical "Les Six," Milhaud was undoubtedly the most prolific, his published works running to nearly 450. He did highly original work in such areas as polytonality and percussion music. His best work is characterized by a Gallic lyricism.

Early Life

Born on September 4, 1892, in Aix-en-Provence, France, Darius Milhaud belonged to a well-to-do Jewish family for centuries settled in Aix and in close touch with the region's cultural life. His father was an amateur pianist, his mother an amateur singer. Piano lessons from his father were followed at age seven by violin lessons from a former Paris Conservatoire prizewinner, Léo Bruquier. In 1902, Milhaud was enrolled at the local *lycée*, where he distinguished himself academically. By the time he was twelve, he was playing second violin in a string quartet with his teacher, taking harmony lessons, and writing a violin sonata. Léo Latil and Armand Lunel, both promising young writers, were his closest friends; later, Milhaud was strongly influenced by friendship with such writers as Francis Jammes, Paul Claudel, and Jean Cocteau. The many friends he made among writers and painters would influence him as much, if not more, than his contemporaries in music.

After passing his baccalaureate examinations at the age of sixteen, Milhaud entered the Paris Conservatoire primarily as a violin student, though he soon came to see composing as his true vocation. In addition to taking the orchestral class of Paul Dukas, he studied harmony with Xavier Leroux and composition with André Gédalge. Milhaud began to travel widely at this time, a habit he would continue throughout his life, despite a severely disabling case of rheumatoid arthritis, which eventually kept him in a wheelchair. He visited Spain in 1911 and Germany in 1913.

Life's Work

Milhaud began composing his first major works while at the Conservatoire. In 1910, he began work on an opera, *La Brebis égarée*, to a libretto by Jammes, for whom he had the opportunity to play and sing the first act. Beginning in 1913, he was engaged in writing the incidental music to Claudel's *Protée*; he composed three different versions of this music during the next six years as he tried to suit it to changing plans for production. The year 1913 also found Milhaud at work on *Agamemnon*, the first of an operatic trilogy based on Claudel's translation of Aeschylus' *Orestia*. He avoided the traditional techniques of incidental music in this work; instead, he employed a novel type of transition from speech to song, one he would also employ in the other two parts of the trilogy.

Milhaud was declared unfit for service on medical grounds when World War I broke out in August of 1914. Returning to the Conservatoire, he was awarded a prize for his two-violin sonata—the only prize, he noted in his 1949 autobiography, that he ever won. In 1915, Milhaud composed *Les Choëphores*, the second part of the *Orestia* trilogy. This work is especially notable for its utilization of a speaking chorus with percussion and for the introduction of polytonality—the simultaneous use of two or more keys—which would remain a distinctive feature of Milhaud's style. In two scenes of *Les Choëphores*, a woman narrator declaims the text against a backdrop of pitchless percussion while the chorus whistles, groans, and shrieks.

In the autumn of 1916, Milhaud entered the propaganda wing of the government; given military standing, he was assigned to the photographic service. Shortly afterward, Claudel, then better known as a diplomat than as a poet and newly appointed ambassador to Brazil, invited Milhaud to accompany him to Rio de Janeiro as his secretary. In 1917, Milhaud began work on the third part of the *Orestia* trilogy, *Les Euménides* (completed in 1922). The sights and native music of Brazil, where he would remain for two years, made an indelible impression on Milhaud. The ballet *L'Homme et son désir* (1918), the two dance suites *Saudades do Brasil* (1920-1921), and random parts of many later works all bear witness to the enormous and productive impact that Milhaud's Brazilian sojourn had upon his work. An encounter with the dancer Vaslav Nijinsky had led to *L'Homme et son désir*, but Nijinsky was no longer able to dance by the time it was completed.

When he returned to Paris in November of 1918, Milhaud was drawn into the Cocteau circle of writers, artists, and composers. Reviewing a concert that included songs by Louis Durey and Milhaud's fourth string quartet, Henri Collet dubbed these two, along with Georges Auric, Arthur Honegger, Francis Poulenc, and Germaine Tailleferre, "Les Six," apparently an arbitrarily chosen French counterpart to the Russian "Five." Their differences in temperament and aesthetic outlook precluded them from working together as a unit for very long. Nevertheless, this rather ill-assorted group decided to capitalize on the "Les Six" designation before eventually going their several ways. They collaborated on a Cocteau ballet, *Les Mariés de la tour Eiffel* (1921), without Durey, and staged a two-year series of Saturday *soirées*. Milhaud wrote the music for another Cocteau ballet, *Le Bœuf sur le toit* (1919), named after a popular Brazilian song and produced on a program that included Erik Satie's *Pièces montées*, Auric's *Fox-Trot*, and Poulenc's *Cocardes*. The press found it all very amusing, and the following year, it was put on as a part of a music-hall show at London's Coliseum.

Milhaud's collaborations with "Les Six" and works of his own such as *Le boeuf sur le toit* soon caused the music public to brand him as an unprincipled and flippant exploiter of fashionable music curiosities. His standing was by no means redeemed by the *Rite of Spring*-like reception of the first performances of the *Protée* symphonic suite in 1920 and of the *Cinq études* for piano and orchestra in 1921. The long-postponed *L'Homme et son désir*, danced by the Ballet Suedois in 1921, occasioned a similar uproar. Even a relatively conventional piece as *La Brebis égarée* caused a riot when it was staged in 1923 at the Opéra-Comique. To make matters worse, critics refused to take seriously, as Milhaud intended them to be, the song cycles *Machines agricoles* (1919), composed of extracts from a catalog of agricultural machinery set to music, and *Catalogue de fleurs* (1920), musical settings to poems by Lucien Daudet inspired by a florist's catalog.

Billy Arnold and his band provided Milhaud's first exposure to jazz when Milhaud visited London in 1920 for a performance of *Le Bœuf sur le toit*. He soon began to steep himself in all of the American popular music he could find. His friends Clément Doucet and Jean Wiener played a variety of transatlantic blues and ragtime imports. In 1922, Milhaud embarked on a tour of the United States. In addition to making his podium debut as conductor of the Philadelphia Orchestra for a program he chose, appearing as a pianist, and lecturing at various colleges, he was taken to Harlem to hear jazz firsthand. His announcement to reporters that jazz was the American music that most stimulated him became front-page news. Fired by his exposure to authentic black jazz, Milhaud composed the ballet *La Création du monde* (1923), which is certainly one of his masterpieces.

Milhaud continued to travel restlessly during the early 1920's; in addition to the United States, he visited Italy, Sardinia, Palestine, Turkey, and Russia. Part of this travel involved his honeymoon; he had married his cousin, Madeline, an actress. *La Création du monde* was followed in 1924 by two more ballets: *Salade* and *Le Train Bleu*. *Salade* eventually became *Le Carnaval d'Aix* for piano and orchestra. In 1925, Milhaud completed the comic opera *Esther de Carprentras*, which was commissioned by the Princess de Polignac, the heiress to the Singer Sewing Machine fortune. Also in 1925, he completed *Les Malheurs d'Orphée*, with a libretto by Lunel. This was the first of several chamber operas that were counterparts to his six chamber symphonies composed between 1917 and 1923. Relatively short in duration, each is scored for a minimum of instrumentalists and singers.

Christophe Colomb, the most imposing collaboration between Milhaud and Claudel, was completed in 1928. Partly expressionistic and partly symbolic, it is an opera on a vast scale. It contains references to the Wagnerian leitmotif, the medieval mystery play, and the Greek chorus. An offstage orchestra, forty-five vocal soloists, numerous nonsinging actors, and a huge chorus were necessary for its execution. The opera was successfully produced in Berlin in 1930—complete with film inserts—but it would not be taken up again for thirty years. Almost every facet of Milhaud's musical personality can be found in this work. The same concentrated musical vitality is not to be found in his later large-scale stage works.

Christophe Colomb was quickly followed by another ambitious opera, *Maximilien*, which was completed in 1930 and staged in Paris in 1932. In 1929, Milhaud had also begun a career as a writer of film scores. He would eventually write more than twenty-five, but none of them was a major success. In 1932, Milhaud also returned to writing incidental music for the theater, eventually providing scores for thirty-odd dramas.

By the 1930's, Milhaud had attained international prominence and respect. He was regularly asked to appear at big music festivals, world's fairs, and other important occasional events. Continuing to combine frequent composition with extensive traveling during the 1930's, Milhaud often appeared as both conductor and pianist at, for example, the Florence and Venice music festivals. He participated in a congress of music critics convened by the government of Portugal in 1932. The year 1937 saw Milhaud making a number of contributions to the International Exposition, including music for Claudel's *Fête de la musique*.

Milhaud had suffered bouts of illness on several occasions during his travels. Always notably overweight, he began to suffer increasingly from rheumatoid arthritis. In an effort to relieve his pain, Milhaud tried such things as acupuncture and faith healing in addition to consulting conventional physicians. Nothing worked, and he was doomed to suffer pain, which was often severe, for the rest of his life. While he was ailing in 1930, Milhaud's son Daniel was born.

Milhaud was bedridden at home in Provence during the first year of World War II. After the fall of Paris, he and his wife realized that they had to leave France. Reaching New York in July of 1940, Milhaud and his wife, after recuperating at the home of friends, bought a second-hand automobile and drove cross-country to Oakland, California, where Milhaud was to teach at Mills College. He taught there for the next thirty-one years.

Before fleeing France, Milhaud had begun the first of a series of twelve symphonies for full orchestra. Of these, No. 3 (1946) is a choral hymn of thanksgiving for victory, No. 4 (1947) is an epic of the 1848 Revolution in Europe, and No. 8 (1957) is a portrait of the Rhone River. Milhaud was seriously ill during 1946, but, by the end of the summer of 1947, he was well enough to return to France. There, he suffered a relapse and was forced to spend much of his time indoors. After August of 1947, despite indifferent health, he combined his post at Mills College with that of professor of composition at the Paris Conservatoire. Among his successful pupils were Morton Subotnick, Steven Reich, Dave Brubeck, Howard Brubeck, William Bolcom, Ben Johnston, Seymour Shifrin, and Betsy Jolas. Together with his wife Madeline, he became a prime mover at the music school connected with the summer festival at Aspen, Colorado.

During the latter part of his career, Milhaud received many commissions and composed as prolifically as before. In 1952, he composed the opera *David*, with a libretto by Lunel, for the Festival of Israel in honor of the three-thousandth anniversary of King David's founding of Jerusalem. Milhaud made a special journey to Israel as part of his preparation for this work. In spite of his ill health, he continued an active schedule of composing and teaching until long after his seventieth birthday, which was marked by a number of new recordings and enthusiastic celebrations in France. Ill health finally forced him to resign his post at Mills College and move to Geneva in 1971. Tribute was paid to him in Brussels, Aix, Rome, Nice, and elsewhere on his eightieth birthday. His last work was *Ani maamin, un chant perdu et retrouvé*, a cantata written for the 1973 Festival of Israel. Milhaud died in Geneva on June 22, 1974.

Summary

Darius Milhaud composed his most enduring works while he was still a comparatively young man. Undoubtedly, his best work was done by the beginning of World War II. After the war, the distinct decline in quality, if not in quantity, may be attributed in part to increasing age, infirmities, and professional commitments. Nevertheless, the real cause of this decline was the war, which cut him off from one of the two primary sources of his inspiration—the Provençal landscape of France and its popular music (the other source of his inspiration being his Jewish heritage). Milhaud's unselfconscious and spontaneous utilization of folk materials give his best work a freshness and an element of Mediterranean lyricism that is conspicuously absent elsewhere. As a folklorist, Milhaud successfully crossed the borderline between popular culture and high art.

In Milhaud's Provençal landscapes, no less than in those of Paul Cézanne, there is the imprint of the familiar features of the Provençal scene: the dry air, the harsh light, the jagged shape of rocks and trees, and the noisy blend of colors. Both Milhaud and Cézanne achieved a remarkable combination of earthy solidity and rustic simplicity. This achievement would not have been possible in Milhaud's case were it not for the new dimension of polytonality that he added to the harmonic language of his time. As he saw it, polytonality was a melodic, tonal antidote to the disintegration of the diatonic system. It was not an end in itself, but rather a means of creating the unique atmosphere in which Milhaud created his best music, in which he captured the Mediterranean spirit of Provençal better than any other composer.

Bibliography

Bolcom, William. "Reminiscences of Darius Milhaud." *Musical Newsletter* 7 (Summer, 1977): 3-11. An affectionate memoir by one of Milhaud's students, who was later an important composer in his own right.

Brody, Elaine. *Paris: The Musical Kaleidoscope, 1870-1925*. New York: George Braziller, 1987. This excellent study chronicles an important chapter in French musical history. Particularly good on the growth of a specifically French musical nationalism and on the new importance of ballet and its function as a focus for artists, writers, musicians, and impresarios.

Collaer, Paul. *Darius Milhaud*. San Francisco: San Francisco Press, 1988. Edited and translated by Jane Hohfeld Galante. This work is valuable for its complete catalog of Milhaud's works, editions, discography, writings, and translations.

Harding, James. *The Ox on the Roof: Scenes from Musical Life in Paris in the Twenties*. New York: St. Martin's Press, 1972. In this book about "Les Six," Harding maintains that the group, even though it did not found a school or stimulate disciples, contributed much to the musical flavor of the 1920's.

Milhaud, Darius. *Notes Without Music*. Edited by Rollo H. Myers. Translated by Donald Evans. London: Dennis Dobson, 1952. On the first page of this autobiography, Milhaud proclaims the mainsprings of his musical inspiration: He is a Frenchman from Provence and a Jew in religion.

Palmer, Christopher. *Darius Milhaud*. London, 1976. The standard treatment in English of Milhaud and his work.

L. Moody Simms, Jr.

JOAN MIRÓ

Born: April 20, 1893; Barcelona, Spain
Died: December 25, 1983; Palma, Majorca, Spain
Area of Achievement: Art
Contribution: The work of Miró, Spanish painter, sculptor, and ceramist, is acclaimed for its highly individualistic style, abstract as well as figurative, and is characterized by its vivacious fantasy. Many critics regard Miró as the greatest artist of the Surrealist movement.

Early Life

Born in Barcelona, Joan Miró was the first son of Michel Miró Adzirias and Dolores Ferrá. Descending from a strong family tradition of craftsmanship, Miró's father was a prosperous goldsmith and watchmaker, his paternal grandfather a blacksmith, and his maternal grandfather a cabinetmaker. The young Miró, although a poor student at school, began to draw at the age of eight and announced soon thereafter that he wished to become a painter. In 1907, he was enrolled at the Escuela de Bellas Artes (school of fine arts), the same official academy in Barcelona where, some twelve years earlier, Pablo Picasso had studied. Modesto Urgell and José Pascó, his teachers at the school, recognized Miró as a promising pupil and encouraged his interest in primitive painting.

Miró's family, convinced that an artist's life was too precarious, insisted that he take an office job; he obediently accepted a job as a store clerk in 1910, when he was seventeen years old. Bored, depressed, and demoralized by the position, however, he suffered a nervous breakdown, and his father sent him to recuperate at a farm overlooking the coastal plain, south of Tarragona. This farm and the nearby hill town of Montroig (red mountain) were to become places of great importance and inspiration in Miró's life.

The artist's parents eventually realized that they had no choice but to allow their son to pursue an artistic career, and in 1912 he was enrolled in a Barcelona art school operated by the architect Francesc Galí. During his years at Galí's school, where he painted his first canvases, Miró discovered the work of Claude Monet, Vincent van Gogh, Paul Gauguin, and Paul Cézanne, as well as the Fauves and cubists. In 1915, however, dissatisfied with traditional art instruction, Miró established himself in a studio that he shared with his friend, E. C. Ricart. During this time, Miró's paintings, influenced by van Gogh and the Fauves, and later by the expressionists, were already marked by a hint of humor. Among these early canvases were his first *Self-Portrait, Portrait of Ricart,* and *The Chauffeur,* all dating from 1917, some expressionist nudes, and *Landscape with a Donkey.* The dealer José Dalmau took an interest in his work and gave Miró his first showing at the Galeria Dalmau in Barcelona in 1918.

Life's Work

After his first exhibition in Barcelona, Miró's work exhibited a dramatic change. He began a series of paintings that combined minutely realistic detail with light and subtle color. Critics have compared the earliest of these, *Montroig Landscape* (1919), with works by the Italian primitives. Among Miró's neoprimitive yet sophisticated Catalan landscapes is *The Olive Grove* (1919).

In 1919, Miró briefly visited Paris, to which he would return every year from then on. There he was welcomed by Picasso, whom he had seen previously in Barcelona, but whom he had never dared to approach. Picasso, who in 1921 purchased Miró's second *Self-Portrait*, introduced him to the avant-garde poets Pierre Reverdy, Max Jacob, and the Dadaist Tristan Tzara. It was during this Paris visit that Miró also became acquainted with the work of Henri Rousseau. After his return to the Barcelona area later in 1919, his works, though still faithful to reality, began to show cubist influences, especially in his basic drawing style, which became more angular and formalized, with greater emphasis on planes. A series of still lifes, among them *Still Life with Toy Horse* and *Table with Rabbit*, both completed in 1920, combine cubist influences with colorful imagery inspired in part by Catalan folk art and the Catalan landscape. These still lifes were shown in Miró's first Paris exhibition, held in 1921 at the Galérie La Licorne.

The outstanding work of Miró's early career, and later referred to by Miró as "the crowning work" of his life, was *The Farm*, completed in 1922, a painting on which he had worked for nine months. (It was later purchased by Ernest Hemingway.) The work possesses Miró's typical freshness of approach, and, while it reflects his admiration for Rousseau, it also reveals an intricate calculation of compositional effect. It marks the end of Miró's "poetic realist" period.

Several months of doubt and self-searching followed the completion of this work. The artist finally emerged from his despair after meeting in Paris with the painter André Masson, and the writers Jacques Prévert and Henry Miller, among others. In *The Farmer's Wife* and *The Carbide*, both of 1922-1923, realism blends with a strong element of fantasy and greater intensity of mood.

By the early 1920's, Miró had become acquainted with the Dadaist poets. During this period, he also met the painter Max Ernst and the poet André Breton and through them was introduced to Surrealism. In 1923, during a stay in Montroig, Miró worked on two canvases (completed in 1924) that determined the future course of his art: *The Tilled Field* and *Catalan Landscape* (*The Hunter*). In the former there is still Miró's favorite sunshine-yellow tonality, but there is also a wild, almost Boschlike transposition of images and animal shapes loosely derived from nature. In the latter canvas, Miró moved closer to a kind of Surrealist abstraction, his imagery sometimes suggesting organic forms observed through a microscope, sometimes evoking the sense of realistic objects through symbolic shapes. Among the signers of Breton's "Surrealist Manifesto" of 1924, Miró was hailed by the poet as "the most 'surrealist' of us all." One of Miró's most engaging paintings of 1924-1925 (and one of his most significant works) was *The Harlequin Carnival*, with its tiny allusive figures, more "signs" than forms, and its playful poetic fantasy and festive color.

In 1925 Miró participated in the first Surrealist group exhibition, held at the Galérie Pierre, Paris. There he was impressed by the work of Paul Klee. The following year Miró, in collaboration with Max Ernst, worked on costumes and settings for Serge Diaghilev's production of *Romeo and Juliet*. This concession to so-called "bourgeois" modernism, however, infuriated Breton and the orthodox Surrealists, who condemned him for his lack of seriousness. Miró's essentially intuitive approach was indeed far removed from the more rigid, intellectual attitude of Breton, although the two were able to maintain a friendly relationship. Miró painted one of his most celebrated and impressive pictures in 1926—*Dog Barking at the Moon*. Sometimes interpreted as symbolizing the link between the physical and the intellectual world, the painting has also been regarded as an almost absurdist statement about the human condition.

In 1928, Miró was married to Pilar Jonosca and traveled to Holland. His admiration for Jan Vermeer and the intimate realism of the Dutch genre paintings led to a series of works entitled *Dutch Interiors*. Next, Miró deliberately sacrificed elegance of line and festiveness of color in such subsequent works as *Spanish Dancer* (1928) and his series of dream-vision "Imaginary Portraits." In the early 1930's, he began to experiment with collages, *papiers collés*, lithography, and etchings, and, in years to come, he illustrated many books with color lithographs. He exhibited his first Surrealist "Sculpture-objects" at the Galérie Pierre in 1931. They were characterized, like his paintings, by great freedom of form and mocking fantasy. The best known of these sculptures of the 1930's is *Objet poétique* (1936), a construction of found objects, including a derby hat, a toy fish, a doll's leg, and a map, topped by a stuffed parrot.

Miró exhibited with the Surrealist painters in the Paris Salon des Indépendents in 1932, and in 1933 produced some of his most masterful paintings, including *Composition*, a large elegant canvas in which silhouetted free forms, analogous to some of Jean Arp's reliefs of the same period, were executed in rich black against subtle background tones. Like others of Miró's best paintings of the early 1930's, this work contains an intense primitivism that links it to the prehistoric cave-paintings of northern Spain.

A brutal eroticism accompanied by monstrous forms invaded Miró's work beginning from about 1934, accompanied by a note of intense anxiety—reflecting his awareness of the imminence of civil war in Spain—that appeared in his paintings of 1935-1936. Although rarely overtly political, Miró, like Picasso and unlike Salvador Dalí, supported the Spanish Republic in its resistance of Fascism. In 1937, the year of Picasso's *Guernica*, Miró worked for five months on *Still Life with an Old Shoe*, a painting in which he expressed his anguished feeling for his country and the poverty of the Spanish people. His large mural, *The Reaper*, painted for the Pavilion of the Spanish Republic at the Paris Exposition of 1937 was an anguished and savage protest, as was his anti-Franco poster of that year, *Aidez l'Espangne* (help Spain). In *Nocturne* (1938), Miró's favorite yellow-colored earth is overwhelmed by a stark, black sky, relieved only by some amorphous stellar shapes.

Between 1936 and 1940, Miró lived in France and did not return to Spain. In 1939, when residing in the village of Varengeville, Normandy, he abruptly turned away from his so-called "wild" paintings and the horrors they evoked and began a series of small lyrical paintings on burlap. These were followed by a group of twenty-three gouaches entitled *Constellations*, on which he was working when the Nazis approached Paris in 1940. At this time, Miró managed to get himself, his wife, and their one child, Dolores, on the last train leaving for the Spanish border. The family went first to Montroig, then settled in Palma, Majorca, with Miró's wife's family.

From 1942 to 1944, Miró, having returned to Barcelona, painted almost entirely on paper. In 1944, he began to work in ceramics, in collaboration with the Catalan ceramist Joseph Lloréns Artigas. Miró divided his time between Barcelona and Paris from 1944 on. His painted compositions became more elaborate, often containing repetitious and self-perpetuating imagery. Such paintings as *Woman* and *Little Girl in Front of the Sun* (1946), however, did exhibit much of his former energy and exuberance.

In 1947, Miró, now world famous, went to the United States for the first time and was impressed by the country's vitality. He received commissions for two large murals, one of which was eventually hung in the Cincinnati Art Museum, and the other, executed in 1950, was commissioned for the Graduate Center at Harvard University in Cambridge, Massachusetts. In 1956, Miró settled once again in Palma, Majorca, where he lived and worked until his death. In 1957-1958, he designed two walls for the garden of the United Nations Educational, Scientific, and Cultural Organization headquarters in Paris. A series of large painted mural compositions followed in 1961-1962; the unifying motif of these was the development of a single line on a monochrome ground.

Following his ceramic sculpture of the early 1950's, some of which displayed a primitive totemic quality, sculpture in bronze played an important role in Miró's work in the 1960's and 1970's. His sculptures were included in a large Miró show at the Galérie Pierre Matisse, Paris, in the spring of 1973.

Summary

Although Joan Miró himself rejected any attempt to categorize his art, especially disdaining the label "abstract," the artist is, nevertheless, most often identified with the abstract Surrealist movement, of which he was one of the most original and sensitive exponents. His highly personalized idiom, replete with great charm and wit comparable in a general way to the art of Klee, while remaining entirely and recognizably his own.

Miró's free-form, associational, highly colored, and decorative art has influenced countless other artists in both the fine and the applied arts, who have profited from the imaginative possibilities of his artistic language. A Catalan who always clung proudly to the language, culture, and landscape of his native province, Miró worked forms of nature into his own personal vocabulary of sign images.

Many future currents of painting were anticipated in Miró's work. Several critics have even maintained that it is Miró, and not Henri Matisse or Picasso, who was the most visionary of the early modern masters. The beauty of nature, rustic folklore, symbols of age-old fertility cults, subtle psychological experiences, and highly sophisticated literary concepts were all embraced within Miró's cosmic scope. What is likely to assure the artist's immortality is his irony, risqué puns, humor, vitality, and the fascinating realm of assorted creatures that were produced by his inexhaustible imagination and reproduced upon his canvases.

Bibliography

Greenberg, Clement. *Joan Miró*. Reprint. New York: Arno Press, 1969. In this 133-page work containing a list of exhibitions, a bibliography, and numerous monochrome reproductions, Greenberg ranks Miró with Matisse, Picasso, and others as one of the formative masters of modern painting. He describes the artist's early years, the influences of cubism and Surrealism, his mastery of Art Nouveau, and his reach beyond Surrealism to comedy and hedonism in his later years.

Miró, Joan. *Joan Miró: Selected Writings and Interviews*. Edited by Margit Rowell. Translated by Paul Auster and Patricia Mathews. Boston: G. K. Hall, 1986. Rowell, in this work, offers the reader a fascinating firsthand account of the complex weaving together of the life and work of an artist. Through the artist's letters, statements, interviews, notebook entries and poems, Miró is allowed to speak for himself. The lengthy work contains photos of the artist, some monochrome reproductions, and a biographical chronology.

Penrose, Roland. *Miró*. New York: Harry N. Abrams, 1970. A biography of Miró that is interspersed with critical commentary and numerous reproductions, both in color and black-and-white. Includes a bibliography, a list of the illustrations contained in the book, and an index.

Perucho, Joan. *Joan Miró y Cataluña*. New York: Tudor, 1968. Perucho
succeeds admirably in analyzing the impact of Miró's native land on the
artist's life and work in this book. The work, written in interfacing Spanish, English, French, and German text, contains a chronology of the artist's life and work, an index of works, a bibliography and many black-
and-white and color plates.

Soby, James Thrall. *Joán Miró*. New York: Museum of Modern Art, 1959.
Soby maintains, in this somewhat dated book, that Miró was one of the
most instinctively talented artists of his generation and that he advanced
the art of his predecessors (such as Picasso) in a new and valid direction.
Although brief, this interesting book also contains a list of exhibitions, a
bibliography, and numerous black-and-white and color reproductions.

Stich, Sidra, ed. *Miró: The Development of a Sign Language*. St. Louis,
Mo.: Washington University, 1980. The aim of this well-written exhibition catalog is to clarify the origins of the many elements of Miró's style
and subject matter. It examines the sources of the artist's neoprimitivism
and clarifies the nature and consequences of his contribution to a sign
language, a pictorial element envisioned at a primary sensory level. This
very brief work also contains numerous monochrome reproductions of the
artist's works.

Genevieve Slomski

YUKIO MISHIMA
Kimitake Hiraoka

Born: January 14, 1925; Tokyo, Japan
Died: November 25, 1970; Tokyo, Japan
Area of Achievement: Literature
Contribution: Mishima was a writer of great power, whose life became a performance, ultimately a tragic performance. At the time of his suicide, he was widely regarded as a leading candidate for the Nobel Prize in Literature.

Early Life

Yukio Mishima was born Kimitake Hiraoka in Tokyo, Japan, on January 14, 1925. His father was Azusa Hiraoka, a senior official in the Ministry of Agriculture. His mother was Shizue (Hashi) Hiraoka. Because of his father's position, the boy was able to attend the prestigious Gakushuin (the Peers' School). He proved a fine scholar and was cited for excellence by the emperor himself. During his schoolboy days, his complex nature was already evident. He was a gentle, bookish child, with a delicate constitution. Nevertheless, he was drawn to stories that portrayed the valiant deaths of warriors or their ritual suicides. This fascination with ritualized death persisted throughout his work and life.

Mishima began to write at an early age and was publishing short stories in the magazine *Bungei Bunka* (literary culture) before the age of sixteen. In 1944, he entered the University of Tokyo to undertake the study of law. He was graduated in 1947, but his education was briefly interrupted by his conscription into the army in February, 1945. He saw no action in the closing months of the war, and his period of active service was short. Still, it was to affect him profoundly in the years to come. In *Taiyō to tetsu* (1968; *Sun and Steel*, 1970), he describes the process by which his personal philosophy of physical prowess and the beauty of violent death began to emerge as he underwent the rigors of military training. In 1947, he received a position in the Ministry of Finance, but he resigned it in the following year to devote himself exclusively to writing.

Life's Work

While he was still a schoolboy, Mishima met Yasunari Kawabata, who was to receive the Nobel Prize in Literature in 1968. The elder writer not only served as a literary influence but also became a lifelong friend. Mishima's decision to use a pseudonym may have been prompted by the subject matter of his first, and very successful, novel, *Kamen no kokuhaku* (1949; *Confessions of a Mask*, 1958), an autobiographical tale of a shy, sensitive young man who is wrestling with his homosexual and sadomasochistic impulses. Critics have suggested that this novel set the tone for the rest of

Mishima's fiction: He had adopted not only a new name but also a new personality. Henceforward, he would mask his timidity, vulnerability, and aestheticism with an arrogant, even a provocative, persona. While retaining the love for fine prose and for the Japanese and Western classics that he had shared with Kawabata, he began to affect a strident manliness. He sought the ideal of male beauty and, through a regimen of weight lifting, transformed his puny physique. He studied boxing and karate until he achieved proficiency in both. He made himself into an excellent swordsman and imbibed deeply the tradition of the samurai.

Throughout the 1950's and 1960's, Mishima produced a succession of critically acclaimed novels, including *Shiosai* (1954; *The Sound of Waves*, 1956), *Kinkakuji* (1956; *The Temple of the Golden Pavilion*, 1959), *Utage no ato* (1960; *After the Banquet*, 1963), and *Gogo no eikō* (1963; *The Sailor Who Fell from Grace with the Sea*, 1965). On June 1, 1958, he married Yoko Sugiyama. He eventually became the father of two children—a daughter, Noriko, and a son, Iichiro.

Mishima was prolific in genres other than the novel. He wrote many short stories, most of which are uncollected or collected in Japanese editions only. A collection in English translation, *Death in Midsummer and Other Stories*, appeared in 1966. Among the stories in this volume is one of Mishima's most celebrated, "Yūkoku" ("Patriotism"), the haunting and prophetic story of a young army officer and his wife. When a group of his close friends rebel against their military command, he is torn by his loyalty to them and to the nation. As an honorable alternative, he chooses a warrior's form of suicide. His wife assists him before killing herself. Every detail of the preparations and of the acts themselves is graphically described.

Mishima also became one of Japan's leading playwrights. By his early thirties, he had published some thirty plays, several of which are available in English. His modernized versions of traditional Japanese No plays were very popular. These can be sampled in the 1957 collection in English, *Five Modern Nō Plays*. His play *Sado kōshaku fujin* (1965; *Madame de Sade*, 1967) employs the Western setting of revolutionary France. When many of his plays were produced, Mishima himself directed them.

He grew increasingly versatile in his work, while he grew increasingly flamboyant in his life. He became a motion picture actor, screenwriter, and director—even appearing in a gangster film. He became a recording artist. For a time, he achieved more fame as a television celebrity than he had gained from his many literary prizes and awards. He built an Italianate villa in Tokyo and filled it with English antiques. He enrolled his wife in classes in Western cooking. His writing began to contain more allusions to French literature than to Japanese literature. Yet he came to oppose the Westernization of Japan, even to hate it. In a stream of essays and articles, he advocated a return to the samurai tradition. He organized a small private army made up of young apostles from the university. Mishima named this group the Tate No Kai (Shield Society). His elitism, his militancy, and his idealization of the old Japan disturbed many people. The Shield Society stirred memories of the military adventurism that had led Japan into World War II. Still, Mishima's charismatic personality and provocative behavior made him fine copy for journalists and a much sought-after guest for television shows.

He ended his life with a *beau geste*. On November 25, 1970, he and four members of the Shield Society invaded the headquarters of the Eastern Ground Defense Forces, took the commanding officer hostage, and demanded that the troops be assembled. Japan's constitution, forced upon her at the end of the war by the victorious Allies, was for Mishima the codification of the pernicious Westernizing of his country. From a balcony, he harangued the twelve hundred soldiers for their failure to rise in rebellion against the constitution. The men responded to his speech with laughter and derision. He then knelt and, in the traditional seppuku ceremony, committed suicide. He disemboweled himself with a dagger, and one of his followers beheaded him with a sword.

Mishima completed his tetralogy *Hōjō no umi* (*The Sea of Fertility: A Cycle of Four Novels*) on the last day of his life. The novels in the tetralogy are *Hara no yuki* (1969; *Spring Snow*, 1972), *Homba* (1969, *Runaway Horses*, 1973), *Akatsuki no tera* (1970; *The Temple of Dawn*, 1973), and *Tennin gosui* (1971; *The Decay of the Angel*, 1974). Critical opinion on this work remains divided, some critics seeing the tetralogy as the summation of Mishima's career while others see a decline from his earlier achievements.

Summary

Yukio Mishima had written his own death scene in his 1960 story "Patriotism." He had later dramatized his death by adapting "Patriotism" as a film, which he directed and in which he acted the leading role. So prophetic was the suicide scene that Mishima's family had the film suppressed after his death. The form of suicide Mishima chose, seppuku, is significant. It tests the warrior's courage and tenacity because, after driving the knife into his belly, he must draw it slowly from one side of his abdomen to the other until his intestines spill out of his body. The act requires physical strength as well as strength of purpose. That seppuku is incomprehensible to the Western mind is precisely the point Mishima was making.

It could be argued that, with the few exceptions which immediately come to mind (for example, Miguel de Cervantes, Ernest Hemingway), the lives of writers are no more dramatic than those of the general population. As a class, writers are more likely to be observers and commentators than active participants. Mishima is, however, such a striking exception to this rule of thumb, that his fascinating life and horrifying death may tend to overshadow the fact that he is probably Japan's greatest postwar writer.

Bibliography

Keene, Donald. *Dawn to the West: Japanese Literature of the Modern Era, Fiction.* New York: Holt, Rinehart and Winston, 1984. A massive study of the fiction produced since the Japanese "Enlightenment" in the nineteenth century. The last fifty-eight pages of the text are devoted to Mishima.

——————. *Modern Japanese Literature: An Anthology.* New York: Grove Press, 1956. Pieces compiled by Keene from various genres. His last selection is "Omi," extracted from *Confessions of a Mask.* The evaluation of Mishima in Keene's long introduction is of historical interest, because it was made so early in the novelist's career.

Nathan, John. *Mishima: A Biography.* Boston: Little, Brown, 1974. The author of this biography, a translator and professor of Japanese literature, was acquainted with Mishima. He provides a full and detailed account of Mishima's life. Includes illustrations and a selected list of Mishima's principal works.

Petersen, Gwenn Boardman. *The Moon in the Water: Understanding Tanizaki, Kawabata, and Mishima.* Honolulu: University Press of Hawaii, 1979. Pages 201-336 are devoted to Mishima. A partial chronology and a general bibliography are provided.

Pronko, Leonard C. *Guide to Japanese Drama.* Boston: G. K. Hall, 1973. An entry in the Asian Literature Bibliography series. Here, Mishima is considered exclusively as a dramatist. Pronko devotes several pages to discussions of *Five Modern Nō Plays* and *Madame de Sade.*

Ueda, Makoto. *Modern Japanese Writers and the Nature of Literature.* Stanford, Calif.: Stanford University Press, 1976. A study of eight major writers of modern Japan. Pages 219-261 are devoted to Mishima. Although many of the novels are discussed, Ueda places special emphasis upon *The Temple of the Golden Pavilion.*

Yamanouchi, Hisaaki. *The Search for Authenticity in Modern Japanese Literature.* Cambridge, England: Cambridge University Press, 1978. Chapter 6, "A Phantasy World: Mishima Yukio," argues essentially that Mishima's alienation from the external world drove him to create a world not only for his literature but also for his life.

Yourcenar, Marguerite. *Mishima: A Vision of the Void.* Translated by Alberto Manguel in collaboration with the author. New York: Farrar, Straus & Giroux, 1986. In this short work, first published in French in 1980, the distinguished novelist Yourcenar explores Mishima's life and works, with the emphasis on the latter.

Patrick Adcock

FRANÇOIS MITTERRAND

Born: October 26, 1916; Jarnac, France

Areas of Achievement: Government and politics

Contribution: Elected President of France in 1981 and again in 1988 with the
backing of a coalition of the Left, which he had played a strong role in
forging, Mitterrand was also a minister of several governments in the
Fourth Republic and a Resistance leader in World War II.

Early Life

François Maurice Adrien Marie Mitterrand was born and spent his early
life in Jarnac, a town of five thousand people not far from Cognac in southwest France. He was the fifth of eight children in a close-knit family. His
mother, Yvonne, was devoutly Catholic. His father, Joseph, was the station-
master of the town of Angoulême. Joseph inherited his wife's father's
vinegar-making business and became president of the Union of Vinegar-
Makers of France.

At age nine, Mitterrand was sent to a boarding school run by priests of the
Diocese of Angoulême. There he was a loner and often sick. A devout
Catholic, he sometimes thought about becoming a priest. He enjoyed reading
philosophy and the French classics. At the Facultés de Droit et des Lettres in
Paris in 1934, he enjoyed lengthy student discussions about literature. In
1938, at age twenty-one, he published in a small student journal an attack on
the French and British governments for appeasing Adolf Hitler.

In September, 1938, newly graduated, Mitterrand was called up for compulsory military service. He was a sergeant in September, 1939, when
France declared war on Germany and spent that winter manning a section of
the Maginot line. Wounded in May, 1940, he was taken prisoner by the
German army. His third attempt at escape succeeded in December, 1941. He
worked for a period in a Vichy department servicing French prisoners of war
and received a Vichy decoration which was later controversial. When the
Germans occupied all of France in November, 1942, Mitterrand began the
full-time Resistance work for which he later received several decorations.

In 1943, Mitterrand resisted Free French efforts to pressure him to merge
his network with a similar one headed by General Charles de Gaulle's
nephew. A meeting with de Gaulle in Algiers ended in hostility. Mitterrand
became a lifelong virulent critic of de Gaulle. In March, 1944, when the
three main Resistance organizations to help escaped prisoners of war were
merged, Mitterrand became the leader of the unified group. Nominated by
de Gaulle to be temporary secretary general in charge of prisoners of war
and deportees, from August 19, 1944, he was briefly part of an ad hoc
government for France.

Mitterrand then became editorial director of a publishing house and resumed his legal studies. He wrote articles for the journal of the Federation of Ex-Prisoners of War, wrote a pamphlet, and joined with left-wing Resistance leaders to stop a Communist takeover of the Resistance. Although he was more in the Center than the Left, from then on he made common cause with the Left. In 1945, he married Danielle Gouze. They had two sons. A third child died soon after he was born in 1945.

Life's Work

From 1945 to 1957, Mitterrand was in and out as a minister in eleven of the many governments of the Fourth Republic. In November, 1946 he became deputy for Nièvre in central France. His first position as a minister was in 1946. He was information minister in 1948 at the start of television transmissions, but most of his several ministerial posts dealt with colonial affairs, in which he tried to hold on to the empire by giving more internal autonomy to the colonies. Intermittently, he was out of the government.

Mitterrand became a friend of Pierre Mendès-France when they both collaborated with the new weekly journal, *L'Express*. When Mendès-France was premier (1954-1955), Mitterrand became minister of the interior. As such, he favored keeping Algeria for France, while proposing some reforms. In February, 1956, under Socialist Premier Guy Mollet, Mitterrand was minister of justice. He left the government in June, 1957, and did not hold office again until he was elected president in 1981. In 1957, he was called to the bar.

In September, 1958, the public voted to abolish the Fourth Republic. When Mitterrand lost his seat in the Gaullist 1958 election landslide, he was president of his party and one of the recognized leaders of the Left. From March, 1959, until 1981 Mitterrand held the position of elected mayor of Château-Chinon and other local offices. In April, 1959, he was elected a member of the senate. His career seemed back on track until autumn, 1959, when events made it seem as if he had contrived a fake attempt to assassinate him, in order to discredit Algerian hard-liners. The facts never were made clear.

In bad repute as a politician, Mitterrand began practicing law and wrote a short book, *La Chine au défi*, published in 1961. Throughout the de Gaulle administration, he scathingly criticized de Gaulle's policies. Under a new electoral process begun in 1962, Mitterrand once more became deputy for Nièvre. He wrote regularly for *L'Express*, contributed to *Le Monde*, and in 1964 published a book, *Le Coup d'État permanent*, criticizing the de Gaulle regime and its constitution. In 1965, when the Communist Party decided not to run a candidate against de Gaulle, Mitterrand ran. His first move was to form the Federation of the Democratic and Socialist Left, grouping the Socialist Party, the Radical Party, and a paper organization that Mitterrand headed. In the final round in December, 1965, Mitterrand received 44.8 percent of the votes.

In the summer of 1966, Mitterrand created a shadow cabinet. In December, 1966, his organization signed an electoral pact with the Communist Party. By the end of the March, 1967, elections, the Left had 193 seats in the National Assembly. In February, 1968, the two wings of the Left agreed on a common policy platform. What put Mitterrand in political limbo was his televised announcement, during the height of the student-worker rebellions in May, 1968, proposing to form a ten-member caretaker government. His bid for power offended many people, and the Left lost one hundred seats in the June elections. In 1969, Mitterrand's book, *Ma part de vérité, de la rupture à l'unité*, was published. In it, he who had been such an anti-Communist in the Fourth Republic, openly embraced Marxist concepts. At the same time, he attacked the Soviet Union's intervention in Czechoslovakia. In 1970, Mitterrand published a short book, *Un Socialisme du possible*. In the summer of 1971, he was elected first secretary of the Socialist Party. In 1972, the Socialist and Communist parties signed a formal agreement on what was termed a Common Programme. Mitterrand ran for president in 1974, receiving wide support. In 1973, he called for direct elections to the European parliament.

Mitterrand made a number of trips to various parts of the world. His meetings with political leaders in the United States and the Soviet Union in 1975 were described in detail in his book, *L'Abeille et architecte: Chronique* (1978; *The Wheat and the Chaff*, 1982). He put his faith in Eurosocialism as an antidote to the excessive power of American capitalism. In 1977, the Union of the Left was ruptured. In his book *Ici et maintenant* (1980), Mitterrand charged that the rupture was the result of a change of policy by the Communist Party in the Soviet Union. The Right won comfortably in the 1978 elections.

Despite efforts to replace him, he retained his hold on the Socialist Party. In 1981, he ran again for president. This time he won, with "110 propositions for France," including nationalization, a wealth tax, increase of public service jobs, abolition of the death penalty, increased rights for women, criticisms of both the Soviet Union and the United States, support for more aid to Third World countries, decentralization of French government and pluralization of television and radio, more rights and benefits for workers, and unified secular public education. He also hoped to scale down the nuclear program.

President Mitterrand appointed a very moderate government led by the Center-Right of his party, but he also included four Communists, in relatively minor posts. Pierre Mauroy, social-democratic mayor of Lille, became premier. While nationalizations of industry were put into effect, the minimum wage was raised, a wealth tax was added, and strong support was given to the arts, the government soon had to cope with rising inflation and unemployment. The first reactions were Keynesian policies of massive public spending and easier credit. Large street demonstrations against the government's efforts to weaken the autonomy of Catholic schools forced it to back down. In mid-1982, Mitterrand announced a plan to devalue the franc, freeze wages and prices, and cut his budget. He lowered domestic interest rates. By 1984, his popularity had dropped sharply, but the economy was better by 1985. While having problems of his own in the South Pacific, Mitterrand was critical of the Latin American policy of the United States and provided weapons to the Sandinistas in Nicaragua. In Paris, new projects were aimed at developing the workers' East Side. Eventually a new concert hall was built at Parc des Vincennes, and a new opera house was built on the site of the old Bastille prison. Controversy arose over the design by Chinese-American I. M. Pei for a seventy-foot-high glass pyramid as the new entrance to the Louvre.

In 1986, when the Right won the elections for National Assembly, Mitterrand made Jacques Chirac premier. The French called it cohabitation and liked it. Few changes were made in foreign policy. Chirac aimed to privatize many of the sixty-five state-owned companies and began the process, but problems multipled. The extreme Right wanted more restrictions on immigrants. Students revolted when efforts were made to make admission to the state-run universities more difficult. French competitiveness in world markets was declining. Chirac bore the brunt of popular discontent. Mitterrand stayed above the fray and became more popular than ever.

In 1988, at the age of seventy-two, Mitterrand ran again for president, promising to privatize some industries and to move to the Center. He won. The new premier was Michel Rocard, who fellow Socialists believed was an apologist for capitalism. He was Mitterrand's main rival in the Socialist Party. Mitterrand has been hopeful about greater economic unification of Europe, expecting Paris to be the center. In 1988, the French economy was booming, but unemployment was still high.

Summary

François Mitterrand developed the French Socialist Party into a large, broadly based, national party aimed at social justice and brought it to national power after years of Gaullist rule. This accomplishment entailed a short-term collaboration with the Communist Party that helped him in the latter's decline. Then Mitterrand moved toward the center, while still embracing Socialist principles. Unlike his three predecessors as president, Mitterrand is a veteran politician. In this capacity, he is tough and clever as well as ambitious and vain. As a private person, he is intellectual, almost mystic, a solitary dreamer. His inconsistencies have made some people distrust him. By 1988, though, many French people saw him as a father figure.

A long-term critic of de Gaulle and of the constitution of the Fifth Republic, once president himself he made no move to diminish the constitutional power of the presidency. He has been more of a friend of a unified Europe than the Gaullists had been. By 1988, his government seemed pro-American. He has always been a man of ambiguities, but then France itself is a country of ambiguities. Whereas de Gaulle was known in some circles as a monarch, some have called Mitterrand "the prince."

He has been all his life an indefatigable traveler, going to China to meet Mao Tse-tung in 1961. A learned man, he has read deeply and written extensively, hoping to provide a testament for Socialists everywhere in the world. He has written many articles and books, which may turn out to be his most lasting testament.

Bibliography
Balassa, Bela. *The First Year of Socialist Government in France.* Washington, D.C.: American Enterprise Institute, 1982. A pamphlet analyzing the Mitterrand government's first-year achievements from an American point of view. *Le Monde* is cited as a major source.
MacShane, Denis. *François Mitterrand, a Political Odyssey.* London: Quartet Books, 1982. This biography gives a readable, thorough account of Mitterrand's career up to 1981 and includes the 110 Propositions as an appendix.
Mazey, Sonia, and Michael Newman, eds. *Mitterrand's France.* London: Croom Helm, 1987. The two principal authors are lecturers at the Polytechnic of North London. The chapters analyze promises and accomplishments of the Mitterrand administration. Each chapter has a bibliography related to the policy discussed in the chapter. The "conclusion" credits Mitterrand's government up to 1986 with some modest achievements but also with some serious failures. Appendices give election results for 1981 and a chronology of major political events in France from 1981 to 1986.
Nay, Catherine. *The Black and the Red: François Mitterrand and the Story of an Ambition.* Translated by Alan Sheridan. New York: Harcourt Brace Jovanovich, 1987. Written in a more novelistic style than many biographies, this book contains references that readers outside France might find puzzling. The book has notes with references but no bibliography.
Ross, George, et al., eds. *The Mitterrand Experiment: Continuity and Change in Modern France.* New York: Oxford University Press, 1987. This book evaluates Mitterrand's achievements before he was reelected in 1988.
Singer. Daniel. *Is Socialism Doomed? The Meaning of Mitterrand.* New York: Oxford University Press, 1988. As the title indicates, this book evaluates Mitterrand's policies. Analysts have frequently expressed the opinion that Mitterrand was originally more Right than Left. In the early

postwar years, he was strongly anticommunist. To some, his embrace of the Left was political opportunism.

Williams, Stuart, ed. *Socialism in France: From Jaurès to Mitterrand.* New York: St. Martin's Press, 1983. This book puts Mitterrand's socialism in perspective.

Corinne Lathrop Gilb

MOBUTU SESE SEKO

Born: October 14, 1930; Lisala, Belgian Congo (now Zaire)

Areas of Achievement: The military, government, and politics

Contribution: Mobutu is one of the first major African leaders to come to power since the early 1960's. His Pan-Africanism has gained for him much power in the Third World and his anticommunism has pleased major Western powers. He has been president of Zaire since 1965; as such he has remained a stable Western ally in Central Africa.

Early Life

Mobutu Sese Seko, christened Joseph Désiré Mobutu, was born into the Bangala People in Équateur Province in the northern Belgian Congo. He came from middle-income parents who sent him to good primary (Léopoldville Mission School) and secondary (Coquilhatville Mission School) schools in the provincial capital. After finishing secondary school in Coquilhatville, he went to Brussels to attend the Institut d'Études Sociales de l'État in 1948. He was selected by the Belgian authorities to attend the institute because of his good grades and superior intellect. When he returned to the Congo in 1949, he enlisted in the Belgian-controlled colonial army, the Force Publique. During his enlistment, he was sent to Luluabourg to receive training in clerical, accounting, and secretarial work at the École des Cadres. Seven years later, in 1956, Mobutu was honorably discharged from the Force Publique. At that time he held the rank of sergeant major, the highest rank a Congolese could hold in the colonial military.

Earlier, while Mobutu was in the army, he was a free-lance writer. After he was discharged, he obtained employment with a left-wing newspaper in Léopoldville (now Kinshasa). The Belgian Socialists supported this paper called *L'Avenir.* His writings were rather moderate, despite the politics of the paper. He later moved to another paper, *Actualités africaines,* where he became an assistant editor. He was promoted to chief news editor and then editor in chief in 1958. Mobutu's journalism career reached its apex when he attended the World's Fair in Brussels in 1958 as a representative of Belgian colonial newspapers. When he returned to the Congo, he briefly worked for Inforcongo, the official government information agency.

Over the course of several years, Mobutu became increasingly interested in politics and affairs of the state. He rose quickly in a new national party, the Mouvement National Congolais (MNC), founded in 1958. He was a supporter of Patrice Lumumba, the leader of the militant faction of the MNC. When the party split in 1959, Lumumba appointed Mobutu as head of the party office in Brussels. This position allowed him to be a delegate to the Round Table Constitutional Conference held in the Belgian capital in January, 1960. Later he was a delegate to the Round Table Economic Conference in Brussels in April and May, 1960. Soon thereafter, these appointments would help him in his rise to the presidency of Zaire. Mobutu is regarded as one of the founding fathers of modern-day Zaire.

Life's Work

Mobutu rose to prominence in the newly decolonized Congo as a military leader. He was appointed secretary of state for national defense in Lumumba's cabinet in 1959. He was quickly demoted, however, to the rank of colonel as a result of the Congolese army revolting against its Belgian officers, only eight days after independence had been declared on June 30, 1960. Lumumba trusted Mobutu and wanted him as a colonel so he could try to preserve the new government from the field. He served under General Victor Lundula and was relatively successful in commanding some authority over the rebellious Congolese forces. He did this by obtaining for them food and pay and enlisting their allegiance to their homeland.

Though Mobutu was successful in this new endeavor, the country was still in chaos. A new civil war had erupted because several groups wanted their own forms of independence, separate from Lumumba. The situation further deteriorated when Belgium sent troops to the Congo to protect Belgian nationals from the army mutineers. Lumumba then, in turn, asked the United Nations to intervene, because he feared that the Belgians would reassert their authority over the government as a result of the civil war. Lumumba then admitted several groups of Soviet and Czechoslovakian technicians. Moreover, there was much disagreement between Premier Lumumba and President Joseph Kasavubu, the post-independence leaders.

During this time, Lundula had been ousted from command of the army, and Mobutu took full control. It is then that he led a *coup d'état* on September 14, 1960, in which he ousted both Kasavubu and Lumumba from their positions. He announced that the army would rule while trying to "achieve a political agreement between the factions." He also promised that his army would try to guarantee the security of the people and their property. As a result of Mobutu's strong action, he was immediately condemned by the Soviet Union and Czechoslovakia. He then deported all Eastern Bloc technicians. His actions, however, were praised by the Western press and Western governments, because he presented a welcome alternate to Lumumba's Socialist tendencies. As a result of this coup, Mobutu emerged as a leader. The world recognition that he received remains, and his position of prominence is almost unmatched by any other modern-day African leader.

Meanwhile Mobutu backed Kasavubu over Lumumba, because he feared Lumumba's Socialist leanings would destroy his homeland. Mobutu seemed to hold a joint power seat with Kasavubu, because Mobutu made it well known that he would not tolerate any challenges to his authority by either

Lumumba's followers or the U.N. forces still present in the Congo. Mobutu and Kasavubu further consolidated their power by issuing a warrant for Lumumba's arrest, charging him with having misused his powers while he was premier. The United Nations objected, but Mobutu had Lumumba kidnapped and taken to an outlying province and killed, many say with the complicity of the U.S. Central Intelligence Agency (CIA). In 1961, Kasavubu promoted Mobutu to major general and appointed him commander in chief of all Congolese forces. Thus, Mobutu wielded considerable power and let Kasavubu work with the politicians while he ran the nation's army.

Several years later, in June, 1964, the U.N. troops were withdrawn from the Congo. Nevertheless, another power struggle erupted in the Congo, this time between Kasavubu and Moise Tshombe, the new premier. Again, Mobutu staged a coup on November 25, 1965, and took over the government as new president for not more than five years. He declared that the "race for the top is finished . . . our political leaders had engaged in a sterile struggle to grab power without consideration for the welfare of the citizens." There was no opposition to the takeover, and there were no arrests. Mobutu, at age thirty-five, was president of a major African nation. After 1965, the year of his ascension to power, Mobutu consolidated his power and made the lives of his potential adversaries very difficult. One such man, a former politician, Nguza Karl I Bond, has described Mobutu as a man of state who keeps secrets. He also describes him as a tyrant and a dictator who runs a reign of terror. In addition, he accused Mobutu and his family of raiding the country's coffers to build their own personal fortunes. Some earlier men who resisted Mobutu's rule tried to assassinate him in 1966 and were later hanged. It is apparent that once Mobutu had tasted power, he would take all steps to get rid of any threat to his power. He was once overheard to say concerning the severe death sentences he imposed on enemies, "I have no lessons to receive from humanity."

Even though it was known that Mobutu did not like political parties or anyone deviating from his idea of the "best Zaire," he still had to try to legitimize his power in the highly politicized bastions of the Zairian cabinet and government. He at first proceeded with caution until he had built up his loyal forces; then, he rewarded them for their loyalty by letting it be known that opposition would be dealt with very severely. This was further enforced by his desire for a single-party system that would help routinize and institutionalize his consolidated power. It was a presidential system, but many have labeled Mobutu's government as nothing short of a monarchy.

In economic terms, Mobutu has brought Zaire, with its rich deposits of minerals and copper, to the forefront of African nations. Mobutu has been criticized for exploiting his country to some Western economic interests and in response has nationalized copper production in the country—a radical step that angered many world leaders. It showed, however, that Zaire, Africa, and the Third World in general were tired of being pushed around by multinational corporations of the Western world and that Zaire could stand up to the rest of the world. This, along with his "authenticity campaign" in 1972, gained for him wide respect in both Africa and the Third World.

Summary

Mobutu Sese Seko is a very powerful, egotistical, domineering, ruthless man who loves his country, but more so, his great power. He is one of the most powerful men in Africa, with great wealth. He was once called "the [Ferdinand] Marcos of Africa." Mobutu was one of the first modern-day African leaders to advance the idea of rejecting European names and culture. In 1972, he called for all Zairians who had European names to adopt African names. Similarly, the previous year, the Congo was renamed Zaire in what he called a "national authenticity" campaign to Africanize Africa. He came onto the political scene at the right time—at the end of colonial rule—and has been in the diplomatic limelight ever since. Mobutu has a Pan-African style of rule in that he tries to do what is best for Africa on the whole; he believes that whatever is good for Zaire is good for Africa. In some ways, he has become a major power broker in Africa as well as on the international stage. He controls through economic aid in an attempt to limit the sphere of influence that industrialized nations seek to have over Africa.

Mobutu's country is in a strategic geographical location in that it borders ten other nations and has precious mineral deposits and oil wells. Zaire is in the middle of Central Africa, thus making it easier for Mobutu to hold out his hand to help the rest of Africa. Mobutu has chosen to be more in the Western sphere than the Soviet and has aligned himself with the United States. In addition, Mobutu is vehemently anticommunist; thus he is seen as a "safe" African leader and receives both military and economic support from the West.

Bibliography

Bohannan, Paul, and Philip Curtin. *Africa and Africans*. New York: Waveland Press, 1988. The book focuses on African history, colonialism, and independence. The section on Africa since independence covers the circumstances under which Joseph Mobutu changed his name to Mobutu Sese Seko, and the country's name from the Congo to Zaire. It also discusses his insistence that his people change their names to "authentic" African forms.

Callaghy, Thomas M. *The State Society Struggle: Zaire in Comparative Perspective*. New York: Columbia University Press, 1984. This book is very theoretical and analytical. It examines the concept of the nation of Zaire and the politics of its leaders. The author explores the development of Mobutu's absolutism and its effective utilization.

Gran, Guy, ed. *Zaire: The Political Economy of Underdevelopment.* New York: Praeger, 1979. An excellent book on Zaire in the realm of political economy and the role that Zaire plays in the game of international politics and its relation to the Western world and the African continent. It also deals with factionalism and internal political struggles.

Taylor, Sidney. "Lt.-General Joseph Mobutu." In his *The New Africans: A Guide to the Contemporary History of Emergent Africa and Its Leaders.* New York: G. P. Putnam's Sons, 1967. The book includes biographies of important men in the Congo Democratic Republic. Examples of other leaders listed are Jean-Marie Kikangala and Felicien Kimvoy. Each biography contains the major contributions and other information about the leaders.

Young, Crawford, and Thomas Turner. *The Rise and Decline of the Zairian State.* Madison: University of Wisconsin Press, 1985. Young and Turner shed new light on Mobutu's political policies at the time of Zaire's revolt from Belgian control. In addition, they examine the economic decline as well as the purported corruption of the Mobutu family.

Alphine W. Jefferson

MOHAMMAD REZA SHAH PAHLAVI

Born: October 26, 1919; Tehran, Iran
Died: July 27, 1980; Cairo, Egypt
Areas of Achievement: Government and politics
Contribution: Mohammad Reza ruled Iran from 1941 to 1979. His reign coincided with major changes in the social and economic life of Iran, although his despotic rule, sustained by brutal repression, and the corruption that accompanied his modernizing program contributed directly to the Islamic Revolution of 1979.

Early Life

Mohammad Reza was the eldest son of the preceding ruler, Reza Shah Pahlavi, and was born when the latter, then known as Reza Khan, was a colonel in the Cossack Brigade of the last ruler of the Qajar Dynasty. In 1921, Reza Khan participated in a *coup d'état* aimed at introducing much-needed reforms and reducing foreign (especially British) influence in the country's internal affairs. In 1925, he had himself proclaimed shah, taking the dynastic name of Pahlavi. As heir-apparent, Mohammad Reza underwent strict training under the eagle eyes of his harsh and overbearing father. Although Reza Shah himself had no experience of the world outside Iran, he sent his heir abroad to complete his education.

In 1936, Mohammad Reza was summoned home to enter the Military Academy in Tehran and to continue his apprenticeship as his father's heir. It was also arranged that he should marry Princess Fawzia, the sister of King Farouk I of Egypt. They were married in 1939, and a daughter, Shahnaz, was born in 1940; but Fawzia returned to Egypt in 1947, and there was a divorce in the following year. In 1951, Mohammad Reza married Soraya Esfandiari, daughter of one of the Bakhtiyari Khans and a German woman. The couple were said to be very much in love, but no heir was produced and Soraya had to compete for her husband's affections against Mohammad Reza's relatives and courtiers in a court riddled with intrigue and backbiting. A divorce was announced in 1958. In 1959, Mohammad Reza married a commoner, Farah Diba, who presented him with two sons and two daughters.

Life's Work

Reza Shah shared with his countrymen deep-seated suspicions of both Great Britain and Russia, and during the course of the 1930's he had leaned increasingly in the direction of the Third Reich, which sedulously wooed him and flattered his vanity. At the outset of World War II, therefore, the British and the Russians demanded an end to Iran's German connection. Unwilling to comply, Reza Shah was compelled to abdicate and was taken into enforced exile in Sôuth Africa, where he died in 1944.

Initially, the British contemplated restoring the former Qajar Dynasty, but, in the end, the Allies decided that Mohammad Reza would do as well as any other puppet. He was, therefore, permitted to succeed to the throne, although for the duration of the war the real rulers of the country were the British and Soviet ambassadors. As soon as the war was over, the occupying British troops were withdrawn, but the Soviet Union showed an obvious unwillingness to withdraw Red Army units stationed in the northwest of the country. The prime minister, Ahmad Qavam, one of the ablest Iranian statesmen of the twentieth century, maneuvered the Soviet government into recalling its forces, but he was then compelled to call upon the Iranian army to reintegrate the dissident provinces by a show of force (undertaken with excessive brutality), which inevitably brought the Shah, as supreme commander, to the fore. The so-called liberation of Azarbaijan (August, 1949) greatly boosted the public image of both the Shah and the army. Shortly afterward, Qavam was forced to resign the premiership under pressure from the hostile Majlis (the Iranian parliament, established by the constitution of 1906).

Mohammad Reza had always hated and feared Qavam, and it was with undisguised pleasure that he now saw him leave the political stage. Henceforth, he would begin to participate more actively in politics. He appointed General Ali Razmara as prime minister (June, 1950-February, 1951), but the latter almost immediately became embroiled in controversy over the status of the Anglo-Iranian Oil Company, regarded by virtually all Iranians as a symbol of quasi-colonial domination. When the new premier was assassinated by a religious fanatic, his opponents openly rejoiced. Nevertheless, there were those who whispered that the order for his death had emanated from somewhere within the palace.

Following Razmara's assassination, the issue of oil nationalization came to dominate both Iran's internal politics and its international relations, leading to the emergence to prominence of Mohammad Mosaddeq and to his stormy premiership (March, 1951-August, 1953). Despite his antecedents as a descendant of the former Qajar Dynasty and as an old-style landowner and bureaucrat, Mosaddeq was an object of intense popular adulation, especially among the more politically sophisticated people of Tehran who shared his animus against both the Pahlavi Dynasty and the British. For a short while, it seemed that Mosaddeq would become the charismatic leader of a new, forward-looking, and progressive Iran; as he proceeded, in the face of hostile world opinion, with the nationalization of the Anglo-Iranian Oil Company, his authority and influence grew accordingly. The British reacted by persuading the United States' government (at the height of the Cold War) that Mosaddeq was becoming dependent upon the support of the Communist-led Tuda Party, itself seen as the cat's-paw of the Soviet Union. Mohammad

Reza had long sensed the threat to the monarchy posed by Mosaddeq's popularity, and so he and a palace clique, together with a number of senior generals, entered into a conspiracy, masterminded by the Central Intelligence Agency (CIA), which led to Mosaddeq's ouster, despite the fact that he was the country's duly constituted prime minister. Mosaddeq was put on trial, imprisoned, and later exiled to one of his estates, where he died in 1967.

The Shah began to assume a greater direction over the day-to-day running of the government. By 1960, underlying discontent with the regime for its failure to address fundamental social and economic concerns was being openly aired, despite the ever-increasing ruthlessness of the secret police. To head off opposition, Mohammad Reza ordered the creation of two political parties, one to head the government and the other to serve as a loyal opposition; while each vied with the other in fulsome flattery of the ruler, the elections of 1960 were so blatantly rigged and the public outcry so vociferous that even the Shah was forced to denounce them. Under pressure from the Kennedy administration, which wanted a program of liberalization and reform for Iran, Mohammed Reza appointed as prime minister in May, 1961, a former Iranian ambassador to Washington, Ali Amini. An economist by training, Amini had experience in government going back to the time of Qavam.

Like Qavam and Mosaddeq, Amini was a statesman of vision whose premiership offered the last chance for prerevolutionary Iran to evolve along the lines of a liberal parliamentary democracy, but his period in office (1961-1962) proved tragically brief. He prepared a far-reaching program of reforms, and it was under him and his able Minister of Agriculture, Hasan Arsanjani, that the government promulgated its first land reform decree of January, 1962, the opening phase of a program of land redistribution later co-opted by the Shah in a relentless propaganda campaign in which he was represented as the emancipator of the peasantry. Amini could never overcome the liability that he lacked the nationwide support that Mosaddeq had undoubtedly enjoyed, and he suffered from the additional disadvantage that Mohammad Reza disliked and mistrusted him. The two were bound to part company, sooner or later. The break, when it came, was over military expenditure. Amini the economist knew that the military budget was excessive when the country was in the midst of a grave fiscal crisis, but, to the Shah, the army was sacrosanct. Amini resigned in July, 1962.

Between 1962 and 1977, Mohammad Reza's rule became increasingly despotic: His will was law, his policies were not to be questioned, and any form of opposition or criticism was regarded as treason, to be stamped out without mercy by the secret police. Isolated from reality by his obsequious entourage and flattered and cajoled by Western leaders, who regarded Iran as an island of stability in the turbulent Middle East, he grew megalomanic in his ambition and his delusions of grandeur.

After Amini, no prime minister possessed the moral courage or the independence to challenge the Shah's will. Asadollah Alam (prime minister from 1962 to 1964) was a close confidant and a born courtier, who in 1963 presided over the savage repression of opposition to the Shah's so-called White Revolution. His successor, Hasan Ali Mansur, was assassinated in January, 1965. Mansur was followed by Amir Abbas Hoveyda, a technocrat who was to hold the premiership longer than any other Iranian prime minister of the twentieth century (January, 1965-July, 1977). Dismissed in response to mounting criticism of the government and imprisoned for alleged corrupt practices, he was still incarcerated when the revolutionaries seized power in 1979 and duly had him executed.

Amid increasing repression, Mohammad Reza had celebrated in 1971 what was styled "Five Thousand Years of Iranian Monarchy" in tawdry ceremonies at Persepolis. Even then, some otherwise friendly foreign journalists had commented unfavorably on the obvious signs of Napoleonic delusions of grandeur. Thereafter, with Iran replacing Great Britain as "policeman" of the Persian Gulf, with the Nixon administration agreeing to provide Iran with unlimited military hardware (short of nuclear weapons), and with the steep rise in the world price of oil, the Shah—engaged in an incredible buying spree, especially of the latest weaponry—was boasting that by the year 2000, Iran would be a power of world class, economically and militarily second to none save the superpowers. In reality, by the late 1970's Iran was suffering from an overheated economy, staggering inflation, massive social dislocation, the breakdown of public services, a monstrous military budget out of all proportion to the country's needs, and mounting fury against the regime and its foreign supporters, especially the Americans, who were in large measure blamed for these developments, since most Iranians since the overthrow of Mosaddeq in 1953 regarded their ruler as an American puppet.

As successive governments between 1977 and 1979 lost control of the situation, Mohammad Reza found that, since he had killed, imprisoned, or driven into exile his liberal or democratic critics, leadership of the opposition had passed to the implacably hostile Muslim clergy, and especially to the charismatic figure of Ayatollah Ruhollah Khomeini. By the end of 1978, the Shah's government had, quite literally, disintegrated, and on January 16, 1979, he fled the country, never to return. He died in Egypt on July 27, 1980, an exile like his father.

Summary

A man of limited imagination and serious character flaws, Mohammad Reza Shah Pahlavi pursued with vigor his father's goal of subverting the spirit of the constitution of 1906 in the interests of Pahlavi dynasticism and a twentieth century version of monarchical absolutism, which was, in effect, dictatorship. In achieving this goal, he undoubtedly benefited from the circumstances of the Cold War, which enabled him to convince the United States and its allies that he was indispensable as a stabilizing factor in the Middle East. As in the case of other Western-backed dictators, it was to be his own people, driven to desperation by the excesses of the regime, who would eventually overthrow him.

Coinciding with a peculiarly challenging and volatile period of modern Iranian history, involving wrenching social and economic changes that would have occurred with or without the Shah's leadership, the reign of Mohammad Reza brought great material benefits to the urban-based elite and to sections of the burgeoning middle class, while creating uncertainty, dislocation, and often new forms of economic hardship among those at the lower end of the social ladder. A ruthless foe to genuine democratic institutions and to the free expression of opinion, Mohammad Reza directed his security forces to eliminate all semblances of legitimate oppositional activity, which they did with extraordinary brutality. In consequence, the only effective leadership left to defy the regime came from the ideologically conservative but well-organized and widely respected Muslim clergy. The Islamic Revolution of 1979 was a direct consequence of the Shah's determined elimination of all other forms of opposition during the preceding two decades. In retrospect, Mohammad Reza's career may be viewed as a monumental failure and a classic object lesson in the limitations of dictatorship.

Bibliography
Abrahamian, Ervand. *Iran Between Two Revolutions*. Princeton, N.J.: Princeton University Press, 1982. This is an important and in some respects definitive account of the period between the Constitutional Revolution of 1905 and the Islamic Revolution of 1979. The greater part, however, deals with the reign of Mohammad Reza and is especially detailed regarding the years 1946 to 1953 and the politics of the Mosaddeq premiership.

Hambly, Gavin R. G. "The Reign of Muhammad Riżā Shāh." In *The Cambridge History of Iran*, edited by Peter Avery and Gavin R. G. Hambly, vol. 7. Cambridge, England: Cambridge University Press, 1990. This narrative account of the period 1941-1979 argues that only under the leadership of the three independently minded and charismatic prime ministers—Ahmad Qavam, Mohammad Mosaddeq, and Ali Amini—was there any hope of Iran evolving along the path envisaged in the constitution of 1906.

Hoveyda, Fereydoun. *The Fall of the Shah*. Translated by Roger Liddell. New York: Wyndham Books, 1980. Fereydoun Hoveyda was brother to Amir Abbas Hoveyda. Fereydoun was Permanent Representative of Iran to the United Nations between 1971 and 1979. His assessment of the factors that contributed to the collapse of the Shah's regime are based upon an insider's knowledge and experience.

Katouzian, Homa. *The Political Economy of Modern Iran: Despotism and Pseudo-Modernism, 1926-1979*. New York: New York University Press, 1981. This constitutes the best detailed account of the Shah's reign available. In this penetrating study, Katouzian shows the Shah's modernization program to have been a facade masking brutal repression and the staggering corruption of a venal elite.

Keddie, Nikki R. *Roots of Revolution: An Interpretive History of Modern Iran*. New Haven, Conn.: Yale University Press, 1981. This is an outstanding work of synthesis, an interpretation of recent Iranian history from the beginning of the nineteenth century down to the Islamic Revolution of 1979. Especially useful in the perspective that it provides for the Pahlavi period.

Radji, Parviz C. *In the Service of the Peacock Throne: The Diaries of the Shah's Last Ambassador to London*. London: Hamish Hamilton, 1983. Parviz Radji was the Iranian ambassador to Great Britain between 1976 and 1979. In his diaries, he conveys with considerable frankness his growing dismay at the crass stupidity and lack of vision that characterized the *ancien régime* in its last days.

Rafizadeh, Mansur. *Witness: From the Shah to the Secret Arms Deal, An Insider's Account of U.S. Involvement in Iran*. New York: William Morrow, 1987. Rafizadeh was a member of the notorious Iranian secret police, in which he rose to be station chief in the United States. From this vantage point, he obtained insights into the working of the Iranian government and the court enjoyed by few other outsiders.

Reeves, Minou. *Behind the Peacock Throne*. London: Sidgwick and Jackson, 1986. Reeves was an Iranian woman who, after employment in the foreign service and in Empress Farah's Organization for the Protection of Children, served in the empress' private office from 1976 until 1979. Her memoirs provide an insider's impression of life in the Pahlavi court.

Gavin R. G. Hambly

PIET MONDRIAN

Born: March 7, 1872; Amersfoort, The Netherlands
Died: February 1, 1944; New York, New York
Area of Achievement: Art
Contribution: Mondrian was of paramount importance to the initiation of geometric abstraction for modern art during World War I. He was the principal voice and exemplar of neoplasticism in Dutch painting as well as one of the founders of the Dutch modern movement in architecture and design known as de Stijl, a movement that influenced the International style in building construction during the 1920's and 1930's.

Early Life

Pieter Cornelis Mondriaan, Jr. (Piet Mondrian), was born in Amersfoort, a central Netherlands town, where his father was headmaster at a Dutch reformed grammar school. Piet Mondrian, as he was known, lived only eight childhood years in Amersfoort, after which his family moved east to Winterswijk near the German border. There his father began duties as headmaster of a Calvinist primary school. Mondrian finished early formal education at that school by 1886. Of special importance for his future, he developed an interest in drawing there as a student, from self-training plus guidance from his father, who was a competent draftsman. He received his first painting instruction from an uncle, Fritz Mondriaan, a professional painter of landscapes who, though based at The Hague, spent numerous summers at his brother's home in Winterswijk. Not surprisingly, early lessons for Mondrian from his uncle included landscape composition. Other documented training in art was received from the Doetinchem artist Johan Braet van Ueberfeldt.

By age fourteen, young Piet Mondrian (he shortened his first name and dropped the second "a" from his last name by 1912) was already consumed with the notion of becoming a painter. His father did not concur and initially prevailed, insisting that his son prepare for a stable profession. Mondrian worked diligently toward, first, a diploma to teach drawing at grammar school levels and then an additional certificate as a secondary school drawing teacher. By 1892, he taught briefly in Winterswijk but less thereafter. Still, his teaching certificates served as exemptions from preparatory courses when he was enrolled at the National Academy in Art in Amsterdam in 1892. There he joined all-day classes in painting and in 1894 added night classes in drawing.

Frustrated by the academy's curriculum and his own money problems, Mondrian withdrew from school for a year. During 1895-1896 and for several years afterward, Mondrian intensified his interest in landscape studies, notably undramatic rural scenery. In Mondrian's early years of academy training his approach was patient, sober, neutral, and objective regarding figuration, a manner that Mondrian carried over to his landscapes. All in all, his was hardly an early life prophetic of a brilliant career as a major figure in twentieth century modernism.

Life's Work

Mondrian's naturalistic paintings and his life remained relatively undistinguished from 1898 until about 1908. During this period, the channel of success for a picturesque landscape painter such as Mondrian included joining various art organizations in cities such as Amsterdam and submitting works to their frequent exhibitions. Mondrian did so, occasionally faring well, but by 1908 other forces were stirring within him and around him that began to change his painting interests forever.

That year he met the painter Jan Toorop, an exponent of Art Nouveau. Mondrian was not swayed by the sinuous excess and thick symbolism in Toorop's work, but his light palette and immersion into theosophy intrigued Mondrian. Soon considerations about the mystical apprehension of God caused the artist to clarify his painting goals. He realized that his current search for an imitation of the divine, present in his naturalistic, or luminist, paintings, actually lay within himself. Slowly but progressively Mondrian set about painting the divine absolute without references to externalized objects.

This procedure required a different pictorial language, one faithful to his new direction yet intelligible to the art-viewing public as well. The direction was one of liberation, exploration, experimentation, and a brighter palette, and it continued up to World War I. From 1908 to 1911 and again in 1913 and 1914, Mondrian painted for long periods during summers at Domburg in the coastal area of The Netherlands called Zeeland. There he continued a preference for single motifs such as mills, lighthouses, church towers, dunes, beaches, and individual stemmed flowers. These paintings were composed of a minimum of strokes, some wide, most gestural, and, again, almost all in brighter, stronger color, leaving behind for good the dark, rather brooding spell of his previous works.

Between 1909 and 1912, at least a dozen paintings and watercolors evidence a metamorphosis wherein a flowering tree is interpreted first in the Fauve manner, next with arbitrary smoldering color, and then as a type of turgid, brittle expressionism, followed by a version as a formalized system with curving webs of criss-crossing branches with spaces infilled with flat color. The last paintings in this series were completed during a trip to Paris in 1912. In them, the tree motif was simplified still more radically into a lattice of laterally repeated branches, some ellipsoidal. At that point, what seemed a conclusion of natural synthesis became an altered visual problem begging further resolution; that is, object representation changed to a schematicized incomplete grid on a flat background.

Part of this transformation from object-oriented art to linear abstraction was the result of Mondrian's exposure to the laboratory-like Paris development of analytical cubism by Pablo Picasso and Georges Braque between 1909 and 1911. Yet Mondrian's own development may not have needed such contact. Whatever the case, world events affected his next potential spheres of influence. A trip home to The Netherlands in 1914 for the impending death of his father was prolonged for four years by the outbreak of World War I. The involuntary detention nevertheless had beneficial ramifications for Mondrian. He grew distant from cubism, believing that its experimental progress stopped prematurely and that it could have advanced to the logical elimination of all subject matter. In The Netherlands from 1914 to 1915, Mondrian resumed his experimental synthesis of form in sparse compositions of varied colors and line-enhanced rectangles. His goal was to achieve what he termed "pure reality" and to represent ideas by pure plastic means—hence neoplasticism, in which all visual information is reduced to activities coded by colors to shapes. Reality now meant, not the picture as an open hole in the wall, but picture making, that is, line, color, shape, texture, composition, rhythm, balance, and the like.

Slowly formulating that position, Mondrian refined it into the concept of dynamic movement of color and shape and then enlarged upon it with the idea of balanced but unequal opposition. The latter was realized by almost exclusive use of rectilinear planes rendered in primary colors and divided by black borders of right angles. *Oval Composition with Bright Colors* (1914) is typical of this radical approach, although a few curved lines remained. Within a year, even curvilinear marks had been eliminated, and the resolution of Mondrian's compositions from then on reflected the rectangle of the picture plane, with architectonic structure dominant.

During this same period, Mondrian met Barth van der Leck, a painter exploring problems related to his own. Through Leck, Mondrian met artist and critic Theo van Doesburg, who was eager to launch both a new architecture and design movement and a journal to promote it. Both he called *de stijl*, meaning "the style." De Stijl championed machine forms and simplicity. Essays by Mondrian were published in the journal.

Possessing nearly obsessional concentration in his search for spiritual expressions of dynamic grid oppositions, Mondrian spent the rest of his career exploring their possibilities. Much of that life (1919 to 1938) was spent in Paris, where Mondrian's presence and active career seemed to encourage the spread of abstraction. His work in general saw the black grid simplified and become bolder, wider, and filled with a reduced palette of the primary colors plus white and gray. The archetypical example of this phase of his work remains *Composition in Red, Yellow, and Blue* (1930).

In 1938, sensing the approach of another war in Europe, Mondrian left Paris and sailed to London, where he lived and worked for two years. With the onset of the Blitzkrieg, the artist changed countries for the last time to the United States, specifically New York City, and did so with no regrets.

In 1941, Mondrian's work experienced another change: The black line network was exchanged for one in yellow and, in some work, for a yellow grid containing small bars of primary colors. Mondrian enthusiasts attribute the transformation to the artist's admiration for the dense but dynamic horizontal and vertical structure of Manhattan, particularly when it is illuminated at night. Additional stimuli proved to be the accelerated pace of life and, above all, the syncopation of jazz, a music form both new and intoxicating to the artist. So fond was Mondrian of the new music that he named his last two major paintings, *Broadway Boogie-Woogie* and *Victory Boogie-Woogie*, both from 1942-1943, in its honor.

During this same brief time span, Mondrian was given his only one-person exhibition, thanks to the Valentine Dudensing Gallery in New York City. In late January of 1944, Mondrian developed pneumonia, and, though medically treated, he died early on February 1 at Murray Hill Hospital.

Summary

In probably no other single artist can the metamorphosis of specific naturalistic motifs into geometric abstraction be traced and studied more clearly than through Piet Mondrian. What is more important, the transformation of his motifs was not the result of clinical deductive reasoning as they may appear, but the search for spiritual equivalents and a universal language for natural form. In his patient, methodical way, he quietly launched one of the most important arms of twentieth century nonobjective painting, that of geometric abstraction.

As a founding member of de Stijl, his ideas regarding neoplastic painting as well as geometric abstraction in sculpture and architecture were published in the Dutch post-World War I journal *De Stijl*. Consequently, Mondrian's ideas were extended to Germany, where they were eagerly received by Walter Gropius during his formation of the Bauhaus. During the heyday of that astounding school of architecture, design, and art, Mondrian's ideas were indirectly spread throughout much of Western civilization.

Reared in a milieu of landscape and cityscape painting, Mondrian had turned away from those genres by 1909. Yet his move to New York in 1940 subsequently witnessed interpretations of Manhattan important as a heroic finale to his career and highly significant in the ongoing development of abstract painting. Mondrian's work and presence in the United States during the early 1940's inspired emerging young painters soon to launch the major movement of abstract expressionism. Finally, Mondrian's influence impacted still later twentieth century painting movements such as color-field abstraction and hard edge abstraction (or, minimal art) as well as optical painting (or, op art).

Bibliography
Blotkamp, Carel. "Mondrian's First Diamond Compositions." *Artforum* 18 (December, 1979): 33-39. The article responds to data and opinions in the catalog of a 1979 exhibition at the national Gallery of Art in Washington, D.C. Blotkamp convincingly refutes catalog author E. A. Carmean's contention as to the sources for Mondrian's diamond, or lozenge, paintings, saying that they were likely based on Mondrian's wartime conversations with de Stijl artists and not on Postimpressionism and the slightly later cubism.

Champa, Kermit S. "Mondrian's Broadway Boogie Woogie." *Arts Magazine* 54 (January, 1980): 170-176. An in-depth examination of Mondrian's most important painting from the artist's New York period.

Friedman, Mildred, ed. *De Stijl, 1917-1931: Visions of Utopia*. New York: Abbeville Press, 1982. This catalog's essays reveal the planned interconnectedness of de Stijl's total design and its prophecy of machine form, efficiency, and dignified simplicity.

Jaffe, Hans Ludwig C. *Piet Mondrian*. New York: Harry N. Abrams, 1970. The book combines an overview of the artist's life, including biographical photographs, student-era paintings, and an in-depth discussion of a key series in which the tree motif evolves into a nonobjective painting mode. It includes description and analysis for most of Mondrian's major paintings.

Mondrian, Piet. *Piet Mondrian, 1872-1944: Centennial Exhibition*. New York: Solomon R. Guggenheim Foundation, 1971. The catalog lists 131 works dated from 1889 to 1944 and illustrates the most familiar pieces. Also includes an interview with one of Mondrian's closest friends.

Rembert, Virginia Pitts. "Mondrian's Aesthetics, as Interpreted Through His Statements." *Arts Magazine* 54 (June, 1980): 170-176. Art historian Rembert maintains that Mondrian's aesthetic reasoning was not only the operative beginning of his paintings but also valid art in itself and equal to the paintings.

Seuphor, Michel. *Piet Mondrian: Life and Work*. New York: Harry N. Abrams, 1957. A monographic study composed of a poignant text interspersed with appropriate illustrated works, most in acceptable color. The book is valuable as an explanation of Mondrian's concepts of neoplasticism and his identification with theosophy and as an exploration of his major painting themes.

Welsh, Robert P. *Piet Mondrian's Early Career: The "Naturalistic" Periods*. New York: Garland, 1977. This published dissertation addresses the artist's art training in the 1880's, when he came under the spell of painting styles in contemporary France. Exhaustive research is evident, covering Mondrian's long gestation as a painter of humble landscape imagery.

Tom Dewey II

CLAUDE MONET

Born: November 14, 1840; Paris, France
Died: December 5, 1926; Giverny, France
Area of Achievement: Art
Contribution: Monet was considered the most important of the Impressionist
painters. He began to reject the illusion of deep space in painting; this
visually flatter approach to painting was subsequently pursued by Paul
Cézanne, then other artists, for nearly a hundred years and came to domi-
nate modern art through the first half of the twentieth century.

Early Life
Oscar-Claude Monet was born in Paris, France, on November 14, 1840.
In 1845, his family moved to Le Havre, where his father worked as a ship
chandler and grocer; the family spent weekends at the beach resort of Sainte-
Adresse. In school, Monet studied drawing under François-Charles Orchard.
He exhibited some of his caricatures in an art supply store, where he met
Eugène Boudin, who influenced the young Monet to do on-site pastel draw-
ings and oil paintings of landscapes.

In 1858, a year and a half after the death of Monet's mother, one of his oil
landscapes was shown in a municipal exhibit in Le Havre. A year later he
moved to Paris and studied at the Académie Suisse; there he met Camille
Pissarro, who was to become a profound influence on Monet's painting. In
1861, he was conscripted into the military and sent to Algeria, but, after a
six-month convalescence from illness, his Aunt Sophie Lecadre paid for his
release from the remaining five years of military duty.

Monet returned to Paris in 1863 and studied under Charles Gleyre; he soon
met Jean-Frédéric Bazille, Pierre-Auguste Renoir, and Alfred Sisley. He had
only sporadic success during the next two decades and salon juries seldom
accepted his work for exhibition. Often destitute, he moved around Europe
frequently, but he often returned to set up a studio in Paris for brief periods.
He married his model, Camille, in 1870, and later, unable to pay his hotel
bill, he moved to London to avoid serving in the Franco-Prussian War. In
London, he studied paintings by John Constable and J. M. W. Turner. In
1871, Monet's father died just before the end of the Franco-Prussian War,
and by 1872 Monet was again living in Paris.

Monet, along with Pissarro, Sisley, and Renoir, began to exhibit with a
group of independent artists outside the salons. At the first group exhibition
in 1874, a critic caustically named the group "Impressionists," after Monet's
painting *Impression: Sunrise.* In 1879, his wife Camille died, leaving him
with two sons.

Though Monet had enjoyed sporadic sales, his paintings began to sell
more consistently after the first New York exhibition. This exhibition was

arranged by Durand-Ruel in 1886 at about the same time that Émile Zola's novel *L' Œuvre* (*His Masterpiece*, 1886), which was loosely based on Monet, was published. In 1887, Monet began to have consistent success in Paris, London, and New York markets. The following year, 1888, Monet refused the Legion of Honor in London and began his *Haystack* series. Monet was successful enough by 1890 to buy a house at Giverny, and he began to improve its garden, which later became the source of so many paintings. In 1892, he married Alice Hoschedé, with whom he had lived for years.

Life's Work

Monet chose landscape as the dominant theme in his subject matter. Monet lived in an art world that had begun to reject the Renaissance paradigm in favor of more modern ideologies. Thus, his choice of landscape solved three problems: It subordinated man to nature; it set up a situation in which the two most obvious devices of Renaissance perspective—linear perspective and the shading of volume—were of little value; and it allowed him to explore his interest in the effects of sunlight reflecting off the surface of objects.

After Copernicus had convinced most of Europe that the earth revolved around the sun—rather than vice versa—man gradually came to view himself as less significant, a slight distortion in the infinite tapestry of the universe. Landscape is the centerpiece of nature and tends to de-emphasize man as the center of attention. Consequently, Monet seldom centered his painting on a figure or a group of figures as Renaissance painters had done.

Linear perspective had been the mainstay of the Renaissance system of perspective, but linear perspective is of real value only when used to depict architecture and man-made environments. Linear perspective exploits straight lines and parallel lines to gain its illusion of depth, but there are no straight or parallel lines in the landscape; thus Monet found it to be of little value in his vision of painting. *La Grenouillere* of 1869 illustrates that Monet was departing the rational space of Renaissance painting and "seeing" the world, in a manner influenced by Rembrandt, as flickering sunlight ricocheting off the surface of a variety of objects. These changes that Monet brought to painting through his view of the landscape all tended to drive the illusion of deep space from Monet's paintings and to depict shallower space; his paintings looked flatter as his career progressed.

Monet integrated his figures into the background; often they were hardly noticeable distortions in the overall vision of the landscape. He also began to reject the Renaissance method of shading volume. Monet seldom shaded trees, objects, or figures with strong dark and light sides, and this rejection of shading made his figures appear flatter, less volumetric. The invention of photography was also a factor that influenced Monet to reject the shading of volume.

Photography was fairly common during the late nineteenth century, and Monet and the Impressionists were influenced by the "believability" of photographs. These painters noticed that photographs seemed to create credible illusions of the exterior world, in spite of the flat manner in which figures were depicted. There was often no dark and light side to photographed objects and figures, because early photographers had a tendency to stand with their backs to the sun, which front-lighted the figure evenly from one side to the other: Front-lighted figures in a photograph look quite flat compared to the painter's traditional volumetric rendering. This flattening and integration of the objects and figures into the background accentuated the flatness of Monet's painting. Renaissance painting had been perceived as a stagelike space, drawn in perspective and depth, but Monet and the painters who followed him thought of their paintings more as the curtain in front of this stage, and they began to value the actual surface of the canvas—the flat picture plane.

The shading of volume tends to de-emphasize color in favor of dark light structure, but Monet no longer used strong darks and lights to create the illusion of volume; in 1885, he used bright saturate color in *Poppy Field in a Hollow near Giverny*. Thus, Monet's vision liberated future painters from the classical dictate that dark and light structure was more important than color structure. He might well be called "the first colorist."

Monet maintained a solid unity of painting technique, and he treated all the images in his painting in a similar fashion. Water, trees, people, and landscape were painted in the same objective manner, using the same technique and the same thick encrusted paint surfaces. This thick paint also helped to destroy the illusionistic depth in painting and accentuated the viewer's tendency to perceive Monet's paintings as flat surfaces. Because of his application of thick paint, the flat surface of the painting could no longer be pushed from the viewer's consciousness, and the physical presence of the paint surface assumed more importance. These paintings were no longer Renaissance illusions in which the viewers "look through" the surface to "see" objects. The viewer was forced to an awareness of the canvas as a physical entity.

In 1892, Monet began a major series of paintings of Rouen Cathedral. He painted mostly frontal views of the flat façade, and his choice of subject matter again served to keep the painting flat and the picture plane visually intact. He painted on several of these paintings each day. Each individual painting was worked during the same time period each day so that the light and shadow did not change during the entire course of the painting. The light depicted on these façades indicates the time of day at which they were painted: Those façades lighted in cool color, from the side, seem to indicate morning or evening periods; those lighted with warm color, from above, imply midday. Because he captured the time of day in which each painting was executed, the *Rouen Cathedral* series—like the *Haystack* series begun in 1888—creates a sensation of the passage of time. Seen together as a series in one body, the changing direction and temperature of light, as seen at different times of day, is evocative of different slices of time.

Monet's second wife, Alice, died in 1911, and, after a long period of grief, Monet continued to work at his painting in spite of cataracts and failing eyesight. He enjoyed the esteem of his peers and financial success during his later years. He lived well into the twentieth century and concentrated on the *Water Lily* series from 1902 until his death at Giverny on December 5, 1926, at the age of eighty-six.

Summary

Claude Monet was the most influential of the Impressionist painters, and it was Monet and the Impressionists, followed by Paul Cézanne, who made the transition from the Renaissance system of perspective to modern art. Monet broke free of the dominant Renaissance vision in painting and thus set the direction for modern art. Italian Renaissance painters had perceived man as the center of the universe: They had created a method of perspective, depicting the world as centered around man himself, which appeared to be so self-evidently true that it had dominated European vision and painting from the fifteenth century to the last half of the nineteenth century. For more than four hundred years, painters could seem to find no acceptable alternatives to this Renaissance system of perspective. Toward the end of the nineteenth century, however, Monet and the Impressionists discovered a powerful alternative to this Renaissance vision—a new and realistic depiction of the world, which has come to be called "Impressionism."

It was Monet who was most instrumental in the rejection of Renaissance linear perspective and the shading of volume in objects and figures. The rejection of these two elements has given direction to art through the twentieth century: Few modern artists used either of these devices. This rejection of the main elements of Renaissance painting led to a flatter picture plane, and this flat picture plane became the dominant theme of modern art. In addition to this, Monet's ability to evoke a sensation of the passage of time seems now to be almost prescient—a harbinger of the modernist obsession with the element of time in painting.

Bibliography

Herbert, Robert L. *Impressionism: Art, Leisure, and Parisian Society.* New Haven, Conn.: Yale University Press, 1988. Herbert lectured on Impressionism for twenty-five years before he wrote this excellent history. He documents Monet's contributions and influence on the school and covers society's role in shaping the vision of an artist as well as the artist's effect on society. This 323-page book has a clearly diagrammed three-and-a-half-page chronology; it is well indexed and opulently illustrated with 311 illustrations, most of which are in color.

House, John. *Monet: Nature into Art*. New Haven, Conn.: Yale University Press, 1986. This very useful book covers Monet's life, career, choice of subject matter, composition, technique, color, and attitudes. Features a thorough bibliography, many color illustrations, and a short index covering mostly names, paintings, and places.

Rewald, John, and Frances Weitzenhoffer, eds. *Aspects of Monet*. New York: Harry N. Abrams, 1984. This is an excellent anthology of papers written by some of the best-known experts on Monet. These papers were delivered at a symposium in Paris in 1981 and cover the entire spectrum of Monet's activities from his early to his late works. Contains many illustrations, some of which are in color.

Seitz, William C. *Claude Monet*. New York: Harry N. Abrams, 1960. The author was a respected painter and art historian who directed a major Monet exhibition at the Museum of Modern Art in New York while he was a curator there. Seitz writes with the insight of a painter and the discipline of an art historian. Contains forty-eight color plates, numerous black-and-white photographs, and a four-page chronology.

Stuckey, Charles F., ed. *Monet: A Retrospective*. New York: Park Lane, 1985. An anthology of what critics have written about Monet's work, from Zola in 1866 to Clement Greenberg in 1957. Begins with an excellent condensed five-page chronology of the artist's life and is well illustrated with hundreds of black-and-white reproductions as well as 122 color plates. The index covers only names, paintings, and places.

William V. Dunning

JEAN MONNET

Born: November 9, 1888; Cognac, France
Died: March 16, 1979; Montfort-l'Amaury, France
Areas of Achievement: Diplomacy, economics, government, and politics
Contribution: Monnet has justly been called "the father of Europe," in recognition of the importance of his role in the foundation of the European Coal and Steel Community, Euratom, and the Common Market. He worked primarily as an adviser rather than as the holder of powerful political positions; his ideas and plans have been instrumental in shaping Europe's postwar moves toward economic and political integration.

Early Life

Jean Monnet was born on November 9, 1888, into a family of winegrowers in Cognac, a small town set amid the vineyards of the Angoulême region of France. In contrast to other European leaders of his generation, his formal education was minimal. He left school at the age of sixteen, never to return. Instead, he spent the next decade traveling the world selling his family's brandy. Long stays in the United States and Canada left him fluent in English and cosmopolitan in outlook as well as increasingly prosperous. During this period, he also began to form the network of friendships and contacts among leading figures in all areas of public life around the world that would serve him so well throughout his career.

A short, compact, highly animated and energetic man, Monnet was never a towering intellect who dazzled people with the brilliant originality of his ideas. Nor was he an imposing physical presence or an impressive public speaker. He had instead solid common sense, enormous tact and discretion, and a remarkably clear vision of what he wanted to accomplish and how to go about realizing his goals most efficiently.

Life's Work

During World War I, Monnet advised both his own government and that of Great Britain on economic matters. The experience convinced him of the importance of rational economic planning and of the necessity of countries cooperating with one another rather than trying to achieve their economic goals unilaterally. His success in coordinating economic aspects of the Anglo-French war effort, particularly shipping, led to his being given the post of Deputy Secretary-General of the League of Nations after the war ended in 1918.

In 1923, problems in the family brandy business led Monnet to resign his position with the League of Nations and return to private life. After reorganizing the family concern, he began working in investment banking. His career as a businessman took him to Sweden, China, and the United States over the following decade and a half. Then, in 1938, the gathering clouds of World War II led Monnet back into public service. Working in the United States on behalf first of the French and then of the British government, he was instrumental in convincing American leaders of the importance of shifting American economic resources over to military production even before the war began. He is credited with coining the phrase "arsenal of democracy" to describe the role that the United States would have to play in defeating the challenge of Fascism and with helping to prepare it to play that role successfully.

In the spring of 1940, with the deadly thrust of the Nazi war machine spreading despair throughout France, Monnet seized upon a bold idea to prevent an ignominious French surrender to Adolf Hitler and keep the French people in the war even after their homeland had fallen. He suggested that France and England merge, that their people share a common citizenship, and that the war be carried on under the direction of a cabinet composed of French as well as English leaders. Winston Churchill, the English prime minister, quickly agreed and formally extended an offer of joint citizenship to the French. This breathtakingly bold idea for submerging ancient national rivalries and loyalties in a new supranational entity was not to come to pass, however, as the French government opted for surrender instead.

Throughout the remainder of the war, Monnet used his diplomatic skills to smooth relations between the English and Americans on the one hand, and the French forces of resistance to Hitler on the other. This proved to be a difficult task, as the most important French leader was the proud and prickly General Charles de Gaulle, whose single-minded French nationalism was a striking contrast to Monnet's broadly international outlook.

At war's end, with France prostrate and impoverished, Monnet was able to convince its government that economic recovery would require careful planning and direction. He worked out a system of planning in which leaders of government, business, and labor unions would sit down together and decide where resources and investments could best be utilized. Monnet became the first director of France's enormously successful postwar planning commission in 1947 and did much to launch France on the road to the prosperity of the second half of the twentieth century. Under his guidance, resources were used not only to relieve current suffering but also to rebuild, reshape, and modernize the entire French economy.

After World War II, all over Europe there was much sentiment in favor of some sort of European unification. Such unification, it was argued, could help strengthen Europe against the Russian menace, could promote the more rational and efficient development of Europe's economic resources, and, most important, could help defuse the murderous national resentments and ambitions that had so often led to war in the past. A number of approaches to unification were proposed and even attempted in the late 1940's and early

1950's, but none succeeded in overcoming the tremendous psychological, political, economic, and military obstacles that blocked the path.

Monnet, long an enthusiastic advocate of supranationalism, argued that the best way to overcome the hatreds and divisions of the past was to unite the peoples and nations of Europe around mutual striving toward a common goal. In this they could begin to see that they had common interests and could form the habit of working together to further them. A common goal required a common institution to coordinate and direct the peoples' efforts. Monnet had few illusions about the possibility of eliminating greed or aggression from human nature. He was convinced, however, that the experience of living and working together under common institutions and common rules could slowly create habits of cooperation and of the peaceful settlement of disputes. His example was the civilized, peaceful lives shared by people within each sovereign country. His goal was to build common institutions for all Europe.

In the spring of 1950, Monnet presented his friend, the French Foreign Minister Robert Schuman, with a plan for beginning the economic integration of Europe. It called for the establishment of a supranational authority to coordinate, direct, and plan the coal and steel production of Europe. The member nations would have to agree to yield some of their sovereign authority over their most significant resources and industries. Monnet argued that in doing so, they not only would ease the staggering task of rebuilding Europe's blasted economies but also would deprive themselves of the independent power to arm against and strike at their neighbors, since coal and steel are the indispensable sinews of modern warfare. Individual governments, he pointed out, would no longer have the ability to control these parts of their nations' economies.

Here at last was a viable proposal for beginning the process of European integration. Monnet's plan quickly led to a treaty between France, West Germany, Italy, Belgium, The Netherlands, and Luxembourg, forming the European Coal and Steel Community. This community, which went into effect in 1952, stripped away all the members' quotas, tariff restrictions, artificial monopolies, discriminatory freight rates, and other nationalistic regulations—regulations that had long strangled the heavy industry of the members in the name of protecting each from the competition of the others. Monnet, as the first president of the Community's High Authority, directed it through its formative years. As he had predicted, economic integration was an enormous success. Trade between the six member countries rose dramatically as did overall production and prosperity.

During the early 1950's, Monnet also attempted to further European integration by advancing a plan for military unification in the form of an integrated army known as the European Defense Community. His hopes, however, were dashed in 1954 when the government of France rejected the project. In 1955, convinced that the Coal and Steel Community was functioning well, Monnet resigned from its High Authority. Its presidency was the last significant political office that he would ever hold, but its abandonment was far from the end of his career. Indeed, the influence that he had on events in Europe continued to be enormous. Throughout his career, he was most comfortable, and most effective, standing slightly in the background, acting as an adviser, allowing others to put his ideas into effect and take the credit for them, rather than doing it himself.

Upon leaving the Coal and Steel Community, he founded the Action Committee for the United States of Europe, which he would lead from 1955 until its dissolution twenty years later. The Action Committee was a group of experts, labor leaders, and political figures who shared Monnet's dream of a united Europe and his conviction that the path to the achievement of this goal lay in the building of institutions that would accustom the Europeans to working together. It became a veritable cornucopia of ideas, suggestions, and plans designed to further the integration of Europe. The work of Monnet's Action Committee, combined with his own tireless lobbying, was indispensable in laying the groundwork for the treaties forming Euratom and the Common Market in 1957. These new organizations extended the Coal and Steel Community into the development of nuclear energy and into far more ambitious economic integration of the six, creating a real European Community.

By the end of the 1950's, the integration of Europe was an irreversible reality but was far from complete. Monnet was highly disappointed by the refusal of the other European nations, particularly Great Britain, to join the six nations of the European Community. In addition, the economic integration represented by the Common Market fell far short of the political and cultural unification that was Monnet's ultimate goal. During the 1960's and 1970's, Monnet continued to advance the cause of European unification through his Action Committee, through his writings and speeches, and above all through his quiet but effective work of advising and persuading. By the time of his death in 1979, Great Britain, Ireland, and Denmark had all joined the European Community, and the negotiations for the addition of Portugal, Spain, and Greece were virtually completed. Meanwhile such developments as a European Monetary System for the community and direct elections of delegates to its legislature appeared to justify Monnet's optimism about the future of European unification.

Summary

Throughout his life, Jean Monnet believed in the ability of human beings to address their problems successfully through rational planning and through the building of institutions that would in turn build habits of cooperating with one another in the pursuit of common goals rather than fighting against one another. Rarely holding any office that gave him power, Monnet worked by preference through advising and persuading others to make such plans and to build such institutions. The economic planning that he suggested helped to lead the Western democracies to victory in the two world wars of the first half of the twentieth century. After World War II, he went on to play a key role in reviving and reshaping the economy of France. His tact and his negotiating skills were instrumental in convincing French businessmen, labor leaders, and politicians to accept the idea of a planned economy.

Monnet's most important role was his leadership in the movement toward European integration. He was able to translate what appeared to be hopelessly idealistic dreams of overcoming deeply embedded nationalistic prejudices into solid, workable plans. No less important, he inspired others with his vision and his enthusiasm. The Common Market and its success are, in a real sense, the offspring of Monnet.

Bibliography
Beloff, Max. "Jean Monnet's Europe and After." *Encounter* 48 (May, 1977): 29-35. In large part a response to the criticisms of Monnet presented by Douglas Johnson (see entry below), this article emphasizes the important and constructive role played by Monnet in European affairs throughout his life.
Bromberger, Merry, and Serge Bromberger. *Jean Monnet and the United States of Europe*. New York: Coward-McCann, 1969. The Brombergers, French journalists, admire Monnet enormously and present a full and sympathetic picture of his career in this popular biography. Despite the authors' advantage of having Monnet's cooperation, however, their work is not very accurate or even well written. The lack of a bibliography, citations of sources, or an index further limits the volume's scholarly usefulness.
Johnson, Douglas. "A Certain Idea of Europe." *Times Literary Supplement* (December 10, 1976): 1530-1531. Johnson, in this review article occasioned by the publication of Monnet's autobiography, makes it plain that he does not share Monnet's faith in the potential advantages of European integration. Johnson attacks him harshly for being unrealistic and egotistical, both in his writing and throughout his career.
Mayne, Richard. "Gray Eminence." *American Scholar* 53 (August, 1984): 533-540. A brief, sympathetic examination of Monnet's importance behind the scenes in the movement to unify Europe. Mayne stresses Monnet's remarkable ability to get what he wanted done while allowing others to take the credit.
_____. *The Recovery of Europe, 1945-1973*. Garden City, N.Y.: Anchor Press, 1973. This book, by an English journalist who knew Monnet well and admired him intensely, contains an excellent scholarly account of

Monnet's role in Europe's most significant economic and political events following World War II. Meticulous notes and a good bibliography and index enhance the value of this volume.

Monnet, Jean. *Memoirs*. Garden City, N.Y.: Doubleday, 1978. Monnet presents a readable and extremely detailed account of his public career, but there is little about his private life here. Indeed, Monnet shows himself to be too tactful and reserved even to make strong judgments about the figures with whom he wrestled in politics. The book is well indexed.

"What Jean Monnet Wrought." *Foreign Affairs* 55 (April, 1977): 630-635. This anonymous article reviewing Monnet's *Memoirs* stresses his role in the founding of the European Community. It also raises serious questions about whether Monnet's approach, centering on the building of supranational economic institutions while leaving national governments intact, will ever produce the true European unity of which Monnet dreamed.

Garrett L. McAinsh

EUGENIO MONTALE

Born: October 12, 1896; Genoa, Italy
Died: September 12, 1981; Milan, Italy
Area of Achievement: Literature
Contribution: Montale is the foremost Italian poet of the twentieth century and the recipient of the Nobel Prize in Literature in 1975. With his contemporaries Giuseppe Ungaretti and Salvatore Quasimodo, Montale created a modern Italian poetry of international significance: honest, poignant, serious, and wise.

Early Life

Eugenio Montale was born in Genoa, Italy, on October 12, 1896. His father owned an import firm and would take the family—Montale's mother and his three elder brothers and one elder sister—to his native place of Monterosso on the Ligurian coast every summer. Montale returned there each summer through his first thirty years. He loved both the lonely splendor of the Italian coastline and the activity of turn-of-the-century Genoa. While he knew the local dialects and grew familiar with the typical mix of rich and poor in the city, he also became entranced by the beauty of the small coastal villages. The formative influences of these places would later color his poetry.

Montale did not attend a university. He was drawn toward a musical career as a singer, but the death of his teacher and his father's objections dissuaded him. Montale went through his early life with no clear idea of a career. His mother died, and he was, as the youngest, the favorite son. He was called up to serve in the army for two years in 1917. He went to Parma for training and then to the front in Trentino.

After World War I, he returned to Genoa and stayed there until 1927, cofounding the Turin review *Primo tempo* (1922) and becoming acquainted with the writers and critics of the day. Being unemployed for most of the time, he read voraciously: Poets such as Stéphane Mallarmé, Paul Valéry, and Charles Baudelaire, as well as the "prose-poet" Maurice de Guérin, Henry James, and philosophers such as Henri Bergson and Benedetto Croce captured his attention. Montale used the libraries, held long discussions with friends, and began to send out poems, essays, and reviews to the literary and popular press. He was quick to appreciate the quality of Italo Svevo, writing an "Omaggio" (homage) in 1925 that virtually created Svevo's Italian reputation. Montale became famous with the publication of his first book, *Ossi di seppia* (1925; *Bones of the Cuttlefish*, 1984). In 1927, he left Genoa for Florence, where he remained for some twenty years before going on to Milan and a full-time appointment as a literary editor for the newspaper *Corriere della sera*.

Life's Work

Montale's poetry draws upon the stark, rocky coastal landscapes of his youth. The poetry flourished throughout his career as a journalist and developed along with his interest in music and painting. *Ossi di seppia* gathered these interests and fused them in a mature, poised, stylish poetry of compact and passionate lyricism, bringing together evocations of youthful energy, the vivid landscapes of Monterosso, and the sense of an inimical world. It was a unique, unrepeatable achievement, mixing tones of longing and loneliness, isolation and love, in acknowledgment not only of the remorselessness of material existence but also of human care and hope for the safety of others. Montale is unflinching in his understanding of human vulnerability on the cosmic scale and is reminiscent of the grim, visionary Italian poet Giacomo Leopardi in his tenacity and depth. Memories, suspended emotions, symbolic presences of sea and coastline—Montale shares certain tonalities with T. S. Eliot. He resolutely refuses easy consolations and brings himself to terms with a world between the wars, in which living is compared to following a wall "with bits/ of broken bottle glass on top" ("Meriggiare pallido e assorto"). Correspondingly, Montale's versification surprises, with lines suddenly extending or contracting and with dissonant half-rhymes and old rhythmic effects. He departs from traditional prosody as he draws upon his memories of youth. Yet, the knowledge that the period of youthful innocence is over and that prosodic traditions have been broken as well lends a startling immediacy and a resilient vitality to his first book.

Upon arriving in Florence in 1927, Montale began work for the publisher Bemporad, but a year later was made director of the famous and prestigious literary and scientific library, the Gabinetto Vieusseux. He was the only candidate for the post not a member of the Fascist Party. In 1938, when Fascism had become much more powerful, his abstention from overt political life worked against him. He resigned from his post at that time rather than be coerced into joining the Party. He married, and throughout World War II, he lived in occupied Florence. He was by then writing for various important Florentine journals, and Einaudi published his second book of poems, *Le occasioni* (1939; the occasions). Here, Montale's most famous poems ("Dora Markus," "Motetti," "La casa dei doganiari," and "Eastbourne") reveal a great personal depth, focused on the love of a woman Montale's persona names Clizia. She is both a real, suffering person and a symbolic force crystallizing life and poetry, transforming fiction and reality. The volume marks the increased extent of the autobiographical aspect in Montale's poetry. Separation and loss, reunion and longing are the fundamental areas of experience explored in the most poignant and intimate fashion. Montale does not romanticize, but he maintains a deeply satisfying fusion of the experience of love with the moral and political dilemmas of the time. His poetry is attentive to the zeitgeist, but it is made more human, more sensitive, and more credible by the strength of love that runs through it. The language is spare; the certainties of Europe and his love are threatened by war and adversity. A number of actual women are given Beatrice-like significance in the poems, but the fragmented sense of their actuality and vulnerability illuminates the atmosphere of incipient tragedy. Underlying the poems runs a tone of anger and protest against human destruction.

If Montale's early life in Liguria, Monterosso, and Genoa had encouraged his introspection and self-absorption, the two decades he passed in Florence fostered his cultural awareness of humanism, literary ideas, and intellectual traditions. He was at this time writing reviews and essays on various literary subjects, and he translated into Italian Christopher Marlowe's *The Tragicall History of Dr. Faustus* (1604), William Shakespeare's *The Comedy of Errors* (1592-1593), *Julius Caesar* (1599-1600), *Hamlet* (1600-1601), *The Winter's Tale* (1610-1611), and other works. As his literary taste expanded and the range of his cultural appreciation widened, Montale was also producing poetry that was to appear in his third book. Between 1940 and 1942, he produced a sequence published in Lugano, Switzerland, in 1943 entitled "Finisterre." In 1948, on January 30, an opportune meeting with Guglielmo Emanuel, the editor of the national daily *Corriere della sera*, resulted in Montale being asked to provide immediately an article on the assassination of Mahatma Gandhi, which had just occurred. In two hours, Montale had the piece ready, and it appeared (anonymously) the next day. As a result, Montale was offered a permanent post on the paper, and he moved to Milan.

Montale's third volume, *La bufera e altro* (1956; *Eugenio Montale: The Storm and Other Poems*, 1978), gathers work written throughout the 1940's, in which lyrical and autobiographical qualities are mixed with political and historical concerns. He regarded it as his best book, and poems such as "L'anguilla" ("The Eel") and the "Finisterre" cycle are brilliantly realized. "Primavera hitleriana" ("The Hitler Spring") is an evocative and sinister depiction of Adolf Hitler and Benito Mussolini meeting in Florence. A sequence of poems sprang from Montale's visits to England and Scotland, as his attention to his immediate location, in Ely or Glasgow or Edinburgh, is disturbingly haunted by the vision of the woman he loves and his craving to rejoin her. Montale visited the Middle East (with his wife), and as his love poetry deepened and grew in poignancy and poise, his resolute refusal to engage directly in political life was reconfirmed. The book ends with two "provisional conclusions": "Piccolo testamento" (small testament) and "Il sogno del prigioniero" (the prisoner's dream), in which Montale's stoical adherence to spiritual independence rejects all recourse to the securities of either the Catholic church or Communism, the two political regimes then dominant in Italy. The mature restraint in these poems is a register of Montale's historical as well as his spiritual condition.

Montale's volume *Satura* (1971) contains poems previously published as

"Xenia" (1964-1967), written on the death of his wife, Drusilla Tanzi, and published in translation in 1970, together with miscellaneous other poems. The elegies are profoundly moving and reminiscent of Thomas Hardy in their hallucinatory power. They were written when Montale was in his seventies. The honorary degree of doctor of letters was awarded to Montale by the Universities of Rome, Milan, and Cambridge. In 1967, he was made a life-senator. The Nobel Prize, awarded in 1975, was a recognition of his life's achievement in poetry, which, though limited to a handful of books, has been compared to that of T. S. Eliot and Ezra Pound. He died in Milan, an elder statesman of Italian literature, in 1981.

Summary

Throughout his working life, Eugenio Montale was a professional journalist as well as a major poet. His published criticism includes work on modern Italian, British, and American literature, as well as essays on Dante, Giovanni Boccaccio, and a wide range of others. He published a book of stories, *La farfalla di Dinard* (1956; *Butterfly of Dinard*, 1971), and collections of essays and articles have also appeared. His achievement as a critic of literature and music and as a storyteller has added to his stature as a man of letters, but it is as a poet of lyric depth and lonely honesty that his moral and political significance is to be found. No one has written so well of the common ground between solitude and love. Concurrently, Montale's intellectual experiences brought about a cultured wisdom that tempered the oblique idiosyncrasies of his style. The intensity of Montale's poetry, its quartzlike beauty, suggests the strength of his character. In contradistinction to T. S. Eliot, Montale consistently refused to come to a point of certainty: His conclusions are deliberate and arrived at with difficulty, but if they are tempered, they are always provisional. Throughout a long life spanning both world wars and the Italian experience during the twentieth century, Montale exerted an immense influence on contemporary poets. As a critic and journalist, a senior figure in the Italian literary world, and a very modest man of great skeptical intelligence, he came to be seen as "the poet" of modern Italy.

Bibliography

Gatt-Rutter, John. "Manichee and Hierophant: Montale's Negative Epiphany." In *Writers and Politics in Modern Italy*. London: Hodder and Stoughton, 1978. A useful discussion of the poem "Nel silenzio" from *Satura* (1971) brings out the relation of Montale's rhetorical devices to the "political structure" of his poetry, determining its "oracular force" as a consequence of its "metaphysical affirmative."
Huffman, Claire. *Montale and the Occasions of Poetry*. Princeton, N.J.: Princeton University Press, 1983. Six interconnected essays offer close

discussions of individual poems, drawing upon Montale's essays, interviews, and letters. Much Italian literary criticism of Montale is also made available in this extremely helpful book. Includes copious annotations and an index.

_____. "T. S. Eliot, Eugenio Montale, and Vagaries of Influence." *Comparative Literature* 27 (1975): 193-207. A carefully judged comparative study of poetic influence. Montale wrote with great sympathy on Eliot and translated his poetry.

Leavis, F. R. "Xenia." *The Listener* (December 16, 1971): 845-846. The great English moralist and critic appraises Montale's elegaic poems in this highly astute and sensitive critique.

Praz, M. "Eliot and Montale." In *T. S. Eliot: A Symposium*, compiled by Richard March and Tambimuttu. London: Editions Poetry, 1948. An early comparative study of the vision and understanding demonstrated by two of the greatest twentieth century poets.

Singh, G. "Eugenio Montale." In *Italian Studies*, edited by E. R. Vincent. Cambridge, England: W. Heffer and Sons, 1962. An essay providing a general overview of Montale's work and achievement.

_____. *Eugenio Montale: A Critical Study of His Poetry, Prose, and Criticism*. New Haven, Conn.: Yale University Press, 1973. An indispensable, full-scale study of Montale's work, discussing his biography, literary background, affiliations, and influences, and providing critical analysis of the poems in each of Montale's books. Contains a bibliography and indexes.

Katherine Kearney Maynard

MARIA MONTESSORI

Born: August 31, 1870; Chiaravalle, Italy
Died: May 6, 1952; Noordwijk aan Zee, The Netherlands
Areas of Achievement: Education, science, and social reform
Contribution: The first woman to earn a medical degree and to practice
  medicine in Italy, Montessori became a spokesperson for human liberation
  and a pioneer in "scientific pedagogy." She developed an educational
  theory based upon children's spontaneous desire to learn in a prepared,
  free, child-centered environment that won international acclaim during
  her lifetime and enjoyed continued success after her death.

Early Life

Maria Montessori was born in the town of Chiaravalle, Italy, on August 31, 1870, the year of Italian unification. She was the only child of Renilde Stoppani Montessori, an educated, patriotic daughter of a landed family, and Alessandro Montessori, a conservative civil servant. The family moved to Rome in 1875. There Montessori attended a public elementary school and, at age thirteen, elected to study mathematics at a technical school. After graduating from technical school with high marks, Montessori attended a technical institute from 1886 to 1890. Then, to the shock of her father and the Italian academic community, she decided to study medicine and to become Italy's first female medical doctor. Montessori's ultimate graduation from the Medical College in Rome as a doctor of medicine and surgery in 1896 was a triumph of self-discipline, persistence, and courage.

Upon graduation, Montessori was chosen to represent Italian women at an international women's congress in Berlin, where her speeches on behalf of educational opportunity and equal pay for women won much praise. In November, 1896, Montessori was appointed a surgical assistant at a hospital for men, a medical assistant at the university hospital, and a visiting doctor at a women's and a children's hospital, all in Rome; in addition, she opened a private practice. She also continued her research at the psychiatric clinic of the University of Rome. As a voluntary assistant there, Montessori visited mental asylums to select patients for treatment at the clinic. Sorely troubled by the neglect of retarded children in the city's asylums, Montessori increasingly directed her research toward possible treatment of these children. Her determination that the best treatment was not medical, but pedagogical, turned Montessori's gaze to the study of educational theory and method.

Montessori undertook this new project with her customary energy and thoroughness, auditing education and physical anthropology courses at the university in 1897-1898 and reading all the pedagogical theory advanced over the last two hundred years. Ultimately, Montessori combined the century-old pedagogical ideas of Johann Heinrich Pestalozzi and Friedrich

Froebel (both of whom stressed the interrelationship of sensory, intellectual, and moral education and the need to move from the concrete to the abstract) with the early nineteenth century reformer Édouard Séguin's graduated exercises in sensory and motor development for retarded children and the new measurement techniques of physiology and anthropology. She tested her ideas about special education for retarded children at the psychiatric clinic, at national medical and teachers' conferences, on public lecture tours around Italy, and finally, in 1900, as the director of a new Roman medical-pedagogical institute for teachers of retarded children. In the demonstration school attached to this institute, Montessori experimented with new teaching methods and materials to foster sensory, motor, and intellectual skills in retarded kindergarten and primary students. The results were impressive: Under Montessori's care, many of the supposedly unteachable children mastered basic skills, learned to read and write, and even passed the examinations given to all Italian elementary-school students. In two short years, Montessori had become the most successful and famous educator of retarded children in Rome. At last she was ready to devote her attention to the education of all children.

Life's Work

In 1901, at the age of thirty-one, Montessori resigned her directorship of the medical-pedagogical institute, gave up her medical practice, and launched a new career. She reasoned that if her classes of retarded children could outperform normal children on standard tests, there had to be something dreadfully wrong with normal elementary education. Simultaneously reading voraciously in educational philosophy and observing in local primary schools, Montessori was struck by the disjunction between the two: While educational theorists preached the need for individual development and freedom to learn, educators practiced a deadening rote instruction, physical restraint and silence, and reliance on external rewards and punishments. Montessori became convinced that her new methods and materials, if "applied to normal children, would develop or set free their personality in a marvelous and surprising way." As a lecturer in the Pedagogic School of the University of Rome from 1904 to 1908, she refined her view that education should develop from the nature of the child rather than the other way around, as in traditional elementary education. She called this innovative approach "scientific pedagogy," but it was at least as concerned with spiritual/moral development and human autonomy as with scientific observation and prediction. Montessori was increasingly certain that her scientific/mystical pedagogy could reform not only the schools but also all of society.

Montessori won the opportunity to prove her theory's worth in 1907. A group of bankers had recently renovated a tenement house in a poor section of Rome and wished to establish a day-care center in the building, to keep the children of working parents from destroying the property. They turned to Montessori to direct the children's center. To the surprise and dismay of her faculty colleagues, she accepted the challenge with alacrity and transformed the empty room and fifty undisciplined, culturally disadvantaged, preschool children into a research laboratory and subjects. There she would observe the children's natures, test various approaches and materials, and ultimately develop the Montessori method.

In this unusual laboratory, Montessori quickly discovered that the children possessed a natural desire to learn and actually preferred challenging educational materials to frivolous toys. The previously unruly children developed tremendous powers of concentration and displayed great contentment when they were permitted to work with interesting, self-correcting materials, such as blocks or cylinders of graduated size, bells along a scale, or colors arranged according to the spectrum. Moreover, learning became joyful and easy when these didactic materials and exercises were introduced in an order that logically developed and coordinated sensory, motor, and intellectual skills. The teacher had only to demonstrate (never to preach) the proper use of the materials to a few children and then stand back and watch them teach themselves and one another. With special child-sized furniture, cupboards, dishes, and washstands, the children eagerly learned to choose and put away their own materials, fix their own lunches, and wash up. Even more impressively, these four- and five-year-olds painlessly and happily "exploded into writing and reading" in less than two months, through the carefully designed sequence of graduated exercises. In her Children's House in the slums of Rome, Montessori demonstrated that children's "spontaneous activity in a prepared environment" was more effective than the traditional coercive methods and rote instruction. Her respect for children's autonomy, desire to learn and grow, and inner dignity yielded rich rewards.

From the very start of the experiment at the Children's House, Montessori had encouraged community involvement. Uniquely at the time, she invited the working-class parents to visit the school often and confer about their children's progress. In an inaugural address at the opening of a second Children's House only three months after the first, Montessori stressed the community's ownership of the school, which she hoped would not only free working mothers from undue stress but also transform the local environment and thus redeem "the entire community." Montessori did not rest there. She also invited the attention and support of the wider community of educators, journalists, philanthropists, and religious and political leaders. Particularly after the children's miraculous initiation into writing and reading gained highly favorable press notices, a group of dedicated young women encircled Montessori and gradually relieved her of many daily operations in the schools. They also frequently served as missionaries for her method, setting up new Children's Houses in other Italian cities and towns. Meanwhile, convinced of the educational and social value of her work, Montessori began a lifelong campaign to publicize and spread her method.

This campaign was truly launched with the publication of Montessori's first book about education, *Il metodo della pedagogia scientifica applicato all'educazione infantile nelle case dei bambini* (1909; *The Montessori Method*, 1912). In her book she outlined the history of her "scientific pedagogy" and its realization in the Children's Houses, described her noncoercive methods and self-correcting materials in detail, postulated the existence of "sensitive periods" or stages of development in young children, and restated her basic belief in education as spontaneous self-development in a prepared but free environment.

This mixture of pedagogical theory and practical details also marked Montessori's other books in these years: *Dr. Montessori's Own Handbook* (1914), originally published in English as a concise summary of her theory and method, and *L'autoeducazione nelle scuole elementari* (1916; *The Advanced Montessori Method*, 2 vols., 1917), which introduced materials for teaching grammar and mathematics to older primary students. These books enjoyed great popularity in more than twenty languages; *The Montessori Method* alone sold five thousand copies in four days in the United States and became the second nonfiction bestseller of 1912.

Montessori's true genius for promotion, however, was manifested in her personal appearances to deliver public lectures and give teacher-training institutes around the world. Her deep conviction in the worth of her method and her charming personality led many who came to hear a celebrity leave converted to the Montessori movement. At the age of forty, Montessori decided to devote all of her time to foster that movement. Over the next forty years, she traveled intensively and extensively, to reach those who could not attend her teacher-training institutes in Italy. Everywhere the pattern followed that of her triumphal visit to the United States in 1913: Enthusiastic advance publicity drew huge crowds to Montessori's public lectures and institutes, which in turn sparked the formation or growth of Montessori societies and schools. With or without government sponsorship, Montessori schools were established in the United States, Great Britain, Italy, The Netherlands, Spain, Switzerland, Sweden, Austria, France, Australia, New Zealand, Hawaii, Mexico, Argentina, Japan, China, Korea, Syria, and India, and the movement continued to gain momentum and scope throughout Montessori's life. At the age of sixty-nine, Montessori spent the years of World War II in India, where she personally trained more than one thousand new teachers. Her striking success in this region that was new to her simply redoubled her energy; she returned to India in 1947 and Pakistan in 1949. Montessori was just planning a lecture tour in Africa, when she died suddenly at Noordwijk aan Zee in The Netherlands on May 6, 1952, at the age of eighty-one.

Summary

Wherever she went and whomever she addressed over a long and phe-
nomenally active career, Maria Montessori stressed two interrelated themes:
the desperate need for educational reform to develop the true potential of all
children and the equally important need for human liberation around the
world. While she believed fervently in the power of education to transform
individuals and society, she never neglected other social issues and approaches to her desired goals. From her early advocacy of women's rights as
a young medical doctor, through her proposal for an international "White
Cross" to nurse and teach the children of war in 1917, to her frequent calls
for recognition of the rights of children in the family and the dangers of
international competition in the 1920's and 1930's, Montessori proved herself to be a tireless and determined spokesperson for the powerless. While
she refused to politicize her educational method and movement—and accepted simultaneous support from the Italian government, the Viennese socialist government, and the Dutch liberal government in the 1920's—there
was never any doubt about Montessori's fundamental respect for human
dignity. She was invited to speak to the League of Nations in Geneva in 1926
on "Education and Peace" and lectured on the same subject at the United
Nations Educational, Scientific, and Cultural Organization (UNESCO) in
1947. Her long insistence on the interdependence of humanity won for Montessori the French cross of the Legion of Honor in 1949 and a nomination for
the Nobel Peace Prize in 1949, 1950, and 1951.

These were fitting tributes, for Montessori was, throughout her life, a
bridge between worlds. Her equal faith in science and spirituality allowed
her to translate between the early nineteenth century visions of moral education of Pestalozzi and Froebel and the twentieth century cognitive psychology of Jean Piaget (who was an active sponsor of the International Montessori Association). That special combination of scientific pragmatism and
spiritual mysticism also permitted Montessori to appeal to an extraordinarily
wide audience, ranging from the British Psychological Society of the Royal
Society of Medicine to the Theosophical Society of India. She moved easily
between the academic and nonacademic worlds, addressing scholars, teachers, social reformers, and working-class parents with equal success. Above
all, Montessori's determination to achieve order and harmony without
sacrificing freedom in education, society, and her own life served as an
inspiration for advocates of human liberation, social justice, and peace
around the world.

Bibliography

Hainstock, Elizabeth G. *Teaching Montessori in the Home*. New York: Ran-
      dom House, 1968. This clear, attractive book introduces the Montessori
      method to parents and provides recipes for Montessori materials and ex-

ercises to develop practical skills, finger dexterity, and sensory and intellectual abilities.

Kocher, Marjorie B. *The Montessori Manual of Cultural Subjects: A Guide for Teachers*. Minneapolis: T. S. Denison, 1973. This is a well-organized and clearly written guide to the Montessori method and materials, designed for teachers. The large quantity and fine quality of the illustrations (photographs and drawings) is especially helpful.

Kramer, Rita. *Maria Montessori: A Biography*. Chicago: University of Chicago Press, 1976. Part of the Radcliffe biography series, this is a densely packed, long, critical biography. Kramer devotes roughly a third of the book to Montessori's "Early Struggles," a third to "The Children's House," and a third to "The Method and the Movement."

Orem, R. C., ed. *Montessori: Her Method and the Movement; What You Need to Know*. New York: G. P. Putnam's Sons, 1974. This collection of essays by various Montessori teachers and advocates summarizes the essentials of the Montessori method in readable style and argues for the "relevance of Montessori to contemporary America."

Standing, E. M. *Maria Montessori: Her Life and Work*. Fresno, Calif.: Academy Library Guild, 1957. This was the authorized, first biography of Montessori, by one of her followers. While the descriptions of the life and work are highly appreciative and uncritical, the book contains many first-hand observations. The final comparison of Montessori and Froebel is especially illuminating.

Eve Kornfeld

AKIO MORITA

Born: January 26, 1921; Nagoya, Japan

Areas of Achievement: Business and industry

Contribution: Together with his mentor and business partner, Masaru Ibuka, Morita turned a tiny precision-instrument factory into the Sony Corporation, one of the largest industrial firms in the world and home of one of the best-known brand names in the world of business.

Early Life

Akio Morita was born in 1921 of a prominent family in Nagoya, the fifteenth-generation heir to one of Japan's oldest sake-brewing families. He grew up in an affluent household that mixed native traditions with an easy familiarity with Western ways. While the family was devoutly Buddhist, holding religious services at home, the young Morita could play tennis on the family court, go for Sunday outings in an open Model T Ford, and listen to Western classical music on an imported Victrola. In his autobiography, Morita writes that as a youngster he was intrigued by electrical devices such as the vacuum tube, which could take old scratchy, hissing records and turn them into beautiful sounding music.

Before long the intrigue turned into an obsession, and he was making his own crude radio and electric phonograph as well as a primitive voice-recording device. His scientific tinkering may have been responsible for his somewhat spotty academic record: While he excelled at mathematics and science, he received less than average grades in other studies. Still, by dint of a determined effort during a year of intense study with tutors, he managed to gain admission to the prestigious Eighth Higher School. With a mixture of self-mockery and pride, he relates that he became the lowest-ranking graduate of his middle school ever to be admitted to the science department at the Eighth Higher School.

Morita continued to develop his scientific skills, from 1940 to 1944, as a disciple of Tsunesaburo Asada, a distinguished specialist in applied physics at Osaka Imperial University. Upon graduation in 1944, Morita entered the navy as a technician-lieutenant and engaged in research on heat-seeking devices in the one year that remained in the Pacific War. It was during that period that he met a brilliant electronics engineer, Masaru Ibuka, thirteen years his senior.

Ibuka, though working on the same military project, was a civilian and owned his own precision-instrument company. Those who know both men frequently comment on their differing personalities. Ibuka is invariably described as shy, retiring, and more typically Japanese, while Morita is a dynamic super-salesman, bold and outspoken. Nevertheless, the two were to become the closest of friends, colleagues, partners, and cofounders of the Sony Corporation.

Life's Work

The story of Sony begins when Morita and Ibuka set up a shop repairing radios and making vacuum-tube voltmeters on the seventh floor of the charred, gutted ruins of a department store in Tokyo's Ginza shopping district in the grim days immediately after the end of the war. With a total capitalization of five hundred dollars—a loan from Morita's father—the business was formally incorporated as Tokyo Tsushin Kogyo (Tokyo Telecommunications Engineering Company) in May, 1946. The world-famous name "Sony" would come later.

There were false starts in the early years—experiments with manufacturing an electric rice cooker proved a failure, for example. In the meantime, when it became necessary to vacate their Ginza premises in 1947, they moved to the Gotenyama district on the southern edge of Tokyo, an area still devastated from the wartime bombing but once renowned for its cherry blossoms. The headquarters of the Sony Corporation remains to this day in Gotenyama.

The first major breakthrough product that Morita and Ibuka produced was a tape recorder, manufactured for the domestic market in 1950. When sales for the machine proved disappointing, it was Morita who decided to bypass the powerful trading companies, which customarily acted as middlemen, and instead set up the company's own distribution system. Morita himself personally visited Japanese schools to show how the product, then virtually unknown in Japan, could be used as a teaching tool, and before long nearly a third of Japan's elementary schools had purchased the devices. More important, the gamble to ignore traditional marketing practices had paid off and from then on it was the company's policy to manage its own sales, a factor that business analysts regard as crucial to Sony's later success.

The next milestone in the company's history has turned into one of the enduring legends of Japanese business history. In 1952, Ibuka (as president of the company) went to the United States to explore the possibilities of obtaining a patent owned by the Western Electric Company (WEC). When prospects for a deal seemed worth pursuing, the task was delegated to Morita, the more business-savvy vice president, who traveled to the United States for the first time in 1953. The negotiations with WEC—and with the Japanese government to take valuable currency out of the country to pay for patent rights—took a year to complete, but by 1954 Morita had successfully completed the deal. For twenty-five thousand dollars—a princely sum in a Japan which had yet to commence its "economic miracle"—Tokyo Telecommunications purchased a license to the transistor. WEC had used the transistor to make hearing aids; Ibuka and Morita had another idea that would tap a much larger consumer demand: a transistorized radio.

One year later, after much work to modify the newly acquired transistor for use in a radio, Morita and Ibuka put the first transistor radio on the market in Japan. Though the new product sold well, they were not satisfied; only the radio tubes had been transistorized. After successfully applying the new technology to the loudspeaker and transformer, the company introduced the world's first pocket-sized transistor radio in 1957.

It was about this time that Tokyo Telecommunications changed its name. Morita insisted that the firm's name was cumbersome in either Japanese or its English version. Someone looked up the Latin word for sound. "Sonus" sounded nice, but they were searching for something that was a little more catchy. Briefly Morita and Ibuka toyed with "Sonny," but the overtones of mischievous little boys did not seem appropriate. The word "Sony" was selected, first as the name for the transistor radio and then in January, 1957, as the name of their firm.

The tiny device was an instant success, and for the first time Sony was able to establish a market in the United States, a major turning point in the fortunes of the company. Morita considered offers from an American firm to market the miniaturized radio in the United States under an American brand name. It was tempting for the still tiny Japanese firm to rely on a large American firm to sell the radios in the unfamiliar American market, but Morita rejected the offer, calculating that it was time for Sony to establish its own name abroad no matter how great the obstacles might be.

Accordingly, in 1960, Sony America was established. From its first showroom on Fifth Avenue in Manhattan and very soon from Sony retailers all across the country, Americans gradually became familiar with the company's product line, which soon expanded into transistorized (solid-state) television. It took a decade for the American operation to become profitable, but by the end of the 1960's Sony had sold more than a million micro-televisions in the United States. The 1970's would see the introduction of the Trinitron color television, followed by a succession of other products, including the Betamax videocassette recorder and the Walkman portable stereo.

Morita also guided the establishment of Sony's first major joint-venture agreement, with the American television network CBS in 1966. Other joint ventures and cross-licensing agreements followed, bringing the Japanese firm more and more deeply into both North America and Europe. Further integration occurred when Sony began not only to sell but also to manufacture in the United States—in 1972, Morita presided over the groundbreaking ceremonies of its San Diego, California, television plant, which soon employed more than one thousand workers.

As president of Sony America, Morita took up residence in New York City with his wife and three children in 1962. This allowed him not only to directly manage the affairs of Sony in the United States but also to immerse himself in Western society and deepen his understanding of Western culture. One of his sons was graduated from Georgetown University. Regarding education, Morita noted that, contrary to Japan, many of the business elite in the United States did not possess a university education, an observation that prompted him to write, in 1966, a book entitled *Gakureki Muyouron* (college education is not always necessary). It became a best-seller in Japan.

In the course of his residence abroad, Morita accumulated a wide circle of friends not only in the business world, but among the leaders of the world political and cultural communities as well. He is always in great demand as a speaker and is known for his lively wit and the frank expression of his views. In an era when "trade friction" has dominated American-Japanese economic relations, Morita is an articulate spokesman for the prevailing Japanese view that the declining competitive position of the United States in world markets can best be explained not by unfair Japanese practices but by shortcomings in the American economy. While praising the innovative accomplishments of American science and technology, Morita faults the way American business is mesmerized by short-term profits to the neglect of long-term growth. Morita served as president of the Sony Corporation from 1971 to 1976 and has served as chairman of the board and chief executive officer since 1976.

Summary

Akio Morita is one of the best-known businessmen in the world, and the Sony label, established by Morita and Ibuka, is one of the best-known commercial names in the world. The two built the Sony empire from nothing in 1946 to its first billion-dollar sales year in 1973, and then to a five-billion-dollar year in 1984. In doing so, they made a major contribution in changing the image enjoyed by Japanese manufactured products throughout the world. At the time when Sony was first introduced to the West, Japanese goods invariably evoked adjectives such as "cheap" and "shoddy" among the consuming public outside Japan. In 1969, after only a decade of experience in international markets, Sony could take pride that the American Apollo mission carrying the first men to the moon carried Sony tape recorders.

By emphasizing reliability and quality and by producing attractive consumer merchandise at highly competitive prices, Sony, along with a few other companies, caused the "Made in Japan" label to become a symbol of excellence. In addition, Sony proved false the stereotype of Japanese industry as imitators. Its modification and improvement of the transistor and its discovery of radically new uses of that invention proved that the Japanese were skilled at innovation and adaptation.

Bibliography

Abegglen, James C., and George Stalk, Jr. *Kaisha: The Japanese Corpora-*

tion. New York: Basic Books, 1985. Though not exclusively devoted to Morita or Sony, this book does discuss them in the course of explaining how marketing, money, and manpower strategy made the Japanese world pacesetters.

Frailey, Fred, with Mary Lord. "Sony's No-Baloney Boss." *U.S. News and World Report* 101 (November 17, 1986): 57. A brief profile of Morita and Sony that gives some background of the company and of Morita. Morita is quoted about his future plans for Sony.

Kamioka, Kazuyoshi. *Japanese Business Pioneers*. Union City, Calif.: Heian International, 1988. In addition to general comments on characteristics of business and management styles in Japan, this book includes chapters devoted to eight corporate leaders in Japan, including Morita.

Lyons, Nick. *The Sony Vision*. New York: Crown, 1976. An informal company history that is made interesting because Lyons interviewed key Sony figures including Morita and Ibuka. The book, however, suffers from the fact that the author has little or no specialized expertise concerning Japan. Contains interesting illustrations.

Morita, Akio, with Edwin M. Reingold and Mitsuko Shimomura. *Made in Japan: Akio Morita and Sony*. New York: E. P. Dutton, 1986. A highly personalized account of the life and times of Morita and Sony. The book, in addition to autobiographical information, includes extensive commentaries by Morita on such topics as management, the difference between American and Japanese business styles, and world trade.

Weymouth, Lally. "Meet Mr. Sony: How the Japanese Outsmart Us." *The Atlantic* 244 (November, 1979): 33-34. Although brief and somewhat dated, this is a fine interpretive examination of the importance of Sony and Morita.

John H. Boyle

GAETANO MOSCA

Born: April 1, 1858; Palermo, Sicily
Died: November 8, 1941; Rome, Italy
Areas of Achievement: Political science, government, and politics
Contribution: Mosca was one of the founders of modern political science. His writings on the concept of elite rule were crucial contributions to a modern theory of government. Mosca combined a university position with an active political life, serving in the Italian parliament for fifteen years and eventually opposing Benito Mussolini and Fascism.

Early Life

Gaetano Mosca was born in Palermo, the capital city of the island of Sicily, on April 1, 1858. He was one of seven children in a middle-class family; his father was an administrator in the postal service. Mosca's Sicilian background played a crucial role in his later intellectual development. Sicily entered the Kingdom of Italy in 1861 with hopes for the island's resurgence as part of a newly unified country; however, the northern rulers proved to be every bit as harsh and corrupt, and as insensitive to Sicily's needs, as their Bourbon predecessors. Indeed, for much of the 1860's, and occasionally over the next two decades, Sicily rebelled against northern rule and was placed under martial law. Elections, when held, were fraudulent, results falsified, and coercion openly practiced.

All of this imbued the young Mosca, a bright and energetic student, with the strong distrust of politics common to most Sicilians. In the late 1870's, Mosca entered the University of Palermo, where he studied law. His degree, awarded in 1881, was based on a thesis whose central theme was nationalism. Mosca argued that national identity was largely a political myth of less real importance than people's regional or even local allegiances. This emphasis on the true rather than the apparent in politics remained with Mosca for the rest of his life.

In 1883, Mosca moved to Rome to take up advanced study in politics and government administration. The following year, he published a treatise on the theory of government, which was quite well-received and established something of a name for the young and clearly talented Mosca. Though he hoped for a position in the national university system, Mosca had to return home to Palermo for financial reasons and spent one year teaching history and geography in a local secondary school.

The call to the university, however, came soon afterward, and in 1885 Mosca became a lecturer in constitutional law in Palermo. He stayed two years, publishing monographs on constitutional issues while at the university. Disappointed at not receiving a full professorship, Mosca competed in a national civil service examination and won a position as editor of the official publications of the Italian Chamber of Deputies. He moved to Rome in 1887, took up his new duties, and embarked on further, direct study of the operation of government within the halls of parliament itself. This experience culminated in the publication of his first major work, *Elementi di scienza politica* (elements of political science), in 1896. In this book he outlined both a theory of government and a scientific methodology for the study of politics. These two issues would remain constant features in Mosca's later writings.

Life's Work

The most productive period of Mosca's life coincided with one of the most turbulent periods of European history: 1895 to 1925, the years of *la belle époque*, its disintegration in World War I, and the rise of Fascism on the Continent. A single concept informed all of Mosca's adult work—the existence and importance of minority rule in government and politics. Indeed, for the forty years of his active intellectual life, Mosca continued to elaborate and expand on this one idea.

Underlying his work was a simple and profoundly modern conception of the purpose of political science: to examine government, not as the state appears or according to what it claims to do but rather as it really operates. In particular, Mosca maintained that modern governments, behind the appearance of majority rule and representative democracy, were really the expression of the power of a small, well-organized minority.

Mosca embarked on a detailed historical investigation into government in the past to see if minority rule was a constant feature in human societies. He insisted on grounding all political theory in actual history rather than on subjective impressions. This approach marked the first serious effort to give the study of politics a real methodology akin to that of the natural sciences. Mosca, first in the 1896 *Elementi di scienza politica* and then as a university professor in Turin from 1898 to 1923, looked at government over a wide sweep of time, starting with the Greek city-states, and then studying the Roman Empire, European feudal societies, absolutist monarchies on the Continent, representative government in England, and finally ending with considerations on democracy in the United States. His conclusion was simple and profound: "Everywhere and in every time," Mosca wrote in *Elementi di scienza politica*, "all that is called government, the exercise of authority, command and responsibility, always belongs to a special class that always forms a small minority." Mosca labeled this minority the "political class," though it is better known today as a ruling elite.

In his teaching at the University of Turin and also at Italy's most prestigious private academy, the Bocconi in Milan, Mosca developed his ideas on the "political class." His mature writings focused on the formation and organization of elite rule in modern society. Mosca maintained that the concentration of power in the modern state and its vast influence over the lives of its citizens made elite rule the most important single issue for contemporary political science.

Initially, Mosca's contention that minority rule was a permanent feature of society made him a strong critic of what he considered to be the democratic pretensions in modern representative government. Most people, he believed, had neither the resources nor the education to rule adequately; as a result, they were thoroughly unqualified to govern themselves. Indeed, Mosca, as a Deputy to the Italian Chamber from 1909 to 1919, was one of only two representatives to vote against the extension of the suffrage to all adult males shortly before World War I.

Mosca offered an original and telling criticism of modern democracies with the assertion that the electors' free choice among candidates—an essential foundation of democratic theory—was quite simply "a lie." He pointed out how various groups in society—politicians, influential social and economic figures, and trade unions—had a determinate voice in the selection of those candidates who would appear before the electorate. The influence of these groups guaranteed the reproduction of the already established ruling elite.

Mosca also argued that increasingly complex technology was an important element in maintaining elite rule in contemporary societies. Knowledge of such technology and mastery of certain vital productive skills, what Mosca referred to as both "personal merit" and "special culture," gave certain individuals and social groups great influence in the political affairs of society. Additionally, Mosca noted that the consent of the governed was crucial to the maintenance of minority rule. Governing elites justified their position in society by developing and disseminating "political formulas," which legitimized their rule and gave their power a "moral and legal base." Mosca left this potent insight undeveloped, turning his attention instead to how elites organize themselves. Modern political and social theorists have used Mosca's conception of political formulas as a springboard for their own work on the social function of ideology.

Mosca found nothing morally objectionable in his assertion that all societies were governed by a ruling minority—for him, this was merely a statement of historical fact. Mosca did distinguish between good and bad forms of elite rule. Minority government was good when it blocked the emergence of disruptive elements and deviant behavior, both of which threatened society's existence; the political class was also "good" when it allowed for a gradual renewal of the ruling elite without violent clashes or revolutionary change. Minority rule was bad when it tended to confer too much power in the hands of one social group, leading to despotic or even dictatorial rule.

Mosca most clearly revealed the prejudices that underlay his claim to an objective theory of government. Mosca was a social and political conservative, a middle-class gentleman and intellectual who mistrusted both the masses and the privileged. Mosca's ideal government was one in which other middle-class, university-trained intellectuals (men like himself) would manage the state. World War I demolished the possibilities for this kind of enlightened elite rule. Mass politics were the order of the day after 1919, and Italy was the first European country to experience the rise of Fascism out of the ruins of a representative democracy.

Mosca was a senator in the Italian parliament from 1919 to 1925, and directly witnessed the destruction of parliamentary rule at the hands of Mussolini. This experience led Mosca to a final development in his theory of government—the advocacy of a mixed form of political rule. The second edition of his *Elementi di scienza politica*, published in 1923 (and issued in an English translation in 1939 with the title *The Ruling Class*), included Mosca's writings on the need to include in the governing minority members of all the major "social forces" in society. Mosca was most concerned to keep political power separate from clerical influence and to avoid mixing politics with either military or economic strengths. Mosca maintained that only a balance of social forces would ensure that elite rule would tend toward social stability and block the drift toward dictatorship. Therefore, Mosca ended his academic and political career strongly supportive of one interpretation of a classic element in democratic theory—the separation of powers.

Summary

The tragedy of World War I and, immediately afterward, the rise of Fascism in Italy forced many European intellectuals, Gaetano Mosca included, to choose among the alternatives outlined in their academic studies. Despite his constant focus on elite rule, Mosca, to his great credit (and unlike the other elite theorists Vilfredo Pareto and Robert Michels), moved increasingly toward an acceptance, albeit a reluctant one, of mass parliamentary democracy. In 1925, Mosca opposed a law granting Mussolini full executive and legislative powers; he then resigned his seat in the senate and spent the rest of his active life teaching political theory at the University of Rome. He retired from teaching in 1933 and in 1937 published a collection of his lectures, *Storia delle dottrine politiche* (history of political theory), which included a strong criticism of the Fascist racial theory of government. Mosca died at his home in Rome late in 1941.

With his theory of a "political class" and elite rule and the outlines of a historical methodology for the study of government, Mosca offered the beginnings of a truly modern science of politics. The real significance and fuller development of political science along the lines sketched out by Mosca waited another decade after his death, but modern political theorists of elite rule and democracy owe much to the work of Mosca.

Bibliography

Albertoni, Ettore A. *Mosca and the Theory of Elitism*. Translated by Paul Goodrick. Oxford: Basil Blackwell, 1987. A good introduction to the work of Mosca, written by one of the foremost Italian specialists. Includes a bibliography of Mosca's principal works, a list of critical studies in English and Italian, a summary of the major interpretations of Mosca's theories, and a brief biography.

Bellamy, Richard. *Modern Italian Social Theory: Ideology and Politics from Pareto to the Present*. Cambridge: Polity Press, 1987. Bellamy presents a concise treatment of several major Italian social theorists, including Mosca. The combination of intellectual history and political theory gives this book strengths that few others in the field achieve.

Bobbio, Norberto. *On Mosca and Pareto*. Geneva: Librairie Droz, 1972. A short paper on the two major Italian theorists of elite rule in modern societies, written by the leading contemporary political philosopher in Italy. Bobbio contrasts the political implications (and actions) of these two men whose understanding of elite theory was so similar.

Hughes, H. Stuart. *Consciousness and Society: The Reorientation of European Social Thought*. New York: Alfred A. Knopf, 1958. One of the best and most succinct accounts of Mosca's work in English. Of particular value is Hughes's approach, which situates Mosca in the context of general intellectual trends and social theory in Europe from 1890 to 1930.

Meisel, James H. *The Myth of the Ruling Class: Gaetano Mosca and the "Elite."* Reprint. Westport, Conn.: Greenwood Press, 1980. The new edition of the 1958 volume, which was the one of the first critical studies in English. Meisel's book contains detailed treatments of Mosca's work and thought.

David Travis

ROBERT MUGABE

Born: February 21, 1924; Kutama, Southern Rhodesia (now Zimbabwe)

Areas of Achievement: Government and politics

Contribution: Mugabe rose rapidly in the struggle for independence in southern Africa during the 1960's to become a prominent nationalist leader and statesman during the later part of the 1970's and the 1980's. Mugabe participated actively in the Lancaster House negotiations that led Rhodesia (Zimbabwe) to majority rule in April, 1980, and became the first black prime minister of Zimbabwe and its first executive president.

Early Life

Robert Gabriel Mugabe was born in Kutama, near Salisbury (modern Harare), in Sinoia district, Southern Rhodesia, in 1924 (some biographers cite the year 1928 for his birth). His father was a Catholic mission-trained carpenter who also owned a considerable number of cattle, which the young Mugabe tended with his friends. Although a gentle and quiet boy, Mugabe is said to have loved boxing and wrestling. He completed his primary education in such Catholic schools as Empandeni and a Jesuit institution in Matabeleland. In 1950, he continued his studies in South Africa and was graduated as a schoolteacher from St. Hare University College. Immediately following his graduation, Mugabe taught school in Zimbabwe from 1952 to 1955 and then moved to Northern Rhodesia (now Zambia), in 1955, and to Ghana, during its transition to independence (1956-1960), continuing his teaching career in both British colonies.

Developing an interest in politics, Mugabe returned to his fatherland in 1960 and became information and publicity secretary of the (African) National Democratic Party, which had initiated negotiations toward independence with the British government. Yet as the self-governing whites banned the party in 1961, Mugabe joined Joshua Nkomo's Zimbabwe African People's Union (ZAPU), becoming his deputy. As a result of political differences and perhaps leadership styles, however, Mugabe defected from the party and joined Ndabaningi Sithole's Zimbabwe African National Union (ZANU) based in Tanzania. Before escaping to Tanzania in 1963, however, Mugabe was accused of calling the Rhodesian Front "a bunch of cowboys" and was arrested and imprisoned in 1962-1963. In Tanzania, he became secretary general of ZANU. In August, 1963, he dared to return to Southern Rhodesia but was arrested in December and spent the next ten years in and out of jail, in a permanent state of detention. In jail, Mugabe found time to take advanced courses in business and law through correspondence and received six degrees, including a master's and a bachelor's degree in law and a bachelor's degree in public administration.

Life's Work

Since 1965, Southern Rhodesia had become independent following a unilateral declaration of independence by the white population. The rebel colony, however, did not receive international recognition. Meanwhile, the white regime, under severe United Nations (U.N.) sanctions, imprisoned most nationalist leaders. In 1974, Ian Smith, the rebel white prime minister, declared a general amnesty and freed all political prisoners, including Mugabe. Mugabe took refuge in Mozambique and assumed leadership of ZANU's guerrilla wing, the Zimbabwe African National Liberation Army (ZANLA), which, along with ZAPU (based in Lusaka, Zambia), began inflicting severe casualties and economic and political damage on the Rhodesian white regime, particularly after Mozambique gained its independence in mid-1975. By 1976, it looked as if international pressure and nationalist guerrillas had succeeded in convincing the white minority regime to negotiate toward majority rule. In fact, the British government arranged such negotiations in Geneva, which Mugabe and Nkomo attended as leaders of their newly formed Patriotic Front (PF). Of the two, Mugabe was the more outspoken critic of the Smith regime at the conference. Unfortunately, the talks ended, and Mugabe returned to Mozambique convinced that only military action could bring down the white regime in Rhodesia.

Inside the former British colony, however, several black political leaders were willing to compromise with Smith. Thus, in 1978, Smith (and his Rhodesian Front) and Bishop Abel Muzorewa (leader of the United African National Council), as well as Sithole, agreed on the formation of a government that would lead to majority rule. Mugabe and Nkomo did not participate in the negotiations and therefore condemned them and their outcome. Notwithstanding their objections, elections followed, making Muzorewa the winner and the Prime Minister of Zimbabwe-Rhodesia. In 1979, however, Muzorewa and Smith repudiated their "internal political settlement" and accepted a new round of negotiations sponsored by the British government at Lancaster House in London from September to December 1979. Both Mugabe and Nkomo, urged by the frontline states, attended the talks, which endorsed national elections and a bicameral assembly—a house of parliament with one hundred seats, twenty of which would be reserved for the white minority, and a forty-member senate. Following the talks, however, Mugabe announced that he and his followers would run independent of the ZAPU wing of the PF as candidates for parliament. ZANU's political strength was such that it captured fifty-seven of the eighty seats reserved for the black parties in the February, 1980, elections. Nkomo's party won twenty, while Muzorewa's secured only three seats. On April 18, 1980, Mugabe became prime minister and immediately formed a coalition government that included five ZAPU members in a cabinet of twenty-five ministers.

Thereafter, Mugabe followed a policy of reconciliation with both white and African political opponents, particularly Nkomo, and slowed down the implementation of his socialist goals and the breakup of the large white farms. Abroad, he followed a nonaligned policy, reserving his harshest criticism for South Africa. The attempt to merge and disband ZANU and ZAPU guerrilla forces, however, proved to be an almost impossible task. ZAPU military elements were accused of terrorizing the countryside in southwest Matabeleland Province through intimidation and murders of white settlers. The ZAPU cabinet ministers, including Nkomo, were allegedly plotting to overthrow Mugabe and his government and were therefore dismissed in 1982. Nkomo became an outspoken critic of ZANU, but in the 1985 elections, Mugabe demonstrated his strength by winning sixty-six seats. He also won two extra seats when a white member of the Conservative Alliance of Zimbabwe (successor to the Rhodesian Front) and a ZAPU delegate switched sides. Tensions between Mugabe and Nkomo were so high that the latter's passport was confiscated as he tried to leave the country in 1985. (He eventually escaped to Great Britain through Botswana but returned home soon thereafter.) The murder of fifteen white missionaries in November of 1987 in Matabeleland, however, compelled the government to arrest several ZAPU members, including some ministers who were subsequently exonerated and released by the High Court. In spite of all the political turmoil, ZANU's leadership was so strong that on December 3, 1987, after a change of the constitution, Mugabe became the first executive President of Zimbabwe, forcing President Canaan Banana to step down. In September of that year, the president had also succeeded in compelling parliament to rescind the provision guaranteeing the twenty seats for the white minority. Meanwhile, reconciliation talks between ZANU and ZAPU had been going on since 1986, after Nkomo condemned the murders in Matabeleland. As a result, on January 2, 1988, a new cabinet, representing all ethnic groups in the country, was announced and, in April, 1988, the two parties fused into ZANU-PF, making Mugabe president and first secretary of the new front and Nkomo and Simon Muzenda co-vice presidents and second secretaries, while agreeing to work toward a one-party state based on Marxist-Leninist principles.

In late 1988 and early 1989, however, the stability of Mugabe's government was threatened by corruption charges involving the selling of state cars at a profit by government officials, including five ministers. Eventually, all of them resigned and one of the officials committed suicide from an overdose of an insecticide, after Mugabe forced all of them to appear before a judicial inquiry commission. The inquiry was embarrassing to the government, and critics of Mugabe accelerated their inflammatory rhetoric. It was this atmosphere that led to the formation of a new party in 1989, the Zimbabwe Unity Movement (ZUM), by a founding member of ZANU, former

Secretary-General Edgar Tekere, whose platform was "anti-corruption, anti-one-party state, and pro-economic growth." Political analysts, however, do not consider ZUM a serious challenge to Mugabe. (Tekere had been implicated in a murder and expelled from ZANU.)

Summary

Robert Mugabe's popularity, despite his autocratic rule in Zimbabwe, is based on many factors. As elsewhere in revolutionary Africa, former guerrilla leaders become extremely popular when they turn statesmen. In fact, his leadership of the ZANU military wing based in Mozambique during the war of liberation has been given much more credit for weakening the Smith regime than ZANU, in spite of the fact that the latter was led by a more seasoned politician, Nkomo. Nkomo, however, was perceived as being manipulated by and the favorite of the West, particularly during the last years of the struggle, in spite of his party's assistance from the Soviet Union. Mugabe, on the contrary, notwithstanding his ties with China, was viewed in the country as a determined "man of his own," with Zimbabwean black people's welfare as his uncompromising goal. His stature was enhanced by the fact that ZANU was predominantly a party of the Shona, who constitute 75 percent of the country, while ZAPU received more of its support from the Ndebele, who make up only 20 percent of the country's population.

Mugabe is, furthermore, one of the most educated African leaders in Africa and the most educated among the frontline presidents. He understands the workings of the capitalist system and the impact of socialist principles and objectives. Thus, his pragmatic approach, mixing capitalism (liberalization of the economy) with socialism (slow and extremely careful nationalization), has been able to maintain an acceptable level of productivity not lower than that of the preindependence period. This method has attracted investors while preventing the flight of needed skilled manpower.

Mugabe's unending emphasis on reconciliation, his strong support for and participation in the Southern Africa Development Coordinating Conference, and his tough stand on South Africa, which advocates "punitive sanctions" against apartheid, have made him a popular president, who will most likely succeed in making Zimbabwe a one-party state. His foreign policy has mostly been nonaligned. His attitude toward the Soviet Union (which he did not invite to participate in the independence celebrations) can be characterized as cool and that toward the United States as lukewarm because of the latter's cozy relations with South Africa. The United States is uncomfortable with Mugabe's Marxist-Leninist philosophy. His pragmatic approach, however, has made him a more acceptable statesman than, for example, António Agostinho Neto, Joao dos Santos, Samora Moises Machel, or Joaquim Chissano.

Lately, Mugabe's problems have come from the corruption of his government officials, the military assistance to the Mozambique Liberation Front against the Mozambique National Resistance (an assistance that has become costly in human and economic resources), his insistence on a one-party state (a Catholic Bishops' pastoral letter criticized him openly in November, 1988), and his feud with Nkomo. Yet, he has faced these problems squarely, as he and President Daniel arap Moi of Kenya, for example, decided to mediate the Mozambique conflict in 1989. He settled his differences with Nkomo in early 1988 and showed his integrity when he ordered an inquiry of the corruption charges. It seemed likely, however, that his survival would be determined by the domestic economic conditions and the rapidly changing situation in southern Africa. Throughout the years, his own integrity has remained unquestionable. Mugabe is a quiet man; his personality has been shaped by Catholic discipline and influenced by his readings of the works of Karl Marx and his encounter with the philosophy of the African National Congress and Mahatma Gandhi in South Africa as well as by his admiration for Kwame Nkrumah, for whom he worked in Ghana.

Bibliography

Astrow, André. *Zimbabwe: A Revolution That Lost Its Way?* London: Zed Press, 1983. One of the best accounts of the Zimbabwe revolutionary movements, although it portrays Mugabe as one who compromised his principles to accommodate imperialist capitalism in the former British colony.

Gifford, Prosser, and Wm. Roger Louis, eds. *Decolonization and African Independence*. New Haven, Conn.: Yale University Press, 1988. The chapter on Zimbabwe outlines the context in which Mugabe assumed power. It provides a sympathetic account of Mugabe's leadership of ZANU.

Lipschutz, Mark R., and R. Kent Rasmussen. *Dictionary of African Historical Biography*. 2d ed. Berkeley: University of California Press, 1986. An impartial, nonanalytical treatment of Mugabe.

Martin, David, and Phyllis Johnson. *The Struggle for Zimbabwe*. London: Faber & Faber, 1981. One of the most important sources for the understanding of the war of liberation in Zimbabwe and the crucial role Mugabe played as leader of ZANLA, the military wing of ZANU.

Rasmussen, R. Kent. *Historical Dictionary of Rhodesia/Zimbabwe*. Metuchen, N.J.: Scarecrow Press, 1979. A quick and easy reference source on the historical, political, and economic development of Rhodesia/Zimbabwe, including a biographical sketch of Mugabe.

Stoneman, Colin, and Lionel Cliffe. *Zimbabwe: Politics, Economics, and Society*. New York: Pinter, 1989. One of the most comprehensive recent works on Zimbabwe and a good analysis of Mugabe's Marxist philosophy. The work is part of Pinter's series on Marxist regimes.

Ungar, Sanfor J. *Africa: The People and Politics of an Emerging Continent.* New York: Simon & Schuster, 1985. Here Mugabe is described as "quiet, pensive, austere . . . and probably the best-educated head of any government in Africa, aloof, undecided, [a man] whose style looks less like caution than like a failure of leadership."

Mario Azevedo

EDVARD MUNCH

Born: December 12, 1863; Løten, Norway
Died: January 23, 1944; Ekely, Norway
Area of Achievement: Art
Contribution: The dramatic paintings and graphics of Munch not only reflected his inner torments and emotions but also proved highly influential on artistic developments in the late nineteenth and early twentieth centuries. In addition to becoming his native country's most famous artist, Munch served as one of the main progenitors of expressionism.

Early Life

Born December 12, 1863, in Løten, Norway, Edvard Munch was the second of five children born to Christian Munch and his wife Laura Cathrine Bjølstad. Munch's father was a doctor who in 1864 moved his family to Oslo, then called Christiania, where he earned a fairly meager living in one of the city's poorer districts. A sickly, lonely child, Munch experienced two early tragedies that haunted the rest of his life—the deaths of his mother in 1868 and of his beloved elder sister Sophie in 1877, both victims of tuberculosis. His mother's sister Karen moved into the household to care for the children, and she provided Munch with a degree of warmth and encouragement that his strict and deeply religious father failed to do. All the Munch children grew accustomed to drawing as a means to pass the long winter nights. Recognizing her nephew's talents, Karen Bjølstad encouraged his interest and bought him painting materials.

Munch's father decided that his son's abilities would enable him to pursue a career in engineering, so Munch was enrolled at the Technical College in 1879. Poor health prevented his attending regularly, and the young Munch became determined to follow a career in painting, a decision that a family friend, C. F. Dirike, helped convince the elder Munch to accept.

In 1880, Munch left the technical school and began painting seriously. The following year, he was enrolled in the School of Design to take classes in drawing and modeling under the direction of sculptor Julius Middlethun. With six other young aspiring artists, Munch rented a studio in Christiania's art district in 1882 and soon became the prize pupil of Christian Krogh, a naturalist painter who was the leader of the town's artistic community. During these years, Munch was also befriended by a distant relative, Frits Thaulow, who had close connections with many French painters. Thaulow provided financial support that allowed the young Munch to make his first trip to Paris in 1885. During his three weeks there, he studied the masterpieces in the Louvre and the salons and found himself particularly impressed by the landmark works of Édouard Manet.

As early as 1883 Munch had participated in a group exhibition in Oslo and had managed to sell a few works, but his early career remained hampered by his environment. Norway in the late nineteenth century remained culturally conservative and unreceptive to the new trends then revolutionizing the art world. Local critics attacked Munch's work as sloppy, unfinished, and unrealistic.

During this period, Munch fell under the influence of the bohemian movement in Oslo, led by the anarchist writer Hans Jaeger. This group of young writers and artists deliberately shocked bourgeois society with their unconventional ideas and behavior and their attack on nearly all sacred traditions. Munch never embraced their program totally, but he was nevertheless influenced by their avant-garde attitudes.

Life's Work

In 1885, shortly after his return from Paris, Munch began work on three paintings that became hallmarks of his mature style: *The Morning After*, *Puberty*, and *The Sick Child*. The last of these three, clearly inspired by memories of his sister's death, created an uproar when shown at the Annual State Exhibition in 1886. Critics assailed his works as laughable and the product of a madman. Still, during the years 1889-1891, Munch received three grants from his government that enabled him to escape the narrow cultural confines of Norway and study abroad.

Following his first one-man show in Oslo in 1889, Munch utilized the first of his state grants to leave for study in Paris. The death of his father later in the year, coupled with this move, opened a new era in Munch's life, a peripatetic existence in which he absorbed many of the dramatic new ideas of late-nineteenth century European culture. He initially was enrolled in the Parisian art school of Léon Bonnat, who was a strict academician. Munch soon quarreled with Bonnat, whose commitment to realism he found unchallenging. He moved to St. Cloud, where he shared a room with Danish poet Emmanuel Goldstein. There he developed a new artistic commitment to abandon his earlier naturalism in favor of mood painting, depicting themes such as suffering and love.

Munch returned to Norway periodically and in 1892 held his second one-man show there, which resulted in his receiving an invitation from the Berlin Artists' Union to exhibit his works in the German capital. The resulting show created such an uproar that conservatives in the union forced it to close after one week. Nevertheless, the 1882 Berlin exhibition made Munch famous throughout Germany and a hero to the more avant-garde artistic community there. He spent much of the next sixteen years in Germany and became associated with Berlin's bohemian circles.

From 1892 until 1908, Munch embraced a restless life-style, living mainly in hotel rooms and traveling constantly. His artistic output remained prolific, and dozens of exhibitions of his work were held in major cities across Europe. During the 1890's, he began work on graphics, a field he found both challenging and rewarding, enabling him to reach a wider audience and give new expression to some of his familiar themes. He eventually mastered all graphic techniques, with his greatest output being in lithographs.

Beginning in 1893, Munch embarked upon an artistic project that he called *The Frieze of Life*, conceived as a series of paintings to present a picture of life, love, and death. Many of the works were inspired by his early childhood experiences and reflected his preoccupation with illness, anxiety, and emotional trauma. He worked on this series periodically for more than thirty years and hoped to have all of it eventually collected in one great hall, an aspiration that remained unfulfilled.

Munch's mature style, which developed throughout the 1890's, followed his determination to make his works explore man's inner psyche. He kept notes of his visual experiences and most often drew from memory. Mood dominated Munch's paintings and graphics more than any other artistic element; he frequently gave his works a bold simplicity that enabled them to convey his emotional reactions. Sometimes he went weeks without painting and then would work in a frenzy of activity late into the night, rapidly putting on the canvas visual images that had been building in his mind.

Certain themes and subjects consistently appeared in Munch's work throughout his long career, many of them reflecting his traumatic childhood and his own introverted nature. Many dealt with death, illness, and isolation. Others were blatantly erotic in nature. Munch became a revealing portraitist and also produced a remarkable series of self-portraits between 1880 and 1943. Other Munch paintings concentrated on the landscape of his beloved Norway. In the early 1900's, he turned to a new theme, depicting members of the working class. Throughout the entire era he was never totally committed to a single style, and he refrained from joining any one of the numerous schools of art that developed during his lifetime. He remained a supreme individualist, letting his art convey his attitudes and emotions.

Although Munch remained devoted to his aunt and sisters, he deliberately avoided permanent entanglements in his personal life. A lifelong bachelor, he early decided against marriage, citing his family history of tuberculosis and mental illness and also fearing that a wife and children would hinder his artistic development. His most serious affair, with Tulla Larsen, ended disastrously, when she threatened suicide and accidentally shot Munch in the hand, permanently paralyzing one of his fingers.

In the early 1900's, Munch's nomadic life-style, coupled with overwork and excessive drinking, threatened his mental stability and led to irrational behavior. He became quarrelsome and consumed by feelings of persecution, an emotion perhaps fed by the continued rejection of his work by Norwegian critics. Despite increasing financial security and a growing reputation in Germany, Munch suffered a nervous breakdown in Copenhagen in late 1908 and voluntarily checked himself into a clinic run by Dr. Daniel Jacobsen. After eight months of treatment, he emerged fully recovered physically and mentally. He abandoned his wandering life in favor of a more stable existence in Norway. Munch's new self-confidence and more optimistic attitude were reflected in his subsequent works, which were less somber and violent.

Although he occasionally traveled throughout Scandinavia and the continent, Munch spent most of his time after 1908 in Norway. One of his major projects during the initial years after his return concerned a series of murals he painted for the Great Hall of the University of Oslo, an undertaking that caused a fierce controversy in which his designs were initially rejected and only approved five years after he entered the competition. These strikingly modern murals consumed most of Munch's time until their completion in 1916.

Munch eventually bought or rented several manors in Norway to provide himself with sufficient space for his work. In 1916, he purchased Ekely, an estate on the outskirts of Oslo, which remained his principal home until his death.

Gradually his native country extended official recognition for his accomplishments, purchasing several of his works for the National Gallery and subsequently awarding him the Grand Cross of the Order of Saint Olav on his seventieth birthday. Yet in spite of his growing prominence, Munch preferred to live a hermitlike existence at Ekely. He saw only a few friends and lived a spartan life surrounded by his paintings and graphics, which he called his children.

In 1930, a blood vessel burst in Munch's right eye, which prevented him from working for almost a year. He had troubles with his vision for the rest of his life. Nevertheless, Munch continued to work twelve hours or more a day. In 1937, the Nazi regime in Germany included Munch on a list of "degenerate" artists and confiscated eighty-two of his works on exhibit in German museums. After the Nazi occupation of Norway in 1940 Munch was left alone. He continued painting and printmaking and refused all contact with the invaders.

Munch died of complications resulting from bronchitis on January 23, 1944. In his will he unconditionally bequeathed all of his work in his possession to the city of Oslo. This collection formed the basis for the museum in his honor that opened in Oslo in 1963.

Summary

During a career that spanned six decades, Edvard Munch produced a remarkable collection of paintings, drawings, and graphics that made him one of the leading figures of modern European art. His works were highly personal, reflecting his inner torments and anxieties and providing glimpses into the psychological aspects of man's nature. His most famous painting, *The*

Scream (1893), foreshadowed the horrors that awaited mankind amid the brutality and existential dilemmas of the twentieth century.

In contrast to his tragic contemporary, Vincent van Gogh, Munch managed to survive despite threatened sanity and emerge a stronger figure who vigorously continued to work into his eighties. His bold use of lines and colors, combined with the psychological implications of his work, clearly made him one of the chief influences on the emerging artistic movement called expressionism. His influence, first greatest in Germany, spread throughout Central and Eastern Europe and was eventually recognized throughout the Continent and the United States.

In his writings, Munch maintained that art resulted from man's desire to communicate with others, and throughout his long life his profoundly personal paintings and other artistic works reflected his desire to share his own grief and joys with his fellowman. His monumental body of work always retained the integrity of his purpose and provided the twentieth century with a poignant glimpse into the dilemmas and perplexities that confronted humanity in an increasingly unsettled and threatening world.

Bibliography

Amman, Per. *Edvard Munch*. Thornbury, England: Artlines UK, 1987. This monograph contains a brief introductory essay on Munch's life and significance, a chronological table of major events in his life, and more than eighty pages of enlarged reproductions of his major works.

Dunlop, Ian. *Edvard Munch*. New York: St. Martin's Press, 1977. Dunlop provides a biographical sketch of Munch's life and forty color prints of the Norwegian artist's key works, accompanied by commentary.

Heller, Reinhold. *Munch: His Life and Work*. Chicago: University of Chicago Press, 1984. This recent, well-researched biography is thoroughly documented and contains copious excerpts from Munch's letters and other writings. It includes a select bibliography and 180 illustrations.

Hodin, J. P. *Edvard Munch*. New York: Oxford University Press, 1972. A volume in Oxford's respected World of Art series, this monograph by an author noted for his Munch studies provides a sympathetic account of the artist's life and works. The format is basically chronological, with separate chapters devoted specifically to Munch's graphics and his general style. Contains a short bibliography and 168 illustrations.

Stang, Ragna. *Edvard Munch: The Man and His Art*. Translated by Geoffrey Culverwell. New York: Abbeville Press, 1979. Probably the most impressive and comprehensive survey of Munch's life and works, lavishly illustrated. The text is accompanied by numerous quotations from Munch's writings as well as comments by his contemporaries. The author played a key role at the Munch museum in Oslo.

Tom L. Auffenberg

BENITO MUSSOLINI

Born: July 29, 1883; Predappio, Italy
Died: April 28, 1945; Giulino di Mezzegra, near Dongo, Italy
Areas of Achievement: Government and politics
Contribution: Mussolini was the first Fascist dictator. He founded the Fascist
Party in 1919 and led it to power in Italy in October, 1922.

Early Life

Benito Amilcare Andrea Mussolini was born on July 29, 1883, outside the village of Predappio, fifteen miles from Forli in the region of Romagna. His mother, Rosa, was a schoolteacher and a devout Catholic, who was able to provide modest support for the family. His father, Alessandro, had a much greater influence upon Mussolini's character and outlook. His father, a blacksmith who drank more frequently than he worked, was a passionate character who was committed to an anarchistic nonideological vision of socialism. Life in the Mussolini household was tumultuous, and young Benito received harsh discipline but little affection. He later expressed pride in the fact that he was a loner who did not make friends. He assuaged his own deep inferiority complex by dominating others.

In imitation of his father, Mussolini became an instinctive and perpetual rebel. He was expelled from a Catholic boarding school at the age of ten for stabbing a fellow student. He continued his schooling, despite additional disciplinary interruptions, until he received his educational diploma in 1901. Apart from his rhetorical skill, his academic performance was rather mediocre.

After leaving school, Mussolini's reputation as a promiscuous and brutal misanthrope flourished, but he accomplished little else. In 1902, at the age of eighteen, he fled to Switzerland to avoid induction into the army and worked intermittently as a laborer. He came into contact with exiled Russian Marxists and, under their influence, became a Marxist, though an eclectic one. His most consistent and persistent idea, the use of violence as a political weapon, predated his Marxism. In 1905, he took advantage of a general amnesty to perform his military service so that he could return to Italy.

After leaving the military in 1906, Mussolini passed a test to teach French on the secondary level and earned the title "professor." He taught at several places without much success. In 1909, he was hired to edit a socialist weekly in the Austrian province of Trentino, but his intemperate writing landed him in jail, an experience with which he was not unfamiliar. Expelled from Austria, he returned to Forli where he edited a socialist weekly.

In 1910, he married Rachele Guidi, the daughter of his father's mistress. Rachele was a simple peasant, completely uninterested in politics and her husband's subsequent career. Though he and Rachele had five children, he was notoriously unfaithful.

Mussolini's extreme radicalism and opposition to reformism isolated him from the leaders of the Italian Socialist Party, but he gained notoriety when he was jailed for his violent opposition to Italy's 1911 war against Turkey for Libya. After his release from prison, he led the left wing in an attack against the party's moderate leaders and, with their expulsion, became a member of the party directorate and editor of the national Socialist newspaper, *Avanti!*

Life's Work

In *Avanti!* Mussolini derided parliamentary activity and advocated revolution. In private, he expressed his desire to be the "man of destiny," who would dominate the passive people. He was disillusioned when he failed to win the support of the people of Forli in the parliamentary race in 1913 and when the Socialist Party did not seize the opportunity provided by the massive but disorganized unrest of "Red Week" in June, 1914. The outbreak of World War I a few weeks later led to his break with the party if not with a vague idea of socialism. Believing that the war itself could be the catalyst for change, on October 18, 1914, without consulting the other party leaders or his coeditor, he published an editorial in *Avanti!* calling for Italian entry into the war.

Unable to win the party over to his new position, Mussolini was expelled and forced to give up the editorship of *Avanti!* On November 15, he launched his own paper, *Il Popolo d'Italia.* The paper was financed by France and other belligerents, but money also came from the Italian government and rich industrialists. Money, however, played no part in Mussolini's defection.

Italy's entry into the war in May, 1915, against the wishes of the parliamentary majority, through the damage done to Italy's political, economic, and social stability, ultimately provided the conditions that contributed to the rise of Fascism. Mussolini's political activities, however, were interrupted when he was conscripted in September, 1915, and sent to the front. After recovering from wounds received in February, 1917, when a mortar exploded, he was discharged, and he returned to his newspaper. His politics remained very fluid and opportunistic but were permeated with a hyper-nationalism.

At a meeting in Milan on March 23, 1919, Mussolini formally established the movement that would in November, 1921, become the Fascist Party. The miserable performance of the nascent party in the November, 1919, election and the failure of the sit-down strikes of 1920 led Mussolini to change his tack. Repudiating the remnants of his socialism, Mussolini recruited a militia of black-shirted hooligans who, with the avowed purpose of saving Italy from Bolshevism, terrorized the Left. Consequently, he received strong financial support from industrialists and large landowners frightened by the specter of social revolution. The Fascists won their first parliamentary seats in the May, 1921, election. With only thirty-five seats, however, their real strength was in their use of terror.

The anarchy created by the Fascists paved their way to power. The weakness of the government coupled with the collapse of the Left created a vacuum. Only the king, Victor Emmanuel III, and the army stood in Mussolini's way. Many generals sympathized with the Fascists, but to preclude the opposition of those who did not, Mussolini unequivocally expressed his support for the monarchy.

Confident that there would be no opposition, Mussolini mobilized his Blackshirts on October 27 to march on Rome and seize power. The twenty-six thousand badly armed and disorganized Fascists would have been no match for the army, and Mussolini, himself, remained close to the Swiss border in case the coup miscarried. Victor Emmanuel, however, fearing that a divided army might not be able to resist successfully and that he might be replaced as king by his pro-Fascist cousin, the Duke of Aosta, changed his mind about approving Premier Luigi Facta's declaration of martial law. In the face of this weakness, Mussolini would accept nothing less than the power to form a government. When the king submitted and confirmed this with a telegram, Mussolini made his "march" on Rome in a sleeping car on October 29.

Mussolini moved toward his goal of a one-party state gradually. His initial cabinet included representatives from all the parties except the Socialists and the Communists. After Mussolini promised to respect the law, his cabinet was not only confirmed by the parliament but also given the power to rule by decree for a year. Mussolini then proceeded to purge the police and the bureaucracy. A Fascist Grand Council, which in 1928 officially became the supreme organ of state power, was established as a shadow government and the Blackshirts were transformed into a state militia. The Acerbo Law, passed by parliament in July, 1923, promised the party with a plurality of the vote two-thirds of parliament's seats, but it was unnecessary. Through terror and intimidation the Fascists, in April, 1924, were able to win 65 percent of the vote.

When the Socialist leader, Giacomo Matteotti, denounced the tactics of the Fascists, he was murdered in June by associates of Mussolini. The crime left Mussolini vulnerable, but the failure of his opponents to seize the initiative allowed him to move against them. In 1925, Mussolini abolished political liberties and, finally, outlawed the Socialist Party. By the end of the year, he had reduced the parliament to impotence by making himself head of the government, answerable only to the king, and had replaced elected officials throughout the peninsula with administrators appointed by himself. In October, 1926, he outlawed all anti-Fascist parties and then set up a secret police organization to cow the nation. By 1928, in fact and in law, Mussolini, as leader of the Fascist Party, had become the omnipotent head of the Italian state.

As he consolidated his power, Mussolini ushered in a transformation of Italian society that he labeled the corporate state. The interests of the state were dominant. Strikes were banned, and the interests of workers and capital were supposedly mediated through organizations called corporations. The party, however, dominated the corporations and the interests of workers received short shrift. With the Fascists supporting the interests of capital, the standard of living of Italian working people declined after 1922. Mussolini claimed that a Chamber of Corporations would eventually replace the old flawed parliament, but the project was not implemented until 1939 and even then was only window dressing for his dictatorship.

Mussolini pursued an adventurous and aggressive foreign policy. He conquered Ethiopia in 1936, supported the Nationalists in the Spanish Civil War, and took control of Albania in April, 1939. Alienated from the British and the French over Ethiopia and cooperating with Adolf Hitler in Spain, Mussolini signed the Axis Pact with Germany in October, 1936. The association with Nazi Germany eventually led to the importation of anti-Semitic laws into Italy, a military alliance, the May, 1939, Pact of Steel, and, finally, defeat.

Mussolini's fate was sealed when he entered the war on June 10, 1940. He erroneously believed that a German victory was inevitable and wished to participate in the division of the spoils. The war, however, continued, and a series of humiliating Italian defeats in Greece, on the Mediterranean, and in North Africa led to the supplanting of Italy in those theaters by the Germans. Increasingly the Germans transformed Italy itself into a fiefdom. Mussolini's dynamism had faded with time, and it was now sapped by defeat and a recurrent ulcer.

The defeat of the Axis forces in North Africa and massive labor unrest in the north of Italy led to a rupture in the Fascist movement. Hoping for a separate peace, leading Fascists began plotting against Mussolini. The court circle, too, began working to replace Mussolini with Marshal Pietro Badoglio. The king's hesitation vanished with the Allied invasion of Sicily and bombing of Rome. The Grand Council of the Fascist Party, attempting to retain control of the government, on the night of July 24 and the early morning of July 25, revolted against Mussolini. That morning, Victor Emmanuel removed Mussolini from office but replaced him with Badoglio.

Mussolini, whose exit was welcomed by most Italians, was held in police custody until his rescue by German rangers on September 12. Flown to Hitler's headquarters, Mussolini denounced Italy's September 8 surrender to the Allies and, reverting to the socialist sentiments of his earliest Fascism, attempted to rally the working class to a new social Fascist regime. Mussolini was escorted back to Italy, where he proclaimed an Italian Social Republic for the north of Italy, headquartered at Salò on Lake Garda. Mussolini was a largely impotent puppet of the Germans, but he was able to revenge himself against five of the Fascist leaders who had revolted against him. Among them was his son-in-law and former foreign minister, Galeazzo Ciano, who was executed on January 11, 1944.

In April, 1945, the end was in sight. The Allies were advancing, partisan activity was increasing, and German forces in Italy were attempting to arrange terms with the Americans. Mussolini was incapacitated by indecisiveness. He met with leaders of the resistance in Milan but decided against surrender. He headed toward his vaunted but nonexistent Valtelline redoubt, and his vacillations cost him any chance that he might have had to cross into Switzerland. On April 27, he and his mistress, Clara Petacci, finally joined a German column headed for Austria. At Dongo, near the head of Lake Como, the Germans were stopped by a partisan brigade and Mussolini, disguised as a German, was discovered. When the partisans sought instructions from the indecisive National Liberation Committee in Milan, the Communists seized the initiative. Walter Audisio was dispatched from Milan to carry out the death sentence. Mussolini and Clara Petacci, who had insisted on being with her lover, were stood against a low wall at Giulino di Mezzegra and shot on April 28. Their bodies, along with those of fifteen other executed Fascist leaders, were brought back to Milan, where the corpses of Mussolini and Petacci were hung by their feet from a girder on the Piazalle Loreto for public display and excoriation.

Summary

Benito Mussolini's egotistical quest for personal power led to a regime of which the only coherent themes were power and violence and finally resulted in the execution of the dictator and the defeat of Italy. Mussolini and his movement left behind some architectural remains and the Lateran Pact of 1929, a rapprochement between the Catholic church and the Italian state, with which it had been at odds since the Italian kingdom seized the Papal States in 1870. The onetime revolutionary, however, did not transform the class structure or the distribution of wealth in Italy but, rather, reinforcd it. He left behind him conditions and structures that would promote class antagonism and produce, after his demise, Western Europe's largest Communist Party.

Mussolini's movement had, at best, an ad hoc program. More than anything it was his personal vehicle to power. Unfortunately, in his egotistical quest, he was able to play on the emotions and fears that many Italians experienced in the turmoil following World War I. Many believed that Italy had been inadequately rewarded for its war effort, but, after Mussolini's enterprise, Italy was stripped of all its colonies and was smaller than it had been when he came to power. Mussolini did temporarily crush the Left and, perhaps more permanently, cemented Italy's class structure in place, but when defeat loomed, the Italian establishment deserted him and sought a new protector against the Left in the conquering Americans.

Bibliography
Cassels, Alan. *Fascist Italy.* 2d ed. Arlington Heights, Ill.: Harland David-son, 1985. This is a short but balanced and cogent study of Fascist Italy and Mussolini. Contains a very useful critical bibliography.
Gregor, A. James. *Young Mussolini and the Intellectual Origins of Fascism.* Berkeley: University of California Press, 1979. A flawed revisionist work by a political scientist whose enthusiasm for intellectually formulated po-litical constructs or models here takes precedence over the evidence of historical data. Gregor views Mussolini as the creative formulator of a theory of modernization rooted in, but transcending, Marxism.
Halperin, S. William. *Mussolini and Italian Fascism.* New York: Van Nos-trand Reinhold, 1964. This is an excellent brief treatment supplemented by key documents. It is well written and clearly developed. Halperin, a respected academic, offers sound and insightful observations.
Joes, Anthony James. *Mussolini.* New York: Franklin Watts, 1982. This book, written by a historian for a popular audience, is a revisionist ap-proach to Mussolini. Joes attempts to offer a positive assessment of Mus-solini, depicting him as the leader who saved Italy from Bolshevism and restored order, prosperity, and self-respect to the country.
Mack Smith, Dennis. *Mussolini.* New York: Alfred A. Knopf, 1982. This book, written by a prominent English historian of Italy, is an excellent source. Although it presumes a certain amount of contextual knowledge, it is the best comprehensive biography of Mussolini written in English. Mack Smith convincingly portrays Mussolini as a violent and demagogic opportunist bent on attaining and retaining personal power.

Bernard A. Cook

GUNNAR MYRDAL

Born: December 6, 1898; Gustafs, Dalecarlia, Sweden
Died: May 17, 1987; Stockholm, Sweden
Areas of Achievement: Economics and sociology
Contribution: Myrdal, who received the Nobel Prize in Economic Sciences, is among the most important intellectual figures of the twentieth century. He was one of the primary forces responsible for the development of the welfare state in his native Sweden, and his study of American racial relations contributed to the dismantling of legal segregation in the United States. His analyses of the Third World—its poverty and other problems—have been equally influential.

Early Life

Gunnar Myrdal was born in the rural parish of Gustafs, in the province of Dalecarlia in central Sweden on December 6, 1898. His father was a farmer and a railroad employee. The eldest of four children, Myrdal, a brilliant and an ambitious student, attended Stockholm University, where he received a degree in law in 1923. Finding the practice of law in itself unsatisfactory, he returned to the university to study economics and received a doctorate in that discipline in 1927. His abilities being obvious, he was retained at the university after graduation, becoming first a lecturer and then, in 1931, a professor. In 1933, he became the Lars Hierta Professor of Political Economy at Stockholm, a position he held for many years.

In 1924, he married Alva Reimer, a fellow student at Stockholm University. Alva Reimer Myrdal had an equally distinguished academic and public career, and the Myrdals often worked together on various social and economic subjects. In 1934, they published *Kris i befolkningsfrågan* (crisis in the population question), which analyzed the reasons for the low birth rate in their native Sweden. Their recommendations included government loans and subsidies to married couples in order to encourage them to have children, as well as the building of public housing and provisions for child care. Since they believed that children should be desired by their parents, however, they also urged the necessity of sex education and family planning. Soon the Myrdal name became famous, so famous that a home planned for large families was known as a Myrdal house, a long couch was a Myrdal sofa, and, used as a verb, the name became a slang term for the procreative act itself. The Myrdals eventually had three children.

Life's Work

Although trained in economics and deeply interested in mathematical models and their application to economic issues, Myrdal early came to believe that too often pure economic theory ignored the more important cultural, historical, political, and societal influences. He became a leading advocate of the multidisciplinary and multicausational approach in the analysis of society, and he is considered to be a major proponent of the institutionalist school. A strong believer in stating his own value premises, Myrdal argued that it was impossible to approach any study without values and preconceptions and that it was thus necessary that the student or observer make those values and preconceptions explicit. Pretensions to simple empiricism or objectivity—an impossibility to Myrdal—could only result in chaos. Intellectually a child of the eighteenth century Enlightenment, Myrdal had great faith in human reason and rationality, and he believed that such reason must be used for the general improvement of society. Never simply an academic, Myrdal regularly served the Swedish government in various executive and legislative capacities and is considered one of the formative influences on the development of the welfare state in that country. During the worldwide economic depression of the 1930's, Myrdal urged additional government spending to combat its effects, a position often popularly associated with the ideas of John Maynard Keynes.

Myrdal was a recipient of a Rockefeller Foundation Fellowship in 1929, beginning a long, fruitful, and sometimes contentious relationship with the United States. He was a great admirer of Presidents Thomas Jefferson and Abraham Lincoln, and he spent much time in the United States. Myrdal approved of American idealism and openness, but he was not uncritical of various institutions and practices which he believed perverted those positive values. In 1938, he was chosen by the Carnegie Corporation to direct a study of the plight of blacks in the United States. The result was *An American Dilemma: The Negro Problem and Modern Democracy* (1944). It was a work which was not only an analysis of the black community but also a profound commentary on the conflict and tensions between the ideals of equality as expressed in the Declaration of Independence and the discrimination that blacks suffered in American society. Myrdal was selected to lead the project in part because of his previous academic and political accomplishments, in part because, as an outsider, he had the appearance of being more objective; thus, the study's findings would be more acceptable.

It was several years before the fourteen-hundred-page work was finally published, in 1944. Its appearance had been delayed by the outbreak of World War II, which prompted Myrdal to return to Sweden for a time. *An American Dilemma* was never a best-seller. Its initial printing was only twenty-five hundred copies. Yet it eventually went through more than thirty editions. More important, it was a major influence on the emerging civil rights movement, culminating in the landmark case of *Brown vs. the Board of Education of Topeka, Kansas*, which saw the United States Supreme Court ban segregation in public schools. In its unanimous decision, rendered in 1954, the court specifically cited Myrdal's work as supporting the argument that the separation of races was inherently unequal and much to the detriment of black students. When *An American Dilemma* first appeared, Myrdal expressed opptimism regarding the future relations of the races in the United States. Because of the slow pace of integration and the intractable problems of economic deprivation, Myrdal later became more pessimistic regarding America's dilemma.

Toward the end of World War II, Myrdal traveled throughout the United States as an economic adviser to the Swedish government. As did many other economists, Myrdal predicted the return of the Depression of the 1930's once the war concluded. In his opinion, the depths of the new economic crisis would be compounded as a result of the lack of government planning in the United States. In 1945, Myrdal was appointed minister of commerce in the first postwar Swedish government. His great faith in planning and his reputation for seeking solutions in extensive government actions made his term as minister of commerce controversial. Also, Myrdal pursued a policy of increased trade with the Soviet Union, a move resented in some quarters, including the United States. Yet, as American idealism and self-interest led to the development of the Marshall Plan in 1947, trade with the Soviet Union became of less consequence, and Myrdal resigned from the Swedish cabinet, accepting instead a position in the United Nations as the secretary general of the European Economic Commission. Here, too, however, the Cold War dogged Myrdal: Europe remained divided, and the commission proved to be of less consequence than he had hoped.

In 1953, Myrdal spent six weeks in Southeast Asia and was struck by the various economic problems in the region. Alva Myrdal, who had also worked for the United Nations, was appointed Sweden's ambassador to India in 1955. Although husband and wife were often apart because of their separate careers, Myrdal was able to spend some time in India with Alva. His Asian visits led to a deep interest in the poverty endemic in Asia. In 1958, he published *Rich Lands and Poor: The Road to World Prosperity.* That work proved to be a preliminary study of Third World poverty, a study which culminated ten years later in a monumental three-volume, twenty-three-hundred-page work entitled *Asian Drama: An Inquiry into the Poverty of Nations* (1968), the subtitle suggesting a comparison with Adam Smith's eighteenth century classic, *Inquiry into the Nature and Causes of the Wealth of Nations* (1776). Like his earlier *An American Dilemma*, *Asian Drama* saw many years of gestation and the contributions of many scholars before its publication.

Consistent with his multicausational analysis of societies and their institutions, and expressing his belief in the need for Southeast Asia to modernize through rational planning and development, social discipline, and changed attitudes, Myrdal criticized earlier theories and programs that had posited that Asia could easily adopt and adapt to Western models of development. Although Myrdal urged more capital investment by the West, *Asian Drama* was more descriptive than prescriptive and caused its reviewers considerable difficulty. While all recognized its scope and its analytic significance, many claimed that Myrdal had become both discouraged and pessimistic. The magnitude of the problems was so profound—a rapidly increasing population, inefficient agricultural and unsuitable educational systems, and the lack of effective governments to make the necessary changes—that Myrdal seemed to be saying that little could be usefully done by the industrialized nations of the West in assisting the East. Others noted that Myrdal's own stated values were perhaps too Western for the varied Asian cultural experience, and still others pointed out that *Asian Drama* failed to discuss the more encouraging experiences of Japan, Taiwan, and South Korea. Nevertheless, the work was a milestone in its discussion of the problems of poverty that faced one-quarter of the earth's population.

Summary

Two years later, in *The Challenge to World Poverty: A World Anti-Poverty Program in Outline*, published in 1970, Gunnar Myrdal returned to the subject matter of *Asian Drama*. Some modern observers of the Third World had expressed optimism over indications of increased food production through the introduction of new and hybrid crops and the possibility of population reduction through birth-control programs. Myrdal was not convinced and reiterated his demand for structural changes in the developing world: land and educational reform and attitudinal and social changes. The so-called Green Revolution and Western programs to limit births were, in his opinion, too ephemeral, too transient, and too superficial. Myrdal, with his multi-disciplinary and multicausational approach, had long doubted the efficacy of simple solutions. He agreed with the Keynesians and their belief in deficit funding, but only during times of crisis. Over the long run and for more permanent solutions, structural changes in the economy and society were required, an argument he had earlier made in *Challenge to Affluence*, an analysis of the economy of the United States, published in 1963.

In the late 1960's and the 1970's, Myrdal pleaded publicly for massive increases in spending to solve the combined urban and poverty problems of the United States. The programs of Lyndon Johnson's Great Society and its successors were simply inadequate. He hoped to revise and update *An American Dilemma*, expressing both optimism regarding American idealism and pessimism over the slow rate of change in solving the crucial problem of American racism. Yet his major work was done. By 1975, his health had declined, although he continued to speak and lecture in the United States and Sweden for many years. In 1974, he shared the Nobel Prize in Economic Sciences with his antithesis, the conservative Austrian economist Friedrich von Hayek. Later Myrdal said that he should have rejected the award because economics was not a science, what with its many value judgments, a position he had maintained for many years. Although wealthy from his many writings, he continued a rather simple life-style until his death in Stockholm in 1987 at the age of eighty-eight.

Myrdal's legacy is a rich and varied one. In the United States, perhaps his most enduring contribution is in the area of race relations. *An American Dilemma* not only influenced policymakers and fellow scholars but also, as Myrdal's ideas were disseminated in textbooks and popular studies, helped to shape the attitudes of several generations of American students. Myrdal's massively documented study of racial discrimination thus played a significant part in forcing American society to acknowledge a great injustice and begin to redress it.

Bibliography

Dykema, Eugene R. "No View Without a Viewpoint: Gunnar Myrdal." *World Development* 14 (1986): 147-163. The author of this study of Myrdal's intellectual approach discusses the latter's belief in the importance of stating one's values before attempting any analysis of social problems. Dykema, while sympathetic to Myrdal's positions, also argues that Myrdal perhaps too often reflects the Western belief in human rationality, sometimes at the expense of differing value systems from other cultures.

Maddison, Angus, ed. *"Myrdal's Asian Drama": An Interdisciplinary Critique.* Leige, Belgium: Ciriec, 1971. This volume is a collection of articles devoted to Myrdal's *Asian Drama.* Originally presented at a conference in Montreal, the papers reflect the diverse background of their authors, all of whom had varied responses to Myrdal's long analysis of the many problems of Southeast Asian societies.

Myrdal, Gunnar. *Against the Stream.* New York: Pantheon Books, 1973. Myrdal never wrote his autobiography, arguing in the preface to this collection of articles that his life had focused more on the problems that interested him than on his experiences and on persons he knew. He stated that this volume should be read as a substitute for his memoirs.

Sherman, Howard. "Gunnar Myrdal: Economics as Social Relations." *Journal of Economic Issues* 10 (June, 1976): 210-214. This article announced that Myrdal had received the Veblen-Commons Award. Sherman, a Marxist scholar, praises Myrdal for his critique of the neoclassical economists and his work on American racism but criticizes Myrdal for not making use of the concepts of class conflict and socialist revolution.

Walsh, Francis P. "The Most International Swede." *Contemporary Review* 224 (March, 1974): 113-120. In this venerable British journal, the author, in the year that Myrdal received the Nobel Prize, summarizes, in an interesting and readable fashion, Myrdal's long and varied career.

Eugene S. Larson

SAROJINI NAIDU

Born: February 13, 1879; Hyderābād, India
Died: March 2, 1949; Lucknow, India
Areas of Achievement: Government, politics, women's rights, education, and literature
Contribution: Naidu demonstrated that strong-willed women can develop the statesmanship necessary to assume leadership of a nation. Her poetry, while overlooked in the West, is regarded as some of the most important in India.

Early Life

Sarojini Chattopadhyay was born in Hyderābād, the capital of the princely state of Hyderābād (Deccan) in the south-central part of India, on February 13, 1879, to Aghorenath Chattopadhyay and Vardha Sundari. Her parents were members of an old priest-caste (Brahman) family in the northeast province of East Bengal (now called Bangladesh). Her parents migrated to Hyderābād because of a teaching position that Sarojini's father, who had received a doctor of science degree from the University of Edinburgh, had obtained. Her father, an ardent educationist, considered radical by his contemporaries because of his advocacy of education for women, hired private tutors to teach English, French, and, later, Persian to his daughter. Sarojini proved to be a child prodigy. She was graduated from one of the toughest school systems in the country with a first class education when she was eleven years old and won a scholarship from the King of Hyderābād (the Nizam) to continue her college education in England. England found the sixteen-year-old too young for college, so Sarojini was asked to attend classes in King's College, London, for a year; later, she was formally admitted to Girton College of the University of Cambridge.

Sarojini's life in England was far from happy. She was uncomfortable with the English image of her as an exotic—almost extraterrestrial—quiet girl, rather aloof, draped in the colorful clingy silks of the Orient, wearing her thick dark hair long and straight, timorously looking at the strange, cold world around her with two compellingly beautiful eyes, and always writing poetry. She enjoyed, however, the opportunity of meeting Arthur Symons, a member of the Rhymers' Club founded by William Butler Yeats in 1891, and Sir Edmund Gosse, a prominent literary figure of the day. The former introduced Sarojini to the English world through his introduction to the first volume of her poems, *The Golden Threshold* (1905), while the latter offered practical advice on how to express her unique poetic sensibility.

Life's Work

Sarojini had changed her name from Chattopadhyay to Naidu when the

English reviewed her poems favorably and the Indians exultantly in 1905, the year of their first publication. The very next year saw the need for a new impression, which was followed by two more, in 1909 and 1914, respectively. In the meantime, Naidu was busy rearing her four children and putting together a new volume of poetry. *The Bird of Time* (1912), with new editions in 1914 and 1916. A third volume, *The Broken Wing*, was published in 1917, and a fourth, *The Feather of the Dawn*, was posthumously issued in 1961.

Naidu was apologetic about the songlike nature of her poetry. "I sing just as birds do," she wrote to Symons, without a "voice," probably implying the awesome prophetic voice of a God thundering through a burning bush— a voice that, presumably, alone can transmute the flimsy material of a song into the weighty substance of great poetry. In her self-effacing humility, she forgot the tradition, exemplified by the Old Testament Song of Solomon and Walt Whitman's "Song of Myself," great poetry in the form of song. Her songs, after all, are songs of life, love, death, and destiny—themes the human race has always considered substantial. Further, they add a new note to the repertoire of poetry as song through a harmonious fusion of otherwise intransigent traditions, their "Eastern-ness" meticulously transposed into the Western medium of English prosody. Such a fusion is evident in the way she weaves magical strands around her themes "like a pearl on a string" ("Palinquin-Bearers") or elevates them to mystical heights "And scale the stars upon my broken wing!" ("The Broken Wing"). In these songs, it looks as if, in P. E. Dustoor's words, "an English garden has exotically put out the most dazzling tropical blooms."

The dazzling English garden of Naidu's consciousness slowly started turning into a blighted one with the fast-changing historical events under the leadership of Mahatma Gandhi and his satyagraha movement. In Sanskrit, *satya* means "truth" and *graha* is the act of "grasping." Satyagraha is a blanket term that Gandhi used for all forms of peaceful efforts to gain independence from the British rule organized through the Indian National Congress, one of the major political parties in India. Naidu joined the party wholeheartedly. She represented the people of India in negotiating with the British government in England as a member of the Home Rule League (1919) and the Round Table Conference for Indian-British cooperation (1931). She also led demonstrations against the government policies at home and was imprisoned three times: in 1930, 1932, and 1942. She visited the major sections of the African continent in 1924, 1929, and 1931, lending the imperial subjects moral support and political guidance. In 1928-1929 she visited the United States to mobilize American support for the independence struggle.

Fighting the battle outside the country, Naidu realized, would not be productive if she did not address the problems inside it. As a woman, she knew of social injustices to women that tradition had helped institutionalize, such as prohibition of remarriage for widows, child marriage, polygamy, and deprivation of education for all women. She organized women's groups, especially for the promotion of education, and raised the consciousness of the women she addressed as speaker to a wide range of women's groups. Curiously enough, she found it harder to convince the "civilized" English about women's rights than the "primitives" at home.

Above all, Naidu gave her full attention to the most sensitive issue of her day: the crisis between the Hindu religious majority and the Muslim minority. A Hindu herself, she was singularly equipped with a heightened awareness that helped her appreciate the experiences of both as one. She did not arrive at this ability because she was a mystic, although three of her poems were included in *Oxford Book of English Mystical Verse* (1927), but because she had retained the resilience of the truly primitive imagination that is able to take consciousness back to its undifferentiated origins. Past and present were copresent in her consciousness, not with the discrete linearity of two neighbors but rather like the commingling of waters. It was this unifying consciousness that gave her the courage to be a friend to Mohammad Ali Jinnah, the Muslim leader who was a devout follower of the Congress but, later, had to dissociate himself from it and espouse the cause of the rival political party, the Muslim League. She remained his friend without losing her loyalty to the Congress at a time when Jinnah came to be looked upon as intransigent and fanatical by the leaders of the Congress. In 1947, when she became the governor of the United Provinces (now Uttar Pradesh) in north-central independent India, her inauguration ceremony was blessed by the representatives of all the religions of India. During her governorship, she restrained the majority from treating the minority as a poor relation, especially on issues concerning language, which took on epic proportions in the first decade of India's independence.

Although a dynamic woman, Naidu, strangely enough, had always been physically ill. Her health started deteriorating close to her birthday in 1949 and worsened in March. On March 2, 1949, she asked the nurse attending her to sing a song for her. As the nurse's song ended, Naidu breathed her last. It is ironical that her active public life began with the publication of a book of songs and ended with a song. Perhaps she saw life itself as a song.

Summary

Sarojini Naidu led a full and successful life. It was full because it was authentic in the Sartrean existential sense of choosing freely and accepting the consequences of one's choice. Such behavior is unlike that of the multitude who let externals—social constraints for example—choose for them; consequently, they live the lives of others, which creates emptiness instead of adding fullness. One glorious example of an authentic choice in Naidu's life is her choice of husband: Govindarajulu Naidu, a person of a non-Brahman caste. This act alienated her from family, friends, and society— especially the Indian society of her time—yet she wore her choice with pride all through her life. Her life was successful not only because she made it through these "outrageously" authentic choices but also because she produced spectacular, though "mundane," results because of them. She won the Kaisar-i Hind award from the Nizam of Hyderābād in 1908, became a fellow of the Royal Society of Literature in 1914, was elected president of the Indian National Congress—the first woman to hold that elective office—and finally became, in 1947, the governor of the most politically active state in India, another first for a woman. Today she is known as the "Nightingale of India." February 13, her birthday, is celebrated as women's day throughout the country.

Bibliography
Azad, Abul Kalam. *India Wins Freedom: An Autobiographical Narrative.* Introduction and explanatory notes by Louis Fischer. New York: Longmans, Green, 1960. Ghost-written by Humayun Kabir. Contains little discussion of Naidu but gives useful insights into the political controversies of the time by a contemporary who, like herself, fought for India's freedom with heart in pain and mind in conflict.
Baig, Tara Ali. *Sarojini Naidu.* New Delhi: Publications Division, Ministry of Information and Broadcasting, Government of India, 1974. A smaller version of the biography by Padmini Sengupta, cited below, this source is slightly different because of the author's personal reminiscences of Naidu. Included are interesting but defensive comments on the place of women in India and a few citations about Naidu from the police records of British India.
Gandhi, Mahatma. *An Autobiography: The Story of My Experiments with Truth.* Translated by Mahadev Desai. Boston: Beacon Press, 1957. Almost a classic for a student of the freedom movement in India. A "spiritual" profile of its ethos, excellent for understanding popular Indian philosophy and the soul-searching that accompanies political activity.
Morton, Eleanor. *The Women in Gandhi's Life.* New York: Dodd, Mead, 1953. The women surrounding Gandhi are portrayed as they figure in his life chronologically. Naidu appears six times. Tara Ali Baig and Padmini Sengupta, two other women writers cited in the bibliography, are amiably critical of Indian society's treatment of women, as was Naidu herself. Useful sourcebook for feminist connections to the Indian freedom movement.
Sengupta, Padmini. *Sarojini Naidu.* New York: Asia Publishing House, 1966. A well-written and more comprehensive biography of Naidu than the one by Baig, cited above. Follows the life of the subject chronologi-

cally but fails to convey her dynamism as effectively as one might expect from a book of this length. Provides useful bibliographical footnotes and a fairly comprehensive bibliography. A must for the researcher on Naidu.

Srinivasa Iyengar, K. R. *Indian Writing in English*. 2d rev. Eng. ed. New York: Asia Publishing House, 1973. A pioneering work, this comprehensive study of Indian writing in English is almost a definitive work on the subject. Very useful for a study of the poetic talents of Naidu. Contains a good bibliography and well-organized index.

Abdulla K. Badsha

GAMAL ABDEL NASSER

Born: January 15, 1918; Alexandria, Egypt
Died: September 28, 1970; Cairo, Egypt
Areas of Achievement: The military, government, and politics
Contribution: Nasser was a member of the Free Officers Society that came to power in Egypt in 1952 via a military coup. Subsequently Prime Minister and President of Egypt, Nasser was a major player in the Arab-Israeli conflict.

Early Life

Gamal Abdel Nasser's father, Abdel Nasser Hussein, was born of a fairly well-to-do family from the village of Beni Murr near Assyut, was educated in a Western primary school in Assyut, and eventually became district postmaster in Alexandria. Little is known about Nasser's mother except that she was the daughter of a local contractor and died young. Nasser was the first of four sons, born in Alexandria. His father remarried, and consequently Gamal was reared for a good part of his life by an uncle in Beni Murr. He attended nine different schools, most in Cairo, spent a term at the University of Cairo (1936) in the law curriculum and then was accepted into the military academy after a first-time rejection. He was graduated at age twenty. During his high school years, he took part in many demonstrations and was wounded by a bullet at age seventeen. He was also known to like American motion pictures. Politically, he was an admirer of Napoleon I and Kemal Atatürk and possessed an extreme dislike of the British army, whose presence in Egypt he never accepted. He married a woman who was from a Persian-Egyptian family.

The students at the military academy during the 1930's found themselves involved in intense discussions about Egypt's problems and destiny. Grievances about poverty, imperialism, and the power of the landed aristocracy occupied much of their time. In fall, 1938, Nasser began to plan a revolutionary organization which, by 1942, had many cells across Egypt. Because of a heavy-handed British policy over Egypt during World War II, many of the military-revolutionaries favored Germany, although no serious plans for an alliance ever materialized. Close relations were also established with a religious fundamentalist group known as the Muslim Brotherhood. Eventually, the Egyptian and general Arab failures in preventing the partition of Palestine in 1947 and then being defeated by Israel in 1948 led to the formation of a larger Free Officers Society. In 1948, Nasser was a lieutenant colonel of infantry and was wounded during the First Palestine War.

Life's Work

In 1950, General Muhammad Neguib, who was regarded as a military hero, was chosen by the young officers as their leader, largely to convey a sense of legitimacy to their organization. On July 23, 1952, after a period of restlessness and demonstrations in Cairo, eleven members of the Free Officers Society staged a bloodless coup against King Farouk I. A revolutionary executive committee was formed, later to be called the Revolutionary Command Council (RCC). Neguib became prime minister, war minister, commander in chief, and RCC chairman in September, 1952, and appeared to be the leading figure. Nasser, however, played a significant role as he represented the views of the younger and less affluent officers. Nasser was the recipient of three million dollars of clandestine support from the United States' Central Intelligence Agency before the July 23 coup, as he was viewed as pro-Western and democratic, yet this was not to be the case.

Nasser believed that democracy had to be established in Egyptian life, which, in particular, focused on social democracy, meaning the uprooting of class distinctions, wealth, and privilege. Nasser's vision of the state also focused on suppressing "sensational" dissent. As a result, most of the press was censored and eventually nationalized in 1960.

During 1953, Nasser and Neguib found themselves in direct opposition over the future of Egypt. Nasser wanted revolutionary reforms, while Neguib stuck to a more reformist line. In January, 1953, Nasser was instrumental in forming the Liberation Rally, an organization designed to mobilize the masses and a forerunner of the Arab Socialist Union. Egypt was declared a republic on June 19, 1953. In February, 1954, Nasser's and Neguib's forces almost forced violence into the streets, but Nasser prevailed and Neguib resigned. Nasser became prime minister and imposed a series of laws restricting opposition to his regime. Political parties were banned and even groups that had supported the Free Officers Society, such as the Muslim Brotherhood, were broken up.

The RCC came more under Nasser's domination as he began the process of creating an authoritarian-mobilizational regime that would feature frequent popular rallies and referenda to demonstrate popular support. Islam also came under the control of Nasser within Egypt, with religious leaders being reduced to mouthpieces for the government, while Pan-Islamism was preached as part of an antiimperialist foreign policy.

In January, 1956, Nasser presented a new constitution that proclaimed the abolition of imperialism, feudalism, monopoly, and capitalist influence. Egyptians were given basic human rights, but the ban on political parties continued. Nasser and three RCC officers had the right to nominate members to the 350-seat National Assembly. The assembly had a useful life of only two years, until February, 1958, when it was suspended because of unification with Syria. Power actually centered on Nasser's National Union, which provided the ideology for Egypt's future.

In February, 1958, Syria and Egypt agreed to form a single country, called the United Arab Republic (UAR), of which Nasser was president. At first this was desired by the Syrian Baathists out of regard for the principles of Arab unity and the desire to see rapid economic development. Real unity, however, never materialized, as the Syrians came to object to the heavy-handed attempt to implement Nasser's reforms in Syria. The UAR broke apart in September, 1961. Afterward, the power of the National Union was increased to include elements from various social groups, and its name was changed in 1962 to the Arab Socialist Union, representing a form of "one-party democracy," modeled probably on Turkey before 1945. Nasser, how-ever, was not an Eastern Bloc-type socialist, as indicated by the dissolution of the two Communist parties of Egypt in 1965.

One of Nasser's most significant reforms in theory was found in agricul-ture. In September, 1952, Nasser sponsored the land reform that confiscated land from estates of more than two hundred acres and distributed it to poor peasants. The shortage of arable land and Egypt's increasing population since the turn of the century made it difficult to provide land for all who needed it. Only one in five who needed land received it. The Nasser govern-ment continually reduced maximum acreages of individual ownership, from two hundred to one hundred acres in 1961 and down to fifty acres in 1969. These reforms, however, did destroy the material base for the two thousand wealthiest landlords in Egypt.

Nasser envisioned many big industrial projects for Egypt, which were to be largely state-directed, as extensive restrictions on private enterprise, even nationalization was part of his economic policies (Egyptianization). The fo-cal point of these projects was the plan for the Aswan High Dam, which was conceived as a symbol of the 1952 Revolution as well as a source of hydro-electric power for industry and land reclamation in agriculture.

Nasser's anti-Western attitude foreclosed the possibility of Western aid for the dam's construction. After nationalization of the Suez Canal in July, 1956, as a means to obtain capital for construction, and an invasion from Great Britain and France during the Suez War of October, 1956, the funding for the dam eventually came from the Soviet Union, which loaned Egypt $300 million for construction costs and supplied a corps of advisers. The artificial lake created by the construction of the dam was named for Nasser.

The anti-imperialist position adopted by Nasser lent itself naturally to support from the Soviet Union. Nasser, after seizing power, moved away from any pro-Western military agreement. On the other hand, he opposed the North Atlantic Treaty Organization (NATO) policy of trying to contain Soviet expansion in the Middle East. He attended the first meeting of the Afro-Asian excolonial states meeting in Bandung, Indonesia, in April, 1955, which marked the beginning of the "non-aligned movement." Nasser be-came acutely interested in Soviet support as he saw Soviet interests in Asia parallel his own: support of anti-imperialism, nonalignment, and Third World independence.

In September, 1955, the first arms agreement between Egypt and Czechoslovakia was announced, with the latter acting as a surrogate for the Soviet Union. Before 1958, Nasser's biggest ideological enemy in the Middle East was the Hashemite regime in Iraq, which was supported by the United States and was a member of the Baghdad Pact Organization. In July, 1958, King Faisal II and his government were overthrown in a pro-Nasser coup, and Iraq moved toward a revolutionary position. The Soviet Union became more interested in Egypt after 1960, when the Sino-Soviet split led Albania to close a Soviet naval base there. Major arms agreements were made during 1964, and Nasser visited Moscow in August, 1965.

The Palestine/Israel problem was one of Nasser's obsessions. He indicated that "when the Palestine crisis loomed on the horizon, I was firmly convinced that the fighting in Palestine was not fighting on foreign territory. Nor was it inspired by sentiment. It was a duty imposed by self-defense." He viewed the issue of Palestine through the prism of colonialism. Israel had been successful, Nasser believed, only because it was a neocolonialist state. Through liberation of Palestine, however, Nasser saw the possibilities of uniting the Arab peoples and restoring some of the greatness of the medieval Arab past, when Arab civilization was dominant on a worldwide basis.

Nasser often deceived himself and was subject to hyperbole regarding the basis of the conflict and the results. After blockading the Strait of Tiran and Gulf of Aqaba to Israeli shipping during 1955 in addition to nationalizing the Suez Canal, Egypt was invaded by Great Britain, France, and Israel. Israel captured the Sinai Peninsula, while France and England occupied the Suez Canal zone. Nasser's interpretation of the defeat in Sinai during October, 1956, was that Egypt withdrew its forces before the actual fighting began. Nasser convinced himself that whatever success Israel achieved in 1956 was the result of air defenses provided by the French. Hence, by May, 1967, Nasser was willing to take new risks to defeat Israel, impelled by the belief that Israel was now alone.

On May 14, 1967, Nasser began moving his forces into the Sinai Peninsula and on May 16 demanded that United Nations Emergency Forces stationed in the Sinai and at Sharm el-Sheik be removed. Secretary General of the United Nations U Thant complied without debate, thus ushering in the crisis leading to the Six-Day War. Nasser was convinced that Israel was about to attack Syria. Nasser created a military alliance with Syria, Jordan, and Iraq, and prepared for war. A blockade was reintroduced at the Strait of Tiran. In his May, 1967, speeches, Nasser constantly raised the issue of the destruction of Israel: "The battle will be a general one and our basic objective will be to destroy Israel."

Israeli forces staged a preemptive strike against Egypt, Syria, and Jordan on the morning of June 5, 1967, destroying the combined air forces of the three states and defeating the Arab alliance in six days. Israel emerged occupying all of the Sinai, the West Bank and Gaza Strip, and the Golan Heights, taken from Syria. Nasser, in response to this overwhelming defeat, resigned in a national radio broadcast on June 9. He blamed the Egyptian defeat on collusion between Israel and the United States. A massive outpouring of Egyptian public support, partially engineered by the Arab Socialist Union, made Nasser's resignation short-lived, indicating that the resignation speech was not serious and merely a tactic for maintaining popular support.

In October, 1962, Nasser had introduced Egyptian troops into Yemen to support the Yemeni Arab Republic, an effort which had a destabilizing effect on the Arabian peninsula as well as inter-Arab politics. The campaign in Yemen was very costly for Egypt, as one-third of the Egyptian army eventually became engaged in the conflict. Nasser used Yemen as a training ground of sorts for his troops. After his defeat in the Six-Day War, Nasser was forced, in September, 1967, to remove all Egyptian forces from Yemen.

The disengagement in Yemen allowed Nasser to step up his confrontation with Israel along the Suez Canal, which began again in the summer of 1968 and eventually matured into the War of Attrition. Nasser's theory was to wear down Israel by manpower losses and perpetual mobilization. Egyptian losses were significant, however, as Israel staged aerial raids on Egyptian bases and cities, with the result being the virtual abandonment of Egyptian cities along the Suez Canal. During the course of these confrontations, Nasser consistently rejected plans for phased Israeli withdrawals. He insisted on his interpretation of United Nations Security Council Resolution 242, which called for the withdrawal of Israeli forces from occupied territories.

From the mid-1950's until his death, Nasser was a strong supporter of the Palestinian cause, although he held the Palestinian resistance movement in check until after his defeat in 1967. The Palestine Liberation Organization (PLO) was created under Egyptian auspices in 1964 but became independent of Egyptian control only after 1967. Late in 1967, Nasser took Yasir Arafat, PLO leader, with him to Moscow. During September, 1970, Nasser negotiated preliminary arrangements for the removal of Palestinian guerrillas from Jordan into Lebanon.

Nasser had sensitive health problems from the fall of 1969 until his death a year later. On September 11, 1969, he suffered a heart attack and was incapacitated thereafter. During his last year of life, he became increasingly cranky and mistrustful and refused to take advice from his staff. He appointed Anwar el-Sadat as vice president on September 20, 1969, who succeeded him as president upon Nasser's death of a second heart attack on September 28, 1970. He was survived by his wife and four children.

Summary

Gamal Abdel Nasser had an enigmatic political career. He had many political setbacks yet was durable as the President of Egypt. He seemed to defy the laws of political gravity, especially after defeats in 1956 and 1967 at the hands of Israel. He was known in the West for a biting and belligerent rhetoric. Before his unexpected death, however, he was viewed as a likely candidate to make peace with Israel. Nasser was in such a position because of his legacy from the 1950's, when Egyptians began to regard him as the savior of the Egyptian Revolution by his nationalization of the Suez Canal.

In the realm of foreign policy, Nasser has been criticized for having opened Egypt and the Middle East to Soviet penetration. The ultimate reason for such penetration may be linked to the failures of the American administration to understand Third World frustrations as embodied in Nasser. The involvement of the Soviet Union in Middle East politics, however, guaranteed Nasser and his successors that Israel could never absolutely "win" a Middle East war because of the threat of Soviet intervention.

Nasser reestablished the long-held Middle Eastern idea of Arab unity, epitomized in the union established between Syria and Egypt in 1958. This union, however, failed after three years. Nasser's attempt to bring Yemen under his control also failed. He did establish links with Gaafar Nimeiry's Sudan and Muammar Qaddafi's Libya, both regarded as left-wing regimes of the late 1960's.

Nasser left Egypt in poor financial condition, racked by losses connected with the Arab-Israeli wars. He succeeded, however, in several areas, including the building of schools and medical clinics around the country and making fresh water more easily available. His socialism was effectively ended in 1968, when the difficulties of war began to erode the Egyptian economy, and by the Sadat regime, which restored contacts with Western countries.

Bibliography

Baker, Raymond. *Egypt's Uncertain Revolution Under Nasser and Sadat.* Cambridge, Mass.: Harvard University Press, 1978. A useful institutional examination of Egypt's difficulties under two regimes.

Copeland, Miles. *The Game of Nations.* New York: Simon & Schuster, 1969. This work focuses on foreign policy before 1967 and identifies Nasser as one of the authors of terrorism in the Middle East.

Dekmajian, R. Hrair. *Egypt Under Nasir.* Albany: State University of New York Press, 1971. A study of Nasser that examines issues such as myth in politics, charismatic leadership, and the theory of routinization of charisma within the Egyptian revolution.

Goldschmidt, Arthur, Jr. *Modern Egypt: The Formation of a Nation-State.* Boulder, Colo.: Westview, 1988. An important general work that embodies the latest historiography on the subject.

Laqueur, Walter, and Barry Rubin, eds. *The Israel-Arab Reader*. New York: Pelican, 1984. This work contains significant speeches by Nasser related to the Arab-Israeli wars.

Mansfield, Peter. *Nasser's Egypt*. Baltimore, Md.: Penguin, 1965. A straightforward account of Nasser's policies through 1965.

Rubenstein, Alvin Z. *Red Star on the Nile: The Soviet-Egyptian Influence Relationship Since the June War*. Princeton, N.J.: Princeton University Press, 1977. A very useful, detailed study of Soviet-Egyptian relations, with particular emphasis on Nasser's foreign policy.

Vatikiotis, P. J., ed. *Egypt Since the Revolution*. New York: Praeger, 1968. This work contains articles that deal with the economy, politics, and culture under Nasser. Although a bit dated, it is still useful as it represents a diversity of views.

Waterbury, John. *The Egypt of Nasser and Sadat: The Political Economy of Two Regimes*. Princeton, N.J.: Princeton University Press, 1983. This is a technical analysis of the performance of the Egyptian economy, with useful evaluations of development projects.

Stephen C. Feinstein

GIULIO NATTA

Born: February 26, 1903; Imperia, Italy
Died: May 2, 1979; Bergamo, Italy
Areas of Achievement: Chemistry, education, and technology
Contribution: Natta was awarded the Nobel Prize in Chemistry in 1963 for his work on macromolecular synthesis with total control of the relative spatial orientation of groups of atoms that are bonded to the polymer chain. This important development revolutionized the plastics industry and made possible the use of polymers in widespread applications, such as plasticware, laundry detergents, and antiknock admixtures to high-octane fuels.

Early Life

Giulio Natta was born on February 26, 1903, in Imperia, on the Italian Riviera, to Francesco Natta, a prominent attorney and judge, and Elena (Crespi) Natta. He was educated in the nearby city of Genoa. Natta claimed that his interest in chemistry began at the age of twelve, when he found that he could not put his chemistry book aside: "From then on, chemistry was my love," he said. He was graduated with honors from Genoa's high school of science in 1919, at the age of sixteen. Initially, he was enrolled in the pure mathematics course at the University of Genoa but found that mathematics was too abstract. As his father had taken up the challenge of putting the ideals of justice into practice, so also was Giulio attracted by the application of the concepts of chemical theory to the solution of practical questions, and this led him to transfer to the Polytechnic Institute of Milan, where he studied chemical engineering. He received his doctorate degree in chemical engineering from the Polytechnic Institute in 1924, five years after his high school graduation.

In his Nobel presentation on December 12, 1963, Natta stated that he first became interested in the spatial relationships of atoms and in structural chemistry in general while he was still a student and apprentice of a Professor Bruni in 1924. It was then that Natta learned the techniques of structure elucidation by X-ray analysis. This analytical procedure was complemented by his study of analysis by electron diffraction at Freiburg, Germany. While in Freiburg, Natta came to know Hermann Staudinger, who was pioneering the analysis of polymers by chemical methods, and he was so influenced by Staudinger that he resolved to investigate the structure of polymers using electron diffraction and X-ray techniques.

On April 25, 1935, Natta married Rosita Beati, a literature teacher at the University of Milan. They had two children, Franca and Giuseppe. He remained close to his wife throughout his life, and it was through her influence and background in literature that the word "isotactic" was coined to describe the structure of the particular form of polypropylene that he had prepared and that marked the beginning of his prizewinning research. Natta's need to combine theory with practical applications was a basic driving force throughout his life. He utilized the techniques of X-ray analysis and electron diffraction, both of which he had learned at a very early stage in his career, throughout his research.

Life's Work

After obtaining his doctorate in chemical engineering in 1924, Natta remained at the Polytechnic Institute of Milan as an instructor. His talents as an educator were quickly recognized and marked by his rapid rise through the academic ranks. In 1925, he was made assistant professor of analytical chemistry and was promoted to professor of general chemistry in 1927. During this period, Natta's research centered on the application of X-ray analysis to the structure elucidation and crystallinity of inorganic substances. He used X-ray analysis to investigate the properties of industrial catalysts. In 1932, he visited the University of Freiburg in Germany to learn the new technique of electron diffraction and immediately began to utilize this new method in his work. His interaction with Hermann Staudinger inspired his idea to apply these analytical techniques to the investigation of macromolecular structure.

Natta returned to Milan in 1933 and then accepted a position as professor and director of the Institute of General Chemistry at the University of Pavia, where he remained for two years. He became professor of physical chemistry at the University of Rome in 1935, professor and director of the Institute of Industrial Chemistry at the Turin Polytechnic Institute in 1937, and then professor and director of the Industrial Chemistry Research Center at the University of Milan in 1938.

Because of his close ties to industrial applications of chemistry research, Natta was asked by the Italian government, under Benito Mussolini, to initiate research and development on the production of synthetic rubber, and he successfully implemented the industrial production of butadiene-styrene rubbers at Ferrara during World War II. His earlier work on industrial catalysts also led at this time to his development of catalytic processes for production of methanol and other alcohols, as well as formaldehyde and butyraldehyde. After the war, Montecatini, a large Italian chemical company in Milan, funded much of Natta's research. The low cost and availability of petroleum stimulated his work in the use of petroleum as a raw material base for industrial chemicals and monomers used in plastics production.

Natta became immediately interested in the work of Karl Ziegler, who had succeeded in preparing high molecular weight polyethylene using transition metal compounds as catalysts, in 1952. Since Ziegler was working on ethylene polymerization, Natta turned his attention to propylene, which has one more carbon than ethylene. Propylene had the advantage of being much cheaper than ethylene, as it was a by-product of the petroleum and propane refining processes.

All Natta's previous research knowledge and industrial experience came to bear on this effort. In 1954, Natta announced that he had succeeded in preparing a new polypropylene that was far superior in physical properties than previous methods could produce. He used X-ray and electron diffraction techniques to show that his polymer had a greater degree of crystallinity than could be obtained previously. In fact, all the methyl groups, which are bonded to the backbone of the polymer chain, where shown to be oriented so that they were all on the same side of the chain. The new class of polymers, where the stereochemistry (the relative spatial arrangement of atoms and groups) could be controlled, were called stereoregular polymers. Further research with a variety of vinyl polymers and catalyst systems led to the total control of macromolecular stereochemistry during the polymerization process. Isotactic polymers, with pendant groups all on the same side of the chain, and syndiotactic polymers, with pendant groups alternating from side to side with each monomer unit, could now be prepared readily and inexpensively.

Natta became a member of the National Academy of Sciences of Italy in 1955. He visited the United States in 1956, and showed several articles made from isotactic polypropylene, including a cup, a washing-machine agitator, and pipes, at a press conference. Montecatini was producing the polymer on an industrial scale in 1957, and the patented process was licensed throughout the world.

He continued research in the area of polymer science and made many other notable contributions. These included the stereospecific polymerization of butadiene to give polybutadiene, which had a configuration analogous to natural rubber. The copolymerization of ethylene with other monomers gave unusual rubber materials in that no double bonds were present in the macromolecule. He also developed the asymmetric synthesis of polymers, where an optically active macromolecule can be produced from optically inactive monomers. To mimic biological processes in this way was a remarkable and insightful achievement. In the 1960's, Natta was continuing this extensive work with the polymerization of nonhydrocarbon monomers, such as benzofuran, and vinyl ether.

Numerous gold medals were awarded to Natta in recognition of his scientific contributions, including the First International Gold Medal of the Synthetic Rubber Industry (1961), the Society of Plastics Engineers Gold Medal (1963), the Lavoisier Medal from the French Chemical Society (1963), and the Perkin Medal (1963). He also received honorary degrees from the University of Turin (1962) and from the University of Mainz (1963). Natta was awarded the Nobel Prize in Chemistry, jointly with Ziegler, in November,

1963. Arne Fredga of the Royal Swedish Academy of Sciences observed, during the formal presentation, that nature's monopoly on stereospecific and asymmetric polymerization had been broken.

In the last twenty years of his life, Natta became increasingly limited in his activities by Parkinson's disease. He could still go for long walks in the woods and hunt for mushrooms with his wife, but his other hobbies, mountain climbing and skiing, were impossible. Natta also had an interest in fossils and kept a collection of petrified fish. He continued his impact on chemistry education as coeditor of the book *Stereoregular Polymers and Stereospecific Polymerizations* (1967) and was coauthor of *Stereochimica: Molecole in 3D* (1968; *Stereochemistry*, 1972) with Mario Farina; he retired in 1972. Natta died in Bergamo, Italy, on May 2, 1979, following complications from surgery for a broken femur.

Summary

The driving force in Giulio Natta's scientific achievements was the desire to apply the theories of chemistry to practical applications. His background in engineering and chemistry provided him with the intellectual tools required to transform ideas into reality. He was known as "the wizard of plastics" and was one of the foremost personalities in leading the world into the age of plastics. The explosive expansion of the plastics industry and the use of plastics in every facet of life brought about an environmental stress as the result of the quantities of durable waste accumulating in dump sites. Legislation has been aimed at limiting the type and quantities of plastics waste. Many industrial projects in the plastics industry have been initiated to develop product biodegradability and the recyclability of polymers.

The impact of Natta's contributions can hardly be overstated. Much of the plasticware used in household goods, scientific and medical laboratories, microwavable containers, detergents, pipes, and antiknock additives are a direct result of his work. He laid the foundations for understanding the relationships between polymer structure and the resulting physical properties of polymers. These discoveries influenced the development of the entire plastics industry. The advancement of technology in many other fields, such as the aerospace industry, computers, and the automotive industry, are directly related to the availability of inexpensive, lightweight materials that outperform metals, wood, and paper in terms of strength, durability, heat resistance, and other physical properties.

Bibliography

"Giulio Natta." In *Contemporary Authors*, edited by Hal May, vol. 113. Detroit, Mich.: Gale Research, 1985. Contains an obituary notice with a brief overview of Natta's contributions to science.

"Giulio Natta." In *Current Biography Yearbook 1964*, edited by Charles

Moritz. New York: H. W. Wilson, 1964. Contains much of the biographical material available on Natta. The article mentions some of his coworkers by name and lists the early trade names of some of the plastics produced industrially by Montecatini and others. References at the end of the article provide a few other sources.

McGraw-Hill Modern Scientists and Engineers. Vol. 2. New York: McGraw-Hill, 1980. The section on Giulio Natta summarizes Natta's scientific achievements and lists a reference on Hermann Staudinger, who influenced Natta's interest in high polymers, as well as references to the polymerization process in general, to rubber, and to stereochemistry.

Natta, Giulio, and Ferdinando Danusso, eds. *Stereoregular Polymers and Stereospecific Polymerization.* London: Pergamon Press, 1967. This book is a compendium of the publications by Natta. Since most of Natta's research was published in Italian, or languages other than English, the book is an invaluable source to anyone wishing access to Natta's original work.

Natta, Giulio, and Mario Farina. *Stereochemistry.* Translated by Andrew Dempster. London: Longman, 1972. An excellent source on the technical aspects of stereochemistry for a college-level student. Many parts can be read with a minimal background in chemistry. Shows the clarity of thought that Natta had in visualizing molecules in three dimensions and contains many illustrations. Discusses the entire field of stereochemistry and is not limited to the polymer aspects. Biological considerations are extensively treated.

Wasson, Tyler, ed. *Nobel Prize Winners.* New York: H. W. Wilson, 1987. The chapter on Natta gives the English translation of the formal presentation speech made by Arne Fredga of the Royal Swedish Academy of Sciences as well as Natta's Nobel lecture. An extensive list of references are cited at the end of the lecture, and these are followed by a condensed biographical sketch, which details the awards and honors received by Natta.

Massimo D. Bezoari

LOUIS-EUGÈNE-FÉLIX NÉEL

Born: November 22, 1904; Lyons, France

Area of Achievement: Physics

Contribution: By applying revolutionary viewpoints to old ideas of physics, Néel discovered new forms of magnetism, including antiferromagnetic and ferrimagnetic materials. His work greatly strengthened modern magnetic theory and has added fundamentally to computer-memory techniques and to the use of high-frequency waves. For his scientific zeal, he was awarded the Nobel Prize in 1970. Additionally, he has had tremendous importance in the establishment of various research centers in Europe.

Early Life

Louis-Eugène-Félix Néel was born in Lyons, France, on November 22, 1904. He was quite precocious as a child, and his exceptional ability in mathematics became evident early in his schooling. As a result of his outstanding examination scores and teacher comments, he was admitted to the École Normale Supérieure in Paris, which he attended from 1924 to 1928. In the latter year, he received a lectureship at the school, during which time he further developed his abilities in mathematics and physics, and began formulating his ideas on magnetism. In 1932, he obtained his doctorate of science from the University of Strasbourg.

Working in the laboratory of Pierre Weiss at Strasbourg, Néel started his original research in 1928 on basic problems of magnetism, a subject which would consume his interests until 1939. While working on his doctoral thesis, he had found extremely original possibilities in the works of Werner Heisenberg on ferromagnetism and in Heisenberg's idea that the field was a result of actions over small distances between neighboring atoms. Néel's work suggested that there should also be interactions between closely packed atoms that would cause an antiparallel alignment of the magnetic moment of individual atoms. In a series of papers published from 1932 to 1936, he described the characteristics of those materials he would name "antiferromagnets" (originally he had called the phenomenon constant paramagnetism). For that excellent series of researches, he was appointed professor of physics at the faculty of science at Strasbourg, where he served until 1945. For a brief period, his tenure was interrupted by World War II, during which he served the government as an investigative scientist. His main topic of research was the means of defending ships from floating German magnetized mines. To counteract them, he invented a new method of protection, known as neutralization, which gave the ship a permanent magnetization in a direction opposite to the terrestrial magnetic field.

In 1947, he became professor of physics at the University of Grenoble. In

1940, he had gone there, being the principal agent in establishing the Laboratoire d'Électrostatique et de Physique du Métal. He served as director of the Polytechnic Institute until 1956, when he created and formed the Centre d'Études Nucléaires de Grenoble. Subsequently, he represented France at the Scientific Council of the North Atlantic Treaty Organization.

Life's Work

During his tenure at Pierre Weiss's laboratory, Néel came into contact with the current theory for the properties of matter, that of ferromagnetism's being a result of a uniform imaginary molecular field resulting from interactions of individual atoms. No origin for this field had been discovered, so Néel introduced the idea of local molecular fields, resulting from close neighboring atoms, abandoning the notion of a general field. Accompanying this idea with that of time-varying fluctuations in the heat energy of the field, Néel found that he could account for constant paramagnetism, in elements such as manganese and chromium, changing to a temperature-dependent paramagnetism, via an interaction that would cause an antiparallel alignment of the magnetic moments of closely spaced atoms. He referred to this as antiferromagnetism. He considered that, at low temperatures, atomic moments within a crystal lattice would couple together, dividing the atoms in a typical crystal into two types, one with magnetic moment pointing in the reverse direction of the other set. The atoms in these sublattices, as they were called, were opposite in orientation to their neighbors. When the temperature increased, Néel found, this ordered orientation of magnetic moments seemed to disappear, the temperature where the disruption becomes complete being known now as the Néel temperature. Néel noted that, from his analysis, two conditions for ferromagnetism had to occur: Atoms must have a net magnetic moment, a result of unfilled electron shells, and the quality known as the exchange integral between nearby atoms must be positive. Néel argued that, for nonferromagnetic materials that did contain magnetic atoms, the exchange integral would be negative, and the maximum number of antiparallel moments would have the lowest available energy state. He called these materials antiferromagnetic. Above the Néel temperature, the susceptibility, or ability to hold a magnetic field, of an antiferromagnet, behaves according to the well-established Curie-Weiss law for magnetic susceptibility-temperature interactions of molecular regions.

While developing his theory of antiferromagnetism, Néel also became interested in the properties of very fine-grained ferromagnets, the material of a size necessary to be resolved with a microscope. In 1941, he set out to explain, based on his understanding how these minute particles must act in a magnetic field, the "magnetic memory" exhibited in diverse forms found in nature, including lavas, both granitic and basaltic. He found that the locked-in memory tied the time of cooling of the sample below the temperature necessary to keep the magnetic atoms totally disrupted in orientation to the absolute age of the sample. This type of memory allows geologists and archaeologists to retrace the history of paleomagnetism, or how the nonconstant earth's field varies with the passage of four billion years.

While working on the memory idea, Néel discovered a new class of permanent magnets, whose properties are a result of the very fine grains enclosed together. Materials of this sort he called "ferrimagnets," the term describing such compounds as the ferrites, a class of compounds with a general structural formula of divalent metals, such as copper, magnesium, nickel, or iron, combined with oxygen in the form $MOFe(2)O(3)$. These compounds exhibit a spontaneous magnetization at room temperature of a low value; that is, they develop a field by themselves without any outside influence. Above the Curie point, where materials lose their ability to hold a magnetic field, the magnetic susceptibility does not obey a simple Curie-Weiss law but rather follows a nonlinear curve when susceptibility is plotted against temperature. Néel resolved the problem by developing an unbalanced antiferromagnetic structure he called a "ferrimagnet."

In 1956, Néel's concepts were used by others on the garnet ferrites of the rare earths, which were found to be extremely useful in technological applications in high-frequency engineering. Equally important today is the discovery that ferromagnetic oxides and spinels can be tailored to suit the job based on the theoretical descriptions of the magnetic properties as proposed by Néel. Such materials are fundamental to core memories in computers, magnetic tapes, and the ideas of domain memories.

In the 1950's and 1960's, Néel was concerned primarily with theoretical problems, which have formed the main subjects of more than 150 publications. One series of his researches derived from the importance of the role of the internal demagnetizing fields in the properties of ferromagnetic substances. Néel developed a theory of magnetization for monocrystals based on the idea of the existence of various modes and phases of sublattices and interacting atoms. He showed that, in a perfect crystal, a number of phases coexist, the number being based on external conditions. He suggested that each phase was composed of what are known now as elementary domains, whose spontaneous counteractions, such as magnetizations, are aligned parallel. In simple cases, Néel was able to detail the subdivision of a ferromagnetic substance into those domains. The domain formation was found to have a special form, known as "Néel's spikes," around inclusions or cavities within the mineral, and a different form within very thin layers of walls of separation between the elementary domains (called Néel walls). Néel also published numerous papers on the theory of Rayleigh's laws, magnetic viscosity, internal dispersion fields, superantiferromagnetism, and hysteresis.

Besides his great discoveries in magnetism and solid-state physics, for which he received the Nobel Prize in Physics, Néel has also been of tremendous importance in the establishment of great research centers in Europe. In 1940, he went to Grenoble and established the world-famous laboratory there, which, in 1946, became one of the external laboratories of the Centre National de la Recherche Scientifique, expanding rapidly and giving rise to several new laboratories. Since 1946, he has been professor at Grenoble and the director of the laboratory, during which time Néel's school has become internationally recognized for excellence in magnetism research. Néel has been the director of the Centre d'Études Nucléaires de Grenoble, which he founded in 1956, and which has strong programs in neutron diffraction, crystal growth, Mossbauer studies, high-strength magnetic fields, high-level pressure studies, and very low-temperature physics. In 1967, he was one of the principals in the decision to install the Franco-German high-flux reactor in Grenoble. He has been the director of the Polytechnic Institute of Grenoble, a member of the Consulting Committee on Higher Education, and a director of the Centre National de la Recherche Scientifique.

Summary

Louis-Eugène-Félix Néel's contributions to physics have been numerous and innovative; he has virtually rewritten the knowledge of how magnetic fields are generated, maintained, and modified in diverse natural materials. From his studies of permanent magnetism in ferromagnets, his discoveries have led to the understanding of how antiferromagnetism and ferrimagnetism work, and to further work on more quantum-related topics such as superantiferromagnetism. In physics alone, his ideas have made possible the development of a modern, quantum-level understanding and theory of atomic magnetism, a perception that has led to further advances in such diverse fields as aircraft and electronic high-frequency oscillatory controls, transference of information at exceedingly high rates of data turnover, and the development of magnetic "memory cores" for modern computer technology.

Outside the area of physics proper, his hand has guided the development of successful laboratories in France, enhancing national prestige with developments in fields ranging from cryogenics to nuclear technology to the education of new generations of scientists. For his many contributions, he has been awarded numerous awards and honors, all graciously received, including his being named a Nobel laureate in physics.

Bibliography

Abro, A. d'. *The Rise of the New Physics: Its Mathematical and Physical Theories*. New York: Dover, 1952. A detailed history of the rise of twentieth century physics, this two-volume set covers all the developments of physics in the twentieth century. Contemporaries of Néel, and developments in magnetism, are related to electrical and solid-state physics. Some difficult mathematics.

Burke, Harry. *Handbook of Magnetic Phenomena for Electronic Engineers.* New York: Van Nostrand Reinhold, 1986. Providing an excellent overview, this book covers all the known phenomena associated with magnetism. Burke explores the diverse relationships between magnetism and the particles of nature. Measurement techniques are detailed. Thorough discussions, with well-conceived illustrations.

Cotterill, Rodney. *The Cambridge Guide to the Material World.* New York: Cambridge University Press, 1985. Providing a comprehensive survey, this work details the physics and chemistry of the crystalline and non-crystalline worlds on an atomic and superatomic level. The role of magnetism is intertwined throughout the text, being an integral element in explaining such topics as crystals, ceramics, conductors, and electrical interactions in living matter. Well illustrated, and well written.

McKeehan, Louis W. *Magnets.* New Jersey: Van Nostrand Reinhold, 1967. Deals with the history of magnets, from their first use in the ancient world to the sophisticated developments of modern times.

Massey, Harrie S. W. *The New Age in Physics.* New York: Harper & Row, 1960. Deals with the major topics explored in physics throughout the twentieth century. A detailed section on electrons views the magnetic properties of matter, with well-written descriptions of paramagnetism and ferromagnetism, and the science of magnetic properties of matter at low temperatures. Well written, with a wide range of interlocking topics.

Schneer, Cecil J. *The Evolution of Physical Science: Major Ideas from the Earliest Times to the Present.* New York: University Press of America, 1984. This work illustrates how science is performed, how scientific discoveries are made to bring order out of disorder. Provides a chapter on magnetism, giving basic reading for understanding Néel's ideas. Supplemental readings provided for each major scientific theme.

Arthur L. Alt

JAWAHARLAL NEHRU

Born: November 14, 1889; Allahabad, India
Died: May 27, 1964; New Delhi, India
Areas of Achievement: Government and politics
Contribution: Nehru led India through the difficult transition from colony to
   independence, providing the critical political skills for his close friend and
   mentor, Mahatma Gandhi. Upon India's being granted independence on
   August 15, 1947, Nehru became India's first prime minister. Following
   Gandhi's assassination in January, 1948, Nehru placed India firmly in a
   nonaligned, democratic path, ruling the country until his own death on
   May 27, 1964.

Early Life

Jawaharlal Nehru was born into an affluent, prominent Kashmiri Brahman
family on November 14, 1889. Nehru's father was both a barrister and
prominent politician, and Jawaharlal was groomed for a similar role from an
early age. Given the family background, young Nehru was reared in an An-
glophile atmosphere, tutored by a succession of British nannies and teachers.

At thirteen, under the influence of his tutor, Ferdinand Brooks, Nehru
joined Annie Besant's Theosophical Society. In May, 1905, Nehru arrived at
Harrow School in London to prepare for college. Following three years of
study at Harrow, Nehru began his studies in 1907 at Trinity College, Cambridge. Following completion of his undergraduate studies, in 1910 Nehru
moved to London to begin his bar studies at the Inner Temple.

Nehru returned to India in September, 1912. Given his family interests in
Congress Party politics, young Nehru soon became involved in Allahabad's
political scene, though at the time the Congress Party was fairly obscure.
Nehru attended the Congress Party's Bankipore meeting as a delegate in
October, 1912. He worked as a junior barrister under his father's supervi-
sion, but he was not drawn to the practice of law as a profession.

Nehru married Kamala Kaul, the daughter of an orthodox Brahman Kashmiri family, on February 8, 1916. In November, 1917, their daughter Indira
was born, who would herself later become Prime Minister of India.

Life's Work

Despite India's contributions to the Allies in World War I, the nation was
disappointed by Britain's subsequent Government of India Act of December 23, 1919, feeling that it fell far short of Indian desires for home rule.
Nehru by this time had determined to work with Gandhi, who had returned
to India from South Africa in January, 1915. Gandhi's satyagraha (nonviolence) campaign began in March, 1919, and Nehru fully supported it.
Nehru believed that Gandhi's policies offered "a method of action which was

straight and open and possibly effective." The relevance of Gandhi's policies was highlighted by the massacre on April 13, 1919, at Amritsar, when troops under General Reginald Dyer opened fire, killing hundreds of unarmed civilians. Nehru's father had continued to rise in Indian politics; in November, 1919, he was elected to the presidency of the Congress Party.

In June, 1920, Nehru met with a crowd of peasants who had marched fifty miles to Allahabad to acquaint the politicians with the appalling conditions of their lives. Nehru was sufficiently moved by their tales of exploitation by the large landowners that he began to interest himself in the plight of the peasantry. Nehru began to understand that in the countryside might be built a base of political support for a national movement, rather than largely relying on the cities. He quickly became very popular among the peasantry as a politician who, despite a background of affluence, was genuinely concerned with their problems. Nehru now busied himself with spreading Gandhi's satyagraha policies throughout the countryside.

British authorities were sufficiently vexed by the Nehrus' activities that on December 6, 1921, they took father and son into custody. Jawaharlal was released in March, 1922, when it was discovered that he had been wrongly convicted. Upon his release he worked to urge Indians to boycott foreign goods, resulting in his rearrest and sentencing on May 19, 1922, to a twenty-one-month prison term. Nehru was again released early, in January, 1923. Nehru was arrested yet again in September, 1923, but given a suspended sentence.

Nehru now believed that Congress Party policies needed a body of regular, disciplined volunteers; he accordingly founded the Hindustan Seva Dal in December, 1923, a body under congressional control that was to recruit and train patriotic Indians. Within the month, Nehru was formally elected General Secretary of Congress.

Nehru's wife's health began to deteriorate; she was diagnosed as having tuberculosis. In March, 1926, the entire family moved to Switzerland in order to facilitate her recovery. The Nehrus settled in Geneva; while Kamala underwent medical treatment, Jawaharlal busied himself observing the International Labor Office and the League of Nations, both headquartered in the city.

Nehru was a keen political observer of the European political scene and during his twenty-month stay in Europe, visited a number of the European capitals. During the summer of 1926, he visited Italy, observing the effects of Fascism there. During September he again went to England, while that autumn a trip to Berlin impressed him with German industrial might. In February, 1927, Nehru went to Brussels as an Indian National Congress Party representative to attend the International Congress of Oppressed Nationalities Against Imperialism. Nehru pursued some academic interests while in Switzerland, becoming enrolled in the University of Geneva's International Summer School. During November, 1927, Nehru and his family went to Moscow for the tenth anniversary celebrations of the establishment of Soviet power, giving Nehru a chance to observe firsthand the workings of a socialist state.

Upon his return to India in December, 1927, Nehru threw himself into Congress political work, immersing himself in it for the next two years. In answer to the hotly debated question of whether India should seek either dominion status within the British Empire or complete independence, Nehru at the Madras Congress in December, 1927, forwarded a resolution that this "Congress declares the goal of the Indian people to be complete National Independence." The same month he formed the first of his pressure groups within Congress, the Republican Party of Congress. Nehru contributed extensively to the popular press, particularly the *Hindu* and *Tribune*. His untiring efforts were rewarded with election to the presidency of Congress in 1929. At Congress' annual meeting that December, Nehru moved the main resolution, that Congress now stood for complete Indian independence. The resolution passed overwhelmingly.

Nehru's predicament was that he was drawn to both Gandhian principles of nonviolence and socialism. His interest in socialism had been strengthened by his visit to the Soviet Union, which he saw as a nonimperialist nation attempting to implement true equality. His closeness to Gandhi, however, made him constantly aware of the ethical strength embodied in his nonviolent principles.

Direct conflict with the British government erupted with Gandhi's famous March, 1930, "March to the Sea" to manufacture salt in violation of a government monopoly. Both Gandhi and Nehru spent much of the next few years in and out of British jails; Nehru served nearly four years during the period 1930-1935. While in prison he wrote *Glimpses of World History* (1934-1935), a series of letters to his daughter Indira that contemplated the entire sweep of human history. Nehru also wrote *Jawaharlal Nehru: An Autobiography* (1936) and many articles during this period of confinement. Nehru was to spend nearly nine years total in prison between 1921 and 1945, but he never allowed himself to become embittered by the experience; instead, he tried to put his time to good use.

A great personal loss was the death of his father on February 6, 1931. As his wife's health deteriorated, Nehru became more and more concerned; following an early release from prison in September, 1935, he flew immediately to Europe to be with his wife, who had earlier gone there for medical treatment. His wife died in Lausanne on February 29, 1936. With his wife's death, Nehru threw himself into political work. Following his return to India, by February, 1937, he had visited every province in India, giving him a broad perspective of the country's problems. Subsequent elections strengthened Congress' power. Congress now faced growing unrest from the Muslim

League, led by Mohammad Ali Jinnah.

The next major issue facing Congress was the declaration by Great Britain on September 3, 1939, of Indian belligerency in the war against Adolf Hitler without Indian consent. As a member of the Working Committee, Nehru drew up a protest, but this was contrary to the emergency acts passed by the government, and on October 31, 1940, Nehru was immediately arrested and sentenced to four years' imprisonment. Despite the severity of the British crackdown, Nehru and five hundred Congress colleagues were released in early December, 1941.

Given the seriousness of the British position in the Far East with the Japanese advances since December, 1941, Churchill's government began to deal seriously with India. Sir Stafford Cripps arrived in India on March 22, 1942, with a compromise offer from His Majesty's government. In return for wholehearted Indian support of the war effort, India would achieve independence after the war. Nehru and Gandhi were arrested after rioting erupted in August, 1942, after the proposal was rejected. Nehru wrote *The Discovery of India* (1946) during this period of confinement, which lasted from August, 1942, to June, 1945.

Upon release, Nehru continued to agitate for complete independence. Clement Atlee's government had declared in December, 1945, its support for Indian independence, but increasing Muslim resistance to inclusion in a Hindu state made negotiations increasingly difficult. Nehru in August, 1946, was invited as the president of Congress to form an interim cabinet. In early 1947, the British government declared its intention to quit India by June, 1948, and the friction between the Muslim League under Jinnah and Congress increased.

India was formally granted independence on August 15, 1947. Fighting between the areas assigned to an independent Muslim Pakistan and a Hindu India forced a migration of hundreds of thousands and resulted in many deaths. Prime Minister Nehru and Gandhi attempted to stanch the bloodshed but were largely unsuccessful. Gandhi himself was assassinated on January 25, 1948.

Nehru's troubles as prime minister were immediately increased in 1947-1948 by the problem of conflicting Indian-Pakistani claims to Kashmir, with firefights occurring along the disputed frontier. India also experienced increasing tension with China, especially after China's invasion of Tibet in October, 1950. After a revolt in Tibet failed in 1959, the Dalai Lama with 100,000 followers found sanctuary in India. Chinese and Indian troops subsequently fought a series of fierce border skirmishes in the autumn of 1962.

India's postcolonial domestic problems were immense. In order to improve the economy, Nehru's government on April 1, 1951, inaugurated its first Five Year Plan, with an emphasis on increasing agricultural output. The government also instituted a Community Development Program to raise the living standard of the countryside. In 1955, the Untouchability Act was passed to attempt to ease life for India's most degraded citizens.

Nehru's popularity remained high; he was reelected in March, 1957, and to a third five-year term in March, 1962. Nehru's nonaligned stance slowly won for him grudging admiration, even in the fiercely anticommunist United States. He visited the United States in 1949 and 1956; President Dwight D. Eisenhower returned the courtesy in 1960. His emphasis on India's need for both democracy and socialism has increasingly proven a model for the Third World since Nehru's death on May 27, 1964. With brief exceptions, his descendants ruled India up until 1989.

Summary

Jawaharlal Nehru had an influence far outside India's borders. In pursuing democratic, nonaligned policies, Nehru's India provided a pattern for the newly emerging postcolonial nations of Africa and Asia. With Gandhi's untimely death, Nehru was the one Indian political leader who had been sufficiently closely associated with the Mahatma to be accepted as his most capable disciple and successor. In the postwar, postcolonial era, Nehru, as leader of the world's largest democracy, faced the staggering problems brought about by the ending of the British Raj. Despite Nehru's cosmopolitan background and his close friendship with many Englishmen, he did not want to turn an independent India into an Asian replica of Great Britain.

Nehru's acute observations of both the European and Soviet political systems led him to attempt to combine the best features of both in India. Given India's industrial weakness, Nehru believed that a centrally planned economy would provide the most immediate results. In politics, Nehru believed that the British parliamentary system and a multiparty structure provided a better model for India than the Soviet one-party state. Nehru was also an innovator in international relations. Nehru attempted to draw closer to other Asian states attempting to maintain an equal distance between the American and Soviet blocs, believing that India's immense size made it the natural leader in south Asia.

The political dynasty that Nehru founded remained remarkably stable in Indian politics. When his grandson, Rajiv Gandhi, resigned as prime minister, on November 29, 1989, a Nehru had ruled India for all but five of its forty-two years of independence from Britain. While Rajiv was not able to carry on that heritage, his mother, Indira Gandhi, governed India from January, 1966, with a brief break in 1977-1979, until her assassination by Sikh extremists on October 31, 1984. For whatever future direction the nation may take, many of Nehru's values continue to guide the country's destiny.

Bibliography

Brecher, Michael. *Nehru: A Political Biography.* New York: Oxford University Press, 1959. A massive, scholarly examination of Nehru's life and political philosophy. The work is especially valuable for its setting of Nehru's life in the larger context of India's resurgent nationalism under British rule from the nineteenth century onward.

Collins, Larry, and Dominique Lapierre. *Freedom at Midnight*. New York: Simon & Schuster, 1975. Based on extensive use of both primary and secondary sources, this work is a very readable account of India's push toward independence and the immediate postindependence era. The book succeeds in putting Nehru's accomplishments in the larger perspective of twentieth century Indian politics, though the account ends with Gandhi's assassination.

Gopal, Sarvepali. *Jawaharlal Nehru: A Biography*. 3 vols. Cambridge, Mass.: Harvard University Press, 1976-1984. As one of India's most respected historians, Gopal was chosen to write Nehru's official biography and enjoyed access to Nehru's papers and associates. While the work is extremely thorough, it suffers from a slight lack of relative objectivity about its subject.

Nehru, Jawaharlal. *Jawaharlal Nehru: An Autobiography*. New ed. London: The Bodley Head, 1985. The bulk of this work was written by Nehru during his confinement June, 1934-February, 1935, with additional material added later by the author to cover events up to 1940. The tone is both thoughtful and reserved, and is marked by a remarkable lack of rancor toward the British.

Pandey, B. N. *Nehru*. London: Macmillan, 1976. Pandey, a member of the University of London's School of Oriental and African Studies, conducted extensive interviews in India with members of Nehru's family, friends, and politicians.

Shorter, Bani. *Nehru: A Voice for Mankind*. New York: John Day, 1970. A fairly intimate biography of Nehru that serves as an introduction to the man, his work, and the history of India. Includes an index and photographs.

John C. K. Daly

WALTHER HERMANN NERNST

Born: June 25, 1864; Briesen, Prussia
Died: November 18, 1941; near Bad Muskau, Germany
Area of Achievement: Chemistry
Contribution: Nernst won the Nobel Prize in Chemistry in 1920 for his statement of the third law of thermodynamics. Yet his equation for the electrode potential of a voltaic cell is his best-known contribution and appears in nearly all general chemistry texts.

Early Life
Walther Hermann Nernst, born in 1864, in the town of Briesen, in what was then Prussia, was not from a family of scientists. In fact, he displayed a talent for the arts and maintained a lifelong interest in the theater. Yet he was inspired by the chemistry master at the *Gymnasium*, where he finished at the top of his class, to become what is now called a physical chemist. During his early school and undergraduate years, the German chemical industry became world-dominant in dyestuffs and pharmaceuticals. The discovery by Friedrich Wöhler in 1828 that urea could be synthesized from inorganic materials had inspired German scientists to design chemical processes to manufacture products previously obtainable only from biological sources. There developed a strong relationship between German industry and the universities to foster this revolutionary notion of basic research aimed at the creation of new products. Industry established and maintained its own research laboratories for the development of these products. The professors from these technical universities did consulting work, which furthered the opportunities for graduating scientists and engineers. Capital was provided and controlled by the various German governments through ministers of higher education, who believed strongly in this emerging pattern. It was in this atmosphere that Nernst began his career in higher learning.

It is important to note that there was an increased emphasis on basic research as Nernst began his undergraduate education. Otherwise, Nernst might never have been able to devote almost his entire career to the fundamental research that brought him to such important discoveries. Much freedom was enjoyed by university students of that time. They attended lectures and laboratory sessions at a variety of institutions, if they chose, until they believed themselves to be qualified to sit for examinations. Nernst was no exception to this practice. He attended lectures at Zurich, Berlin, Graz, and Würzburg, and he was attracted to the outstanding scientists of the day. Nernst first began research at Graz in 1886 under Ludwig Boltzmann, a champion of the atomistic viewpoint. Nernst soon moved to Würzburg, where he continued his research under Friedrich Kohlrausch on electrical currents in solutions.

Life's Work

Ultimately Nernst was to become the world's authority in the field of electrical currents in solution. Michael Faraday had suggested in his publications of the mid-nineteenth century that ions were produced by electric currents in solution. Svante Arrhenius, however, suggested that these ions could be produced by the dissociation of a salt in forming a solution. These ions then were free to move between electrodes as current carriers, suggesting an electrical nature of salts before dissociation. That is, the nature of chemical bonds was somehow electrical. At the invitation of Friedrich Ostwald, Nernst accepted a position at the new Physico-Chemical Institute in Leipzig. He continued to study the nature of ions in solution, but he now began to include the ideas of Hermann von Helmholtz and Rudolf Clausius and to investigate the behavior of ions in a chemical reaction in solution. Helmholtz and Clausius had clarified the concept of spontaneity in a physical process as related to the external work capability of the system. Nernst realized that the idea of external work capability of a chemical system is related to the electrode potential of the reaction embodied in the configuration of a voltaic cell. A voltaic cell is superbly adapted to demonstrate this relation of external work and the electrical potential generated between ions in relation to an electrode. The electrode either donates or accepts the electron charge while, perhaps, it is even involved in the reaction. Nernst supplied the equation that related the concentrations of ions to the external work capability of a cell, which is a means of separating a reaction into donating and accepting cell halves. The overall cell potential, as a combination of these half-cell potentials, is a measure of the chemical potential of the reaction and hence the external work capability. This external work capability has since become known as free energy. The free energy change in a chemical reaction is related to the equilibrium constant for the reaction, or the point of equilibrium as it was then known.

This research earned for Nernst a lectureship at Leipzig. In a few years, however, he accepted a lectureship at Göttingen. The attraction was a promise of his own department and eventually an assistant professorship. Göttingen had a very high reputation among German universities. More offers prompted the creation of a chair of physical chemistry at Göttingen for Nernst, and Nernst accepted in 1894. During his time at Göttingen, Nernst wrote a physical chemistry text entitled *Theoretische Chemie vom Standpunkte der Avogadroschen Regel und der Thermodynamik* (1893; *Theoretical Chemistry from the Standpoint of Avogadro's Rule and Thermodynamics*, 1895), which was widely used and went through ten editions. He remained there for fifteen years, during which time he also met and married Emma Lohmeyer, the daughter of a local physician, and together they had five children. They eventually settled into a mansion that was provided by the Ministry of Education. Directly connected was a new electrochemical laboratory of which Nernst became the director. The Nernsts hosted many social functions, many of which were for the research assistants at the laboratory. There were as many as forty young people there working for doctorates, and an extension was eventually added to keep up with the work in progress.

Nernst was compelled to leave Germany because of a war-crimes scare following World War I. After returning to Germany, he moved to Berlin, where new labs were under construction from the rubble left after the war. The prominence of Germany in academics was manifested by a succession of Nobel Prizes in the years following the war. This dominance was to last for many years. A revolution was taking place, and Nernst was at the center of it.

Alfred Bertholet's explanation of chemical spontaneity in 1867, although of profound impact, was not complete. Bertholet said that spontaneous chemical reactions are those that are exothermic. This theory required much additional work to define the concepts that made it possible to formulate a complete statement of chemical spontaneity. Statements by Sadi Carnot (1824) and Clausius (1850) were crucial to the equations of Helmholtz and Oliver Gibbs. Carnot's cycle defines a heat engine, operating between two specified temperatures, that converts a given amount of heat into the maximum amount of useful work possible. This heat engine applies to physical as well as chemical processes. Clausius introduced the entropy term S, which is a disorder function that defines the unavailable energy in the process of heat energy conversion to useful work. The equations of Helmholtz and Gibbs were to follow. They state that this maximum amount of useful work is the difference between the total heat energy and that amount that is unavailable for useful work. Nernst's heat theorem states that, in the equations of Helmholtz and Gibbs, the total heat energy in a chemical reaction and the maximum work available are identical at the absolute zero of temperature. Nernst stated that the specific heat of substances in the condensed phases would become zero at the absolute zero of temperature and therefore S would become zero. With a better understanding of absolute zero, the heat theorem became the third law of thermodynamics: The entropy, S, of a substance (in a perfect crystalline state) may become zero at the absolute zero of temperature, if the absolute of temperature can be reached. S means disorder and thus it is what goes to zero at the absolute zero of temperature instead of energy. It follows, then, that S has a finite positive value at temperatures above absolute zero. Chemists were then able to determine the free energy changes for chemical reactions at a variety of temperatures. This permits the calculation of the equilibrium distribution of mass between reactants and products.

After having received the Nobel Prize for his heat theorem, Nernst spent two years as president of the National Physical Laboratory. He did not like this assignment and returned to the academic life as head of the physics department at the University of Berlin. During his last years, he purchased a one-thousand-acre estate at Zibelle. He held bird shoots and began to raise carp in some of the ponds available on the grounds. The Nernsts permanently retired to Zibelle in 1933, though Nernst maintained an apartment in Berlin for use during his frequent attendance at university functions. He suffered a heart attack, from which he never recovered, and died on November 18, 1941.

Summary

The impact of Walther Nernst on the evolving science of physical chemistry cannot be overemphasized. His contribution to thermodynamics is well established. A knowledge of the equilibrium distribution constants for chemical reactions is of inestimable value to the design of commercial manufacturing processes. Nernst also wrote the equation for predicting the potential of a voltaic cell in terms of ion concentrations. This equation is essential to the prediction of spontaneity of chemical reactions that can be expressed as electron exchange.

Nernst also sponsored a discussion group every Friday afternoon in his laboratory in the University of Berlin. The group included world-class physicists and chemists such as Albert Einstein as well as research students. Recent publications and new research findings were brought in for discussion. Nernst's sponsorship of these weekly colloquia may be his one underrecognized contribution to the revolution in physics and chemistry in the early twentieth century.

Bibliography

Atkins, P. W. *The Second Law.* New York: W. H. Freeman, 1984. This book is excellent for the lay reader, outlining the physical meaning of entropy and its relation to chemical reactions. The author uses the steam engine as an example of the workings of the second law of thermodynamics.

Glasstone, Samuel. *Thermodynamics for Chemists.* New York: D. Van Nostrand, 1947. Author provides the reader with an excellent reference to the third law of thermodynamics that is closer to that of the chemists of Nernst's time.

Mahan, Bruce H. *Elementary Chemical Thermodynamics.* New York: W. A. Benjamin, 1963. This text contains an excellent mathematical discussion of the second law of thermodynamics. Discusses the molecular interpretation of the third law and its relation to the specific heat of substances. The reader is introduced to the voltaic cell as the vehicle for illustrating the second law as Nernst did in his Nobel address.

Mendelssohn, Kurt. *The World of Walther Nernst: The Rise and Fall of German Science, 1864-1941.* Pittsburgh: University of Pittsburgh Press,

1973. Provides a thorough portrayal of Nernst's life against the background of the spectacular growth of German science. The development of the university-industry reciprocal relationship is examined.

Pimentel, George C., and Richard D. Spratley. *Understanding Chemistry.* San Francisco: Holden Day, 1971. Chapter 9 offers an excellent step-by-step derivation of the first law of thermodynamics. The voltaic cell is used as a means of introducing the second law. Chapter 10 describes the relationship between free energy and equilibrium.

Robert E. Whipple

PABLO NERUDA
Neftalí Ricardo Reyes Basoalto

Born: July 12, 1904; Parral, Chile
Died: September 23, 1973; Santiago, Chile
Area of Achievement: Literature
Contribution: Neruda is the greatest modern poet to have combined a personal and lyrical mode with a political voice in a way that spoke to and for a popular mass readership. Rooted in Chile, his poetry has a universal human significance marked by the award of the Nobel Prize in 1971.

Early Life
Pablo Neruda was born Neftalí Ricardo Reyes Basoalto, in the small town of Parral in southern Chile, on July 12, 1904, the son of José del Carmen Reyes and Rosa de Basoalt. His mother, a schoolteacher, died of tuberculosis not long after he was born. Neruda began writing poetry at the local schools but kept it hidden from his schoolmates and his relations, who were mainly agricultural or manual workers, and his father, a tough railroad worker. The family moved to Temuco in 1906, and Neruda grew up in a frontier atmosphere, becoming familiar with the forests and the native Indians who inhabited them. His father remarried, and Neruda grew close to his stepmother, a quiet, unassuming peasant woman named Trinidad Candia Marverde. The headmaster of the local school was the poet Gabriela Mistral, who encouraged the literary talent he saw in the boy. Neruda's reading at this time was eager and indiscriminate. He grew to be a tall, slim youth and began translating Baudelaire and winning various local poetry prizes.

In 1921, he left high school and went to the teachers' college in Santiago (the capital of Chile) but much preferred talking about literature in the cafés to studying French. He had submitted his earliest poems for magazine publication when he was only fifteen, signing himself "Pablo Neruda." His range of literary acquaintances widened, but his early poetry, *Crepusculario* (1923), remained provincial and sentimental. At twenty, however, he published *Veinte poemas de amor y una canción desesperada* (1924; *Twenty Love Poems and a Song of Despair*, 1969, 1976) and established his reputation as a love poet.

Neruda worked fanatically, earning money writing articles for newspapers and journals and writing translations. He edited his own magazine, wrote short stories and an immature episodic novel, and began work on a larger sequence, *Residencia en la tierra* (3 vols., 1933, 1935, 1947; *Residence on Earth and Other Poems*, 1946, 1973). Yet his love affairs left him unhappy, and he remained poor. It was not until 1927 that Neruda successfully gained an appointment with Chile's Ministry of Foreign Affairs and became the honorary consul to Rangoon, Burma. He was neither a trained diplomat nor an outstanding linguist, but, as a gregarious, charismatic, presentable, and accomplished writer who had a proven ability to move his readers, he fulfilled the requirements of an ambassador for his country.

Life's Work

The sense of political solidarity that Neruda came to affirm was gained through years of isolation and a continuous balancing of powerful emotions of love, with rich, dark, sometimes surreal journeys of the imagination. Personal loneliness and a fond memory of his home were counterpointed in his verse. He traveled to various parts of the world on his first trip to the East and sent articles back to the Santiago daily newspaper *La Nación*. In Burma he encountered professionally the remnants of ancient cultures and the continuing exploitation of colonial occupation, and his personal anxieties found a counterpart in society at large. He attempted to maintain contact with friends and writers in Chile and was published in Spain, but in Burma he was depressed.

While visiting India to cover a political meeting in Calcutta in 1929, the enormous crowds that he encountered in the subcontinent brought him to greater depths of despair. He continued writing the *Residence on Earth* poems. In 1930, Neruda became Consul to the Dutch East Indies and married a Dutch woman, Maria Antonieta Haagenar. In 1932, they returned, briefly, to Chile. Though Neruda's poems were by now being published and republished, they would not bring him a living wage. In 1933, he took up another consular appointment in Buenos Aires and in 1934 yet another in Barcelona. His bureaucratic experience had not made him a happy man, but now things were to change. He moved on to Madrid, where the Spanish poet Federico García Lorca (whom he had met in Buenos Aires) introduced him to a new public. He separated from his first wife and later was happily married to Delia del Carril, with whom he remained until the 1950's. His great work *Residence on Earth* was now published, and an international audience was responding to Neruda with vital enthusiasm. Concurrently, Neruda was becoming more thoroughly intellectually politicized, as he was introduced to the social struggles that underlay the Spanish Civil War. García Lorca, who had become a friend of Neruda, was murdered by the Fascists, and Neruda found comradeship with the French left-wing Surrealist writers Louis Aragon and Paul Éluard, and with the Peruvian Cesar Vallejo. He allied himself with the political struggle of the Spanish Republic.

Neruda returned to Chile, and through 1937 and 1938 supported the struggle of the Spanish Republic and the left-wing Chilean government, giving lectures and readings. He began work on a long poetic sequence that was to comprise his greatest work, *Canto general* (1950). In 1939, he traveled to Paris to assist the Spanish Republican refugees in flight to Chile.

Neruda's life continued to be peripatetic. He returned to Chile in 1940 and went on to Mexico. He became more deeply acquainted with meso-America, traveling throughout the Caribbean, Guatemala, and Cuba. Though he wrote a "Song to Stalingrad" in 1942, he became fascinated by the fate of man in the Americas, and a climb to the ruined Inca city of Machu Picchu, on October 22, 1943, resulted in one of the most profound meditative poems of the century, a key poem in the *Canto general* sequence: "Alturas de Machu Picchu" (1950; "The Heights of Machu Picchu," 1966). When the poem was written, in 1945, Neruda had returned to Chile, been elected a senator, won the National Literary Prize, and officially joined the Communist Party. The political forces of the right were growing more powerful, and the leftist President González Videla became a puppet for international monopolists. Neruda, who had at first supported Videla, was now seen as a dangerous rebel. The Communist Party was made illegal and Neruda, to avoid arrest, took refuge among the rural and urban proletariat of the country before fleeing on horseback to Mexico. The poetry of *Canto general* that was written through 1948-1949 exhibits much of the rage and protest of the persecuted poet.

Neruda made his way to Paris and the Soviet Union. His poetry had by now been published in countries throughout the world. He was internationally honored. He returned to Mexico, where *Canto general* was published (with illustrations by the great mural artists Diego Rivera and David Alfaro Siqueiros), and though he was awarded global public recognition (the Soviet edition of *Canto general* ran to 250,000 copies), he was still banned in his native Chile. He met Matilde Urrutia in Mexico, and a stunning series of love poems, *Los versos del Capitán* (1952; *The Captain's Verses*, 1972), followed. After a worldwide reading tour, Neruda and Matilde heard that he was no longer under arrest in Chile. He returned there in 1952.

His poetry turned now to the commonplace and everyday objects of the *Odas elementales* (1954; *The Elemental Odes*, 1961), simple poems of praise and delight that pleased critics and general readers of his work alike. He was equally acclaimed in capitalist and communist worlds. He separated from Delia del Carril in 1955 and remained in love with Matilde Urrutia for the rest of his life. He did not stop traveling: to South America, the Soviet Union, China, and elsewhere. His vanity was appealed to wherever he went, and his gregarious love of life was indulged alongside his enthusiasm for collecting things. Royalties from book sales at last began to bring him some money, and he built a house on Isla Negra that became his favorite retreat, filled with the books and things he had collected over the years. He continued to produce poetry of great tenderness and exquisite sensuality, such as *Estravagario* (1958; *Extravagaria*, 1974) and *Cien sonetos de amor* (1959; *One Hundred Love Sonnets*, 1986). He also began work on his autobiographical *Confieso que he vivido: Memorias* (*Memoirs*, 1977), published posthumously in 1974.

In the late 1960's, Neruda began writing for the theater, with a Spanish translation of William Shakespeare's *Romeo and Juliet* and *Fulgor y muerte de Joaquín Murieta* (1967; *Splendor and Death of Joaquin Murieta*, 1972). He also maintained his political activities, becoming the Communist candidate for the presidency of Chile. He renounced his candidacy, however, to campaign in support of his friend Salvador Allende. After Allende's victory, Neruda, although suffering from cancer of the prostate, agreed once again to act as Chilean ambassador to France.

Neruda was awarded the Nobel Prize in 1971, and his acceptance speech presents a moving vision of a future world free of exploitation. He was seriously ill, though, and returned to Chile for the last time in 1972, to find his country poised upon disaster. Opposition to Allende from both outside and inside Chile was growing, and Neruda himself was becoming weaker. He attempted to rally friends abroad to support the Chilean government and wrote a vehement diatribe calling for the extermination of Richard M. Nixon. He was also working on his memoirs and the eight books of poetry he had planned to publish on his seventieth birthday. Disaster overtook the country, however, with Allende assassinated, the government broken, and a military dictatorship instated under Augosto Pinochet Ugarte. Neruda died in a hospital in Santiago, on September 23, 1973.

Summary

Since his involvement with the Republicans during the Spanish Civil War in the 1930's until his death, Pablo Neruda's political commitment and personal sincerity were constant, unwavering even as the popularity of his work developed internationally. His loneliness drove him into himself, to explore his own imagination and his past, while the solidarity that he felt with other living things drove him to celebrate life with an infectious enthusiasm and an effusive sense of riotous abundance. Poetry was not the pursuit of an elite for Neruda. In *Canto general*, he took his beginnings and his bearings from Chile but opened out to hymn the Americas in general, in all their detail, animals, flowers, history, and politics, and opened further to consider their place in the global context.

A hugely prolific poet, Neruda was the most magniloquent Latin American writer to span the literature of the century, beginning in provincial Chile, centering on Europe, then returning to take his place on the global stage. Even those who consider his political beliefs misguided or naïve grant the earthly vitality and vivacious sensuality of his celebrations and the profundity of his meditations.

Neruda believed that poetry was as essential for human life as bread and that it was not the property of scholars or booksellers but the inheritance of humanity. In the end, his accommodative vision contemplated the certainty of his own death, but he continued to write, leaving numerous posthumous works. He was a love poet, a public poet, and a poet of the natural world. He identified himself with his native place, but he aligned himself with all mankind.

Bibliography
Costa, René de. *The Poetry of Pablo Neruda.* Cambridge, Mass.: Harvard University Press, 1979. A good introductory critical study of Neruda's poetic achievement as a whole.
Durán, Manuel, and Margery Safir. *Earth Tones: The Poetry of Pablo Neruda.* Bloomington: Indiana University Press, 1981. A detailed survey of individual books of Neruda's poems, including the posthumous works. Separate areas covered include Neruda as a poet of nature and of the erotic, the public, and the personal.
Gallagher, D. P. "Pablo Neruda." In his *Modern Latin American Literature.* New York: Oxford University Press, 1973. A judicious essay discussing Neruda's relation to modernism, his love poetry, and his communism that suggests a link between *The Elemental Odes* and the mode of "magic realism" favored by other Latin American writers.
Riess, Frank. *The Word and the Stone: Language and Imagery in Neruda's "Canto general."* London: Oxford University Press, 1972. An extremely useful in-depth study of the forms and imagery in Neruda's most ambitious poetic sequence.
Rodman, Selden. "Pablo Neruda's Chile." In his *South America of the Poets.* New York: Hawthorn Books, 1970. A helpful essay, with illustrations by Bill Negrón, introducing Neruda's native land.
Willard, Nancy. *Testimony of the Invisible Man: William Carlos Williams, Francis Ponge, Rainer Maria Rilke, Pablo Neruda.* Columbia: University of Missouri Press, 1970. This book is particularly useful as it considers Neruda in the company of three other internationally respected modern authors and thereby highlights his individual characteristics.

Katherine Kearney Maynard

PIER LUIGI NERVI

Born: June 21, 1891; Sondrio, Italy
Died: January 9, 1979; Rome, Italy
Area of Achievement: Architecture
Contribution: Nervi was actually an engineer, but one whose goal was to create aesthetically pleasing structures. His importance lies in the fact that he was among the first in modern times to reunite architecture and engineering.

Early Life

Pier Luigi Nervi was born in the village of Sondrio in the Italian Alps to the local postmaster and his wife. Nervi remained thoroughly Italian throughout his life, and his work symbolizes the confluence of two major factors: his upbringing amid the aesthetic richness of Italy and his engineering education. Significantly, some of Nervi's first major works were large domes that may be said to have been influenced by earlier domes such as St. Peter's in Rome and the dome of the cathedral of Santa Maria del Fiore in Florence. As a youngster, he attended the Ginnasio-Liceo Muratori in Modena. In 1913, Nervi was graduated from the Civil Engineering School of Bologna, where he learned the basic principles of structures (and at the same time satisfied his childhood fascination with mechanical things). His schooling, however, treated art and science as two distinct endeavors—an approach that seemed illogical to Nervi.

Upon graduating from Bologna, Nervi gained employment as a civil engineer with the Societa per Costruzioni Cementizie. The Societa provided him with much experience in reinforced concrete, a structural material that he would eventually master. Nervi remained with the Societa until 1923 (his tenure having been interrupted by World War I when he served with the Italian Army's Engineering Corps), when he left in order to work full-time in a firm he had founded in 1920. As a partner in this firm, Nervi and Nebbiosi, he built several structures that drew international attention for their originality and beauty.

It is significant that Nervi began his career just as new materials and a new architectural movement were gaining momentum. During the first decade of the twentieth century, reinforced concrete gained recognition as an important new structural material through the works of François Hennebique, Auguste Perret, Robert Maillart, and others. Furthermore, by the early 1920's the outlines of the modern architectural movement were being clarified by pioneers such as Walter Gropius, Ludwig Mies van der Rohe, and Le Corbusier. In April, 1924, shortly after joining Nervi and Nebbiosi on a full-time basis, Nervi married Irene Calosi, and they eventually had four sons, Antonio, Mario, Carlo, and Vittorio.

Life's Work

One of Nervi's first major works was the Municipal Stadium in Florence. As with all of Nervi's work, the stadium design began with a concern for economy, and Nervi won the design competition because of the low cost of his project. The outstanding feature of the stadium is the grandstand roof: a shell extending over the seating on cantilevered beams. It clearly demonstrates, at an early point in Nervi's career, his ability to achieve both beauty and economy with reinforced concrete.

In 1932, Nervi joined with a cousin to form a new firm. This firm won a competition announced by the Italian Air Force in 1935 to build a series of airplane hangars. The hangars, as designed by Nervi, were to become landmarks of reinforced concrete construction. The problem posed by the hangars was how to span an area 330 feet by 135 feet with no internal supports. Nervi chose to make a vaulted roof with concrete ribs, which were cast in place and then covered with tiles. One problem with this type of construction was the vast amount of timber required for the concrete forms. Nervi solved that problem in a second series of hangars that he built beginning in 1940, by using precast concrete ribs for much of the roof's span. Driven by the need for greater economy in both material and timbers, Nervi had thus created a light but incredibly strong vaulted structure, which only required a roof covering and walls in order to make a hangar. When the Germans destroyed these hangars by demolishing the supporting columns, many of the roofs remained intact after they fell.

In the mid-1940's, Nervi developed an important new type of reinforced concrete, which he called "ferro-cement." Ferro-cement consists of several layers of fine steel mesh sprayed with a cement mortar. For heavier uses, it sometimes has reinforcing rods between the mesh layers. Ferro-cement is very thin—slightly thicker than the mesh itself—and its great strength and elasticity make it ideal for constructing thin shells and slabs. Since the mortar can be sprayed directly onto the mesh, structures can often be built of ferro-cement without the use of forms. In cases in which Nervi did use forms, he made them of ferro-cement instead of wood, thus giving him greater flexibility in shaping cast concrete pieces.

In the late 1940's, Nervi was faced with a new challenge: to build Salone B, 243 feet by 310 feet, for the Turin Exposition Hall of 1948-1949. Again, Nervi's was the most economical proposal submitted. He had only eight months in which to complete the building, and he used ferro-cement to help him meet that demanding schedule. To form the roof vaulting, he made prefabricated sections of corrugated ferro-cement, which were then lifted into place. The troughs and peaks of the corrugated pieces were then filled with cast-in-place reinforced concrete to form integral ribs—the main load-bearing structural members. Thus, the roof vaulting was a combination of ferro-cement and reinforced concrete.

For the half-dome at one end of the hall, Nervi introduced another innovation. He used precast, panlike units made of ferro-cement, which created troughs between them when laid side by side. The units had been cast in concrete molds, which had been built from a model of the half-dome. The precast units, in the shape of diamonds, were then lifted into place and supported by scaffolding while the roof was completed. Into the troughs between the units, Nervi laid reinforced concrete in order to form the supporting ribs of the half-dome. Thus, the reinforced concrete ribs together with the precast units formed the entirety of the half-dome. Nervi also used this system on Salone C of the Turin Exposition Hall and later on a number of other domes, vaults, and ceilings. In addition to being light, strong, and easy to build, the crossing ribs and diamond-shaped panels created a pleasing visual effect.

In addition to his busy schedule with these and other projects, Nervi began teaching in 1947. He joined the faculty of architecture at the University of Rome and remained there until 1961. During the academic year 1961-1962, he was the Charles E. Norton Professor at Harvard. Nervi's diligence allowed him to maintain this demanding schedule. He always started work promptly at 8:30 A.M. and only took time out to teach or to visit one of his building sites.

In 1952, Nervi devised yet another construction technique for use in building the Tobacco Factory in Bologna. The five-story building was to be large in measure and thus represented a significant challenge. Nervi once again won the design competition on the basis of the great economy of his design, which was, in turn, based on movable forms. Avoiding a costly timber framework, Nervi made ferro-cement forms that resembled inverted rectangular pans. The forms rested on wheeled scaffolding that could be raised and lowered by hydraulic jacks. The troughs between adjacent forms created strengthening ribs in the floor, when filled with cement. After the concrete pillars for a given floor were in place, the builders raised the ferro-cement forms into place and poured the reinforced concrete floor on top of them. Once the concrete had hardened sufficiently, the builders lowered the forms and wheeled them to the next bay. Nervi carried this time- and money-saving technique one step further in the Gatti wool factory in Rome. In this building, the forms were shaped so as to locate the strengthening ribs along the lines of greatest stress. This technique added to both the efficiency and the beauty of the building.

The 1960 Olympics in Rome created for Nervi the opportunity to achieve some of his most spectacular structural engineering—but not at the cost of aesthetics. Nervi designed three structures for the Olympics: the Palazzetto dello Sport, the Palazzo dello Sport, and the Stadio Flaminio. The Palazzetto, though smallest, has perhaps the strongest impact from both inside and outside. The flute-edged roof of the Palazzetto was constructed in typical

Nervi style. He used precast, diamond-shaped units to form the shell of the roof. As in some of his earlier structures, these pieces were joined by cast-in-place ribs that gently curved outward from the center in left- and right-handed curves, thus intersecting to create the diamond pattern. The ceiling's visual effect was one of a light and elegant webbing. The ribs carry their load to Y-shaped buttresses, which also carry the line of the shell to the ground. The outside view of the larger Palazzo is spoiled, however, by a gallery all the way around it which conceals the lines of the structure. Inside, however, Nervi created a much different look from that in the Palazzetto by using precast, corrugated sections (resembling those in the Turin Exhibition Hall) which radiate out from the center. As in the Turin Exhibition Hall, he filled the troughs and peaks in the corrugation with cast-in-place concrete. Although the outside surface of the corrugations have been covered in order to create a smooth surface, the inner view is quite striking.

Pier Luigi Nervi received many honorary degrees and awards during his lifetime, including honorary membership in the American Academy and National Institute of Arts and Letters (1957). He died at the age of eighty-seven in his home in Rome.

Summary

The two primary motivating factors in Pier Luigi Nervi's designs were economy and art. He produced his first major work during the Great Depression and remained quite busy throughout World War II and after. The resultant search for economy not only won many design competitions but also produced new construction techniques and forms. His concern for art probably stemmed from his upbringing in Italy and his consciousness of the many beautiful structures to be found there.

Nervi achieved his desired economic and aesthetic ends largely through the repeated use of three structural elements: precast corrugated beams, precast ceiling panels, and ferro-cement. Using these elements in combination with techniques of his own device (such as forms on movable scaffolding), Nervi avoided the use of expensive timber forms and framework, speeded construction time, and gave himself much freedom in shaping the lines of a structure. In the process, he also created very light but strong roof spans, enclosing and beautifying large indoor spaces. By always striving for economy and beauty, Nervi reached a high point in building with concrete. Although trained as an engineer, he did not let mathematics and scientific theories dominate his work. Through his buildings, he proved that structure can be art.

Bibliography

Huxtable, Ada Louise. "Geodetic and Plastic Expressions Abroad." *Progressive Architecture*, June, 1953: 111-116. This brief article summarizes

Nervi's contributions to the field of structural engineering, emphasizing ferro-cement. It also summarizes some of his most important works (as of 1953) and illustrates one of his hangars, the Gatti wool factory, and Salone B of the Turin Exposition Hall.

_____. *Pier Luigi Nervi*. New York: George Braziller, 1960. Part of the Masters of World Architecture series, this short book provides a concise, yet thorough account of Nervi's life, work, and place among the world's architects. Roughly one-half of the book is devoted to photographs and drawings of his major works, both in progress and completed. The book contains a complete list of his works and bibliographies of books and articles written by and about him.

Nervi, Pier Luigi. *Structures*. Translated by Giuseppina and Mario Salvadori. New York: F. W. Dodge, 1956. In this book, Nervi explained in his own words, clearly and simply, the principles behind the structures that he built. He also pointed out why he thought beauty was unavoidable in finding a solution to structural problems. The reader will also find discussions of the role of economy in design, the advantages and behavior of reinforced concrete, and a separate chapter on ferro-cement (with photographs of several boats that Nervi built with hulls of ferro-cement).

_____. *The Works of Pier Luigi Nervi*. Translated by Ernest Priefert. London: Architectural Press, 1957. With a preface by Nervi and an introduction by Ernesto N. Rogers, this is probably the best illustrated book available on the work of Pier Luigi Nervi. The bulk of the volume (almost 140 pages) consists of black-and-white photographs and line drawings of Nervi's works. Useful explanatory notes accompany many of the illustrations.

"Pier Luigi Nervi." *Architectural Forum* 99 (November, 1953): 141-148. This article highlights Nervi's structural innovations—precast corrugated beams, precast ceiling panels, and ferro-cement forms—and then illustrates their use in Nervi's projects.

Smith, G. E. Kidder. *Italy Builds: Its Modern Architecture and Native Inheritance*. London: Architectural Press, 1955. This work begins with a brief and very general overview of the influences in Italian architecture. The remainder of the book is then devoted to a discussion of modern architecture in Italy. Most of Nervi's major works, as of the date of publication, are included. Reasonably well illustrated; includes an index and a useful bibliography.

Brian J. Nichelson

OSCAR NIEMEYER

Born: December 15, 1907; Rio de Janeiro, Brazil

Area of Achievement: Architecture
Contribution: Perhaps the most widely known of Brazilian architects, Niemeyer is one of a key group of architects who gave a distinctly Brazilian flavor to the modern international architectural style.

Early Life

Oscar Niemeyer Soares Filho (commonly known as Oscar Niemeyer) was born to a well-to-do Rio de Janeiro family. Little has been written of his childhood, but it is clear that his early career was an undistinguished one. At the age of twenty-three, after completing Barnabitas College, he entered the National School of Fine Arts in Rio de Janeiro to study architecture. While still a student, he insisted upon joining the office of Lucio Costa, a well-known architect and city planner. Niemeyer continued in Costa's office after completing his architectural studies (in 1934), but prior to 1936 his work drew little notice.

In 1936 a dramatic transformation occurred in Niemeyer's career. He joined a group under Costa's direction that had been formed in order to design a new building for the Brazilian Ministry of Education and Health. When the group submitted its design in May, 1936, Costa suggested that Le Corbusier be invited to Brazil in order to evaluate the design. Le Corbusier stayed for nearly a month, working in close cooperation with Costa's group. During that time he had a profound impact on Niemeyer and the other architects in the group. Many consider his 1936 visit to Brazil to be the launching point for modern architecture in that country.

In 1939, Costa left the design group for the Ministry of Education and Health building, and the remaining architects then elected Niemeyer to take Costa's place as head of the group. This sign of acclaim, in addition to several projects that Niemeyer had undertaken on his own, signaled the start of a promising career—a career that was to afford Niemeyer unusual opportunities for developing and expressing his creativity.

Life's Work

The first project of Niemeyer actually to be built was a maternity clinic and day nursery he designed for a philanthropic institution known as "Obra de Berco." The design problem was complicated by the need to accommodate a number of diverse functions—medical care, staff areas, nursery—but Niemeyer handled the problem in a way that reflected the modest means of the Obra de Berco, while maintaining a friendly, almost anti-institutional atmosphere. On the northern side of the building, Niemeyer put vertical louvers on the outside of the building as protection from the sun. Several years after completion of the building, Niemeyer found that the louvers were not working as designed, so he replaced them at his own expense.

Niemeyer remained involved with the Ministry of Education and Health building through its completion in 1943. The design team finally adopted a variation of a plan proposed by Le Corbusier, and it proved quite successful. The building drew worldwide attention as the first public building to embody the concepts of the modern architecture movement. The design team, sensing that this building was to be a proving ground for modern architecture in Brazil, spent many years perfecting the design, and it is generally conceded that they were successful.

After completing the Ministry of Education and Health building, Niemeyer began to experiment with different forms more widely. He began to break out on his own, away from what had by then become the conventional "new"architecture. Rather than striving for austere and highly rational designs, Niemeyer became more preoccupied with aesthetics. The first example of his new direction comes from a group of buildings that he built on the shores of Lake Pampulha: a casino, a yacht club, a restaurant, and a church. In these buildings, Niemeyer continued to use plastic forms but, in a major departure, not always for functional elements. His use of contrasting room heights, floating ramps, and a variety of means for modulating light all indicated his break from the functionalism and rationalism of the natural sciences.

The church at Lake Pampulha, named for Saint Francis of Assisi, was both the most striking and the most controversial building of the group. Niemeyer chose paraboloid vaults as the main structural elements of the church. By thus creating walls and ceiling with one continuous structural component, he created both a unified and an economical structure. Although criticized roundly by some observers, Niemeyer refused to be inhibited by this subject. The Church of Saint Francis of Assisi is quite in keeping with his style of this period.

Niemeyer's commissions increased after World War II, and with them his fame. The Boavista Bank building marked his return to downtown Rio de Janeiro and clearly illustrates the influence of Le Corbusier (in the cubism of the building's exterior) as well as the freely curving forms of Brazilian architecture. One striking feature of the building in which many elements of Niemeyer's style come together is a two-story, undulating wall of glass blocks. This wall forms the backdrop for the main banking floor and is stunning in its structural and visual effect.

By 1950, Niemeyer had firmly established himself as one of the world's premier architects. By the middle of the decade, he had more than sixty commissions on the drawing board at one time. Some of his projects dating from this period include the United Nations Building in New York (he was a member of an international team of architects), the Sul American Hospital in Rio de Janeiro, the Aeronautical Training Center in São José dos Campos, and the Museum of Modern Art in Caracas. In September, 1956, Niemeyer embarked upon perhaps the largest and most important project of his career: creating a new capital city for Brazil.

In 1955, Juscelino Kubitschek had been elected President of Brazil, and he quickly set out to accomplish a number of reforms. One of those reforms was to be the relocation of Brazil's capital to the interior of the country. This new capital was to be built from scratch and was to be called Brasilia. Kubitschek and Niemeyer had formed a close relationship years earlier and so Kubitschek came to his architect friend for help in this massive undertaking. By 1957, Niemeyer had been appointed chief architect for the Authority for the New Capital of Brazil (NOVACAP). In that capacity, he was responsible for the design of all the important federal buildings. With the help of Lucio Costa and sixty young architects, Niemeyer completed the final drawings in only two years. Construction also proceeded at a hectic pace, and, on April 21, 1960, Brasilia became the capital city of Brazil.

The scale of the project is hard to imagine: to design and build a city and government center with an initial population of 500,000. Laid out on Costa's plan based on the form of a curved cross, the city was intended to be a fully working metropolis from the start. Niemeyer was directly involved in all the major projects, including the congress buildings, the supreme court and presidential offices, the Cathedral and Chapel of Our Lady of Fatima, the presidential residence (Alvorada Palace), the foreign office, the Brasilia Palace Hotel, and the National Theater.

Brasilia did not come cheap, however, and the city took a political toll on Niemeyer's patron, President Kubitschek, who decided against seeking re-election in the October, 1960, election. In the meantime, Niemeyer had been injured in an automobile accident. After a lengthy recovery, he continued his work around the world, having lived in Israel, Paris, and again returning to Rio de Janeiro.

Summary

Oscar Niemeyer and other Brazilian architects were influenced by Le Corbusier, but they built upon that foundation in order to establish a clearly Brazilian style of achitecture—one held in high esteem in international architectural schools. Niemeyer found new, highly imaginative (hence, not strictly rational) uses for freely curving architectural forms. He also took conventions of the modern style, such as lifting buildings off the ground, and gave them his own form as seen in the stylistic "V" shaped stilts he often used.

Another important aspect of Niemeyer's work is his ability to adapt his buildings to the climatic, physical, and economic setting of Brazil. He used the *brise soleil* (literally "sun breakers") in a variety of ways that enhanced both a building's appearance and the comfort of its occupants. Not only was such a solution more economical than air conditioning but also it served as a minimum barrier between the indoors and the outdoors. Breezes were allowed to enter Niemeyer's buildings, where they were channeled through the building to create a more comfortable environment. Niemeyer did not neglect Brazil's history either. Many observers see a baroque influence from Brazil's colonial period. Furthermore, Niemeyer capitalized upon a suggestion by Le Corbusier to use the traditional Portuguese blue ceramic tile (normally associated only with colonial-era buildings) as a finishing material. Niemeyer used these *azulejo* tiles, as they were known, extensively, and on some buildings, notably the Church of Saint Francis of Assisi, created striking murals. In this manner, Niemeyer adapted the international modern style of architecture to his native and beloved Brazil.

Bibliography

Joedicke, Jürgen. *A History of Modern Architecture.* Translated by James C. Palmes. New York: Frederick A. Praeger, 1959. Joedicke establishes the setting of the architectural world within which Niemeyer worked. He discusses the intellectual and social factors behind the modern movement, new materials, the early pioneers and later masters, and a summary of contributions to the movement from countries around the world (including Brazil).

Mindlin, Henrique E. *Modern Architecture in Brazil.* New York: Reinhold, 1956. Mindlin's book is most useful in providing a historical overview of Brazilian architecture in general, with a focus on modern architecture. The reader thus gains a good feel for Niemeyer's place among the architectural exuberance evident in Brazil. The bulk of the book examines the work of Brazilian architecture, classified by building type.

Niemeyer, Oscar. *Oscar Niemeyer.* Introduction and notes by Rupert Spade. London: Thames and Hudson, 1971. The strength of this book is that it allows the reader to see Niemeyer's work. The almost one hundred pages of glossy plates include photographs (many in color) and drawings of the plan and elevations of many of the buildings. In addition, useful explanatory notes accompany the illustrations for each project, thus interpreting Niemeyer's work. Spade's introductory comments also shed light on Niemeyer's life and work.

_____. *Oscar Niemeyer: Works in Progress.* Edited by Stamo Papadaki. New York: Reinhold, 1956. A continuation of the work cited below, this book covers what was perhaps Niemeyer's most fertile period: 1950 to 1956. It clearly demonstrates how busy he was during the 1950's. Plentifully illustrated with photographs (often of scale models, since many of the projects were not complete at the time of publication) and drawings, this book is an important visual record of this period of Niemeyer's career. Unfortunately, it stops before he became involved with Brasilia.

_____. *The Work of Oscar Niemeyer.* Edited by Stamo Papadaki. New York: Reinhold, 1950. After a few introductory remarks by Papadaki and a foreword by Lucio Costa, the bulk of this book is devoted to chronicling all of Niemeyer's projects through 1950. The Obra de Berco nursery and day-care center, the buildings at Lake Pampulha, the Boavista Bank, and many other buildings that contributed to Niemeyer's rise to fame are illustrated (with both photographs and drawings) and interpreted here.

Papadaki, Stamo. *Oscar Niemeyer.* New York: George Braziller, 1960. One of the books in the Masters of World Architecture series, Papadaki's book is a concise account of Niemeyer's life and work. It puts him in proper context within both Brazil and the international modern architecture movement. Roughly half the book is devoted to photographs and drawings of Niemeyer's projects. The chronology and bibliographies of works by and about Niemeyer are all quite useful.

Brian J. Nichelson

MARTIN NIEMÖLLER

Born: January 14, 1892; Lippstadt, Germany
Died: March 6, 1984; Wiesbaden, West Germany
Areas of Achievement: Church reform and social reform
Contribution: Niemöller, a leading religious opponent of the National Socialist regime, helped to organize the Confessing church in 1934, a body within the German Evangelical church that formed the center of Protestant resistance in the Third Reich. After his liberation from eight years in a concentration camp, he became a prominent figure in the restored German Evangelical church and the World Council of Churches, best known for his outspoken opposition to West German rearmament, nuclear armament, and his advocacy of pacifism.

Early Life

Friedrich Gustav Emil Martin Niemöller was born in Lippstadt, Westphalia, on January 14, 1892, as the second of six children of a Lutheran pastor. He was educated in public schools, first in Lippstadt and, after age eight, in Elberfeld, where his father moved to a new parish. In the Niemöller family the practice of the Protestant religion went hand in hand with German nationalism. Following an early fascination with the sea, young Niemöller joined the imperial navy upon graduation from the Elberfeld Gymnasium, an academic secondary school, in 1910. Talented, ambitious, and imbued with the teaching from home that a good Christian is a good citizen and as such a good soldier, he quickly advanced in his naval career. After first being trained on a battleship, he was transferred to submarine service in 1915. Two years later he was put in command of a submarine and led several missions against the British and the French. During his submarine service, he was awarded the Iron Cross First Class. After the war, he resigned from the navy in March, 1919.

Disillusioned by Germany's defeat and antagonistic to the democracy of the Weimar Republic, Niemöller briefly tried farming but soon concluded that the postwar inflation made the purchase of a farm impossible. He married Else Bremer, who was to be his supportive wife and mother of seven children until her death in a car accident in 1961. Having repeatedly faced the meaning of life and death in war, drawing on his religious upbringing, and hopeful that the church could help regenerate German spiritual life, he began to study theology in 1920 with the intention of entering the ministry. At the same time, he remained captivated by right-wing political sentiments. In March, 1920, he and other nationalist students formed the Academic Defense Corps during the monarchist Kapp Putsch against the Weimar government. After the failure of the coup, Niemöller and his compatriots battled communist insurgents in the Ruhr region before resuming their studies.

Throughout much of his life, Niemöller saw himself both as a good Christian and as a supreme German patriot.

While a student and then during his mandatory service as a curate, he helped supplement his family income by working as a platelayer and accountant on the German railroad. Once he got closer to finishing his studies, he was reluctant to take a parish of his own because of the difficult economic conditions in Germany. Instead, late in 1923, he became manager of the Inner Mission of Westphalia and was thus put in charge of the administration of church social welfare for an entire province. Over the next seven years, this work gave him invaluable organizational experience as well as heightened awareness of the meaning of the "social gospel."

Life's Work

By 1931, Niemöller was eager to accept a church of his own. He was appointed third pastor to a church in Berlin-Dahlem, one of the richest and most fashionable parishes in Germany. Within months he became senior pastor upon the death of the incumbent, and two years later he found himself a national figure in Germany. The two sides of his personality continued to show: He was a committed Christian caring for the souls of his parishioners and a man of deep political convictions. He identified most closely with nationalist conservatives who loathed the Weimar Republic and, on several occasions from 1924 to 1933, even voted for the National Socialist Party. He was impressed with a part of the National Socialist program that advocated freedom for all religious denominations and the idea of "positive Christianity." Adolf Hitler, however, upon becoming chancellor in January, 1933, attempted to achieve dominance over the Evangelical Church (Lutheran and Reformed) by promoting the neopagan movement of the German Christians and the appointment of Pastor Ludwig Müller, a National Socialist follower, as Reich bishop.

Disillusioned by such blatant interference in church affairs, Niemöller attacked the religious policies of the government. In September, 1933, he and others established the Pastors' Emergency League to assist non-Aryan pastors or those married to non-Aryans, such as Christian Jews, who were threatened with dismissal, and to serve as an organizational network for the clergy, who resisted the inroads of the regime in church work. In the following year, Niemöller and his allies set to work creating a new church structure by adding lay support to the efforts of the clergy. At two synodal meetings at Barmen and Berlin-Dahlem, they organized free synods, in opposition to those dominated by the Reich bishop, and thus laid the groundwork for the Confessing church. Informed by Karl Barth's theological declaration that drew a sharp distinction between the true church and the German Christians, the Confessing church claimed to be the duly constituted Protestant church in Germany. It managed to maintain itself as the sole coherent opposition among Protestants to the religious policies of the Third Reich.

Niemöller's outspoken criticism of National Socialist religious policies and fearless defense of the independence of the church focused national attention on his person and earned for him Hitler's personal wrath. Disagreement with the regime's religious policies and racial measures as they affected Christian Jews, albeit much less so Jews in general, did not lead Niemöller to dissent from the government's political and foreign policies. In the fall of 1933, he sent a congratulatory telegram to Hitler, on behalf of the Pastors' Emergency League, when Germany left the League of Nations. He also approved of German rearmament. In the following year, he authored his autobiographical *Vom U-Boot zur Kanzel* (1934; *From U-boat to Pulpit*, 1936), which revealed his singular patriotism, bringing him considerable fame in Germany and abroad. None of this, however, saved him from repeated arrest by the Gestapo and permanent imprisonment starting in July, 1937. Early in 1938, he was tried on charges of violating the law and engaging in treasonous activity. He mounted a defense stressing his patriotic service in war and peacetime, which resulted in a reduction of charges and a minimal sentence. Expecting to be released, he was immediately rearrested and sent to the Sachsenhausen concentration camp near Berlin as Hitler's personal prisoner. In June, 1941, he was transferred to the Dachau concentration camp near Munich. At the end of the war, he escaped execution and was freed while on transport to the Austrian Tyrol.

Having become aware of the full magnitude of the crimes committed by the Hitler regime only after his release, Niemöller concluded that the renewal of the German church and its acceptance by foreign churches required unconditional penance. He became a driving force behind the Stuttgart Declaration of Guilt issues in October, 1945. In the presence of ecumenical representatives, twelve leaders of the German Evangelical church confessed that the church shared with the German people responsibility for the endless suffering caused to many peoples and countries and accused themselves of not acting more courageously to prevent it. In sermons and speeches, especially before student audiences, Niemöller explicitly asserted that his confession included responsibility for the murder of five to six million Jews, but he rejected the political conception of collective guilt. Because of his international reputation, he was named president of foreign affairs of the German Evangelical church in 1945. Very soon he became an active participant in the emerging World Council of Churches and was appointed its copresident in 1961. In addition, he also served as president of the Evangelical church of Hesse and Nassau from 1947.

The concentration camp experience and contact with foreign inmates at Dachau had broadened Niemöller's narrow German vistas. The ecumenical work that he engaged in and the regular contact with non-Germans both in occupied Germany and on his frequent travels abroad completed his development from a German nationalist into an internationalist. Taking the role of the church as a moral force in society very seriously, he felt an obligation as one of its leaders to speak out boldly on current issues of concern. In 1946, he was among the first prominent Germans to criticize the treatment of German prisoners of war in British camps. He clashed with the occupation authorities over their policies of denazification and dismantling. He actively worked for the release of Waffen Schützstaffeln Gestapo officers and several prominent Nazis when he believed that their sentence outweighed their alleged crimes. Fearing that the division of Germany might become permanent, he opposed the creation of the Federal Republic of Germany in 1949. He vehemently objected to German rearmament in the early 1950's, incurring the wrath of Chancellor Konrad Adenauer, who called him an enemy of the state.

While the Cold War raged, Niemöller met with the patriarch of Moscow in 1952 and soon joined the communist dominated World Peace Council. He angered many in the West with his contacts in East Germany and his insistence that the vitality of Christianity was much greater there under communism than in materialist West Germany. His attack on racism as a threat to world peace won for him wide support, but his antinuclear stance raised much objection. Having learned from Otto Hahn that nuclear weapons could extinguish higher life on the planet, he declared himself a convinced pacifist in the mid-1950's. His controversial if not iconoclastic pronouncements tended to lose friends for him and to diminish his organizational influence. In 1956, he was removed as head of the church's foreign affairs office. In 1964, he retired from the presidency of the Hesse and Nassau church, and in 1968 he relinquished his leading position on the World Council of Churches. He continued his active involvement in the German and European peace and antinuclear movement in sermons, speeches, and writing until only a few years before his death in 1984.

Summary

Martin Niemöller, who never really liked theology and considered philosophy useless, was a practical man of action. Imbued with strong religious convictions, he had boundless energy and demonstrated remarkable commitment applying Christian principles to life in society. He once remarked that he developed from an ultraconservative into a revolutionary and, if he were to live to be a hundred, he might become an anarchist. He never fully internalized a Western liberal worldview and regarded West German democracy as imperfect. Much of his life his commitment was that of a Christian and a German nationalist; after World War II it became that of a Christian and an internationalist who continued to love his homeland deeply. Above all, he came to believe that Christian spirituality transcended national boundaries and could unite believers under different political systems.

Niemöller's most notable historical achievement was the dedication to Christian ideals that he showed and the leadership role that he performed during the early years of National Socialist rule in Germany—one of the most troubled times for modern Christianity. He committed his life to creating the German Protestant church's resistance to the Hitler regime. His courage and fearless defense of Christian beliefs inspired others to carry on when he was incarcerated and gave him a reputation much beyond Germany's borders. The moral prestige that he commanded as a Protestant resister and imprisoned martyr enabled him to play a prominent role during the aftermath of the war, when the German Evangelical church was struggling to reconstitute itself and restore its moral prestige. He is remembered for his untiring effort to establish ecumenical ties with churches in the West and the East. His relentless promotion of international peace and antinuclear campaigns helped to shape in no insignificant way the climate of public opinion in West Germany and Europe for the concrete steps toward nuclear disarmament taken by the United States and the Soviet Union during the 1970's and 1980's. It was indicative of Niemöller's international stature that he was honored for the promotion of world peace by being awarded both the Lenin Peace Prize in 1967 and the Grand Cross of Merit, West Germany's highest recognition, in 1971.

Bibliography

Bentley, James. *Martin Niemöller, 1892-1984*. New York: Free Press, 1984. This definitive biography draws on archival sources and also relies heavily on information obtained from interviews with Niemöller. It is well written and covers all phases of his life and career. Its principal weakness lies in the absence of an adequate historical context for its subject.

Davidson, Clarissa Start. *God's Man: The Story of Pastor Niemöller*. New York: Ives Washburn, 1959. A more captivating journalistic partial biography than Dietmar Schmidt's book noted below. Davidson met Niemöller and his family and presents a sympathetic portrait of a man whom she much admires. Includes a bibliography.

Helmreich, Ernst Christian. *The German Churches Under Hitler: Background, Struggle, and Epilogue*. Detroit: Wayne State University Press, 1979. The most important scholarly treatment of German churches during the Third Reich. It also summarizes developments before and after the National Socialist era. Essential for putting Niemöller in the broader context of church history.

Schmidt, Dietmar. *Pastor Niemöller*. Translated by Lawrence Wilson. Garden City, N.Y.: Doubleday, 1959. An informed journalistic account of Niemöller's life and work through the late 1950's by a close associate. It offers insights into its subject's complex personality but does not purport to be a completely impartial biography. Contains a short bibliography.

Spotts, Frederic. *The Churches and Politics in Germany.* Middletown, Conn.: Wesleyan University Press, 1973. Based on unpublished sources, this detailed study of the West German churches in the postwar period analyzes such issues as denazification, reunification, and political attitudes of church leaders. Niemöller's role is put in the broader context of German church development.

George P. Blum

VASLAV NIJINSKY

Born: March 12, 1890; Kiev, Ukraine, Russian Empire
Died: April 8, 1950; London, England
Area of Achievement: Dance
Contribution: With the impresario Sergei Diaghilev, who enlisted him as a premier dancer in the Ballet Russe company, Nijinsky established the popularity of Russian ballet throughout the Western world in the second decade of the twentieth century. As a choreographer, he was also very instrumental in adapting dance movements to the new music of the twentieth century, especially that of Russian composer Igor Stravinsky.

Early Life

Vaslav Nijinsky was born in Kiev when his dancer parents were on tour in the Ukraine. Both of his parents, Eleonora Nikolayevich and Thomas, were Polish, and when young Vaslav was two they took him to Warsaw for baptism in the Catholic religion. Vaslav was the second of three children. An elder brother, Stanislav, was mentally retarded following a fall at age six. The youngest was Bronisława, who became a celebrated ballerina in St. Petersburg. After Thomas deserted the family, Eleonora took the children to St. Petersburg and enrolled Vaslav, then age nine, in the Imperial School of Ballet. The celebrated dancer Nicholas Legat noticed his athleticism and recommended his admittance. He began his studies there in 1898, graduating in 1907. He quickly caught the eyes of the critics with his exceptional leaping ability. Aside from dance, Nijinsky was a poor student and was teased by other boys for his Tatar-like features. Young Nijinsky never made a real friend there.

In 1902, Nijinsky's dance instructor was Mikhail Obukhov, who protected him from the cruelty of the other boys. During these years Nijinsky also learned how to play the piano, flute, balalaika, and accordion. In January, 1905, Nijinsky was caught in the crowds during the demonstrations against the government when Cossacks attacked. On this "Bloody Sunday," Nijinsky was bloodied by a knout from one of the Cossacks. He was not politically inclined and spent most of his hours devoted to music. He was not an avid reader but was absorbed by Charles Dickens' *David Copperfield* (1849-1850), which he and his sister read together. He also read Fyodor Dostoevski's *Idiot* (1868; *The Idiot*, 1887). He was very moved by the main character in this last story, Prince Myshkin, a Christ-like simpleton with whom he apparently identified. His favorite composers were the Russian Nikolay Rimsky-Korsakov and the German Richard Wagner.

Life's Work

When American dancer Isadora Duncan visited the Russian capital, Nijinsky was fascinated by her. The choreographer Michel Fokine decided to stage a short ballet in her honor and chose Nijinsky for a small part. His manner and style were very appealing to the St. Petersburg critics, who were more attracted by the dramatic abilities of dancers than by their technique. Famed dancer Tamara Karsavina was so attracted by the splendor of his leaps that she promised to dance with him. His first real applause came on January 31, 1906, during a special dance for eight people inserted into the Mozart opera *Don Giovanni* at the Mariinsky Theater. Nijinsky was the only one who had not yet graduated, but he stole the short dance to take his first solo bow. Weeks later the program was repeated, and this time the dancers included the acclaimed Anna Pavlova.

Several small parts followed that year, and, after his graduation performance on April 29, even the most celebrated Mathilde Kchessinskaya expressed a desire to dance with him. He was readily admitted to the Imperial Ballet Company, and that summer he vacationed at Krasnoe Selo, where he danced with Kchessinskaya before the military troops. Following a solo dance before Czar Nicholas II, the emperor presented him with a gold watch. Before autumn he was contacted by his father and visited him in Nizhni Novgorod. They danced together and had a very friendly reunion. That was to be the last time that they met.

Back in St. Petersburg, the family moved to a well-to-do district near the Hermitage. Nijinsky was only a member of the Corps de Ballet, but he accepted offers to instruct children in the art of dance, for which he received one hundred rubles an hour. When his first season began he had opportunities to dance solo pieces and a *pas de deux* with Karsavina. In the winter, his roles increased in importance and frequency, and he soon found a patron in Prince Pavel Dmitryevich Lvov. The prince introduced him to Diaghilev in the early winter of 1908.

It was not until Nijinsky first danced with the Diaghilev company in the Russian season in Paris in 1909 that audiences noticed his greatness. He soon became the showcase for Russian dance throughout Europe and South and North America. He was the "Favorite Slave" in *Le Pavillon d'Armide*, the "Poet" in *Les Sylphides*, the "Golden Slave" in *Schéhérazade*, "Harlequin" in *Carnaval*, and the transformed "Puppet" in *Petrushka*. Nijinsky developed a reputation for being exotic and otherworldly. Critics found his dancing technically perfect and his performances highly dramatic. Diaghilev saw in him also a choreographer and trained him as such. Their relationship became intimate, and, after Nijinsky became seriously ill with typhoid fever, Diaghilev nursed him back to health.

Nijinsky returned from Paris to dance the season with the Imperial Ballet Company, but when he danced in a shocking costume designed by Alexander Benois for the ballet *Giselle*, the theatrical authorities demanded that he alter it. When he refused, they gave him the option of apologizing or resigning from the company. He resigned. There is some suspicion that the affair was staged by Diaghilev to free the dancer from his five-year contract with the Imperial Ballet Company. Following his resignation in January, 1911, he returned to France that spring to join the next season with Diaghilev full-time. On April 9, the company abandoned its summer status, and at Monte Carlo Diaghilev formed the permanent Ballet Russe. Fokine's *Specter of a Rose* was first performed there as Nijinsky's most famous role of a phantom was danced opposite Karsavina. Upon reaching Paris, the company thrilled French audiences with marvelous tableaux of Russian life in Fokine's choreography of Stravinsky's *Petrushka* with Nijinsky as the puppet. So popular were the dancers that the company was invited to London to celebrate the coronation of King George V.

The Ballet Russe was equally popular in the following year, but in Paris Nijinsky the dancer also became Nijinsky the choreographer. Fokine's work had worn thin with Diaghilev, and the famed dancer choreographed Claude Debussy's *Afternoon of a Faun*. He reversed many of the classical postures as he struggled to create new dance forms, consciously breaking with the past. These new movements themselves were controversial, but the closing scene displayed an erotic episode that scandalized the audiences. Nevertheless, the reaction was a mixture of damnation and enthusiastic praise. Among the latter was a newspaper letter of sculptor Auguste Rodin. If the controversy over the Debussy piece was well known, it was soon eclipsed by one of greater dimensions. This was the reaction to Nijinsky's choreography of Stravinsky's *The Rite of Spring*, in which Nijinsky danced the leading role. The spasmic and frenzied motions were ill understood even by his followers, and audiences were repelled by the cacophonous rhythms of the composer. When it was first performed in Paris on May 29, 1913, it produced a near riot in the theater. That season, Nijinsky also choreographed *Jeux*, a ballet performed in modern dress that was never popular.

There followed tours to London and to South America. A year earlier, when the company was in Budapest, Nijinsky met Romola de Pulszky, a famous actress and daughter of the founder and first director of the National Gallery of Hungary, Karoly de Pulszky, a Pole whose family had long resided in Hungary. Attracted to Nijinsky, she was determined to become a member of the Ballet Russe. She took dancing lessons and, using her family influence, persuaded Diaghilev to take her to South America as a student dancer. En route to Argentina she and Nijinsky fell in love, and four days after landing they were married in Buenos Aires. So enraged was Diaghilev that he dismissed his famous star.

An independent Nijinsky and his bride went to London, where he started his own short-lived company. They then returned to Budapest, where their daughter Kyra was born. While in Hungary, they were caught in the maelstrom of World War I. As a Russian citizen, Nijinsky was declared a prisoner of war and detained. Nevertheless, Diaghilev, who was planning an American tour for the Ballet Russe, had a change of heart and negotiated for his release. When the couple arrived in New York early in 1916, the impresario met them with flowers, and a reconciliation took place. In autumn the company took a second tour of the United States, and the Nijinskys simply stayed there between tours. It was during the second American season that Nijinsky choreographed his last ballet, *Tyl Eulenspiegel*, at the Metropolitan Opera House in New York. In 1917, Nijinsky embarked on a four-month dancing tour of the United States and joined Diaghilev in Spain by June. There they planned another tour of South America, where Nijinsky last danced with the Ballet Russe on September 26 in Buenos Aires.

One year later in St. Moritz, Nijinsky fell into severe depression. In 1919, he was diagnosed as an incurable schizophrenic. Romola stayed close to him for the next thirty-one years while he was in and out of asylums. In 1928, the Nijinskys sat in Diaghilev's box to watch the Ballet Russe perform in Paris. When World War II began, the couple was again stranded in Hungary, and Nijinsky rejoiced upon seeing Russian armies arriving in 1945. Two years later, the couple moved to London, where Nijinsky died after a kidney illness on April 8, 1950, at age sixty. Nijinsky was given a Roman Catholic funeral and buried outside London. Three years later, Serge Lifar arranged for the transfer of the body to Paris, at which time Bronisława Nijinska insisted upon a new funeral in the Russian Orthodox rite.

Summary

An assessment of Vaslav Nijinsky's impact necessarily includes both his dancing and his choreography. Parisian audiences were astonished by the gracefulness of his leaps. Until he performed with the Ballet Russe, Western audiences were unaccustomed to admiring the beauty of male dancers such as Nijinsky and others in the troupe. Nijinsky and his generation of dancers had already changed the image of the male dancer at home in St. Petersburg with the Imperial Ballet Company. Before this time, it was not unusual for females to assume male dancing roles. At other times, the male was expected to render mere support for the female star. After Nijinsky's era, the female was not eclipsed, certainly, but the famed Polish dancer made it possible for later male stars such as Rudolph Nureyev and Mikhail Baryshnikov to emerge.

Nijinsky was equally innovative in choreography, but his contribution here was more by design than by instinct. A keen student of music, he was one of the first to appreciate the direction in which modern rhythms should take the art of dance. Hence Nijinsky choreographed *Afternoon of a Faun, Jeux, The Rite of Spring*, and *Tyl Eulenspiegel* in the new style for the Diaghilev company. These may have been the first truly creative ballets of the twentieth century. He surely surpassed his rival, Fokine, by using a bolder and more daring style. There was a sense of mystery to his dance and choreography that seemed to suit the new music of Igor Stravinsky and other modern composers. Nowhere was this match so evident as in Stravinsky's *The Rite of Spring*, a ballet that has become standard fare throughout much of the world.

Bibliography

Buckle, Richard. *Diaghilev*. New York: Atheneum, 1979. Especially useful in the section entitled "The Fokine-Nijinsky Period" in this, the latest and most definitive biography yet written of Diaghilev.

——————. *Nijinsky*. New York: Simon & Schuster, 1970. This work presents the basic information about the subject and is the standard, reliable work.

Gelatt, Roland. *Nijinsky: The Film*. New York: Ballantine Books, 1980. Gelatt wrote the text, and the book has sixty-two pages of photographs from the film. Other photographs are of Nijinsky himself.

Krasovskaia, Vera. *Nijinsky*. Translated by John E. Bowlt. New York: Schirmer Books, 1979. First published in Russia in 1974, this is the first Russian account of Nijinsky to be translated into English. Somewhat anecdotal and without a bibliography, the narration is a revealing portrait by another well-known dancer. Contains many photographs.

Nijinska, Bronisława. *Bronislava Nijinska: Early Memoirs*. Edited and translated by Irina Nijinsky and Jean Rawlinson. New York: Holt, Rinehart and Winston, 1981. A charming, readable account of her brother's life as well as her own. The work reveals a magnificent eye for detail.

Philip, Richard, and Mary Whitney. "The Living Legend of Nijinsky." In *Danseur: The Male in Ballet*. New York: McGraw-Hill, 1977. Containing an easy-to-read summary of Nijinsky's career, this narrative stresses his innovations and influence. The text also contains twelve full-page photographs of the dancer and a bibliography.

John D. Windhausen

KITARŌ NISHIDA

Born: May 19, 1870; Unoke, near Kanazawa, Japan
Died: June 7, 1945; Kamakura, Japan
Areas of Achievement: Philosophy and religion
Contribution: Nishida is widely considered to be the foremost philosopher of modern Japan. He created his own highly original and distinctive philosophy, based upon his thorough assimilation of both Western philosophy and methodology and the Zen Buddhist tradition.

Early Life

Kitarō Nishida was born on May 19, 1870, in the Mori section of the village of Unoke in Ishikawa Prefecture, located near Kanazawa on the Sea of Japan. He was the eldest son, the middle child out of five. Nishida's family moved to Kanazawa in 1883. There Nishida entered the local school, the prefectural normal school, which boasted an enterprising Western-style school system. Typhus forced his withdrawal from the school one year later, and he studied privately with several teachers for the next two years. In July, 1886, Nishida entered the Middle School attached to the Ishikawa Prefectural College. After completing his preparatory work there, Nishida entered the Fourth Higher School in July, 1889. While attending the Fourth Higher School, Nishida lived in the home of the mathematician Hōjō Tokiyoshi. His interest in Zen Buddhism, of which his mathematics teacher was an adept, dates to this period of his life.

Despite the urging of Hōjō that he become a mathematician, Nishida specialized in philosophy. He left the Fourth Higher School shortly before his graduation in 1890. The circumstances surrounding his departure remain mysterious. Lack of formal graduation from high school forced Nishida to enter the philosophy department of Tokyo Imperial University as a special student in September of 1891. There he was exposed to contemporary European thought. Nishida was graduated from Tokyo Imperial University in 1894. He encountered difficulties in finding employment because of his irregular academic background and was unemployed for nearly a full year after graduation. He took a room in the house of a painter named Tokuda Kō; during this time he wrote a study of Thomas Hill Green, a British Hegelian. He then obtained a position with a meager salary at a prefectural middle school on remote Noto Peninsula.

Nishida married the daugher of Tokuda Kō, Tokuda Kotomi, in May of 1895. His first daughter, Yayoi, was born in March of 1896. Together, Nishida and Kotomi had eight children: six daughters and two sons. Shortly after his marriage, Nishida's religious interests deepened. Upon returning to Kanazawa in 1896 to take a teaching position at the Fourth Higher School, Nishida began Zen meditation. A diary begun in 1897 provides an account of his rigorous introspective regimen. This spiritual discipline intensified in 1897 to 1899, when Nishida was alone in Yamaguchi, separated from his wife as a result of a serious disagreement with his father.

Life's Work

After teaching as a part-time professor at Yamaguchi Higher School from 1897 to 1899, Nishida returned to teach again at the Fourth Higher School in Kanazawa. There he taught psychology, ethics, German, and logic for ten years, from 1899 to 1909; at this time, he developed the basic philosophical views that he would broaden and deepen for the rest of his life but never abandon. In addition to teaching, Nishida was active in establishing extracurricular literary groups. His most ambitious project was the establishment of a student residence and study center called San San Juku. San San Juku served as a meeting place for students to discuss problems of religion and literature with invited lecturers from various religious sects and denominations. This institution became a lasting one of the Fourth Higher School in Kanazawa.

In January of 1907, Nishida's daughter, Yūko, died of bronchitis. In June of that same year, another daughter, only one month old, died. Nishida himself fell sick. In the face of these tragedies, Nishida encouraged himself toward greater self-reliance. He also disciplined himself to increase the level of his intellectual output. The fruit of this discipline was the publication of his first book, *Zen-no-kenkyū (A Study of Good*, 1960), in January of 1911. Nishida's lifelong concern was to provide a Western philosophical framework for Zen intuition. *A Study of Good* launched this project. It included a theory of reality, a study of ethics, and the skeleton of a philosophy of religion. One of Nishida's most central philosophical concepts, that of "pure experience," is introduced in this first major work. Nishida defines "pure experience" as direct experience without deliberative discrimination and without the least addition of one's own fabrications. Unlike many practitioners of Zen, Nishida does not give the impression of being anti-intellectual. "Pure experience" is not in opposition to thought and intellect but rather lies at the base of all the oppositions produced by the mind, such as those of subject and object, body and mind, and spirit and matter. Nishida was inspired by the American philosopher William James and found in Henri Bergson a kindred spirit, but if he borrowed anything from either, it became thoroughly assimilated into his own philosophy. The publication of *A Study of Good* in 1911 was hailed as an epoch-making event in the introduction of Western philosophy into Japan. The academic world perceived it to be the first truly original philosophic work by a Japanese thinker in the modern period (which began in 1868 with the Meiji Restoration). All prior attempts at combining traditional Japanese thought with Western philosophy had been patently eclectic.

Following one year at Gakushūin University in Tokyo, Nishida was appointed assistant professor of ethics at Kyōto Imperial University in 1910. In August of 1914, he was relieved from his chair of ethics in the Faculty of Letters and called to the first chair of the history of philosophy in the philosophy department of the University of Kyōto. There he taught until his retirement in 1928. Many brilliant students flocked to his classes. Together with Hajime Tanabe, he established what has come to be known as the Kyōto, or Nishida-Tanabe, school of philosophy. Around 1910, Nishida's philosophy was influenced by his study of Bergson and the German Neo-Kantians, especially Wilhelm Windelband, Heinrich Rickert, and Hermann Cohen. His thorough assimilation of the logical epistemology of Neo-Kantian transcendentalism and his own critique of its fundamental principles enabled Nishida to discover a deeper significance in Immanuel Kant's philosophy and the transcendental method of German idealism. This achievement enabled him to bring his earlier concept of "pure experience" to a higher level. In his second major work, *Jikaku ni okeru chokkan to hansei* (1917; intuitions and reflection in self-consciousness), Nishida strove to eliminate psychologism from his thinking. In this work, he defined the ultimate character of self-consciousness as "absolute free will." "Absolute free will," when genuine, transcends reflection. It cannot be reflected upon, for it is that which causes reflection.

In August of 1918, Nishida's mother died; disaster struck again when his wife, Kotomi, suffered a brain hemorrhage in September of 1919. Kotomi was paralyzed for the remaining six years of her life. In June of 1920, Nishida's eldest son, Ken, died of peritonitis at the age of twenty-two. During the next several years, three more of his daughters fell ill with typhus. In January of 1925, Kotomi died after a prolonged period of suffering. She was fifty years old. Nishida's diary reveals that these personal tragedies affected him deeply. Nevertheless, he disciplined himself to maintain his philosophical activity. His next two works, *Ishiki no mondai* (1920; problems of consciousness) and *Geijutsu to dotoku* (1923; *Art and Morality*, 1973), offered progressive refinements of the concepts of "pure experience" and "absolute free will."

The epoch-making *Hataraku-mono kara miru-mono e* (1927; from the acting to the seeing self) formulates the concept of *basho no ronri* ("logic of place"). It is Nishida's notion of "place" and his "logic of place" that distinguish him in the history of philosophy. In this work, he discusses a realm of reality that corresponds to his own mystical experience. Indeed, with his concept of "place," Nishida provided a conceptual and logical framework for a philosophical position that is usually categorized as mysticism in the West. According to Nishida, the "true self" is revealed in the "place" of "absolute nothingness." The concept of "absolute nothingness" has clear roots in Buddhist tradition. This "nothingness" is not relative nothingness, nothingness as contrasted with phenomenal existence; rather, it is absolute nothingness, that wherein all phenomenal existences appear as determinations of it. "Absolute free will" emerges from creative nothingness and returns to creative nothingness.

Retirement from his teaching position at the University of Kyōto in 1928 did not slow Nishida's productive pace. His postretirement works include *Ippansha no jikakuteki taikei* (1930; the self-conscious system of the universal), *Mu no jikakuteki gentei* (1932; the self-conscious determination of nothingness), *Tetsugaku no kompon mondai* (2 vols., 1933-1934; *Fundamental Problems of Philosophy*, 1970), and *Tetsugaku rombunshu* (7 vols., 1937-1946; philosophical essays). In this last stage of his philosophical development, Nishida was concerned with "the self-identity of absolute contradiction," or "the unity of opposites." This concept was discovered through his investigation of the relationship between the self and the world. Nishida used this concept to probe what he considered to be one of the fundamental problems of a philosophy of religion: the contradictions of an existence in which the satisfaction of desire means the extinction of desire and in which the will makes its own extinction its goal. These contradictions undergird religious experience, for it is only in the awareness of the absolute contradictoriness and nothingness of the self's existence that human beings are able to touch God and the absolute.

Nishida's first grandchild was born in October of 1928. He married again in December of 1931; his second wife's name was Koto. For perhaps the first time in his life, Nishida's family life became serene. The retired professor enjoyed the visits of his children and grandchildren immensely. There were no further deaths in the family until February of 1945, when his favorite daughter, Yayoi, died suddenly. Nishida found World War II to be a profoundly distressing event. He managed, however, to continue his philosophical writings at his home in Kamakura despite the destruction in Tokyo and other major Japanese cities. He died suddenly in early June of 1945, only two months before Japan's surrender.

Summary

Kitarō Nishida is widely recognized as the first genuinely original Japanese philosopher of the modern period. He departed from the crude eclecticism of his predecessors and almost singlehandedly created an indigenous Japanese philosophy. His true significance will probably not be determined until a comprehensive, global history of modern ideas is written. Nishida is the only Japanese philosopher of recent times around whom a philosophical school has been formed. Most of the leading philosophers of twentieth century Japan were influenced by him, either as a result of being his student or through assimilation of his thought.

Since the late 1950's, Nishida's works have begun to be known outside

Japan. Although his thought has been severely criticized by Marxist and other antimetaphysical thinkers, on the whole Nishida's philosophy has been favorably received by the Western world. He is recognized as one of the first philosophers to offer a system that transcends the distinctions between Eastern and Western philosophy. He is further credited with having given Oriental thought a logical foundation with his "logic of nothingness."

Bibliography
Abe, Masao. "Nishida's Philosophy of 'Place.'" *The International Philosophical Quarterly* 28 (December, 1988): 355-371. Abe's intended audience is composed of professional philosophers. Nishida's concept of "place" distinguishes him in the history of philosophy.
Knauth, Lothar. "Life Is Tragic—The Diary of Nishida Kitaro." *Monumenta Nipponica* 20 (1965): 335-358. A study of Nishida's life, based on his diary. Discussions of Nishida's personal and family life, his professional life, his reading interests, and the development of his philosophical ideas are included.
Merton, Thomas. "Nishida: A Zen Philosopher." In his *Zen and the Birds of Appetite.* New York: New Directions, 1968. A brief introduction to Nishida's philosophy for Westerners. It would be helpful to know something about Western philosophy and have some knowledge of Zen before reading this article.
Piovesana, Gino K. "The Philosophy of Nishida Kitarō, 1870-1945." In his *Recent Japanese Philosophical Thought, 1862-1962: A Survey.* Tokyo: Enderle Bookstore, 1963. An introduction to Nishida's thought, with some helpful introductory comments that suggest how to approach the demanding aspects of Nishida's works. Includes an index and a bibliography.
Piper, Raymond Frank. "Nishida, Notable Japanese Personalist." *Personalist* 17 (1936): 21-31. The only English-language article on Nishida written while he was still live, it is a study of Nishida's philosophy based on the author's acquaintance with *A Study of Good.*
Shibata, Masumi. "The Diary of a Zen Layman: The Philosopher Nishida Kitarō." *The Eastern Buddhist* 14 (1981): 121-131. A study of what can be learned about Nishida's Zen practice and his thoughts about Zen from the pages of his diary.
Shimomura, Torataro. Introduction to *A Study of Good*, by Kitarō Nishida. Translated by V. H. Viglielmo. Tokyo: Japanese Government Printing Bureau, 1960. Nishida's thought is related to the Japanese philosophy that preceded him. This article also contains brief overviews of Nishida's life and of his later philosophical development.
Viglielmo, Valdo Humbert. "Nishida Kitarō: The Early Years." In *Tradition and Modernization in Japanese Culture*, edited by Donald H. Shively. Princeton, N.J.: Princeton University Press, 1971. A detailed account of

Nishida's early life, from birth to approximately thirty-three years of age. Viglielmo is a noted Nishida scholar, and this well-written work does nothing to detract from his reputation.

Ann Marie B. Bahr

KWAME NKRUMAH
Francis Kwia Kofi

Born: September 18, 1909; Nkroful, Gold Coast
Died: April 27, 1972; Bucharest, Romania
Areas of Achievement: Government and Politics
Contribution: Nkrumah was the first statesman to lead an African country to
independence after World War II. As the first major proponent of Pan-
Africanism, he gained both continental and international stature. He
served as Prime Minister of the Gold Coast, Prime Minister of Ghana
after its independence, and President of Ghana. After the coup that deposed him, he was named titular copresident of Guinea, a recognition of
his status as an international leader and world statesman.

Early Life

The man who would one day be internationally known as Kwame
Nkrumah was born in Nkroful in the British West African colony of Gold
Coast on Saturday, September 18, 1909. Although he was christened Francis
Kwia Kofi, his African name, Kwame, is indicative of the day on which he
was born as was the local custom. Despite the fact that he was his mother's
only child, he grew up in a large family of fourteen people, including children of his father by other wives. Nkrumah's father was a goldsmith and
jeweler; his mother was a retail trader. He was baptized a Roman Catholic,
and at his mother's insistence he attended the nearby Roman Catholic mission schools at Esima and Sekondi-Takoradi. Nkrumah did so well in school
that he was sent to the Government Training School in Accra. He was
graduated from Achiomota College, where he was trained as a teacher, in
1930 and taught at Catholic junior schools and a seminary until 1935. While
at school, Nkrumah met Kwegyir Aggrey, the school's first African staff
member. It was Aggrey who guided Nkrumah's mind toward the issues to
which he would later devote his life. At the same time, another major influence came into Nkrumah's life. Nnamdi Azikiwe, a Nigerian journalist, who
would later become Nigeria's first president, fired Nkrumah's enthusiasm for
nationalist struggle. He would also have a direct impact on the next phase of
Nkrumah's life. He suggested that Nkrumah attend Lincoln University in the
United States. From Lincoln, Nkrumah received a bachelor of arts degree in
economics and sociology in 1939, a bachelor of theology degree in 1942,
and an honorary law degree in 1951. In addition, Nkrumah received a master's degree in education from the University of Pennsylvania in 1942 and a
master of arts in philosophy from the same school in 1943. He finished all
the requirements for the doctoral degree except the dissertation. After having
worked his way through school for ten years, exhausted and homesick as
well as excited about the political stirrings in Africa and Europe, Nkrumah

decided to return to Africa via Europe.

In May of 1945, Nkrumah left the United States for Europe. Landing in England, he decided to continue his studies by enrolling at University College and the London School of Economics, but, having become radicalized politically, abandoned this pursuit in order to devote his energies full-time to a publication he had founded called *The New African*. Moreover, his increasing revolutionary consciousness made the liberation of Ghana specifically and Africa generally his primary goals. Thus, he joined several Pan-African groups in London. Because of his political activities in the United States (where he had been president of the African Students' Association of North America) and Europe (where he was a leader in the West African National Secretariat), Nkrumah was invited to return to the Gold Coast in 1947 as general secretary of the United Gold Coast Convention (UGCC), the nationalist party popular throughout the land. Nkrumah heeded the call of his people and returned to Ghana.

Life's Work

When Nkrumah returned to the Gold Coast, the colony was experiencing very bad economic conditions and the social situation was in chaos. These difficulties would eventually help him into power. The main source of these problems rested with the coca tree disease "swollen shoot." The government considered this a major issue because coca was the main export. The government's solution to the problem was to cut out the diseased trees to protect the others. Farmers resented this policy because it threatened their whole livelihood. This policy was particularly offensive because the price of coca was rising after a long period of low prices during the 1930's. The economic result of the government's farm policies was severe inflation and high prices while wages remained low. In addition, there were other problems associated with the presence of both European and Syrian merchants dominating retail and commercial trade. Moreover, soldiers returning from overseas were disillusioned with the government's failure to fulfill its promises of better housing and more jobs. Indeed, the government's failure to pay attention to these issues and the problems they engendered caused the people to resent further the British and their colonial leaders, including the UGCC.

The failure of the older leaders of the UGCC to address these issues and their continued association with the British led Nkrumah to form his own party in June of 1949. Indeed, the Convention People's Party (CPP) was an attempt by the young leaders, including Nkrumah, seen by the people as the "petit bourgeois," to overcome the soft and satisfied image of the older elite, which was identified as the "grand bourgeois." Nkrumah's charisma, speaking ability, and charm had pulled many people into the UGCC; when he formed his own party, they followed him, as did most of the colony's activists and local leaders. The CPP elected Nkrumah president and life chairman; from that position he stressed West African unity at first and then called for the unity of the entire African continent, or Pan-Africanism. With the UGCC weakened by Nkrumah's departure, the CPP emerged as the colony's main political organization. The planks in its political program were indicative of its ability to articulate the hopes and needs of the people. The party's goals were to achieve "self-government now" as well as to end all forms of oppression and establish a democratic government. The party also called for complete unity of the colony by ensuring the rights of local chiefs and all ethnic groups. The CPP appealed to workers and soldiers by advocating the interests of the trade union movement as well as the right of the people in the Gold Coast to live and govern themselves. Its final goal, the realization of West African unity, reflected Nkrumah's Pan-African ideals.

In an effort to coerce the government to accept constitutional reform, the CPP called a general strike in 1948. Nkrumah and the other leaders were arrested. The British allowed an election and used trucks with sound systems to drive about the colony and denounce the CPP. Despite these and other tactics, Nkrumah's party won thirty-three of thirty-eight seats in the governing body. Thus, he and the leaders were released from jail. In some ways, this election became Nkrumah's mandate to lead his people to independence. The CPP continued to gain power and popularity under limited British self-government. In his first speech after the election, Nkrumah called himself "a friend of Great Britian" and spoke of the Gold Coast becoming a dominion within the Commonwealth. During this period of limited self-government, internal rivalries caused accusations against Nkrumah and his party. Some called him a Communist, others hailed him as a puppet of the British. Nkrumah was in a difficult position as he tried to work with the British while keeping the trust and support of his people. Nkrumah continued to enjoy the support of the youth groups and the military as well as many local factions. He appealed to the Africans because he continued to remind them of their own glorious history and their dignity.

Nkrumah's rise to power was swift. After a second arrest and imprisonment in 1950, he rose from leader of government business to prime minister. While still prime minister in the British colonial government, Nkrumah made his date with destiny when he called for the independence of the Gold Coast within the British commonwealth on July 10, 1953. Nkrumah would serve as prime minister for the Gold Coast from 1952 to 1957 and then of Ghana from 1957 to 1960. He changed the name of the colony to Ghana in an attempt to move away from British influences and English titles. In 1957, he married Fathia Halen Ritzk, and the couple eventually had three children. In 1960, he became president of the independent republic and was granted the title *ossaggeto*, which means redeemer.

Having achieved the independence of Ghana, his first political goal, Nkrumah turned his energies toward a second major issue, the unity of

Africa. In April of 1958, he convened a conference of eight states, and from this group, the Organization of African Unity (OAU) was born. In turning his attentions away from the problems of Ghana, Nkrumah let too much responsibility be taken by his ministers. In turn, several of his closest friends had to be dismissed for corruption, graft, and mismanagement. In addition, there were demonstrations by the soldiers, displeasure at his policies in the farming sector, and ethnic tensions. The people of Ghana were so displeased that they formed an organization, Ghana Shifimo, to address their concerns. The group's inception was unlawful, and its threatened violence and bombing of indiscriminate areas presented major problems. Nkrumah's reponse was repression. He had its leaders detained under the Preventive Detention Act of 1958. By 1960, more than 318 detention orders had been issued, and this act was extended to the Ghana Shifimo.

Many people believed that Nkrumah had responded properly to the growing violence, social unrest, bombings, and assassination attempts on his life. Others believed that he had lost touch with the people. Frustrated and depressed, Nkrumah withdrew more and more from public life. Much of the political unrest was the result of general dissatisfaction with the CPP and its monopoly on power. In dismissing some of his ministers, Nkrumah addressed some of the peoples' complaints; however, the task of bringing a colony into the world body of nations as a free and equal partner proved harder than Nkrumah had realized. Ghana was independent, but it was not free of the problems of nationhood.

When Ghana first became independent, its economy was strong. As in times before, it relied heavily on the export of coca. In his attempt to make Ghana more self-sufficient, Nkrumah forced farmers to diversify their crops. The growing unhappiness with his farm policies, a chronic shortage of trained personnel, and the breakdown of the traditional British civil service all undermined many of his reforms. The decline in the world price of coca, large-scale smuggling, and the recently minted cedi, Ghana's currency, which had no attachment to the international standard, combined to make Ghana unable to pay its debts to various international bodies. This caused Ghana additional problems, and cries of incompetence and mismanagement arose. In some ways, Nkrumah was the appropriate person to lead his African country to independence; however, many speculate that he was not the best choice to handle the day-to-day operations of a fragile government.

On February 24, 1966, a long-planned military coup deposed Nkrumah. At the time, Nkrumah was in North Vietnam attempting to create a peaceful solution to the conflict there. Many speculate that he was aware of the coup before he left Ghana. He was deliberately out of the country both to avoid what would have been a very bloody civil war and to protect his good name and international stature. In some ways, he let the coup occur in recognition of his failure to address the problem of a crumbling economy and massive unrest as well as political turmoil over his increasingly repressive measures. After the coup was announced, Nkrumah continued his travels throughout the Eastern Bloc and accepted exile in Conakry, Guinea, where President Ahmed Sékou Touré named him copresident in a gesture of solidarity and in recognition of his status as the redeemer not only of Ghana but also of much of Africa.

Summary

Kwame Nkrumah was an international statesman, politican, and philosopher. He was a visionary who led a nation and influenced a continent toward independence. His two main goals were the independence of Ghana and the liberation of Africa. At some level he was able to achieve both. Nkrumah was a very intelligent and articulate man who was able to formulate a strategy that was appropriate for both the time and place to achieve his lifelong goals. His insistence on nonviolent civil disobedience as well as his appeal to the righteousness of political freedom for African people were good tactics in the context of the colonial regime. Like most great statesmen, Nkrumah appeared to be the right man for the right time. In some ways he was profoundly affected by the injustices he witnessed as a small child while the British controlled his people. His intelligence and willingness to leave home and study in the United States and Europe made him ripe for the roles he would later occupy in life. His vast knowledge and his reading of a variety of political philosophies were to become the tools he used to orchestrate his people's independence. Nkrumah was a farsighted man who brought free education, health care, and other social services to his nation. In addition, he repaired the physical infrastructure of roads, bridges, and dams in an attempt to assist Ghana in claiming its place among the modern nations in the world. His most important role was his insistence on the unity of Africa and the creation of the OAU. His basic philosophies and approach became a model for the rest of emerging Africa and the globe. In many ways, he is the father of modern political struggle.

Bibliography

Ames, Sophia Ripley. *Nkrumah of Ghana.* New York: Rand McNally, 1961. This short biography contains interesting anecdotes about and insights into the personal side of Nkrumah, the statesman and politician. It also looks at the development of his philosophy.

Bretton, Henry L. *The Rise and Fall of Kwame Nkrumah: A Study of Personal Rule in Africa.* New York: Praeger, 1966. This work presents a rather critical look at both the personal and political Nkrumah. The author examines what he calls Nkrumah's "political machine" and the effects of his personality cult on the government and politics of Ghana.

Hodgkin, Thomas. *Nationalism in Colonial Africa.* New York: New York

University Press, 1957. In this political analysis of Africa, Hodgkin looks at Africa's many different political organizations and documents their evolution. He takes a close look at Ghanaian leaders such as Danquah and Nkrumah and examines how their views and visions of Ghana differed.

Nkrumah, Kwame. *Africa Must Unite*. New York: International Press, 1963. In this work, Nkrumah discusses African history and the evolution of its distinct political institutions. Nkrumah also gives insight into the governmental systems of Ghana and other African nations. He examines how colonialism affected Africa negatively and asserts that Ghana will redeem the entire continent.

_____. *The Autobiography of Kwame Nkrumah*. Edinburgh: Thomas Nelson and Sons, 1957. In this balanced and expressive autobiography, Nkrumah presents in detail his life from birth to the declaration of Ghana's independence. It also gives much insight into the various local and international personalities who admired both the man for his charisma and the politician for his skill.

_____. *Revolutionary Path*. New York: International Press, 1973. This work was compiled during the last two years of the author's life. It was written as a result of a request for a single book that would contain documents relating to the development of Nkrumah's thoughts. It is very informative for understanding Nkrumah's political motivations and his vision for Africa.

Omari, T. Peter. *Kwame Nkrumah: The Anatomy of an African Dictatorship*. New York: Africana, 1970. This work looks at the rise and fall of Nkrumah as well as critiques his use of power and the treatment of his political adversaries.

Powell, Erica. *Private Secretary (Female)/Gold Coast*. New York: St. Martin's Press, 1984. This is a unique biography of Nkrumah written by the white female British private secretary who worked for Nkrumah for more than a decade. She brings to her story the insight of a loyal assistant and the criticisms of a trusted friend. It has interesting personal anecdotes and political insights about Nkrumah and the people he knew.

Rooney, David. *Kwame Nkrumah: The Political Kingdom in the Third World*. New York: St. Martin's Press, 1988. This work is the story of Nkrumah's life from birth to death. The author's goal is to provide an objective account of Nkrumah's life in view of recent developments in Africa and the history of Ghana. It presents a detailed discussion of the complex cultural, psychological, sociological as well as political factors that influenced Nkrumah's development.

Alphine W. Jefferson

JULIUS NYERERE

Born: March, 1922; Butiama, Tanganyika (now Tanzania)

Areas of Achievement: Government and politics

Contribution: Nyerere peacefully brought an end to the British United Nations Trusteeship of Tanzania and became the founding father of independent Tanzania. Throughout the 1960's, 1970's, and 1980's, he opposed racial oppression and discrimination of all types.

Early Life

Julius Kambarage Nyerere was born in the village of Butiama in Zanakiland, Tanganyika, in March, 1922. He was named for his father, Chief Nyerere Burito, who ruled the surrounding area. Nyerere grew up in the sheltered, peaceful, safe world of the Zanaki. He learned Zanaki traditions and was initiated into manhood. His basic values are African and never changed, though he added Western values and skills to this foundation later in life. Nyerere's father sheltered him from the humiliations and dehumanization of the colonial system until he was certain that his son had developed self-assurance that no insult or mistreatment could destroy. His father believed that this was important for a man destined to lead his people.

Nyerere took Zanaki values to school with him, such as the notion that a leader's first duty is to serve his people; that group interests are more important than individual interests; and that social welfare depends on cooperation, not competition. He attended Mwisenge Elementary School, Tabora High School, and Makerere College. While at Makerere, he discovered political science. He stated that "John Stuart Mill's essays on representative government and on the subjection of women . . . had a terrific influence on me." He won an essay contest by applying Mill's ideas to his own society. He was graduated from Makerere in 1946 and wanted to continue his education but did not have an opportunity to do so until awarded a scholarship to the University of Edinburgh in 1949.

While seeking opportunities to continue his studies, Nyerere taught school and worked as a political organizer for the Tanganyika African Association (TAA). Simple, clear explanations came naturally to him, and this earned for him the title *mwalimu*, meaning teacher. When he combined this skill with politics, he became the "fighting professor of Tanzania."

Nyerere arrived in Edinburgh in 1949 and was impressed by Scottish politicians' ability to overcome clan divisions, thereby uniting their people. He used much of what he learned from the Scots later to unify Tanganyika's Africans. Pursuit of an arts degree at Edinburgh allowed Nyerere to formulate his own philosophy. His studies convinced him that only independence could remove the menace of colonialism.

Life's Work

Shortly after returning to Tanganyika in 1952, Nyerere married Maria Gabriel. They moved to Zanakiland, and Nyerere made a house for his new bride using traditional building techniques. To neighbors who were shocked that a university graduate would perform such work, he replied that "everyone who has an education must work." Nyerere assumed teaching duties at St. Mary's and tried to ascertain the political consciousness of his fellow Africans. He learned that in 1951, Europeans had taken large tracts of land from Meru tribesmen and evicted them. This caused bitter resentment and protest. Fear that the British would treat other tribes as callously spread. Nyerere saw in this crisis an opportunity to organize Africans and unite them.

Nyerere was elected president of the TAA in 1953, and by July 7, 1954, he had organized the TAA into a political party known as the Tanganyika African National Union (TANU). *Saba saba*, or the seventh day of the seventh month, is celebrated as a national holiday that rivals independence day. A few months after its formation, TANU voted to send Nyerere to the United Nations to address the United Nations Trusteeship Council on the Meru Land Case and on independence. Upon his return from the United Nations, Nyerere resigned his teaching position and began to work full-time for TANU. His career as a national and international politician had begun.

He argued for prohibition of land alienation, cessation of foreign immigration, expansion of education and technical training, and encouragement of trade unions and cooperatives. His logical, reasoned arguments won wide support for his position and the restoration of Meru land to the Meru people. Nyerere stated that he believed in the brotherhood of the races and that any European or Asian who accepted the principle of "one man, one vote" would be welcomed as a citizen of an independent Tanganyika.

Nyerere admired Mahatma Gandhi and wanted to achieve independence without bloodshed. *Uhuru na kazi*, meaning freedom and work, became TANU's slogan and rallying cry. The party's ranks swelled as peasants joined forces with the educated elite. Nyerere soon headed a popular grassroots movement capable of mobilizing mass support for its policies. Without doubt dissension existed—the militants wanted to abolish the office and power of the chiefs; wealthy Africans clashed with egalitarian idealists. In the early days, however, the dream of *uhuru* was enough to keep them together. Nyerere was convinced that a national movement had to represent all interests. TANU was fighting to build a democratic state in which each person had one vote and in this regard everyone would be equal. Since most Tanganyikans spoke Swahili, communication was not a major problem and this helped unify Tanganyika.

When it became clear to the British that Nyerere had emerged as the spokesman for Tanganyika's African majority, they tried to silence him by appointing him to the legislative council on a temporary basis. He surprised everyone by using this opportunity to attack the government's educational policy. He declared the policy inadequate, because 64 percent of school-aged African children were not in school, and no provision was made for their education. He also attacked a proposed increase in civil servant salaries, stating that salaries should be frozen and the difference applied toward the education of African youth. As rejected patrons, the British were bitter toward Nyerere, but the African masses hailed him as their champion. He became a folk hero, and the more the British attacked him the more popular he became.

By 1957, Ghana had become the first African nation to achieve independence from Great Britain. Kenya was embroiled in the Mau Mau Rebellion, and most whites in Tanganyika resigned themselves to the inevitability of majority rule. The "winds of change" were sweeping across Africa. Thus, no one was surprised that, when the colonial government called for elections in 1958, every candidate nominated by TANU won. Nyerere's party gained control of the legislature, so Great Britain began immediate preparation to hand over power without bloodshed. By 1961, Tanganyika had achieved internal self-government and full independence. Nyerere predicted that independence did not mark the end of his nation's problems. He began to work on his greatest challenge: eliminating poverty for the majority of Tanganyikans.

A dedicated Pan-Africanist, Nyerere convinced Karume, the leader of revolutionary Zanzibar, to combine Tanganyika and Zanzibar into a single nation now known as Tanzania. In 1963, he helped form the East African Community, which had a common currency, postal service, and airline. Irresolvable differences caused the community to collapse in 1976. Thus, the dream of transforming Kenya, Uganda, and Tanzania into one large nation died too.

Nyerere has emerged as a spokesman for Africa's oppressed. He finances refugee camps for displaced Africans and settles them on their own farms. Nyerere backed the Mozambique Liberation Front (FRELIMO) for fourteen years while Mozambicans fought to overthrow Portuguese colonial rule. He provides school and training facilities for the African National Congress (ANC) of South Africa as it strives to end apartheid and usher in power sharing in South Africa. As part of this effort, he inspired the formation of the Southern African Development Coordination Council (SADCC). This is an organization of the frontline African nations that border South Africa. It seeks to support the ANC, resist South Africa's efforts to destabilize her neighbors, and attract foreign capital to develop these states. Nyerere has been one of the most outspoken opponents of apartheid and has used a very high proportion of Tanzania's income to defeat this system.

Diplomatically, Tanzania is nonaligned. Most of its development aid comes from Western nations. China won Nyerere's admiration and support by financing construction of the Tanzam railroad when no other country would assist.

Nyerere coined the slogan *uhuru na kazi*. He also devised the policy of *ujamaa*, or African socialism, which he used to organize and mobilize the masses. Nyerere's socialism is based upon the African concept of the extended family. Land is owned collectively by the state, and individuals lease it as long as they demonstrate that they are improving it or productively using it. This policy also encourages collective production of wealth and the collective pursuit of prosperity. More than 80 percent of all Tanzanians have been moved into nucleated villages so that the government can provide them with clean water, health care, agricultural advice, and other services. Difficulties in gaining voluntary compliance caused this *ujamaa vijijini*, or collective village, scheme to be abandoned.

Nyerere teaches Tanzanians that they cannot rely upon money to develop their country, because they are poor. Money, he argues, "is the weapon of the rich." He advises Tanzanians to learn to work intelligently and to combine this with much hard work to develop their country. Education is a key factor to this development, and it is free up through university level for those who qualify. Yearly Nyerere educates quadruple the number of Africans that were educated annually by the former colonial regime.

By encouraging Tanzanians to modernize agriculture and grow enough food crops to feed themselves as well as manufacture cloth and other items used often, Nyerere is teaching self-reliance. Compulsory military service has been used to instill discipline and has made Tanzania a formidable regional power, as the country's easy victory over Uganda in the 1977-1978 Uganda-Tanzania War proved. Nyerere has taught Tanzanians to value sharing, education, hard work, and honesty and to fight all forms of discrimination. This has provided Tanzania a stable foundation on which to build their future. Perhaps the greatest lesson that Nyerere taught Tanzanians was not to covet power. In 1985, he voluntarily stepped down, making way for Ali Hassan Mwinyi to become, democratically, the second head of state of Tanzania. This proved that a *coup d'état* is not necessary to effect a transfer of power in Africa. It also demonstrated that a former head of state can live out the balance of his life in peace in his own nation if he managed it well.

Summary

Julius Nyerere peacefully achieved independence for Tanzania in 1961. Using a unique form of socialism based upon traditional African values and the close bonds of the family, he instilled a spirit of close cooperation, sharing, and love that he called *ujamaa*. Because he led by persuasion rather than force, he is affectionately known as *mwalimu*, or the teacher. Unlike Gandhi, he used peace wherever possible but force without fear where needed, as demonstrated by his support for African freedom fighters from Mozambique, Angola, Zimbabwe, Namibia, and South Africa for more than a decade. His calm, humor, self-control, and personal honesty and integrity, and his devotion to the education, freedom, and development of Africa and Africans assure Nyerere pride of place in African and world history. The development of humans remains his guiding star and the highest ideal of independent Tanzania.

Bibliography
Duggan, William Redman, and John R. Civille. *Tanzania and Nyerere: A Study of Ujamaa and Nationhood.* Maryknoll, N.Y.: Orbis Books, 1976. Contains substantial biographical information on Nyerere. Follows the emergence of an independent Tanzania and Nyerere's part in that emergence. Includes an extensive bibliography, index, notes.
Graham, Shirley. *Julius K. Nyerere: Teacher of Africa.* New York: Julian Messner, 1975. An inspiring picture of a man born to privilege who risked everything to champion the rights of all and to build a nation where all share equally its benefits and shoulder its responsibilities.
Hatch, John. *Two African Statesmen: Kaunda of Zambia and Nyerere of Tanzania.* Chicago: Henry Regnery, 1976. Contains little-known facts about the British Labor Party's role in the independence of both Zambia and Tanzania. A sympathetic portrait by a British Labor Party official who knew both leaders.
Nnoli, Okwudiba. *Self Reliance and Foreign Policy in Tanzania.* New York: NOK, 1978. An in-depth look at Tanzania's foreign affairs that places Nyerere in context. The president is discussed in a very favorable way. Includes an index.
Smith, William Edgett. *We Must Run While They Walk: A Portrait of Africa's Julius Nyerere.* New York: Random House, 1971. A warm, endearing portrait of the man behind Tanzania's freedom movement. The influence of his father, his brother Edward, Oscar Kambona, Rashidi Kawawa, Abeid Karume, and others on Nyerere is assessed. It is enjoyable and easy to read.

Dallas L. Browne

HERMANN OBERTH

Born: June 25, 1894; Hermannstadt, Siebenburgen, Transylvania
Died: December 29, 1989; Nürnberg, West Germany
Area of Achievement: Aeronautics
Contribution: Oberth is one of the three great pioneers of the sciences of
astronautics and modern rocketry. Along with Konstantin Tsiolkovsky and
Robert Goddard, he is credited with developing the principles behind
rocket-powered flight beyond Earth's atmosphere, liquid-fueled rockets, a
manned Earth orbital space station, and manned interplanetary flight.

Early Life
Hermann Julius Oberth was born on June 25, 1894, in Hermannstadt,
Siebenburgen, Transylvania, a part of what is modern Romania. His father,
Julius, was a physician who stressed learning to his son from an early age.
The younger Oberth attended elementary and high school in the town of
Schaessburg until 1913, when he entered the University of Munich to study
medicine, as had his father. Oberth, like fellow rocketry pioneers Konstantin
Tsiolkovsky in Russia and Robert Goddard in the United States, was heavily
influenced in his formative years by the emerging genre of science fiction
in the late nineteenth and early twentieth centuries that detailed possible
methods of traveling into space. Indeed, in his later years Oberth acknowledged that his mother's gift of Jules Verne's books in his eleventh year
helped shape the course of the rest of his life.

When World War I started in 1914, the twenty-year-old Oberth joined the
German army's medical service. This experience gave him a strong distaste
for the healing arts and convinced him to pursue another area of endeavor
as his life's work. Turning to his childhood fascination with the concept
of spaceflight, he chose mathematics and physics to be his new fields of
study.

After leaving the army medical service, Oberth returned to the University
of Munich and began his studies. He also studied at Göttingen and Heidel-
berg before receiving his schoolmaster's diploma in July, 1923. Returning to
Siebenburgen, he began work as a fifth-grade teacher of mathematics and
physics. Later he taught in the German town of Mediasch, where he made
his home until 1938. He later took German citizenship. It was during his
service in Germany in World War I that he unsuccessfully proposed that the
German government build liquid-fueled bombardment missiles, the forerun-
ners of the modern Intercontinental Ballistic Missiles.

Oberth continued to read and theorize about the prospects of rocket-
powered space flight. This avocation led to the publication of his first and
most well known work on astronautics, *Die Rakete zu den Planetenräumen* (1923; the rocket into interplanetary space). It was this seminal work's

worldwide popularity that gave Oberth an international reputation as an expert in astronautics.

Life's Work

Oberth's *Die Rakete zu den Planetenräumen* and an expanded version of the book published in 1929, *Wege zur Raumschiffahrt* (*Ways to Spaceflight*, 1972), put forth numerous ideas that were to form the basis of the German missile program in World War II and the ongoing American and Soviet manned and unmanned space programs. These included the theory that a liquid-fueled rocket could propel an object through the airless void of space and that the vehicle could develop sufficient velocity and centrifugal force to counterbalance Earth's gravity and remain in orbit around the planet. He also theorized that the vehicle could move quickly enough to break free of Earth's gravity and move into interplanetary space.

Moving beyond the theory of propulsion, Oberth hypothesized the potential effects of space travel on the human body and was the first to coin the phrase "space station" to mean a permanent manned facility in Earth orbit. Although he developed his theories independently of his peers, Oberth's two books confirmed both Tsiolkovsky's theoretical work on rocket propulsion and Goddard's practical experience in rocketry, and moved Oberth to the pinnacle of the rapidly developing field. Both before and after the publication of his first books he maintained active correspondence with both men until their deaths.

In 1928, Oberth was given the chance to put the theories he had developed into practice when he became the technical adviser to the famous film director Fritz Lang and the Ufa film company for the motion picture *Die Frau im Mond*. As part of his service to Ufa, he was asked to build and fly a liquid-fueled rocket to promote the film. Unfortunately, the rocket Oberth constructed was unable to fly, and the film company ran out of development funds before he was able to correct the design. Oberth was, however, able to test-fire a rocket engine successfully in 1930 as part of the project.

An active and vocal proponent of space exploration, Oberth helped found in 1929 the Verein fur Raumschiffahrt (VfR), Germany's first society for space travel. In addition to Oberth, who was elected the society's first president, the group's first members included such pioneers of aeronautics and rocketry as Willy Ley and an eighteen-year-old student of Oberth by the name of Wernher von Braun. The VfR's development paralleled the founding of similar groups elsewhere in the world, including the Moscow Group for the Study of Reactive Propulsion, whose members included the future chief designer of the Soviet space program, Sergei Korolev, and aircraft designer Andrei Tupolev. The VfR and other of these groups both built and flew rudimentary rockets and sponsored public displays on rocketry such as the one built by Oberth and von Braun in a Berlin department store to educate the public about their work.

In 1930, the VfR was given a parcel of land outside Berlin to conduct practical experiments in rocketry. This empty field, which was once an ammunition dump for the German army, was called Raketenflugplatz Berlin (rocket field Berlin). Oberth and the VfR spent the next two years conducting experiments there before the German army developed an interest in their work and recruited several of the VfR's members into service developing ordnance. During this period, Oberth supported himself by teaching mathematics and physics at the technical universities in Vienna and Dresden, as well as by publishing his research in astronautics in numerous books and articles. In 1941, he went to work for his former student von Braun as a member of the team of scientists at the German rocket-development center in Heeresversuchsstelle, Peenemünde.

At Peenemünde, von Braun and Oberth developed and then successfully launched the Vengeance weapons, the V-1 and V-2 rockets. The V-1 "Buzz Bomb" was a short-range, rocket-powered winged bomb, while the V-2 was a powerful ballistic missile able to span hundreds of miles to deliver its deadly payload. With the approval in June, 1943, of Adolf Hitler, the V-2 went into mass production. The first operational V-2 missile was launched on September 8, 1944, at London, England, from The Hague, The Netherlands.

In 1943, Oberth transferred to the Rheinsdorf aircraft facility near Wittenberg, Germany, where he remained for the duration of World War II. After the war, he left Germany unnoticed by the Allies and moved to Switzerland, where he lived in seclusion until 1949. Oberth's research into rocketry resumed in 1949 at Oberried am Brienzer Lake and, later, for the Italian navy at La Spezia, Italy. During these years, he also gained considerable recognition from the growing international community of rocket scientists. His theories were being put to use by both the United States with its early V-2 tests and its own Viking rocket, and by the Soviet Union under Sergei Korolev and his larger, more powerful rockets.

During these years and later, Oberth continued to publish both technical materials and popular treatises on practical concepts of space travel. His later books and articles, including *Menschen im Weltraum* (1954; men into space) and *Stoff und Leben* (1959; matter and life), were well received both by the scientific community and by the general public. He was the recipient of numerous awards during his long career, including the REP Hirsch Award of the Société Astronomique de France, of which he was the first to be so honored in 1925, and the coveted Galabert Prize in 1962. As one of the pioneers of space travel, he was also invited to lecture and participate in many international conferences and programs on astronautics and rocketry. One of the honors he is known to have most prized, however, was having been invited to participate in the realization of his dream of interplanetary space travel as a witness to the launch of Apollo 11, the first manned landing on the moon, in 1969.

In 1955, Oberth again went to work for his former student von Braun at the Technical Feasibility Studies Office of the Ordnance Missile Laboratories in the United States. In 1956, he transferred to the Army Ballistic Missile Agency with von Braun to assist in the development of the Redstone Rocket, one of the United States' first liquid-fueled boosters and the backbone of the early U.S. space program. Two years later, Oberth returned to Germany in semiretirement.

Summary

Hermann Oberth was one of the first great idealists of space travel in the modern age. He, along with his contemporaries Tsiolkovsky and Goddard, had the knowledge and the passion to take the fantasy of science fiction and turn it into the reality of science fact. Through their vision, they forged a new understanding of their world. Oberth's theories, enumerated in his books, showed how the laws of physics could be put to use to conquer the heavens. He theorized about the first space station and gave a detailed, startlingly accurate account of how microgravity would affect the human body on long space voyages. These writings, along with his seminal works about reaction propulsion of a space vehicle and liquid-fueled rockets, gave future engineers and scientists a path to follow in making space travel a reality.

While his work at Peenemünde helped develop weapons of destruction, he was a man who believed deeply in the peaceful pursuit of space. He urged international cooperation between the United States and the Soviet Union in the early days of the space race, even going so far as asking Nikita Khrushchev to allow him to work with Sergei Korolev in the development of the Soviet space program. One of Oberth's most direct contributions to the progress of space travel was the encouragement he gave to the rocketry enthusiasts of his day, such as Wernher von Braun. Von Braun took the knowledge he gained from Oberth, expanded upon it, and made space travel a reality by developing the launch vehicles that carried men to the moon and the unmanned probes that traveled beyond the solar system.

Bibliography

Braun, Wernher von, and Frederick I. Ordway III. *The History of Rocketry and Space Travel*. 3d rev. ed. New York: Thomas Y. Crowell, 1975. As one of the unequaled giants in modern rocketry, von Braun brings to this well-written and easily understandable compendium a unique and fascinating perspective. An excellent starting point for the layperson for information on the early days of the American space program.

Hurt, Harry, III. *For All Mankind*. New York: Atlantic Monthly Press,

1988. Gives an overview of the American space program through the Apollo lunar landings. An accompanying volume to a documentary on the men who flew the lunar landing missions.

Huzel, Dieter K. *Peenemünde to Canaveral*. Englewood Cliffs, N.J.: Prentice-Hall, 1962. This insider's account of the German rocket program during World War II is fast-paced and reads like a novel. Of interest to anyone who wishes to learn more about the proving ground for much of the technology in use in the modern space race.

McAleer, Neil. *The Omni Space Almanac: A Complete Guide to the Space Age*. New York: World Almanac, 1987. A compendium of information about the major developments of the space age, with emphasis on the modern years and their import for the future.

Oberth, Hermann. *Man into Space: New Projects for Rocket and Space Travel*. Translated by G. P. H. De Freville. New York: Harper & Brothers, 1957. This book, one of Oberth's last, is a scholarly approach to space travel, written on the eve of the modern space age. While it contains some technical information, the book is written in easily understandable language for the layperson or amateur space enthusiast.

Stuhlinger, Ernst, et al., eds. *Astronautical Engineering and Science: From Peenemünde to Planetary Space, Honoring the 50th Birthday of Wernher von Braun*. New York: McGraw-Hill, 1963. Written by von Braun's colleagues from Peenemünde, the U.S. Army missile program, the Marshall Space Center, and Cape Canaveral, this collection of essays on space technology and exploration is excellent. Oberth contributed a paper on an electrical rocket engine that is well written and informative.

Eric Christensen

ÁLVARO OBREGÓN

Born: February 19, 1880; Hacienda Siquisiva, Sonora, Mexico
Died: July 17, 1928; Mexico City, Mexico
Areas of Achievement: The military, government, and politics
Contribution: Obregón emerged from humble beginnings to become the most
successful and celebrated general of the Mexican Revolution. Elected
President of Mexico after ten years of civil war, Obregón worked from
1920 to 1924 to pacify his country by a program of demilitarization, sup-
port for public education, and recognition by the U.S. government.

Early Life
Álvaro Obregón, the eighteenth and youngest child of Francisco Obregón
and Cenobia Salido, was born to a respectable family fallen on hard times.
Francisco had been a successful businessman but lost most of his holdings
because his business partner had supported the emperor Maximilian. The
family was reduced to living on their Sonoran ranch, which was ruined by a
series of disasters, including Indian uprisings and floods. Francisco died a
few months after his youngest son's birth.

Obregón spent his early years at Siquisiva, living there until his mother
moved the family to the town of Huatabampo, Sonora. Three elder sisters,
Cenobia, María, and Rosa, assisted his mother in rearing him. He would
remain close to his sisters for the rest of his life. These sisters, all schoolteachers, gave him his essential education. He received little formal education, attending the primary school in Huatabampo, run by his brother José,
for only a few years. He was a voracious reader and largely self-educated.

By the age of thirteen Obregón had left school in order to begin making a
living. He tried his hand at various jobs and money-making schemes: growing tobacco and making cigarettes, organizing a family orchestra, photography, and carpentry. He discovered that he had natural mechanical talent and
began to get jobs taking care of machinery on large plantations in the region.
In his early twenties, he turned to farming, after also having been a traveling
salesman and schoolteacher.

In 1903, Obregón married Refugio Urrea, by whom he would have four
children. By 1906, Obregón had become successful enough to buy a small
farm of his own. He gave this place a whimsical name, "La Quinta Chilla,"
which translates as "the broken down farm" or "penniless farm." In 1907
tragedy struck. His wife and two of his children, including the eldest, died.
His sisters stepped in to help rear his remaining children. In 1909, Obregón
achieved his first real success, inventing a chickpea planter which was soon
adopted by most of the local growers. This allowed him to become modestly
prosperous. After an unsuccessful attempt to gain a state office, Obregón, by
a small margin, was elected *presidente municipal* (mayor) of Huatabampo

during the presidency of Francisco Madero. His interests as mayor centered on public education and public works.

Life's Work

Obregón did not participate in Madero's 1910-1911 rebellion against Porfirio Díaz, citing his parental responsibilities as his reason for abstaining. Later he would regret his actions, which he considered cowardly. When the next opportunity came to fight, he came forward. In April, 1912, he was called upon as mayor to raise troops to fight Pascual Orozco, then in rebellion against Madero's government. Obregón recruited three hundred men and was named Lieutenant Colonel of the Fourth Sonoran Irregular Battalion. During the following months, Obregón demonstrated his courage and natural military ability in the successful campaign against Orozco, earning the rank of colonel.

Obregón had no previous military training or experience but from the first displayed a natural talent for tactics and leadership. He was shrewd, intelligent, and blessed with a prodigious memory. He used these talents to his advantage. Obregón's forte was in assessing troop and material strengths, evaluating terrain, and patiently waiting to do battle when the enemy could be maneuvered into maximum disadvantage. He was a master of the bluff and used his superior knowledge of the situation to trick the enemy into defeating itself. Obregón was also an innovator. His men were using individual foxholes for protection several years before World War I made this technique well known. A pilot in Obregón's army made the first aerial bombardment of gun emplacements in 1914. Such abilities and innovations permitted Obregón a string of uninterrupted victories during the Mexican Revolution.

In December, 1912, Obregón returned to farming, only to take up arms again after Madero's overthrow by General Victoriano Huerta in February, 1913. By August of 1914, Obregón, fighting for the constitutionalist cause organized by Venustiano Carranza, had fought his way from Sonora to Mexico City. Along the way the victorious warrior was made first a brigadier general (May, 1913), and then commander in chief of the Army of the Northeast by Carranza, the head of the constitutionalist forces.

The young general was an attractive figure. Obregón was taller than average and stockily built. His wide, handsome face, with large green eyes, brown hair, and light complexion, reflected his Hispanic heritage. He possessed a lively and creative intelligence and, despite his lack of formal education, was renowned for his prodigious memory. He had a reputation of being a cheerful, frank, and congenial person with a good sense of humor. He was a good conversationalist, much given to telling jokes and humorous stories, often with himself as the butt of the humor. He was abstemious in his personal habits, neither smoking nor drinking. Yet, Obregón was a man of contradictions, and there was a darker side to his personality as well. His genial demeanor masked a driving ambition and ruthlessness. He would not hesitate as the revolution progressed to deal harshly with his enemies and former allies if he deemed it expedient.

After the victory over Huerta, the constitutionalist forces fell into factionalism. General Obregón attempted to serve as conciliator between Carranza, Pancho Villa, and Emiliano Zapata, but without success. Obregón had to defeat Zapata and Villa's forces in battle to end their challenge to Carranza's dominance. He accomplished this but at great personal cost. It was during this campaign, at the Battle of León in June, 1915, that Obregón was wounded and lost his right arm. He became not only the revolution's most successful general but also something of a martyr.

After recovering from his wound, Obregón continued his campaign against Villa. He was made secretary of war by Carranza in March of 1916 to facilitate the campaign. Nevertheless, a rift was growing between the first chief of the Revolution and his best general. By 1916, Obregón's military successes, his reputation as a peacemaker and negotiator among the revolutionaries, his position in the government, and his personal charisma had given him a powerful position. Carranza began to see Obregón as a potential rival and to fear his growing power. For his part, Obregón was increasingly critical of his chief's lack of social conscience. Yet, each needed the other, and this postponed an open break between them until 1917.

Obregón used his position as secretary of war to begin the reorganization and professionalization by which he planned to eliminate the military from politics. He took an active, though indirect, interest in the constitutional convention which met in Querétaro from December, 1916, to January, 1917. Although not a delegate and frequently absent on military business, Obregón associated himself at the convention with the radicals, who were responsible for the inclusion of innovative articles in the constitution regarding the Church, labor, and landownership. Obregón emerged from the convention with a reputation as a champion of radical causes.

Having waited until the ratification of the new constitution and Carranza's election as president under it, in May, 1917, Obregón resigned from the cabinet and returned to private life. He and his second wife, María Tapia, whom he had married in 1916, returned to La Quinta Chilla. There, Obregón pursued numerous economic activities. He grew chickpeas, founded a cooperative agricultural society for chickpea growers, acquired additional land, raised cattle, and opened an import-export firm. He grew wealthy from his business interests and began to age rapidly, growing fat and gray by the age of forty.

By 1919, Obregón was preparing himself to run for the presidency. He had not directly challenged Carranza, preferring to bide his time until the 1920 election. President Carranza, however, attempted to block Obregón's ambitions, believing that his former subordinate lacked both an understanding of national problems and a program for dealing with them. Obregón increasingly saw Carranza as an obstructionist and reactionary who lacked commitment to the revolutionary principles embodied in the constitution. The showdown began when Obregón announced his candidacy in June, 1919. Carranza realized that Obregón, an energetic and effective campaigner, was the popular candidate and would win unless he could be eliminated from the race. Therefore, in April, 1920, Carranza pushed Obregón and his supporters into armed rebellion, hoping to eliminate the threat once and for all. Within a month, however, Carranza was dead, and the rebels triumphed. This paved the way for Obregón's landslide election to the presidency.

Obregón was inaugurated President of Mexico on December 1, 1920, inheriting a nation in chaos. While committed to implementing the provisions of the 1917 constitution, he was at heart a pragmatist. His main objective as president was the pacification of Mexico after ten bloody years of civil war. To achieve this, he needed to strengthen the central government, eliminate the military from politics, and begin the economic and social regeneration of Mexico. Strengthening and legitimizing the regime was of paramount importance if the revolution was to endure. To do this, Obregón had to compromise the constitution's nationalist principles regarding foreign investors and make an accommodation with the United States. The Bucareli Agreements of 1923 granted concessions to American companies and investors but obtained American recognition. This was an important deterrent to the success of future rebellions against the regime, because American arms and support would be withheld from the rebels. He began the forced professionalization of the army, making limited but significant gains in depoliticizing its leadership. To check the power of the military, he built new bases of regime support among urban labor and the rural peasantry by beginning the implementation of the labor and agrarian reforms outlined in the constitution. Obregón reduced military spending and increased the government's commitment to education, hoping to build Mexico's future on an educated citizenry. Obregón's presidency paved the way for the more rapid and complete implementation of the constitution under his successors.

After defeating a major military rebellion in 1923, Obregón finished his full term of office—the first Mexican president to do so since 1910—and handed power to his elected successor Plutarco Elías Calles. He then returned to farming. Helped by government loans, he further expanded his business interests. For a time he was content living in Sonora, enjoying his return to private life surrounded by his wife and children, but by 1926 he was spending increasing amounts of time in the capital. In October, 1926, the congress, after stormy debate, changed the constitution to pave the way for Obregón's reelection as president. This triggered discontent among the military chieftains. After having dealt harshly and efficiently with them, Obregón ran unopposed in 1928. He did not, however, live to take office a second time. After surviving a series of assassination attempts in 1927 and 1928, President-elect Obregón met his death at a banquet in Mexico City in July, 1928. José de León Toral, a young Catholic fanatic posing as a caricaturist, shot Obregón at point blank range as he sat at the head table. In keeping with his wishes, Obregón was buried in his home state of Sonora.

Summary

Álvaro Obregón's career represented both the good and bad aspects of the Mexican Revolution. He was a member of the new elite, which came to power as a result of the revolutionary struggle. A moderately successful farmer before the Revolution, he considered himself a citizen-soldier compelled to arms in order to champion the interests of the Mexican people. He risked his life to topple the entrenched interests that had perpetuated a life of misery for so many of his countrymen. He supported the writing of a constitution that would build a new, more equitable Mexico from the ashes of the old regime. As president, he worked to institutionalize the revolutionary regime and to build the mechanism needed to create that new nation. He is justly considered one of the great heroes of the Revolution.

He was, however, a flawed hero. Obregón also used the revolution for self-aggrandizement. The upheaval created opportunities for him to feed his driving ambition for power and influence. He used his success as a military leader to become the most powerful man in Mexico, despite the fact that he considered the military in politics to be the major threat to the stabilization of the country. He ruthlessly eliminated his rivals for power if they did not step aside. He forced the amending of one of the most cherished provisions of the revolutionary constitution—prohibiting the reelection of presidents to prevent dictatorships—because it stood in the way of his personal ambition. In the end, he met the fate of most revolutionary generals who survived the Revolution, death by assassination in the political struggles that followed.

Bibliography

Bailey, David C. "Obregón: Mexico's Accommodating President." In *Essays on the Mexican Revolution*, edited by George Wolfskill and Douglas W. Richmond. Austin: University of Texas Press, 1979. A short piece focusing on Obregón's contributions as president of Mexico. Bailey believes that Obregón's willingness to compromise made possible the institutionalization of revolutionary goals.

Dillon, E. J. *President Obregón: A World Reformer.* Boston: Small, Maynard, 1923. An idealized and uncritical study of Obregón by a journalist who traveled with his retinue. Dillon presents Obregón as a statesman who, among others, holds out hope for the future of Western civilization.

Dulles, John W. F. *Yesterday in Mexico: A Chronicle of the Revolution, 1919-1936.* Austin: University of Texas Press, 1961. Dulles uses interviews with survivors, published memoirs, and newspaper accounts to construct a narrative of the rise and fall of the three great Sonoran revolutionary leaders: Obregón, Huerta, and Calles. Valuable for its coverage of Obregón's presidential years.

Hall, Linda. *Alvaro Obregón: Power and Revolution in Mexico, 1911-1920.* College Station: Texas A&M Press, 1981. Extensively researched and well balanced, this is the best work in English on Obregón. Hall covers Obregón's rise to presidential power through military success and political infighting. Unfortunately, Hall does not extend the work to Obregón's presidency.

――――――. "Alvaro Obregón and the Agrarian Movement 1912-20." In *Caudillo and Peasant in the Mexican Revolution,* edited by David Brading. Cambridge, England: Cambridge University Press, 1980. An article focusing on Obregón's relations with the peasantry. Hall sees Obregón not as a typical caudillo but as a leader with broader based support.

Hansis, Randall. "The Political Strategy of Military Reform: Alvaro Obregón and Revolutionary Mexico 1920-1924." *The Americas: A Quarterly Review of Inter-American Cultural History* (October, 1979): 197-233. Highlights Obregón's program of military reform during his presidency.

Lieuwen, Edwin. *Mexican Militarism: The Political Rise and Fall of the Revolutionary Army, 1910-1940.* Albuquerque: University of New Mexico Press, 1968. This work describes how the revolutionary army of Mexico seized power, the role it played in social reform, and how it was gradually forced to surrender its power to civilian politicians. Obregón as president was a key figure in professionalizing and depoliticizing the army, although the task would be completed by his successors.

Ruiz, Ramón Eduardo. *The Great Rebellion: Mexico, 1905-1924.* New York: W. W. Norton, 1980. Contains a chapter devoted to Obregón. Ruiz sees him not as a revolutionary nor even much of a reformer, despite his political reputation. Instead, he finds Obregón's political philosophy (as reflected in his actions) to be more in keeping with nineteenth century liberal notions about individualism and capitalism.

Victoria Hennessey Cummins

SADAHARU OH

Born: May 10, 1940; Tokyo, Japan

Area of Achievement: Sports

Contribution: Oh hit more home runs, 868, than any other man in organized baseball while playing twenty-two years with the Yomiuri (Tokyo) Giants in the Central League in Japan. When he retired, he also held the Japanese career records in runs batted in, runs scored, and total bases as well as the second highest marks in doubles and games played.

Early Life

Sadaharu Oh was born in the Sumida-ku section of Tokyo, Japan, on May 10, 1940. His father was a Chinese immigrant restaurant owner. During the war, his father was imprisoned for several months and permanently scarred during questioning as a possible Chinese agent. Oh is still technically a Chinese national with permanent working rights in Japan. His heritage and the availability of food gave him the size (5 feet, 10 inches, and 175 pounds) that made him very large for Japanese players and certainly contributed to his power hitting.

The family survived the fire-bombing of Tokyo, though their restaurant was destroyed and had to be reestablished after the war. During the occupation, Oh's elder brother was a star on an amateur baseball team and introduced him to baseball. Since he had never seen a left-handed batter, Oh first batted right-handed even though he pitched left-handed. When Oh was in the eighth grade, he was converted to a left-handed batter at the suggestion of Hiroshi Arakawa, a major league outfielder.

Oh's father had high ambitions for his sons. The eldest son became a medical doctor, and Oh was being prepared for a career as an engineer. He did not, however, make a high enough score on the entrance exam to get into the exclusive local high school and instead was accepted at Waseda Commercial High School, far across the city. High school baseball is one of the major sporting events in Japan, and Waseda always had a good team. Oh was persuaded, as a highly rated young player, to travel long hours to and from school to participate.

The climax of the high school baseball season each year is the National High School Tournament at Koshien Stadium in Osaka. There are fifty thousand spectators for each game and each is nationally telecast. In 1956, Waseda reached the national finals for the seventeenth time in thirty-eight years. They won their first game, but Oh, the starting pitcher in the second game, was unable to do well and the team was eliminated. The next year, Waseda reached the finals again, and this time Oh was their only pitcher. He had two badly injured fingers on his pitching hand with deep blisters that bled as he pitched. He managed to pitch three straight complete games to reach the climactic game. Oh won the final game 4-2 and was lauded by the newspapers for his fighting spirit. Soon afterward, he was refused the right to participate in the Kokutai (National Amateur Athletic Competition), because he was a Chinese national. In his last year in school, Waseda was beaten in their last game in Tokyo and failed to reach the Koshien tournament.

Life's Work

In 1959, Oh joined the Yomiuri Giants, signing a bonus contract for sixty thousand yen after a bidding war in which considerably higher sums were offered by other teams. He began practice as an eighteen-year-old rookie on the veteran team of the Japanese leagues and was almost overwhelmed by all the activity, particularly since Shigeo Nagashima, a college graduate and the most popular player in Japanese baseball history, had enjoyed a brilliant rookie year in 1958. Quickly Oh earned a reputation for being very hardworking, even for a Japanese player, all of whom worked much longer hours than American players. During the first year, he lived in the dormitory for younger players. Often he practiced from eight o'clock until noon with them, in the afternoon with the Giants, and in the evening he played in a game. Throughout his career, he never took less than forty minutes of batting practice on a game day and carefully drank a secret blend of Korean ginseng before each game. The first year Oh batted .161 with only seven home runs and twenty-five runs batted in in ninety-four games, making the Giants decision to convert him to a first baseman seem quite questionable. Though he did so poorly, it was prophetic that his first hit was a home run. The next year he did improve to .270 with seventeen home runs and seventy-one runs batted in, leading the league in bases on balls for the first of nineteen times. The third year, Oh slumped again to .253 with only thirteen home runs and fifty-three runs batted in.

In the spring of 1962, Manager Kawakami of the Giants hired Hiroshi Arakawa as his batting coach. For the next nine years, Arakawa would almost completely dominate Oh's life. He had been told to turn Oh into a .280 hitter with twenty home runs a year, a goal that Arakawa considered modest from the start. The training regimen established included work in the traditional Japanese martial arts and philosophy and orders to give up visiting the bars in the Ginza and all tobacco products. Then began intensive instruction for both of them in Zen and in the martial art called Aikido, the latter under the direction of the founder of the school Ueshiba. Aikido is based on the idea that the power of the opponent is absorbed and put to one's own use. Arakawa would always emphasize that Oh should use this technique with the pitcher, so that each at bat would be like a samurai sword fight or a sumo wrestling match—a battle between two individuals that affects all that is around them.

Arakawa also began instructing Oh in his theory of hitting, which was down swinging, or hitting downward through the ball, so that it was met at the nadir of the swing as it started upward, with the wrists exploding forward after contact was made. Moving pictures of Oh after he established his style show a swing that looks remarkably like that of a professional golfer with an elaborate backswing, downswing through the ball, and a high follow-through. The wrist explosion technique is very similar to the technique of Hank Aaron, the greatest American home run hitter.

In spite of Arakawa's help, the early part of 1962 was a disaster for Oh. Then in June, Arakawa ordered Oh to bat one-footed, holding his right, or front, foot off the ground. It was an extreme measure to solve a hitch, a double back-swing, that Oh had developed. Because he would have fallen down if he tried a double back-swing, it worked. He got a single and a home run the first two at bats, and Oh's famous "flamingo," or scarecrow, stance was born. By the end of the year, Oh was hitting .272 and led the league in home runs (38), games played (134), runs scored (79), total bases (281), runs batted in (95), walks (84), and intentional walks (9). It was a stunning turn-around. There developed the so-called O-N Cannon, the middle of the order for the Giants featuring first baseman Oh and third baseman Nagashima. They were the equivalent of Babe Ruth and Lou Gehrig for the Yankees, completely dominating the batting crowns for Japan's leagues.

From 1962 to 1979, Oh dominated Japanese baseball, leading the league each year in at least one, and usually in several, categories. He was extremely durable, playing every game eleven of his twenty-two years and never missing more than ten games in a season. He led the league in home runs thirteen straight times and fifteen in total. In 1964, he hit 55 home runs in a 140 game season, equal to Ruth's pace in his 60 to 154 games. From 1962 to 1980, he never hit less than thirty home runs in a season, including two other fifty-plus seasons and ten more in the forties. In the same years that he led in home runs, he also led the league in runs scored, thus benefitting from Nagashima's runs batted in ability. Oh himself led the league in runs batted in thirteen times, including a run of eight straight as Nagashima aged and retired. Oh also led the league in bases on balls nineteen times out of twenty-two years, including sixteen years in intentional walks. This occurred because of his fearsome reputation and his excellent eye. He was often compared to Ted Williams for his refusal to swing at a ball that was out of the strike zone. Surprisingly, he never led the league in strikeouts, and, as he matured, his strikeouts decreased. Five times he hit more home runs than he struck out, a very unusual feat for a power hitter in any league. He also led in total bases twelve times, in hits three times, and in doubles once. The most underrated part of Oh's game was his fielding. Nine times he won the golden glove as the first baseman with the highest fielding average, and his career fielding average was .994. He was the Gil Hodges of Japan, a fine power hitter who was slow afoot but graceful and quick and so knowl-edgeable about the game that he almost never made an error. Yet in Oh's autobiography, or in any other publication in English, this ability is never mentioned. Philosophically, Oh was a hitter who played first to be allowed to hit.

From 1965 to 1973, the Giants won both the Central League pennant and the Japan Series, the longest run of success in Japanese baseball history, surpassing the runs of the great Yankee teams of the 1930's and 1940's. In 1973 and 1974, Oh reached his zenith with back-to-back triple crowns, leading the league both times in home runs, runs batted in, and batting average, something no other player has ever done in any league.

By 1975, Oh's goal became surpassing Babe Ruth in home runs and, if possible, his friend Hank Aaron, who was still playing and with whom Oh put on some famous home run exhibition contests. On October 11, 1976, Oh hit home run number 715, surpassing Ruth. In the same month, Aaron re-tired, giving Oh a definite goal for the overall record. On September 3, 1977, Oh hit his 756th home run, surpassing Aaron. There was a tremendous outpouring of acclaim, particularly throughout Asia, where he was seen as a continent-wide hero. By the time Oh retired, he had hit 868 home runs with an average of one home run to every 10.7 at bats, a better average than either Ruth or Aaron. He had been an All Star for eighteen years and most valuable player in Japan's Central League nine times.

When Oh began to have vision and coordination problems, he tailed off to .236 in 1980, though he still hit thirty home runs. He retired at the end of the year and was named assistant manager of the Giants. At the end of the 1983 season, he became the manager. Originally, like so many other all-stars who became managers, he had problems, but in 1988 he led the Giants to their first pennant in several years and seems to have built another dynasty. His managerial style is a combination of Japanese hard work and discipline with the understanding of how to use star players to the best of their ability.

Summary

By consensus, Sadaharu Oh was the greatest player in Japanese baseball history, the only one whom all observers agree could have been a star in the American major leagues. He hit more home runs, 868, than any other man in organized baseball while playing twenty-two years with the Yomiuri Giants in the Central League in Japan. When he retired, he also held the Japanese career records in runs batted in, runs scored, and total bases as well as the second highest marks in doubles and games played.

No one ever dominated an organized baseball league so completely for so long. Ruth won twelve home run titles and Aaron won four, but Oh won that title in the Central League fifteen times. His domination in runs batted in is actually even more astounding: He won the title thirteen times. His 2,504 bases on balls are more than 400 more than any other player, and no American player has won the Most Valuable Player Award more than three times—Oh won it nine times.

Philosophically and psychologically, Oh's dedication to Japanese self-discipline and martial arts was quite significant in enhancing not only his own reputation but also that of those aspects of life. Yet at the same time, his continuing status as a Chinese national remains one of the principal symbols of the Japanese internationalization movement. Nothing can be more symbolic of the tremendous popularity that Oh, more than any other player and manager, brought to Japanese baseball than the Tokyo Dome, which opened in the spring of 1988. It is the "House that Oh built."

Bibliography
Deford, Frank. "Move Over for Oh-san." *Sports Illustrated* 47 (August 15, 1977). This is an excellent summary of Oh's life and hitting techniques. It emphasizes heavily his Chinese heritage and the discrimination that has been occasioned by that heritage. It was written just before Oh broke Aaron's record.
Obojski, Robert. *The Rise of Japanese Baseball Power.* Radnor, Pa.: Chilton Books, 1975. Much more popularistic than Whiting, this book deals often with Oh. There is, however, no specific section outlining his life and accomplishments.
Oh, Sadaharu, and David Falkner. *Sadaharu Oh: A Zen Way of Baseball.* New York: Time Books, 1984. This is Oh's autobiography, written while he was still an assistant manager. He emphasizes Japanese philosophy and martial arts as well as baseball. In many ways it is a tribute to Arakawa, but it also includes excellent statistics and an appendix giving the opinions of many American major leaguers about Oh. It is by far the most comprehensive of all books.
Whiting, Robert. *The Chrysanthemum and the Bat: Baseball Samurai Style.* New York: Dodd, Mead, 1977. This is the best overview of Japanese baseball in English. It devotes one section to Oh who, though not yet retired, is seen as the most outstanding of all Japanese players. He also appears many other times in the book. It is only here that one can learn that Oh was extremely well-paid with a total income of some $400,000 a year in the mid 1970's. Oh is also shown as modest, hardworking, and extremely popular.
_____. "The Master of Besaboru." *Sports Illustrated* 71 (August 21, 1989): 68-69. This is a short section of a major summary of Japanese sports. It is the best commentary in English on Oh's managerial style. Oh is the only Japanese baseball player or manager mentioned by name.

Fred S. Rolater

JAN HENDRIK OORT

Born: April 28, 1900; Franeker, The Netherlands

Area of Achievement: Astronomy
Contribution: Oort is one of the most significant astronomers of the twentieth century. He was the first to postulate the vast swarm of comets known subsequently as the Oort cloud. He was one of the pioneers of radio astronomy, and he is one of the leaders in establishing the structure of the Milky Way Galaxy.

Early Life
Jan Hendrik Oort was born in Franeker, The Netherlands, on April 28, 1900, the son of Abraham Hermanus Oort, a physician, and Ruth Hannah Faber Oort. His grandfather, a professor of Hebrew at the University of Leiden, was one of the translators of the Bible into the Dutch Leiden edition.

Following his graduation from the Leiden *Gymnasium* in 1917, Oort enrolled in the University of Gröningen, where he studied under the prominent astronomer Jacobus Kapteyn. He spent the years 1922 to 1924 in the United States as a research assistant at Yale University and became familiar with Harvard University astronomer Harlow Shapley's study of the Galaxy. Upon his return to The Netherlands, Oort began working at the University of Leiden, an association that would last throughout his career. He was appointed an instructor in 1926, after receiving his Ph.D. from the University of Gröningen with a dissertation on high-velocity stars.

Oort married Johanna Maria Graadt van Roggen on May 24, 1927. In that same year, he began establishing his reputation as a major scholar with the presentation of two papers on the rotation of the galactic system.

Life's Work
Although it hardly reflects the full range of his accomplishments in the world of astronomy, Oort's name and reputation are guaranteed longevity through the Oort cloud—the conglomeration of comets he hypothesized in 1950—and, to a lesser extent, by the Oort constants of galactic rotation and Oort's limit, the value of density near the Galaxy's midpoint. Despite the public recognition inherent in the name of the comet cloud, however, Oort's greatest achievements lie in his contributions to an understanding of the structure and function of the Galaxy.

Oort began his career by studying under Jacobus Kapteyn, one of the pioneers of galactic research. By 1922, Kapteyn had spent sixteen years mapping the galaxy. Although Kapteyn's map showed the Galaxy as only half its actual size, he was correct in his assessment of its shape as a disk with a central bulge narrowing toward the edges (something like a discus). After sharing the Bachiene Foundation Prize in 1920 for his paper on stars of the F, G, K, and M types, Oort turned his attention to Kapteyn's researches. Oort began studying stars of high velocity, which had proved difficult to reconcile with a galactic model that had the Sun near its center. His analysis of high-velocity stars and his close observation of Shapley's work during his research assistantship in the United States convinced Oort that the Galaxy was much larger than Kapteyn had assumed.

Oort's two 1927 papers furthered the work of Bertil Lindblad of the Stockholm Observatory. The papers argued that the Galaxy rotates not as a unit but more like the solar system, with those stars far from the center moving slower and those close to the center, faster. Through elaborate calculations involving rotational velocities of various stars, Oort was able to estimate the galactic mass, the number of stars, and the dimensions of the Galaxy. As Bengt Stromgren observed in awarding the Vetlesen Prize to Oort, ". . . it was only through Professor Oort's detailed analysis . . . that the hypothesis was finally proved. This is an example of one paper changing the whole outlook of the astronomical community."

In 1935, Oort was promoted to professor of astronomy, and, during that decade, he turned his attention to the distribution of stars in the Galaxy, realizing that Kapteyn's problem had been the interstellar dust that obscures the view of the distant parts of the Galaxy. Although Oort's theory of galactic structure was accepted by the scientific community, it was not possible to test his hypothesis until the development of radio astronomy. During World War II, with the occupation of The Netherlands by the Nazis, the Leiden Observatory was closed, and Oort and his colleagues continued their work only with the greatest of difficulties. Nevertheless, one of the most important discoveries for modern astronomy was made by Oort's colleague Hendrik Van de Hulst. Van de Hulst's work was based upon the principle that the hydrogen atom periodically emits radio waves at a constant wavelength of 21 centimeters. Though this characteristic is useless in local applications, in the vastness of space there is a sufficient number of atoms to be measured. Immediately following the war, Oort and Van de Hulst began working toward a test of Van de Hulst's hypothesis, but it was not until 1951 that they were able to do so. The theory, which had been independently reached by the Soviet scientist I. S. Shklovsky, proved to be true and, coupled with the building of large radio telescopes, led to the establishment of radio astronomy, the most important step in studying the Galaxy. The 21-centimeter waves pass through the dust and gas and allow astronomers to "see" as they cannot with optical telescopes. Meanwhile, also in collaboration with Van de Hulst, Oort, who had been appointed director of the Leiden Observatory following the war, in 1946 published a study of the clouds of gas and dust and subsequently showed that these clouds surrounding bright, hot stars can provide the material for the spontaneous formation of new stars.

In 1950, Oort made public the theory that led to the naming of the Oort cloud. His observations of the actions of nineteen long-period comets led him to the conclusion that there is a vast body of comets—in the trillions—consisting largely of debris from the disintegration of a planet. As a result of gravitational forces from various stars, comets are periodically thrust into orbits that bring them into the solar system. Oort theorized that there must be a swarm of these comets extending almost to the nearest stars, but their tie to the solar system suggests that they were formed soon after the planetary system itself. It is again a measure of Oort's careful reasoning and analysis that his theory is accepted almost universally despite the total absence of visual evidence.

By 1954, Oort and Van de Hulst had completed a map of the spiral structure of the Galaxy's outer region based on their radio-wave analysis. Oort also showed that the part of the Galaxy that is visible is far too small to account for its gravitational attraction on distant stars—evidence of a black hole in the Galaxy. In 1956, Oort and Van de Hulst revealed the discovery of radio signals produced by ionized hydrogen in space. Further investigation showed that these emissions occurred across the Galaxy, and, using the 21-centimeter wavelength, they established the rotational period of the Galaxy at 225,000,000 years.

In 1956, with T. Walraven, Oort engaged in the first extensive examination of the light polarization in the Crab nebula, a gaseous mass assumed to be the result of the fabled supernova of A.D. 1054. In a 1957 article in *Scientific American*, Oort argued that the light of this nebula consists of synchrotron radiation produced by high-velocity electrons spiraling about large magnetic fields, in accordance with a theory of Shklovsky. This phenomenon is believed to be responsible for the significant radio-wave radiation from the Crab nebula and other radio sources in space.

In the late 1950's, Oort and Australian Frank Kerr discovered that the galactic core consists of "turbulent" hydrogen that is constantly expanding outward only to be replaced by other hydrogen falling back into the center from the top and bottom of the central bulge. Oort's observations suggest that a massive explosion in the core of the disk, perhaps ten million years ago, produced this turbulence. Further radio analysis allowed him to establish the Galaxy as a rapidly whirling disk with a jagged edge produced by the juxtaposition of rapidly rotating material on the inside and material of slow rotation on the outside. In 1964, Oort and G. W. Rougoor discovered a ring of neutral hydrogen 3,000 parsecs from the galactic center. These gases, which form the spiral arms of the Galaxy, are expanding rapidly outward and also provide support for the hypothesis of a major explosion.

Oort then began studying the space through which the Galaxy moves, both on its own and as part of the cluster of galaxies to which it belongs. His most significant observation was the nearly limitless clouds of hydrogen through which the Galaxy moves. He hypothesized, from the fact that the densest part of this hydrogen corona was above, that the Galaxy was moving upward. He also theorized that while some gas was absorbed and other gas was moving outward, the fact that some was moving inward would double the mass of the Galaxy every three billion years and also effect a change in its shape.

In addition to his duties in Leiden, Oort served from 1935 to 1948 as general secretary of the International Astronomical Union and from 1958 to 1961 as its president. He has been the recipient of numerous honorary degrees and other awards, including the 1942 Bruce Medal from the Astronomical Society of the Pacific, the Gold Medal of the Royal Astronomical Society in 1946, and the Vetlesen Prize (established to supplement the Nobel Prizes in areas where they are not awarded) in 1966.

Summary

Jan Hendrik Oort's long and distinguished career has been characterized by steady progress toward the solutions to the problems which he has undertaken. From the beginning, he demonstrated the ability to work well with his colleagues and students. From his first modification of Kapteyn's galactic model, he demonstrated the capacity for detailed and painstaking research even—as in the case of the German Occupation—in the face of exceptional difficulty. While the ever more sophisticated methods of modern astronomy have modified or enhanced some of his theoretical work, his methods were so precise, his research so painstaking, and his arguments so convincing that the scientific mainstream accepted his theories even when no direct visual evidence existed.

Highly respected by his contemporaries, Oort has cast a long shadow. His galactic formulations and his pioneering work in radio astronomy, his postulation of the comet cloud and his analysis of the Crab nebula, his administrative work, and his encouragement of others justify Carl Sagan's assertion that "Jan Oort . . . perhaps more than any other person in the twentieth century has revolutionized our knowledge of the Galaxy."

Bibliography

Pfeiffer, John. *The Changing Universe: The Story of the New Astronomy.* New York: Random House, 1956. A good popular introduction to radio astronomy. The author devotes several pages to the work of Oort and Van de Hulst.

Ritchie, David. *Comets: The Swords of Heaven.* New York: New American Library, 1985. One of the better books to capitalize on the arrival of Halley's Comet. Contains a brief discussion of the Oort cloud.

Sagan, Carl, and Ann Druyan. *Comet.* New York: Random House, 1985. In one of his best-selling scientific works, Sagan and his novelist wife have assembled an impressive study of comets from both a scientific and a cultural perspective. Their discussion of Oort and the Oort cloud is outstanding. Profusely illustrated, this is a truly beautiful book.

Stromgren, Bengt. "An Appreciation of Jan Hendrik Oort." In *Galaxies and the Universe*, edited by Lodewijk Woltjer. New York: Columbia University Press, 1968. The Vetlesen tribute to Oort by the eminent Danish astronomer is an excellent commentary on Oort's career to that point.

Struve, Otto. "The Origin of Comets." In *The Origin of the Solar System*, edited by Thornton Page and Lou Williams Page. New York: Macmillan, 1966. This article, which first appeared in 1950, summarizes one of Oort's papers, which concluded with the theory of the comet cloud.

Tayler, R. J. *Galaxies: Structure and Evolution*. London: Wykeham, 1978. This book in the Wykeham Science series is aimed at high school seniors and first-year undergraduates. The book presents the full mathematical details and applications of both Oort's constants and Oort's limit.

Daniel J. Fuller

ALEKSANDR IVANOVICH OPARIN

Born: March 2, 1894; Uglich, Russia
Died: April 21, 1980; U.S.S.R.
Areas of Achievement: Biochemistry, botany, and biology
Contribution: Oparin was the principal pioneer in theorizing on the origins of life on Earth from inorganic matter. Of major importance also were his works which dealt with the biochemistry of plant material, from which he successfully developed the principles of Soviet biochemistry based on biocatalysis.

Early Life
Born on March 2, 1894, in the small village of Uglich, near Moscow, Aleksandr Ivanovich Oparin was the youngest of three children in a typical Russian family. Because the area lacked a secondary school, Oparin's family moved to Moscow when he was nine, making it possible for him to continue his education. Details of his younger years are scant until he reached college age. Attaining a complete secondary education, in which he distinguished himself by his abilities in science, Oparin decided to attend Moscow State University. There he became interested in plant physiology, studying in the natural sciences department of the physico-mathematical faculty. While at the school, he became associated with and greatly influenced by K. A. Timiryazev, who had known Charles Darwin and was a determined exponent of his theory of evolution. Oparin himself was drawn to Darwin's theory of natural selection, a viewpoint that would dominate his later career and be a special feature of his theory of the beginnings of life.

Life's Work
Impressed with the ideas inherent in contemporary Darwinian thinking, particularly that of selection for characteristics best adapted to a specific environment, Oparin began to extend the theory of evolution to the possible biochemical origin of life. Graduated in 1917, Oparin worked in several research institutes and institutions of higher learning, doing research under A. N. Bakh in biochemistry and botany. In 1922, his ideas, already in a concrete form, were presented at a meeting of the Russian Botanical Society, causing quite a stir, particularly among critics of the idea that life could form from nonliving chemicals. The entire topic of life's original beginnings had been ignored for years because of a basic biological assumption that "life begets life," which was prevalent since Louis Pasteur's experiments put the final demise to the idea of spontaneous generation of organic bodies, and also because of the tremendous philosophical and religious issues inherent in the subject. With the collapse of the vitalistic theory, removing the need for a spiritual force animating matter to distinguish it from nonliving material,

Great Lives from History

it became possible to explain life exclusively in terms of chemistry and physics, an outlook readily adopted by members of the physical sciences.

Oparin's theory was based on three premises, derived from his ideas on how life might have arisen in the primitive conditions that existed on Earth some three billion years previously. He assumed that the first organisms arose between 4.7 and 3.2 billion years ago in the ancestral world seas. The oceans, in the process, had derived the necessary chemicals for complete organic synthesis from the primordial atmosphere, consisting of methane, hydrogen, ammonia, and water, much like the atmospheres today encircling the giant planets Jupiter and Saturn. These earliest organisms would not have been able to synthesize their own food but rather must have been hetero-trophs, deriving nutrients from the surrounding medium or from consuming each other—this was in conflict with the then-current idea that all the early life-forms were autotrophs, making their own food supplies. Second, Oparin speculated that there was a virtually unlimited, continual supply of energy usable by the organisms, most likely in the form of sunlight, particularly ultraviolet, but also possibly from other sources (including volcanoes, light-ning discharges in electrical storms, meteoric actions, and cosmic rays). Since this energy was continually added, life forming was not limited by the second law of thermodynamics acting in a closed system. Finally, Oparin postulated that life had to be characterized by a high degree of structural and functional organization before it could be called alive. This last point stood strongly at odds with the prevailing view that life was basically molecular in nature. To back up his arguments, he showed, by using well-known chemi-cal reactions, how molecules might combine to form the important organic molecules and amino acids needed. Through painstaking laboratory experi-ments, he was able definitively to answer his critics, particularly as to the feasibility of reactions being caused by energy from either electrical storms or ultraviolet radiation from the sun. His findings, although they did not answer the question of how primitive organisms could reproduce, suggested that the necessary degree of order in protein structure probably resulted from restrictions imposed on the binding of amino acids through their shapes and electric charge distribution. Oparin showed conclusively that enzymes, as proteins, functioned much more efficiently in synthetic cells than in an ordi-nary aqueous solution. This idea was critical to later experiments with mi-croscopic droplets, called "coacervates," of gelatin and gum arabic that demonstrated that the droplets, in a water and sugar solution, would grow and continually reproduce by budding.

Oparin's basic theory, published in 1924, reached the general public in 1936 in *Vozniknovenie zhizni na zemle* (*The Origin of Life*, 1939). This single work stimulated great interest and was first tested analytically in 1953 by S. L. Miller and Harold Urey. These two scientists used a mixture of Oparin's gases to simulate the early atmosphere of primordial Earth with electrical discharges, simulating lightning bolts for energy that ran through the circulating gases. After the test period of two weeks, the chemicals that were turning the water turbid were found to be compounds of sugars, complex carbohydrates, and amino acids, the latter being the basic material for producing proteins and enzymes. Additional confirmation of Oparin's idea came almost at the same time, with the discovery of fossilized amino acids in rocks dating some three billion years old. C. Ponnamperuna complemented Oparin's theory by performing the same experiments but altering the original mixture of gases, adding other compounds and molecules quite regularly found in volcanic discharges. He showed that, in support of Oparin's ideas, one could easily make nucleotides, dinucleotides, and ATP (adenosine triphosphate, the energy molecule in the cells)—more organic materials necessary for life. Oparin himself carried the work forward when he was able in the laboratory to polymerize adenine to form droplets that he called protobionts. These droplets carried out many of the normal processes associated with life such as absorbing molecules from the surrounding media, metabolizing those molecules, recombining the ingredients in their own structures, and reproducing by division. Oparin believed that these early creations were alive because of their spectacular ability to reproduce and to take in and use foodstuffs.

In 1929, Oparin became professor of plant biochemistry at Moscow State University. In 1935, he helped found, with the botanist Bakh, the Bakh Institute of Biochemistry at the Academy of Sciences of the Soviet Union in Moscow. He was appointed by the government to be deputy director of the institute until 1946, when he became the director, a position he held until his death in April, 1980. From 1948 to 1955, Oparin also served as the academician-secretary of the department of biology of the Soviet Academy of Sciences. For his work, he was the noteworthy recipient of the A. N. Bakh Prize in 1950 and the Élie Metchnikoff Gold Prize in 1950.

Summary

Aleksandr Ivanovich Oparin became one of the best-known Soviet biochemists internationally. After being graduated from Moscow State University in biological chemistry, he helped cofound the Institute of Biochemistry. His main works dealt with the development of biochemical principles necessary for processing plant raw materials, processes vital to the economy of his country. He became greatly interested in the enzymatic activities in plants, the study of such enzymes leading to his work on the origin of terrestrial life. He was able to show through scientific experiments that biocatalysis was the basis of the production in nature of a large number of food products, the combined operation of molecules and enzymes together being necessary for the formation of starches, sugars, and other carbohydrates and proteins found in usable plants. Virtually alone, he developed the principles of Soviet technical botanical biochemistry.

He is best known worldwide for his hypotheses on the origin of life on the planet, first made available in 1922, and for *The Origin of Life*. According to his theory, life originated on Earth as a result of evolution acting on molecules formed from simpler combinations created in Earth's primordial atmosphere by violent energy discharges. Such complex molecules, raining down on the oceans, came together to react and produce structures with the basic characteristics of life, including, as he showed in the laboratory, the ability to grow, metabolize, and reproduce. Subsequent work by others has given credence to many of his ideas.

As a result of his work, Oparin was elected president in 1970 of the International Society for the Study of the Origin of Life, becoming honorary president in 1977. Over the years, he has been a member of numerous scientific societies, including the academies of Bulgaria, East Germany, Cuba, Spain, Italy, and the Leopoldine German Academy of Researchers in the Natural Sciences. He received numerous awards and medals including one as Hero of Socialist Labor (1969), the Lenin Prize (1974), five Orders of Lenin, two other Soviet orders, and many foreign awards. He was a member of the Soviet Committee in Defense of Peace and a member and vice president of the International Federation of Scientists. Oparin's participation contributed to his belief in world peace and a harmony well worth looking for overriding the magnificence of nature.

Bibliography

Bernal, J. D. *The Origin of Life*. Cleveland: World Publishing, 1967. Provides a detailed review of the known characteristics of life and the various solutions that have been proposed to account for its origin. Many ideas are presented as extensions of those of Oparin. The importance of primeval conditions is stressed. Includes an extensive bibliography and a very usable glossary of necessary terms.

Cairns-Smith, A. G. *The Life Puzzle: On Crystals and Organisms and on the Possibility of a Crystal as an Ancestor.* Edinburgh, Scotland: Oliver and Boyd, 1971. An investigative account of how life could have arisen from developments within crystalline matter. Stressing the relationships between inorganic crystals and organic forms, the author clearly presents the rationale for the belief that life could arise from nonliving forms.

Calvin, Melvin. *Chemical Evolution: Molecular Evolution Towards the Origin of Living Systems on the Earth and Elsewhere.* New York: Oxford University Press, 1969. An older book that presents in detail the evidence, both chemical and physical, for life arising in the past from inorganic materials. Traces the early finds of fossils to substantiate ideas such as Oparin's.

Fox, Sidney W. *Molecular Evolution and the Origin of Life*. San Francisco:

W. H. Freeman, 1972. This well-written work presents a detailed view of how, once chemical molecules of sufficient complexity are formed, processes associated with evolution take over to lead to life. Fox details many theories of life's formation, including the data and problems with each theory. Includes comprehensive references.

Futuyma, Douglas J. *Evolutionary Biology.* Sunderland, Mass.: Sineuer, 1986. A detailed explanatory treatment of how evolution works, starting from the formation of life molecules through the processes that have acted on Earth for four billion years. Encompasses a wide range of evolutionary thought and covers Oparin and others speculating on life's origins. Very well written and illustrated.

Hoyle, Fred. *The Intelligent Universe.* New York: Holt, Rinehart and Winston, 1983. A very enjoyable and well-illustrated book that explains how life might have formed anywhere in the universe as a result of chemical reactions occurring on Earth and in the depths of space. Presents scenarios dealing with the evolution of life under diverse conditions and the possible transmittal of life elsewhere in the galaxy.

Oparin, Aleksandr Ivanovich. *The Origin of Life on the Earth.* Edinburgh, Scotland: Oliver and Boyd, 1957. The original work on the possible causes and mechanisms for organic molecule formation early in Earth's history. Presents all Oparin's major ideas, including a discussion of molecular formation, energy sources, and reactions observed in the laboratory.

Arthur L. Alt

JOSÉ CLEMENTE OROZCO

Born: November 23, 1883; Ciudad Guzmán, Mexico
Died: September 7, 1949; Mexico City, Mexico
Area of Achievement: Art
Contribution: Orozco was one of the greatest muralists of the twentieth century and was considered the foremost to work in fresco. He was among the earliest Mexican artists to break away from European conventionalism and treat purely Mexican themes: The silent, suffering masses became a recurring interest in his art, reflecting his deep humanitarian concern and empathy for his people.

Early Life

José Clemente Orozco was born into a respected middle-class family on November 23, 1883, in Ciudad Guzmán in the coastal state of Jalisco in west-central Mexico. When he was two, the family moved to Guadalajara and then in 1890 to Mexico City, where he would grow up with his sister, Rosa, and brother, Luis. While attending primary school, Orozco passed by the workshop of Mexico's finest engraver, José Guadalupe Posada, and frequently stopped to watch as Posada produced caricatures for news stories, illustrations for children's books, and traditional Mexican folk art. By Orozco's own admission, it was Posada's work that first awakened his own artistic talents and taught him his earliest lessons about using color. He began to sketch and soon was enrolled in night classes in drawing at the Academy of Fine Arts of San Carlos, but Orozco's art studies were interrupted in 1897 when his family sent him to the School of Agriculture in San Jacinto.

Orozco was bored with his agrarian training, but it did give him some practical experience, and he was able to earn money drawing topographical maps. During this period, an accident damaged his eyes (he wore thick glasses), and his left hand became a fingerless stump (probably the reason for his preoccupation with hands in his paintings). He next entered the National Preparatory School, where he studied architecture for four years, but his obsession with painting eventually led him back to the Academy of Fine Arts in 1905. Since his father had died, Orozco earned his way by working as a draftsman and doing architectural drawings. At the academy, he had only a brief introduction to the methods of Antonio Fabrés, a masterful academic Spanish painter, but embraced wholeheartedly the latter's insistence on intense training, discipline, and photolike exactness in reproducing nature.

While at the academy, Orozco met Gerardo Murillo, recently returned from studies in Rome and Paris. A radical student who rejected conventional artistic views and Mexican subservience to Spain and Europe, Murillo had taken an Aztec name, calling himself "Dr. Atl." Atl's violent anticolonial views began to sway Orozco and other students away from dependence on a European style and toward Mexican-oriented themes in art. For the first time, Mexican painters began to look to their own country for inspiration, and a purely Mexican style of art began to emerge. For Orozco, a strong, dramatic style began to overwhelm his earlier traditionalist training.

Life's Work

In 1910, with Atl as their leader, Orozco and other emerging "Mexican" artists gave their first exhibit at a state exhibition to celebrate the first hundred years of Mexican independence. Originally, the exhibit was to feature only Spanish artists, but Atl objected and conducted negotiations that enabled the group to show their art also. The exhibit—the first of Mexican artists—met with unexpected success. The group next formed a society called the Artistic Center and secured wall space from the government to paint murals. Just as work was beginning at the amphitheater of the National Preparatory School, the Revolution of 1910 began on November 20, and the project was necessarily shelved.

Orozco showed little interest in the new government of Francisco Madero, believing it offered nothing new. When student strikes closed the academy, he spent the winter of 1911-1912 doing anti-Madero caricatures for an opposition newspaper, claiming he was an artist and had no political convictions. When the academy reopened in 1913, Orozco gave the new curriculum a try but soon left, unimpressed, disliking the emphasis on French Impressionists. He began to find inspiration for his developing expressionist style in the brothels and dark streets of the Mexico City counterculture and produced a series of watercolors of prostitutes—who became a major symbol in his art—and their environs known collectively as the *House of Tears*.

Civil war erupted in 1914. Orozco's damaged hand foiled every attempt to draft him, but he produced satirical caricatures for *La Vanguardia*, a prorevolutionary newspaper, which supported the cause of General Venustiano Carranza and was edited by Dr. Atl. There were moments when Orozco could not help but be amused by the confused antics of the dissident generals, but the violence, bloodshed, terror, and mutilated and mangled bodies he personally observed were what he remembered and what affected his art. In 1916, Orozco had his first one-man exhibit, which included *House of Tears*, and, the following year, he produced a series of watercolors called *Sorrows of War*.

Critics and moralists did not react favorably to his work, and insecure politicians winced at his earlier published cartoons and caricatures. Orozco found it opportune to spend several years in the United States. He lived in San Francisco and New York, where he had a brief meeting with David Siqueiros, another of Mexico's emerging artistic giants. These years were not happy ones for Orozco, but what he observed was not lost on his artist's eye.

In 1920, Orozco returned to Mexico, where he found the new government of Álvaro Obregón sympathetic with the old ideas of the Artistic Center. The "Mexican Muralist" movement began in 1922 when Orozco, Diego Rivera, Siqueiros, and others were commissioned by the minister of education to adorn the walls of the National Preparatory School. Lacking experience, the artists' first results were disappointing, and much in the murals betrayed a European rather than Mexican style of execution. The murals were disliked and defaced by students, who drove Orozco and Siqueiros out. In 1926, Orozco was invited back to complete his frescoes. He gradually developed his own personal, distinctive style, exemplified in the finest of his early work, *The Trench*, and also in *Cortes and Malinche*. During this period, Orozco also completed *Omniscience* (1925) in the House of Tiles, and *Social Revolution* (1926) in Orizaba at the Industrial School.

The agitation caused at home by the unpopular art and views of Orozco and his fellow artists, as well as a growing family (he had married Margarita Valladares on November 23, 1923) that was becoming more difficult to support (his third child had just been born), prompted him to leave for New York, where he arrived in December, 1927. He was promised a three-month subsidy by the secretary of foreign relations. While in New York, he met Mrs. Alma Reed and Madame Sikelianos, whose spacious house on Fifth Avenue had become an international salon for intellectuals, poets, artists, and revolutionaries. The women were interested in Orozco's paintings and sketches of revolution and exhibited them in their house; they also influenced him with their own interest in Greek culture and classical scholarship. Through their patronage, Orozco became better known. An exhibition at the Marie Sterner Gallery (1928) was followed by a showing of his earlier fresco studies for the National Preparatory School by the Art Students' League (1929). Reed dedicated her new Delphic Studios to Orozco and exhibited his paintings of New York and Mexico.

In 1930, Orozco received his first commission to do a mural in the United States from Pomona College in Claremont, California, which wanted a Mexican artist to decorate the student refectory. There he would execute his *Prometheus*, departing temporarily from Mexican subjects and social criticism in favor of a classical and more universal theme (reflecting the influence of Reed's salon). The colossal figure of the immortal, self-sacrificing Titan, leaning on one knee, his curved body and muscular shoulders stretching upward with their burden, recalls Michelangelo and El Greco. Holding it aloft in his hands, the bright gift of fire emerges from the browns and grays of the lower mural to offer liberation, enlightenment, and purification. Yet, fire can also destroy. Fire became a major symbol in Orozoco's work. The *Prometheus* is less stylized and more expressionistic than earlier frescoes. At the time, only his sponsors were pleased with the result, and Orozco earned little money for his efforts.

Unfortunately, Orozco became overly technical in his next set of murals at the New School for Social Research (1930-1931) in New York City. Influenced by a then-current theory known as "dynamic symmetry," his execution of themes concerned with universal brotherhood, world revolution, and arts and sciences was rigid and mechanical, a disappointing sequel to the *Prometheus*. Orozco followed this project with a brief trip to Europe to see the great paintings in the museums and churches of England, France, Italy, and Spain. When he returned, he began decorating the library at Dartmouth College in New Hampshire (1932-1934), where he incorporated much of what he had recently observed overseas, presenting his worldview in two main scenes entitled *The Coming of Quetzalcoatl* and *The Return of Quetzalcoatl*. The Mexican Revolution, the Great Depression, and an impersonal, industrialized urban society had provoked Orozco to contrast a primitive, non-Christian paradise of the past with a modern-day, Christian, capitalist hell.

By 1934, Orozco's reputation had been firmly established. He triumphantly returned to Mexico and painted a huge single mural, *Catharsis*, in the Palace of Fine Arts. In 1936, he was in Guadalajara, where he executed what most consider his greatest murals at the University of Guadalajara, the Governor's Palace (1937), and in the chapel at the orphanage of Hospicio Cabañas (1938-1939). Historical themes illustrating inhumanity developed in earlier works are repeated here, with greater negativity. In the Hospicio dome, Orozco painted the *Man of Fire*, the logical culmination of his art and thought, and a composition some regard as unique in the history of art. Here is represented a figure engulfed in flame with light radiating all about him—embodying hope, salvation, and creativity, it is a meditation on human existence itself.

No later murals match the emotional intensity of the Guadalajara group, and universal themes took a second place to nationalistic ones, perhaps because of World War II and contemporary events in Mexico. Orozco painted frescoes in the Ortíz Library (in Jiquílpan) in 1940 and, during the same year, painted a mural for the New York Museum of Modern Art, which he entitled *Dive Bomber*, a work not as powerful in form as his others, more abstract and with delicate colors. Returning to Mexico City in 1941, he adorned the walls of the Supreme Court Building. He never finished his project in the Chapel of Jesus Nazarene (1942-1944). His last murals were at the National School of Teachers (1947-48), the Museum of History at Chapultepec (1948), and in the Government Palace in Guadalajara (1948-1949). In 1947, he received his government's highest award for cultural achievement during the preceding five-year period. While Orozco's murals constitute the heart of his work, his easel paintings alone would have established his reputation as a great artist. His *Zapatistas*, for example, captures some of the essence of his murals but lacks the grandeur that only a large-scale painting can convey. The abstract quality and hint of mysticism in his work toward the end of his life suggest to some that he was on the verge of an artistic breakthrough when he died on September 7, 1949, at age sixty-five.

Summary

José Clemente Orozco was one of the monumental painters of the twentieth century and was foremost in reviving and perfecting the art of the mural, especially frescoes. He was one of the small group of Mexican artists who were the first to break with European colonial tradition and produce a purely Mexican, nationalistic art. Orozco believed that his paintings should convey ideas rather than stories. The bold form, social content, mordant colors, and revolutionary nature of his paintings made him unpopular in his own country, but Orozco persevered, developing his own expressionistic style. He finally found fame in the United States, where his work took on a more mature and international flavor, represented best in his work at Pomona College and, especially, the Dartmouth murals. His genius was finally recognized internationally.

A sensitive man who was deeply disturbed by the Mexican Revolution, the Great Depression, World War II, and other less traumatic but nevertheless horrifying aspects of the human condition, Orozco empathized with the suffering masses, decried inhumanity, and viewed modern industrial society as a seemingly godless, capitalistic wasteland compared to the paradise of primordial, non-Christian times. Yet in his paintings there is usually a glimmer of hope—if humankind will recognize and be guided by it. His greatest work was produced in Guadalajara from 1936 to 1939, culminating in what is perhaps his most representative painting, the *Man of Fire* in the dome of the Hospicio Cabañas. Few artists have had such an impact on their craft, yet because of Orozco's Mexican origins and socialistic tendencies, his name is not as well known as that of other artistic giants of this century, who are from Europe and the United States.

Bibliography

Charlot, Jean. *The Mexican Mural Renaissance, 1920-1925.* New York: Hacker Art Books, 1979. Contains two chapters on Orozco and some illustrations. Good brief survey of his role in Mexican mural painting by a French muralist who knew him.

Edwards, Emily. *Painted Walls of Mexico.* Austin: University of Texas Press, 1966. A survey from prehistoric to modern times. Includes a general discussion of Orozco's life, highlighting the major events and contributions. Contains some illustrations.

Fernandez, Justino. *A Guide to Mexican Art from Its Beginnings to the Present*. Translated by Joshua C. Taylor. Chicago: University of Chicago Press, 1969. Under the section on "Contemporary Art," this work devotes pages 161-170 to Orozco's life and work. Contains some illustrations. Good for a quick summary.

Helm, MacKinley. *Man of Fire: J. C. Orozco*. Reprint. Westport, Conn.: Greenwood Press, 1971. An interpretative memoir by a person who knew Orozco. The earliest major work on the artist, MacKinley's book attempts to understand the man and his art.

Orozco, José Clemente. *An Autobiography*. Translated by Robert C. Stephenson. Austin: University of Texas Press, 1962. Orozco's own account of his life to 1936. Indispensable but lacking pertinent detail.

——————. *José Clemente Orozco*. Introduction by Alma Reed. Mt. Vernon, N.Y.: William Edwin Rudge, 1932. An illustrated collection of Orozco's work to 1932. Minimal textual matter.

Reed, Alma M. *Orozco*. New York: Oxford University Press, 1956. A biography written by Orozco's New York patron and friend, who first introduced him to American art circles and was largely responsible for launching his international career.

Robert B. Kebric

JOSÉ ORTEGA Y GASSET

Born: May 9, 1883; Madrid, Spain
Died: October 18, 1955; Madrid, Spain
Areas of Achievement: Philosophy and journalism
Contribution: Ortega's books, journalism, and lectures commanded attention
   throughout Europe. His renown helped to bring Spain out of a long period
   of cultural isolation, and his thought contributed greatly to his country's
   intellectual reawakening.

Early Life

José Ortega y Gasset was born in Madrid, Spain, on May 9, 1883. His
father, José Ortega y Munilla, was a novelist and had formerly been editor
of *El Imparcial*, a leading Madrid newspaper founded by his grandfather. He
was first taught by private tutors. Subsequently, like so many European
intellectuals before him, he was schooled by Jesuits, at the College of Mira-
flores del Pala in Málaga. He later studied at the University of Madrid and at
the universities of Leipzig, Berlin, and Marburg in Germany. In 1904, he
received a doctorate in philosophy and literature from the University of
Madrid, and in the German years that followed he deeply imbibed neo-
Kantian philosophy. Ortega was named professor of metaphysics at the University of Madrid in 1910-1911. His association with that institution was to
continue until 1936, when he went into self-imposed exile during the Spanish Civil War.

The same year that he received his chair, he founded *Faro* (beacon), a
philosophical review. Shortly thereafter, he founded a second, *Europa*.
These were the first of many periodicals he was to found during his long
journalistic career. By roughly the age of thirty, Ortega was well launched
upon his multifaceted career as philosopher, journalist, author, educator, and
statesman. Having spent the years 1905-1907 at German universities, he had
become conversant with northern European ideas. He believed that Spanish
thought would tend to be superficial as long as Spain remained cut off from
the cultural roots of Europe. In his own journals and in the newspapers, he
tirelessly argued for a reintegration. By the time Spain's intellectual reawakening came to pass, Ortega was famous throughout the Spanish-
speaking world.

Life's Work

For several years, Ortega had been writing on Spanish problems, in his
own reviews and in *El Imparcial*, but it was a speech he made in 1914 that
catapulted him into national prominence. The speech, entitled "Old and New
Politics" and delivered at the Teatro de la Comedia, denounced the mon-

archy. Shortly thereafter, the League for Political Education was founded, and Ortega participated in the establishment of its monthly organ, *España*.

Also in 1914, Ortega published *Meditaciones del Quijote (Meditations on Quixote*, 1961), which contains the germs of his philosophy. The work contrasts the depth and profundity of German culture with the perceived superficiality of Spanish and Mediterranean culture. At this same time, the German writer Thomas Mann was exploring in fiction the different frames of mind in northern and southern Europe. In 1917, Ortega conducted a lecture tour in Argentina. Upon his return to Spain, he became one of the founders of the liberal newspaper *El Sol*. The paper was intended to counter the conservatism of *El Imparcial*, which his father had once edited.

The 1920's were a period of great literary productivity for Ortega. The title of *España invertebrada* (1921; *Invertebrate Spain*, 1937) is a metaphor for the nation's lack of an intellectual elite that could lead it out of its morass. Many essays that Ortega originally wrote for *El Sol* appear in this book and in *El tema de nuestro tiempo* (1923; *The Modern Theme*, 1931). The latter explores the different concepts of relativity that have influenced the author and states his philosophy more systematically than do his first two books. Also in 1923, Ortega founded yet another magazine: *La Revista de Occidente*, a literary monthly that soon came to be held in very high regard. It was in this journal that many European writers first appeared in Spanish.

By the end of the decade, Ortega and his fellow philosopher Miguel de Unamuno y Jugo were recognized as the foremost intellectuals in Spain. In 1928, Ortega again traveled in South America, where he was even more popular than Unamuno. His reception there was tremendously enthusiastic, but he soon returned to Spain to participate in the revolution that would lead in 1931 to the exile of King Alfonso XIII. In the same year, principally because of his work in the Association for Service to the Republic, he was elected deputy for Leon.

Ortega's political career was short-lived. In 1929, he had published *La rebelión de las masas (The Revolt of the Masses*, 1932), destined to become a best-seller in its English translation. This book, like the earlier *Invertebrate Spain*, had predicted that the hegemony of mass man would have dire consequences. When the republican movement rapidly proceeded far to the left of mere liberalism, Ortega broke with it. He also did not support the loyalists when civil war finally came. He fled to France instead.

His stated longings for the leadership of an intellectual aristocracy misled the theoreticians of the Falange, the Spanish Fascist organization. They believed that his sympathies were being altered in their favor, while he still desired a rule of enlightened liberalism. After the forces of Francisco Franco had triumphed, Ortega was offered a position as Spain's official philosopher. The regime also offered to publish a deluxe edition of his works, provided that he would delete certain essays and certain passages from others. He declined and remained abroad. He moved to Argentina, where earlier he had been well received, and in 1941 became professor of philosophy at the University of San Marcos, in Lima, Peru. This was a difficult period for Ortega. All of his political impulses were liberal, but he feared the results of an undifferentiated egalitarianism. Thus, he was condemned by the Right and Left alike. He did not return to his native country until 1945.

During his exile of almost a decade, Ortega had also lived in The Netherlands and Portugal. Upon his return to Spain, he chose not to reclaim his chair at the University of Madrid, although technically he still held the rank of professor there. Instead, he and Julián Marías founded a private institution of higher learning, the Instituto de Humanidades in Madrid.

In the same year (1948), his influential treatise on modern art, *La deshumanización del arte, e Ideas sobre la novela*, 1925, was translated into English under the title *The Dehumanization of Art and Notes on the Novel*. His interests continued to be wide-ranging. Toward the middle of his career, he had offered his theories on higher education—*Misión de la universidad* (1930; *Mission of the University*, 1944). During the last fifteen years of his life, he also addressed the daunting subjects of love—*Estudios sobre el amor* (1939; *On Love*, 1957)—and history—*Historia como sistema y Del imperio romano* (1941; *Toward a Philosophy of History*, 1941).

Ortega y Gasset was an intensely private man. Beyond his writings, he revealed little of himself to his readers. He was described physically by observers as a small, well-proportioned man, with dark olive features and bright, arresting eyes. During his last years, he lectured throughout Europe. He died in the city of his birth on October 18, 1955.

Summary

José Ortega y Gasset is acknowledged to be a beautiful stylist. Some critics have found his individual books disappointing and have implied that his style is superior to his thought. Julián Marías, however, who edited several volumes of his posthumous works, asserts that, despite surface indications, Ortega's philosophy is highly systematic. He saw no transcendent purpose in life and, since it consists of the present only, he argued that one should approach life as one approaches a game. Ortega's insistence that man must remain totally free, so that he can create his own life, has caused his name to be linked with existential philosophy. He held life to be the relationship between the individual and his environment—that is, each person is the ego plus its circumstances. He believed, therefore, that Aristotelian reason must be sometimes subordinated to the intuition and spontaneous insight that comes from life experiences. His adjective for this kind of biological reason is translated as "vital" or "living." Commentators have identified various influences upon Ortega's thought, foremost among them the differing relativities of Albert Einstein and Oswald Spengler.

Ortega's extensive use of the essay form meant that of necessity he often could not rigorously pursue ideas to their ultimate conclusions, in the manner of a dissertation. Yet his breadth of interests and mastery of language have earned for him a readership much larger than most serious philosophers can attract. An excellent example of both the benefits and hazards of his method is *The Dehumanization of Art and Notes on the Novel.* While it is one of the most influential statements on the art of the twentieth century, it is also—say many commentators—widely misunderstood. In books, journals, magazines, and newspapers, Ortega tirelessly sought to Europeanize Spain. Certainly not the least of his accomplishments was his profound effect upon the culture of his nation.

Bibliography

Díaz, Janet Winecoff. *The Major Themes of Existentialism in the Work of José Ortega y Gasset.* Chapel Hill: University of North Carolina Press, 1970. Examines Ortega's major works against the background of the existentialist tradition. Also contains a survey of the critical reaction to these works.

Ferrater Mora, José. *Ortega y Gasset: An Outline of His Philosophy.* London: Bowes & Bowes, 1956. This sixty-nine-page book uses a biographical method as the best approach to Ortega's nonsystematic philosophy.

Frank, Joseph. *The Widening Gyre: Crisis and Mastery in Modern Literature.* New Brunswick, N.J.: Rutgers University Press, 1963. In his chapter "The Dehumanization of Art," Frank notes that the influential essay of that name is universally accepted as a defense of modern art, while Ortega insisted that he was acting as neither judge nor advocate. Frank attempts to reassess Ortega's observations from a more balanced perspective.

Gray, Rockwell. *The Imperative of Modernity: An Intellectual Biography of Ortega y Gasset.* Berkeley: University of California Press, 1989. Coming as it does almost thirty-five years after the death of the subject, this biography benefits from the accumulated scholarship.

McClintock, Robert. *Man and His Circumstances: Ortega As Educator.* New York: Teachers College Press, 1971. This massive work (648 pages) studies Ortega's role as an educator. McClintock emphasizes the philosopher's view of the future of Western society.

Marías, Julián. *José Ortega y Gasset: Circumstance and Vocation.* Translated by Frances M. López-Morillas. Norman: University of Oklahoma Press, 1970. This exhaustive study (479 pages) originally appeared in 1960 under the title *Ortega, Revista de Occidente.* The work is considered the single most important treatment of Ortega's philosophy.

Ouimette, Victor. *José Ortega y Gasset.* Boston: Twayne, 1982. This is a comprehensive survey of Ortega's works, including the collections of his later and posthumous essays. Ouimette argues that, while Ortega almost always fails to see his insights through to their logical conclusions, he is consistently evocative.

Patrick Adcock

WILHELM OSTWALD

Born: September 2, 1853; Riga, Latvia
Died: April 4, 1932; Grossbothen, near Leipzig, Germany
Areas of Achievement: Chemistry, physics, and philosophy
Contribution: Ostwald's most notable work was in the field of chemistry, in which he is considered to be the "father" of physical chemistry and in which he was awarded the 1909 Nobel Prize. He was later nominated for a second Nobel Prize, this time in physics, for his work in the field of color science.

Early Life

Friedrich Wilhelm Ostwald, son of Gottfried Wilhelm and Elisabeth Leuckel Ostwald, was born in Riga, Latvia, on September 2, 1853, and spent the first thirty-four years of his life there and in nearby Dorpat (now Tartu). At the *Realgymnasium* at Riga, Ostwald required seven years to complete the curriculum normally finished in four. This delay can be attributed to the wide range of his interests, because during this period young Ostwald pursued studies in music, becoming proficient on both piano and viola; studied painting and handicrafts under the tutelage of his father; and set up a private laboratory in which he experimented in chemistry and physics, became an accomplished amateur photographer and film processor, and manufactured fireworks. The near disasters that accompanied the fireworks project taught him the need for more than a recipe and a desire. He knew he needed an understanding of what was occurring.

In 1872, following graduation from the *Realgymnasium*, Ostwald left Riga to attend the University of Dorpat and studied chemistry under Carl Schmidt and Johann Lemberg and physics with Arthur von Öttingen. More focused on his pursuits, Ostwald finished this part of his chemical education in only three years. Thereafter, he took positions as an unpaid assistant, first to Öttingen and later to Schmidt. Ostwald credited these two men as the main influences on his chemistry. Ostwald also realized the need for a strong mathematical background and proceeded to teach himself from a textbook by Karl Snell. Ostwald later gave Snell credit both for his sound mathematics and for his direction into the field of philosophy. He was awarded the doctorate in chemistry by the University of Dorpat in 1878 with a dissertation whose subject was optical refraction as a way to assess chemical affinity. Ostwald stayed in Dorpat, assisting at the university and teaching at the *Realgymnasium*.

In 1880, Ostwald married Helen von Reyher. Their marriage produced two daughters and three sons. His son, Karl Wilhelm Wolfgang, followed in his father's footsteps and was a prominent chemist, and one of his daughters, Grete, published an Ostwald biography, *Wilhelm Ostwald: Mein Vater*

(1953; Wilhelm Ostwald, my father). In 1881, Ostwald returned to Riga as professor of chemistry at the Polytechnic Institute. While holding this position, Ostwald began making scientific contributions that brought him to the attention of the world's chemists.

Life's Work

The branch of chemistry known as physical chemistry originated in a series of lectures on chemical affinity that Ostwald presented at the University of Dorpat in 1876. Notes from that series were expanded by research and reading and published as Ostwald's first book, *Lehrbuch der allgemeinen Chemie* (1885-1887; textbook of general chemistry), which presented a new organization of chemistry.

In 1881, Ostwald accepted the professorship of chemistry at the Riga Polytechnicum. At Riga, Ostwald became interested in Svante Arrhenius' ionic dissociation theory, and in 1886 Arrhenius accepted an invitation to work with Ostwald. The two worked closely, but on different problems, for years. Jacobus H. van't Hoff's publications on chemical dynamics were also noted by Ostwald. It was the importance of these new concepts of Arrhenius and of van't Hoff that Ostwald recognized and promoted in his writing. The controversy generated by Ostwald's "new chemistry" brought him wide recognition and the appointment as professor of physical chemistry at the University of Leipzig in 1887.

Ostwald organized the Department of Physical Chemistry and spent the years until 1906 strengthening it. The department was at its prime in 1899, and it was common to have forty students from around the world in Ostwald's laboratory. Research on such a large scale required special methods, and those developed by Ostwald are still seen in university research groups. Mature scientists acted as assistants to Ostwald and as liaison officers between Ostwald and the students. Each problem to be studied was chosen by consultation between Ostwald and the student. There were weekly seminars to present and discuss research progress. This way Ostwald exerted his influence on each investigation, though he did not directly participate in each one.

Many to-be-famous chemists worked in Ostwald's laboratory. Among them were Arrhenius (Nobel Prize in 1903), van't Hoff (Nobel Prize in 1901), Walther Hermann Nernst (Nobel Prize in 1920), and Americans Theodore William Richards, Arthur Amos Noyes, and Gilbert Newton Lewis. This succession of scientists solidified physical chemistry as a new branch of chemistry.

Ostwald was greatly involved with communicating knowledge. He published forty-five books, five hundred scientific papers, and fifty thousand reviews and in 1887 founded, jointly with van't Hoff, the *Zeitschrift für physikalische Chemie* (journal of physical chemistry). Ostwald continued as editor of this publication through the first one hundred volumes, stepping down in 1922. In 1894, Ostwald's *Die wissenschaftlichen Grundlagen der analytischen Chemie* (*The Scientific Foundations of Analytical Chemistry Treated in an Elementary Manner*, 1895) appeared and revolutionized analytical chemistry. From that time on, analytical chemistry was taught in terms of physical chemistry, and the measurement of physical properties became the common thread in all of chemistry.

Ostwald's 1901 discovery of a method to manufacture nitric acid is his only notable commercial contribution. The process freed Germany from dependence on foreign sources of nitrates for munitions manufacture, an important freedom to have as the world was building toward war.

At the turn of the century a confrontation occurred between two camps in the scientific world. Ostwald headed the "energetics" and Ludwig Boltzmann, also at Leipzig, headed the "atomistics." Ostwald and his followers claimed to represent "science without suppositions" and demanded that science be purely descriptive and deal only with correlating observable data. As late as 1904, Ostwald did not believe in the existence of atoms and would not use them, even as models, in explaining chemical observations. At some later date, he did relent and accept atoms as models, but he never did rely on them in his own work.

Ostwald was also involved outside chemical research, teaching, and publication. He published books and lectured internationally about methods of teaching, philosophy, painting, and educational reform and published a number of biographies. These activities caused Ostwald to be away from Leipzig much of the time and strained the relationship between Ostwald and his colleagues. This strain was relieved in 1906 when he admitted that he had become exhausted and had lost all interest in doing chemistry and resigned.

Ending his career at the university did not mean a quiet retirement. He had shown an interest in philosophy in publications at the turn of the century, and through these works, and others, Ostwald founded a branch of philosophy — natural philosophy. He led the movement for monism, a doctrine that stated that there is only one kind of substance or ultimate reality, and that reality is one unitary organic whole with no independent parts. To Ostwald, the ultimate was energy, as it had been in all of his chemical researches. He wrote and spoke widely on this topic from 1910 to 1914, when World War I brought the effort to an end.

Ostwald put his organizational abilities to work on the national and international scale. In Germany, he founded what became the Kaiser Wilhelm Institute, a national bureau of chemistry. He served on the International Commission for Atomic Weights from 1916 to 1932. He cooperated in the founding of the International Association of Chemical Societies in 1911.

The importance of Ostwald's discoveries in catalysis to the war effort is ironic, because he was an ardent pacifist. He considered war a horrible waste of energy and regularly attended and addressed peace congresses. His pleas for voluntary disarmament fell on deaf ears, however, and war came. Ostwald took no part in the war and was mentioned by some as a candidate for a Nobel Peace Prize.

Always interested in painting, Ostwald, in 1914, turned his skills to the study of color. He devised ways of measuring color, invented the instruments needed, set the standards, and wrote books that were accepted as the classics in the study of color. Ostwald believed that his work on color was his greatest contribution, and there were those in agreement who nominated him as a candidate for a Nobel Prize in Physics. Ostwald died on April 4, 1932, at his home, "Landhaus Energie," at Grossbothen, near Leipzig.

Summary

Wilhelm Ostwald contributed to scientific knowledge with several very sound pieces of chemical research, but his major impact was by way of his organizational skills, his skills as a systematizer, and his writing skills. Chemical knowledge in the 1880's was expanding at a fast pace and was branching out into considerable new ground. The niche that Ostwald chose to fill was that of synthesizer of this new knowledge to the end that it could be taught and built upon.

Wilder D. Bancroft, a student of Ostwald in 1892, distinguished three classes of scientists. The first group is composed of those who make great discoveries, the second those who see the importance and bearing of the discoveries and promote them, and the third the group who have to have discoveries explained to them. Ostwald stood at the head of the second group as a great protagonist and inspiring teacher, more greatly loved and greatly followed than any chemist of his time.

In matters not strictly in the field of chemistry, Ostwald also had vital ideas. He preached the need to conserve natural energy resources, promoted the organization of scientific work as the means to attain solutions to problems, and recognized that new ideas need a champion to push for their acceptance. In each of these ideas, Ostwald stands out as being well ahead of his time.

Bibliography

Bancroft, Wilder D. "Wilhelm Ostwald: The Great Protagonist." *The Journal of Chemical Education* 10 (1933): 539-542, 609-613. Bancroft was a doctoral student with Ostwald in the late 1880's and writes about Ostwald as chemist, as teacher, and as synthesizer of diverse information. This is the best and most personal comment, published in English, about Ostwald. This was published just following Ostwald's death.

Farber, Eduard. *Nobel Prize Winners in Chemistry.* New York: Henry Schuman, 1953. This text contains a chapter concerning Ostwald. Within the chapter there is a short biographical sketch, a description of the prizewinning chemistry, and an analysis of the consequence of that chemistry.

Harrow, Benjamin. *Eminent Chemists of Our Time*. 2d ed. New York: D. Van Nostrand, 1927. Although Ostwald is not treated in a separate chapter in this text, much of his impact on the structure of chemistry in his day is shown through the discussions of his contemporaries.

_____. "The Meeting of Ostwald, Arrhenius, and van't Hoff." *The Journal of Chemical Education* 7 (November, 1930): 2697-2700. Utilizing the recently published autobiography of Ostwald, Harrow concentrates on the details dealing with the way in which a remarkable friendship grew among the three founders of physical chemistry. This short article gives a close look into the meetings that led to Nobel Prizes for each of these men.

Hauser, Ernst A. "The Lack of Natural Philosophy in Our Education: In Memoriam of Wilhelm Ostwald." *The Journal of Chemical Education* 28 (September, 1951): 492-494. This article concerns itself with the philosophical aspect of Ostwald's life. It contains an extensive quotation translated from Ostwald's *Grundriss der Naturphilosophie* (1908).

Jaffe, George. "Recollections of Three Great Laboratories." *The Journal of Chemical Education* 29 (May, 1952): 230-238. Jaffe was the last personal student of Ostwald and writes of his recollections of the man and the laboratory. Jaffe also met van't Hoff and Arrhenius during this period and writes about the interrelationship of these three winners of the Nobel Prize in Chemistry.

Moore, Forris J. *A History of Chemistry*. 3d ed. New York: McGraw-Hill, 1939. Presents a concise biography of Ostwald and places his work in the context of the developing chemistry of that era.

Wall, Florence E. "Wilhelm Ostwald: A Study in Mental Metamorphosis." *The Journal of Chemical Education* 42 (January, 1948): 2-10. As the title suggests, this article follows the life of Ostwald from his earliest years through his chemical interests and on to the later eclectic years. There is a very good listing of relevant literature included with this article.

Kenneth H. Brown

J. J. P. OUD

Born: February 9, 1890; Purmerend, The Netherlands
Died: April 5, 1963; Wassenaar, The Netherlands
Area of Achievement: Architecture
Contribution: Oud is one of the founders of functional modern architecture, which through subtle techniques he imbued with an elegance and style achieved by few other architects. With a pronounced social commitment, Oud specialized in handsome yet low-cost housing and public buildings.

Early Life

Jacobus Johannes Pieter Oud showed an interest in architecture at an early age. Possibly because of the ferment involving architectural styles at the turn of the century as well as a decided turn toward social commitment by the more progressive European states, an architect friend of his father suggested the son concentrate on the technical rather than aesthetic aspects of architecture. Consequently, Oud studied at the Rijks Normal School for Drawing Masters in Amsterdam and the Technical School of the University of Delft. He then worked as a designer with architectural firms in both The Netherlands and Germany. His basic training was thorough, especially in the technical aspects of architecture and in the knowledge of building materials. While still a student, Oud designed his first building for a member of his family.

While at Delft, Oud came under the influence of Hendrik Petrus Berlage, an early functionalist and considered to be the father of modern Dutch architecture. Berlage emphasized structural rationalism in architecture involving simplicity of form and clarity of structure. According to Berlage, the aesthetic qualities of a building should derive from these guidelines and the building materials themselves rather than from deliberate ornamentation. A pioneer in city planning and an early environmentalist, Berlage stressed continuity and harmony in the urban fabric. His most noted building, the massive Stock Exchange in Amsterdam, while completely modern in concept, in its use of plain and glazed brick, hewn stone, and iron visually was in harmony with the existing buildings of the old city. Probably the greatest influence Berlage had on his pupil was his firm belief that architecture is art, not technology and engineering. It was an admonition that Oud never forgot.

Life's Work

In 1913, Oud established himself as an independent architect. His early designs were derivative, reflecting Berlage's influence: handsome and functional but not particularly distinguished. The change came in 1915, when Oud became aware of the work of the cubists and their message that it was not the object that was important but the emotion it transmitted to the spectator. To impart the message effectively, the cubists designed a universal language of fundamental forms: the cube, sphere, triangle, and circle. At this time, Oud met the aesthetic theorist Theo van Doesburg. Their friendship and collaboration effected the change in Oud's architectural style. In 1917, with other architects and artists, notably the abstract painter Piet Mondrian, they formed a revolutionary art group called *De Stijl* (the style) and published a magazine by the same name. Although Oud would become known as a *De Stijl* architect, the greatest influence on him would come from Mondrian's adaptation of cubism called neoplasticism. Neoplasticism did not make use of figurative elements but restricted design to the right angle in horizontal-vertical relation to the frame using primary colors together with white, black, and grey. In 1917, Oud designed a group of seaside houses for an esplanade above the beach at Scheveningen which were little more than cubic masses clearly showing the influence of neoplasticism. The project was never executed and probably could not have been without extensive modifications. The one building that Oud designed and had built completely in the neoplastic manner was the Café de Unie in Rotterdam, now destroyed.

In 1918, Oud became the architect for the City of Rotterdam; he was commissioned to help solve an acute housing shortage. At the time he had become aware of the *Neue Sachlichkeit* (new reality) movement in architecture—precursor of the International Style—and its message that the course of architecture would be determined by social and technological forces necessitating the development of the techniques of standardization and mass production.

Between 1918 and 1925, various socialistic Dutch governments sponsored comprehensive building programs whose primary objective was making housing for everyone a social right. The programs helped Oud achieve the architectural designs for which he is best known: three low-cost housing projects. All showed the *De Stijl* influence yet demonstrated the basic precept of functionalism, namely that form follows function, and as such Oud's designs were integrated into the broader more practical idiom of the International Style. The projects were working-class housing in the Hook of Holland (1924), residential housing in Kiefhoek (1925), and experimental housing the Weissenhof Settlement, Stuttgart, Germany (1927). Oud's sound technical training enabled him to make the often impractical *De Stijl* ideas reality. Although starkly austere, the designs of all three projects differed from the often impersonal rectangular International Style in that they bore the unmistakable Oud touch: meticulous workmanship, exquisite proportioning, and subtle, integrated ornamentation. Rounded corners softened the angularity of the buildings of the Hook of Holland project; integrated gardens lent a bucolic aspect to the Kiefhoek development; and even though the Weissenhof project, with its severe carefully syncopated geometric forms, most clearly showed the cubist influence, it was limited to the street façade.

The rear had charming gardens overlooked by traditional balconies. It was at Weissenhof that Oud raised the minimal worker's dwelling to a work of art. The Stuttgart exhibition, coordinated by Mies van der Rohe, was devoted to single family houses designed by the leading architects of the time, including Walter Gropius and Le Courbusier. Oud's project was among the most admired, and in 1932, when the New York Museum of Modern Art mounted its seminal exhibit that defined modern architecture and the International Style, Oud was one of four European architects whose works were displayed.

In 1933, Oud resigned as architect for the City of Rotterdam and resumed private practice. In 1938, his admirers were startled and some outraged by his design for a massive building in The Hague housing the offices of the Shell Oil Company. The *De Stijl* manner had given way to monumentality, symmetry, and ornamentation. Over a concrete skeleton, Oud fashioned a mantle of wheat-colored, hand-fired bricks, sandstone, and Majolica in novel decorative patterns. Toward the end of his life, Oud explained that his stockpile of ideas needed to be expanded and that the dispute between the old-fashioned and modern in architecture must end. It is a tribute to the greatness of Oud as an architect that in his Shell building he anticipated and was a pioneer in a movement in architecture beginning in the 1940's called "The New Empiricism" marked by a movement from established modernity and the enrichment of newer structures with patterns and traditional styles.

Between 1938 and his death in 1963, Oud either designed or designed and completed fourteen major projects. Among these was the charming Bio Resort Village near Arnhem for spastic children and the Congress Building in The Hague, a major complex incorporating assembly halls, theaters, recreational areas, and a hotel. The "village" is an exercise in miniature of city planning as can be seen in the organic relationship of the buildings. The cubist influence can be seen in the geometric forms of the buildings. Oud's fondness for integrated ornamentation can be seen in the mosaic that he commissioned from the Dutch artist Karel Appel and incorporated into the circular conical-roofed central administration building.

In 1955, Oud was given an honorary doctorate by the Technical University of Delft. The year before, he had moved to Wassenaar near The Hague, where he continued to practice architecture until his death in 1963.

Summary

J. J. P. Oud's greatness is derived from not only his skill as an architect in the modern manner but also his demonstrating that such architecture, while functional, can also be handsome and individualistic. Because of the relatively small number of buildings designed by Oud, there is a tendency among some critics to dismiss him as a major architect. What is overlooked is that in his work Oud was always the artist and the meticulous craftsman.

Each work was an individual creation, not to be altered to meet later exigencies. To be admired is Oud's strong social commitment, especially in the design of public housing that was not only serviceable and handsome but also, through techniques such as prefabrication and the innovative use of space, remarkably inexpensive. Another indication of Oud's greatness as an architect is his versatility, his ability to move from the stark rigidity of neoplasticism to the more traditional New Empiricism with no loss of artistic integrity.

Bibliography
Museum of Modern Art. *Modern Architecture International Exhibition.* New York: Museum of Modern Art, 1932. Although Oud's professional career had not reached the halfway point at the time this important exhibition was mounted, the projects for which he is most admired were completed. The book has a well-written essay by Russell Hitchcock on Oud, especially on his development as a *De Stijl* architect. The book contains a series of excellent black-and-white photographs of Oud's major works.
"Recent Works of a Pioneer: J. J. P. Oud." *Progressive Architecture* 42 (June, 1961): 72. Enthusiasm for Oud's earlier works often obscures the fact that he worked steadily until the time of his death on major projects that would have daunted a much younger man. Photographs and models for his Resort Village in Arnhem and the Congress Hall in The Hague, unfinished at the time of Oud's death, illustrate his mastery of conceptualizing large complexes.
Tafuri, Manfredo, and Francesco Dal Co. *Modern Architecture.* Translated by Robert Erich Wolf. New York: Harry N. Abrams, 1980. Throughout his professional life, Oud either worked with or was influenced by other artists and architects. This work is particularly valuable in differentiating modern architecture with which Oud is associated from earlier movements. It also gives details on the influence of other architects such as Berlage and the nature of his associations with the *De Stijl* group.
Wiekart, K. *J. J. P. Oud.* Translated by C. de Dood. Amsterdam: J. M. Meulenhoff, 1965. Probably the only available work in English on Oud that spans his entire career. Contains an excellent monograph on Oud's aesthetic and professional development. Of particular interest are the details of Oud's designing techniques: his attention to the most minute details in a design, even to the size of kitchen tiles; his selection of materials; and his specifications of workmanship. Contains an extensive bibliography, a list of all of Oud's projects and completed works, and forty-four black-and-white photographs of completed works, projects, and plans.
"The Work and Writings of J. J. P. Oud." *Architectural Design* 33 (July, 1963): 308-309. Oud was a prolific writer as well as a shrewd and witty

observer. Unfortunately, few of his writings have been translated from Dutch and German, both of which he utilized. This article contains selections from his writings dating from 1918 to 1957 and gives a valuable insight as to his reasons for modifying his architectural styles. There are twelve photographs of his works, including furniture and the delightful but now-destroyed Café de Unie.

Nis Petersen

VIJAYA LAKSHMI PANDIT

Born: August 18, 1900; Allahabad, India

Areas of Achievement: Diplomacy, government, and politics
Contribution: Pandit served as post-independence India's foremost diplomatic representative, holding the highest positions in international councils and in many ways helping to reconcile the bitter and deep disputes between India, its neighbors, and its former rulers.

Early Life

Vijaya Lakshmi Pandit was born on August 18, 1900, the eldest daughter of Motilal Nehru, a prosperous attorney, in the city of Allahabad. Her name at birth, Swarup Kumari ("Beautiful Princess"), was changed, according to the Hindu custom, upon her marriage at the age of twenty to Ranjit Sitaram Pandit, but as a child and throughout her life she was known by the nickname "Nan." Her elder brother, Jawaharlal Nehru, served as India's prime minister, and Pandit, along with her entire family, was an active participant in the Indian political struggles of the day to separate India from the British Empire.

Pandit's early life reached a watershed in 1920 during the turmoil following the Amritsar Massacres. The action by British General Reginald Dyer of allowing his troops to fire on demonstrators protesting British rule, killing 372 and wounding thousands, caused Pandit, along with the other members of her previously politically moderate family, to shift her allegiance to Mahatma Gandhi's satyagraha movement, which aimed through nonviolent methods to force the British from India completely. Given Pandit's upbringing with a Westernized and Anglophilic environment, however, such a high degree of political involvement might not have been expected. Still, while embracing the West, her family were members of the Kashmiri Brahman, and the family was correspondingly conservative in attitude.

Pandit was educated at home by English governesses and later attended finishing school in Switzerland. She was taken by her father on a visit to England when she was five and was encouraged in her studies, but it is unlikely that she hoped for any kind of scholarly future—within the family most expectations were for Jawaharlal. She did begin writing for Hindu periodicals at about the age of fifteen, at much the same time as the divisions between Indian nationalists and the British were gaining strength. This division, marked by the participation of her father in the Indian National Congress meetings of 1915, led to Pandit's first introduction to Gandhi.

Pandit's marriage, unlike that of many upper-class Hindus of the time, was not arranged. Her husband was an attorney and as well a highly educated scholar who had studied abroad. He shared the Nehru family's political

interests, and the couple worked together in Allahabad toward Indian independence. Pandit, her husband, her brother, and his wife journeyed to Switzerland in 1926, where they were joined by Pandit's father the next year.
Pandit's three daughters—Chandalekha, born in 1924, Nayantara, born in
1927, and Rita Vitasta, born in 1929—were in their own right to carry on
the family traditions of active political involvement in Indian politics. Further, after her sister-in-law's death, Pandit was to help rear her niece, Indira
Gandhi, India's future prime minister.

Life's Work
It was during the 1920's that Pandit, by then accustomed to the highest
levels of political discourse, began her own active participation. By the end
of her public career, she had held more key diplomatic and political positions, both appointed and elected, then any other Indian woman of the twentieth century. Pandit's background in Indian politics lay in both Gandhi's
"Quit India" movement, directed against the British, and in the All-India
Women's Conference. This latter affiliation culminated in her organization,
with her sister-in-law Kamala Nehru, of the women's general boycott of
British goods, which spread outward from Allahabad throughout the entire
province now known as Uttar Pradesh. She spoke vigorously at public gatherings, advocating the complete withdrawal of the British.

It was not until the 1930's, however, that Pandit's activities began seriously to alarm the British. In January, 1932, she and her sister Krisha (also
a member of the All-India Women's Conference, and Pandit's junior by
seven years) were forbidden to take part in any more political meetings,
under threat of confinement. On Independence Day, January 26, 1932, the
two deliberately participated in just such a meeting and were promptly arrested by the British authorities. This marked Pandit's first term of imprisonment, when she was sentenced to serve one year. The political punishment
was served at Lucknow Prison and was extremely rigorous.

Released in 1933, Pandit rejoined the independence movement. Her political fervor had been heightened not only by her imprisonment but also by the
public reaction that had followed her father's death in 1932. The funeral had
been marked by the presence of Gandhi, whose eulogy for Nehru was heard
by thousands gathered on the banks of the Ganges River. It had become clear
that the politicization of India against the British occupation was increasing
at a very swift pace.

While it would be incorrect to speak of this period of Indian history as
somehow indicating the "inevitable" withdrawal and defeat of the British,
once the influential Indian upper classes had reached out and connected with
the middle and lower classes on a unified political basis, the relatively small
British ruling class was faced with very difficult choices. In an attempt to
maintain the status quo, there were increased numbers of political arrests,

interdictions of free speech, and military action. In response, the Indian political activists used Great Britain's own traditions. The independence movement participants chose to join the existing governmental bodies, campaigning in and winning election after election, leaving the British in a position of appearing to oppose legitimately chosen representatives with legitimate grievances.

Pandit's participation within government began when she stood as the Congress candidate for the Allahabad Municipal Board and won. In 1935, a year later, she was elected Chairman of the Board and served two years. During her membership, her chief concern was with local public institutions, particularly in the social services areas. In the time she was a member of the board, she was instrumental in turning the local "night schools" into the focus of Allahabad's advanced study of literary and political issues. This change in emphasis reflected a worldwide movement in adult education, and allowed, often for the first time, workers in the city access to education beyond a primary or vocational level.

In 1936, Pandit won a seat during the general elections of that year, standing for Kanpur. In that rural district, she won a majority of about ten thousand from an electorate of thirty-eight thousand. In 1937, still representing the Congress Party, she capped her local governmental career by her unopposed election as the Minister of Local Self Government and Public Health for the United Provinces.

During the 1930's, Pandit consolidated her political position, standing firmly for the independence goals of the Congress Party and as well for the rights of women within the "new" India. It was a time of advancement for women throughout the world, but it is significant that within India women, from the first of the independence movement, were an integral part. Rather than having to assert a separate role, Indian women political activists were accorded a fully equal position in the struggle against British rule. Not only were they admitted to strategic and political associations but also they suffered the same consequences in terms of imprisonment and censure by the British. Thus, women's rights in India have not generally been a separate issue, at odds with mainstream political objectives. Pandit's place within India was won with the assistance of the emerging political power of the Congress Party and the leaders of India. Consequently, after independence, her role as ambassador must be seen as fully representative of India nationalist political opinion and not as a concession to her position as Prime Minister Nehru's sister.

When independence came in 1947, Pandit's career as an international spokeswoman for India was well under way. After her husband's death in 1944, which had left her without financial resources, she had decided to go to the United States and lecture; she was accepted as India's representative at the Pacific Relations Conference held by the Council for World Affairs. Her background as the former president of the All-India Women's Conference (1940-1942) had validated her right to speak at such an international meeting and marked the beginning of her association with world figures. At the end of the war, she became the leader of the Indian delegation to the inaugural meetings of the United Nations (1946) and continued to serve in that position in 1947 and 1948. Her prestige was such that in 1949 she was appointed Indian Ambassador to the United States, where she remained until 1951.

In 1947, however, she served as Indian Ambassador to the Soviet Union, initiating a pattern that typified her public life. Pandit frequently held more than one post for the government at a time, and the 1940's and 1950's saw her moving between one responsibility and another. For example, in 1952 she headed the Indian "Goodwill Mission" to China during the extremely tense political atmosphere that had resulted from Sino-Indian border disputes and that same year was again leader of the Indian United Nations delegation. During the Eighth Assembly (1952-1953), she was elected president of the General Assembly and had become the acknowledged leader of the newly emerging Arab-Asian bloc.

It was in 1954 that Pandit served in what may have been the most remarkable position of her career. In that year, she became India's High Commissioner to Great Britain, consolidating the former colony's new status as an independent and equal state within the community of nations. Her work in the United Kingdom marked the conclusion of much of the enmity that had resulted from the conflict of the two nations and can be viewed not only as the high point of her career but also as an illustration of the ways in which colonial relationships could develop into effective partnerships.

Summary

While Vijaya Lakshmi Pandit was most actively representing India internationally during the 1950's, it was after the death of her brother that it became clear that she saw herself first and foremost as a servant of India, rather than as a world figure. When she left the High Commission to Great Britain in 1961, it had been her intention to resume private life, but she soon realized that this would be impossible. Between 1961 and 1964, she was her brother's unofficial link to European opinion, most significantly during private talks with Chancellor Konrad Adenauer. By 1963, she gradually reentered official life, serving as leader of the Indian United Nations mission. She was eventually recalled to India to become the appointed governor of Maharashtra Province.

This largely ceremonial position occupied her only until it became clear that her prestige and the respect in which she was held made it necessary that she stand in the by-election at Phulpur, for the seat her brother had held until his death. Pandit won the election with a huge majority of more than fifty-eight thousand votes, preserving the seat for the Congress Party and continuing thereby to ensure the presence of her family in Indian politics.

Pandit's position in Indian government virtually paralleled that country's own growth and development in the twentieth century. From her early life as a traditional member of the upper classes, through her participation in the effort to free India from the British, to her successful attempts to have India received into the community of nations, Pandit always stood for the betterment of the people of India.

Bibliography

Andrews, Robert Hardy. *A Lamp for India: The Story of Madame Pandit.* Englewood Cliffs, N.J.: Prentice-Hall, 1967. A very admiring biography, with photographs and an index, which takes the story of Pandit's life past her brother's death, particularly noting her role as negotiator during the Pakistan-Indian conflicts of the 1960's.

Bowles, Chester. *Ambassador's Report.* New York: Harper and Bros., 1954. This former Ambassador of the United States recounts his time spent in India during the early 1950's and provides an insight into Pandit's circle during the post-independence period. Contains many unique photographs that more than convey the flavor of the period.

Brittain, Vera. *Envoy Extraordinary: A Study of Vijaya Lakshmi Pandit and Her Contribution to Modern India.* London: Allen & Unwin, 1965. A well-written, accessible biography by a contemporary and friend. This account is intended for the general reader with some knowledge of the times and concentrates on the feelings and personal behavior of Pandit.

George, T. J. S. *Krisna Menon: A Biography.* London: Jonathan Cape, 1964. This biography of Pandit's sometime friend and sometime enemy contains in-depth discussion of the United Nations period and is particularly useful when discussing how the conflicts between the two emerged.

Guthrie, Anne. *Madame Ambassador: The Life of Vijaya Lakshmi Pandit.* New York: Harcourt, Brace & World, 1962. Intended for younger readers, the author relies heavily on anecdotal accounts and personal information. Still, her retelling of Pandit's early life and how she gradually became political is most evocative.

A. J. Plotke

FRANZ VON PAPEN

Born: October 29, 1879; Werl, Westphalia, Germany
Died: May 2, 1969; Obersasbach, Baden-Württemberg, West Germany
Areas of Achievement: The military, government, and politics
Contribution: After serving six months as German chancellor in 1932, Papen masterminded the backstairs appointment of Adolf Hitler to power on January 30, 1933. In the years that followed, he served the Third Reich as vice-chancellor (1933-1934) and ambassador to Austria (1934-1938) and Turkey (1939-1944).

Early Life
Franz von Papen was born in Werl, Westphalia, on October 29, 1879. A child of aristocratic privilege, he grew up the third of five children in a Catholic family that traced its noble ancestry back four centuries. As a younger son with no claim to the family estate, he was guided into a military career by his father, a retired officer. Beginning at age eleven in Bensberg Cadet School and culminating with three years of training at Gross-Lichterfeld Academy near Berlin, the young Papen dutifully learned the military discipline and bearing, commitment to national service, and loyalty to the Hohenzollern monarchy that were to shape his political outlook and future. After graduation in 1898, he was posted to his father's former regiment in Düsseldorf, the Fifth Westphalian Uhlans, as a second lieutenant. There he developed the professional expertise, social graces, and personal contacts essential for a successful military career in imperial Germany.

His marriage in 1905 to Martha von Boch-Galhua, the daughter of a wealthy and influential Saarland industrialist, added important new dimensions to Papen's life. Besides responsibility for a wife and eventually five children, the marriage brought him into contact with Francophile in-laws who persuaded him to view French culture and Franco-German friendship in a more positive light. His father-in-law's admiration for the German General Staff also encouraged Papen to seek appointment to this powerful military circle, a goal he realized in 1913 with his promotion to captain.

By prewar standards, Papen's military career was modestly successful. Peacetime promotion came too slowly for this ambitious young officer, however, and so he used his personal contacts to secure appointment to the German embassy in Washington as military attaché. He was expelled in 1915 for directing anti-Allied espionage and sabotage operations covering the United States and Canada. Much to Papen's future embarrassment, moreover, check stubs documenting agent payoffs were confiscated from his luggage by British authorities during his return to Germany and reproduced in a British white paper that questioned his personal integrity and respect for international law.

Papen fought with conspicuous courage on the Western Front in World War I, winning the Iron Cross (First Class) in 1916 while commanding a regiment on the Somme River. Transferred to Turkey in 1917, he served bravely in the Middle Eastern campaign as both a political officer and field commander, attaining the rank of major. With the collapse of the Central Powers in 1918, Papen was forced to return to civilian life in Germany.

Life's Work

Unable to remain idle for long, Papen turned to politics in 1921, trading in the life of a country gentleman on his Westphalian estate for a seat in the Prussian state diet representing the Catholic Center party. The Westphalian Centrists who recruited him were impressed by Papen's conservative orientation, agricultural interests, strong Catholic beliefs, independent wealth (inherited mostly from his wife's family), and influential contacts.

They were less familiar with his political views. An obdurate reactionary, Papen bitterly rejected the new Weimar Republic and parliamentary democracy in favor of the discarded military monarchy of the kaisers. He believed that true political leadership had to come from an experienced ruling elite standing above partisan, interest-oriented parties. In his mind, the fundamental duty of government was not to promote majority rule or social reform but to defend the authoritarian state from the dangers of socialism and Asiatic Bolshevism. Measured even by the standards of conservative Westphalian Centrists, Papen's views were narrow and extreme.

Yet this extremity was not immediately apparent to party leaders. In the early 1920's, he worked hard for Centrist causes, especially agricultural issues important to him and his Westphalian constituents. By 1924, however, as his dissatisfaction with the Center Party's republican ties mounted, Papen turned his energies to separating the Center Party from its Socialist and democratic allies and aligning it with the conservative Right. His uncompromising persistence in this crusade gradually alienated party colleagues and cost him his diet seat between 1928 and 1930, and again in 1932.

Exclusion from Center Party politics did not end Papen's public career. Even as Germany was slipping into the Great Depression, he kept in touch with forces of the Right through private associations such as the Herrenklub in Berlin. To those who would listen, he repeatedly warned of the dangers of communism, urged rapprochement with France—something most conservatives eschewed—and called for the establishment of an authoritarian dictatorship of the Right. Yet he rarely attracted wider attention in the years between 1928 and 1932.

It thus came as a stunning surprise in June of 1932 when President Paul von Hindenburg, the aging World War I hero, asked Papen to form a national government. In reality, it was not Hindenburg who had picked Papen but General Kurt von Schleicher, a backstairs intriguer who planned to use the little-known Papen as a figurehead chancellor for a cabinet under his command. Papen accepted the offer, noting in his memoirs that he could hardly disobey an order from his wartime commander Hindenburg, a man he deeply admired.

Yet Papen's "cabinet of barons" did little during its six-month tenure to ease Germany's growing political crisis. The new chancellor negotiated the end of reparations, but neither this nor his reactionary domestic policies produced enough political or popular support to end the parliamentary stalemate paralyzing the German government. Above all, Papen failed to deal decisively with the growing National Socialist movement. Like his predecessor, he was also handicapped by his dependence on presidential emergency powers rather than a Reichstag majority. As Germany's domestic crisis worsened, Schleicher finally realized that he had misjudged Papen's usefulness and, over the angry objections of President Hindenburg, brought the Papen government down in December.

In the critical weeks that followed, as Schleicher formed his own government and struggled to cope with the Depression and the Nazis, Papen embarked on a fateful venture that was to bring Adolf Hitler to power. Determined to regain power and repay Schleicher's disloyalty, he secretly reopened negotiations with Hitler and the Nazis toward the formation of a new government of national concentration. He arduously patched together a coalition of three Nazis and eight non-Nazis headed by Hitler as chancellor and himself as vice-chancellor. Then he convinced the reluctant Hindenburg to accept and support it. In the end it was Papen more than any other person who masterminded Hitler's legal appointment as German chancellor on January 30, 1933.

Shortly thereafter, Papen predicted that "in two months we'll have pushed Hitler into a corner so hard he'll be squeaking." Yet the new vice-chancellor did not know Hitler as well as he believed. Within weeks all the safeguards he had erected to contain Nazi excesses were brushed aside, and Hitler was wresting absolute power into his own hands. The vice-chancellor and non-Nazi cabinet members were left reeling, often confused or bypassed by the lightning pace of events. Thus the conservative revolution envisioned by Papen actually took place according to the revolutionary precepts of Hitler and the Nazis.

In the tragedy that followed, Papen seemed unable to separate himself from the dictatorship he had helped to install. Because he saw only what he wanted and dismissed Nazi excesses as temporary, he defended Hitler's coalition throughout the Nazi consolidation of power in 1933-1934. His negotiation of a concordat between Germany and the Vatican in 1933 may even have helped in the process by winning the Catholic church's blessing for the Third Reich. Papen did, to be sure, speak out courageously against Nazi illegalities and cruelty on June 17, 1934, at the University of Marburg. Thereafter he kept silent, intimidated perhaps by threats of Brownshirt violence.

Papen claims in his memoirs that he served Hitler and the Third Reich out of a sense of national loyalty, a loyalty instilled in him by his aristocratic origins, military service, and deep Catholic faith. Whatever the reasons, he did publicly represent Nazi Germany for most of its existence. When Hitler offered him the post of Ambassador to Austria in 1934, he accepted, working for four years to improve Austro-German relations, strengthen the Austrian Nazis, and prepare the groundwork for the 1938 Anschluss that unified the two countries. When Hitler sent him as ambassador to Turkey in 1939 during the Albanian Crisis, he took up his new duties eagerly, engaging once again as he had earlier in espionage activities. This time, however, his intrigues were more successful, providing Germany with invaluable intelligence on Allied operations in the Middle East.

Captured by U.S. forces at the end of the war, Papen was held for trial at Nürnberg, where he was cleared of all charges by the War Crimes Tribunal. He was subsequently sentenced to eight years' hard labor by a Bavarian denazification court, but punishment was suspended in 1949. Papen devoted the last years of his life to writing his memoirs, trying unsuccessfully to rehabilitate his reputation, and seeking the pension he believed due him for service in the Prussian army.

Summary

Franz von Papen's archaic aristocratic creed and reactionary political views remained unchanged throughout his entire life. These combined with his vanity and lack of political acumen made it relatively easy for others to use him for their own questionable purposes. His mistake was to believe that he, relying on his social charm and aristocratic standing, could outplay his rivals at their own game. Without the selfish machinations of this shortsighted, devious man, National Socialism might not have found the road to power in 1933. Papen compounded his fateful mistake by refusing to recognize the Third Reich for what it really was: a criminal conspiracy. His myopic support made it easier for other conservatives, aristocrats, and officers to tolerate National Socialism, even when they found certain aspects distasteful. In the end, Papen's biography demonstrates not only the importance of reactionary monarchists in Hitler's rise to power but also the susceptibility of people like Papen to political manipulation and expedience.

Bibliography

Blood-Ryan, H. W. *Franz von Papen: His Life and Times*. London: Rich & Cowan, 1940. One of several contemporary journalistic biographies covering the pre-1940 period. The absence of footnotes and a bibliography, glaring omissions, and the anti-German predisposition make it necessary to use this work with caution.

Dorpalen, Andreas. *Hindenburg and the Weimar Republic*. Princeton, N.J.: Princeton University Press, 1964. Possibly the best general discussion of Papen's role in 1932 and 1933, especially for his maneuvers to bring Hitler to power at the head of a coalition of the Right. Carefully documented, extremely well written, highly analytical, and accurate.

Papen, Franz von. *Memoirs*. Translated by Brian Connell. New York: E. P. Dutton, 1953. The most important primary source available on Papen's life and politics. Filled with inaccuracies, attributable partly to the destruction of Papen's papers at the end of the war and partly to his notoriously subjective approach, it nevertheless provides a valuable insight into this debonair nobleman's outlook and life.

Shirer, William L. *The Rise and Fall of the Third Reich*. New York: Simon & Schuster, 1960. Shirer incorporates Papen's role into a broader history of the Third Reich, focusing appropriately on his role as chancellor, political mediator, and ambassador. In Shirer's view, this vain and incompetent man was "more responsible than any other individual for Hitler's appointment as Chancellor."

Turner, Henry Ashby, Jr. *German Big Business and the Rise of Hitler*. New York: Oxford University Press, 1985. Shows convincingly that big business played a far smaller role in Papen's actions than many historians have believed.

Wheaton, Eliot B. *Prelude to Calamity: The Nazi Revolution 1933-35, with a Background Survey of the Weimar Era*. Garden City, N.Y.: Doubleday, 1968. Provides a brief analysis of Papen's role in Nazi politics and assesses him as an amateur who underestimated Hitler.

Rennie W. Brantz

BORIS PASTERNAK

Born: February 10, 1890; Moscow, Russia
Died: May 30, 1960; Peredelkino, near Moscow, U.S.S.R.
Area of Achievement: Literature
Contribution: Pasternak was a leading Russian poet, a particularly gifted translator, and a writer of prose, most notably the novel *Doctor Zhivago*, for which he was offered the Nobel Prize in 1958. His highly cultured talent managed to find both expression and influence despite severe adversity in the Soviet literary climate.

Early Life

Boris Leonidovich Pasternak was born on February 10, 1890, in Moscow, the first child of Leonid Osipovich Pasternak, an artist renowned for his portraiture, and Rosa Isidorovna Pasternak (née Kaufman), a talented pianist. In their youth, Boris, his brother Alexander, and his two sisters, Josephine and Lydia, were exposed to a richly cultured environment of art, music, and literature. The famous author, Leo Tolstoy, was an admirer of Leonid's work and sat for one of his most prominent portraits. The Pasternaks were, as a result, visitors on several occasions to Tolstoy's Moscow residence and to his estate near Tula. The effect of this contact was to be felt in Pasternak's later religious and philosophical views. The German poet Rainer Maria Rilke, who twice visited the Pasternaks, influenced young Boris to appreciate the role of the poet in society—a role he later assumed. It was the eccentric composer Aleksandr Scriabin who most determined Pasternak's youthful endeavors. Under his influence, Pasternak studied music composition while attending Moscow's German Classical Grammar School. At school, Pasternak enjoyed foreign languages, especially German, and philosophy. He took an interest in the poetry of the Russian Symbolists Innokenty Annensky and Aleksandr Blok. Through his father he met the founder of the Soviet literary doctrine of Socialist Realism, Maxim Gorky, both in Moscow and in Berlin, to which the Pasternaks traveled in 1905 after the failed Russian revolution attempt of that year. In 1907, the family returned to Moscow, and in 1908 Pasternak was graduated from school with a gold medal for excellence.

In 1909, Pasternak entered Moscow State University as a law student, but he soon transferred to philosophy. He began to participate in a literary circle called "Serdarda," which was devoted to poetic innovation. Other members of this group, notably Sergei Makovsky and Sergei Bobrov, recognized Pasternak's talent for poetry and urged him to give up his work in music composition to focus on poetry. In 1912, Pasternak traveled to Germany to study philosophy under the Neo-Kantian leader Hermann Cohen at the University of Marburg. He was unhappy over his relationship with Ida Davidovna Vysofskaya, the daughter of wealthy family friends. He had fallen in love with her while tutoring her. She visited him in Marburg and there rejected his proposal of marriage. He then withdrew from the university and returned to Moscow, intent on devoting himself more exclusively to literary pursuits.

Life's Work

In 1913, Pasternak had five of his poems published in a Moscow almanac called *Lirika*. The group that sponsored this almanac soon merged with a Futurist group, Centrifuge, through which Pasternak came under the influence of Vladimir Mayakovsky, the revolutionary poet who had been a passing acquaintance of Pasternak in school. In 1914, Russia's participation in World War I began, and Pasternak was drafted for service; he was soon exempted, however, because of his leg, which had improperly healed after a fracture sustained in a fall from a horse in 1903. In 1914, his first collection of verse, *Bliznets v tuchakh* (twin in the clouds), was published, and, while staying on the estate of the Lithuanian poet Jurgis Baltrushaitis, he translated Heinrich von Kleist's *Der zerbrochene Krug* (1808; *The Broken Jug*, 1930) into Russian. By the time his translation was published with Gorky's personal editorship in *Sovremennik* (the contemporary) in 1922, Pasternak was roundly acclaimed as an author and a poet. Early prose writings such as "Apellesova cherta" (1918; the mark of Apelles) and especially "Detstvo Liuvers" (1922; the childhood of Liuvers), with its depiction of a child's growing awareness of an adult world, established Pasternak as a leading stylist. His collections of verse, *Poverkh bari erov* (1917; *Above the Barriers*, 1959, 1964) and *Sestra moia zhizn* (1922; *My Sister, Life*, 1959, 1964), demonstrated his transcendence of Mayakovsky's revolutionary Futurism and his coming into his own as a major modern poet.

Like many of the leading artistic intellectuals with whom he was acquainted, Pasternak's initial enthusiasm for the Russian Revolution of 1917 was short-lived. In 1921, his parents and his sisters emigrated to Germany, never to return. He remained in the family house in Moscow with his brother Aleksandr and, in 1922, married a talented painter, Evgenia Vladimirovna Lourié. Together they traveled several times to Germany and to France, where he met with prominent émigré poets such as Andrei Biely, Vladislav Khodasevich, and especially the ill-fated Marina Tsvetayeva, with whom he was to maintain a long mutual admiration by correspondence. Pasternak's son Evgeny was born in 1923.

After a successful collection of lyric verse published in 1923, *Temy i variatsii* (*Themes and Variations*, 1959, 1964), Pasternak attempted to explore the revolutionary ethic in the narrative poems "Devyatsot pyaty god" (1926; the year 1905) and "Lyutenant Shmidt" (1927; Lieutenant Schmidt). In his prose story "Vozdushnye puti" (1924; aerial ways) and in his novel-in-verse *Spektorsky* (1931), however, Pasternak's problems in viewing the poet as a revolutionary became clear. Pasternak's poet-heroes were prone to passivity in the buffetings of historical change. They martyred themselves to serve as witnesses to the personal consequences of global events. In this they presaged the character of Yuri, his hero in *Doktor Zhivago* (1957; *Doctor Zhivago*, 1958).

In 1931, Pasternak left his wife and took a residence with Zinaïda Nikolaevna Neuhaus, the wife of an acquaintance. He published his unconventional autobiography *Okhrannaya gramota* (*Safe Conduct*, 1945) in the same year. Travel to the Caucasus and meetings with Georgian poets inspired the verse collection *Vtoroye rozhdeniye* (1932; *Second Birth*, 1959, 1964). Yet the increased strictures on literature after the formation of the Union of Soviet Writers in 1932 kept Pasternak from publishing original work throughout the remainder of the 1930's. Although he did serve as a delegate of the Union of Soviet Writers to a Paris conference in 1935, he was privately dismayed at Stalinist tyranny in the arts. On one occasion detailed by the poet Osip Mandelstam's widow, Joseph Stalin personally telephoned Pasternak to gain assurance that Mandelstam "was a great poet." Inevitably Mandelstam perished in the labor camps. Pasternak was able to find a safer livelihood by translating into Russian the works of Johann Wolfgang von Goethe, Friedrich Schiller, George Gordon, Lord Byron, John Keats, Paul Verlaine, and especially William Shakespeare, the major tragedies of whom he published during World War II.

Pasternak married Neuhaus in 1934, and a second son, Leonid, was born three years later. In 1937, he refused to sign a letter in *Pravda* denouncing the purged General Mikhail Tukhachevsky, but colleagues protectively signed his name anyway. In 1939, his mother died in London, and Tsvetayeva returned from emigration only to commit suicide in the Yelabuga labor camp two years later. The need to impress literature into the service of the country during World War II enabled the publication of Pasternak's own patriotic collections *Na rannikh poezdakh* (1943; *On Early Trains*, 1959, 1964) and *Zemnoy prostor* (1945; *The Vastness of Earth*, 1959, 1964). The postwar clampdown, however, ceased for Pasternak all but the publication of translations until the death of Stalin in 1953.

In 1945, Pasternak's father died in Oxford, England. The next year, Pasternak fell in love with Olga Vsevolodovna Ivinskaya, a worker in the offices of the literary journal *Novy mir* (new world). In 1947, he excused himself from participating in the Union of Soviet Writers' condemnation of Anna Akhmatova and Mikhail Zoshchenko. Soon after Ivinskaya's arrest in 1949, Pasternak had a serious heart attack, and while convalescing he worked on the poems and the prose of his novel *Doctor Zhivago*. Ivinskaya refused to incriminate Pasternak in "activities against the state" and was transferred to a labor camp only to be released in 1953. The stress of Pasternak's literary plight, combined with his being torn between his family and his lover, eroded his health and necessitated prolonged periods of rest.

The thaw that followed the death of Stalin and Nikita S. Khrushchev's subsequent denunciation of the cult of Stalin in 1956 gave Pasternak hope that his novel *Doctor Zhivago*, which he had completed the previous year, would be accepted for publication. Indeed several of the poems that were to accompany it were accepted and published by *Znamya* (the banner) in 1954. Thus encouraged, he sent a complete manuscript to Feltrinelli Publishers in Italy. When Communist Party officials decided not to allow the publication of *Doctor Zhivago* in the Soviet Union, Pasternak tried to recall his manuscript from Italy, but Feltrinelli published it anyway in 1957. The novel, describing the harried life of Dr. Yuri Zhivago, a physician and poet caught up in the monumental events of Russia's first third of the twentieth century—war, revolution, civil war, and the radical transformation of Russian society—was an international sensation. Translated into many languages, *Doctor Zhivago* was admired by all who appreciated the travail inflicted by the clash of political ideologies on sensitive and creative individuals of conscience. Abroad Pasternak was acclaimed. In Stockholm, the Nobel Prize Committee voted to award him the 1958 Nobel Prize in Literature. Within a day of this announcement letters denouncing Pasternak as a "Judas who has shut his eyes to the transformation of his country by victorious socialism" appeared in the Soviet press. Not only was he expelled from the Union of Soviet Writers but also a petition of more than eight hundred Moscow writers requested that the government deprive him of his Soviet citizenship. Ill and harassed, Pasternak telegrammed to Stockholm his refusal to accept the Nobel Prize, and, a few days later, wrote a letter to Khrushchev asking that he not be separated from his native land.

In the year and a half left in Pasternak's life, he tried to have his works *Kogdá razguliayetsa* (1959; *When the Skies Clear*, 1959, 1964), a collection of reflective verse, and *Avtobiograficheskiy ocherk* (1958; *I Remember: Sketch for an Autobiography*, 1959) published in the Soviet Union as they had been abroad. His historical drama *Slepaya krasavitsa* (1969; *The Blind Beauty*, 1969) was left incomplete at his death. In his last days the Soviet authorities cut off his royalties from foreign publications and continued their personal harassment of his family and his loved ones. He died of a weakened heart and of lung cancer on May 30, 1960. At a sparsely attended funeral his poem "Hamlet" from the *Doctor Zhivago* cycle was read. His home in the writer's colony at Peredelkino has become a kind of shrine for visiting literati, students, and tourists.

Summary

Boris Pasternak left a legacy of poetic achievement. Through his poetry he labored to create something profound and beautiful—a different way of appreciating reality given to the reader. He was unable to make his poetry adapt to the rigors of social utility and so he escaped into translation, the competence of which still enriches Russian-speaking peoples everywhere. The work for which he is best known is his novel *Doctor Zhivago*, the political impact of which stands in ironical juxtaposition to its content—a veritable paen to the apoliticality of artistic achievement. Banned from publication in its native land for almost a quarter century—only in 1989 was a Russian version printed in the Soviet Union—*Doctor Zhivago*'s characters and poems are nevertheless widely known and held in high esteem.

Bibliography
Barnes, Christopher. *Boris Pasternak: A Literary Biography.* Vol. 1. Cambridge, England: Cambridge University Press, 1989. Barnes's study may be termed a second-generation biography, building on others done soon after Pasternak's death and having available more recently published memoirs (such as the memoirs of Ivinskaya, who was arrested and sent back to the camps after Pasternak's death), and archival materials. Volume 1 of this work covers Pasternak's life and works to 1928, and volume 2 will cover the rest. Detail is superb.

Dyck, J. W. *Boris Pasternak.* New York: Twayne, 1972. This is an important overall survey of Pasternak's life and works that endeavors to explain Pasternak's complexities of both philosophy and style to the layperson. A useful chronology of Pasternak's life is included for ease of reference.

Gifford, Henry. *Pasternak: A Critical Study.* Cambridge, England; Cambridge University Press, 1977. Gifford's work frames the events of Pasternak's life well within the literary context of his times. The chronological table, for instance, lists the suicides or grim deaths of a dozen of Pasternak's literary compatriots. The literary works are deeply and clearly analyzed, with citations given in both Russian and English.

Hingley, Ronald. *Pasternak: A Biography.* London: Weidenfeld & Nicolson, 1983. Hingley's biography focuses on Pasternak's personal motivations for his reactions to the forces that molded Soviet literature and, indeed, Soviet culture in this century.

Hughes, Olga R. *The Poetic World of Boris Pasternak.* Princeton, N.J.: Princeton University Press, 1974. An examination both thematic and structural of Pasternak's peculiar perception as expressed in his poetry is the strength of this work by Hughes. The scholarly apparatus of this work is particularly useful, with the frequent Russian citations given insightful translations.

Mallac, Guy de. *Boris Pasternak: His Life and Art.* Norman: University of Oklahoma Press, 1981. This is a very detailed narration of Pasternak's life with included critical treatments of his works. The book is wonderfully illustrated as well and features the most complete capsulized chronology available.

Payne, Robert. *The Three Worlds of Boris Pasternak*. New York: Coward-McCann, 1961. This work, by a very experienced biographer, was produced soon after Pasternak's death. It attempts to sketch Pasternak's life as a poet, prose writer, and political figure for the lay audience, giving insightful explanations of Russian historical context.

Lee B. Croft

VALLABHBHAI JHAVERBHAI PATEL

Born: October 31, 1875; Nadiād, Gujerāt, India
Died: December 15, 1950; Bombay, India
Areas of Achievement: Government and politics
Contribution: Patel's uncanny ability to inspire political cooperation among
disparate personalities and groups served as the single most important
element in the post-independence Indian government's successful integration of the various princely states into a single national unit.

Early Life
Vallabhbhai Jhaverbhai Patel was born in the province of Gujerāt, the son
of a fairly prosperous farmer of the peasant class. Within the family there
was a tradition of opposition to the occupying British administration; Patel's
father had been involved in the Mutiny of 1857, although it has never been
clear how far his participation went. Nevertheless, Patel, along with his
elder brother Vithalbai, were sent for their educations to the Nadiād and
Baroda high schools, where the standard subjects were presented. After this
level of education, Patel very much wished to study law and to that end
inquired about the various criteria that would be necessary in England. The
reply to his letter was apparently addressed to him by his initial, and his
brother, who was also considering law, prevailed on Patel to sponsor his
study in England first.

While Vithalbai studied in England, Vallabhbhai studied for and passed
the local district pleaders' examinations and set up his first practice at
Godhra. He later moved his practice to Borsad, where he specialized in
criminal law. To a degree this specialization was less a matter of personal
interest than of opportunity, since the Borsad region was notorious as a
criminal center.

In 1913, Patel was finally able to attend the Middle Temple in London,
where his already well-developed legal talents allowed him to be called to
the bar in two rather than the customary three years. When he returned to
India, he decided to establish his practice at Ahmadabad, where as a defense
counsel he was very much sought after. His practice very quickly made him
quite wealthy, and, since much of his prosperity was dependent on the goodwill of those connected with the British administration, he was more than a
little reluctant to participate in activities that might have jeopardized the
relationship. Patel was during this period fully Westernized in attitude and
behavior and was quite willing to allow the debates about nationalism and
independence to take place without him.

At least part of Patel's reluctance to involve himself in the political controversy was his doubt that men such as Gandhi could succeed against the
pragmatic British. Thus, while Patel actually met Gandhi in 1915, it was not

until some two years later that Patel was able to reconcile his personal doubts as to Gandhi's nonviolent campaign with his understanding of the campaign's potential implementation. It was in 1917, at the time that Gandhi refused to abide by a judicial order, that Patel realized that other areas of Indian life might be equally susceptible to a policy of refusal. It was this realization that spurred Patel's organization of the no-tax campaign for Gandhi, his participation as an advocate representing those accused by the British authorities of taking part in self-government activities, and his prominent role in local Gujerati politics. Between about 1917 and 1928, Patel's activities in support of Gandhi's effort to gain Indian freedom gradually expanded outside the province of Gujerat, and his reputation as a pragmatic and astute political strategist was enhanced nationally.

Life's Work

After Patel's four-year term as president of the Ahmadabad municipality (1924-1928), he began to try to apply the principles of public responsibility and governmental obligation to a wider area. Committed to the ideas of Indian self-government, he led a massive civil disobedience campaign in the district of Surat in 1928, largely on behalf of small landowners of the class from which he had come. In this case too, the matter at issue seems to have appealed to his legal experience, in that the farmers, having been severely overtaxed and underrepresented, chose tax refusal as the best method of fighting the injustice.

While Patel customarily chose legalistic and specific methods of depriving the British authorities, his methods were not without risk. His actions during the national civil disobedience campaign of 1930 caused his first imprisonment by the British, and he was jailed again in January, 1932. His prominence within the independence movement was recognized in 1931 when he was elected president of the Congress Party.

Patel during the 1930's was largely responsible for the strategic foundations that were to allow the Congress Party to form an effective government as the British were gradually forced from power. His position on the 1935 parliamentary subcommittee meant that he, along with others similarly involved in long-range political planning, was to guide most of the decisions about the ways in which Hindus and Muslims within India were to cooperate within the government. Unfortunately, Patel and the subcommittee chose not to share their power with Muslim proponents of independence, a decision that was to have brutal consequences after partition.

Up until the outbreak of the war, Patel continued his work within the Congress Party, but when war was declared in 1939 all Congress ministries resigned and effectively cut off Patel and the party from further hope of reconciliation under any circumstances. Patel was again imprisoned, in 1940. By that time the activities of Congress and the independence movement generally had reached such a pitch that approaches to the Japanese were made in an attempt to force the British from India. The 1942 "Quit India" movement was the culmination of Congress' hostility toward the British occupation, and the campaign's planning was in very large part that of Patel. For the campaign, along with what Great Britain perhaps properly viewed as extraordinary disloyalty in time of war, Patel and other Congress leaders were imprisoned until June, 1945.

Thus, it was only in 1945, after some twenty-five years of active resistance, that the British finally began negotiations that would lead to their departure from India. At that time, and until the final transfer of power in August, 1947, Patel played his most important role, both behind the scenes and as a member of the interim form of government that was established in 1946. Eventually, Patel was to become, first, minister for the states and then deputy prime minister. The second position, which he achieved directly after independence, gave him authority over home affairs, information and broadcasting, and the matters that concerned the Indian states.

It was during the period immediately following independence that Patel's talents in organization, conciliation, and political compromise were most used by President Jawaharlal Nehru and the Congress Party generally. His pragmatism and sense of expedience in service of the goals of creating a unified India were of enormous value. The civil disorder that followed independence could have aborted Indian political unity completely; instead, Patel, as deputy prime minister, insisted on and achieved a level of discipline within the government that has not subsequently been matched. This discipline was especially important following partition, when the bitterness and violence that partition caused among both Muslims and militant Hindus threatened to destroy India altogether.

As part of his responsibilities as deputy prime minister, Patel was in charge of maintaining civil order as much as possible. In a real sense, his position may have been unique within modern politics. Essentially, as one of the leaders of a national revolution as expressed through the "Quit India" movement, he was then called upon to restructure the revolution, halt the protests that had almost become a way of Indian life, and rechannel an entire pattern of conduct directed against authority; in short, he was asked to create methods for a newly independent nation to function within its ideology.

Without Patel, it is unlikely that India would have survived the extremely difficult period after partition. Further, he also had the responsibility for somehow unifying the Indian princedoms, which composed in large measure the political superstructure that had sustained the independence movement. That superstructure was certainly unwieldy, and the powers of the princes were such that very few were willing to give them up easily; Patel, however, was determined that the nearly six hundred different jurisdictions be forced into orderly and mutually supportive units.

If Patel's work in maintaining order was difficult, the work he undertook to reorganize the princely political states was virtually overwhelming, although for rather different reasons. Since the eighteenth century, most of these states had been granted treaty privileges that gave them legal paramountcy within their borders. These rights were not automatically transferred to a central Indian government when independence came, and as a result each had to be dealt with separately by the Nehru government. Patel's methods of dealing with the states was utterly straightforward—they were merged into larger administrative units, the larger states became provincial units, and princes themselves were retired or became elected officials. In some cases Patel took military or police action against recalcitrant states, and the central government occupied the district. The entire national realignment took him two years, but at its conclusion India was indeed a single, independent nation, and the real threat that it would simply collapse into anarchy was past.

In this administrative work, Patel had the support of Nehru and the other members of the government, but it is doubtful that he was entirely influenced by Nehru's sometimes more expedient point of view. Patel was ruthless in his belief that the consolidation of the various political structures had to be accomplished as quickly as possible. He was not prepared to allow any interference with the achievement of that end goal, regardless of whether it might be temporarily desirable. Perhaps of greater importance, given the likelihood of such a philosophy being perverted toward personal gain, Patel was instead completely focused on the benefits to be accrued for India. He was ready to abandon his own views when they came into conflict with the greater ambitions that the Congress held for the nation.

Summary

Vallabhbhai Jhaverbhai Patel, called "Sardar," or leader, by his peers, was that most unique political figure, the intellectual pragmatist. In his early life, he put his family responsibilities before his own preferences; in his active life within the Congress Party and later the Indian government, he was able to see consequences and effects of actions where others saw only short-term benefits or losses. In the largest sense, Patel was India's *éminence grise* after independence, allowing Nehru to present as accomplished fact what Patel forced into creation: a unified India.

Patel's private behavior was always secondary to the necessities of public life, so much so that he gained a reputation for both cynicism and coldness. He has been compared to Otto von Bismarck in his ruthless suppression of the princely resistance; if the comparison is apt, then it is so because after independence India desperately needed a Bismarck. He was in many ways an idealist, but of a kind specifically necessary to his time and completely without the sentimentality that did affect other Congress leaders. Patel took up the cause of an independent India early in his life and never varied his belief that it was both politically and emotionally achievable. His early training and natural disposition toward order, when combined with an overwhelming sense of public duty and responsibility, illuminated the path for India to follow into the modern political structure.

Bibliography
Ahluwala, B. K., ed. *Facets of Sardar Patel*. Delhi: Kalyani Publishers, 1974. A collection of personal and political assessments of Patel and of all facets of his life, this volume tries to present the whole man within the context of his political importance. Included are reminiscences by Vapal P. Menon, B. Shiva Rao, and the Earl Mountbatten of Burma. An invaluable portrait of Patel as both his friends and opponents saw him.
Menon, Vapal P. *The Transfer of Power in India*. London: Longmans, Green, 1957. In this volume, written at the behest of Patel, Menon examines India's constitutional history and the mechanisms that Patel and others used to effect a transfer of power from Great Britain to the centralized Indian government. Menon's account is straightforward, devoid of unnecessary wordage, and a valuable and scholarly record of events that were at the time often confusing.
Moraes, Frank. *Witness to an Era: India 1920 to the Present Day*. London: Weidenfeld & Nicolson, 1973. Moraes, former war correspondent for the *Times* of India, was present at almost every step of India's road to independence and offers a personal account of the leadership of the movement. His insights and recollections of Indian life before and after independence are accessible, and his understanding of Patel's difficult position enlightening.
Patel, Sardar. *Sardar Patel: In Tune with the Millions*. Edited by C. M. Nandurkar. Ahmadabad: Navajivan Press, 1975. A chronological collection of Patel's speeches and writings during the period 1947-1950. Nandurkar has selected those writings that shed the most light on Patel's work across India to unify the nation and has traced Patel's attitudes toward those who placed personal gain above that unity. While a difficult volume if used as an introduction to Patel, it provides much primary information to the way in which Patel's mind worked and his hopes for India's future.
Subramanya Menon, K.P. *Homage to Sardar Patel*. Bombay: Patel Institute, 1976. Menon's extensive examination of the relationship between Nehru and Pandit and his role as the "Bismarck of India." Menon dwells on Patel's devotion to India and his loyalty to principle, although he points out it was often at odds with Nehru's convictions.

A. J. Plotke

PAUL VI
Giovanni Battista Montini

Born: September 26, 1897; Concesio, near Brescia, Italy
Died: August 6, 1978; Castel Gandolfo, Italy
Areas of Achievement: Religion and church reform
Contribution: Paul VI convened the last three sessions of the historic Second
Vatican Council (1962-1965), which brought the Roman Catholic church
into constructive engagement with the modern world. His abiding concern
for the poor and for human rights and social justice and his extensive
travels reinforced the progressive influence of the Vatican Council.

Early Life
Giovanni Battista Montini was born on September 26, 1897, in Concesio,
a small village near Brescia, in the province of Lombardy, Italy. He was the
second son of Giorgio and Giuditta Alghisi Montini. The Montinis were a
prosperous aristocratic family, deeply devoted to the Roman Catholic
church. Giorgio was one of the founders of Sa Paolo Bank of Brescia, La
Scuola Publishing Union, and the Morcelliana publishing house. A successful journalist, he edited the daily *Il Cittadino di Brescia* between 1881 and
1912. Giorgio was also very active in Italian politics, defending the interests
of the Catholic church. Pope Benedict XV appointed him to the leadership of
the Catholic Electoral Union of Italy. After World War I, when Catholics
were allowed to participate in Italian politics, Giorgio Montini became active
in the Popular Party. He was elected to represent Brescia in three legislatures
prior to the party's suppression in 1926 by Benito Mussolini. Giovanni's
mother, Giuditta, was also from an aristocratic family. She was noted in
Brescia as a leader of the Catholic women of the area and for her generosity
to the poor. Thus, Giovanni's parents provided a home atmosphere that
emphasized education and a lively interest in the social and political issues
of the turn of the century.

Giovanni suffered from chronic ill health as a child. Much of his early
education was provided at home. Until 1914, he was enrolled at the Institute
Cesare Arici, an elementary school operated by the Jesuits. Between 1914
and 1916, he was privately tutored in preparation for final examinations at
the Liceo Arnaldo de Brescia, which he passed with "highest honors." Because of his health, Giovanni was not called up for military service along
with his classmates in 1916. Instead, he began studying for the priesthood.
He was ordained on May 29, 1920. After his ordination, Father Montini took
up the study of philosophy at the Jesuit Gregorian University in Rome, while
simultaneously becoming enrolled at the University of Rome.

Father Giovanni Montini's talents and potential were soon recognized by
those close to the papal throne. In 1922, during the first year of Pope

Pius XI's reign, he was asked to prepare himself for service in the Vatican's diplomatic corps. It was the first step in a career that led to his election as Pope Paul VI, forty-one years later.

Life's Work

Montini's first appointment in the Vatican's diplomatic corps came in 1923, when he was sent to Warsaw, Poland, as attaché on the staff of the apostolic nunciature (papal ambassador). Ill health cut short his appointment. Within a year, he was back in Rome. It was a propitious move, for it returned Montini to the very center of power at the Vatican. He rose steadily over the next thirty years from one post to another in the Vatican Secretariat of State. In addition to his duties at the secretariat, Montini was active in the Catholic student movement during the 1920's and 1930's. In 1924, he was appointed chaplain at the University of Rome. During the following year, he was appointed national ecclesiastical assistant to the Federation of Italian Catholic University Students (FUCI), a post he held until early 1933. During those years, Montini led the FUCI in active opposition to the Fascist University Youth. The struggle for the hearts and minds of Italian youth was often a violent one. By his leadership, Montini won the respect and admiration of many individual Catholic students who would later play key roles in postwar Italian politics.

In 1937, Cardinal Eugenio Pacelli, secretary of state, appointed Montini to his personal staff. The two worked closely together. In 1938, when Pacelli was appointed the papal legate to the Eucharistic Congress in Budapest, Hungary, Montini accompanied him. Their collaboration continued after Pacelli's election as Pope Pius XII in 1939. They worked together so harmoniously that the Roman press referred to Montini as "the right eye of the Pope." Pius appointed Montini undersecretary of state in 1939, acting secretary of state for ordinary (that is, nondiplomatic) affairs in 1944, and prosecretary of state in 1953. Pius wanted to elevate him to the Sacred College of Cardinals, but Montini declined the honor.

Throughout his years in Rome, Montini served the poor as a parish priest. It was in recognition of his interest in the working classes that Pius appointed him Archbishop of Milan in 1954. For the next nine years until his election as pope, Montini labored to win the workers of Milan to the Catholic church. It was not an easy task. Milan during the 1950's was a heavily industrial area and a regional stronghold of the Communists.

With the death of Pius XII in 1958, Cardinal Angelo Giuseppe Roncalli was elected Pope John XXIII. Montini's name was the first on a list of twenty-three prelates named by John to the Sacred College of Cardinals in December, 1958. Montini supported the progressive policies of the new pope, including John's call for an ecumenical council to revitalize the Roman Catholic church. The first session of the historic Second Vatican Council convened on October 11, 1962. On June 3, 1963, shortly before the second session was to convene on September 29, John died. On June 21, the College of Cardinals chose Cardinal Giovanni Montini to succeed John as Pope Paul VI.

Paul's background in diplomacy prepared him for the difficult task of leading the Roman Catholic church during the remaining years of the Second Vatican Council and afterward. His leadership was conservative in that he sought to keep the Church faithful to past traditions, except where those traditions were hopelessly out of tune with the twentieth century. The progressive nature of Paul's leadership both during and after the Second Vatican Council can be seen in the reforms he instituted and the causes he championed. Among the former were creation of a Synod of Bishops, replacement of the Latin Mass with the vernacular, and reforms of the papal curia. Even his style was progressive. He was the first pope whose reign was covered by television, as he led the papacy into the center of world religious and political affairs. He traveled extensively, being the first pope to travel by airplane.

Paul also used his influence to promote the cause of human rights and social justice, values he learned in his parents' home and which he never abandoned. In 1967, he issued a papal letter, *Populorum Progressio* (progress of the peoples), which was such a departure from the Vatican's traditional conservative stance on social justice that *The Wall Street Journal* called it "warmed-over Marxism." In the interest of world peace and social justice, Paul addressed the United Nations General Assembly in 1965 and made journeys to Asia, Africa, and Latin America.

Paul was noted for his faithfulness to what he believed to be right, even when it put him at odds with his own clergy and laity. In March, 1964, against the strong opposition of the German bishops, Paul welcomed a delegation from the West German Social Democratic Party (SPD) to the Vatican. It was a recognition of both the efforts of the SPD on behalf of German workers and the progress the SPD was making in moving away from its Marxist origins.

Paul's conservatism can be seen in his steadfast resistance to all efforts to change the Church's position on such key teachings as artificial birth control and priestly celibacy. In July, 1968, he issued the papal encyclical *Humanae Vitae* (of human life), which upheld the Church's ban on all forms of artificial birth control. In *Sacerdotalis Caelibatus* (sacerdotal celibacy), issued in June, 1967, Paul reaffirmed the church's stand on clerical celibacy, while condemning the "spiritual and moral collapse" of priests who abandoned their ministries for marriage. Both encyclicals evoked some of the most serious attacks on papal authority in modern history, but Paul stood firm.

Paul is perhaps best remembered as the "pilgrim pope," who reached out to Christians as well as nonbelievers with an ecumenical spirit. He met with the Greek Orthodox patriarch of Constantinople while on a pilgrimage to the

Holy Land in 1964 and again in 1967 while on a journey to Turkey. In 1969, he visited the headquarters of the World Council of Churches in Geneva, Switzerland. Yet his ecumenism was not restricted to Christians alone. He reached out to Jews, nonbelievers, and adherents of non-Western religions, also. He established a Vatican Secretariat for Nonbelievers and a Secretariat for Relations with Non-Christian Religions. Throughout his pontificate, Paul followed an exhausting schedule. When he died on August 6, 1978, at Castel Gandolfo, his summer retreat, he was one of the most significant popes of the Roman Catholic church in modern history.

Summary
Paul VI was undoubtedly one of the most significant popes of the twentieth century. It was John XXIII who called for the changes that brought the Roman Catholic church into the modern world, but it was Paul who saw the changes implemented. His constructive and conservative leadership enabled the Church to undergo revolutionary changes without being rent asunder or breaking its continuity with the past.

Paul's personal contribution, aside from his conservative leadership, was to make the Church an active participant in the struggle for social justice and world peace. On May 15, 1971, the eightieth anniversary of Pope Leo XIII's historic social encyclical *Rerum Novarum* (new things), Paul issued a papal letter calling upon all people, whatever their religious beliefs or positions in life, to seek out practical means by which they could work for world peace and justice. Yet, he did more than call for involvement. He set an example that others could follow.

In one respect, however, Paul's legacy was a mixed one. By upholding the Church's traditional stance on such controversial issues as birth control and clerical celibacy, he contributed, some believe, to the weakening of papal authority. Others believe just as strongly that by his defense of what he held to be true doctrine, he enhanced papal authority within the Church. Perhaps the Second Vatican Council and Paul's strong leadership enabled the Roman Catholic church to change without experiencing the physical schism and fragmentation that had rent a more rigid Church in the sixteenth century.

Bibliography
Andrews, James F., ed. *Paul VI: Critical Appraisals*. New York: Bruce, 1970. Seven distinguished Catholic and Protestant scholars, theologians, and journalists assess Paul's policies on such key issues as birth control, celibacy, and ecumenism. It also contains a brief biography and a chronological outline of his reign through 1969.
Clancy, John G. *Apostle for Our Time: Pope Paul VI*. New York: P. J. Kenedy & Sons, 1963. Published in the year Paul began his reign, this standard biography is especially good for his early life. The influence of

his parents in developing his concern for social justice is well covered. Clancy is clearly one who admired Paul.

Gremillion, Joseph. *The Gospel of Peace and Justice*. New York: Orbis Books, 1976. Part 1 is a summary and analysis of Catholic social teaching during the reigns of John XXIII and Paul VI. Part 2 contains some 550 pages of papal documents (for example, *Humanae Vitae* and Paul's address to the United Nations) in English.

Hebblethwaite, Peter. *The Year of Three Popes*. Cleveland, Ohio: William Collins, 1979. Although a somewhat dry and fact-laden account of the careers of Paul VI, John Paul I, and John Paul II, this book is particularly good for an understanding on how a pope is elected. It provides a balanced and sympathetic assessment of Paul's reign.

Holmes, J. Derek. *The Papacy in the Modern World, 1914-1978*. New York: Crossroad, 1981. This is a highly readable history of the Papacy during the years when Giovanni Montini rose from parish priest to supreme pontiff. The latter chapter covers the Second Vatican Council.

Serafian, Michael. *The Pilgrim*. New York: Farrar, Straus and Giroux, 1964. A critical analysis of Paul's role in the Second Vatican Council by a Roman Catholic diplomat writing under a pseudonym. The emphasis is on Paul's role during the second session of the Council.

Waibel, Paul R. "Politics of Accommodation: The SPD Visit to the Vatican, March 5, 1964." *The Catholic Historical Review* 65 (April, 1979): 238-252. This essay provides an example of how Paul could influence the course of politics within a nation simply by granting an audience to a visiting delegation. Paul's act meant that the Geman bishops could no longer influence Catholic voters not to vote for the Social Democrats.

Paul R. Waibel

WOLFGANG PAULI

Born: April 25, 1900; Vienna, Austria
Died: December 14, 1958; Zurich, Switzerland
Area of Achievement: Physics
Contribution: Pauli's discovery of the exclusion principle, which asserts the individuality of electrons, revolutionized atomic physics. He is also responsible for the electron theory of metals, which led to the development of transistors, and for proposing the existence of neutrinos.

Early Life

Wolfgang Pauli was born on April 25, 1900, in Vienna, Austria. His father, also named Wolfgang, was a distinguished professor of colloid physics at the University of Vienna. Although Pauli received his formal education in the Viennese school system, he was also informally instructed by his father, who often discussed questions relating to physics with his son. Because of his proficiency in higher mathematics, he read such works as Camille Jordan's *Cours d'analyse* (1882) during dull classroom periods in high school. Yet it was Albert Einstein's theory of relativity that had the most profound effect on Pauli's development. Once he was satisfied that he understood Einstein's theory and had acquired an adequate background in classical physics, he decided to embark on a career as a physicist.

When he was nineteen, Pauli enrolled at the University of Munich. His mentor at this time was Arnold Sommerfeld, the most prestigious teacher of theoretical physics in Germany. Under Sommerfeld's supervision, Pauli acquired the analytical skills that he was to put to good use years later. At the age of twenty, Pauli was assigned the task of submitting an article on relativity theory for the *Encyklopädie der mathematischen Wissenschaften* (encyclopedia of mathematical knowledge). Pauli's article became a 250-page monograph which is both an informative introduction to relativity theory and a history of the mathematical foundations of the theory. The art with which Pauli presented science in this early work was to characterize everything that he wrote thereafter.

At the same time that he was working on the relativity theory, Pauli also became familiar with the quantum theory at the University of Munich. He was strongly influenced by the different approaches to the structure of the atom to which Sommerfeld had introduced him. Whereas Niels Bohr's theory attempted to reconcile the differences between the laws of quantum theory, Sommerfeld's theory tried to interpret atomic phenomena through the direct application of integral numbers. The revolutionary nature of quantum theory was quite shocking to someone such as Pauli, who had been steeped in classical physics.

In 1921, Pauli became an assistant in theoretical physics at the University of Göttingen. Not only did he meet the noted physicists Max Born and James Franck, who were teaching there at the time, but also he came into personal contact with Bohr, who delivered a series of lectures there in 1922. Pauli was particularly impressed with Bohr's attempts to explain why electrons in an atom are distributed in definite groups throughout the atom's structure instead of clustering within the shell closest to the nucleus.

Life's Work

After obtaining his doctorate, Pauli immediately initiated the projects from which emerged his most significant hypothesis. In 1922, Pauli tried to explain why the spectrum lines of atoms do not always split into three lines when exposed to a strong magnetic field. After spending considerable time probing this phenomenon, known as the Zeeman effect, Pauli postulated that the quantum properties of the atomic core were permanent. This theory had far-reaching consequences, both for Pauli's own research and for the field of physics in general, because it suggested that every electron could be described by quantum numbers. Pauli was not any closer to solving the Zeeman effect a year later, when he went to the University of Hamburg as an assistant in theoretical physics. Soon after his arrival there, he was promoted to the position of assistant professor, and he spent the next few months reexamining the standard explanations for the anomalous splitting of the spectrum lines.

In 1925, Pauli's research culminated in an argument that he proposed in an article in *Zeitschrift für Physik* (periodical for physics). In this article, he stated that a new quantum theoretic property of the electron was necessary before the Zeeman effect could be properly understood. The publication of this opinion gave him the resolve he needed to complete his research into the phenomenon. That same year, Pauli discovered the final clue to the problem's solution in a paper by the English physicist Edmund Stoner. By way of explaining Stoner's rule, Pauli developed his famous exclusion principle, which states that no two electrons can have the same energy in an atom. Pauli's description of the exclusion principle in the *Handbuch der Physik* (handbook of physics) in 1926 paved the way for the development of mathematically consistent quantum mechanics through research conducted by Werner Karl Heisenberg, P. A. M. Dirac, and Erwin Schrödinger.

Pauli left Hamburg in 1928 to assume the position of professor of theoretical physics at the Federal Institute for Technology in Zurich, Switzerland, which became his home for the next twelve years. Together with his friend George Wentzel, a professor at the University of Zurich, Pauli taught a seminar for many years in which all areas of theoretical physics were discussed. During his first ten years in Zurich, he was fortunate enough to have students such as R. Kronig, Rudolf Peierls, H. B. G. Casimir, and V. F. Weisskopf as his assistants, all of whom later went on to become prominent physicists in their own right.

While Pauli was in Zurich, he produced one of his most important theories, the neutrino hypothesis. In a letter that he wrote to Lise Meitner in 1930, he reported that a neutron is emitted along with an electron when certain subatomic particles decay. Although Enrico Fermi later christened this neutron the "neutrino," it is also referred to in some circles as the "Paulino," since Pauli made this observation before Sir James Chadwick had discovered the neutron in the nucleus. Pauli published his proposal in the report of the Solvay Congress in 1933.

Much of Pauli's research in this period was also devoted to the development of relativistic quantum electrodynamics in an effort to explain the infinite self-energy of the electron. This work led Pauli into a study of wave mechanics. In an article Pauli wrote for *Handbuch der Physik* in 1933, he expanded the scope of wave mechanics to include not only a single particle but the interaction of an indefinite number of particles as well.

In the late 1930's, Pauli's work began to take him away from Zurich. Between 1935 and 1936, he was appointed visiting professor of theoretical physics at the Institute for Advanced Study in Princeton, New Jersey. Then, in 1940, the Institute for Advanced Study once again summoned him to Princeton, largely because of the Nazi invasion of Norway and Denmark. In 1945, while he was still a temporary member of the institute's faculty, Pauli received a Lorentz Medaille and, later, the Nobel Prize in Physics.

In 1946, at the end of the war, Pauli returned to Zurich with his wife, Franciska, whom he had married in April, 1934. He spent the remainder of his life in a heavily forested area called "Zollikon," where he often took long walks. During this time, he also became a Swiss citizen.

In the last years of his life, Pauli began to reflect seriously on the meaning of scientific activity; this new interest manifested itself in a number of essays, lectures, and a book coauthored with C. G. Jung—*Naturekklärung und Psyche* (1952). He even looked to Chinese philosophy for answers. Actually, though, Pauli had hoped all along that physics would reveal the harmony between God and nature. Pauli became seriously ill in December, 1958, and he died on December 14.

Summary

Wolfgang Pauli's impact on the world of physics can be traced to the scientific method that he employed throughout his career. His solid background in classical physics, which he had acquired from his father and from his own reading, became the standard against which he weighed all hypotheses, his own as well as those of others. As a student at the University of Munich, Pauli was willing to exchange some of the principles of classical physics for the quantum theory of Niels Bohr and Sommerfeld only after he was convinced that quantum theory could solve some of the mysteries of the atom, such as the Zeeman effect. For the most part, though, his classical training acted as a buffer, protecting him from obscure argument and superficial speculation.

Pauli's research laid the foundation for a new physics at the same time that it was shaking the very foundation of the old. His exclusion principle demonstrated the individuality of electrons and thus solved a problem—the Zeeman effect— that had puzzled physicists since Pieter Zeeman first observed it in 1892.

The principles of relativistic quantum electrodynamics, which had been the focus of much of Pauli's work, were finally accepted after twenty years of skepticism and inquiry. Pauli's discovery of the neutrino set the stage for further investigations by Sir James Chadwick and Enrico Fermi. Finally, his hypothesis for the permanence of quantum numbers permitted the development of a periodic table.

Yet Pauli's influence goes beyond physics. His concern with finding an ethical basis for scientific inquiry had a lasting effect on both his students and his colleagues. He was truly, as Victor Weisskopf eulogized at Pauli's funeral, "the conscience of theoretical physics."

Bibliography

"Atom Bomb Nobelists." *Science News Letter* 48 (December 1, 1945): 141-142. Announces the awarding of the Nobel Prize in Physics in 1945 to Wolfgang Pauli. Explains very clearly what Pauli meant by the "rugged individualism" of electrons.

Current Biography: Who's Who and Why. New York: H. W. Wilson, 1947. A short but fairly detailed account of Pauli's life and work. A very good introduction to his career.

Fierz, Marcus. "Wolfgang Pauli." In *Dictionary of Scientific Biography*, vol. 10. New York: Charles Scribner's Sons, 1974. An excellent account of Pauli's most important hypotheses and their impact on the field of physics. The entry also discusses Pauli's philosophical views regarding science. The scientific sections are fairly technical and would, therefore, appeal to a reader with a solid background in physics.

Fierz, Marcus, and V. F. Weisskopf, eds. *Theoretical Physics in the Twentieth Century: A Memorial Volume to Wolfgang Pauli.* New York: Interscience, 1960. Contains a series of articles ranging from first-person accounts from Pauli's coworkers to a complete listing of Pauli's books, articles, and studies. Provides useful insights into Pauli's personality as well as short, technical discussions of his theories, some of which are in German.

Goudsmit, S. A. "Pauli and Nuclear Spin." *Physics Today*, June, 1961: 18-21. Written by one of Pauli's colleagues, the article disputes Pauli's contention that Goudsmit and Ernst Back had been influenced by a paper of Pauli published in 1924 regarding the angular momentum of the atomic nucleus.

Alan Brown

IVAN PETROVICH PAVLOV

Born: September 26, 1849; Ryazan, Russia
Died: February 27, 1936; Leningrad, U.S.S.R.
Areas of Achievement: Physiology and medicine
Contribution: Pavlov is best known for developing the theory of conditioned reflexes, which he demonstrated by teaching a dog to salivate when it heard a bell. He also performed important experiments to determine the connection between human behavior and the nervous system; he won the Nobel Prize in Physiology or Medicine in 1904 for his work on the digestive tract.

Early Life

Ivan Petrovich Pavlov was born on September 26, 1849, in Ryazan, Russia, the eldest son of parents of peasant stock. His father, Peter Dmitrievich Pavlov, was a village priest, who emphasized family, hard work, reading, and education. His mother, Varvara Ivanovna Pavlov, supported his father in these efforts. Pavlov was born into a large family of eleven children, six of whom died in childhood.

Pavlov's education began when he was seven years old; at home, he was taught to read and write. When he was ten years old, he had an accident that weakened him physically, and the effects of the accident lasted throughout the remainder of his childhood. When he was eleven years of age, his parents entered him in the second grade at the local parish school to begin his formal education. Four years later, in 1864, he entered the theological seminary of Ryazan, where he received a classical education of the day in preparation for the priesthood. It was there that he developed his first genuine interest in science. In 1870, he decided not to become a priest and left the seminary to enroll at the University of St. Petersburg, where he studied science. There he pursued inorganic chemistry, organic chemistry, and physiology under such renowned professors as Dmitry Mendeleyev, Aleksandr Butlerov, and Ilya Tsion.

Pavlov completed his studies at the University of St. Petersburg in 1875 and entered the Medico-Chirurgical Academy (later renamed the Military Medical Academy), where he worked as a laboratory assistant while earning his medical degree. In 1877, he published his first work of substance; the subject was the control of blood circulation by reflexes. He completed his course of study and became a full physician in 1879 at thirty years of age. Four years later, in 1883, he completed his dissertation. In the meantime, he met and married Serafima Karchevokaya, a friend of Fyodor Dostoevski. Theirs was a good, supportive marriage.

Life's Work

Pavlov's three main areas of investigation and physiological inquiry include blood circulation, food digestion, and conditioned reflexes. These three matters provide a convenient way of discussing his life's achievements, as he took these up in turn.

After completing his medical dissertation in 1883, Pavlov and his wife spent two years in Germany, where Pavlov studied cardiovascular physiology under Carl Ludwig and gastrointestinal physiology under Rudolf Heidenhain. Upon his return to St. Petersburg in 1886, Pavlov began his first major, sustained research; his efforts were directed to understanding cardiac physiology and regulating blood pressure. His success is greatly attributable to his surgical skills. Pavlov was able to enter a catheter into the femoral arteries of dogs and cats with little pain and no anesthesia; thus, he was able to observe and record the effects of various stimuli on the blood pressure of the animals. By working carefully and repeatedly, he was eventually able to determine which nerves controlled the pulsation and magnitude of the heartbeat. Dissection further assisted him in verifying his findings, as did the use of drugs, cutting nerves, and making permanent openings into the digestive tract.

At about the time Pavlov completed his work on blood circulation, he was appointed to a position at the Military Medical Academy, where he had earlier been a medical student. First, he served as an instructor of pharmacology; he then became director of a new surgical department of the school called the Institute of Experimental Medicine, where he conducted his scientific studies for the next several decades. To his credit, Pavlov was consistently humane in his treatment of his subjects, that is, his dogs and cats. His leadership provided for a system under which pain during surgery and other study was minimized, and the animals received the best of care after procedures were completed.

Pavlov had already been at work on the digestive tract before he finished his work on blood circulation. For some ten or twelve years after the formation of the Institute of Experimental Medicine under his direction in 1891, Pavlov and his researchers determined a number of things about the digestive system. They were able to do so primarily because Pavlov perfected a surgical technique of creating a kind of separate stomach in dogs, which made it possible for investigators to monitor secretions and other activity of the digestive process. He was able to determine the function of nerves in controlling digestion, and he discerned a wealth of other information about processes of the alimentary canal. In 1888, he discovered the secretory nerves of the pancreas; in 1889, he studied the function and activity of other gastric glands. His work on digestion continued for decades, but in 1897 he published his findings on the principal digestive glands. This demonstrated existence of secretory nerves to the digestive tract resulted in Pavlov's receiving the Nobel Prize in Physiology or Medicine in 1904.

Pavlov and researchers under his guidance at the Institute of Experimental

Medicine never discontinued their study of digestion. Yet at some point in the early 1900's, Pavlov became absorbed with the effects of the brain upon learned behavior. He became almost completely concerned with what came to be known as his theory of conditioned reflexes. Early in his career, Pavlov had realized that dogs would secrete saliva and other digestive fluids throughout the alimentary canal before they actually received food. He noticed this occurrence when dogs would hear the timely approach of laboratory assistants who might or might not be bringing food to the animals. In one of the most famous scientific experiments ever conducted, Pavlov trained (that is, he conditioned) dogs to salivate at the sound of a bell, when they learned that the bell indicated that food was soon coming. Some critics immediately dismissed his theory, or at least the relevance thereof, claiming that Pavlov had simply given terminology to what every dog trainer already knew. In general, though, Pavlov had demonstrated clearly that there is an explicit connection between physiological function and learned behavior, the ramifications of which have never been fully explained. His experiment, perhaps, left more of a mark on psychology than it did on physiology. In general, he showed that the theory of muscular reflexes of the nervous system could be expanded to include mental reflexes; thus, his experiments put forth the question as to what extent human behavior is controlled by learned mental patterns and responses.

Beginning in 1918 and for several years thereafter, Pavlov studied the behavior patterns of several mentally ill patients in an attempt to treat them. He believed he could alter the behavior of the insane by using a physiological method that primarily involved removing the patient from any physiological stimuli which might be considered harmful. In other words, insanity was treated with quiet and solitude.

At the end of his career, Pavlov used his beliefs about conditioned reflexes to explore the differences between mankind and animals. He came to regard human language itself as the most advanced and complicated form of conditioned reflex. He found both in mankind and among the animals a commonality in some matters of reflexes but not in all. Man is thus viewed as a kind of advanced species, different from other creatures primarily because the brain and nervous system accommodate more complicated, conditioned reflexes. Pavlov remained in general good health until 1935, when he first began to fall ill. He recovered somewhat to live until February 27 of the next year, when he died of pneumonia.

Summary

Given the extreme advance of modern medicine in the second half of the twentieth century, Ivan Petrovich Pavlov's discoveries about blood circulation and digestion seem to be rather basic, if not primitive, contributions to modern science. Such a judgment, however, does injustice to both Pavlov and his work. Readers should remember that in the late 1800's, medicine had only lately rediscovered that the blood circulates. For Pavlov to succeed in determining causes for both the rhythm and strength of the heartbeat was quite a feat in the medicine of his time. Pavlov's perfection of surgical techniques and his enthusiasm for studying the previously unexamined matter of digestion also qualify him as one of the great scientists of the twentieth century. His humane treatment of the animals that served as the subjects of his studies further adds credit to his name.

In his personal life, Pavlov must be repeatedly credited for doing what he believed was morally right regardless of consequences. In 1895, he had open conflict with his superior at the Military Medical Academy, and consequently his promotion from professor of pharmacology to professor of physiology was delayed for two years. His most noteworthy of moral actions occurred, however, in his resistance to the Communists after their rise to power in 1917. In 1922, because of a food shortage, Pavlov requested permission of Vladimir Ilich Lenin to relocate the Institute of Experimental Medicine abroad. Lenin denied the request but did offer Pavlov more food for himself. Angrily, Pavlov refused to accept the food until it was available for everybody working at the laboratory. He later publicly accused the Bolsheviks of conducting a social experiment with Communism, and he added that for the value of this experiment he would not sacrifice so much as a frog's hind leg; the statement became the most famous he ever uttered. In 1924, when the sons of priests were collectively expelled from the Military Medical Academy, Pavlov resigned from the Institute of Experimental Medicine, a division of that school, reminding the government that he, too, was the son of a priest. The government permitted these instances of resistance undoubtedly because it thought Pavlov's theories and research into human behavior would be useful for its own purposes. At the same time, Pavlov gradually mellowed toward the government and its policies, although he never joined the Communist Party.

Pavlov was wrong in thinking that psychology would eventually become a subset of physiology. This, however, does not undercut the validity of his theory of conditioned reflexes; nor does it diminish the effects of his own theories on later thinkers in other disciplines of study. Pavlov's works provided the foundation upon which the subsequent study of human behavior has been conducted. His methods and approaches, though not all of his theories, are still intact and in practice in research laboratories throughout the world.

Bibliography
Babkin, Boris P. *Pavlov: A Biography.* Chicago: University of Chicago Press, 1949. Babkin, who was one of Pavlov's pupils, has provided one of the best biographies of Pavlov. Much of the biography is given to personal

anecdote. Babkin also uses information gathered from A. A. Savich, one of Pavlov's colleagues, and Pavlov's widow.

Gantt, W. Horsley. "I. P. Pavlov: A Bibliographical Sketch." In *Lectures on Conditioned Reflexes*, by Ivan Petrovich Pavlov. Translated by W. Horsley Gantt. New York: International, 1928. Gantt, a friend and student of Pavlov, has written an excellent short biography of the scientist. Information about Pavlov's life is accurate and is provided in some detail. Modern readers of biography will not appreciate the patronizing, self-serving flavor of Gantt's approach.

_____. "Physiology Since Pavlov." *The New Republic* 105 (1941): 728-731. In this article, Gantt traces developments in physiology in the five years following Pavlov's death. He reports on the connection between the amount of external stimulus and brain activity; he also takes up the formation of neuroses.

Grigorian, N. A. "Ivan Petrovich Pavlov." In *Dictionary of Scientific Biography*, edited by Charles Coulston Gillispie, vol. 10. New York: Charles Scribner's Sons, 1974. After a brief biographical sketch, this article provides a straightforward account of Pavlov's work, emphasizing his methodological innovations. Strongly disputes the popular image of Pavlov as "a mechanist who saw complex behavior as the sum of individual conditioned reflexes." Includes a bibliography.

Pavlov, I. P. *Conditioned Reflexes: An Investigation of the Physiological Activity of the Cerebral Cortex*. Translated by G. V. Anrep. New York: Dover, 1960. Anrep's translation of Pavlov's work on conditioned reflexes is one of the best and most reliable available. Pavlov's own lectures, rendered into English here, remain the best introduction to the man and his life and theories. The book contains a rather extensive bibliography for those who would further study conditioned reflexes.

Straus, Erwin. *The Primary World of Senses*. Translated by Jacob Needleman. New York: Free Press, 1963. One of Straus's main objections to Pavlov's theories is that "man thinks, not the brain." The critic's perspective essentially is that of a psychologist.

Wells, Harry K. *Ivan P. Pavlov: Toward a Psychology and Psychiatry*. New York: International, 1956. Wells primarily treats Pavlov in the light of the theories of Sigmund Freud; he defines the roles of psychology and psychiatry in the context of theories presented by both thinkers.

Carl Singleton

ANNA PAVLOVA

Born: February 12, 1881; St. Petersburg, Russia
Died: January 23, 1931; The Hague, The Netherlands
Area of Achievement: Dance
Contribution: Pavlova was widely regarded as the greatest embodiment of ballet in her lifetime, and she became a symbol of the best the ballet has known after her death. She spread knowledge of and interest in ballet through her worldwide tours.

Early Life

Anna Pavlovna Pavlova was born in St. Petersburg (now Leningrad), on February 12, 1881. Her parents were poor, and her father died when she was only two. Her mother sent her to live in the country with her grandmother. In Ligovo, she led a simple life with a grandmother who was totally devoted to caring for her. Her favorite amusement was seeking flowers in the woods. She developed a deep love of nature and of this landscape in particular. When she was eight years old, her mother took her to see the ballet at the Maryinsky Theater. The performance of *La Belle au Bois Dormant* (Sleeping Beauty) captured her imagination, and she told her mother that she wanted to become a ballerina and dance that role. At Anna's insistence, her mother applied to the Imperial Theater School, but she was told they would take no children under ten. After waiting for two years, they applied again. She passed the examination and entered the school in 1891.

At the school, her teachers were Christian Johannsen, a former pupil and dancer of the Danish master, Auguste Bournonville, and Pavel Gerdt. She also studied with E. P. Sokolova, a former prima ballerina of the Maryinsky, and Enrico Cecchetti, the great Italian teacher. The Imperial Theater School gave instruction in general education and religion as well as dance. The full program took seven years to complete. In addition to ballet, the students learned historical and national dances and practiced long hours on their own. Pavlova was graduated and made her debut at the Maryinsky on June 1, 1899. She immediately moved into small parts rather than the *corps de ballet* and moved steadily through the ranks of the company from second soloist (1902) to first soloist (1903), ballerina (1905), and prima (1906). Before becoming a ballerina, she spent more time studying with Cecchetti to perfect her technique. By that time, she had appeared in all the major ballerina roles and had attracted a loyal following.

Life's Work

Two of the great themes of Pavlova's life became apparent very early in her career. In 1907, she created the title role in *The Dying Swan*, choreographed by Michel Fokine, and in 1908, she began to tour abroad. Throughout her life, though she performed with companies and organized and led her own, she was best known for her solo and duet roles, in which her individual artistry as a performer shone clearly. Her tours throughout the world helped to make ballet universal and an international language of art.

In her early years as prima ballerina with the Maryinsky company, she created her major solo roles. In 1907, she premiered Fokine's *Pavillon d'Armide*, in 1908, *Egyptian Nights*, and also in 1908, Fokine's second version of *Chopiniana*. After she began to tour outside Russia in 1908, she remained a member of the Maryinsky company but spent continually less time there. Eventually, she would return only after long tours and would study again with her teachers to refresh her technique. Her performances at the Maryinsky ended when she officially left the company in 1913.

Her first foreign tour took her to Scandinavia, Leipzig, Prague, and Vienna. She was immediately successful and acclaimed wherever she performed. In Stockholm, young men unharnessed the horses from her carriage and led it back to her hotel themselves—a tribute paid to only a few nineteenth century ballerinas and an exuberant beginning to her international career. In 1909, she performed with Sergei Diaghilev's company, the Ballets Russes, in Paris. She made her debut in Berlin, in 1909, and in New York and London, in 1910, all with the Ballets Russes. Her last appearance with Diaghilev's company was in London, in 1911. London was to be her home; in 1912, she and her husband, Victor Dandré, purchased Ivy House on Hampstead Hill. She had a particular love for the gardens and pond at the home.

She formed her own company in 1914, a more difficult path to choose than to stay within the Maryinsky or to continue with Diaghilev. Yet, she assembled a company and led it on world tours as though given a mission to take ballet and her own dancing presence to every country on the earth. Her company repertoire was drawn from the classics, sometimes in abbreviated versions. The choreography was by Jean Coralli, Marius Petipa, and Lev Ivanov. The repertoire also included the dances by Fokine in which she created her great roles. Newer work was contributed by Uday Shankar, among others. Her attention to Shankar, an Indian artist studying painting in London, led to their performances together of dances inspired by classical Indian dance. Pavlova encouraged Shankar to leave ballet and develop and renew the Indian art form. As Shankar was greatly responsible for the renaissance of classical dance in India, Pavlova can be credited with urging him to do so.

Pavlova's repertoire also included works that she herself choreographed. Among the most popular was *Autumn Leaves* (1919), set to music by Frédéric Chopin, the only full company ballet she choreographed. Similar to her other works, it developed from an intense appreciation of nature. All of her work was inspired by nature, and her artistic gift was to appear actually to become the flower, dragonfly, swan, or human emotion that she portrayed. To her audience, she seemed to create a miracle in each performance, transcending her own being and transporting the members of the audience from their own time and place as well. She believed that expressing beauty so that the audience might experience it in an immediate way was the goal of her art and also the source of hope for humanity.

As her performances featured duets and solos, Pavlova had a series of male partners who were famous dancers in their own right. The first was Mikhail Mordkin, who partnered her at the Maryinsky; Laurent Novikov became her partner in 1911 and Pierre Vladimirov in 1927. Although her first set of dancers were mostly Russian, once she fully organized her company they were drawn mainly from England and other European countries. The company members were influential in spreading her philosophy and style and the Cecchetti-influenced technique. Many European dancers left the company to remain as teachers and performers in the United States, and many Americans who returned home after being in her company gained fame on their return. They became important not only in ballet but also in theatrical and popular dance.

Pavlova's touring was tireless and covered great distances on the globe at a time when the only means of travel was ocean liner. She and her company spent the period of World War I in South America, where they had been conducting an extensive series of performances when the war broke out. Her company danced not only in the great capitals of Europe but also in provincial towns. Their travels also took them to then-exotic places such as Egypt and Australia.

Pavlova made one film and a series of test shots in Hollywood. In 1915, she portrayed Fenella in *The Dumb Girl of Portici*. The test shots, filmed in 1924, included excerpts from some of her most popular dances: *Christmas*, *The Dying Swan*, *Oriental Dance*, *Rose Mourante*, *Fairy Doll*, *The Californian Poppy*, and *Columbine*. These were arranged for a film, *The Immortal Swan*, in 1956, the twenty-fifth anniversary of her death.

This pioneer of world dance suffered somewhat from the fluctuations of fashion. She kept to her classical repertoire throughout the time that Diaghilev's innovations became popular. Thus, there was little enthusiasm among the patrons of the high culture in London for her production of *Giselle*, for example, in the late 1910's and early 1920's. At that time, most of the classics of Russian ballet, the works of Petipa, were out of favor. After her death, the importance of the classics was restored as they took their places in repertoires alongside modern additions. Pavlova's faith in the classics did not come from a lack of curiosity or a limited imagination; rather, she believed that these ballets and her own dances were the best way to touch the hearts of the broadest range of people. To bring ballet to the world did not mean to her to limit it to an aesthetic elite. In 1915, she considered experimenting with dance without music but decided it would be too strange to attract "the masses." She wanted to reach the people and was in turn embraced by them. She truly believed that she could provide joy for the people of the world and through dance give them relief from the sorrows of life.

Her wide appeal affected many future dancers and dance lovers. Sir Frederick Ashton, who was to become one of the great twentieth century ballet choreographers, saw her dance when he was a young man in Lima, Peru; her performances helped lead him to a life in ballet. He always considered himself a follower of the tradition of the great Russian choreographers Fokine and Petipa, but with a sense of theater that might be traced to Pavlova. He remembered her exceptionally expressive hands and feet and the sensitivity and unique "plasticity" of her movement. Although questions have been raised about the purity of her technique—was hers the greatest or was it merely equally great as that of other ballerinas?—Ashton and other exemplars of ballet, such as Margot Fonteyn, have maintained that her technique was fine but so surpassed by her magical presence that it cannot be considered separately. Hers was a total performance. Ashton claimed that she was the "greatest theatrical genius" that he had ever seen and that she was able to create more beauty and emotion from her slight dances than could be achieved in full-scale ballets.

Pavlova's death came tragically early, in 1931, after she became ill while on tour in The Netherlands. She continued with her rehearsal preparations despite her illness. One of her company members who was with her at the time recalled that after she was forced to bed by a high fever, doctors pierced her back in order to drain fluid from her lungs; she died soon after this treatment. It is said that her last words were a request for her swan costume. At her funeral in London near Ivy House, she was mourned by many who had never known her but had believed in the beautiful legend she had become.

Summary

Anna Pavlova became the image and spirit of ballet during her lifetime. Her name continues to be synonymous with greatness not only as a dancer but also as an artist who gave her whole life to her art. There was nothing in her life that did not contribute in some way to her perfection of her dancing or to the furthering of the art. She traveled at least three hundred thousand miles at a time when travel was difficult. While acknowledged as the world's greatest dancer, she took her performances to remote places and was said never to find them anything less than stimulating and a source of joy. She called herself "a sower." Through her work and her travels, she not only allowed vast numbers of people to share the pleasure of her performances but also spread the knowledge and love of ballet. She was physically beautiful but did not stop at portraying prettiness; according to Ashton, her performances could make the audience uncomfortable because of her powerful presence and uncompromising presentation of emotional truth. She stirred her audiences more than she entertained them. Even in choreography that would not have been meaningful without her performing it, she created profound illustrations of life. No one could be indifferent to her. As a woman leading her own company around the world with her husband assisting, she presented a strong image of courage and confidence. It is to her credit, through her own performances and the legend she created, that ballet is performed and applauded on every continent.

Bibliography
Algeranoff, Harcourt. *My Years with Pavlova*. London: William Heinemann, 1957. A narrative by a company member of Pavlova's work with her companies on tour.
Beaumont, Cyril W. *Anna Pavlova*. London: C. W. Beaumont, 1938. A brief biography and appreciation of Pavlova by a ballet lover who admired her greatly and promoted her legend after her death.
Dandré, Victor. *Anna Pavlova in Art and Life*. London: Cassell, 1932. A detailed biography by Pavlova's husband. In this book, Dandré frequently tries to correct what he believes to have been mistaken ideas about Pavlova's life.
Fonteyn, Margot. *Pavlova: Portrait of a Dancer*. New York: Viking, 1984. A remarkable collection of photographs from all stages of Pavlova's life accompanies a text drawn greatly from Pavlova's interviews and letters. The commentary by Dame Margot Fonteyn is helpful but never intrusive and serves to illustrate the continued admiration for Pavlova in the ballet world.
Lazzarini, John, and Roberta Lazzarini. *Pavlova: Repertoire of a Legend*. New York: Schirmer Books, 1980. A large-format picture book that focuses on photographic studies from Pavlova's repertory. The authors are the curators of the Pavlova Society and offer reliable discussion of the works.

Leslie Friedman

PELÉ
Edson Arantes do Nascimento

Born: October 23, 1940; Três Corações, Minas Gerais, Brazil

Area of Achievement: Sports
Contribution: Probably the greatest soccer player of all time, Pelé starred on the Brazilian national teams that won the World Cup in 1958, 1962, and 1970. Following his retirement, the New York Cosmos of the North American Soccer League lured him to the United States, where he did much to popularize soccer.

Early Life

Pelé, christened Edson Arantes do Nascimento, was born October 23, 1940, in Três Corações, Minas Gerais. His father, João ("Dondinho") Ramos do Nascimento, was a popular minor league soccer player in a nation where soccer was a consuming passion. The young black considered Dondinho the greatest player in the world and wanted to be like him, but his mother, Celeste Arantes, hoped for a better career for her son than that of itinerant soccer player. Although Edson attended school until the fourth grade, it held little interest for him. At age ten, he quit school and, when not working as a two-dollar-a-month shoemaker's apprentice, spent his days playing soccer with the neighborhood boys. The games provided a carefree interval in a life of poverty and insecurity, made worse when his father suffered a serious knee injury.

Young Edson had natural gifts unlike anything his chums brought to their makeshift field. In Bauru, São Paulo, he and his friends played in the streets, with sticks or rocks marking the goals and rags tied up with string serving as the ball. One day they pilfered a cargo of raw peanuts and then roasted and sold them in the streets to raise money for a real ball and some faded uniforms. A local promoter organized them into a team, and for two years they won the children's championship of Bauru. By this time, Edson had acquired his famous nickname: "Pelé" is meaningless in Portuguese although probably derived from the verb *pelejar*, to battle. Pelé also caught the attention of Valdemar de Brito, a former member of the Brazilian national team and coach of the Bauru Athletic Club. Brito offered Pelé a contract to play for his club's youth team, and the boy led the team to three championships.

Life's Work

Pelé was almost fifteen when Brito took him to Santos for a tryout with the team there, a major Brazilian club. Although a slender 130 pounds and awed by the big city, Pelé managed to impress the coach. For several months, he played on the junior squad, but, on September 7, 1956, he substituted in the second half for an injured player and scored his initial first-division goal. By early 1957, still only sixteen years old, he was a striker on the starting team, and the goals had begun to accumulate.

Brazilians loved graceful, elegant, attacking soccer, and Pelé gave it to them. As his body matured, he stood five feet, nine inches and weighed 165 pounds. A superb athlete, he had a powerful kick with either foot, remarkable peripheral vision, great leaping ability, and amazing skill in feinting and dribbling. Pelé was creativity on the field, using acrobatic moves to manufacture seemingly impossible shots and passes. Most important, he used his individual skills to improve the play of his teammates.

Pelé won international recognition in 1958, when he was chosen at age seventeen to play on the Brazilian national team in the World Cup competition held in Sweden. Suffering from a knee injury, he did not participate in Brazil's first two games of the tournament. In the quarterfinal match against Wales, however, he gave the Europeans a taste of the spectacular: Receiving a high pass on his chest, he used his foot to lift the ball over the onrushing defender's head and then blasted it past the goalkeeper without the ball ever hitting the ground. The goal gave Brazil a 1-0 victory. He marked three goals in Brazil's 5-2 win over France in the semifinal. Pelé's two goals in the final against Sweden helped give Brazil a 5-2 victory and its first world championship.

Pelé's success in Sweden and the elegance and showmanship of Brazilian soccer made his Santos club a tremendous draw on the international circuit during the following years. A group of Italian clubs offered Santos one million dollars in 1960 for Pelé, and the Brazilian congress responded by declaring him a "non-exportable national treasure." With Pelé leading the way, Santos won the world club championship in 1962 and 1963.

In 1962, Brazil gained its second World Cup triumph, this time in Chile. Pelé scored once and assisted on Brazil's other goal in its 2-0 victory over Mexico in its initial match, but, in the second game against Czechoslovakia, he severely pulled a muscle. Fortunately for Brazil, the team had good depth, and Garrincha, Pelé's sidekick in the forward line, emerged as the star of the tournament. Pelé's injury kept him out of action for several weeks after Brazil's 3-1 defeat of Czechoslovakia for its second consecutive championship.

The 1962 World Cup gave a taste, however, of the new levels of violence to which international soccer had sunk and to which Pelé would be subjected. The increasing intrusion of politics and nationalism into international competition and the financial rewards for success added to the tendency for teams to seek victory at any price. Stars such as Pelé became marked men, subject to brutal, vicious tackling, which in his eyes seemed even worse because his style of play emphasized elegance and agility.

The Brazilian national team headed to England in 1966 in search of its third consecutive world championship, but the fates were unkind. At the peak of his game, Pelé went into the competition on a wave of international acclaim and national euphoria. Brazil's midfielders were past their prime, however, and the tournament was being played in northern Europe, on the English fields where soccer had originated. Sir Stanley Rous, English president of the International Soccer Federation, which conducted the tournament, had allegedly instructed referees to let the northern Europeans play their style of soccer rather than penalizing them for defensive aggressiveness. Brazil defeated Bulgaria 2-0 in its first match, but a savage tackle left Pelé injured for the remainder of the tournament. Without Pelé, the Brazilians then lost to Hungary. Trying to save the team from elimination, Pelé attempted to play against Portugal. Savagely fouled, Pelé was reinjured. In the wake of Brazil's defeat, Pelé's spirit was shattered, and he vowed not to play in another World Cup competition as a protest against the mounting violence.

Back home in Brazil, his love for the game gradually revived, and besides he had contractual obligations with Santos that carried him around the world and earned for both him and the club huge sums for exhibition matches. On November 19, 1969, he scored the thousandth goal of his career against Vasco da Gama in Rio de Janeiro. The country nearly stopped in adulation, he received equal billing in the newspapers with an American moon landing, and Brazil rushed out a postage stamp commemorating his achievement.

The following year brought his crowning feat. Having put the misery of 1966 behind him, Pelé agreed to play once again for Brazil in World Cup competition in Mexico. While he had never been strictly an individualist on the field, Pelé recognized that opponents would attempt to brutalize him again, and so he became the consummate team player in 1970. He flicked pinpoint passes to streaking teammates when defenses collapsed on him; he fought valiantly on defense; and he still marked marvelous goals. The final against Italy pitted the defensive, counterattacking strategy of European soccer with the slashing, offensive flair of the Brazilians. Pelé and his teammates won 4-1, retiring the Jules Rimet cup that belonged to the first country to win three championships.

The triumph in Mexico left Pelé with little to achieve on the field. He announced his retirement from the national team on June 18, 1971, to the consternation of Brazilians who hoped he would help defend the title again in 1974. Then on October 2, 1974, he retired from Santos, intending to devote greater attention to his family. After a secret six-year engagement to Rosemari Cholby, a blond bank employee, the couple had married in 1966; they had two children, Kelly Cristina, born in 1967, and Edson, born in 1970. Pelé's business activities outside soccer were also time-consuming. He had invested in several industries and companies, starred as a detective in a television series, acted in movies, and performed songs that he had written.

Manufacturers of clothing, watches, chocolate, soccer equipment, soft drinks, and bicycles all sought his endorsement. He was probably the wealthiest athlete in the world and certainly the most famous.

As it turned out, his soccer career was not finished. In 1975, he shocked the soccer world by signing a seven-million-dollar, three-year contract to play for the New York Cosmos of the North American Soccer League (NASL). He needed the money to offset business losses but was also motivated by love for his country and for soccer. He saw the Cosmos' offer as an opportunity to be a goodwill ambassador for Brazil in the United States and at the same time popularize soccer there, where it had always been a minor sport. While some Brazilians were initially upset that their hero was leaving to play in the United States, his countrymen came to take great pride in his achievements among the Yankees. During the three seasons he played, Pelé was by far the greatest draw of the NASL. The Cosmos set attendance records wherever they played, and Pelé retained enough of his skills to awe American crowds. When he retired in 1977, his final opponent was the Santos club from Brazil. At halftime, he put on his famous Santos shirt and finished his career playing for his old team. When the match ended, both teams carried him off the field on their shoulders to the chant of "Pelé! Pelé!" from the seventy-six thousand Americans who had braved a rainstorm to witness history.

Summary

Gracious and accommodating to his fans, Pelé was idolized throughout the world. Brazilians regularly talked about electing him president, and Pelé was the most recognized figure in the country. In black Africa he was a demigod, the pride of the entire subcontinent. The Nigerians and Biafrans halted their war for a day so that Pelé could play an exhibition there. Popes and heads of state asked to meet him, curious about the man who attracted such universal acclaim. A few Brazilians quietly criticized him for not being more of a social reformer, for not taking bolder stands on behalf of his country's poor and blacks, but such activism would have been out of character. Instead, he was an outstanding role model for children, setting a good moral example and devoting much time to his fans. He also returned to his studies and received a university degree.

During his twenty-two-year career, Pelé played 1,363 games and scored 1,281 goals, twice as many as anyone else in the world's most popular team sport. From 1957 to 1966, for ten consecutive years, he was the leading scorer in the tough São Paulo League, yet he also stood at the top in 1974, when he retired in Brazil. The youngest to play on a World Cup winner, he was also the only person to win the World Cup three times. In addition, Pelé scored what was reputed to be the greatest goal in the history of the game: Taking the ball in his own penalty area, he dribbled the length of the field, eluding nine defenders, and scored. Brazilian television replayed a tape of that goal every day for the next year. Altogether, Pelé played soccer in eighty-eight different countries. His ability to create goals for teammates and make seemingly impossible shots set him apart as a genius in stark contrast to the trend of modern soccer to become more and more conservative and defensive, avoiding risk and subduing individualism. That genius and his long career exalted Pelé above all others who have played the game.

Bibliography
Bodo, Peter, and David Hershey. *Pelé's New World*. New York: W. W. Norton, 1977. A biography that focuses primarily on Pelé's years playing for the Cosmos.

Lever, Janet. *Soccer Madness*. Chicago: University of Chicago Press, 1983. In this study of soccer's sociological impact on Brazil, Lever discusses Pelé's popularity and his symbolic importance to the game and his country.

Morris, Desmond. *The Soccer Tribe*. London: Jonathan Cape, 1981. Morris portrays soccer as a tribal sport that demands intense loyalties from players and fans. He makes numerous references to Pelé.

Pelé, with Robert L. Fish. *My Life and the Beautiful Game: The Autobiography of Pelé*. New York: Doubleday, 1977. Movingly written by Fish, this book is the place to start for anyone interested in Pelé.

Rosenthal, Gary. *Everybody's Soccer Book*. New York: Charles Scribner's Sons, 1981. A good history of the World Cup, including references to Pelé's participation.

Rote, Kyle, with Basil G. Kane. *Kyle Rote Jr.'s Complete Book of Soccer*. New York: Simon & Schuster, 1978. This general overview of soccer contains numerous references to Pelé, particularly in the chapter tracing the history of the World Cup.

Thébaud, François. *Pelé*. Translated by Leo Weinstein. New York: Harper & Row, 1976. A French sports writer who saw Pelé play many times and interviewed him wrote this biography and analysis of Pelé's place in the soccer pantheon.

Trevillion, Paul. *"King" Pelé*. London: Stanley Paul, 1971. This short biography is aimed at juvenile readers and contains illustrations and a section on soccer techniques.

Kendall W. Brown

P'ENG TE-HUAI

Born: c. October 24, 1898; Shihhsiang, China
Died: November 29, 1974; Peking, China
Area of Achievement: The military
Contribution: P'eng was a soldier for his entire adult career, all but the first few years of that career spent in the highest echelons of the Chinese Communist army. Despite making an immense contribution to the military victory of communism in China, P'eng became the victim of political purges carried out by Mao Tse-tung in 1959 and spent his last years in official disgrace.

Early Life

P'eng Te-huai was born in Hunan Province, China, very near to the village birthplace of his later comrade-in-arms Mao Tse-tung. One's class background could be very important in later years, especially in the Cultural Revolution, in determining one's political reliability—the presumption being that higher social origins made one more unreliable. P'eng described his family as "lower-middle peasant," and clearly his family suffered severe hardships in his youth. It is not surprising then that he made the same career choice as other impoverished peasant boys—military service. At the age of eighteen, he joined one of the many warlord armies that dominated the political and military scene in China from 1916 to 1928. He was to remain a soldier for the next forty-three years of his life, until he fell victim to purges carried out by Mao in 1959.

In 1922, P'eng was able to gain admission to the Hunan Provincial Military Academy to receive professional training. After nine months of training, P'eng was graduated and was appointed captain and commander of the very unit he had joined as a recruit seven years earlier. In 1926, the army that P'eng served went over to the Nationalist army under Chiang Kai-shek, who had just launched the Northern Expedition aimed at eliminating the warlord menace. Though not an official member of the Nationalist army, P'eng regarded himself as a "follower" for the next two years, during which time he rose to the rank of colonel in the Nationalist army. In early 1928, he applied for membership in the Chinese Communist Party (CCP), and in April of that year his entrance into the Party was approved. What prompted his transfer of allegiance from the Nationalist (KMT) cause to the Communists was not ideology so much as a rebellious spirit and the conviction that the CCP and not the KMT was committed to a struggle against rural poverty.

Life's Work

Much of P'eng's career, especially his later years, would be characterized by an antagonistic relationship with his fellow Hunanese, Mao Tse-tung. In the earlier years, conflicts, while frequently evident, were moderated. Building an army from scratch, challenging the much superior forces of the KMT, and, in the 1930's, mobilizing resistance against the invading Japanese—these challenging tasks overshadowed the factional struggling that often went on behind the scenes.

Though not one of the founders of the Chinese Red Army—it was organized in the year before P'eng joined the CCP—P'eng was one of the major figures in developing the guerrilla tactics that the CCP used to defend itself against the "annihilation campaigns" launched against it by Chiang Kai-shek's forces in the period from 1930 to 1934. Like nearly all the subsequent leadership of the CCP, P'eng was present on the yearlong (1934-1935) retreat called the "Long March," which took the Communists on a six-thousand-mile journey from their bases in the south of China to a new headquarters in Shensi Province. They had barely dug in at their new base at the city of Yen-an when war erupted with Japan.

The eight-year-long Sino-Japanese War, 1937-1945, would prove to be a key factor in determining the fortunes of the CCP. At the beginning of the war, the CCP, weak and exhausted after having barely survived the ordeal of the Long March, controlled the single base at Yen-an and commanded the allegiance of no more than a million Chinese. At the end of the war, in 1945, the CCP, thanks to perfecting tactics of guerrilla warfare and mobilizing masses of China in the patriotic resistance cause, had expanded its network of bases to nineteen and controlled a population of about one hundred million. Throughout that war, P'eng was deputy commander of the Eighth Route Army, the formal designation of the Chinese Red Army. While the commander, Chu Teh, was a towering figure in the army and highly respected, P'eng is often given credit for carrying the main responsibility of the frontline direction of the war of resistance against Japan.

The defeat of Japan did not bring peace to China for long. In 1946, one year after Japan's surrender, a three-year civil war between Chiang's Nationalists and Mao's Communists swept over China. The now largely expanded Communist armies were reorganized and named the People's Liberation Army (PLA); Chu continued as commander, with P'eng as his deputy. As commander in chief of the First Field Army, P'eng was responsible for the victorious offensive against the KMT armies in the northwest of China.

In 1950, one year after the establishment of the People's Republic of China (PRC), China found itself involved in the Korean War. As American forces drove into North Korea toward the Yalu River boundary with the PRC in November, 1950, P'eng was called upon to lead the "Chinese People's Volunteers" into engagement with American forces. For the next three years, until the war ended in a stalemate in 1953 near the original thirty-eighth parallel, P'eng remained in Korea directing the Chinese effort there. He was the only first-rank PLA veteran to participate in the Korean War. In

1954, P'eng became both the de facto commander in chief of the PLA and the minister of defense. One year later he was elevated to the newly created rank of marshal.

It was exactly at this time that P'eng launched a campaign to modernize the army, a venture that was eventually to arouse Mao's suspicion. To modernize meant to professionalize and that required trimming the ranks of the PLA, which had ballooned in size. What was needed, P'eng believed, was a relatively small, highly trained elite establishment rather than a mass army steeped in guerrilla traditions. Compulsory military service was substituted for the old "volunteer" system. Insignia of rank were introduced in the PLA, and distinctive uniforms and caps, modeled on those of the Soviet Red Army, were issued. It is a wonder that P'eng's reforms saw the light of day, for they contradicted Mao's dicta that men were more important than weapons, that the guerrilla traditions of the Yen-an days had to be preserved, that political indoctrination was more important than technical training, and that political commissars were at least as important as good professional officers.

The chairman's response came in 1958, when Mao moved to check P'eng's professionalization drive by promoting his own militia movement under the slogan "Every man a soldier." While only a limited number of the so-called core militiamen would be issued rifles and live ammunition, a second armed force was being created. In addition to this frontal challenge to P'eng's professional military convictions, Mao's Great Leap Forward, launched in 1958, caused the rift between Mao and P'eng to widen. Inspection trips into the countryside in that year caused P'eng to recoil at the veritable chaos caused by the sudden rush into the communes and frenzied campaigns to increase steel production in the backyard furnaces that became the hallmark of the Great Leap Forward.

The issue came to a head at historic meetings attended by the entire top level of party leadership in the resort area of Lushan in the summer of 1959. By that time, bogus statistics and heroic slogans could no longer conceal the economic dislocations and plunging national morale that were the main legacy of the Great Leap Forward. It was P'eng who stepped forward at the conference to offer the most frontal challenge to Mao's personal leadership and policies by anyone from the Party's inner circle in the twenty-four years since the chairman had assumed unchallenged control during the Long March.

Many ranking Party members endorsed P'eng's views, and in fact the Party did move decisively away from the Great Leap Forward programs after the Lushan Conference. Nevertheless, Mao had a score to settle with his defense minister, and he moved swiftly to force P'eng into ignominious retirement in September, 1959. During the next seven years, from 1959 to 1966, he was mentioned only once in the official media.

A worse fate was to befall P'eng during the Cultural Revolution. In December, 1966, as that decade-long upheaval began to sweep over China, P'eng was arrested. The final eight years of his life were a nightmare of imprisonment, physical abuse, and character assassination—as it was for most of Mao's rivals in the Party. P'eng died of the effects of his imprisonment and medical neglect on November 29, 1974, an all but forgotten "nonperson." In 1978, two years after Mao's death and the end of the Cultural Revolution, China's new leadership, under Teng Hsiao-p'ing, posthumously "rehabilitated" P'eng and restored his good name.

Summary

In his judiciously balanced biography of P'eng Te-huai, Jürgen Domes argues that much of P'eng's success as a military leader must be explained by his character. He won the loyalty of his subordinate officers and troops because of his personal qualities. He led a simple, frugal life, worked hard, and was straightforward in his dealings with both superiors and subordinates. While P'eng was courageous in battle and a good campaigner and tactician, Domes concludes that he was "at best a fair if not a mediocre strategist."

P'eng's career is of great interest as a case study in intraparty conflict. Mao's purge of P'eng from the very highest ranks of the military establishment in 1959 came at a time when there was widespread dissatisfaction with Mao's policies and tyrannical methods. Mao's response to P'eng's challenge was to issue an ultimatum to the Party leadership: If it and the PLA accepted P'eng's views, Mao would split the Party by going to the countryside and mobilizing the peasants in his own private army to maintain control. The specter of such a civil war was apparently enough to isolate P'eng from his supporters and leave him to face Mao's wrath alone.

P'eng's fate illustrates the ability of the government of the PRC to reverse the public image of one of its most important leaders overnight. From being recognized as a hero of the revolution for decades, P'eng was transformed overnight into an archvillain, a "great conspirator, a great ambitionist," who had joined the movement only to advance his career and achieve fame for himself. Then, after Mao's death, P'eng's reputation was soon elevated to almost superhuman heights. The power of a regime to manipulate personal images in such an arbitrary fashion should give caution to those seeking to separate fact from fiction in the careers of men such as P'eng.

Bibliography

Domes, Jürgen. *Peng Te-huai: The Man and the Image*. Stanford, Calif.: Stanford University Press, 1985. This brief volume, the only biography of P'eng in English, is an engrossing study of the man and his relationship to the political and military development of China with an especially good analysis of the intraparty conflict which swirled around P'eng and Mao after 1959.

Griffith, Samuel B., II. *The Chinese People's Liberation Army.* New York: McGraw-Hill, 1967. A well-respected standard authority on China's army written by a United States Marine Corps general with long years of experience in China and considerable academic expertise as well. Includes valuable organizational charts and biographical sketches of all important PRC military leaders including P'eng.

Joffe, Ellis. *Between Two Plenums: China's Intraleadership Conflict, 1959-1962.* Ann Arbor, Mich.: Center for Chinese Studies, University of Michigan, 1975. A highly specialized study of the three-year period of conflict touched off by P'eng's challenge of Mao at the Lushan Conference; by a recognized expert on Chinese military history.

Klein, Donald W., and Anne B. Clark, eds. *Biographic Dictionary of Chinese Communism, 1921-1965.* Cambridge, Mass.: Harvard University Press, 1971. Volume 2 contains a richly detailed and largely factual account of P'eng's career, though information on the post-1959 years is scanty. Contains a good bibliography.

Snow, Helen Foster. *The Chinese Communists: Sketches and Autobiographies of the Old Guard.* Reprint. Westport, Conn.: Greenwood Press, 1972. This is a highly personal account of the early years of P'eng and other Communist leaders based on interviews conducted in Yen-an in 1937. Includes a glossary of terms and a chronology.

John H. Boyle

JUAN PERÓN

Born: October 8, 1895; Lobos, Buenos Aires Province, Argentina
Died: July 1, 1974; Buenos Aires, Argentina
Areas of Achievement: Government and politics
Contribution: More than any other figure, Perón dominated the history of twentieth century Argentina. He participated in coups that toppled the government in 1930 and 1943. With support from the armed forces and organized labor, he governed as president from 1943 to 1955 and 1973 to 1974. His legacy continued to divide Argentina long after his death in 1974.

Early Life

Juan Domingo Perón was born in the town of Lobos in Buenos Aires Province on October 8, 1895. His restless father, Mario Tomás Perón, had given up the study of medicine to live as a minor government bureaucrat and tenant rancher. In 1890, at Lobos, he met Juana Sosa Toledo, a farm girl, and they had a son the following year. Juan was the second born, although the couple still had not married. In 1900, the family moved to Patagonia, but four years later his parents sent the boy to Buenos Aires to begin elementary school while living with some of his father's relatives.

Large for his age and increasingly self-reliant, Perón stayed on in the city with brief visits to his family, until in 1911 he entered the Military College, a prerequisite for a career in the armed forces. An average student as a cadet, Perón was commissioned a second lieutenant in 1913. By 1929, he was a captain, and his career had been routine and apolitical. Charismatic, hardworking, and energetic, Perón showed talent as a teacher and athlete. He also received an appointment to the Escuela Superior de Guerra (war academy) for three years of intensive study (1926-1929). On January 5, 1929, he married Aurelia Tizón, from a respectable middle-class Buenos Aires family.

Life's Work

The depression of 1929 provoked a crisis in Argentina that brought Perón into politics. Appointed to the army's general staff, he joined in conspiracies against the government of President Hipólito Yrigoyen, culminating in the 1930 military coup. Although Perón's role was a small one, he did perceive an important lesson: The armed forces succeeded in overthrowing the government, he believed, only because a large number of civilians in Buenos Aires took up arms in support of the coup. The Revolution of 1930 subverted the Argentine political system, and constitutional rule came to an end. Perón became a professor of military history at the war academy, improved his didactic and speaking skills, and published several books. Promoted to lieutenant colonel in 1936, he served as a military attaché in Chile. His wife's death from cancer on September 10, 1938, ended a happy marriage, which had produced no children.

Perón then received orders to go to Italy, an assignment that shaped his political philosophy and later guided his policies as president of Argentina. His experiences in Italy, Germany, and Spain convinced him that some form of Fascism would dominate the future, although his own predilection was for a state similar to Francisco Franco's Spain rather than Nazi Germany. Perón's reading of military theory, much influenced by German writers, had persuaded him that war was an inevitable state of society. He admired the way that Adolf Hitler and Benito Mussolini had mobilized and organized their peoples, especially through the use of trade unions, mass demonstrations, and appeals to anticommunism.

After spending 1939 and 1940 in Europe, he returned to Argentina, was promoted to full colonel, and began to conspire with fellow officers against the civilian government. The conspirators' organization was the Group of United Officers (GOU), an extremely secret faction probably founded by Perón. When President Ramón S. Castillo unconstitutionally tried to name his successor, it provoked the GOU into action. On June 14, 1943, a military faction led by General Arturo Rawson forced Castillo's resignation. Perón, who had been deeply involved in the conspiracy, did not participate in the military action. He usually disappeared when physical danger threatened.

Perón emerged from the coup as chief aide to General Edelmiro J. Farrell, the new minister of war. As the only leading officer who had a clear idea of what to do with the government, Perón appealed for working-class support. On October 27, 1943, he became minister of the National Labor Department and converted it into a nearly independent Secretariat of Labor and Social Welfare. He simultaneously courted factions within the military and gained support from the workers by according them respect. He encouraged them to organize, aided older unions that supported his policies, and oversaw the implementation of new laws favorable to the working class. Anarchist, socialist, and communist union leaders were repressed. In July, 1944, Perón became vice president under President Farrell, while retaining his other positions. Yet his mounting power threatened his rivals and the United States government, which mistakenly considered him a Nazi.

The end of World War II forced the military government to relax its most authoritarian measures, but more political freedom allowed opponents of the regime to organize. Anti-Peronist elements in the military seized power on October 9, 1945, arrested Perón, and imprisoned him on Martín García Island. When the workers saw that the anti-Peronist faction intended to erase most of the gains that Perón had granted, they rallied to his support. Resorting to mass demonstrations and violence on October 17, the working class forced the opposition to back down, release Perón, and permit free elections for the presidency in 1946. Meanwhile, Perón's mistress, actress Eva

("Evita") Duarte, had shored up his courage, but she had nothing to do with the popular demonstrations despite later myths to the contrary. Although Perón and Evita had flaunted their relationship since early 1944, to the scandal of straitlaced Argentines, they married shortly after his release, in part to enhance Perón's chances in the presidential election.

With the campaign under way, both the opposition and the United States government underestimated the depth of Perón's support. His opponents, ranging from the Radicals to the Communists, coalesced in the Democratic Union, confident of victory. Meanwhile, United States Assistant Secretary of State Spruille Braden made public a compilation of anti-Perón propaganda, the "Blue Book," intended to portray Perón as a Nazi and discredit him with Argentine voters. Braden's ploy backfired, however, because Argentine nationalists resented American intervention. Charismatic and forceful, Perón attracted huge crowds and mounting support. In the freest election up to that point in Argentine history, Perón won 54 percent of the popular vote and decisive control of both houses of congress. He took office on June 4, 1946.

On the surface, Perón ruled for the next nine years as a populist president, playing to nationalist sentiments. He used foreign reserves accumulated during the war to repatriate railroads, utilities, and other holdings from foreign investors. For the first time, Argentine manufacturers benefited from a high protective tariff, along with the governmental measures to stimulate industrialization. The government invested great sums in heavy industry, building the nation's first steel plant and subsidizing automobile manufacturing. Perón also spent huge sums to provide new equipment for the armed forces.

Perón called his political philosophy *Justicialismo*, a muddled theory that neither he nor his followers ever clearly defined. It was allegedly a middle position between capitalism and communism. Perón was no democrat despite his reliance upon the working class for support, yet neither did he espouse an ideologically consistent form of dictatorship. While his attitudes favored the lessons learned in Italy and Spain, his only consistent policy was Argentine nationalism, much to the chagrin of the United States. The new constitution of 1949, which abolished the proscription upon a president's succeeding himself and permitted Perón's reelection in 1951, gave women the right to vote and established ten basic rights of workers.

Evita played an important but not crucial role in Perón's rule. She was the de facto head of the labor department, provided an important link to the common people and to female voters, and ran the Eva Perón Welfare Foundation, a graft-ridden charitable institution that enriched its namesake. Evita derived her power from her husband, however, and, as a female involved in politics, was barely tolerated by Perón's military supporters. Her campaign for the vice presidency in 1951 had to be aborted when the military balked. Her death from cancer on July 26, 1952, deeply affected Perón.

Perón's regime was also in crisis. Public spending had outstripped revenues, causing serious inflation. Livestock and grain production fell because of Perón's economic policies. Enemies spread rumors about Perón's alleged sexual orgies with young girls. As discontent mounted, he became more dictatorial inside Argentina but began to soften his xenophobia in the hope of obtaining international aid. Although Perón and the Roman Catholic church had initially supported each other, a bitter conflict broke out between the two erstwhile allies, with the government of Argentina making divorces easy to obtain, legalizing prostitution, and limiting the Church's role in education. When the regime arrested and exiled two bishops, the papacy excommunicated the officials responsible. The next day, June 16, 1955, factions within the armed forces attempted a coup against the Peronist government, but it failed because it lacked the army's support. Perón responded fearfully, however, and made a number of concessions to the opposition. He seemed afraid to fight and claimed later that he was trying to avoid a civil war. When sectors of the army joined a second coup on September 16, 1955, Perón went into exile, leaving a bitterly polarized nation.

Perón first sought refuge in Paraguay, later drifted through Venezuela, Panama, Nicaragua, and the Dominican Republic, and eventually took up permanent residence in Spain. Peronists never abandoned hope, however, that their hero would govern Argentina once again. In 1964, he made a semi-serious attempt to return but upon his arrival in Brazil was prevented from embarking for Argentina and was sent back to Madrid. Even from Spain, however, he exerted great influence over the Peronists, directing their political activities and preventing anyone from challenging his position as leader of the movement. Meanwhile, political chaos engulfed Argentina, with neither the armed forces nor civilians able to govern. Beginning in 1969, terrorism and turmoil mounted until the military decided to permit a free election, even if it might permit a Peronist victory and the return of Perón himself to Argentina.

Perón arrived in November, 1972, too late to be a candidate, but his lieutenant, Hector Cámpora, won the presidency. Cámpora soon resigned, and Perón was elected on September 27, 1973, with his third wife, Isabel Martínez de Perón, as vice president. Yet during his eighteen-year exile, Peronism had changed. Organized labor remained loyal, but many intellectuals, students, and others dissatisfied with Argentine politics, including some terrorists such as the Montoneros and Peronist Youth, also looked to Perón for leadership. Once in office again, Perón sought national reconciliation and seemed committed to democratic rule. The conflicting aims of his own supporters made government difficult, however, and his health failed before he even took office. Perón died on July 1, 1974.

Summary

Juan Perón's first administration attempted to deal with important obstacles to Argentine development. He played to the interests of organized labor and accorded women new political rights. He attempted to break the rural elite's control over the economy by subsidizing industrialization. His nationalism carried popular support. Yet his dictatorial method and lack of fiscal restraint, his grandiose but xenophobic foreign policy, the continued enmity of the rural oligarchs, and the regime's failure to achieve long-lasting social and economic reform undercut his accomplishments. Argentina was far more polarized when he fell in 1955 than it had been when he took office.

By the 1970's, Perón was the only person with a chance of healing Argentina's wounds, and his death, followed by the shortlived rule of his third wife, touched off a downward spiral into military dictatorship, leftist- and state-sponsored terrorism, and military debacle in the Falkland Islands.

Bibliography
Alexander, Robert J. *Juan Domingo Perón: A History.* Boulder, Colo.: Westview Press, 1979. A short biography, with bibliography, by an author who has written extensively on various facets of the Peronist years in Argentina.
Crassweller, Robert. *Perón and the Enigmas of Argentina.* New York: W. W. Norton, 1987. This well-written biography argues that Perón achieved great popularity in Argentina, despite accomplishing little, because he embodied the cultural ethos of Hispanic and creole Argentina. Contains a good bibliography and photographs.
Fraser, Nicholas, and Marysa Navarro. *Eva Perón.* New York: W. W. Norton, 1980. Generally balanced in its treatment of Evita, this biography strips away much of the myth surrounding Perón's wife and shows her political contributions.
Page, Joseph A. *Perón: A Biography.* New York: Random House, 1983. The best biography of Perón available, this is a lengthy, thorough treatment of his entire career and is more sympathetic to its subject than most studies.
Rock, David. *Argentina, 1516-1982: From Spanish Colonization to the Falklands War.* Berkeley: University of California Press, 1985. This excellent overview of Argentine history devotes extensive coverage to Perón, including photographs and bibliography.
Turner, Frederick C., and José Enrique Miguens, eds. *Juan Perón and the Reshaping of Argentina.* Pittsburgh: University of Pittsburgh Press, 1983. Offers the flavor of Perón's thought through translations of speeches, lectures, essays, and addresses.

Kendall W. Brown

AUGUSTE PERRET

Born: February 12, 1874; near Brussels, Belgium
Died: February 25, 1954; Paris, France
Area of Achievement: Architecture
Contribution: Perret's great contribution was the utilization, refinement, and promotion of reinforced concrete, or ferroconcrete, which he was convinced was the building material of the future.

Early Life

Auguste Perret, the eldest of three brothers, was born near Brussels of French parentage. His father, descended from a long line of master stonemasons, had been a successful building contractor in Paris. His involvement in the Communist uprising against the government in 1871 forced him to leave France for Belgium, where he reestablished himself as a contractor. In 1881, however, after a general amnesty, he and his family returned to Paris, where he successfully continued his career as a building contractor, training his sons to do the same.

In 1891, Auguste Perret was enrolled in the École des Beaux-Arts, the leading architectural school of its time. The training was theoretical, and the curriculum stressed classical designs. Perret was a diligent student, earning a series of first prizes. He always considered the architect Eugène Viollet-le-Duc (1814-1879), known for his restoration work on ancient French monuments, to have been his great inspiration. Not only did Viollet-le-Duc respect traditional architecture but also he stressed the importance of unity between design and execution.

While at the Beaux-Arts, Perret continued to work for his father in construction. He left the school without completing the final project for his diploma. The move was deliberate. By law, a licensed architect could not be a building contractor. Perret wanted to build what he designed. Therefore, for the next sixty years one of France's leading architects was known simply as a contractor.

At the time Perret was at the Beaux-Arts, François Hennebique patented a process for creating a concrete frame structure reinforced by embedded iron or steel rods. He constructed several buildings in Paris with a reinforced concrete core but with exposed surfaces covered with traditional building materials. Perret recognized both the potentials and faults of the new material; he was determined to improve it and to utilize it honestly as an inexpensive, versatile, and potentially handsome building material.

Life's Work

Perret's first major use of reinforced concrete was in 1899 at the municipal casino in St. Malo, where he installed a clear span reinforced concrete beam sixty feet long. The pivotal structure, the one to establish Perret's reputation as a great architect, was the rue Franklin apartment house in Paris built in 1903, the first to be built completely of reinforced concrete with its basic lines revealed rather than hidden. The site with its limited area would have been unsuitable for conventional building materials. Using more compact and stronger reinforced concrete solved the problem.

Perret designed what appeared to be a conventional, handsome seven-story and penthouse apartment building architecturally in harmony with those it abutted. Technically, the design was revolutionary. All the light for the apartments came from the street side. Since the walls were non-load-bearing because of the reinforced concrete frame, more window space was available. To secure even more lighting, Perret recessed part of the façade as a light well and compensated for the lost space by cantilevering the lateral bay windows of the apartments. The services were in the rear, where light was secured by embedded hexagonal glass bricks. The interior walls too were non-load-bearing and thus could be rearranged at will. The only concession Perret made to conventional architecture was in covering the exposed concrete with colorful faience tiles. The concrete was not impervious to moisture—a shortcoming Perret was determined to correct. The tiles, however, followed the building lines.

The elder Perret, who had neither sympathy for nor understanding of reinforced concrete and forced the son to use a subcontractor for the rue Franklin building, died in 1905. The firm now became Perret Brothers: Auguste and his two brothers Gustave and Claude. The same year, the new firm built another concrete frame building, a garage. Then for seventeen years, Perret would not build another, although his firm often constructed skeletal reinforced concrete frames upon which a veneer of conventional building material would be placed—a process Perret considered dishonest.

In 1913, Perret was involved in a major building project that would enhance his reputation as an innovative builder, for he had to accept with modification a design already accepted. The building was the Théâtre Champs-Élysées in Paris. Again there were difficulties: groundwater and an irregular building site. Perret overcame the former by floating the theater on a concrete pontoon; he overcame the latter by the use of concealed reinforced concrete arches, which enabled him by the process of cantilevering and suspending to construct three separate theaters, each capable of being used independently.

The war years of 1914-1918, while inhibiting conventional architectural design, afforded Perret the opportunity of improving reinforced concrete and demonstrating its versatility. At the great docks constructed in Casablanca, Morocco, his reinforced concrete vaulting was in places less than two inches thick yet incredibly strong. In a clothing factory completed in 1919, Perret created the greatest amount of unobstructed floor space yet known through the use of gigantic freestanding reinforced concrete arches.

By this time, through consultation and experimentation, Perret had succeeded in making reinforced concrete moisture-resistant. He achieved this innovation by vibrating the composition before it had hardened in order to increase its density. The improved concrete was used to construct in 1922-1923 the church of Notre-Dame at Le Raincy, for many Perret's greatest masterpiece. Dedicated to French soldiers who had fallen in the Battle of Ourq in World War I, built in record time and with limited funds, the church was made entirely of exposed reinforced concrete. In form, the church followed that of the traditional cathedral, but its execution was unique. A single great barrel vault spanned the nave, which was separated from the side aisles by slender columns added for dramatic effect. The glory of the church was the walls constructed of precast concrete grilles in geometric patterns. Into the openwork Perret had inserted colored glass arranged according to the spectrum. The effect was overwhelmingly magnificent. In the words of one critic, concrete had at last come of age.

The time of the building of Notre-Dame at Le Raincy marked a turning point in Perret's professional career. His reputation now firmly established, he could devote himself to honest reinforced concrete constructions. The architectural avant-garde ignored him, but businessmen and governmental bureaucrats liked him, seeing him as a dependable architect who never exceeded cost estimates.

Between 1923 and his death in 1954, Perret completed more than seventy projects in addition to numerous plans. Three bear mentioning because they demonstrate advances in Perret's professional career. The Mobilier National Building of 1934, built to house the costly official furniture and furnishings of the French government, again had to be built on an irregular site and for multiple functions ranging from monumental exhibition halls to domestic quarters for curators. Perret created a harmonious design incorporating features of traditional French architecture. Because of the increased density and strength of the concrete, the unattractive layer of mortar that rises to the surface once concrete is poured could now be removed. Perret executed this innovation through a bushhammering technique, and the concrete looked like traditional dressed stone.

Since the bushhammering revealed the pebble and stone content of the concrete or its aggregate, Perret now sought to improve its appearance. One method involved graduated sizes in the pebbles and stone. Another mixed colored stone chips with a white matrix or cement binder, thus achieving a pointillistic effect. The best examples of his experimentations are to be seen in the composition of the columns of the Museum of Public Works built facing the Place de la Concorde in Paris. Perret's columns harmonized with those on the splendid eighteenth century buildings. By carefully controlled formwork, Perret also succeeded in achieving beautiful profiling for the building in the form of subtle curves.

Perret's last major project was the rebuilding of the port city of Le Havre, whose center had been demolished by Allied bombing during World War II. In his design, Perret showed the influence of the great city planners of the seventeenth and eighteenth centuries whose ideas Perret had adapted to the twentieth. His plan called for grand avenues connecting principal buildings with the spaces between filled with parks, squares, and streets laid out in grid fashion. He designed both the new city hall and the monumental church of St. Michael.

Official recognition and honors for Perret came late. At the age of seventy-one, he was finally permitted to call himself an architect and was made president of the newly formed Order of Architects. He became a professor at the Beaux-Arts, was elected to the Institute of France, and was appointed officer of the Legion of Honor. In 1948, he was awarded the Gold Medal by the Royal Institute of British Architects; in 1953, he was awarded the Gold Medal by the American Institute of Architects. Perret died the following year as he would have wished, in a luxurious apartment in a building he had himself constructed—of reinforced concrete.

Summary

Auguste Perret's professional career as an architect can best be summed up by viewing him essentially as an innovator and compromiser. The innovation was the utilization, refinement, and promotion of reinforced concrete. Through processes such as vibrating, bushhammering, constituting, and profiling, Perret succeeded in making it not only an inexpensive and incredibly strong but also a handsome building material. In a sense, he accomplished in a lifetime for concrete what it had taken countless generations of others to do for stone. As a compromiser, Perret in his designs tried to draw what was useful from the past and adapt it to the present. He viewed much of the work of his architectural contemporaries as unwarranted displays of egotism. He always maintained that the architect was limited by the laws of nature regarding the properties of materials, the vagaries of climate, the rules of optics, and the sense of lines and forms. Ignoring these limitations produced designs that fatigued the eye and were transitory. In the last analysis, what was to be sought was environmental harmony.

Bibliography

Benevolo, Leonardo. *History of Modern Architecture.* Translated by H. J. Landry. 2 vols. Cambridge, Mass.: MIT Press, 1971. Benevolo explains how Perret, despite his reputation as a "classical" architect, through subtle refinements and true originality fits into the 1890-1914 avant-garde movement of European architecture.

Bosworth, William Wells. "Perret, the Innovator, a Professional Study."

American Society Legion of Honor Magazine 26 (Summer, 1955): 141-148. Bosworth knew Perret well. They were both members of the Institute of France. The article has interesting quotes from various authorities on Perret. Bosworth singles out the Museum of Public Works as Perret's most significant work and explains why.

Collins, Peter. *Concrete: The Vision of a New Architecture.* New York: Horizon Press, 1959. The most comprehensive work available in English on Perret. The book is divided into three sections. The first deals with the historic development of the use of concrete; the second with the technological evolution of reinforced concrete or ferroconcrete in the nineteenth century; the third section and principal part of the book deals with the work of Perret. Collins divides Perret's career into two parts: the formative and the definitive, with 1928 as the dividing line. It was in the latter period that Perret came into his own. Of particular value are the 156 black-and-white photographs of all of Perret's principal works as well as related works and designs of other architects.

Goldfinger, Ernö. "The Work of Auguste Perret." *Architectural Journal* 70 (January, 1955): 144-156. Goldfinger knew Perret for nearly a quarter century and had worked in his office. This article is a transcript of a speech Goldfinger delivered to a meeting of the British Architectural Association shortly after Perret's death. Goldfinger divides Perret's career into four parts: search for a medium, adventures in tectonic truth, search for a French style, and the final achievement. The comments of some of the members of the association who also knew Perret are also interesting.

Tafuri, Manfredo, and Francesco Dal Co. *Modern Architecture.* Translated by Robert Erich Wolf. New York: Harry N. Abrams, 1979. The book gives probably the best concise overall account of Perret's career from the building of the rue Franklin apartment house to the plan for the rebuilding of Le Havre. Of particular interest is the description of French politics that prevented Perret from receiving commissions he deserved.

Nis Petersen

PHILIPPE PÉTAIN

Born: April 24, 1856; Cauchy-à-la-Tour, France
Died: July 23, 1951; Port-Joinville, Île d'Yeu, France
Areas of Achievement: The military, government, and politics
Contribution: During World War I, Pétain was one of the few prominent
   military commanders to discard the massive offensive as a desired operational method. His skill at defensive warfare contributed to the Allies'
   eventual defeat of Germany in 1918. Pétain later entered politics and
   served as the controversial Vichy chief of state during the entire German
   Occupation of France.

Early Life

   Henri-Philippe Pétain was the third of five children born to the peasants
Omer-Verant and Clotilde Pétain. Clotilde died in 1857, and Omer-Verant
remarried less than two years later. Three more children followed in rapid
succession as the Pétains managed an austere living in the Artois region of
northern France. Like most peasant children of the middle-nineteenth century, Pétain spent much of his early childhood working on the family farm
and attending a local school.

   At the age of eleven, Pétain left home to attend school full-time. From
1867 to 1875, he lived at the Collège Saint-Bertin, where he received an
education dominated by religious deference and military discipline. Upon the
urging of several maternal relatives, Pétain eventually decided upon a military career. Pétain realized that the first step in this direction was his attendance at the Imperial Special Military School of Saint-Cyr. Despite a poor
performance on the entrance examination, Pétain was admitted to Saint-Cyr
in 1877. Pétain did not excel at Saint-Cyr; the school's engineering curriculum frequently baffled him. Saint-Cyr's moral lessons did, however, help
forge an emerging character. By the time of his graduation, Pétain had
developed a strong sense of duty and honor. Concerned more with these
attributes than career advancement, Pétain entered the army as a second
lieutenant in 1878.

Life's Work

   In the early part of 1914, Pétain was apparently nearing the end of an
undistinguished military career. Since 1878, he had capably served France,
but nothing stood out to indicate greatness. In the age of some of his country's biggest imperial ventures, Pétain had never left France. He had commanded troops, but a majority of his service was as an instructor at the École
de Guerre in Paris. While a teacher, Pétain acquired the reputation of being a
military nonconformist when he condemned the French reliance upon offensive doctrine. Having studied the then-recent Boer and Russo-Japanese wars,
Pétain dismissed large-scale offensive tactics as useless in the era of the

modern machine gun. This position, coupled with his blunt personality, made Pétain extremely unpopular at France's war ministry. His future promotions were therefore severely hindered. By 1914, Pétain was an obscure colonel with thirty-six years of service who awaited retirement in two short years. The outbreak of World War I, however, quickly changed Pétain's military and political destiny. The German invasion of Belgium and France in the late summer of 1914 provided Pétain with the opportunity to practice his unorthodox defensive theories. Pétain was a success, and he gained rapid promotion to the rank of general.

Throughout the war Pétain outperformed his peers. In February, 1916, the Germans launched a massive offensive that threatened the capture of Paris. Standing firm on the Meuse River at the town of Verdun, Pétain organized and inspired the French in a bloody defense that lasted until December, 1916. With this victory, the once unpopular Pétain was now known throughout a grateful France as the "Hero of Verdun."

Appointed the commander of all French armies in May, 1917, Pétain faced another crisis. Approximately 350,000 frontline troops throughout the army had mutinied. Sacrificed in innumerable assaults that served to accomplish no apparent objectives, French soldiers simply left the trenches in droves. Pétain quickly assumed control of a situation that had the potential to spell the defeat of France. Leaders of the uprising were arrested and publicly sentenced to death. Although few of the mutineers were actually executed, this response helped squelch the disorder. In other actions, the commanding general gained the cooperation of his soldiers by visiting their outposts, listening to their complaints, and promising to end useless attacks. Once he had restored order, Pétain led the French army to victory in 1918.

At the close of the war, Pétain remained France's leading military figure. He was made a Marshal of France and placed on the influential peacetime army council, Conseil Supérieur de la Guerre. French citizenry and politicians revered the "Hero of Verdun" and generally followed his military pronouncements. In his most significant decision of the interwar period, Pétain called for the fortification of France's eastern border against future German attacks. Built at the expense of weapons modernization, this costly series of forts and entrenchments—called the Maginot Line—did not include the border with Belgium. Pétain concluded that this heavily forested area between France and Belgium was impregnable and therefore not in need of fortification. In 1940, this assumption would prove tragically incorrect, but in the interwar years France clung to the strategies of its most popular marshal.

Although war minister for a short period in 1934, Pétain remained outside active French politics. His lack of participation did not, however, represent political apathy. He believed that republican politics and socialism were weakening France. Interestingly, he continued to avoid others' attempts to draft him into political office. An ambassador to Spain in 1940, Pétain was called home when Adolf Hitler's German armies easily bypassed the Maginot Line and invaded France through the Ardennes Forest. As the armies collapsed, France turned to Pétain as a symbol of greatness and power to save the crumbling nation. In May, 1940, and at eighty-four years of age, Pétain acquiesced to these wishes. He formed a new government and acquired the authorization to abolish the Third Republic and create a new constitution.

Almost immediately Pétain proclaimed defeat, and he negotiated an armistice with Germany that split France into occupied and unoccupied zones. Pétain remained the "chief of state" of the unoccupied territory, which had its capital at Vichy in southern France. Unlike many resisting Frenchmen, Pétain saw no sense in continuing a guerrilla war after the nation had been defeated. He reasoned that only a functioning French government could help rebuild the shattered country.

Although Pétain was allowed to rule over southern France, Germany exacted many demands upon Pétain's government that forced Vichy into increased collaboration with the enemy. In 1940 and 1941, Pétain maintained some form of autonomy. He was able to purge his cabinet of radical collaborationists such as Pierre Laval and still court the United States as an ally. By 1942, however, Pétain drifted into the role of aging figurehead. Germany installed Laval as first premier, while giving him absolute power to run the government. Decisions now drifted from Pétain's control. By the end of the war, Vichy would cooperate with Germany in such endeavors as Jewish persecution, munitions exchanges, and recruitment of men to serve with the German armies on the Eastern Front.

During World War II, Pétain resisted any idea of fleeing France and what he perceived as his duty. Even as the Allies invaded France and his government collapsed, Pétain desired to remain at his post. Detained by the Germans as they fled eastward in late 1944, Pétain protested this treatment. In April, 1945, his captors relented, and he was allowed to return to France. Once on native soil, Pétain was promptly placed on trial by Charles de Gaulle's new French government for his leadership of the collaborationist government. On August 15, 1945, the deaf Marshal of France was found guilty and sentenced to death and national degradation. De Gaulle commuted the sentence to life imprisonment on the Île d'Yeu off the Mediterranean coast of France, Pétain remained imprisoned on this island until pulmonary failure ended his life on July 23, 1951.

Summary

Philippe Pétain is a controversial figure in French history. During World War I, he received the highest accolades a country can offer. He was then strictly an army officer, and his contribution to the military science of the early twentieth century was enormous. Twenty-seven years later, however, and in the twilight of his life, Pétain suffered national humiliation. Vichy was in shambles, and Pétain bore the stain of leading France along the path of Nazi collaboration.

A stubborn sense of duty had guided Pétain to his greatest triumphs, and it now contributed to the disaster of Vichy. Pétain did not espouse Fascism or even crave power; he simply believed himself the only man capable of saving France. The country needed a leader, and his concept of duty would not permit him to back down from his challenge. He therefore offered himself to the nation as a persevering moral example of past glory. Only by such a sacrifice did Pétain think that he could both acquit his duty and return France to the country's former prominence.

Pétain's estimation of this situation was wrong, and it altered his place in history. The Vichy experiment demonstrated a failed chapter in Pétain's life, but it does not detract from either his military reputation or his personal character. Trained to place duty above self-interest, Pétain left a legacy of having struggled in two separate conflicts to save France. At his death, he was most proud of this simple fact.

Bibliography
Griffiths, Richard. *Marshal Pétain*. London: Constable, 1970. The best analysis in any language of Pétain's military and political career. The book contains eighteen illustrations and a select bibliography.
Horne, Alistair. *The Price of Glory*. New York: St. Martin's Press, 1962. The definitive account of the Battle of Verdun. This book contains an extensive sketch of Pétain and his role during the battle. Horne's treatment of Verdun provides an excellent beginning for studies into the tactics of World War I.
Lottman, Herbert R. *Pétain, Hero or Traitor*. New York: William Morrow, 1985. Based upon previously sealed archives, Lottman's work frequently delves into the personal life and character of Pétain. The narrative reads extremely well, but it lacks both illustrations and bibliography.
Paxton, Robert O. *Vichy France*. New York: Alfred A. Knopf, 1972. This is a comprehensive account of Vichy. The book provides an overview of life, economics, and politics in unoccupied France during Pétain's period in office. The bibliographic essay contains detailed references for further research.
Spears, Sir Edward. *Two Men Who Saved France*. Briarcliff Manor, N.Y.: Stein & Day, 1966. This is a fine account of Pétain during the mutiny of 1917. The volume contains an eyewitness account plus Pétain's own version of the crisis.

Kyle S. Sinisi

JEAN PIAGET

Born: August 9, 1896; Neuchâtel, Switzerland
Died: September 16, 1980; Geneva, Switzerland
Areas of Achievement: Biology, education, and philosophy
Contribution: Piaget was awarded an honorary degree from Harvard University in 1936, the Sorbonne in 1946, and the University of Brussels in 1949 for his work on the evolution of intelligence in the human young. He found in developmental psychology a link between the biological adaptation of organisms to the environment and the philosophical quest for the source of knowledge.

Early Life

Jean Piaget was born the first of three children and only son of Arthur and Rachel Piaget. Arthur was devoted to medieval literature, and Rachel, although energetic and intelligent, suffered from poor mental health. As a young child, Piaget was interested in mechanics, birds, sea shells, and fossils. At the age of ten, he went to Latin School and after school hours helped the director of the Natural History Museum put labels on collections in exchange for rare species, which he added to his own collection. Piaget began writing when he was seven, and a short essay on an albino sparrow was published when he was eleven. By the age of fifteen, he was writing a series of articles in the *Swiss Review of Zoology* and was receiving letters from foreign scholars who expressed a desire to meet him. They did not, of course, realize how young he was.

Piaget might have pursued his career as a naturalist had it not been for several events that occurred when he was between fifteen and twenty years of age. His mother insisted that he take religious instruction, and, by doing so, he became interested in philosophy. His godfather, a philosopher, believing that Piaget's education needed to be broadened, invited him to spend time with him. While Piaget looked for mollusks along a lake, his godfather talked with him about the teachings of Henri Bergson. It was through this experience that Piaget decided to devote his life to a biological explanation of knowledge. Even though he received the doctor's degree in his early twenties in the natural sciences with a thesis on mollusks, Piaget was more interested in the relationship of biology and philosophy. He decided that if he obtained work in a psychological laboratory, he could better research this epistemological problem.

Piaget's first experience in a laboratory was in 1918 in Zurich, where he was introduced to psychoanalysis by Eugen Bleuler and Carl Jung. He pursued psychoanalysis diligently, partly in an effort to understand his mother's illness and partly to use the therapeutic approach with mental patients. In 1919, he went to Paris, where for two years he adapted the clinical technique to questioning schoolchildren at the Alfred Binet Institute. His assignment at the institute, given to him by Theodore Simon, was to standardize Sir Cyril Burt's reasoning tests. By listening to the verbal responses of the children, he was able to probe such areas as the child's understanding of space, time, numbers, physical causality, and moral judgment. He became fascinated with the question of why children up to the age of eleven or twelve have great difficulty with certain intellectual tasks that adults assume children should be able to do. He noticed that the difficulty seemed to be the child's inability to relate adequately the parts of the problem to the whole. Logic apparently is not inborn but develops little by little with time and experience. Here was the embryology of intelligence fitting in with his biological training.

Life's Work

Piaget came to believe that knowledge is not a subjective copy of an external world but rather is invented or constructed by the developing human organism. The child assimilates meaningful information from the environment and actively accommodates to that information by adapting to new situations. A person's intellectual or cognitive understanding determines other aspects of life as well: emotions, humor, moral development, and social interaction. Thinking precedes language and derives from human action upon the environment, so, in order to understand the origins of intelligence, it is necessary to study the behaviors of the young child rather than to ask questions of children already in school.

The opportunity to observe infants presented itself when he became the father of three children: two girls and a boy. He and his wife, a young woman he had met at the Jean-Jacques Rousseau Institute in Geneva, where he was named director in 1921, spent considerable time observing the behaviors of their babies and submitting them to various tasks. Three volumes were published dealing with the genesis of intellectual conduct based on these experiments. Other books written during this time are entitled *Le Langage et la pensée chez l'enfant* (1923; *The Language and Thought of the Child*, 1926), *Le Jugement et le raisonnement chez l'enfant* (1924; *Judgement and Reasoning in the Child*, 1928), *La Représentation du monde chez l'enfant* (1926; *The Child's Conception of the World*, 1929), and *La Causalité physique chez l'enfant* (1927; *The Child's Conception of Physical Causality*, 1930). The central theme running through all this work is that in every area of life—organic, mental, or social—there exist totalities qualitatively distinct from their parts and imposing upon the parts a particular organization. Growth or development, with roots in biological morphogenesis, is a striving for the equilibrium of these structures of the whole.

Not only was Piaget director of the Rousseau Institute, a post he held until his death, but also, from 1925 to 1929, he taught classes in child psychology and the philosophy of science at the University of Neuchâtel. In 1929, he became director of the International Bureau of Education, a position he retained for almost forty years. This led to his becoming president of the Swiss Commission of the United Nations Educational, Scientific, and Cultural Organization. At the bureau, he contributed to the improvement of pedagogical methods based on the mental development of the child. In 1929, he was also named professor of the history of scientific thought at the University of Geneva. Ten years later, he became professor of sociology and a year after that, professor of experimental psychology at that same institution. His special research interests between 1929 and 1939 were the study of scientific epistemology, both autogenetic and phylogenetic; the development of the concepts of numbers, space, and time in children ages four to eight; and the formation of the idea of preservation or constancy, which he labeled "concrete operations."

The standardization of Burt's reasoning tests with schoolchildren in Paris, the careful observation of his own children as infants, continued research at the Rousseau Institute, and numerous teaching duties resulted in Piaget's recording voluminous amounts of information on the evolution of thought in the child. Piaget wrote that there are four major stages of cognitive development. These stages are invariant, hierarchical, and seen in children universally. Every normal child goes through the same sequence because every person is genetically programmed to do so. The first is a period of sensorimotor intelligence and takes place from birth to approximately two years of age. The newborn is provided with such reflexes as sucking, swallowing, and crying, the bases of later adaptation tasks. The infant understands the world only as he acts upon it and perceives the consequences of those acts. By the age of two, he begins to invent solutions by implicit as well as explicit trial and error. He can "think" as well as act.

The second stage occurs between the ages of two and seven and is called preconceptual or intuitive intelligence. The advent of language brings mental images of events. Yet the child understands these events only from his own perspective and experience and is therefore unable to take the viewpoint of others. Error is perceptual in nature in that the child is influenced by the way objects appear to him: If a sausage-shaped piece of clay appears to be more when it is broken into small pieces, then it is more. This faulty relation of parts to the whole disappears sometime during concrete operational intelligence, when the child is in elementary school. He now can compare classes and relationships, and thought no longer centers on one salient characteristic of an object. He discovers that things are not always what they appear to be. What he knows, however, is still tied to the concrete world. It is not until eleven years of age or older that he reaches the fourth stage of formal operational intelligence, in which hypothetico-deductive thinking is possible. The orientation is toward problem solving rather than toward concrete behavior. The adolescent is full of ideas that go beyond his present life and enable him to deal through logical deduction with possibilities and consequences.

From 1938 to 1951, Piaget was a professor of psychology and sociology at the University of Lausanne. This post, in addition to his teaching at the University of Geneva and his duties as coeditor of the *Archives de psychologie* and the *Revue Suisse de psychologie*, did not lessen his productivity in research and writing. In the 1940's, his major concerns were the relationship of perception and intelligence and the testing of the claims of Gestalt psychology. By the 1950's and through the 1960's and 1970's, Piaget was surrounded by an ever-increasing number of assistants and colleagues. His professorships, including one in child psychology at the Sorbonne in 1952, and his directorships, including that of director of the International Center for Genetic Epistemology at the University of Geneva funded by the Rockefeller Foundation in 1955, provided him with eager scholars who collaborated with him on his studies. Men and women from around the world and representing many disciplines—biology, psychology, philosophy, mathematics, and linguistics—gathered to learn from him and to engage in research.

Piaget wrote in his autobiography that solitude and contact with nature were as essential to his well-being as hard work. After a morning of interaction with academicians, he would take long walks, collect his thoughts, and then write for the remainder of the afternoon. Summertime found him in the mountains of Switzerland, hiking and writing. He remained physically and mentally active in his eighties.

Summary

Jean Piaget has been called a biologist, a logician, a sociologist, and a psychologist, but he is best known as a genetic epistemologist, for he spent a lifetime studying the origins of human knowledge. Over a seventy-year period, he wrote fifty books and monographs and hundreds of articles, as well as lecturing in French to audiences all over the world. Unlike B. F. Skinner, who focused on environmental influences, or Sigmund Freud, who emphasized emotions and instincts, Piaget selected for his topic the rational, perceiving child who has the capacity to make sense of the world about him. Knowledge is a process, not a product; it is dynamic, never static, self-regulatory rather than imposed from without. Even as mollusks taken from the lake of Neuchâtel and placed in an aquarium change very little after five or six generations, the human organism has a built-in blueprint that determines the course of cognitive evolution, a course not unlike that of the evolution of scientific thought.

Piaget's later writings refined and helped to explain his previous studies, yet it is the earlier works that have received the greatest attention. From these writings, parents have been encouraged to provide a rich, supportive environment for the child's natural propensity to grow and learn. Educators have been exposed to child-centered classrooms and "open education," a direct application of Piaget's views. Lawrence Kohlberg's paradigm of moral reasoning, itself fostering hundreds of studies in moral cognition, has as its basis Piaget's study of the moral judgment of the child. A child prodigy, Piaget used his superior intellect to examine the evolution of human thought from birth to adulthood, and the interdisciplinary nature of his work has, in turn, influenced many areas of inquiry.

Bibliography
Cohen, David. *Piaget: Critique and Reassessment*. New York: St. Martin's Press, 1983. An outline of Piaget's career and the main elements of his theory are given, including the moral development of the child. Several major criticisms are offered as well as studies that run counter to Piaget's ideas.
Flavell, John H. *The Developmental Psychology of Jean Piaget*. Princeton, N.J.: Van Nostrand, 1963. This volume is a groundbreaking attempt to organize, for the English-speaking world, Piaget's ideas from the viewpoint of a developmental psychologist.
Furth, Hans G. *Piaget and Knowledge: Theoretical Foundations*. 2d ed. Chicago: University of Chicago Press, 1981. This book deals with Piaget's basic theoretical positions, including the biological, logical, and epistemological dimensions of human knowledge. Piaget's final work in the area of equilibration is explained in the last chapter.
Piaget, Jean. *The Essential Piaget*, edited by Howard E. Gruber and J. Jacques Venèche. New York: Basic Books, 1977. An anthology of Piaget's writings organized by time periods and topics. Essays published prior to 1922 were translated from the French especially for this volume. The editors' introductory notes to each section are insightful and informative.
_____. "Jean Piaget." In *A History of Psychology in Autobiography*, edited by Edwin G. Boring, Herbert S. Langfield, H. Werner, and Robert M. Yerkes, vol. 4. Worcester, Mass.: Clark University Press, 1952. A fascinating account of Piaget's life and work until 1950. The variety and enormity of his interests and responsibilities come through in this autobiography.

Bonnidell Clouse

ÉMILE PICARD

Born: July 24, 1856; Paris, France
Died: December 11, 1941; Paris, France
Areas of Achievement: Mathematics, physics, and engineering
Contribution: Picard's theories advanced research into analysis, algebraic geometry, and mechanics.

Early Life
Émile Picard's mother was the affluent daughter of a doctor from France's northern provinces. His father, from Burgundy, was a textile manufacturer, who died during the Franco-Prussian War of 1870. Picard demonstrated brilliance early in his life. While in school, he developed interests in varied subjects such as literature, languages, and history. His accomplishments in these areas of scholarship were enhanced by his love for books and reading and by his exceptionally powerful memory. One theme that appears throughout Picard's life is his broad range of interests. He was an athlete as well as a scholar. Throughout his life, he maintained a love for such rigorous physical activities as gymnastics and mountain climbing.

Given the fact that Picard was a generalist, it was difficult for him to choose any one field in academics on which to focus. In fact, he only decided to study mathematics at the end of his secondary studies. The reason for this decision came from his having read an algebra book. After making the decision to study mathematics, Picard committed himself to this pursuit with a devotion that is rarely matched. Indeed, by 1877, at age twenty-one, he had already made a major contribution to the development of a portion of mathematics that focused on the theory of algebraic surfaces. He had also received, by this time, the degree of doctor of science.

Picard's scholarship was recognized by many important members of the academic community. One of the great French mathematicians of the time, Charles Hermite, became his mentor and lifelong friend. In fact, Picard's development as a mathematician was strongly guided by Hermite. In 1881, with support from Hermite, he was appointed to a professorship at the Sorbonne, and during the same period he married Hermite's daughter.

Life's Work
The diversity that marked his life also marked his professional development. His early career emphasized research and focused on algebra and geometry. Some of his major contributions came in the field of algebraic geometry. He soon, however, began to pursue other interests in mathematics. By 1885, he had begun to pursue work in the field of differential and integral calculus. Picard was elected to the chair of this subject at the Sorbonne during this period.

Picard's most famous work came from his investigations of differential equations. Indeed, one theorem for which he is still remembered in modern texts of all languages is Picard's theorem, a method for approximating the solution to a differential equation. More important, however, is the work that Picard did in trying to develop a general framework for finding solutions to differential equations.

In addition to his work in differential equations, Picard did work in complex analysis. In this area, he helped to extend the research of his colleague Henri Poincaré. The work on which he focused involved functions of two complex variables. Picard termed these functions hypergeometric and hyperfuschian. The work that he did here was collected in a two-volume set entitled *Théorie des fonctions algébriques de deux variables indépendantes* (1897, 1906). This work was coauthored by the mathematician Simart.

At the turn of the century, Picard was engaged in the study of algebraic surfaces. This series of investigations was inspired by his previous work on the nature of complex functions. One of the interesting side effects of Picard's career as a generalist is the fact that his investigations frequently led him into other areas of study.

Another interesting facet of Picard's career is the fact that it touched so many areas that one would not expect. For example, he was the chairman of many government commissions, including the Bureau of Longitudes. Also, the quality and the variety of his scholarship led to his permanent election as the secretary to the Academy of Sciences. Picard's wide-ranging scholarship reached even into areas such as physics and engineering. His researches included the application of mathematical methods to physics problems of elasticity, heat, and electricity. One subject to which Picard added significantly was the way in which electrical impulses moved along wires. In engineering, Picard, who had originally begun as a theoretician in mathematics, developed into an excellent teacher and eventually became responsible for training ten thousand French engineers between 1894 and 1937.

It should be emphasized that the quality of Picard's scholarship did not suffer because of its variety. During the course of his career, he was responsible for the development of more than three hundred papers on various subjects. His *Traité d'analyse* (1891-1896) is considered a classic book on mathematics. At one time, this monumental work was considered required reading for obtaining a thorough background in mathematics.

Picard also published materials that were, strictly speaking, outside the realm of mathematics. He was, for example, responsible for collecting and editing the works of Charles Hermite, his mentor. In addition, he published a number of works on the philosophy of science and the scientific method, the majority of these after 1900.

Picard's career was long as well as productive. Many mathematicians find their most productive years early. Picard was a notable exception to this pattern. Again following his early path of intellectual diversity, he made significant contributions to the development of mathematical concepts such as similarity and homogeneity well after he was eighty years old. These concepts are important in algebra and engineering.

Picard's investigations were particularly significant in their effects on his fellows and successors in his field. Among those influenced by him were Henri-Léon Lebesgue, Émile Borel, and Otto von Blumenthal. Picard was one of the most honored scientists of his generation. In 1924, he was elected to the Academy of France. In 1932, he received the Gold Cross of the Legion of Honor. In 1937, he received the Mittag-Leffler Gold Medal from the Swedish Academy of Sciences. All told, he was awarded honorary doctorates by universities in five foreign countries.

In contrast to his almost unbroken string of professional successes, Picard had a personal life that was filled with tragedy. War was a common theme in the litany of misery that filled his personal existence. Besides the death of his father in the Franco-Prussian War, he lost a daughter and two sons during World War I. During World War II, his grandsons were wounded in the invasion of France. The personal tragedy under which Picard lived was emphasized by the fact that he died while France was still under German occupation. Yet he had lived as one of the most productive and honored mathematicians in a period known for the brilliance of its mathematical researchers.

Summary

Émile Picard was, in all ways, a generalist. Many would have termed him a Renaissance man. This diversity of interests was reflected in his work both in and out of mathematics. In mathematics, his research involved such varied areas as geometry, algebra, differential equations, and complex analysis. It is extremely rare to encounter mathematicians in the modern world who make significant contributions in more than one specialty. Picard's most significant work was in differential equations. It is here that the mathematical world outside France most commonly remembers the great Parisian. Modern works still make reference to Picard's theorem for approximating solutions to differential equations and these new efforts still mention Picard groups as a way of categorizing the transformations that can occur in linear differential equations.

In areas outside mathematics, Picard was known as a teacher, writer, editor, and administrator. He published an important survey of mathematics in France. He headed both the Academy of Sciences and the Society of Friends of Science, a group interested in helping needy scientists. Picard was not only a great mathematician and scientist, he was a great man as well. In an age that is characterized by the specialist, it is good to reflect that men such as Picard have lived.

Bibliography

Bell, Eric T. *The Development of Mathematics*. New York: McGraw-Hill, 1940. This is a particularly good discussion of the history of mathematics from a developmental standpoint. Consequently, Picard gets fairly good treatment. This book also discusses Hermite fairly extensively.

_____. *Men of Mathematics*. New York: Simon & Schuster, 1937. Picard is mentioned only slightly in this text. Yet it provides an excellent look at one of his most famous colleagues, Henri Poincaré. It gives a good view of the flavor of the times and the problems that were faced by mathematicians.

Boyer, Carl B. *A History of Mathematics*. New York: John Wiley & Sons, 1968. Picard is referenced several times in footnotes in this work. Why he receives no discussion in the text is hard to understand. These footnotes help to place Picard's work in relationship to other important works of mathematics.

Considine, Douglass M., ed. "Picard's Theorem." In *Van Nostrand's Scientific Encyclopedia*. New York: Van Nostrand Reinhold, 1976. This includes a good discussion of Picard's theorem.

Griffiths, Phillip. "Œuvres de Émile Picard, Tome II." *Dialog Math-Sci Database*, February, 1989. A review of the collected works of Picard. It discusses the material addressed by Picard during his researches. It also includes a good discussion of his life. The review is in English. Unfortunately, the book that it covers is not.

Hadamard, J. "Émile Picard." *Journal of the London Mathematical Society* 18 (1943). This biographical sketch, published not long after Picard's death, is the best description of his life.

Lyndon Marshall

PABLO PICASSO

Born: October 25, 1881; Málaga, Spain
Died: April 8, 1973; Mougins, France
Area of Achievement: Art
Contribution: The most prolific and famous artist of his time, Picasso was crucial to the development of modern art. He was an inventor of cubism and one of the prime practitioners of academic realism, Postimpressionism, art nouveau, expressionism, Fauvism, abstract expressionism, Surrealism, and Futurism. A skilled craftsman, he was the master of many mediums.

Early Life

Pablo Ruiz Picasso first learned how to draw from his father, José Ruiz Blasco, an art teacher and curator of the local museum. Don José was also a skilled painter, and he recognized early that his son possessed considerable artistic talent, potentially vaster than his own. As an old school pedagogue, he saw to it that Pablo became well grounded in the classical style of art, insisting that he copy the works of the masters with meticulous fidelity and pay close attention to the traditional laws of proportion and harmony of color. So formidable a draftsman did Pablo become that Don José abandoned his own painting and gave his son all of his materials. Pablo was then only thirteen years old.

In 1895, the family moved to Barcelona, where Pablo's father was to teach at the local School of Fine Arts and where he had his son enrolled to perfect his skills. Pablo stayed at his father's school for two years and was then sent to continue his studies in the more prestigious Royal Academy of San Fernando at Madrid. Yet Pablo's developing personal style and growing professional confidence put him increasingly at odds with the strictures of art currently taught by his hidebound professors. Taking advantage of a brief illness, he quit the Madrid academy to return to Barcelona.

The art scene in Barcelona was then in the throes of a modernist revolution, just the sort of atmosphere to stimulate experimentation and independence. Despite such positive reinforcement, Pablo still felt constrained. He wanted to leave, to go to London, and he persuaded his father to come up with the money. On the journey to Great Britain, however, he stopped off in Paris. The city so impressed him that he decided to go no farther. Although he returned to Spain from time to time, the French capital henceforth became his home and continued to be so during the most creative periods of his life. At this time, he definitively adopted his mother's maiden name as his own, Picasso being less common than Ruiz. The change also dramatically symbolized the artistic break that he was making with the academic and, for him, stultifying artistic values of his father.

initial association with Paris, and with it a deeper exposure to the
s of Edgar Degas, Paul Gauguin, and Henri de Toulouse-Lautrec, led
asso to modify his artistic style. He eliminated the bright colors from his
lette and began painting in monochromatic blue. At the same time, he
exchanged his carefully modeled figures for flatter, more solid surfaces. The
Blue Period—prompted by the suicide of a friend—is appropriately one of
deep melancholy in which Picasso showed his compassion for the Paris poor,
its downcast and destitute. To emphasize this sense of desolation, Picasso
elongated the bodies of his subjects, making them bony and angular in the
style of El Greco, thereby accentuating their condition of hopelessness.

Picasso, however, could not remain faithful to any one style for long. By
1904, his mood had changed; he had fallen in love for the first time in his
life, and, abandoning his cold colors, he now used warmer, more romantic
tones. His subject matter also became more joyful, as revealed in a series of
paintings of circus performers. These works are painted with great skill and
sensitivity and with more dimensionality than those of his previous period.
Yet soon this Rose Period also disappeared. During a visit to Spain, he used
more earth colors. His figures became more classically ponderous, perhaps
more naïve, in their reflection of prehistoric art. These paintings exude a
strong, sensual vitality. The twenty-four-year-old Picasso seemingly had established himself in a style that he might exploit for years to come. He was
on the verge, however, of a sudden change in direction that would lay the
foundations of modern art.

Life's Work
During the last half of the nineteenth century, French artists had discovered new ways of expression, either by depicting light through color or
by distorting perspective to transform shape and form. Picasso had been
influenced by these new directions but until 1906 had yet to go beyond them.
In that year, however, he began working on a canvas that would end any
associations with the traditional spatial organization of the past. In *Les Demoiselles d'Avignon* (the young ladies of Avignon), painted on a canvas
nearly eight feet square, he showed the distorted anatomy of five nude
women in a jarring assemblage of disorderly facets, triangular and rectangular wedges, and other confusing geometric shapes. Two of the figures are
wearing hideous African-like masks. The other three have eyes on different
levels and noses jutting out like pieces of architecture. The painting has no
rational focus of attention, the viewer being forced to look everywhere as if
at pieces of broken glass. Yet *Les Demoiselles d'Avignon* is now recognized
as the first true painting of the twentieth century. When Picasso showed the
painting to his friends, however—none of whom was exactly a rustic when
it came to accepting new ideas—the reaction was almost universally negative. As a result, Picasso rolled up the canvas and refused to exhibit it

publicly, thereby removing its direct influence on the course of the modern movement. Nevertheless, it had firmly established Picasso's new artistic direction, marking his great adieu to the past.

In embarking on this more hazardous artistic journey, Picasso had been strongly influenced by the works of Paul Cézanne, who in his mature works had also distorted shapes and contours and broken-down images into an infinite series of individual geometric perceptions. Picasso, with the close collaboration of Georges Braque, who had been heading in the same direction, broke down his figures into a series of flat tonal planes that in succeeding pictures became progressively more abstract. He also reduced his palette to only several colors. So close was Picasso's association with Braque that it was often difficult to tell which painter painted which canvas. The outbreak of World War I, and Braque's departure for military service, however, ended their partnership.

Although Picasso continued to paint in the cubistic manner, he also returned to realistic portraiture, thus continuing to fluctuate between the academic realism of his youth and the modernist synthesis of his early adulthood. Many of his more traditional figure paintings reflect his interest in sculpture, frequently the subjects being inspired by classical mythology. Sometimes he would do a portrait in one style and follow it by doing one in another. He reintroduced perspective depth into his later cubist paintings, rendering figures less abstract yet more fantastic, a characteristic that pointed the way to yet another direction.

Picasso's ensuing productivity is almost impossible to classify neatly. Throughout the interwar years, he continued to distort the human anatomy, reemploying a technique he had developed in his early cubist days: the rearrangement of pictorial features so that one part of the anatomy is seen simultaneously from many angles.

Guernica (1937), his most famous painting of this period, shows his preoccupation with violence. The masterpiece, nearly twelve by twenty-six feet, was reputedly inspired by the German bombing of that Basque city during the Spanish Civil War. It is, however, a universal statement of human anguish, heightened by terrorized people and animals. In its exaggerations and distortions—its overlapping planes and absence of modeling—it reveals both the influences of cubism and expressionism, but without the latter style's lurid colors. The painting was Picasso's contribution to the Spanish Pavilion of the 1937 International Exposition held in Paris, where it became the center of controversy.

Picasso had become sufficiently famous that anything he did became noteworthy: his many affairs with women, his membership in the Communist Party, his friendships with writers and movie stars, his habits of work and tastes in food. Dora Maar, his mistress during the *Guernica* days, said that during Picasso's postcubist days, his style was determined by the woman he loved, the place where he lived, the circle of his friends, poets, and his dog.

Picasso lived frugally and was reluctant to sell many of his finished works. Consequently, the greatest collector of Picassos was Picasso himself. When the artist died, the French government in lieu of collecting monetary death duties, selected over a thousand of the choicest paintings, drawings, and pieces of sculpture—about one-fourth of the entire treasure trove—and made them the nucleus of a special Picasso museum in Paris.

Summary

In Western society, which so highly prizes artistic change, diversity, and innovation, Pablo Picasso stands forth as the quintessential creative genius. A master in every medium to which he put his hand—painting, sculpture, graphics, ceramics—he, more than any other single artist of his age, was responsible for altering the way people approach, view, and accept art. Constantly moving from one style to another, he destroyed forever the hold that Renaissance concepts of pictorial space held over artists, especially their devotion to the canon that flat images on a canvas are given dimensionality and perspective through diminution in size and change in coloristic atmosphere. Picasso broke his figures into fragments, split them into geometric shapes, and had them occupy diverse planes, ignoring any rational relationship they had to their environment. He made his images exist independently of nature, giving them no unifying point of view and no fixed perspective. He even made them completely abstract. By forging a new tradition, Picasso revealed a more profound reality. He recognized that the human eye is highly selective, that it often glances at objects haphazardly, focusing on bits and pieces, looking at things selectively, highlighting parts and planes and aspects, and divorcing the particular from the totality, independent of any natural arrangement of shapes and lines and colors. Thus, Picasso was able to transcend the times in which he lived. His talent remained fresh and young throughout his entire professional life of more than sixty years. In addition, his creations, despite their great diversity, always remained unified in the strength of his own remarkable personality and vast talent for regeneration.

Bibliography
Cirlot, Juan-Eduardo. *Picasso, Birth of a Genius*. New York: Praeger, 1972. This sumptuous volume was published on the occasion of the lavish donation of his works that the artist made to the city of Barcelona to memorialize his friend Jaime Sabartés. Thus, it serves as a catalog of that collection but also provides a complete record of the development of the artist during his crucial formative period before the birth of modernism to the period of World War I. The collection is particularly strong in sketches and drawings. Cirlot organizes his study around the way Picasso worked rather than where he worked.

Daix, Pierre, and Georges Boudaille, with Joan Rosselet. *Picasso, The Blue and Rose Periods: A Catalogue Raisonné of the Paintings, 1900-1906*. Translated by Phoebe Pool. Greenwich, Conn.: New York Graphic Society, 1967. More than a listing of the paintings of that important period in Picasso's creative life, this study also deals with the development of the early modern art movement and discusses Picasso's relation to its formation. Lavishly illustrated.

Duncan, David Douglas. *The Private World of Pablo Picasso*. New York: Harper and Bros., 1958. This study is by a famous photographer who, upon Picasso's invitation, lived as Picasso's guest for three months during the artist's seventy-fifth year. The several hundred photos that illustrate Picasso in the act of creativity and at play and relaxation—there is even a shot of him in the bathtub—is a distillation of the more than ten thousand that Duncan took. Duncan's worship of his subject is evident from his opening sentence: "Maybe this is the happiest house on earth." As a photographic record of the object of this veneration, it is a true tour de force.

Elgar, Frank, and Robert Maillard. *Picasso*. Translated by Francis Scarfe. New York: Frederick A. Praeger, 1956. The premise that Picasso's art cannot be understood without reference to the society in which he lived gives shape to this outline of his corpus, in which the biographical study of Maillard is conveniently juxtaposed with a study of his work by Elgar.

Gedo, Mary Mathews. *Picasso: Art as Autobiography*. Chicago: University of Chicago Press, 1980. Gedo looks at the artist from a psychodramatic point of view. She considers how the experiences, emotions, and images of his childhood relate to his artistic vision. She maintains that his frequent change of artistic vision corresponded to some alteration or disruption in his life at the time. This central theme of "partnership" is varied and complex and is more related to other men of genius than to women.

Granell, Eugenio Fernandez. *Picasso's "Guernica": The End of a Spanish Era*. Ann Arbor, Mich.: UMI Research Press, 1967. Through analysis of one of Picasso's masterpieces, Granell seeks to understand the culture and tradition that gave it life, claiming that its inspiration emanates from two Spanish myths: the myth of Epiphany, which expresses the irrational and passive proclivities of Spanish society, and the myth of the bullfight, which expresses the irrational but active attitudes. In any case, the author rejects the common assumption that the painting represents an episode in the Spanish Civil War.

Penrose, Roland. *Picasso: His Life and Work*. Rev. ed. New York: Harper & Row, 1958. Penrose provides an outline of the artist's works from style to style and period to period. While establishing Picasso's talent as a main part of the landscape of modern art, he reveals the artist's lack of interest for that period's continual factional quarrels and any intellectual theorizing.

Wertenbaker, Lael. *The World of Picasso*. New York: Time-Life Books,

1967. A worthy addition to the acclaimed series of the Time-Life Library of Art. The commentary is perceptive and the illustrations first-rate.

Wm. Laird Kleine-Ahlbrandt

LUIGI PIRANDELLO

Born: June 28, 1867; Girgenti (now Agrigento), Italy
Died: December 10, 1936; Rome, Italy
Area of Achievement: Literature
Contribution: Pirandello revolutionized modern drama by creating innovative plays that explored the nature of drama itself. He created an intellectual drama that redefined the nature of the self and examined in detail the effects of relativity on the human psyche.

Early Life
On June 28, 1867, in the midst of a cholera epidemic, Luigi Pirandello was born prematurely at Il Caos, in Girgenti, Sicily. He was a fragile, weak, and lonely child. Unable to communicate with his authoritarian father, he felt isolated and turned rebellious. This feeling of isolation became a central theme in his creative work. Pirandello was also influenced by his Sicilian background. Sicily's hierarchical, almost feudal, society demanded restrictive codes of honor and strict adherence to convention, which led to repressed emotions and acts of violence. This conflict between individual desires and repressive social norms would become a recurring motif in Pirandello's work.

As a student, Pirandello read classical and Italian literature, and at fifteen he wanted to be a poet. His early poetry already showed his preoccupation with the themes of death and madness. After an unsuccessful venture into his father's business, he pursued his academic studies at the University of Rome and at the University of Bonn, where he earned a doctorate in philology.

After completing his education, Pirandello returned to Rome and became involved in the literary circle of the realist author Luigi Capuana. He then began to focus on his prose writing and published a collection of his short stories, *Amori senza amore* (1894; loves without love). In 1893, he began to formulate his artistic credo. He saw modern humanity trapped in a maze and believed that the old social norms were disintegrating, leaving the world in a state of uncertainty.

At twenty-six, Pirandello entered into an arranged marriage with Antonietta Portulana, the daughter of his father's business partner and a woman he hardly knew. Four years later, he began teaching in Rome at the Instituto Superiore Magistero, a teacher's college for women. In 1903, his father's sulfur mine was destroyed in a flood, leaving the family bankrupt. Distraught by these events, his wife was stricken by hysterical paralysis and later went insane. She became obsessively jealous, tried to stab Pirandello, and accused him of incest with his daughter. After many years of torment, he finally put her in a clinic in 1919. From living with a madwoman, he learned that reality was a matter of perception and that in the eyes of his demented wife, he could become many different people. These experiences would influence his writing.

Life's Work

Pirandello soon began to establish himself as a noted writer of short stories, novels, and most significantly, dramas. With his novel *Il fu Mattia Pascal* (1904; *The Late Mattia Pascal*, 1923), he gained recognition both within Italy and abroad. In the novel, he shows how the modern individual tries both to escape the conventional roles placed on him and to free himself from social restraints. The attempt is a failure. Mattia, an insignificant, unheroic man, always questioning his own actions, finds out that he cannot exist outside the bounds of society, nor can he return to a role he once had.

In *Si gira . . .* (1916; *Shoot, The Notebooks of Serafino Gubbio, Cinematograph Operator*, 1926), Pirandello continues to treat the themes of alienation and loss of identity. In this novel, he uses the diary form to trace the fragmented impressions of a cameraman who tries to become a detached recorder of the lives of glamorous movie stars. In *Uno, nessuno centomila* (1925; *One, None, and a Hundred Thousand*, 1933), he foreshadows the modernist novel. The work is composed of long interior monologues, lengthy self-reflexive digressions, and an unreliable narrator who cannot certify what he has seen.

Throughout his career, Pirandello continued to publish short stories, 233 in all. He had planned to do twenty-four volumes but completed only fifteen. His stories reflect a pessimistic worldview tinged with a sense of tragicomic irony. As journeys in search of the unattainable, they bring out the humor in the disparity between human ideals and the cruel realities of experience.

Pirandello was to reach the height of his artistic genius as a dramatist. In 1915, Angelo Musco coaxed Pirandello into writing for the Sicilian theater. Writing plays in the Sicilian dialect, he began to achieve popular success as a playwright, and drama became the perfect medium for him to explore his vision. Between 1916 and 1924, Pirandello made his most significant contribution to modern drama in particular and world literature in general. In *Così è (se vi pare)* (1917; *Right You Are (If You Think So)*, 1952), he shows how a husband who separates his wife and his mother-in-law can lead a whole town into confusion as both the mother-in-law and the husband claim that they are playing along with the deluded perceptions of the other. In this play and in subsequent dramas of this period, Pirandello turns the well-made play of the nineteenth century against itself. His dramas thrust bizarre characters into fantastical situations that lead to explosive climaxes built around ironic twists. As each character gives his own conflicting view of what has happened, the facts blur, and truth becomes a matter of individual perception. Pirandello's plays use passionate confrontations to examine one of the major philosophical issues of modern times: the relativity of truth.

In *Sei personaggi in cerca d'autore* (1921; *Six Characters in Search of an Author*, 1922), Pirandello achieved his greatest success. This play was so unconventional that at its first performance in Rome in 1921, it precipitated a riot in the theater. Pirandello was hissed off the stage and slipped out a back entrance, pursued by a mob crying "Madhouse!" Despite the initial reaction, the play achieved international fame. Between 1922 and 1925, it was translated into twenty-five languages. Pirandello's fame eventually spread to England and the United States, where one theater devoted an entire season to his plays. *Six Characters in Search of an Author* tells the story of six unfinished characters who interrupt the rehearsal of a Pirandello play and insist on acting out their drama. In this play, Pirandello not only examines the psychology of the twentieth century individual but also dissects the nature of theater itself. Theater becomes a distorting mirror through which actions are viewed from various perspectives. Each character interprets his actions differently so that reality becomes a matter of perception. As the professional actors try to play the parts of the characters, the characters begin to see distorted views of themselves as others interpret them. Thus, all human beings are seen as actors who play a variety of roles and who constantly try to adjust their perceptions of themselves to the way others see them.

In *Enrico IV* (1922; *Henry IV*, 1923), Pirandello continues to depict the uncertain nature of the self. The play shows how a man masquerading as an emperor receives a blow on the head, goes insane, and believes that he actually is the emperor. The play depicts the desperate quest of the modern individual to create a life of his own in a world that is constantly changing. It is the tragedy of a man who has remained frozen and static behind a mask while the rest of the world has changed around him.

Pirandello's later plays take on a mythical dimension as he confronts universal problems. In *La nuova colonia* (1928; *The New Colony*, 1958), he treats the impossibility of the Utopian myth. In *Lazzaro* (1929; *Lazarus*, 1952), he focuses on the nature of the religious experience. Finally, in his unfinished work, *I giganti della montagna* (act 1 published in 1931, act 2 in 1934, and act 3 in 1937; *The Mountain Giants*, 1958), he confronts the nature of art itself. His final plays have a more fantastical, visionary, and even allegorical quality.

Pirandello not only wrote plays but also produced and directed them. In 1925, he established the Arts Theater, in which he tried to combine the energetic improvisatory style of Italian acting with the more disciplined approach of the new schools of realistic acting. The Arts Theater toured Europe and South America before it was disbanded in 1928 for financial reasons.

In the latter part of his life, Pirandello achieved popular success. In France, he was awarded the Legion of Honor medal. In the United States, he was greeted with accolades. In Italy, he became a member of the Italian

Academy, and, in 1934, he won the coveted Nobel Prize in Literature. Yet, to the very end, he believed himself to be an alienated man. In his will, he stated that he wanted his death unannounced, his naked body wrapped in a winding sheet, his remains cremated, and his ashes scattered in the wind so that nothing of himself would remain. His ashes were preserved and finally buried in his birthplace in Il Caos. Pirandello was, indeed, what he had called himself, the "Son of Caos."

Summary
    Luigi Pirandello is one of the leading writers of the modernist period. His drama and fiction focus on the relativity of truth and the impossibility of certainty in an age of anxiety. He examines in detail the disintegration of the self, the fragmentation of human experience, the unreliability of rational thought, and the impossibility of language to communicate. His self-conscious, tortuously analytical antiheroes constantly confront the dilemmas of an indifferent universe. His use of parody and farce to undercut the tragedy of existence in a world without hope foreshadows contemporary absurdist literature. The existentialist philosopher and playwright Jean-Paul Sartre found him the most timely dramatist of the post-World War II era. His influence on the French dramatists Jean Giraudoux, Jean Anouilh, and Eugène Ionesco is extensive. More than any other playwright, he is responsible for the self-reflexive theatricality of the modern era that has given us everything from the optimistic panoramas of Thornton Wilder to the absurdist dramas of Samuel Beckett. The famous poet, playwright, and critic T. S. Eliot wrote: "Pirandello is a dramatist to whom all dramatists of my own and future generations will owe a debt of gratitude. He has taught us something about our own problems and has pointed to the direction in which we can seek a solution to them."

Bibliography
Bassnet-McGuire, Susan. *Luigi Pirandello*. New York: Grove Press, 1983. Briefly discusses the political and personal influences on Pirandello's work and concentrates on a detailed analysis of the major plays grouped according to themes. Also touches on Pirandello's one-act plays and mentions his use of stage directions. Contains photographs of international productions and a bibliography.
Bentley, Eric. *The Pirandello Commentaries*. Evanston, Ill.: Northwestern University Press, 1986. A series of articles by an eminent critic and theorist of modern drama, spanning a lifetime's work of penetrating insights into Pirandello's major dramas. The articles include a short biographical profile of Pirandello.
Cambon, Glauco, ed. *Pirandello: A Collection of Critical Essays*. Englewood Cliffs, N.J.: Prentice-Hall, 1967. A diverse collection of critical

articles, including Adriano Tilgher's influential analysis of Pirandello's drama, Wylie Sypher's discussion of Pirandello's cubist approach to drama, Thomas Bishop's article tracing Pirandello's influence on French drama, and A. L. de Castris' dissection of Pirandello's experimental novels. Includes a detailed chronology of Pirandello's life and a selected bibliography of critical works on Pirandello.

Giudice, Gaspare. *Pirandello: A Biography.* Translated by Alastair Hamilton. New York: Oxford University Press, 1975. One of the more comprehensive biographies of Pirandello even though an abridged version of the original. Details much of Pirandello's personal life using quotations from personal correspondence and other primary sources. Includes extensive descriptions of Sicilian life-styles and a good analysis of the political climate in Italy during Pirandello's lifetime.

Oliver, Roger W. *Dreams of Passion: The Theater of Luigi Pirandello.* New York: New York University Press, 1979. This study demonstrates a connection between Pirandello's theory of humor and his drama. Oliver shows how Pirandello makes a distinction between the surface awareness of contrary events in comic situations and a more internal awareness experienced by an audience when it is cognizant of the "sentiment of the contrary." Presents a close analysis of five major plays.

Paolucci, Anne. *Pirandello's Theatre: The Recovery of the Modern Stage for Dramatic Art.* Carbondale: Southern Illinois University Press, 1974. A literary and theatrical analysis of Pirandello's major plays and some of his minor dramas arranged thematically. The introduction discusses most of the major themes in his works, and the individual chapters—each preceded by brief synopses of the plays discussed—focus on the development of those themes.

Starkie, Walter. *Luigi Pirandello.* Berkeley: University of California Press, 1965. A very thorough literary biography. Discusses various literary movements in Italy that influenced Pirandello's writings and outlines the primary themes that run throughout his work. Also discusses Pirandello's place in world literature as well as his influence on other playwrights. Well organized, with a good but dated bibliography.

Paul Rosefeldt

DOMINIQUE PIRE

Born: February 10, 1910; Dinant, Belgium
Died: January 30, 1969; Louvain, Belgium
Area of Achievement: Social reform
Contribution: Pire received the Nobel Peace Prize for his work among World War II refugees in Europe, particularly those who were aged, crippled, or without those skills that could assure them acceptance by a receiving country.

Early Life

Georges Charles Clement Ghislain Eugène François Pire was born in Dinant, Belgium, in 1910, the first of seven children. His father was a schoolmaster in the nearby village of Leffe. Pire was four years old when World War I began. In 1914, German troops marched into Belgium, and Pire fled with his parents to France, where they remained as refugees until 1918. When he arrived in his hometown again after the war, Pire returned to a family house which had been burned to the ground.

Pire attended school in Leffe and, after learning classics and philosophy at the Collège de Bellevue at Dinant, decided in 1926 to become a priest. He was sixteen years old. As Brother Henri Dominique, he entered the Couvent de la Sarte, a Dominican monastery in Huy, where he studied philosophy for four years. Pire took his final vows on completion of his studies in 1932 and during the same year went to Rome to attend the Angelicum, the Dominican university. While pursuing doctoral work there, he was ordained into the priesthood (1934) and became Father Pire. He was ordered back to the Couvent de la Sarte monastery at Huy, where he continued work on his dissertation, receiving the doctorate of theology in 1936. At that time, the assignment came to teach the Dominican brothers at Huy. At the age of twenty-six, Pire believed himself to be too young and inadequate to assume those duties and requested further preparation. He studied social and political sciences at the University of Louvain in 1937 and then returned to Huy to begin work as a teacher of moral philosophy and sociology at the Couvent de la Sarte.

When German troops marched into Belgium in 1940, Pire fled to France with other Belgian refugees. When France itself was occupied, he returned to Belgium and resumed his lectures at Huy.

Life's Work

Aside from teaching, Pire spent the war years trying to obtain sufficient food from the countryside for the children in the villages. He served as chaplain to patriots of the Belgian underground and as an intelligence officer for the resistance, carrying messages and using his proximity to vital information to serve the cause. Pire also assisted downed Allied airmen in escaping German occupied territory and reported German V-1 launches on the Strait of Dover to Allied authorities. For his work, he was honored with several national medals.

Already in 1938, Pire had established a mutual aid society for poor families in rural areas, and, by 1945, his open-air camps in the country had supplied homes for thousands of children from bombed Belgian and French cities and towns. In 1949, on hearing an address by Colonel Edward F. Squadrille, formerly of the United Nations Relief and Rehabilitation Administration, Pire expanded his commitment to charitable work and assistance to the homeless. Squadrille had resigned his post with the United Nations out of frustration, citing enormous difficulties in placing stateless and destitute refugees who were old, handicapped, or without marketable skills. Although most of the eight million displaced persons of World War II had been settled by relief and relocation organizations, approximately 150,000 remained uprooted. These were the "hard-core" refugees who had little to offer receiving countries.

Pire began writing letters to such refugees and visited an Austrian camp in which sixty thousand of them awaited relocation. Noting the toll that years of insecurity, lack of privacy, and reliance on charity had taken on their lives, he began disseminating information about their plight, encouraging more fortunate people to develop relationships by writing letters and sending packages, and calling on others to assist in programs to resolve the displaced persons' problems. In 1950, Pire opened the first of four homes in Belgium for elderly refugees who were no longer able to care for themselves. To rekindle self-worth, these people were encouraged to cultivate old and vanishing skills, such as embroidery, to offer for sale.

The priest's major task was locating refugees in communities where they could participate productively in mainstream European life. Pire believed that reestablishing roots was the fundamental need of displaced persons, and he conceived of small villages near cities where refugees would gradually be integrated into local life. After convincing citizens that their cities would not be negatively impacted by such groups, Pire began establishing his "European Villages," consisting of 150-200 refugees and largely supported by private funds. Eventually there were six such villages, and members ultimately became self-supporting.

It was through his efforts to establish the sixth village that Pire received the Nobel Peace Prize. Short of funds, Pire applied to the Nobel Foundation for support but was informed that the organization only disbursed money as prizes. The priest found a person qualified to nominate him for a prize, and in 1958, Pire received an invitation to come to the Norwegian Embassy to present his work to Nobel Foundation representatives. Later, he traveled to Oslo for further discussions, and, in 1958, Pire was awarded the Nobel

Peace Prize for his efforts to help refugees, especially the "hard core," leave their camps and return to lives of freedom and dignity.

Pire extended his efforts to achieve peace through creating contacts and understanding among people from different parts of the world by beginning his Open Heart to the World organization in 1960. The major operation of the organization was the Mahatma Gandhi International Peace Center, which later became known as the University of Peace. Located in Huy, the university held seminars designed to help men, women, and youth to engage in positive peace activism. Additionally, the organization sponsored the World Friendships initiative, which encouraged exchanges between people of varied backgrounds; the World Sponsorship system, which provided aid for Asian and African refugees; and the Peace Islands in East Pakistan and India, which provided education, medical assistance, and help in developing more effective agricultural methods. Pire died at the age of fifty-eight in Louvain, Belgium, of a heart attack while recovering from surgery.

Summary

Dominique Pire's commitment to social justice pivoted on interaction between individuals of varied backgrounds. Beginning with a recognition of both the fundamental diversity and unity of humankind, Pire promoted the equality of all persons in respect to their dignity and rights. In order to achieve that level of mutual esteem as a practical reality, he developed a style of communication that he referred to as "fraternal dialogue." This form of exchange was characterized by listening, openness, and unselfishness on both sides of the dialogue, and Pire advanced it through his writings and teachings as the sure means of achieving internal as well as external peace.

Pire was one of several post-World War II peace activists who went beyond nationality, race, and creed to seek solutions to the destructive capabilities and the competitiveness that his generation had experienced in human relations. Although his goals were regarded by some as idealistic, the priest's simple and practical program for achieving them united with useful results to gain international recognition. Pire described himself as being pro-humankind and not "anti" anything. Because his agenda included the advancement in dignity of all categories of people, Pire's views obtained widespread currency and support.

Bibliography
Gray, Tony. *Champions of Peace*. New York: Paddington Press, 1976. The story of Alfred Nobel, the Nobel Peace Prize, and its recipients is described in this work. Gray analyzes the political and social milieu in which Pire worked and how that environment impacted the decision to award him the prize.
Houart, Victor. *The Open Heart*. London: Souvenir Press, 1959. Houart fo-

cuses on the evolution of Pire's "European Villages" but includes substantial information on the priest's childhood and early adult years.

Northcott, Cecil. "Profile: Father Dominique Pire." *Contemporary Review* 202 (September, 1962): 130-131. This article deals with the University of Peace and the philosophy and approach of the person who founded it.

Pire, Dominique. *The Story of Father Dominique Pire.* Translated by John L. Skeffington. New York: E. P. Dutton, 1961. This work provides Pire's autobiography and includes editorial comments from Hugues Vehenne, the person to whom Pire told the story. The engaging and reflective account is enriched by photographs of family, friends, refugees, and the villages that Pire founded.

Wintterle, John, and Richard S. Cramer. *Portraits of the Nobel Laureates in Peace.* London: Abelard-Schuman, 1971. The chapter on Pire contains an interesting analysis of how he obtained the Nobel Peace Prize and addresses the question of whether he was an appropriate recipient.

Margaret B. Denning

THE PIRELLI FAMILY

Giovanni Battista Pirelli

Born: December 27, 1848; Varenna, Austrian Empire
Died: October 20, 1932; Milan, Italy

Piero Pirelli

Born: January 27, 1881; Milan, Italy
Died: August 7, 1956; Milan, Italy

Alberto Pirelli

Born: April 28, 1882; Milan, Italy
Died: October 19, 1971; Casciano, Italy
Areas of Achievement: Business, industry, government, politics, invention, and technology
Contribution: The Pirelli family was a group of Italian industrialists who furthered the development, production, and trade of rubber goods, electric wire, and electric cables. The family also figured significantly in nineteenth and twentieth century Italian and international politics.

Early Lives

Giovanni Battista Pirelli was born in Varenna, Como, then part of the Austrian Empire, in December, 1848. He attended schools in Como and later entered the Facolta de Matematica in Pavia, from which he went on to the Politechnico of Milan. During the years of the Italian unification, Giovanni fought with the Italian patriot Giuseppe Garibaldi, serving as a guerrilla Red Shirt at Trentino and in the Battle of Mentana. He later served as a senator in the Italian government.

In 1870, Giovanni traveled to Switzerland and Germany to learn about the rubber industry, which, like other forms of industry, was little developed in Italy. He returned to Milan and, in 1872, started a rubber hose factory to combat domination of the market by the French, Italy's erstwhile enemy. He opened a shop in Milan with forty-two thousand dollars in borrowed capital, thirty-five workers, and some experience in vulcanization, the process whereby rubber is hardened to prevent melting at high temperatures. It was the first business of its kind in Italy and one of the first in Europe.

Life's Work

The firm developed specialties in wires, insulated cables, and eventually automobile tires. It produced some of the earliest telegraph and telephone wires for Italy's new army. In 1879, Giovanni extended his enterprise to the production of electrical conductors. He later produced cables whose design and construction stood far in advance of anything obtainable at the time. In 1883, Milan inaugurated the Edison Central Electric Station, the first station of its scale in Europe. The Pirelli firm supplied the rubber-coated wires used in the new installations, its first customer being the Milanese opera house, La Scala. The company pioneered the manufacture of electric cable and, in 1887, began producing and installing underwater cables as well. The firm had a subsidiary factory in Barcelona for the production of electric cables by 1902, making Pirelli the first Italian industrialist to establish plants outside Italy. In 1917, when a Pirelli engineer patented an oil-insulated cable that could carry far more than the limit then in effect, Pirelli became a leader in the high-tension cable business. The Pirelli firm entered the pneumatic tire business in 1890 with production of its first air-filled bicycle tires. As Italy's automobile industry began increased development, Pirelli moved into the pneumatic automobile tire market in 1899.

Giovanni's son, Piero, joined the firm in 1901. Born in Milan in 1881, Piero received an LL.D. at the University of Genoa. Alberto, a second son, joined the business in 1903. To promote the automobile tire industry, Alberto helped sponsor the eight-thousand-mile Peking-to-Paris automobile race of 1907, which was won by the Italian driver Prince Borghese in a car fitted with Pirelli tires. Alberto built dirigibles for North Pole explorations during the 1920's. The Pirelli *Norge* was the first lighter-than-air craft to succeed in reaching the pole, making a more than eight-thousand-mile voyage from Rome to Teller, Alaska, in 1926. The crew, which included Roald Amundsen, saw and photographed parts of the globe never before seen by human eyes.

By 1914, the Pirelli company was the largest Italian manufacturer of rubber goods. It had built an industrial system that was virtually independent of the Italian state, linking its strength to foreign markets without Italian favors. Pirelli plants could be found in many parts of Italy and the world.

Both Piero and Alberto participated actively in promoting Italian business and international trade. Piero assisted greatly with the development of the Italian telephone service, represented Italy in many important international financial negotiations, and served as vice president of the Confederation of Italian Industries. Alberto was chosen by Benito Mussolini to represent Italy at the important post-World War I conferences. The younger Pirelli brother was a member of the Supreme Economic Committee of Versailles, Italian delegate to the first International Labor Office of Geneva, and a member of the League of Nations Economic Committee. Between 1928 and 1932, Alberto served as president of the International Chamber of Commerce. He served on the Dawes Committee, bringing to bear his concern for the impact of reparations payments on international trade. Alberto became Mussolini's trusted financial and economic adviser. He was a member of the National Council of Corporations and a commissioner of the General Fascist Confederation of Industries, two syndicates through which the Italian government controlled industry.

Giovanni died in 1932. Piero was then serving as managing director of the Pirelli organization and, after his father's death, became chairman of the board. Alberto assumed management of the business that year.

Pirelli plants were destroyed during World War II, but Marshall Plan funds assisted in building five new factories and refurbishing old ones; the business flourished again. To counter the growing communist influence among workers during the 1950's, Alberto began a progressive program that brought higher wages, increased benefits, and greater worker satisfaction to the business, resulting in the decline of communist influence and an increase in worker productivity. Pirelli workers gained a free medical, surgical, and hospital plan, low-cost modern housing options, a free home for retirees on Lake Como, and free vacation camps on the Italian Riviera. During one eight-year period, Pirelli wages increased 96 percent vis-à-vis the 28 percent Italian cost-of-living rise.

By the mid-1960's, Pirelli had become the second-largest tire and rubber company outside the United States and shared a close race with a British company for the position as the world's largest producer of electric cable. It sold more abroad than any other Italian company and had eighty-one plants in thirteen different countries. It was also the second-largest stockholder in Italy's Fiat automobile company.

The Pirelli organization continued innovation in the tire industry. In 1953, radial-ply tires using textile belts were introduced, giving much greater vertical flexibility. During the 1970's, Pirelli improved wet traction by modifying rubber formulas, and the company's methods of measuring vehicle handling came to be considered the most professional in the world. In 1971, the firm merged with Great Britain's Dunlop Holding, Ltd., a union designed to join the resources of Europe's two largest tire and rubber companies, while maintaining their status as separate holding companies and retaining their own trademarks. The merger was dissolved in 1981. Its failure has been attributed to greater competition in the industry and to higher production costs emerging from increased oil prices. Today Pirelli is an international holding company with operations in Europe, North and South America, the Middle East, and New Zealand.

Piero died in 1956. His younger brother, Alberto, retired in 1965 and died six years later after a long illness. The direction of the Pirelli company remained in the hands of Alberto's second son, Leopoldo, who modernized the organization's management structure and conducted the firm as the chief executive of the vast and highly organized stockholder organization that it had already become.

Summary

Giovanni Pirelli, his sons, and the firm they established were both cause and effect in the industrialization of Italy during the late nineteenth and early twentieth centuries. Giovanni brought to Italy the production practices of that part of Europe north of the Alps. His sons Alberto and Piero played a large role in the political and industrial advancement of Italy as a substantial international power.

The Pirelli family, particularly Alberto, pushed rubber technology to the limit. Besides innovative research and application in the tire industry and with rubber-insulated electric cables, the Pirelli organization has produced countless rubber items, including skin diving equipment, raincoats, elastic thread, plastic food bags, baby bottle nipples, rubber hoses, and drive belts.

Bibliography

Coates, Austin. *The Commerce in Rubber: The First 250 Years*. New York: Oxford University Press, 1987. Coates's interesting and comprehensive history of the world rubber industry places the Pirelli organization in the larger context of that trade. The chapter entitled "Europe-electricity and tyres-Pirelli-Dunlop-Michelin" is particularly relevant.

Fortune, Editors of *Businessmen Around the Globe*. Englewood Cliffs, N.J.: Prentice-Hall, 1967. The article on Leopold Pirelli, who assumed leadership of the Pirelli organization in 1965, contains a brief account of Giovanni's founding of the business.

Nobile, Umberto. "Navigating the *Norge* from Rome to the North Pole and Beyond." *National Geographic Magazine* 52 (August, 1927): 177-215. Nobile was an Italian Air Force general who codirected the Pirelli-sponsored dirigible flight over the North Pole. The body of the *Norge* was constructed of rubberized, triple-ply fabric.

Pirelli, Alberto, Josiah C. Stamp, and Count A. de Chalendar. *Reparation Payments and Future International Trade*. Paris: International Chamber of Commerce, 1925. This report by the Economic Restoration Committee of the International Chamber of Commerce contains the study of the possible effects of the German reparation payments on international trade. Pirelli served on the subcommittee and helped compose part 1 of the report.

Ridgeway, George L. *Merchants of Peace: Twenty Years of Business Diplomacy Through the International Chamber of Commerce*. New York: Columbia University Press, 1938. Ridgeway describes the evolution and work of the International Chamber of Commerce, whose president from 1928 to 1932 was Alberto Pirelli. The chapter on the business settlement of reparations also describes the work of the Dawes Committee, on which Alberto also served.

Webster, Richard A. *Industrial Imperialism in Italy 1908-1915*. Berkeley: University of California Press, 1975. Webster's research provides a valuable description of the environment in which Italian companies such as the Pirelli organization worked during the decade preceding World War I. The chapter dealing with non-trust industries is the most pertinent.

Margaret B. Denning

HENRI PIRENNE

Born: December 23, 1862; Verviers, Belgium
Died: October 24, 1935; Ukkel, Belgium
Area of Achievement: Historiography
Contribution: Pirenne altered extant periodization of European history and altered the thinking of medievalists by reminders of the influences of Islam and Byzantium on Western history and of all historians by diverting them from undue emphasis on institutional (legal), political, and religious events. The "Pirenne Thesis" has been a major influence on professional historical thinking.

Early Life

Jean Henri Otto Lucien Marie Pirenne was the first, and ultimately the most distinguished, child born into an unusual bourgeois family on December 23, 1862, in Verviers, Belgium. His father, Lucien Henri, a hard-driving industrialist who operated Belgium's technically most advanced woolen manufactory, was also bookish, polylingual, learned, and widely traveled. Young Henri's mother, Marie Duesberg, was the accomplished daughter of his paternal grandfather's business partner. She came from a less fervently economic, more intellectual lineage than her husband. Since the marriage, which joined Verviers's two most respected families, was less a marriage of convenience than one based on mutual respect and affection, young Henri enjoyed a nourishing familial environment.

Romantic, bookish, but gregarious and observant, Pirenne not only came to know Verviers's urban workers but also explored the surrounding Franchimont region, whose peasants had always been freemen. At seven, his formal education began at the local Collège Communal, pedagogically French, where he displayed a remarkable memory and prizewinning excellence in Latin, German, Greek, French, geography, and history, but notable weakness in mathematics, thus aborting his father's hopes that he would proceed to engineering, helping to upgrade the mill's technology. Pirenne's father, therefore, suggested that his son study law at the University of Liège.

Matriculating in 1879, Pirenne subsequently performed brilliantly in all subjects but swiftly came under the influence of historians Godefroid Kurth and Paul Fredericq: Kurth was fervently Catholic, and Fredericq was vociferously Protestant. Each taught superbly, however, and both, trained in the new critical German historical methodologies, identified with Leipzig's great Theodor Mommsen and Berlin's masterful Leopold von Ranke, helped further a renaissance in Belgian university life. Not less propitious was the amazing Belgian archival collection somewhat earlier assembled by Paris-born and self-taught Prosper Gachard. It was invaluable to the Liège historians—later, most particularly to Pirenne.

In 1881, Pirenne qualified with greatest distinction (by examination) to proceed toward the doctorate; directed by Kurth, he published his first monograph at the age of nineteen in 1882. Completing his doctorate in 1883, he was urged by his mentors to continue medieval studies in Paris at the École Pratique des Hautes Études and the École des Chartres, which, after extensive scholarly travels, he did, again performing with excellence. Essentially his career was well launched with a scholarship to study at the very heart of the modern revolution in historical studies: in Germany at the University of Leipzig, then at the University of Berlin.

Life's Work

Berlin meant Pirenne's direct contact with the elite of nineteenth century historians: Ranke, Gustav von Schmoller, Georg Waitz, and a host of young rising historians. Then in 1885, through the indefatigable efforts of Kurth, Pirenne received a professorship at the University of Liège, teaching Latin paleography and diplomatic as well as historical exercises for the humanities division. Master of French, German, Dutch, Latin, and Greek, he also read Italian and English; master too of paleography, philosophy, and toponomy (the origins of regional place names and languages), he had, as they expected, excelled his mentors. However distinguished a future awaited him at Liège, he was within a year "stolen" by Fredericq for a post in the less distinguished University of Ghent, where he would remain until retirement in 1930. Advancement in academic rank was one reason for the move but was less important than Fredericq himself and the opportunity to teach his own courses on medieval history and the history of Belgium—of which in time he would be applauded as the nation's premier historian.

Two loves pinned Pirenne to Ghent: first, as a medievalist, his recognition of its immense economic importance from the twelfth into the fourteenth centuries—and the economic revivification it again was enjoying while he was there—and second, his marriage in 1887 to Jenny Vanderhaegen, an alert, shrewd, gracious woman who industriously protected and advanced her husband's career. They would have four sons, one a historian of note.

Thus settled, Pirenne extended associational activities promoting collections of Belgian historical documents, added the teaching of urban economic history, and published a series of originally documented monographs, which exposed previous scholarship as myth and thereby promoted controversies of the sort that would mark his entire career. He also produced a monumental Belgian bibliography of extant documents from dozens of fields up to the year 1580 plus a history of Belgium and the Low Countries up to 1830 that instantly won international acclaim. Further, his monographic history on medieval Dinant became a model of urban history because of its concentration upon social, political, legal, and economic affairs—a precursor of total history, later to characterize the Annales school of historical research that has enjoyed international recognition.

Disciplined, a splendid teacher—whose students' scholarly careers confirmed this—active in meliorating German and French scholars after embitterments of the Franco-Prussian War, active also in a host of professional associations, Pirenne, with the publication in the *Revue historique* of his "L'Origine des constitutions urbaine au moyen âge," by 1893 ranked among the greater European historians. Already he had established the thesis that urban development was the key to understanding the history not only of Belgium and The Netherlands but also of European civilization in general. Additionally, besides scores of book reviews, lectures, and meetings, he published eighteen major articles on aspects of the Middle Ages between 1894 and 1899.

Of these articles, the most important conveyed Pirenne's conviction that European urban life, based largely on Roman towns, was virtually extinguished between the sixth and eighth centuries and that a general economic revival in the tenth and eleventh centuries produced and centered on the town, a new institution in the Middle Ages, one that precipitated the decline of feudal institutions and social structure. The second portion of the article (1895) focused on historical forces that he regarded as responsible for the rise of the town and the emergence of the bourgeoisie.

While this so-called mercantile-settlement theory gained some adherents, it initially was rebuffed by most French historians, while those in Great Britain clung to earlier Germanic explanations of town origins. Nevertheless, it commenced another of Pirenne's shifts of historians' emphases. This theory was also incorporated into the first of what eventually became seven volumes of his *Histoire de Belgique* (1900-1932; history of Belgium); the initial volume alone made him Belgium's national historian and a figure of international professional renown, with accompanying honors and awards. His writing continued, of which the most significant was his *Les Anciennes Démocraties des Pays-Bas* (1910; *Belgian Democracy: Its Early History*, 1915). He continued in these works to reject traditional history as mere chronologizing, as a lexicon of biographies, or tales of politics and wars, rather emphasizing that events were best depicted as a complex interweaving of a people's collective activities.

Congenitally optimistic, a meliorist through his professional contacts of Franco-German-Belgian relations, he naïvely dismissed possibilities of war in 1914, let alone the invasion of Belgium, or the instant obedience that German historians lent their government. For passive resistance, both Pirenne and Fredericq were arrested in 1916 and confined in German camps. There, over the next thirty-two months, Pirenne learned Russian, expanded his perspectives beyond Western Europe, and became intrigued with comparative interactions of Eastern and Western cultures.

Free in 1918, Pirenne continued to ask when historically the break came between the Roman world and "the First Europe," a query he answered in his *Les Villes du moyen age: Éssai d'histoire économique et sociale* (1927; *Medieval Cities: Their Origins and the Revival of Trade*, 1925). His next major study, partially completed after his retirement in 1930, *Mahomet et Charlemagne* (1937; *Mohammed and Charlemagne*, 1939), demonstrated that the Roman world lasted longer than traditional histories indicated and that it was Islam, not the Germanic invasions, that finally destroyed it. He was unable to revise the work, for, stricken with pneumonia, this distinguished, indomitable, unassuming man died of heart failure on October 24, 1935, in Ukkel, Belgium.

Summary

In an era of great historians, Henri Pirenne ranks among the greatest for his dramatic and provocative thesis that the accepted periodization of European history was erroneous; that the Roman world lasted centuries longer than had been believed; that its disruption was the work of militantly spreading Islam, not a consequence of the Germanic invaders—who, in his view, assimilated quite readily into Roman civilization; and that the revival of Europe from rather backward agrarianism was the result of a revival of trade, responsibility for which should be assigned to the emergence of new European urban life and the activities of its commercial (or bourgeois) citizenry. While controversy still continues over his thesis and there have been factual revisions of some of its elements, most of its main features are widely viewed as basically sound. Few historical perspectives have so dramatically changed historical thinking and research or so massively shifted the focus of professional attention to economic and social history away from literal chronologization and literal political and institutional history. Historians accept superannuation of their research and syntheses; undoubtedly, Pirenne would have agreed that on very minimal available evidence on the Merovingian and Carolingian periods, he at times both overstated and understated his basic thesis. Yet he unquestionably raised and substantially answered fresh questions on medieval history and decisive changes within the Mediterranean-European world and altered perspectives in the profession to which he so decently and devotedly committed his life.

Bibliography
Boyce, Gray C. "The Legacy of Henri Pirenne." *Byzantion* 15 (1940-1941): 449-464. An early, scholary, well-written, appreciative but by no means uncritical analysis of Pirenne's studies upon medieval studies as well as upon the historical profession in general.
Havighurst, Alfred F., ed. *The Pirenne Thesis: Analysis, Criticism, and Revision.* Boston: D. C. Heath, 1958. With excellent introductory materials, fine footnoting throughout, and excellent bibliographical references,

this brief volume not only includes excerpts from Pirenne's work but also compacts a distinguished range of fine, very readable scholarly reactions to it.

Lyon, Bryce. *Henri Pirenne: A Biographical and Intellectual Study.* Ghent, Belgium: E. Story-Scientia, 1974. A major work and as fine a study as exists on any major modern historian. Contains a superb summation of the strengths, weaknesses, and legacies of Pirenne's work in chapters 11 and 12. Includes photographs, citation footnotes, an excellent select bibliography, and an index.

_____. *The Origins of the Middle Ages: Pirenne's Challenge to Gibbon.* New York: W. W. Norton, 1972. Well written by an authoritative Pirenne expert and medievalist in his own right, this work provides excellent perspective on problems of reinterpreting or delineating the origins of the Middle Ages. Contains a good bibliography and an index.

Pirenne, Henri. *Medieval Cities: Their Origins and the Revival of Trade.* Translated by Frank D. Halsey. Princeton, N.J.: Princeton University Press, 1925. For all of his immense scholarship, Pirenne wrote in order to be read by intelligent publics. It is essential for serious readers to read Lyon's biography; but there is no substitute for reading the master himself. As was usual in his writing, the text itself generally suffices for documentation; there are few notes, only a modest select bibliography and index.

Riising, Anne. "The Fate of Henri Pirenne's Thesis on the Consequence of Islamic Expansion." *Classica et Mediaevalia* 13 (1952): 87-130. Riising, a Danish journalist, here examines in greater detail than anyone the arguments pro and con respecting this critical aspect of Pirenne's major thesis about the severance of Europe from the Roman Mediterranean world in the Merovingian and Carolingian periods. Her purpose, since she agrees that the last word has not been said, is to review the extant evidence, which she manages with great skill and clarity.

Clifton K. Yearley

PIUS XI
Ambrogio Damiano Achille Ratti

Born: May 31, 1857; Desio, Italy
Died: February 10, 1939; Vatican City, Italy
Areas of Achievement: Religion and diplomacy
Contribution: Pius XI was forced to deal with the problems emerging from World War I, especially the rise of communism and the various forms of right-wing totalitarianism (including Fascism and Nazism), along with the economic dislocation that affected Europe throughout the interwar period. His efforts not only allowed the Catholic church to regain respect but also restarted the Church's public involvement in social and political issues.

Early Life

Ambrogio Damiano Achille Ratti was the son of a well-to-do manufacturer in northern Italy. His scholastic brilliance and encyclopedic mind were recognized early and, probably partially through the influence of his uncle, an important priest in his home diocese, Ratti was admitted to the famous Roman seminary of Lombard College and was ordained in December, 1879. While he continued his studies in Rome, taking graduate degrees in canon law, theology, and philosophy, Ratti was also pursuing his hobby of mountain climbing, tackling several technically difficult peaks and later producing a small book of memoirs on the subject.

In 1882, Ratti became an instructor at the seminary in Milan. Seven years later, he transferred to the famous Milanese library, the Biblioteca Ambrosiana, starting the field of work that would occupy him for most of the rest of his life. He reached the pinnacle of his field within the Catholic church in 1914, when Pope Pius X appointed him to serve as the prefect of the Vatican Library.

For reasons known only to himself, the next pope, Benedict XV, chose his librarian to head a diplomatic mission to Warsaw in the spring of 1918, anticipating the formation of a united Poland out of the chaos of war-torn Eastern Europe. The Catholic church would become one of the forces that helped the Poles create a unified nation after having been split by Russia, Austria, and Prussia in the 1790's.

The three years in Poland when Ratti was the apostolic envoy and then nuncio were filled with problems. Besides the great economic problems, Poland also launched an attack on the areas immediately to the east and southeast. Unfortunately, the new Soviet Union was also interested in regaining its lost provinces, and so the two states were quickly fighting each other. Poland lost the war, but Ratti gained some fame for being one of the few diplomats who refused to flee Warsaw when the Soviet troops nearly surrounded the city. This episode also led to Ratti's personal dislike for the

Soviet Union, in addition to the religious objections all Church leaders had for the officially atheistic state.

In recognition of his service, Benedict recalled Ratti late in 1921, made him a cardinal, and posted him to the Diocese of Milan, one of the most important posts within the Church. Ratti had little time to do anything as Archbishop of Milan, however, because of Benedict's death on January 22, 1922. On February 6, Ratti was elected pope, taking the name Pius XI.

Life's Work

Pius started his reign with an important gesture. Ever since the new Italian nation had taken over Rome and the Papal States more than fifty years before, the popes had acted as "prisoners of the Vatican," meaning that they refused to accept the loss of the papal territory, recognize the Italian state, or leave the area of the Vatican. Pius made his first appearance as pope on an outside balcony, as a symbolic opening of the Vatican. Pius was determined to bury the feud with the Italian state, which would enable the Papacy to move on to some of the other problems that it faced in the twentieth century.

Pius was sincere in his desire to reestablish the Vatican as a force in the modern world, and he made more concordats (Church-state agreements) in his reign than had ever been made before, a total of twenty-five. He also opened numerous diplomatic missions to countries with small, almost forgotten, Catholic minorities, especially in the Balkan region. Other signs of Pius' desire to bring the Church into the modern world include his establishment of Vatican Radio (a worldwide shortwave service) in the 1930's, the establishment of new orders within the Church whose prime service goals were to publicize the faith, and his many encyclicals on the state of the world, beginning with *Ubi Arcano Dei* (where God's silence) in 1923, which discussed the state of post-World War I Europe, and ending with his trio of antidictatorial statements in 1937.

Unfortunately, Pius is best known for two of his concordats: the 1929 concordat with Benito Mussolini's Italy and the 1933 agreement with Nazi Germany. The Italian concordat established Vatican City, and some other Church property, as an independent state, while the one with Nazi Germany (which was more of a culmination of a decade-long process than a quick agreement with the new German regime) promised noninterference with the internal workings of the Church; neither concordat, however, would prevent the two Fascist states from persecuting the Catholic church during the 1930's.

Pius' 1937 encyclical *Divini Redemptoris*, refuting the claims of historical inevitability that the Soviets were then making, is still probably his best-known work. Because it is so well known and so often quoted and reprinted, *Divini Redemptoris* overshadows Pius' other social and political commentaries, at times to the point at which he has been accused of ignoring the threats of Fascism in general and Nazism in particular and concentrating only on the threat from the far Left.

Pius did condemn the far Left and not only in *Divini Redemptoris*. He also condemned the left-wing Mexican Revolution in 1937 and the left-wing government in Spain during the mid-1930's. On the other hand, he also restated Pope Leo XIII's 1891 condemnation of the exploitation of the working classes by capital in his 1931 encyclical *Quaragesimo Anno* and condemned Mussolini's Fascism in his other 1931 encyclical *Non Abbiamo Bisogno* and the Nazi movement with the first of his 1937 condemnations, *Mit brennender Sorge*. Both of these last two encyclicals had to be smuggled out of Italy in order to be published. Taking all twenty-nine of the pope's encyclicals together (the most written by one pope until that time and dealing with problems and developments from politics to the film industry), it can be seen that, while he was most concerned about the dangers from the far Left, Pius was also concerned about the other problems facing interwar Europe, including the dangers posed by the Right.

Besides the many social and political problems that Pius saw emerging during his time as pope, he also dealt with a number of other issues. One, as befitting the former head of the Vatican library, was the sponsoring of a number of new intellectual agencies, including the Pontifical Academy of Sciences (which recognizes the achievements of non-Catholic as well as Catholic scientists), the reform of some older ones, and an increased support by the Church to regional literary, religious, and scientific conferences and congresses. Pius also enlarged the Vatican Library and encouraged Catholic seminaries to update their curricula to include more science and social science.

Pius was also interested in opening dialogues with other religious leaders, especially those within the Orthodox churches. While a little progress was made with some of the Eastern Orthodox churches, the effort did not go very far during this period, since neither side was willing to make concessions to the other, nor was the Russian Orthodox church, perhaps the largest of the Orthodox churches and completely under the authority of the Soviet government, interested in making any contacts at all. These attempts mark the start of the dialogue that has lasted until today between the Catholic church and the Orthodox churches.

Late in 1936, the seventy-nine-year-old pope became very sick, and the press of the world set up a sort of "death watch" to cover the expected funeral and subsequent papal election. Pius recovered from that illness by the Easter of 1937 and returned to working full-time. Rumors started circulating in late 1938 and early 1939 that Pius was going to issue a new, stronger, condemnation of either Fascism or Nazism, perhaps both. These rumors increased when the entire Italian episcopate was ordered to come to Rome to hear a major papal address on February 11, and Pius was known to be working hard on the texts of two speeches. What those speeches might have been are unknown. Pius fell ill with a cold on February 7 and died of complications on February 10.

Summary

Pius XI faced many problems during his reign, most of them having to do with the political and social problems that Europe faced during the period between the world wars. He was, perhaps, hampered with a determination to maintain, if not increase, the traditional powers of the pope while having to face the fact that the Papacy no longer had any secular power base. Pius condemned the evils of his time, but, like all the other leaders of the period, secular and religious alike, his reputation has suffered since because he was unable to stop the coming of World War II and the Holocaust that accompanied it.

Autocratic, brilliant, and determined, Pius never stopped working to improve the social and political climate around him until his death. In the short run, Pius can be said to have failed, since World War II and its attendant horrors started six months after his death. The failure, however, was not so much Pius', since he did more than most leaders of the period to point out the evils that were growing, as it was that of Europe as a whole. Unable to recover from the political and economic ruin of World War I, most European societies opted during the interwar period for solutions that would lead to World War II.

Bibliography

Browne-Olf, Lillian. *Pius XI: Apostle of Peace*. New York: Macmillan, 1938. A very sympathetic, well-researched biography of Pius, written just before his death. Writing from the viewpoint of the 1930's, Browne-Olf's judgment of Pius is all the more favorable because of the lack of hindsight that has tarnished the reputations of most of the world leaders from the interwar period.
_____. *Their Name Is Pius*. Reprint. Freeport, New York: Books for Libraries Press, 1970. A study of five of the seven popes who chose the name Pius since 1775. Pius VIII, who was pope for only eight months, and Pius XII, who had just started his pontificate when the book was written, are omitted.
The Daughters of St. Paul. *Popes of the Twentieth Century*. Boston: St. Paul Editions, 1983. A short work that serves as a favorable introduction to the twentieth century popes, laying out the salient facts of each one's biography and life's work.
Kent, Peter C. *The Pope and the Duce*. New York: St. Martin's Press, 1981. This is a monograph on the relationship between the foreign policies of the Vatican and Fascist Italy during the period 1922-1935. The author's thesis

is that these foreign policies at times came together and worked in concert, especially when most of Europe was fearing possible rising support for Communism during the early years of the Depression, although the Vatican ultimately took a strong stand against both Fascist Italy and Nazi Germany, as well as the Soviet Union.

Murphy, Francis X. *The Papacy Today.* New York: Macmillan, 1981. A concise history of the internal and external political evolution of the Papacy during the first eighty years of the twentieth century.

Teeling, William. *Pope Pius XI and World Affairs.* New York: Frederick A. Stokes, 1937. Although this is a very biased work, based on a fundamental anti-Catholic worldview, this work is valuable because it shows how the theory of Pius' alleged pro-Fascist and pro-Nazi views became widespread.

Terrance L. Lewis

PIUS XII
Eugenio Maria Giuseppe Pacelli

Born: March 2, 1876; Rome, Italy
Died: October 9, 1958; Castle Gandolfo, near Rome, Italy
Areas of Achievement: Diplomacy, religion, and theology
Contribution: Pope Pius XII preserved the Church as an institution during the crisis of World War II. He upheld traditional Catholic doctrine in an era of difficult economic, political, and social change.

Early Life

Eugenio Maria Giuseppe Pacelli (the future Pope Pius XII) was born in Rome, Italy, on March 2, 1876. His parents were Filippo Pacelli and the former Donna Virginia Graziosi, and he was the second of their four children. He was baptized March 26, 1876, at the Church of Saints Celso and Giuliano as Eugenio Maria Giuseppe Giovanni. The Pacellis were an old Roman family with a long tradition of service to the Vatican in key positions. Eugenio's grandfather, Marcantonio Pacelli, helped found *L'Observatore Romano* in 1861 and served as Papal Minister of the Interior. Filippo Pacelli, a lawyer, served as Dean of the Lawyers of the Consistory and president of a Catholic action group. His family's traditions ensured that Pacelli was reared in an atmosphere of religious devotion and scholarship. He continued a long tradition of service to the Vatican.

After finishing studies at the Lyceum Visconti with an excellent academic record, Pacelli decided to become a priest in October, 1894. After further education at the Capranica, a Roman college, the papal Athenaeum of St. Apollinare, and the Gregorian University, he was ordained to the priesthood on April 2, 1899. Although serious health problems had threatened his ability to continue his duties, he had achieved his first major goal. His ordination did not end Pacelli's education. He added a doctorate in canon and civil laws to the doctorate in sacred theology that he had already received.

Life's Work

After his ordination, Pacelli served briefly as a substitute canon at the Chapter of St. Mary Major. This period was his only direct experience as a local pastor. In February, 1901, he received an appointment in the Papal Secretariat of State in the section called the Congregation of Extraordinary Ecclesiastical Affairs. This appointment marked the beginning of a long career as a Church diplomat.

Pacelli's intelligence and hard work received quick recognition, and the future Pius XII rose rapidly in rank. He became a monsignor in 1904 and a Domestic Prelate in 1905. On May 13, 1917, Pope Benedict XV consecrated him Titular Archbishop of Sardes. In the reign of Pope Pius XI, the future pope became a cardinal on December 15, 1929. Pacelli was Benedict's nuncio to Munich, Bavaria, and he became Apostolic Nuncio of Germany on June 22, 1920, when the nunciature moved to Berlin. He earned the respect of the German people, who regretted his departure for Rome in 1929.

While Pacelli did not secure the approval of the Kaiser for a peace proposal supported by Benedict, he did secure a "solemn agreement" between Prussia and the Holy See on June 14, 1929, which was ratified on August 14, 1929. While his critics contend that his German experience biased his later actions, the agreement did give the Vatican certain legal rights, which helped protect Church interests in the Adolf Hitler era. During the 1930's, Pius XI used the future Pius XII as Cardinal Secretary of State from 1930-1939. Pacelli did much traveling to represent the Vatican in countries as diverse as Argentina, Hungary, and the United States.

When Pius XI died on February 10, 1939, his successor, Eugenio Cardinal Pacelli, called the consistory that was to elect him pope. Pius XI's trust in the then Cardinal Pacelli had resulted in his appointment as camerlengo. The camerlengo administers the Vatican during an interregnum period. On March 2, 1939, Eugenio Cardinal Pacelli, was elected pope. Many observers believed that this election fulfilled the wishes of his predecessor.

Pius XII was soon required to put his diplomatic talents to use. The outbreak of World War II put the Vatican in a difficult position, since it was an island in Fascist Italy. As war began Pius XII watched in horror as the devoutly Catholic population of Poland suffered under Nazi occupation. By 1942, the Vatican had clear proof that the Jewish population of Europe was threatened.

Despite his pity for the victims of the Nazis, Pius XII decided that the interests of Catholic Europe required that the Vatican maintain strict neutrality. The Vatican's firm neutrality angered Sir Winston Churchill and Franklin D. Roosevelt, and New York's Cardinal Francis Joseph Spellman warned the pope that many American Catholics were seriously alienated by Vatican neutrality.

Unfortunately for his historical reputation, Pius' actions during World War II have obscured his achievement as a scholar, teacher, and theologian. Papal critics who believe that Pius should have been a prophet or martyr during World War II tend to ignore his achievements in other areas and see him as a callous, cold bureaucrat, who preserved the institutional Church at the expense of the ideals of Jesus Christ.

Pius probably took more pleasure in his role as a teacher and theologian than in any other aspect of his papal duties. Among his outstanding pronouncements were *Mystici Corporis Christi* (1943), *Mediator Dei* (1947), *Humani Generis* (1950), *Menti Nostrae* (1950), *Munificentissimus Deus* (1950), *Musicae Sacrae Disciplina* (1955), *Haurietis Aquas* (1956), and *Miranda Prosus* (1957). *Mystici Corporis Christi* attempted to define the nature of the Church's role as the Mystical Body of Christ. *Mediator Dei* served to stimulate the liturgical movement. Pius always had a strong interest in the proper forms for Christian worship. *Humani Generis* hoped to correct what Pius saw as errors in modern theology. In this encyclical, Pius limited the ability of Catholic theologians to question the historical validity of parts of the Old Testament. In *Menti Nostrae*, Pius stressed the necessity of sound education, obedience to proper authority, and holy living for priests. *Munificentissimus Deus*, which may have been the most important encyclical of Pius' reign, proclaimed that the Virgin Mary had been assumed body and soul into heaven. In this encyclical, Pius broke important doctrinal ground. In *Miranda Prosus*, Pius considered both the blessings and the problems that radio and television brought to Catholic life. He urged priests to master the use of communication.

While Vatican II radically changed Catholic life, the teaching of Pius did not lack enduring value. Pius was an important transitional figure, who preserved the Catholic church in an era of economic, political, and social turmoil.

Summary

Pius XII's career reflected the upheaval experienced by European society during the first half of the twentieth century. As a skilled diplomat, he consistently sought peace. As a pastor, he tried to relieve the sufferings of the poor and the persecuted. Since he did not speak out strongly to condemn Nazi atrocities against Jews during World War II, many postwar writers have condemned his failure to protest Fascist actions vigorously and publicly. His critics have contended that strong action by Pius might have saved many innocent Jewish lives.

Pius agonized over his actions in World War II, and he was aware that the strict neutrality maintained by the Vatican during the war angered the Allies and those involved in anti-Nazi movements. His priorities clearly stressed the preservation of the Church as an institution and opposition to the spread of communism. These priorities caused him to believe that condemning Nazi atrocities in the early 1940's would jeopardize the Church, and he also contended that he could not condemn Nazi atrocities without condeming Soviet atrocities.

Given his priorities, Pius' actions are understandable. His long-term, historical reputation, however, has suffered greatly from what critics see as pro-German bias, cowardice, and even anti-Semitism. Many historians share the conviction that Pius could have and should have done more to aid the victims of Hitler and defend the European Jewish community.

Bibliography
Alvarez, David J. "The Vatican and the Far East, 1941-1943." *Historian* 40

(1978): 508-523. This excellent article focuses on the Vatican's relations with Japan and its concern for the Philippines.

Byers, Catherine. "Pius XII and the Jews." *Indiana Social Studies Quarterly* 31 (1978-1979): 57-67. Byers provides an excellent bibliography of writings on the life and pontificate of Pius.

Dietrich, Donald J. "Historical Judgements and Eternal Verities." *Society* 20 (1983): 31-35. Dietrich disagrees with Rolf Hochhuth to some extent. He does, however, believe that Pius should have spoken out against Nazism to his bishops from 1941 to 1943 and to European Catholics generally in 1944.

Friedlander, Saul. *Pius XII and the Third Reich: A Documentation.* Translated by Charles Fullman. New York: Octagon Books, 1980. Friedlander collects German documents from 1939 to 1944. His brief conclusion is unsympathetic to Pius, whom he regards as pro-German and overly anti-Bolshevik. In Friedlander's view, Pius' silence over the extermination of Jews is almost inexplicable.

Herber, Charles J. "Eugenio Pacelli's Mission to Germany and the Papal Peace Proposals of 1917." *Catholic Historical Review* 65 (1979): 20-48. Herber provides a solid account of Pius' role in World War I peace efforts at the behest of Benedict XV.

Hochhuth, Rolf. *The Deputy.* Translated by Richard Winston and Clara Winston. Preface by Albert Schweitzer. New York: Grove Press, 1964. This critically acclaimed drama attacks Pius for his silence during World War II.

Lipstadt, Deborah E. "Moral Bystanders." *Society* 20 (1983): 21-26. Lipstadt supports Hochhuth's accusations against Pius. She states that "by maintaining its thunderous silence and refusing to act, the Vatican bestowed a certain degree of legitimacy on Nazi atrocities and the inaction of other "bystanders."

O'Carroll, Michael. *Pius XII, Greatness Dishonored: A Documentary Study.* Dublin, Ireland: Laetare Press, 1980. O'Carroll attempts to defend Pius against Hochhuth.

Smit, Jan Olav. *Angelic Shepherd: The Life of Pope Pius XII.* New York: Dodd, Mead, 1950. This sympathetic biography was written during the lifetime of Pius.

Tinnemann, Ethel Mary. "The Silence of Pope Pius XII." *Journal of Church and State* 21 (1979): 265-285. In an article focused on Eastern Europe, Tinnemann, a nun, condemns Pius for what she sees as his failure to denounce Nazi atrocities in Germany, Poland, and Czechoslovakia forcefully.

Susan A. Stussy

MAX PLANCK

Born: April 23, 1858; Kiel, Schleswig
Died: October 4, 1947; Göttingen, West Germany
Areas of Achievement: Physics, philosophy, and religion
Contribution: Planck's discovery in 1900 that light consists of infinitesimal "quanta" and his articulation of the quantum theory replaced classical physics with modern quantum physics. This work not only resulted in Planck's receiving the Nobel Prize in Physics for 1918 but also became a major enabling factor in the work of many other Nobel laureates.

Early Life
Born into an intellectual family in Kiel, Schleswig, Max Karl Ernst Ludwig Planck spent most of his early life in Munich, where the family moved in the spring of 1867, when he was nine. Planck's father, Johann Julius Wilhelm von Planck, was a professor of civil law at the university in Kiel, whose second wife, Emma Patzig, was Max's mother. Max's forebears included many lawyers and clergymen, a fact which helps explain Planck's lifelong respect for the law and interest in religion.

In May, 1867, Planck was enrolled in Munich's Konigliche Maximilian-Gymnasium, a classical *Gymnasium*, where he came under the tutelage of Hermann Müller, a mathematician who took an interest in the youth and taught him astronomy and mechanics as well as mathematics. It was from Müller that Planck first learned the principle of the conservation of energy that underlaid much of his future work in thermodynamics and quantum theory.

Upon completion of the *Gymnasium* in 1874, Planck was at a personal crossroads. He was gifted in music and humanities as well as in mathematics and the sciences. He concluded ultimately that his music talents were insufficient to justify his continuing in that field. When he entered the University of Munich in October, 1874, he concentrated on mathematics. At Munich, however, his interest in physics grew, although his mathematics professors tried to dissuade him, arguing that nothing new remained to be discovered in the field.

Planck became ill as he was completing his first year at Munich and missed two years of school. In the winter term of 1877-1878, when he was well enough to resume his studies, he entered the University of Berlin, where he decided to study theoretical physics because of the order and logic that discipline demanded. Planck yearned to study the nature of the universe. Theoretical physics offered him his most sensible foothold for achieving that goal.

In Berlin, Planck studied with Hermann von Hemholtz, Gustav Kirchhoff, and Rudolf Clausius. Only Clausius was a gifted teacher, although the other two were able physicists. Planck learned much on his own through reading. Although his doctoral dissertation, on the second law of thermodynamics, was undistinguished, he was graduated summa cum laude in 1879. He taught mathematics and physics briefly at his former secondary school in Munich and in 1880 was appointed a privatdocent at the University of Munich. At that time, theoretical physics was viewed as an unpromising field, so his future seemed less than bright.

In 1885, Planck became an associate professor of physics at the University of Kiel, where he remained until 1888, when he was appointed assistant professor and director of the Institute for Theoretical Physics, to replace Kirchhoff, who had died. He rose to professor in 1892 and remained at Berlin until his retirement in 1926.

Life's Work

Planck's early work in the laws of thermodynamics and his early interest in the principle of the conservation of energy figured largely in his research from his early teaching days at Kiel through his first decades at the University of Berlin. Although he had been reared on classical physics and was a conservative at heart, Planck began to realize that the laws of classical physics deviated greatly from results obtained in experimental physics. He found the greatest disparities not in the field of optics but in that of thermodynamics. The problems stemmed from the measurement of radiant energy in the frequency spectrum of black bodies.

Kirchhoff deduced that radiant energy is independent of the nature of its radiating substance, reasoning that black bodies that absorb all frequencies of light should therefore radiate all frequencies of light. Energy at that time was considered infinitely divisible, a theory that led to many anomalies and seeming contradictions in physics. The problem arose because the lower-frequency range has a smaller number of frequencies than the higher-frequency range.

Important physicists working on this problem reached conflicting conclusions. Wilhelm Wien devised an equation that explained the emissions at high frequencies but not at low frequencies. John William Strutt, Third Baron of Rayleigh devised an equation that worked for low frequencies but not for high frequencies. Work in the field was at an impasse when Planck devised a classically simple equation that explained the distribution of radiation over the full range of frequencies, basing his equation on the daring supposition that energy is not an indivisible flow but is composed of tiny particles, or "quanta," for the Latin word meaning "How many?" Incidental to this discovery was his discovery of a means of measuring the absolute weight of molecules and atoms, in itself a major breakthrough.

Planck's theory showed that the energy of various frequencies of light from violet to red contain different energies, a quantum of violet containing twice the energy of a quantum of red and requiring twice the energy to radiate from a blackbody, making such radiation improbable. So pristine and uncluttered was Planck's theory that he himself was suspicious of it. Other scientists, however, began to realize its validity, and soon Albert Einstein based much of his work on photoelectric effect, which classical physics could not explain, on quantum theory. Planck embraced Einstein's theory of relativity eagerly because of its absolutism and because of its presentation of the velocity of light.

Now firmly established at the University of Berlin, Planck was instrumental in bringing Einstein to the Berliner Academie in 1914 as a professor without teaching obligations and as director of the embryonic Kaiser Wilhelm Institute for Physics, which Planck himself eventually headed. Planck also nominated Einstein for the Nobel Prize in Physics in 1921, a year in which the award was withheld. In 1922, however, partly at Planck's urging, Einstein received the 1921 prize a year late.

Max Born, Theodor von Kármán, and Peter Joseph Wilhelm Debye began to study the problem of the dependence of specific heat on temperature from the standpoint of quantum theory and soon articulated a law that made it possible to ascertain the variation in specific heat with temperature from the elastic constants in any substance. The field of quantum mechanics became the most important field of physics in the first half of the twentieth century, followed closely by the field of quantum electrodynamics, both developments that evolved from Planck's original insights and from his expression of the ratio between the size of a quantum and its frequency by the symbol h, which expresses a universal quantity.

Planck, a balding, bespectacled man with heavy brows, a dark mustache, and grayish eyes, spent nearly four decades at Berlin, teaching extensively and carrying heavy administrative responsibilities. He apparently was a splendid, well-organized teacher, who was clear in his presentations and interested in students. His life during these years was not easy. His wife died in 1909, and, in the next decade his son was killed in World War I and his two daughters died in childbirth.

With Adolf Hitler's rise to power, Planck decided that he had to remain in Germany, although he deplored what was happening. His respect for the law was deeply ingrained, and he felt duty-bound as a citizen to live within the laws but to work from within to change them. He intervened unsuccessfully for Jewish friends and colleagues who were being sent to death camps.

As a Nobel laureate of enormous prestige, Planck scheduled an interview with Hitler and tried to dissuade him from the genocide that was overwhelming Nazi Germany. Hitler, upon learning why Planck had come to see him, began a diatribe that lasted for hours; Planck's intervention did not deter Hitler from his disastrous course. Before the end of the war, Planck, in his eighties, had lost his home and all of his papers to a bombing raid, had once been trapped for several hours in a collapsed air-raid shelter, and, worst of all, had suffered the execution by the Nazis of his son Erwin, a secretary of state before Hitler's ascension, who had been accused of plotting to assassinate Hitler.

Summary

Max Planck lived for twenty-one years after his retirement. These were troubled years in Germany. The search for the meaning of the universe and for the nature of existence that had led him into physics, where he hoped he would discover absolutes to help answer his questions, persisted in his later years. He wrote on general subjects, developing some of his earlier lectures and essays into fuller works.

In 1930, Planck became president of the Kaiser Wilhelm Society of Berlin, which was renamed the Max Planck Society in his honor. In his final postwar years, he again became president of the society, agreeing as he approached his ninetieth year to assume the post until a permanent president could be found.

Five volumes of Planck's work in theoretical physics were published in English under the title *Introduction to Theoretical Physics* (1932-1933). His highly philosophical *Physikalische gesetzlichkeit im lichte neuer forschung* (1926) and *Das Weltbild der neuen Physik* (1929; combined in *The Universe in the Light of Modern Physics*, 1931) were released and showed a search for absolutes in a broadly religious context, although Planck sought a prime cause more than for an anthropomorphic god.

His general works, *Where Is Science Going?* (1932) and *Weg zur Physikalischen Erkenntnis* (1933; *The Philosophy of Physics*, 1936) were combined with *The Universe in the Light of Modern Physics* and published in English under the title *The New Science* (1959). Planck's autobiography, entitled *Wissenschaftliche Selbstbiographie* (1948; *Scientific Autobiography and Other Papers*, 1949), was published posthumously.

When the Allies came into Germany in May, 1945, Planck, who, with his second wife, had fled to Magdeburg to live with friends after the destruction of their home near Berlin, was again homeless. The area was overrun with Allied soldiers, and Planck had no place to live. American soldiers rescued him and had him sent to a hospital in Göttingen, the city in which he lived for the two and a half years remaining to him. He continued his professional activities, giving his last public lecture—on pseudoproblems—in 1946.

Bibliography

Hermann, Armin. *The Genesis of Quantum Theory (1899-1913)*. Cambridge, Mass.: MIT Press, 1971. This careful study of the pioneering work Planck did in the late 1880's and in the 1890's as he moved toward the discovery of quanta is a complex, thorough book that definitely is best for readers with some background in physics, particularly in thermodynamics and optics.

Hiebert, Erwin N. "The Concept of Thermodynamics in the Scientific Thought of Mach and Planck." *Wissenschaftlicher Bericht, Ernst Mach Institute* 5 (1968). This article demonstrates the marked differences between classical physics as represented by Ernst Mach, a leading Austrian physicist, and the quantum physics of Planck. Mach refused to accept the atomic theory and degraded it as a retrogression that undermined the philosophical development of physics.

Hirosige, T., and S. Nisio. "The Genesis of the Bohr Atom Model and Planck's Theory of Radiation." *Japanese Studies in the History of Science* 9 (1970): 35-47. In this article, Planck is viewed as a catalyst who made Niels Bohr's model of the atom possible. This highly technical article illustrates how quantum mechanics was integral to nearly every major occurrence in physics after Planck's discovery.

Planck, Max. *The New Science.* New York: Meridian Books, 1959. This book is valuable for its preface by Albert Einstein and its splendid introduction by James Franck. This compact volume contains three of Planck's most important general works: *Where Is Science Going?*, *The Universe in the Light of Modern Physics*, and *The Philosophy of Physics.* A reasonable starting point for intelligent readers with minimal background in physics.

Rosenfeld, Leon, et al., eds. *Max Planck Festschrift.* Berlin: Veb Deutscher Verlag der Wissenschaften, 1958. Eleven of this memorial volume's thirty-one essays are in English, including important contributions by Linus Pauling, Herbert Fröhlich, and Hannes Alfvén, each contribution being directly pertinent to understanding Planck's scientific impact.

R. Baird Shuman

GARY PLAYER

Born: November 1, 1935; Johannesburg, South Africa

Area of Achievement: Sports
Contribution: Player is one of only four men to achieve golf's Grand Slam, and at twenty-nine the youngest player to do so. He won numerous championships worldwide and helped to promote golf as an athletic sport.

Early Life

Gary Jim Player was the youngest of three children born to Francis Harry Audley Player and Muriel Marie Ferguson in Johannesburg, South Africa. His father was a foreman in a gold mine for more than thirty years. The Player family was not destitute, but the financial resources were never abundant during Player's childhood. When Player was eight years old, his mother died of cancer. This tragedy proved to be an almost devastating blow to the young Player. Player, however, surmounted the loss. Thus, Player began a lifelong struggle to conquer whatever challenge or challenger loomed in his path. This determination to succeed was fueled by his elder brother, Ian, who encouraged him to excel despite his diminutive stature. Spurred by his determination to triumph over those bigger than himself, which was just about everyone, Player launched himself into athletic competition. Goaded by his brother's fraternal intolerance, Player was ultimately voted all-round athlete at King Edward School in Johannesburg.

Since his father was a two-handicap golfer, it was perhaps inevitable that Player would seek parental approval by taking up the game. In his first round, the unskilled, self-taught player of fifteen shot par on the first three holes. This achievement caught the eye of the club professional, Jock Verwey. Simultaneously, Verwey's daughter, Virginia, came to Player's attention. Virginia Verwey quickly provided Player with a powerful stimulus to pursue the sport.

Verwey put Player to work as an assistant, while providing lessons to the intense young man courting his daughter. Player began to compete at the amateur level, and, even though he had not won a tournament, he was convinced that competition golf was his goal in life. Determined to turn professional, even though he was only seventeen, Player left school. He practiced constantly and followed a carefully constructed plan of physical exercise and diet to compensate for his relative lack of size and strength.

Life's Work

When he was nineteen, Player won the East Rand Open. This victory served to persuade his father to finance his first foray outside South Africa. He entered the Egyptian Match Play Championship that same year (1955).

Player won again and used his prize money to fuel an assault on the British golf tour. Player spent five months on the British tour and posted not a single victory. Still, he did garner enough in prize money to cover his expenses— a considerable achievement.

The next year, 1956, Player won the Ampol Tournament (Australia) and promptly married Virginia. He thereupon began the practice of a lifetime by leaving his young bride to return to the professional circuit. This time, Player made his mark with a win at the British Dunlop Tournament, which he followed with the first of his many victories in the South African Open.

From 1957 to 1959, Player competed around the world from Great Britain to the United States and on to Australia and South Africa. If Player did well in Australia and South Africa, his performance in the United States and Great Britain was rather lackluster. He did win the Kentucky Derby Open (1957) and made a surprisingly good showing in the 1958 U.S. Open. Still, he was only barely making his expenses on the American tour. Yet, if Player was absent from the winner's circle on the Anglo-American tour, he constantly improved the quality of his game. Moreover, his victories elsewhere, when combined with a frugal life-style, an unexpected benefit of his concern with his diet and physical well-being, enabled him to support his growing family and continue to pursue a professional career in golf.

Then came the breakthrough victory in the British Open in 1959. Player became the youngest golfer to capture that Grand Slam event since 1868. In 1961, Player determined to make a concentrated effort on the prize-laden American tour. He entered all twelve tournaments sponsored by the Professional Golfers' Association of America (PGA) between January and April. He finished in the top five in seven of the tournaments and won two—the San Francisco Open and the Sunshine Open. Player then joined the gathering of men in Augusta, Georgia, for the 1961 Masters Tournament.

Player arrived in Georgia fresh from a one-stroke victory over the defending Masters champion, the redoubtable Arnold Palmer. Needless to say, Palmer was expected to retain his title—most especially against a relatively unknown golfer from South Africa. In one of the most dramatic finishes in the history of the competition, however, Player edged Palmer yet again, by one stroke. Player did not win another tournament on the American tour that year, though he did take first prize in tournaments in Japan and Australia. On the other hand, while Player was not victorious in the United States, he was in the money on several occasions. In consequence, he ended the year as the leading money winner on the American tour—a first for an overseas-based player.

The euphoria engendered by his triumph in the American Masters Tournament soon, however, turned to despair. Player was suddenly in the midst of a slump so profound that he went fifteen months without a single win. He became so depressed by his failure that he seriously contemplated leaving the tour and returning home for good. Before he could implement his retirement plans, Player captured the PGA Championship (1962). Player now had three of the four events necessary to achieve the Grand Slam of golf to his credit and every reason to continue with the tour. Player was undoubtedly a force to reckon with on the international circuit during the 1960's. On the American circuit, he shared the honors with Jack Nicklaus and Arnold Palmer, particularly the former, as the essential component of the "Big Three" of the modern era. Furthermore, while Player won far more tournaments away from the American tour than in the United States, he consistently placed in the top five when he did play there. In 1965, Player won the U.S. Open and completed the Grand Slam.

In the years following the completion of the Grand Slam, Player seemed to vanish from the American tour—not in the sense of failing to compete, but rather the absence of victories. Indeed, from 1966 to 1969, Player went without a first-place finish on the American tour. He did repeat his victory in the British Open (1968), however, and announced his pursuit of a second Grand Slam. Nevertheless, throughout this period Player continued to win outside the United States. Moreover, he continued to make money on the American tour by placing near the top in those tournaments he entered.

In 1972, a second victory in the PGA Championship put him on the road to a second, unprecedented, Grand Slam. Unfortunately, he underwent serious surgery in 1973, and for a time he wondered if he would ever recover his skill. If Player, and others, wondered if his career was finally over, the answer came in 1974. In that year, he took the U.S. and British Open championships. A second U.S. Open continued to elude him, however, and Player capped his active career on the American tour with a victory at the American Masters Tournament. At forty-two, Player was the oldest player to accomplish that feat.

In 1985, Player joined the Senior Tour sanctioned by the PGA. Once again he became a fixture in the winner's circle with his triumph in the PGA Senior Championship. In 1988, Gary Player was voted "player of the year" by his competitors on the senior circuit.

Player was always a subject of controversy. He definitely upset the staid world of British golf with his many questions and his requests for free lessons from his fellow professionals when he joined the tour in 1956. In fact, one British professional informed Player that inasmuch as he was so poorly prepared, perhaps he should abandon the game altogether. Player, however, if he was nothing else, was tenacious. Player persevered and survived to confound his critics. He ended most tournaments with a lengthy practice session to correct defects and deficiencies he had observed in the course of tournament play. Informed by seemingly knowledgeable observers that he lacked the physical stamina or the size to prosper on the professional circuit, he intensified his already rigorous physical regime. Moreover, he supplemented his campaign for physical fitness with an attention to his diet that was quite exceptional at the time. Actually, it must be said that Player pioneered the concept of the golfer as an athlete. He ignored the doomsayers and the faint-hearted to pursue his dream of being a "world" golfer. Player's decision did not come without problems. For one thing, continued residency in South Africa meant long periods of inactivity while in transit to almost any tournament. Moreover, travel across multiple time zones exacted a physical toll from Player. A further complication was the effect of international competition on his family. His wife was required to function as a single parent for all practical purposes. Finally, although it was not a problem initially, there was the question of international perceptions of his country. The mere fact that he was a South African citizen subjected Player, over the years, to criticism as the visible representative of a governmental policy (apartheid) that an increasing number of people found objectionable. He was physically abused during the 1969 PGA Championship and was forced to deal with protesters during the 1979 French Open.

Summary

There were more than a few who insisted in 1961 that Gary Player's surprising victory in that year's Masters Tournament was a fluke. Surely, it was asserted, this largely self-taught golfer with a questionable grip and a swing that no one cared to copy was nothing more than a flash in the pan. Yet, in the final analysis, no one can gainsay the fact that in his active career on the international tour Player compiled an impressive record. He won nine major tournament titles as well as the Grand Slam of golf. He not only won more than 120 tournaments worldwide, including twenty-one PGA tour events, but also was the first overseas-based player to head the American money list.

Player began his career determined to be a world golfer, the best there was, and in that he posted a remarkable success. Yet, in typical fashion, Gary Player was not content to rest on his laurels. Once he became eligible to participate in the PGA Senior Tour he returned to vigorous competition with all the enthusiasm he had demonstrated on what he fondly called the "junior" tour. Indeed, the continued expansion of the Senior Tour was largely the result of Player's activities.

Player triumphed over adversity by turning seemingly insurmountable deficiencies into apparent assets. He continued, despite his years and accomplishments, to play the game he truly loved. It is doubtful that his donation of his entire purse from the 1965 U.S. Open (twenty thousand dollars to the American junior golf program and five thousand dollars to cancer research) was simply a public relations gesture. Player most definitely adhered to the principle that from those to whom much is given, much is expected.

Bibliography
Hobbs, Michael. "Gary Player." *Fifty Masters of Golf*. Ashbourne, England: Moorland, 1983. This work offers a technical assessment of Player as a golfer. The centerpiece of the article is an analysis of Player's performance in a 1965 match with Tony Lema.
McCormack, Mark H. *The Wonderful World of Professional Golf*. New York: Atheneum, 1973. A general book about professional golf, this work contains many references to Player and discussion of all the major tournaments up to the time of its publication. Includes a good appendix.
McDermott, Barry. "No Such Word as Can't." *Sports Illustrated* 48 (May 1, 1978): 16-19. A portrait of Player after he had won three tournaments in a row. Describes his family life and exercise and diet regimen.
McDonnell, Michael. "Gary Player." *Golf: The Great Ones*. London: Pelham Books, 1971. This piece, by the golf correspondent for the London *Daily Mail*, attempts to determine exactly what makes Player tick.
_____. "The Man in Black." *Golf Magazine* (November, 1985): 58-59, 94-96. This is a retrospective on Player's career at the moment he was eligible to join the Senior Tour. Once again, the author addresses himself to the why and less to the what.
Moritz, Charles, ed. *Current Biography Yearbook, 1961*. New York: H. W. Wilson, 1962. A fairly in-depth look at Player's life up to 1961.
Player, Gary, with Floyd Thatcher. *Gary Player, World Golfer*. Waco, Tex.: Word Books, 1974. An as-told-to autobiography composed with the help of Thatcher. This work is written in a conversational tone and does not diverge from the portrait that has appeared in countless magazines and interviews.

J. K. Sweeney

RAYMOND POINCARÉ

Born: August 20, 1860; Bar-le-Duc, France
Died: October 15, 1934; Paris, France
Areas of Achievement: Government and politics
Contribution: Poincaré was perhaps the most important political figure of the French Third Republic (1871-1940). He had the distinction of moving from the premiership to the presidency before World War I and back to the premiership twice in the 1920's. He and Georges Clemenceau struggled to defend France against Germany during World War I and by the Treaty of Versailles, and Poincaré attempted to enforce or at least salvage part of the treaty during the postwar decade.

Early life

Raymond Poincaré was born during the summer of 1860 in Lorraine in northeastern France, exactly a decade before the outbreak of the Franco-Prussian War. Nevertheless, his was a secure and comfortable childhood in the bosom of a prosperous bourgeois family. He was a highly competitive and talented student, who started keeping a journal when he, his mother, and his brother fled Bar-le-Duc as the German troops advanced into their province. The brilliant lad would be haunted by the memory of the German occupation for the rest of his life. The evacuation of his province in 1874, after the French had paid a war indemnity of one billion dollars, was also etched in his mind. The young man, a cousin of the distinguished mathematician Henri Poincaré, was educated in Bar-le-Duc and Paris, where he studied law and was admitted to the bar.

Poincaré was introduced to politics in 1886 when he was appointed chief assistant to the minister of agriculture. That same year he was elected to the general council of the Meuse department and the following year to the Chamber of Deputies. During these turbulent years of the Boulanger crisis and the forced retirement of Jules Grévy from the French presidency, he seldom addressed the Chamber. In 1893, he was offered the Ministry of Finance in a "Progressist," or Moderate, government; however, he chose that of public instruction. The government resigned after a few months, but he became minister of finance the following year, when he was only thirty-four. He displayed typical nineteenth century bourgeois liberalism as he favored governmental economy and opposed an income tax. He returned to the education ministry for several months in 1895 and attempted unsuccessfully a reorganization of the French university system. He was highly acclaimed for his many polished and erudite speeches, which he wrote rapidly and delivered from memory. At the funeral of Louis Pasteur in October, 1895, he gave the only eulogy before an immense crowd in front of Notre Dame Cathedral. The premier, the press, and the public acclaimed his oration, but three days later the cabinet fell. Nevertheless, Poincaré's second tenure at the education ministry greatly increased his prestige.

Life's Work

Disenchantment with politics and financial need prompted Poincaré to develop his legal practice and reject cabinet positions from 1896 to 1906. The Dreyfus affair was raging during these years, and he reluctantly but dramatically broke with the "Progressists" in November, 1898, and cautiously supported the Radicals when he realized that Captain Alfred Dreyfus had been unjustly convicted. Early the next year, he and several friends founded the Democratic Alliance, a loose grouping of "liberals" who advocated patriotism, religious and educational freedom, and opposition to socialism. His dissatisfaction with the extreme anticlerical legislation and socialist ties of the Radical cabinets from 1899 to 1905 led him often to abstain from important votes in the Chamber of Deputies. Therefore he was happy to accept election to the senate in 1903. The following year he married the divorcée Henriette Benucci in a civil ceremony, much to his pious mother's displeasure. Benucci's divorce and Poincaré's anticlerical politics prevented a sacramental wedding even if the couple had desired it.

The Agadir crisis with Germany during 1911 undermined the government of Joseph Caillaux and helped provoke a passionate upsurge of French patriotism in many quarters. This carried Poincaré to the premiership in January, 1912. As both foreign minister and premier, he vigorously sought to restrain Russia in the Balkans but also to strengthen the alliance with Russia and the entente with Great Britain. During late 1912, Poincaré began to consider running for the presidency and was elected by the National Assembly to this largely symbolic office.

Poincaré's major domestic goal in 1913 was to increase universal military service from two years to three. The Germans had twice in two years enlarged their standing army until it was virtually double the size of the French. In midsummer, the "three years law" was passed over the opposition of most Radicals and all the Socialists. An income tax and the "three years law" were the chief issues in the 1914 spring elections for the Chamber of Deputies. These were won by the leftists, but the European war prevented a return to two-year military service.

Poincaré was certainly not responsible for the outbreak of World War I, despite some postwar accusations. Poincaré successfully increased presidential power, his major reason for seeking the office, during 1913 and the first three years of war. He played a very active role in military and foreign affairs and was not an impotent "prisoner in the Élysée" palace, as he often complained. He, of course, selected the premiers but also influenced ministerial choices and policy decisions as he presided over the Council of Ministers. Yet the great popularity that he had enjoyed in 1912 and 1913 evaporated, and he was often criticized for his leadership and even ridiculed for his "chauffeur's uniform," which he adopted to visit the troops.

In his memoirs, Poincaré called 1917 the *année trouble* (the confused year), but it was also a troubled year for France, with widespread French mutinies and three ineffectual cabinets. During November, Poincaré was confronted with an unpalatable choice for premier, either the defeatist Joseph Caillaux and a possible compromise peace or the domineering Georges Clemenceau and bloody war until victory. Clemenceau in his newspaper had constantly criticized the government and especially Poincaré. The president, however, inevitably chose the "tiger," who would become a great popular hero as "Father Victory," whereas Poincaré would be somewhat forgotten. Poincaré had very little influence on the peace conference, since Clemenceau, David Lloyd George, and Woodrow Wilson made the decisions. The president thought the final treaty was a poor one and that Clemenceau had won the war but lost the peace.

Centrist cabinets, attempting to lead a rightist Chamber of Deputies after the December, 1919, elections, were confronted with a Germany determined to avoid reparations and a Great Britain concerned about alleged French hegemony in Europe. Several ephemeral ministries were finally replaced in February, 1922, by a Poincaré government that survived for twenty-six onths. He was once again widely popular, for it was believed that he would enforce the Treaty of Versailles. Poincaré is probably best known outside France as the "man of the Ruhr," the Frenchman who occupied the Ruhr Valley and tried to obtain reparations by coercion. There is general agreement that he did this as a last resort. In 1922, French per capita taxes were almost twice those in Germany, and French per capita governmental debt was greater than that across the Rhine River. Poincaré's goals in the Ruhr have been questioned, but undoubtedly he wanted German payments so that the French budget, overburdened by reconstruction costs, could be balanced.

The occupation began in January, 1923, after the Reparation Commission found Germany in default; therefore, Poincaré had sound legal if not wise diplomatic grounds for action. Poincaré's Ruhr policy fractured the entente with the British and triggered vitriolic attacks upon him by Parisian intellectuals and French Communists. Nevertheless, he was generally popular and had a large majority in the Chamber of Deputies. German surrender, Anglo-American hostility, and French fiscal problems led Poincaré to accept an international investigation and eventually the Dawes Plan. Most French conservatives thought he had won the Ruhr "war" but lost the peace. Moreover, Poincaré insisted upon a 20 percent tax rise in March, 1924. The increase was not to pay for the Ruhr occupation, which was profitable, but to cover the budget deficit and reverse the critical decline of the franc.

Not surprisingly, the Cartel des Gauches (cartel of leftists) of Socialists and Radicals won a majority in the 1924 spring elections as Frenchmen voted against Poincaré's higher taxes. The leftist government of Édouard Herriot was divided on financial policy and soon confronted a dangerous flight of capital abroad. The franc, stable since 1924, began to fall precipitously. In April, 1925, Poincaré vigorously attacked Herriot in the senate and provoked his resignation. A series of Cartel ministries failed to stanch the fiscal hemorrhage as the franc fell to fifty to the dollar in July, 1926.

Poincaré, the "man of the Ruhr," now became the "savior of the franc." He was sixty-six years of age but still had an impeccable memory and prodigious energy for work. He formed a government containing Herriot and four other former premiers, representing all parties except the extremes of Left and Right. Following the recommendations of a committee of experts, excise taxes were raised, expenses were reduced, and a budgetary deficit became a surplus. Higher interest rates coaxed fugitive French capital to return, and within several months the franc had risen to twenty-five to the dollar. The premier wisely stabilized it officially in 1928 at that rate. Stabilization was achieved smoothly after Poincaré's supporters in the chamber were successful in the spring elections. The committee of experts had also urged ratification of treaties regularizing the repayment of French war debts to Great Britain and the United States. Poincaré sought ratification by the National Assembly for several weeks in the summer of 1929, but he became seriously ill in July and was forced to resign permanently from the cabinet and active political life.

Summary

Raymond Poincaré has been described as a petit bourgeois, a grand bourgeois, or even a bourgeois king who fought valiantly for his nation. Certainly he exemplified many characteristics of the French bourgeoisie with his probity, diligence, intelligence, dignity, and ardent republican patriotism. He was considered to be a genie who saved France in time of crisis. On the eve of World War I, he incarnated and led the national revival, and in 1923 he attempted to ensure reparations. He was the savior of the franc in 1926, but, more important, he rescued a floundering parliamentary republic.

His career may appear to have been a failure. France was victorious by 1918 but proportionately suffered the heaviest manpower losses. The Ruhr was occupied, but reparation payments were never very productive and ceased by 1932. Then the liberal Third Republic collapsed in 1940 from the onslaught of Adolf Hitler, the very antithesis of Poincaré. Nevertheless, all nations can profit from Poincaré's method of approaching problems with studious, precise analysis and solving them by the honest, equitable administration he practiced throughout his life.

Bibliography
Gooch, George P. *Before the War: Studies in Diplomacy.* London: Long-

mans, Green, 1938. This book contains a lengthy sixty-three-page essay on Poincaré's conduct of foreign policy as premier and foreign minister during 1912. Gooch admires Poincaré's ability and integrity and says that he did not desire or work for war but sought to maintain the balance of power by closer cooperation with Russia and Great Britain.

Huddleston, Sisley. *Poincaré: A Biographical Portrait.* Boston: Little, Brown, 1924. This book by a correspondent of *The Times* of London is not a biography of Poincaré. It is a journalistic account that stresses his honesty, patriotism, incredible memory, and legalistic attitude. It was written during the Ruhr occupation but has limited value.

McDougall, Walter A. *France's Rhineland and Diplomacy, 1914-1924.* Princeton, N.J.: Princeton University Press, 1978. This excellent study describes the failure of the French, in their view, to secure a satisfactory peace and then the failure of their allies to help enforce the treaty. Most of the book is devoted to Poincaré's Rhenish policy and occupation of the Ruhr. The author argues that, as a result of British opposition and German passive resistance, Poincaré sought to revise the treaty. There is an exhaustive bibliography.

Martin, Benjamin F. *Count Albert de Mun: Paladin of the Third Republic.* Chapel Hill: University of North Carolina Press, 1978. This valuable biography of an aristocratic Catholic leader describes his change from a royalist to a moderately conservative supporter of the republic. There is considerable information about Poincaré during the decade before World War I and an extensive bibliography.

Poincaré, Raymond. *The Memoirs of Raymond Poincaré.* Translated by George Arthur. 4 vols. New York: Doubleday, Page, 1926-1931. Covers the years 1912 through 1918. Unfortunately, this English edition of the memoirs has been adapted and compressed, but it does include most of Poincaré's first seven volumes.

Schuker, Stephen A. *The End of French Predominance in Europe: The Financial Crisis of 1924 and the Adoption of the Dawes Plan.* Chapel Hill: University of North Carolina Press, 1976. This superbly researched book presents essential economic information about reparations, the occupation of the Ruhr, the French financial crisis of 1924, and the Dawes Plan. Schuker revises Poincaré's reputation upward and Herriot's downward. There is an extensive bibliography.

Weber, Eugen J. *The Nationalist Revival in France, 1905-1914.* Berkeley: University of California Press, 1959. Weber argues that patriotism became respectable and widespread after 1905 because of domestic and foreign factors. Concern about German aggressiveness resulted in widespread chauvinistic nationalism after November, 1911. Poincaré is often mentioned as a patriotic leader.

Wright, Gordon. *Raymond Poincaré and the French Presidency.* Stanford,

Calif.: Stanford University Press, 1942. Wright's book is not a biography even for the years 1913 to 1920; it is a detailed consideration of Poincaré's attempt to strengthen the presidency without constitutional amendment. Nevertheless, it is a well-documented account of his presidential activities and includes a helpful biography.

Malcolm M. Wynn

GEORGES POMPIDOU

Born: July 5, 1911; Montboudif, France
Died: April 2, 1974; Paris, France
Areas of Achievement: Government and politics
Contribution: Of the eighteen years during which Gaullism was in power in France, Pompidou was premier from 1962 to 1968 and president from 1969 to 1974. Gaullism stabilized France, renewed its pride, and restored its stature in the world.

Early Life
Born of peasant stock in the small village of Montboudif, Georges Pompidou spent much of his early life in nearby Albi, where his mother's family were linen cloth merchants. His father, Léon, and his mother, née Marie-Louise Chavagnac, were both schoolteachers. Molded by the parish church, the communal school, and his parents' wish that he succeed as an educator, Pompidou studied at Lycée d'Albi, Lycée de Toulouse, and Lycée Louis-le-Grand at Paris, emphasizing French literature, Greek, Latin, and history. Having performed brilliantly, he then went to the École Normale Supérieure in Paris. He received his *agrégé des lettres* in 1934, the *diplôme* of the Institute of Political Studies in 1934, and the *breveté* of the Centre des Hautes Études Administratives in 1947.

After obligatory military service, Pompidou was named professor of French, Latin, and Greek at Lycée Saint-Charles in Marseilles in 1935 and then married Claude Cahour, the daughter of a physician. In 1938, he was invited to teach at Lycée Henry IV in Paris. The Pompidous began a social pattern that continued when he was a banker. They frequented art galleries, bookstores, bistros, films, concerts, the theater, and played tennis, skied, and vacationed in Saint-Tropez. Pompidou had a reputation for indolence, but he had leisure time because he did his work quickly, effortlessly, and yet effectively.

In August, 1939, Pompidou was a second lieutenant with the 141st Infantry regiment from Marseilles, assigned first to the Italian frontier, then Alsace, Lorraine, and the Somme. Pompidou heard and was deeply moved by de Gaulle's radio appeal from London urging that Frenchmen outside France continue the war against the Germans, but he went back to Paris to the *lycée* to teach a class preparing students for colonial service. His son, Alain, was born in 1942.

Life's Work
Pompidou was present at de Gaulle's liberation march down the Champs Élysées in 1944, and with the help of a friend was put in charge of school and university problems in de Gaulle's provisional government. From Febru-

ary, 1946, to 1949 he was assistant to the director of the Commission of Tourism for the national government. Although he had not studied law, from September, 1949, to 1954 he was one of a number of *maîtres des requêtes* preparing reports for the Conseil d'État, an administrative court. He became secretary-general in 1951 of his colleagues' association.

In January, 1946, the de Gaulle family put him in charge of their charitable foundation. After de Gaulle organized the Rassemblement du Peuple Français, Pompidou began assisting de Gaulle in various other ways. In 1953 Pompidou handled the negotiations for publication of the first volume of de Gaulle's war memoirs. Working on de Gaulle's finances in 1951, Pompidou met the director-general of the Rothschild Bank and in 1953 helped him become a senator. Leaving the Conseil d'État, in February, 1954, Pompidou became director of a railroad company and, in July, of an import-export company—both affiliates of the bank. In 1956, he became director-general of the bank, and, until 1962, he also administered several of the bank's affiliated companies. Rothschild was especially interested in mining ventures in Africa. While still at the bank, Pompidou resumed giving lectures at the Institute des Sciences Politiques and helped de Gaulle put together his new government in May, 1958.

On leave from the bank, he served from June 1, 1958, to January 8, 1959, as de Gaulle's principal private secretary. While back again at the bank, he was appointed as a member of the Conseil Constitutional. He also continued his writing. He was not a creator of literature, but he was an appreciator. Having specialized in Jean Racine's tragedies, he published *"Britannicus" de Jean Racine* (1944) and edited two books for use in secondary school instruction. While at the bank he edited *Anthologie de la poésie française* (1961), giving much space to Charles Baudelaire. His last book was *Le Nœud gordien* (1974), discussing values and events, with references, among others, to Niccolò Machiavelli, Blaise Pascal, and Paul Valéry. Some effort was made after his death to compile a record of political thought, though he was not prone to original thinking, nor was he given to theorizing. These included a two-volume compilation of his speeches, *Entretiens et discours, 1968-1974* (1975) and *Pour rétablir une vérité* (1982).

De Gaulle had chosen Pompidou as his confidential agent because he made quick decisions; was a good judge of men; was loyal, discreet, and diplomatic; and made himself indispensable by efficiently taking care of numerous details. In 1961, de Gaulle sent him to negotiate in Switzerland with the chiefs of the Algerian rebels. De Gaulle began using Pompidou as de facto premier in March, 1962, and formally made him premier on April 16, 1962. The new premier was assigned jurisdiction over financial and domestic policies and politics while de Gaulle personally directed the army, the department of justice, and colonial and foreign affairs.

Pompidou had not come up through the ranks of politics, but he proved to be skillful at directing election campaigns. He had not had experience in front of television cameras, but he became effective at using that medium. When he began to think of himself as successor to President de Gaulle, this did not please the president, who had valued him for his self-effacing services. By 1966, de Gaulle began to think of replacing Pompidou, especially as Pompidou's public popularity grew. The turbulence of student rebellions and a general strike in May, 1968, gave de Gaulle the occasion he needed. When Pompidou left the government on July 10, 1968, he had been premier longer than any Frenchman except François Guizot.

Pompidou remained on the municipal council at Carjac (Lot) to which he had been elected in March, 1965, and remained a deputy to the National Assembly from Cantal. The other Gaullist deputies made him their honorary president. While Couve de Murville was premier, the Gaullist party organization and parliamentary group were dominated by Pompidou's men.

De Gaulle left office on April 28, 1969. Pompidou was elected president of France on June 15, 1969. His first premier was Jacques Chaban-Delmas, who launched a program for a "new society." Pompidou was more conservative than his premier and gave top priority to making French industries more internationally competitive. He wanted France to grow richer. In 1972, he replaced Chaban-Delmas with Pierre Messmer. While de Gaulle was still alive, until November 9, 1970, Pompidou could not be sure that de Gaulle would not intervene, and he had to satisfy the Gaullists who deplored any deviation from the general's policies. Pompidou's first cabinet was full of the barons of Gaullism. He made a point of making speeches echoing de Gaulle's views about French nationalism and Europe as a combine of nations.

Most of the Gaullist objectives remained, but the language and methods were new. Astute, realistic, down to earth, prudent, calm, courteous, and patient, Pompidou was more pragmatic than doctrinaire. Unlike de Gaulle, he preferred to achieve cordial understandings through negotiations, and he was less likely to resort to de Gaulle's brand of political theater. By temperament he favored stability, tranquillity, and maintenance of the social order. He valued traditions and also believed in freedom, for which he thought the state was essential as a guarantor. Man is neither angel nor beast, he said, but a little of both.

He negotiated with the Soviet Union's Leonid Brezhnev, though he profoundly distrusted communism. He did not share de Gaulle's hostility toward the Anglo-Saxons, but he believed Spain and Portugal would be useful counterweights to the north in the European Common Market. He was criticized by the French Communist Party for supporting American Vietnam policies in 1972. He took an interest in Francophone Africa and thought Israel should trade land for peace. He leaned toward economic liberalism and believed that the solution to France's problems was economic growth, but he did not propose to denationalize state-owned industry. His government promoted new technology. His government also sought to modernize Paris, to make it a counterweight to London in the expanded Common Market. An underground shopping center was placed where Les Halles had been, new office towers rose at La Défense, and the striking Pompidou Center was built. In the midst of all the rebuilding, there was a scandal about real estate speculation. When he died on April 2, 1974, of cancer of the bone marrow, he left an unfinished term as president.

Summary

Georges Pompidou's most notable achievement was as a sustainer of the Gaullist regime. Although he was a banker, he was not a banking technician. Although he worked in government commissions concerned with law, he was not a legal technician. Although he won elections, he was not a politician. His posts were gained through personal contacts. Although he socialized with fashionable and artistic people, he never lost the aspect of a peasant. Although his father was a Socialist, Pompidou was unwilling to complete de Gaulle's plan for greater worker participation in decision-making.

Pompidou was loyal to his friends, able to assess situations quickly and accurately, and able to resolve problems quietly and effectively. These qualities induced de Gaulle to turn to him for help from 1946 onward. De Gaulle believed that his premier was practical and prudent. As president, Pompidou demonstrated that his concerns in foreign affairs were closer to those of Europe and less global than de Gaulle's had been. He continued support for nuclear defense. One of the roles of a president is to symbolize France, and he did do that. Blessed with a keen intelligence, Pompidou loved poetry and understood people.

Bibliography
Alexandre, Philippe. *The Duel: De Gaulle and Pompidou.* Translated by Elaine P. Halperin. Boston: Houghton Mifflin, 1972. This is the best available account in English of the subtleties of personal relationship between the two men. It is highly readable.
Bomberger, Merry. *Le Destin secret de Georges Pompidou.* Paris: Fayard, 1965. This book is very readable and gives a thorough account of his life up to the early stages of his roles as premier.
Roberts, Frank C. *Obituaries from the Times, 1971-1975.* Westport, Conn.: Meckler Books, 1978, pp. 414-418. Written from an American viewpoint, this assessment concentrates on Pompidou's foreign policies as President of France. He improved relations between France and Great Britain, especially in terms of Great Britain's membership in the European Economic Community. The article states that he did not like sweeping social reforms.
Roussel, Eric. *Georges Pompidou.* Paris: Jean-Claude Lattès, 1984. To read

about the rest of Pompidou's career, as well as the earlier stages, turn to this book. It has photographs, lists the ministers of his cabinets when he was premier and president, and contains a bibliography.

Werth, Alexander. *De Gaulle*. Harmondsworth, Middlesex, England: Penguin, 1967. This book is about de Gaulle but contains a number of references to Pompidou, including a short biography. Mention is made that Pompidou was a Socialist in his youth but became a neo-capitalist—that is, someone who believed that modernization of France could best be achieved through a combination of big business and state capitalism. An explanation is given of why de Gaulle picked him to be prime minister, and there is a description of the parliament's initial dissatisfaction with the appointment.

Williams, Philip M. *French Politicians and Elections, 1951-1969*. Cambridge, England: Cambridge University Press, 1970. Williams describes de Gaulle's selection of Pompidou as prime minister and Pompidou's subsequent role in elections and in the events of May, 1968.

Williams, Philip M., and Martin Harrison. *Politics and Society in de Gaulle's Republic*. Garden City, N.J.: Doubleday, 1972. This book contains numerous scattered references to Pompidou, including a description of his conciliatory gestures as prime minister.

Corinne Lathrop Gilb

FRANCIS POULENC

Born: January 7, 1899; Paris, France
Died: January 30, 1963; Paris, France
Area of Achievement: Music
Contribution: Poulenc gradually came to be recognized by many as perhaps the greatest twentieth century exponent of the art song and, toward the latter part of his career, as the composer of deeply felt religious music.

Early Life

Francis Poulenc was born in Paris on January 7, 1899, to wealthy parents. From his father, Émile Poulenc, a manufacturer of pharmaceuticals, he inherited affluence, which allowed him to devote his life to music, and a profound Catholicism, which manifested itself strongly in his music by his late thirties. His musical interests were awakened as a small child by his mother, the former Jenny Royer, an excellent pianist who gave him his first lessons. At eight, Poulenc studied with Mademoiselle Boutet de Monvel, César Franck's niece. About this time, as he later noted, he was profoundly moved upon hearing a composition by Claude Debussy.

In 1915, Poulenc's pianistic education was turned over to the Spanish virtuoso Richard Viñes, who, realizing that Poulenc's ambition was to compose rather than perform, provided him a sound training in the classics and encouraged his interest in modern music. Poulenc had already become acquainted with and been moved by the music of Igor Stravinsky, Erik Satie, and Debussy. An even older musical influence was *Die Winterreise*, Franz Schubert's song cycle, which encouraged Poulenc's lyrical gifts and romantic tendencies as well as his later passion for writing songs. In addition to his musical studies, Poulenc, at his father's insistence, remained in school until he was graduated from the Lycée Condorcet.

Life's Work

Poulenc's first compositions were for the piano, written early in 1917, the year his father died, leaving him financially independent. He achieved success the same year with *Rapsodie nègre*, an unusual work for chamber ensemble which anticipated the Dada movement. The text of this composition consisted of a verse from *Les Poésies de Makoko Kangourou*, supposedly the work of a Liberian black but in fact a hoax. The success of the rhapsody, with its verse of sheer gibberish, attracted the attention of the public and critics to Poulenc for the first time. He never completely abandoned the levity of this piece, continuing to produce from time to time compositions in which mockery and laughter were the keynotes.

In January of 1918, Poulenc was drafted into the French army. After spending six months at Vincennes and three in an antiaircraft battery in the

Vosges, he was in Chalons-sur-Marne when the war ended. Instead of being demobilized, he was sent to Paris to work as a typist in the Ministry of Aviation. He was discharged in October of 1921. While still in the army, he composed a number of tongue-in-cheek works. His three *Mouvements perpétuels* for piano, in which his indebtedness to Satie is obvious, were introduced by Viñes in 1919.

Poulenc's first songs also came in 1919—the cycles *Le Bestiaire* (to poems by Guillaume Apollinaire) and *Cocardes* (to poems by Jean Cocteau), both characterized by a rich irony. It was soon afterward that the critic Henri Collet, in a review of a new music concert promoted by cellist Félix Delgrange, half-jokingly dubbed Poulenc, along with his associates Louis Durey, Georges Auric, Arthur Honegger, Darius Milhaud, and Germaine Tailleferre, "Les Six," a label that stuck with them long after they had drifted apart. The group worked together long enough to create (minus Durey) a scandal with contributions to *Les Mariés sur la tour Eiffel*, Cocteau's rather loony ballet of June, 1921. Of "Les Six," Poulenc for a time was the one who remained most faithful to such principles as directness, simplicity, and economy as well as to the idea of everyday music for ordinary people. All of this was a reaction to German post-Romanticism and French Impressionism.

By 1921, Poulenc, who thus far had produced nothing of substance, had begun to feel a need for some formal instruction. Seeking a sympathetic teacher, he found one in Charles Koechlin, with whom he worked for four years. During this period, he produced his first major work, the music for the ballet *Les Biches*, commissioned by Sergei Diaghilev for the Ballets Russes de Monte Carlo in 1923. Poulenc's score consisted of a suite of dances, each complete and self-sufficient. The ballet was a major success when it was presented in Paris on January 6, 1924. It was also about this time that Poulenc traveled with Milhaud to Rome and Vienna to meet the leading musical figures in those cities.

Poulenc followed *Les Biches* with other important works, also in a light and graceful vein. He wrote *Concert champêtre*, for harpsichord and orchestra, for Wanda Landowska, who introduced it on May 3, 1929, with the Paris Philharmonic, under Pierre Monteux. About this time, he bought an estate at Noizay, on the Loire River near Amboise—more for the sake of privacy than its rural location, he being a boulevardier at heart (he kept a Paris apartment on the Left Bank near the Luxembourg Gardens after 1935). In 1929, Poulenc was the piano soloist in his ballet score *Aubade* for piano and eighteen winds. First presented at the International Society for Contemporary Music festival in Venice on September 5, 1932, Poulenc's Concerto in D Minor for Two Pianos and Orchestra is characterized by its wit projected through a number of popular tunes and rhythms.

Poulenc reached a new maturity around 1935, precipitated by his reacquaintance with the baritone singer Pierre Bernac and the death in a car accident of his friend Pierre-Octave Ferroud. In August of 1935, Poulenc appeared as a piano accompanist of Bernac in song recitals at Salzburg, Austria. It marked the first of many similar recitals in the major music centers of Europe and the United States. These recitals played a major role in Poulenc's growth as a composer of art songs. He maintained that he learned the art of writing songs through his accompaniment of Bernac in the great literature of the French and German schools. From his association with Bernac, Poulenc went on to write songs that won him acclaim as one of the greatest twentieth century composers of such music. His 1935 musical setting of five poems by Paul Éluard was followed in 1937 with a setting for Éluard's cycle *Tel jour, telle nuit*. From the late 1930's to 1956, Poulenc wrote about a hundred songs, most of them to poems by Éluard and Apollinaire. The best of these are noted for the sensitivity and poetic beauty of their melodies and for the rich invention of the piano accompaniment, as well as for Poulenc's gift for projecting subtle nuances, feelings, and atmospheres.

The death of Ferroud in 1935 and a consequent visit to Notre Dame de Rocamadour restored Poulenc to his paternal Roman Catholic faith. The first fruits of this restoration were *Litanies à la vierge noire* (1936), for children's (or women's) voices and organ, and the Mass in G Major (1937) for four-part a cappella mixed chorus. These works give expression to deep religious convictions; they combine serenity with spiritual ardor and humility with sweetness, traits characteristic of Poulenc's greatest religious compositions. In 1938, Poulenc wrote the Concerto in G Minor, for organ and orchestra, for the Princesse Edmond de Polignac, at whose salon it was premiered the same year. Though wit is given free rein, there are solemn, perhaps ominous, passages that portend a new and more serious direction for the composer.

The outbreak of World War II in 1939 called the forty-year-old composer back to the antiaircraft guns. He was in Bordeaux when the French military collapsed the following summer; instead of heading for the border, he returned to Paris. Poulenc remained in occupied France for the war's duration, demonstrating his "resistance" by musical means. The war years invested his music with increasing expressiveness and intensity. In 1943, Poulenc wrote a poignant Sonata for Violin and Piano, inspired by and dedicated to Federico García Lorca, the Spanish poet who had been murdered by the Falangists. Its first performance was given on June 21, 1943, in Paris, with the composer at the piano. During the same year, Poulenc finished *Figure humaine*, one of his greatest works for chorus, to a poem by Éluard. Deeply moving and tragic, this music, which concludes with a mighty hymn to human liberty, expressed the suffering of every Frenchman as well as his will to resist. In 1944, Poulenc completed his first opera, *Les Mamelles de Tirésias*, a one-act Surrealist fantasy based on a play by Apollinaire. It received its first performance in 1947 at the Opéra-Comique in Paris, where it became a center of violent criticism. Satirizing a French campaign to increase the population, it caused shock and dismay by some of the items discussed in the text, such as the way by which one of the characters changes his sex. This latter work, which had its American premiere on June 13, 1953, at the second annual Festival of the Creative Arts in Waltham, Massachusetts, demonstrates that, despite the increasing seriousness and sobriety of purpose in many of his works after 1935, Poulenc had not altogether deserted an iconoclastic attitude and the light touch.

It was from a Bernac-Poulenc recital in Paris just after the war that the general recognition of Poulenc's songs as the finest since Gabriel Fauré's arose. In 1948, Poulenc and Bernac received an enthusiastic welcome on the first of several visits to the United States. The world premiere of Poulenc's piano concerto was given in Boston by the composer and the Boston Symphony on January 6, 1950.

Poulenc spent the years 1953-1956 at work on his first full-length opera, *Dialogues des carmélites*, which deals with the self-sacrifice of a group of Carmelite nuns during the French Revolution. It is possibly Poulenc's greatest single work in any medium. First produced with outstanding success at La Scala in Milan on January 26, 1957, it is characterized by exalted spirituality, expressive lyricism, and shattering tragedy. An American premiere of the opera followed in September of the same year in San Francisco. In 1958, it was telecast by an American television network and received the New York Music Critics Circle Award. Poulenc had no librettist for either *Les Mamelles de Tirésias* or *Dialogues des carmélites*. Preferring to deal directly with the original texts, he skillfully condensed the originals by excising unessential details and repetitions. He retained the beauty and force of the original language and the logic of the original dramatic structure.

Trouble over the rights of *Dialogues des carmélites* in 1954 put Poulenc under severe nervous strain, but he made a complete recovery. In 1958, he composed another unorthodox opera, *La Voix humaine*. A tour de force, but this time on a note of tragedy, it is a one-character opera with a libretto by Cocteau. First heard at the Paris Opéra-Comique on February 9, 1959, it concerns the reactions of a woman who is being spurned by her lover. The heartbreak of the deserted woman is effectively captured by the declamatory style of most of the music. In 1960, Poulenc made another successful tour of North America with Denise Duval.

It is the serious and religious side of Poulenc that is encountered in his last important compositions. The six-part Gloria, for chorus and orchestra, was commissioned by the Koussevitsky Music Foundation and introduced on January 21, 1961, by the Boston Symphony. His last major completed work was the vocalorchestral *Sept Répons des ténèbres* (1961), which was posthumously premiered on April 11, 1963, by the New York Philharmonic to help celebrate its opening season at the Lincoln Center for the Performing Arts. Poulenc was working on a fourth opera based on Cocteau's *La Machine infernale* (1934; *The Infernal Machine*, 1936) when he died.

Poulenc's death from heart failure on January 30, 1963, was unexpected. He had never married. It is said that he loved only one woman in his life. She was Raymonde Linaissier, with whom he had grown up. He was deeply attached to her, but she died prematurely in 1930. Every song Poulenc wrote in which the word "face" appeared in the title was dedicated to her memory. Bernac survived Poulenc by sixteen years and published a useful guide to the songs, most of which he recorded with the composer.

Summary

Francis Poulenc did not care for abstract ideas or philosophy. He was essentially a sensualist and was sentimental as well. A musical natural, Poulenc probably composed more from aural experience and instinct than any other major composer of the twentieth century. During the first half of Poulenc's career, critics frequently failed to consider him as a serious composer because of the directness and simplicity of his writing. Gradually, it became clear that the lack of linguistic complexity in his music in no way indicated the absence of technique or feeling.

In addition to exhibiting a kind of classical simplicity, Poulenc's music often emphasizes the unexpected. Even though these traits can be found in music by Stravinsky, Maurice Ravel, and Satie—all of whom influenced Poulenc's style—he probably came to them more directly through the work of such writers as Apollinaire, Éluard, and Cocteau. They provided an aesthetic with which he could identify and furnished the texts for many of his best vocal pieces.

In Poulenc's music, melody is always the dominant element. His songs often begin immediately with the voice. His religious music, for which he became known as a distinguished master, is imbued with an almost medieval quality of naïveté and candor because of this same lyricism. A five-record collection of all Poulenc's songs (released in France in 1980)—performed by Elly Ameling, Nicolai Gedda, Gérard Sougay, and others—strengthened Poulenc's reputation as perhaps the foremost twentieth century composer of the art song.

Bibliography

Bernac, Pierre. *Francis Poulenc: The Man and His Songs.* Translated by Winifred Radford. New York: W. W. Norton, 1977. The unrivaled interpreter of Poulenc's songs provides a detailed and lucid analysis of all Poulenc's piano-accompanied songs. Having had the unique advantage of concertizing repeatedly with Poulenc, Bernac provides interesting insights in two chapters on Poulenc "the man" and "the composer."

Daniel, Keith W. *Francis Poulenc: His Artistic Development and Musical Style*. Ann Arbor, Mich.: UMI Research Press, 1982. Five biographical chapters are followed by material on Poulenc's style and compositions.

Hell, Henri. *Francis Poulenc*. Translated by Edward Lockspeiser. New York: Grove Press, 1959. First published in France in 1958 as *Francis Poulenc, musicien français*, this is a good study of Poulenc and his work.

Myers, Rollo. *Modern French Music, from Fauré to Boulez*. New York: Praeger, 1971. A good account of French music in the twentieth century. Helps place Poulenc and his music in its historical context.

Poulenc, Francis. *My Friends and Myself: Conversations with Francis Poulenc*. Translated by James Harding. London: Dobson, 1978. Conversations originally broadcast by Suisse-Romande Radio between 1953 and 1962. Poulenc discusses his youth, early studies, "Les Six," his secular and religious works, and friends ranging from Satie and Éluard to Honegger and Stravinsky.

Roy, Jean. *Francis Poulenc: L'Homme et son œuvre*. Paris: Seghers, 1964. Available only in French, this work contains a complete list of Poulenc's works and a discography.

L. Moody Simms, Jr.

LUDWIG PRANDTL

Born: February 4, 1875; Freising, Germany
Died: August 15, 1953; Göttingen, West Germany
Areas of Achievement: Physics and aerodynamics
Contribution: Prandtl was one of the fathers of theoretical aerodynamics and is credited with discovering many of the pivotal concepts upon which modern aviation is based. He was also the founder of the highly acclaimed school of aerodynamics and hydrodynamics at the University of Göttingen and the first director of what would become the Max Planck Institute for Fluid Mechanics.

Early Life

Born in the town of Freising, Germany, on February 4, 1875, Ludwig Prandtl took an early interest in the forces and characteristics of nature as a result of the strong influence of his father, Alexander Prandtl, who was a professor of engineering at a college in Weihenstephan, Germany. Magdalene, Ludwig's mother, played a lesser role in her son's life because of her extended periods of chronic illness. Ludwig took an early interest in science and engineering, deciding in 1894 to study the latter as his major at the Munich Technische Hochschule, a facility for higher education at the time, comparable to a modern college or university. He successfully completed the course of study and, in 1898, went on to earn his doctorate in physics.

Prandtl's doctoral thesis, an experimental study in the distribution of tension and torque along a beam arranged at right angles from its source, became an important work in the field of the mechanics of solids. It was an indication of his exceptional abilities as a scientist that his first major paper—and one in an area that would be of peripheral interest in his later work—would generate significant interest from the contemporary scientific community.

His doctoral thesis and the help of his mentor, a noted German physicist, August Foppl, would earn for him a job upon graduation as an engineer in the Augsburg-Nürnberg Machine Factory. It was at the factory that Prandtl was introduced to the study of the characteristics of the flow of air over objects, otherwise known as fluid mechanics. This emerging science was in its infancy at the turn of the century, with the first practical wind tunnels and heavier-than-air craft only slowly coming into use. (Prandtl himself would later in his life be responsible for the construction of the first functional wind tunnel in Germany in 1909.) Prandtl's own introduction to the field came as a result of a project to refit a vacuum device used in the factory. Prandtl's work at the factory would be the last he would undertake outside the world of academia, but it led to his most important discoveries and to a brilliant career as a founder of an emerging modern science.

Life's Work

In 1901, to allow him to continue his studies into fluid mechanics, Prandtl accepted a position as a professor at the Technische Schule in Hannover. His first observations at Hannover involved the flow of thin liquids through a pipe. He noticed that the shape of the liquid flow did not fully conform to the shape of the pipe through which it flowed. A minute layer of liquid, no matter how low in viscosity the substance, would always form between the interior surface of the pipe and the main body of the liquid. This layer between the wall and the fluid actually controlled the pressure of the liquid flow and, consequently, the rate of flow itself. In practical terms, this boundary of stationary fluid is much the same as the layer of air that forms on a wing or airfoil in flight. This boundary actually helps to provide the lift and drag of an air wing necessary to control its movement through the air. Prandtl's discovery of the boundary theory, as he named it, would be his single most meaningful discovery and would revolutionize powered aviation, leading to major innovations in the streamlining of aircraft wing and fuselage designs.

In 1904, shortly before Prandtl's publication of his paper on the boundary theory, he was invited to head a new Institute for Technical Physics at the University of Göttingen. The institute would serve as Prandtl's primary base of operations for the remainder of his life and would become one of the world's leading centers for theoretical research into fluid mechanics. At Göttingen, Prandtl addressed many of the theoretical questions about manned flight that were arising as a result of the breakthroughs in aviation technology. He conducted research into, among many subjects, the characteristics of airflow around a body traveling at either subsonic or supersonic speeds. He directed research projects by the institute's graduate students into wing drag, the mechanics of solids, and other areas. Part of his work during the years before World War I also involved developing testing procedures for electrical fans for the German government and industry. In 1909, Prandtl married Gertrude Foppl, the daughter of his former mentor August Foppl. The couple eventually had two daughters.

Prandtl's mathematical theories also played a significant part in the advent and popular acceptance of the single-winged airplane. He was himself an advocate of the controversial design concept, in direct conflict with the prevailing opinion held by the aircraft design community in favor of bi- and tri-winged aircraft. He also contributed through his theoretical discoveries to improvements in the design of lighter-than-air craft known as dirigibles, which were commonly in use in the early years of the century as both civilian and military air carriers.

After World War I, in 1918-1919, Prandtl published a breakthrough paper on the way in which air flows around airplane wings of a finite span. The paper, which duplicated and expanded on work done simultaneously by a British physicist named Frederick W. Lanchester, became known as the Lanchester-Prandtl wing theory, one of many theoretical innovations that would bear Prandtl's name over the next several years.

In the mid-1920's, Prandtl and other researchers in Göttingen and elsewhere undertook the study of air turbulence created by a body moving through the air. In conjunction with another scientist, Theodor von Kármán, a former student of Prandtl, he developed a device for analyzing the distance turbulent air travels before its motion is dissipated. Prandtl's paper on the subject, presented in 1933, led to radical changes in accepted theories about air turbulence and to concepts used by pilots around the world. Prandtl also conducted extensive studies into the question of how objects traveling at high subsonic speeds are compressed by the air flow over their surfaces. This theory, known as the Prandtl-Glaubert rule, along with his other research into supersonic airflow, played a vital role in developing successful designs for supersonic aircraft.

During the same period, Prandtl, already a world-renowned pioneer in his field, was named to head a technical facility in Germany that would later be known as the Max Planck Institute for Fluid Mechanics. Part of this facility, following Prandtl's leadership and inspiration, would later become a major engineering design center and, in the 1970's and 1980's, an important contributor of spaceflight hardware and support services to the National Aeronautics and Space Administration (NASA) of the United States and to the European Space Agency.

Although it was not his area of primary investigation, Prandtl was also interested in questions concerning the elasticity and plasticity of a variety of solids, and the reaction of solid structures to torsion forces. In the latter, he developed a soap-film analogy that was found to be exceptionally useful in analyzing the effects of torsion forces on structures with noncircular cross sections. Prandtl's work often centered on the equipment and mathematical models for use in testing natural reactions and design concepts. Such devices include the tubes that bear his name used in the measurement of the static and complete pressure of a liquid flow at any point. He was also instrumental in advancing the development of air-tunnel technology and other equipment used in aerodynamic testing and design.

Unlike many of the scientists in Germany during the years between World War I and the end of World War II, Prandtl managed to avoid responding to political pressure from the ruling Nazi Party and to maintain civilian control over his work. He also continued to publish technical papers on his work regularly and to receive widespread attention from the international scientific community. In later years, after World War II, Prandtl expanded his efforts to include meteorology, a subject on which he published a paper in 1950. On August 15, 1953, Prandtl died in Göttingen, West Germany.

Summary

Ludwig Prandtl was one of a generation of scientific pioneers whose practical innovations during and after the Industrial Revolution made possible many of the conveniences known to modern mankind. As the father of several pivotal theories of fluid mechanics used in the production of aircraft, he helped create the age of rapid, safe air transportation. Prandtl is known as the father of aerodynamics, because he developed some of the fundamental concepts upon which modern air travel is based. There is, however, much more to his story than the list of his singular accomplishments. Prandtl both developed numerous theories and helped create much of the basic methodology used by both his own students and others in the generation of physicists who followed him. Men such as Kármán, although only slightly younger than Prandtl, owed much of their understanding of how to approach theoretical problems to the training and example of Prandtl. Prandtl's contributions extend into education as well as science. He helped build two institutions, the Institute for Technical Physics at the University of Göttingen and the Max Planck Institute for Fluid Mechanics, both of which have made significant contributions to science during and after Prandtl's time.

Beyond his accomplishments, Prandtl was one of a class of scientists in the late nineteenth and early to mid-twentieth centuries who possessed an extraordinarily single-minded drive to advance their areas of investigation. Konstantin Tsiolkovsky in Russia, Pierre and Marie Curie in France, and Robert Hutchings Goddard in the United States were chronologic and spiritual contemporaries of Prandtl, who worked not only to solve individual scientific questions but also to create a new field of study and to advance the broader body of mankind's knowledge. It was the collegial perspective that also helped build an international scientific community that could coordinate and fully exploit limited financial, human, and natural resources to the best, most productive end.

As part of this community, Prandtl focused his efforts on practical, technological questions, the solutions for which could be put to direct use in aircraft design and other areas. Prandtl and his contemporaries were part of the modern class of scientists who used their studies to solve problems that derived from practical, secular needs. In this regard, Prandtl's discoveries are every bit as significant as those of more visible inventors such as Orville and Wilbur Wright.

Bibliography

Lienhard, John H. "Ludwig Prandtl." In *Dictionary of Scientific Biography*, edited by Charles Coulston Gillispie, vol. 11. New York: Charles Scribner's Sons, 1975. This reference series includes concise, well-written biographies of many scientific figures. Listings are generally confined to basic facts about the individual's life and works, with minimal coverage of the motives or reasons behind the person's work.

Liepmann, H. W., and A. Roshko. *Elements of Gasdynamics*. New York: John Wiley & Sons, 1957. This book illustrates the role that Prandtl played in the theory of compressible flow.

Prandtl, Ludwig. *Applied Hydro- and Aeromechanics: Based on Lectures of Ludwig Prandtl*. Translated by J. P. Den-Hartog. New York: McGraw-Hill, 1934. This collection of technical lectures given by Prandtl is one of the earliest English-language versions of his works still readily available.

_____. *Essentials of Fluid Dynamics, with Applications to Hydraulics, Aeronautics, Meteorology, and Other Subjects*. New York: Hafnere, 1952. This technical volume provides an in-depth look at Prandtl's work in fluid dynamics and other areas of interest to him throughout his long career. One of the few more readily available English-language works of Prandtl.

Schlichting, Hermann. *Boundary Layer Theory*. Translated by J. Kestin. 4th ed. New York: McGraw-Hill, 1960. This work includes many references to Prandtl and to his students. Contains a good discussion of his involvement in the viscous flow theory.

Eric Christensen

SERGEI PROKOFIEV

Born: April 23, 1891; Sontsovka, Ukraine, Russian Empire
Died: March 5, 1953; Moscow, U.S.S.R.
Area of Achievement: Music
Contribution: Prokofiev is one of the two most successful Soviet composers of the twentieth century; he also ranks with the half dozen leading composers of the century. Although he first gained notice as an extraordinary pianist, he eventually created masterpieces in most major musical forms; in particular, in *Peter and the Wolf, Alexander Nevsky,* and *Romeo and Juliet,* he wrote three of the most celebrated works of his time.

Early Life
Sergei Prokofiev was born on April 23, 1891, on an isolated estate in the remote Ukraine, where his father managed agricultural production. Born to his parents only after fourteen years of marriage and two earlier pregnancies that had failed, Prokofiev experienced both the advantages and the disadvantages of an only and long-desired child. He enjoyed much attention, stimulating his creativity; he was treated overindulgently, which made him self-centered and demanding. Because of the remoteness of the area, all of his early education was at home, supplemented by summer excursions to Moscow and especially St. Petersburg, his mother's family home, one marked by intellectual upward striving. An enthusiastic amateur pianist herself—she played regularly for her unborn child—she was overjoyed when her five-year-old son said that he wanted to learn the piano. Shortly thereafter he declared that he wanted to write his own music; he proceeded to do so, inventing his own notation in the process. Yet, although his family encouraged this musical precocity, his father insisted that he acquire a rigorous standard academic background. At nine, his parents took him to his first opera; he returned home to write and stage his own opera, with neighbor children and servants taking the roles. The following year he was introduced to the head of the Moscow Conservatory, who recommended that a professional tutor be hired to teach him the fundamentals of composition and theory.

At considerable sacrifice, his parents decided to follow this advice. For two summers, beginning in 1902, they hired the young composer Reinhold Gliere, who proved the perfect mentor for a talented child for whom music was both a complex mathematical game and the basis of a spectacle. At the same time, his father continued to insist on his general education. His mother, however, determined that he was destined for music; from this point she managed his education so that he would qualify for admission to the St. Petersburg Conservatory, the most prestigious in the country, at the earliest possible moment. He took the examinations in August, 1904, and was admitted at the age of thirteen. He would remain there for ten years, though he would gain his first degree in 1911.

As a student, Prokofiev was both precocious and obnoxious; he early formed the habit of doing his exercise compositions the way his professors insisted he do them, while working on his own compositions in private. Entering the conservatory as a prodigy of sorts did little for his social development; in fact, for a while it intensified his obstinacy and irritability, since he felt different from everyone else. Still, Prokofiev grew up at the conservatory, both socially and musically. Socially, he passed through adolescence there, developing a fondness for women, with whom he always got along better than men. Musically, he was instructed by Aleksandr Glazunov, Nikolai Tcherepnin, and Nikolay Rimsky-Korsakov, among others. He largely ignored them, however, concentrating more on developing a reputation as a spoiled prodigy. Within four years, he was performing his own compositions in conservatory and city concert series. He became a sensation; no other conservatory student gained public notice at such an early age. His remaining years as a student saw him building on his early successes. When he left in 1914, he was ready to step into the front ranks of performers and composers.

Life's Work

Before Prokofiev left the conservatory at the age of twenty-three, he had already begun his career as a published composer and had gained a national reputation as a performer. His list of compositions was already impressive: He had before graduation completed a number of piano pieces, including a set of études and three sonatas; two chamber works; a fairy tale for voice and piano; two sets of songs; a sinfonietta; two symphonic sketches; two piano concerti; and an opera. Not all of these saw publication, but the list is intimidating and ambitious. Yet at that point his celebrity was primarily as a performer. He had premiered both of his piano concerti in Moscow and St. Petersburg, causing a sensation with each appearance. These were the most controversial entrances onto the Russian musical scene of the period; single-handedly they catapulted Russian music into the twentieth century. To be sure, he was following the lead of Stravinsky, who had caused a riot with the premiere of *The Rite of Spring* in 1912; that was in Paris, however, and besides Stravinsky had turned his back on Russia. Prokofiev brought the modernist revolution to Russia.

During the four years following—the years of the outbreak first of World War I and then of the Russian revolutions—Prokofiev consolidated his position. Just prior to the beginning of hostilities, Prokofiev toured Europe, in the course of which he met Sergei Diaghilev, the famous impresario of the Ballets Russes and the primary vector of the modernist movement in Paris; he also introduced both his performance technique and his music to Europe.

After hearing the Paris premiere of the second piano concerto, Diaghilev commissioned a ballet score from the young composer. Prokofiev completed a version within a year, but it proved unsatisfactory, whereupon Diaghilev commissioned another. This became *The Buffoon*, which he finished quickly. Simultaneously he developed the *Scythian Suite* out of the rejected ballet, and this was a triumph. He also finished a second opera, *The Gambler*, based on a Fyodor Dostoevski novel but unproduced until 1929; a first symphony, the *Classical*, a sensation then and popular ever since; a first violin concerto, another success; two more piano sonatas; two sets of songs; and a cantata. Yet making a living through music in war- and revolution-afflicted Russia was dubious at best, and in 1918 Prokofiev decided to leave for the West. His visit—intended at first to last only a few months—extended in the end to seventeen years.

Those years constitute Prokofiev's middle period, during which he gradually shed his bad-boy image and established his position as one of the world's leading composers. During that period, he tried living in a variety of places before finally settling on Paris. Before leaving Russia he had introduced his *Classical* symphony (No. 1), modeled on his notion of what Joseph Haydn might have done with the harmonic modifications of the twentieth century. Because of the turmoil in Europe, he traveled across Siberia, itself in disarray because of the revolution; from Japan, where he concertized to replenish his finances, he sailed to the United States. He spent most of the following three and a half years in that country, performing often, introducing his works as he composed them, but getting mixed responses—regularly cool in New York and hot in Chicago. He also traveled to the Continent, where he renewed connections with Diaghilev. The major achievements of his American years were the opera *Love for Three Oranges*, which is still performed and from which a more popular suite was extracted; the ballet *The Buffoon*; and the Third Piano Concerto.

From 1922 to late 1935, Prokofiev lived in Europe, for two years in Austria and then semipermanently in Paris. In 1923, he married Lina Codina, a young American singer of Cuban, Spanish, and Polish background whom he had met in New York in 1918 and with whom he had often performed. The couple had two sons, both born in Paris, Sviatislav in 1924 and Oleg in 1928. Although the strain of supporting a family—which in those days included relatives—at first proved difficult, these years witnessed a series of successes, which confirmed Prokofiev's eminence. In 1927, he returned to the Soviet Union for the first time in nine years, tentatively attempting to repair connections, but the financial attractions of the West still proved too tempting. Thereafter he would return to Russia regularly. Yet for the next several years, his triumphs occurred in the West, which saw several major works premiered: the ballets *Le Pas d'acier* (1927), *The Prodigal Son* (1929), and *On the Dnepr* (1932); the opera *The Gambler* (1929);

the film score for *Lt. Kije* (1933), which also furnished material for a popular suite and which introduced Prokofiev to the medium of film composition; the Fourth Symphony (1930); two piano concerti (1931 and 1932); the Second Violin Concerto (1935); and a profusion of chamber, solo instrument, and vocal works.

By 1935, Prokofiev had decided that his future lay in returning to the Soviet Union. The Depression (1929-1941), while limiting opportunities in the West, had had little effect on the Soviet economy, and Prokofiev had begun to believe that his soul was rooted in Russia. This return inaugurated his Soviet period (1935-1953), the years of his greatest achievements as well as his greatest humiliations. For he returned just as Stalin began putting into practice his program for turning artists into propaganda-mongers. For musicians as for others this meant subordinating creative impulses to socially and politically acceptable work. At first Prokofiev fit smoothly into this regimen. He had always worked well in response to specific directions, and the commissars required much work to order. His first years were extraordinarily productive: He completed the ballet *Romeo and Juliet* (1937) and the three suites drawn from it; *Peter and the Wolf* (1938), a children's fable for narrator and orchestra; film scores for *Queen of Spades* (1938) and *Alexander Nevsky* (1939), the latter also developed into a cantata; and his First Cello Concerto (1939).

These were also the years immediately preceding World War II, years of intensifying tension and suspicion. Some of this fell on Prokofiev because of his long absence from the country during its formative years. As a result, he experienced some negative criticism, hostile reactions he did not expect in his homeland. The outbreak of war affected him both professionally and personally. Like most Soviet artists, Prokofiev was expected to produce works that would help rally the Soviet people. Seizing the opportunity, Prokofiev chose the classic text for an opera aimed at that end, Leo Tolstoy's *Voyna i mir* (1865-1869; *War and Peace*, 1886), although it was not produced until 1946. He also composed a number of classic film scores, most notably that for Sergei Eisenstein's monumental *Ivan Grozny* (1944-1946; *Ivan the Terrible*). With Russian success in the war, he returned to the ballet score *Cinderella* (1945), another wonderful work. The premiere of his epic fifth symphony was appropriately symbolic; its performance was delayed by cannon salvos signaling the beginning of Russia's final victorious offensive of the war.

The war also brought the dissolution of his first marriage and his liaison with and eventual marriage to Mira Mendelson. His remarriage in 1948 accompanied significant changes: He was humiliated before and censured by a congress of Soviet composers as part of Stalin's program to establish absolute rule. Simultaneously his first wife, Russian only by naturalization, was sentenced to hard labor in a Siberian prison camp for supposed disloyalty. His health broke in this crisis; the last five years showed a lingering decline. He continued composing to the end; though his final works are not among his finest, they do include the bold Sinfonia Concertante for Cello and Orchestra (1948); the broad and affirmative Sixth Symphony (1949); the Cello Sonata, his most accessible chamber work; and the somewhat less effective Seventh Symphony (1950). Broken by hypertension and high blood pressure, hounded by the attacks of ideological commissars, Prokofiev died in Moscow on March 5, 1953, at very nearly the same time that his prosecutor, Joseph Stalin, died.

Summary

By all accounts one of the most brilliant and successful composers of the twentieth century, Sergei Prokofiev is in some respects more remarkable because of his interaction with Russian culture and the evolving Soviet state. His cultural heredity determined the orientation of his music and shaped his life. His most popular and enduring works grow out of and reflect the Russian soul: historically in *Alexander Nevsky* and *Ivan the Terrible*, folkloristically in *Peter and the Wolf*, artistically in *Romeo and Juliet* and *Cinderella*, narratively in *Lt. Kije* and *War and Peace*. He is the prototypical iconoclastic Russian artist, shattering idols in an orgy of self-expression yet reserving his best work for command performances and made-to-order scores. Throughout his life he remained Russian, returning home at a hard time because he believed it was home and expending his energies in really trying to express the Russian soul in his music.

Some critics have contended that Prokofiev's return to the Soviet Union and voluntary submission to creative controls stunted his creative growth and limited the music he could have composed. Throughout his career, however, Prokofiev did his best work in response to strict directions. Probably for this reason he is indisputably the master film-score composer; no other craftsman proved more adept at creating the perfect aural analogue for a visual image. Similarly, no other attempt at creating a musical illustration for a fable has succeeded like *Peter and the Wolf*, which has entered the common consciousness as few classical compositions have. Undoubtedly Prokofiev suffered from the strictures clamped on him, but what he achieved is unprecedented and will endure.

Bibliography

Krebs, Stanley Dale. *Soviet Composers and the Growth of Soviet Music.* London: Allen & Unwin, 1970. This is the best general account of the impact of socialist ideology on Russian composers up to 1960. Quite useful because it sets Prokofiev squarely in his cultural context, this work offers interesting comparisons of Prokofiev with other composers. The book perhaps overstresses the negative aspects of Stalinism.

Nestyev, Israel. *Prokofiev.* Translated by Florence Jonas. Stanford, Calif.: Stanford University Press, 1960. An authorized Soviet biography with full apparatus, this work presents much detailed information through the distorting lens of ideological preconception. Nestyev's basic view is that Prokofiev's music was perverted by his stay in the West.

Robinson, Harlow. *Sergei Prokofiev.* New York: Viking, 1987. This book is the single indispensable work on the composer, a complete and even-handed scholarly biography with full critical materials, including an annotated bibliography. Robinson presents all the information available with clarity and grace, leaving readers to draw their own conclusions.

Samuel, Claude. *Prokofiev.* Translated by Miriam John. London: Calder and Boyars, 1971. A readable and well-focused biography, this book is particularly useful for the general reader. It is, however, colored by a pro-Western bias and is somewhat limited in technical musical information.

Savkina, Natalia. *Prokofiev.* Translated by Catherine Young. Neptune City, N.J.: Paganiniana, 1984. A translation of an authorized Soviet biography of 1982, this presents a revisionist Soviet view of the composer and his sufferings under Stalin. More objective and pictorial than Nestyev, this account is slighter and less substantial, and still exhibits a pro-Russian bias.

Seroff, Victor. *Sergei Prokofiev: A Soviet Tragedy.* New York: Funk & Wagnalls, 1968. As the title indicates, this book is less objective biography than the Western entry in an ideological conflict. It is well written, however, and contains some good illustrations.

James Livingston

MARCEL PROUST

Born: July 10, 1871; Auteuil, France
Died: November 18, 1922; Paris, France
Area of Achievement: Literature
Contribution: Proust is the most celebrated French writer of the twentieth century. His masterwork in seven volumes, the novel *À la recherche du temps perdu* (1913-1927; *Remembrance of Things Past*, 1922-1931, 1981) broke new ground in its explorations of the nature of individual identity, its psychology of space and time, and its stylistic and thematic expansiveness. Proust's fiction and his criticism have helped widen the traditional perspectives of literary criticism.

Early Life
Marcel Proust was born in Auteuil, a suburb of Paris, on July 10, 1871. Proust's father, Adrien Proust, a medical doctor and professor, had received the Légion d'Honneur the previous year for his theoretical and practical efforts to halt the spread of epidemics. Dr. Proust's success lent his family stature, but, because Proust's mother was Jewish, he was also something of an outsider in Parisian society. Proust was a weak child, plagued by asthma, which intensified when he was a teenager and limited his activities for most of his life. During his childhood, his family divided its time between Paris, Auteuil, and Illiers, a village southwest of Paris. Despite the security of his father's prestige and his family's wealth, Proust was tormented by his poor health and by a strained, although loving, relationship with his parents. In 1882, he entered the Lycée Condorcet, a private secondary school, where he pursued the chief interests of his life: the theater, reading, and writing. In 1889, Proust received a baccalaureate degree from the *lycée*; in the examinations, he took a first prize in French composition.

Proust had no plans for a career when he left the *lycée*. He spent a voluntary year of military service with the Seventy-sixth Infantry in Orléans, where, despite his weak constitution, he delighted in the routine and the camaraderie. Pressure from his family to settle on an occupation led him to study law at the Faculté de Droit at the Sorbonne and diplomacy at the École des Sciences Politiques, but much of his energy was devoted to the Parisian social scene. Proust began by frequenting bourgeois literary salons, gatherings at the homes of prominent society matrons that attracted figures from the arts. At first, Proust gained entry only to salons linked to school and family friends. Eventually, however, he was accepted into some of the most exclusive salons in the Faubourg Saint-Germain, representing the highest level of French nobility. At the same time, Proust continued writing short stories and essays like those he had contributed to magazines at the *lycée*. He passed the law examination in 1893, but he never practiced the profession.

In the eyes of family members and acquaintances, he was a dilettante. Even the publication in 1896 of his early stories and sketches, under the title *Les Plaisirs et les jours* (*Pleasures and Regrets*, 1948), failed to win for him a reputation as a serious writer. Doubtless his negligent attitude toward an unpaid position at a library, which he often abandoned to travel with friends, suggested that he was more interested in gossip and play than in producing substantial work. The deaths of his father in 1903 and his mother in 1905, however, served as catalysts to Proust's literary efforts.

Life's Work

Despite appearances to the contrary, the influences and the aborted beginnings that would eventually culminate in Proust's *Remembrance of Things Past* can be traced through the ten years before his parents' deaths. The nature of aesthetic experience fascinated Proust. Before the turn of the century, he became interested in the work of the English art critic and historian John Ruskin. Despite Proust's relatively meager knowledge of English, he translated some of Ruskin's work and wrote prefaces, published in 1904 and 1905, that explore the nature of reading and its effect on the reader. Proust valued reading not for its power to educate but for its power to send the reader deep within himself. For Proust, reading is communication "in the midst of solitude," and therefore is divorced from ordinary, daily life. Allied to Proust's conception of reading was his determination to change the assumptions and the nature of French literary criticism. In a book written during this period but not published until 1954, *Contre Sainte-Beuve* (*By Way of Sainte-Beuve*, 1958), Proust takes exception to the views of the most influential nineteenth century French critic, Charles Sainte-Beuve. Proust argues in opposition to Sainte-Beuve that a book should not be judged by its author or an author by his book. Instead, he argues, the author and the book represent two distinct selves. A book presents the elusive inner self that cannot be glimpsed in the daily life of the author, but, in Proust's view, that glimpse should push the reader to plumb his own elusive self. Thus, the key to truth is not in any book, but within each individual.

Remembrance of Things Past, which Proust wrote and rewrote over a span of at least fourteen years, also draws on narrative material from several earlier efforts: the aborted novel *Jean Santeuil* (English translation, 1955) probably written largely between 1895 and 1899, but not published until 1952; "Sur la Lecture" (1905; "On Reading," 1971), his preface to his translation of Ruskin's *Sesame and Lilies* (1865), and *Contre Sainte-Beuve*. In 1909, incorporating parts of these works, Proust wrote the beginning and end of *Remembrance of Things Past*. What he intended in 1912, the year the first volume, *Du côté de chez Swann* (1913; *Swann's Way*, 1922), was published, to be three volumes eventually became seven, as Proust added hundreds of thousands of words. The novel's seemingly infinite expandability reflects Proust's addition of new layers to his narrator's life. The added length intensifies one of the novel's key processes: forgetting and remembering. Proust writes in the last volume, *Le Temps retrouvé* (1927; *Time Regained*, 1931), "[T]he true paradises are the paradises that we have lost."

The plot of *Remembrance of Things Past* is a transmuted version of Proust's life. The narrator begins by remembering a time when his life was disordered, when he was plagued by memories. One memory, an unconscious memory, sparked by a cup of tea and a madeleine, a shell-shaped French pastry, conjures up a vivid memory of his childhood; from that memory, the main narrative begins. The narrator presents his life in a roughly chronological order, with digressions and some hints of the future. His life is one of repeated disappointments in himself and in others: in his parents, in the wealthy bourgeois aesthete Swann, in the aristocratic Guermantes family, and in the enigmatic Albertine, the narrator's great love, who may represent a combination of women the homosexual Proust admired and men he loved. Seemingly like Proust, the narrator feels lost, unsure of his life's work. The novel's sheer mass occasions in its reader the same divorce from the past experienced by the narrator. Finally, in the last volume, the narrator experiences a series of revelations that highlight his error in searching for truth in others instead of seeking it within himself. He discovers himself and his past anew and, in an effort to resurrect all the selves buried within him, he determines to write the book that the reader has now finished.

Remembrance of Things Past is autobiographical, but its clues to Proust's life are of secondary importance. More significantly, drawing in part on the ideas of the French philosopher Henri Bergson, Proust's novel asserts in both its narrative form and its theme the need for a "three-dimensional psychology, one that adds to the traditional points in space and time a movement through time: what Bergson calls 'duration.'" Proust's literary theory and technique might be compared to a cubist painter's representation of movement or changes in perspective in a medium generally considered two-dimensional. In an attempt to create duration in fiction, Proust turned to a variety of techniques, including cutting back and forth between memories in a quasi-cinematic fashion and undermining narrative tension by prematurely revealing future events.

Proust had difficulty finding a publisher for his novel and therefore paid for the printing of the first volume. When it was published, however, its value was soon recognized. Printing difficulties and the outbreak of World War I delayed publication of subsequent volumes until after the war's end, but the delay proved fortuitous because it allowed Proust the time to expand and revise the novel. When he was awarded the prestigious Goncourt Prize in 1917 for the second volume, Proust was lionized.

Stories abound of Proust's eccentricities during the years he spent writing *Remembrance of Things Past*. He usually slept during the day and wrote at night. To shield himself from urban noise, he had a cork lining applied to the bedroom walls of one apartment he occupied during those years. His guilt over his homosexuality sometimes led him toward sadomasochism, but he was not a recluse, as he is sometimes claimed to have been. He emerged often to dine at the Ritz, he still sometimes attended society soirées, and he occasionally patronized the ballet and the theater. His true devotion, however, was to his work. When he was dying of pneumonia, too weak to write in his own hand, he insisted on dictating textual additions to his housekeeper. At Proust's death on November 18, 1922, the last three volumes of *Remembrance of Things Past* remained unpublished. Doubtless Proust would have revised them if he had lived longer, but their published forms complete his design.

Summary

Marcel Proust's *Remembrance of Things Past* is valuable in all its facets: as a panorama of French society of his time, ranging through all economic and social classes and illustrating changes in fashion, technology, psychology, philosophy, and politics; as a treatise on the psychology of the self and the relation of the individual to society; and as an exemplum of literary modernism in its isolation and elevation of the individual consciousness. Proust's influence on both criticism and literature has been powerful. Although no single author can be credited with spawning new schools of criticism, a comprehensive review of criticism would suggest that Proust's experiments with narrative and his three-dimensional psychology deserve some part of the credit for the development of branches of criticism such as structuralism and narratology. In literature, Proust's influence is clearly evident in the work of a number of major figures who have followed him, including Samuel Beckett, whose debt to Proust would be obvious from a look at his characters lost in time even if he had not written about Proust himself, and Alain Robbe-Grillet, whose dismembered narratives and amnesiac narrators represent extreme versions of Proust's narrative cross-cutting and his forgetful narrator. Like the work of most great innovators, Proust's novel *Remembrance of Things Past* is part of a historical complex of interrelated ideas. That complex has shaped the psychology and the values of the twentieth century.

Bibliography

Beckett, Samuel. *Proust*. New York: Grove Press, 1931. A brief but fascinating book by the premier playwright of the second half of the twentieth century, who explores the nature of habit and its role in *Remembrance of Things Past*.

Brée, Germaine. *The World of Marcel Proust*. Boston: Houghton Mifflin, 1966. One of a number of books by a prominent critic of Proust, this work explains the problems and joys of reading Proust.

Genette, Gerard. "Time and Narrative in À *la recherche du temps perdu*." In *Aspects of Narrative*, edited by J. Hillis Miller. New York: Columbia University Press, 1971. A seminal article on Proust's narrative techniques by one of the French literary critics who have helped shape the branch of criticism called narratology.

Kilmartin, Terence. *A Reader's Guide to "Remembrance of Things Past."* New York: Random House, 1983. Four indexes to characters, historical figures, places, and themes in *Remembrance of Things Past*, compiled by the most recent translator of the novel.

Painter, George. *Proust: The Early Years*. Boston: Little, Brown, 1959.

_____. *Proust: The Later Years*. Boston: Little, Brown, 1965. An exhaustive two-volume biography that is especially helpful about Proust's historical context and the correspondences between Proust's life and the plot of *Remembrance of Things Past*.

Poulet, Georges. *Studies in Human Time*. Translated by Elliott Coleman. Baltimore: Johns Hopkins University Press, 1956. A widely cited critical work that helped open a new sphere of inquiry for criticism by identifying one of Proust's methods as the "spatialization of time."

Proust, Marcel. *Letters of Marcel Proust*. Translated and edited by Mina Curtiss. London: Chatto & Windus, 1950. Although not the most recent selection of Proust's letters, this book includes a range of letters from all periods of his life as well as notes and photographs.

Shattuck, Roger. *Proust's Binoculars*. New York: Random House, 1963. A thought-provoking book by a prominent critic of French literature, who here outlines Proust's use of optical and cinematic images and techniques in *Remembrance of Things Past*.

Helaine Ross

GIACOMO PUCCINI

Born: December 22, 1858; Lucca, Italy
Died: November 29, 1924; Brussels, Belgium
Area of Achievement: Music
Contribution: Born into a Tuscan family with almost a dynastic tradition in
musical composition and instruction, Puccini became a leading member of
a talented group of Italian composers of opera in the generation succeeding Giuseppe Verdi. Many of Puccini's operatic works have proved to be
among the most popular in the twentieth century operatic repertory.

Early Life
Tradition and expectation are reflected in the names given the fifth child of
Michele and Albina Puccini: Giacomo Antonio Domenico Michele Secondo
Maria Puccini. The child's great-great-grandfather, Giacomo Puccini, had
studied music at Bologna, then returned to Lucca to become organist and
choirmaster at this Tuscan city's cathedral (San Martino) and prolific composer of sacred and civic music. His son Antonio also studied at Bologna,
returned to Lucca to compose sacred music and assist, then succeed, his
father as choirmaster. His son Domenico followed study at Bologna with a
musical apprenticeship at Naples (under the operatic composer Giovanni
Paisiello), then returned to Lucca to assist his father and compose an occasional opera. Domenico's son Michele studied music first at Lucca with his
father, then at Bologna with a contemporary master of opera, Gaetano Doni-
zetti, and at Naples with Giuseppe Mercadante, composer of operatic and
choral music. Michele then became choirmaster and organist at San Martino
and wrote an opera on a historical theme (1884) and texts on counterpoint
and harmony.

The child Giacomo was therefore expected to study music and his skill
was such—and the family tradition so strong—that at his father's death
(1864), the Luccan authorities reserved the post of organist and choirmaster
until the eight-year-old Giacomo should come of age. By age fourteen, Giacomo was sufficiently adept to become organist at San Martino and other
local churches. He was also pianist for several nearby resorts, taverns, and
(some said) a brothel. Additional funds came from the sale of organ pipes
that he and his friends stole from churches.

Meanwhile, Puccini continued musical studies with his father's sometime
pupils, then entered the local musical academy. There he studied Verdi's
operas—a performance of Verdi's *Aida* (1876) in nearby Pisa inspired in
Puccini a vow of composing opera himself—and composed minor orchestral
and choral works. His final exercise, a *Mass of Glory* (1880), was performed
amid praise for the young musician's skillful writing for chorus and solo
voices. With a relative's aid and a royal scholarship, Puccini, in the fall of

1880, commenced advanced study at the Milan Conservatory. There his work was directed by a leading operatic composer, Amilcare Ponchielli. In July, 1883, Puccini was graduated with the performance of his *Capriccio sinfonico*, which was praised for its orchestration and melody. Now Puccini would compose an opera.

Life's Work

Puccini's first opera, *Le Villi*, with a libretto by the dramatist Ferdinando Fontana, used a story that Adolphe Adam had already exploited for his popular ballet *Giselle* (1841): A peasant girl's spirit haunts the lover who abandoned her. Puccini submitted his work for a Milanese competition and was rebuffed, primarily because his score was illegible. Yet the respected composer Arrigo Boito heard Puccini play his score at the piano, promptly raised funds for a production, and convinced the Milanese editorial firm of Ricordi to publish the opera. *Le Villi* was performed to great acclaim at the Teatro dal Verme in Milan on May 31, 1884.

Sorrow, scandal, and defeat followed. Puccini's mother died in the summer of 1884; shortly thereafter, he eloped from Lucca with Elvira Bonturi Gemignani, who was already married, with two children. (She would not marry Puccini until her husband's death in 1903.) In January, 1885, *Le Villi* was poorly received in Naples and at La Scala, the premier Milanese opera house.

Puccini and Elvira lived in poverty in Milan for the next several years, supported by a stipend from Ricordi, their difficulties compounded by the birth of a son, Antonio, in 1886. Puccini's second opera, *Edgar*, with a libretto by Fontana, intentionally resembled Georges Bizet's popular *Carmen* (1875). Yet while Puccini's score was pleasant, the drama (a fourteenth century youth is seduced by a Gypsy girl) was dull. A lukewarm reception greeted the premiere at La Scala on April 21, 1889.

Encouraged by Ricordi, Puccini had started yet another opera on an unpromising subject. Abbé Prévost's novel *Histoire du chevalier des Grieux et de Manon Lescaut* (1731, 1733, 1753; *Manon Lescaut*, 1734, 1786) had already been the subject of at least three operas, including Jules Massenet's great Parisian success, *Manon* (1884). Puccini's opera had a difficult birth, requiring several librettists. The result was an incoherent plot overwhelmed by music of great passion and memorable melody. The premiere, at the Royal Theater of Turin, February 1, 1893, was a popular success.

Manon Lescaut provided financial freedom. Puccini acquired a villa at Torre del Lago, by a scenic lake between Pisa and Lucca, where he would compose and, for relaxation, hunt wild fowl. In March, 1893, Puccini learned that a rival, Ruggiero Leoncavallo, planned an opera based on Henri Murger's novel and play, *Scènes de la vie de bohème* (1847-1849). Puccini hastened to complete his opera on the same subject, choosing as librettists the noted playwrights Giuseppe Giacosa and Luigi Illica. Both had worked on *Manon Lescaut*; both would collaborate on Puccini's next two operas. *La Bohème* had a favorable premiere at Turin on February 1, 1896, with a conductor, Arturo Toscanini, who commenced a lifelong friendship with Puccini. Critics noted the trivial plot, but all were impressed by this work's drama and powerful music, especially in the heroine's death scene.

Puccini had long been interested in an opera based on Victorien Sardou's play *La Tosca* (1887; English translation, 1925), as popularized by the French actress Sarah Bernhardt. Ricordi acquired the rights to the play, arbitrated quarrels among librettists and composer, and urged completion. Puccini's version of this melodrama set in Rome, 1800, was presented at Rome's Teatro Costanzi, January 14, 1900—and for twenty more performances. Critics have often deplored the plot of *Tosca*, "that shabby little shocker," but none denies the dramatic tension imparted by Puccini's music.

From a factual magazine article by John Luther Long, the American impresario David Belasco produced a popular play (1904) about a Japanese woman's love betrayed by an American naval officer. Puccini saw the play in London, was fascinated by the exotic setting, and his version, *Madama Butterfly*, first appeared at La Scala on February 17, 1904. The critical reception was devastatingly negative (Toscanini hated the opera), but it has become Puccini's most popular. Meanwhile, Puccini's own life came to resemble a melodrama. His constant womanizing drove Elvira to jealous rages; she, in turn, drove Puccini's servant girl to suicide—tragically, for the girl, was innocent of dallying with Puccini. The composer could focus on no project, until 1907, when he saw in New York another Belasco play, *The Girl of the Golden West* (1905). Puccini's version, *Fanciulla*, with libretto by Guelfo Civinini, was presented first at the New York Metropolitan Opera, with Toscanini conducting, December 10, 1910. Technically perfect, the opera was well, but not enthusiastically, received. Igor Stravinsky described it as "a remarkably up-to-date television horse opera," without noting that the plot was far from common in 1910.

Puccini's earlier operas had now become widely popular, frequently performed in Italy, elsewhere in Europe, and in North and South America. Puccini convinced himself that he should now compose a romantic opera similar to the popular operettas of Franz Lehár. A new librettist, Giuseppe Adami, assisted the completion of *La Rondine* (the swallow). Puccini intended a premiere in Lehár's city, Vienna, but war interfered. This slight work was staged to modest acclaim in Monte Carlo, March 27, 1917, and has never been popular. Puccini was already busy with a plan to render in opera the scheme of the French Grand Guignol: a tragedy, a sentimental drama, a comedy. Librettists were found: Adami (again) and G. Forzano. *Il Trittico* (the triptych) was staged in New York, December 14, 1918. The first two episodes—*Il Tabarro* (the cloak), a horrific tragedy, and *Suor*

Angelica (Sister Angelica), a miraculous tale with a heroine bearing some resemblance to Puccini's sister, Mother Superior Iginia—were poorly received. The third, *Gianni Schicchi*, a black comedy based on Dante's *Inferno* (canto 30), was popular. All three episodes have magnificent arias for the female voice. Critics have come to appreciate Puccini's dramatic and musical skill in constructing this complex work.

Puccini chose as his next subject a drama by the Venetian playwright Carlo Gozzi: a bloody, romantic fairy tale set in exotic China. The librettists Renato Simoni and Adami set to work. Puccini composed, while complaining of throat pains. In the autumn of 1924, cancer of the throat was diagnosed. Puccini, accompanied by his son, went to Brussels for radioactive therapy. The treatment seemed successful, but a heart attack brought death on November 29. The body was returned to Milan for temporary burial in the Toscanini family tomb. On the day of national mourning, Benito Mussolini delivered the obituary. In 1926, Puccini was interred at Torre del Lago.

Toscanini conducted the premier of the unfinished *Turandot* at La Scala on April 25, 1926. When he reached the end of Puccini's score, Toscanini turned to the audience, said, "Here ends the opera, which remains incomplete because of the composer's death," and left the stage in silence.

Summary

Turandot was completed from Giacomo Puccini's notes by Franco Alfano and forms part of the standard operatic repertory, as does *Manon Lescaut*. *La Bohème, Tosca*, and *Madama Butterfly* have become favorites with American and European audiences. *Fanciulla* and *Il Trittico* are occasionally presented as curiosities, the latter often to critical acclaim.

Contemporary and later critics debated whether Puccini was the true heir of Verdi. He was not. Puccini's plots lacked the heroic and nationalistic themes that Verdi favored; Puccini was an exponent of *opera verismo*: human characters caught in more or less realistic situations. Indeed, Puccini's best vocal writing was consistently for the vulnerable woman caught in plausible tragic circumstances. Furthermore, the springs of Puccini's music were not fed by Verdi. His skillful orchestral harmonies and lyrical choral passages came from experience, education, and family tradition. Contemporary composers also contributed to Puccini's craft: From *Fanciulla* on, the influence of Claude Debussy and Richard Strauss is apparent, while Stravinskian rhythms enhance *Turandot*. Above all, Puccini learned from Richard Wagner: The continuous melodic line (constant musical background) in Puccini's operas derives from Wagner's *Tristan and Isolde*. Puccini's strong theatrical sense owes something to Wagner's music-dramas, as does Puccini's careful attempt to fit music to words—hence the great emotive power of his music, which often seems to drive his characters to a desired action.

Critics said that a craftsman's operatic music should reflect, not force, the characters' actions. The emotive power of Puccini's music is so strong that his melodies have been appropriated for everything from film soundtracks to television commercials.

Bibliography

Ashbrook, William. *The Operas of Puccini*. Ithaca, N.Y.: Cornell University Press, 1985. A detailed discussion of the composition, structure, and production of each opera, set within the framework of a biography. Includes notes, a bibliography, an excellent index, and full summaries of each opera.

Carner, Mosco. "Giacomo Puccini." In *The New Grove Masters of Italian Opera*, edited by Philip Gosset et al. New York: W. W. Norton, 1983. This is an excellent, brief monograph distilled from the work listed below. Part 1 is a brief biography; part 2 discusses (thematically, not by opera) Puccini's music. Includes photographs of Puccini, a bibliography, an index, and a detailed chronology of Puccini's musical works.

_____. *Puccini: A Critical Biography*. 2d ed. New York: Holmes & Meier, 1977. The standard scholarly discussion, with separate sections on biography, Puccini the artist, and detailed musicological treatment of his works. Includes full reference notes, a bibliography, a detailed index, and selected illustrations, primarily of Puccini and his family.

Marek, George R. *Puccini*. London: Cassell, 1952. An anecdotal biography incorporating substantial material from letters by, to, and about the composer. The other biographies listed here offer a more sophisticated discussion of Puccini's music. Contains an excellent index and selected illustrations of Puccini and his associates.

Mordden, Ethan. *Opera Anecdotes*. New York: Oxford University Press, 1985. A humorous book with a wealth of reliable information. Mordden supplies serious and sound introductory essays to the subjects and personalities treated. Contains an index.

Osborne, Charles. *The Complete Operas of Puccini*. New York: Atheneum, 1982. Similar to the work by Ashbrook, but written with a lighter touch, this biography is organized as background to a discussion of each opera in chronological order. Osborne stresses Puccini's works as musical theater. Contains a brief bibliography, an index, and selected illustrations of items (scores, sets, and the like) pertinent to Puccini's life and work.

Specht, Richard. *Giacomo Puccini: The Man, His Life, His Work*. Translated by Catherine Alison Phillips. New York: Alfred A. Knopf, 1933. A personal assessment of Puccini's work by one who knew the composer (but not well). Specht's study reflects the ambiguity that contemporary Europeans felt concerning Puccini's life, personality, and musical tastes. The index is inadequate and the few illustrations are poorly reproduced.

Weaver, William. *Puccini: The Man and His Music*. New York: E. P. Dutton, 1977. A superb collection of photographs of Puccini, his family, friends and associates, and productions (mostly at the Metropolitan Opera) of his operas. The text should be supplemented by Carner's essay. Contains plot summaries of the operas and a brief bibliography.

Paul B. Harvey, Jr.

SERGEI RACHMANINOFF

Born: April 1, 1873; Semyonovo, Novgorod District, Russia
Died: March 28, 1943; Beverly Hills, California
Area of Achievement: Music
Contribution: Rachmaninoff is best remembered as the composer who was the last great figure in the Romantic tradition and the leading pianist of his era. His music is noted for melancholy and long melodic line.

Early Life
Sergei Vasilyevich Rachmaninoff was born near Novgorod in 1873, the offspring of two noble families. His father was a spendthrift who by 1882 had squandered the family fortune, forcing him to take a flat in St. Petersburg, where he soon deserted his family. Rachmaninoff received a scholarship and attended the St. Petersburg Conservatory. He had shown an early aptitude for the piano. Because of his idle nature, Aleksandr Ziloti, his cousin, suggested that Rachmaninoff study with Nikolai Zverev. In 1885, Rachmaninoff moved into Zverev's apartment. Zverev was a hard taskmaster and, as a result, Rachmaninoff's technique and musical knowledge improved rapidly, especially by playing symphonies in four-hand arrangements and attending concerts.

The Zverevs spent their summers in the Crimea, and it was there that Rachmaninoff, in 1886, first tried his hand at composition. His first surviving composition was the Scherzo in D Minor for orchestra of 1887. In 1888, he studied composition with Ziloti, counterpoint with Sergei Taneyev, and harmony with Anton Arensky. After an argument with Zverev, he went to live with his aunt, Varvara Satin, whose daughter, Natalie, he married in 1902.

In 1890, Rachmaninoff received his first commission for a piano reduction of Peter Ilich Tchaikovsky's *Sleeping Beauty*, though it had to be improved by Ziloti. Rachmaninoff took his graduation examinations one year early and passed with the highest scores. In the summer of 1891, he worked on his First Piano Concerto as well as on the first movement of his Symphony No. 1 in D Minor. For his final presentation at the Conservatory, he presented a one-act opera, *Aleko*, receiving a gold medal for it. That fall he composed his famous Op. 3 for solo piano, *Morceaux de Fantaisie*, in which both the Prelude in C-sharp Minor (No. 2) and the No. 4, the *Polichinelle* in F-sharp Minor, are included. The former piece made him immediately famous. For millions of piano students, this is his quintessential piece because of its melancholia and grandiose style. This piece became the necessary encore at all of his concerts.

It was at this time that Rachmaninoff wrote an orchestral fantasy, *The Rock* (Op. 7), as well as finished his First Symphony, performed on

March 27, 1897. This symphony was a colossal failure, and that deeply disturbed him. So great was his despondency that the Satins sent him for psychiatric treatment with Nikolai Dahl. Dahl's treatment was successful, and he dedicated to Dahl one of his best loved works, the Piano Concerto No. 2 in C Minor, which he introduced on October 17, 1901. It was a great success and marks his return to music as an acknowledged master.

The Piano Concerto No. 2 begins with nine unaccompanied chords on the piano and then the entrance of the orchestra with arpeggios played on the piano. It has a passionate second theme followed by a march and a coda. The second movement, the one that took the world by storm, has a nocturnal Russian-like song in the flutes and broken chords from the piano. The finale of the work is martial in character with bravura passages for the soloist. This work is considered his "signature" piece.

Life's Work

In March, 1902, Rachmaninoff completed his choral work, *Spring*, and in both 1905 and 1906 he won the Glinka Award. During 1905, he and his family left revolutionary Russia and lived in Dresden. It was there that he began sketching his Symphony No. 2 in E Minor, which he conducted in St. Petersburg on February 8, 1908. It is the most celebrated of his symphonic works because of its spontaneity and sincerity, directness and musical balance. Throughout there is a stepwise shape to his themes. This structure is the key to his mature style.

Early in 1909, Rachmaninoff was back in Dresden, where he began a symphonic poem, *The Isle of the Dead*, inspired by Arnold Boeklin's famous painting of the same name. The 1880 painting is a famous mood piece with a dreamlike island cemetery toward which Charon rows a boat across the River Styx, which holds a flag-draped coffin presided over by a mourner. The island rises steeply with grottos in its tall cliffs, bathed in an eerie glow of the setting sun. High, deep-green cypresses crowd the center, and overhead there is an oppressive purple sky. Rachmaninoff set out to capture Boeklin's morbid sensitivity. The gloom is captured by the composer's quote of the *Dies irae* chant in chromatic figures. As Charon's boat nears the isle, the music climaxes in E minor, seemingly reaching out to the high granite cliffs of the painting itself. The 5/8 bars end and the rowboat drifts to its destination. The piece concludes with the soul of the departed recalling its anguished life, used as a contrast of textures between death and life. This piece has had enormous popular success.

In the summer of 1909, Rachmaninoff prepared for his first American tour, and for this occasion he composed his Concerto No. 3 in D Minor, first performed in New York City on November 28, 1909. Although this piece illustrates his great gifts for long phrased melodies, the music has never enjoyed the success of the Second Concerto. In 1910, he completed the

Thirteen Preludes of his Op. 32 and his largest unaccompanied choral work, the *Liturgy of St. John Chrysostom*, Op. 31.

In the winter of 1912, after suffering from a stiffening of his fingers, Rachmaninoff took a vacation in Rome, where he began his largest orchestrated choral work, *The Bells*. The previous summer he had received a copy of Konstantin Balmont's translation of Edgar Allan Poe's poem of the same name. He completed the work while still in Rome. The first movement is full of vigor and a symbol of youth. The second movement, a soprano solo with choral interjections in a rocking figure, is for the golden bells of marriage. He gives this movement a passionate melodic line for the solo voice. The third movement, a scherzo, is without solos and depicts a relentless terror. The finale is quite still and with a solo baritone and recurring chords suggesting the approach of death. In fact, the central part of the section uses a chromatism for Poe's lines about the fiend who dwells in the belfry, and then it ends on the serenity of D flat on the last verse of Poe's poem.

World War I, his father's death in 1916, and the Bolshevik Revolution of 1917 were extremely hard on Rachmaninoff. He and his family left Russia permanently just before Christmas of that year. First they went to Scandinavia, and then to the United States, where he took up a performing career that would last for the rest of his life. During the 1920's and 1930's, he became an incomparable pianist whose theory of a performance centered on making every piece have a culminating point that had to be approached with exact calculation. His playing always had, in addition, a pronounced rhythmic drive, precision, and clarity.

In the United States, Charles Ellis arranged his tours and Victor-RCA did all of his recordings. From 1924 onward, he began to alter his American tours so as to spend time in Europe, first at Dresden; then finally he made Lucerne, Switzerland, his home. It was also at this time that he founded a musical publishing house in Paris called Tair. When, in 1930, he coauthored a letter to *The New York Times* that was critical of the Soviet Union, his music was condemned by the Soviets. In 1931 he resumed composing after a ten-year dry spell. This work was a solo set of variations for the piano on a theme of Marie Corelli and inaugurates his last creative period.

In 1933, Rachmaninoff began work on his *Rhapsody on a Theme by Paganini*, which he finished in August of 1934, giving its first performance on November 7. This piece was an immediate success and is technically his finest work. The rhapsody was written in a loose concerto form of three movements, or twenty-four variations: fast (1-10), slow (11-18), fast (19-24). They are all variations on Paganini's Violin Caprice in A Minor, which Rachmaninoff fully quotes in the second variation. In Variation 7 we get the *Dies irae* theme, which also ends the tenth variation. In Variation 14, the theme is inverted. Variation 17 is a darkly moving passage which leads to the central variation, 18, a highly lyrical modified inversion. Variation 19 starts the last section as a toccata with the rest of the variations increasing in crescendo to the *Dies irae* restatement concluding Variation 24. This is the most melodic and lyrical of all Rachmaninoff's music.

Rachmaninoff returned to Switzerland, and from June to August of 1937 he wrote his Third Symphony. In 1940, he finished his last masterwork, the *Symphonic Dances* of the Op. 45. It was first performed by Eugene Ormandy and the Philadelphia Orchestra on January 3, 1941. Here is a piece of deep chromaticism and contrasting textures. It is especially famous for its long melodic lines in the central section carried by the solo alto saxophone. It ends, humorously, with a quote from his failed First Symphony.

Rachmaninoff's health collapsed in 1942, and in February of 1943 he was brought to his home in Beverly Hills, where he died of lung cancer on March 28, 1943.

Summary

Sergei Rachmaninoff's career has all of the pathos of a Romantic novel wherein the hero is at first accepted, then rejected for another lover, undergoes much travail, and is finally reaccepted. After the ups and downs of Rachmaninoff's career, can anyone wonder why this Romantic hero of music is renowned for his compositions of deep melancholy and a rich lyricism of unremitting sadness? Rachmaninoff's music deeply reflects the inner torment of his own soul's journey through life. It was truly his own life that he saw in Boeklin's picture, *The Isle of the Dead* of 1880, that found such a responsive chord for Rachmaninoff's work of 1909. Perhaps it is because human life oscillates between hope and despair that Rachmaninoff's music will always touch the heart of humanity. Rachmaninoff may be considered the last romanticist. His music is melodic and melancholic. Though he was out of joint with twentieth century music and disliked by two other émigré Russian composers, Sergei Prokofiev and Igor Stravinsky, his music is so lush and beautifully moving that he has found a permanent place in the contemporary repertoire.

Bibliography

Bertensson, Sergei, and Jay Leyda. *Sergei Rachmaninoff: A Lifetime in Music*. New York: New York University Press, 1956. This is the definitive biography of Rachmaninoff and is must reading for anyone interested in the composer. The research on this book is extraordinary and the whole benefits from the intimate recollections of Rachmaninoff's cousin, Sophia Satina.

Cross, Milton, and David Ewen. *Encyclopedia of the Great Composers and Their Music*. Rev. ed. Vol. 2. Garden City, N.Y.: Doubleday, 1962. Pages 598-608 are an excellent and succinct starting place for those who enjoy Rachmaninoff's music. The "analytical notes" on the composer's major works are particularly helpful for the nonspecialist.

Norris, Geoffrey. *Rachmaninov*. London: J. M. Dent and Sons, 1976. This book is well worth the reader's effort. It is conveniently divided into a biography and a thoroughgoing analysis of Rachmaninoff's works, including useful piano parts. Also, there is a biographical calendar and a very useful catalog of his works.

Rachmaninoff, Sergei. *Rachmaninoff's Recollections*. Translated by Dolly Rutherford. Reprint. Freeport, N.Y.: Books for Libraries Press, 1970. This is a controversial book, because, after the composer's many conversations with the editor, the final product angered Rachmaninoff. Nevertheless, it is a very personal account, especially of his early life with a very important chapter on his psychiatric treatment by Dahl.

Seroff, Victor I. *Rachmaninoff*. Reprint. Freeport, N.Y.: Books for Libraries Press, 1970. A popular and very readable account of the composer's life. It is especially noteworthy for its photographic album of the composer.

Donald E. Davis

SIR CHANDRASEKHARA VENKATA RAMAN

Born: November 7, 1888; Trichinopoly (Tiruchirapalli), India
Died: November 21, 1970; Bangalore, India
Areas of Achievement: Physics, physiology, and education
Contribution: Raman, the first internationally acclaimed Indian physicist to be entirely educated within India, was awarded the Nobel Prize in Physics in 1930 for his discovery of important characteristics of light scattering. Raman also made significant contributions to the education of Indian students, establishing the Raman Research Institute in Bangalore in 1948.

Early Life
Sir Chandrasekhara Venkata Raman was born in Trichinopoly, India, on November 7, 1888. He was born into a family of academicians. His father, Chandrasekhara Iyer, was a professor of mathematics and physics, and his mother, the former Parvathi Ammal, was from a family of well-known Sanskrit scholars. His family's income was considered modest at that time in India, and Raman was the second eldest of eight children.

In 1892, while Raman was still a child, his father accepted a position at Mrs. A. V. N. College in the city of Vishakhapatnam, in Andhra Pradesh Province. There, Raman early demonstrated his academic prowess, finishing his secondary education at eleven years of age and immediately entering Mrs. A. V. N. College. Raman completed two years there and entered Presidency College in Madras. Raman continued to manifest his brilliance, receiving his B.A. with honors in English and physics at age fifteen. Raman was not well enough to travel abroad to study as did his peers. Instead, he pursued his postgraduate education at Presidency College, completing his M.A. in 1907, again with honors at the top of his class.

By the time Raman had completed his M.A., he had already begun intense study of available literature on physics, with special interest in the physics of light and of stringed instruments. In November, 1906, Raman saw his first paper published in the British *Philosophical Magazine* on "unsymmetrical diffraction bands caused by a rectangular aperture, observed when light is reflected very obliquely at the face of a prism."

Yet Raman had exhausted the available educational routes in India. Since he was unable to travel, his academic career essentially ended, he applied to take the examination in the Indian civil service, on which he scored top marks. Such positions were highly respected and well paid. Before entering the civil service, Raman married Lokasundari Ammal and in late 1907 moved his new family to Calcutta, where he had been assigned assistant accountant general.

Before the end of 1907, Raman discovered that only a few blocks from his residence was the Indian Association for the Cultivation of Science. The association had fallen on hard times, chiefly because of lack of interest and attention. Raman changed all that, spending nearly all of his spare time at the association for the next ten years and actively pursuing his own research interests in a carefully defined research program that he designed chiefly on his own initiative. During those years, Raman published frequently in his chosen area—primarily the physics of stringed instruments and acoustics—in such publications as *Nature, Bulletin of the Indian Association for the Cultivation of Science, Physical Review,* and the *Philosophical Magazine.*

Life's Work

By 1917, Raman's reputation had been well established so that he was offered the Sir Tarakanath Palit chair in physics at the University of Calcutta. Again, however, Raman was required to study abroad and he refused. Vice Chancellor Asutosh Mookerjee judiciously recognized Raman as the ideal person to occupy the newly established position and was so impressed by Raman's expertise that he waived the requirement, allowing Raman to accept the post.

Raman's move to the University of Calcutta signaled significant changes in his life. He could no longer claim the leadership position at the Indian Association for the Cultivation of Science, and his salary was reduced by at least three quarters. He also moved from a path of studies on the physics of stringed instruments and drums to focus on the physics of light and optics.

Four years after he entered the University of Calcutta, he had become a fully participating faculty member, teaching, lecturing, and helping to establish a fully developed graduate curriculum. For the first time in his career, in 1921, Raman traveled outside India to the Congress of Universities of the British Empire in Oxford. In England, Raman presented the first of his many lectures to be given abroad to the Physical Society about his research activities. On his return to Calcutta, he made the observation that would ultimately lead him to win the Nobel Prize in Physics.

As his ship plowed the blue waters of the Mediterranean Sea, Raman commented on its "wonderful blue opalescence." He also recognized that the blue was a result of the scattering of the light by the water itself and not the reflection of the sky, as was widely accepted at the time. This single observation would focus his career. Even as his ship headed toward home, Raman conducted a simple experiment that confirmed his suspicion. Soon after his return to Calcutta, he published a paper in *Proceedings of the Royal Society* entitled, "On the Molecular Scattering of Light in Water and the Colour of the Sea." He was so delighted at uncovering this apparently pristine area of scientific investigation that he began to focus nearly all of his research in uncovering other aspects of the physics of light.

In 1923, Raman and graduate student K. R. Ramanathan were conducting observations in light scattering through highly purified glycerine, when a phenomenon that would later be called the Raman effect was first discovered. It was a barely detectable trace of light, shifted to either side of the primary optical spectra of the glycerine.

Raman and his associates first suspected that these very weak secondary reflections that were shifted off the primary spectral trace were the result of impurities in the glycerine. They went to great lengths to purify the glycerine before the light was passed through again. Yet the secondary reflections were still present and undiminished no matter how pure the substance. It became obvious to Raman that these secondary reflections were the result of an inherent characteristic of the matter under investigation. Similar results could be observed in liquids, solids, and gases, but the effect was so weak that conventional methods could not magnify the reflections sufficiently for detailed study.

As Raman's group raced to understand the effect, they discovered that if they used a mercury arc lamp, which produced a very intense beam of monochromatic light (light of a single wavelength), they could study the fractional secondary wavelengths reflected. They soon discovered that these secondary reflections revealed aspects of the molecular structure itself. It was a tool of immense importance to physicists and chemists. In 1928, Raman and his colleagues published their results in the *Indian Journal of Physics*. His discovery was of such consequence that, in only a year's time, he was designated a Knight of the British Empire. In 1930, Sir Raman was awarded the Hughes Medal from the Royal Society and won the Nobel Prize in Physics on December 10, 1930, in Stockholm, Sweden.

Raman was ever devoted to the education of Indian students and knew well that the prominence of his nation in the world largely depended on its scientific literacy. Raman would state, "There is only one solution for India's economic problems, and that is science, science and still more science." Raman had already founded the *Indian Journal of Science* and in 1934 would found the Indian Academy of Sciences and its publication *Proceedings*.

In 1933, Raman left his university post to accept the directorship of the Indian Institute of Science in Bangalore. There, he poured the full intensity of his personality to gather a world-class faculty. Unfortunately, his personality did not harmonize with those of the board of directors, and, after only three years as its director, Raman was forced to resign, becoming a professor there. He resigned that post also in 1948.

That year, Raman accepted the directorship of the newly created Raman Research Institute in Bangalore. India had just become independent from Great Britain, and Raman was named national professor. Raman and his students continued studies in optics and reflected light. As he studied the reflection of color from roses in his rose gardens, he became fascinated with the physiology of vision. By 1968, on his eightieth birthday, he had published forty-three papers on vision in a book entitled *The Physiology of Vision*.

Still building the Raman Research Institute and maintaining an active lecture and teaching schedule, he was awarded in 1954 the highest honor of the Indian people—the "Bharat Ratna," or "The Jewel of India." Raman died while still active on November 21, 1970, at the age of eighty-two. He was cremated in one of his rose gardens, as he had requested.

Summary

Sir Chandrasekhara Venkata Raman has been described as one of the last true "natural philosophers of science." He was able to blend a conscious love for nature into a fully developed scientific investigation as was evidenced by his observations of the blue of the sea, of stringed musical instruments, and even of the color of roses and how it relates to the act of vision. Raman's guileless approach to science formed the basis for his life's work, but the consequences of his life's work carried other, far-reaching impressions.

Raman's insistence on remaining in India to complete his education later became the foundation for his motivation to make Indian educational institutions second to none and to provide world-class institutions of learning for Indian students. Raman's influence on science, education, and the spirit of nationalism in the newly independent nation of India was far-reaching. His personal work in establishing so many of India's influential publications and institutions has had a profound impact on India's economic development and social evolution in the world. The Raman effect has experienced a resurgence of interest. With the advent of the laser, a very powerful, monochromatic beam of light, the Raman effect has been used extensively to investigate the molecular characteristics of many substances.

Bibliography

Blanpied, William A. "Pioneer Scientists in Pre-Independent India." *Physics Today* 34 (May, 1986): 36-49. Depicts the life of Raman in a historical perspective in reference to his peers. Demonstrates how Raman influenced his nation's political affairs.

Jayaraman, Aiyasami, and Anant Krishna Ramdas. "Chandrasekhara Venkata Raman, India's Great Savant of Science." *Physics Today* 41 (August, 1988): 56-64. This article was written by one of Raman's close associates and one of his students. It details, in a close and intimate account, the life of Raman. Displays Raman in a very personal way from his early years to his death.

Mehra, Jagdish. "Raman, Chandrasekhara Venkata." In *Dictionary of Scientific Biography*, edited by Charles Coulston Gillispie. New York: Charles Scribner's Sons, 1984. This widely referenced account of Raman's life involves some technical references about his work and chronologically details his life for the general reader. The emphasis is on the details of his life but it does list some relevant equations connected to the Raman effect and other work.

Weber, Robert L. *Pioneers of Science: Nobel Prize Winners in Physics.* London: Institute of Physics, 1980. Details in a chronological order all the winners of the Nobel Prize in Physics to 1980. Provides a sketch of Raman and with the adjoining references shows the applications of his work.

Dennis Chamberland

KNUD JOHAN VICTOR RASMUSSEN

Born: June 7, 1879; Jakobshavn, Greenland
Died: December 21, 1933; Gentofte, Denmark
Areas of Achievement: Exploration, geography, and anthropology
Contribution: A pioneer Arctic explorer, Rasmussen was best known for his
  seven Thule expeditions. In the fifth, the most famous of these, he
  crossed North America from Greenland to the Bering Strait. A celebrated
  ethnographer, Rasmussen studied the folkways of the Eskimos and published many works about the peoples and places of Arctic America.

Early Life
Knud Johan Victor Rasmussen was born on June 7, 1879, in the Lutheran
parsonage at Jakobshavn, Greenland. This Danish settlement was situated
halfway up the western coast of Greenland. The eldest son of Christian
Rasmussen, a Danish missionary in Greenland for twenty-eight years, who
later became a lector in Greenlandic studies at the University of Copenhagen, Knud was exposed to exploration and ethnography in early
childhood. His father took as his parish the entire northern half of colonized
Greenland, often working his way by dogsled up the west coast of the island
to visit his five remote preaching stations. An excellent linguist who later
produced both a Greenlandic grammar and dictionary, the elder Rasmussen
taught Knud to regard all Greenlanders as his brothers, and Knud responded
by learning their ways and developing a love for them that never waned.

Rasmussen's mother was herself part Eskimo. Her father, Knud Fleischer,
had been born in Greenland of Norwegian parents. Becoming a colonial
administrator for the Danes as well as a successful trader, Fleischer married
an Eskimo woman. Young Rasmussen grew up celebrating his dual heritage—the Scandinavian (Danish and Norwegian) and the Eskimo.

Rasmussen recalled his childhood as a happy one. From the parsonage, he
could view Disko Island, the largest off the coast of Greenland, as well as
the great glacier and the spring icebergs. Fascinated by the North, Rasmussen rejoiced in a childhood trip with his father and Riis Carstensen, an
explorer, to visit his uncle, Carl Fleischer, who headed the Danish settlement at Qeqertak. This Greenland childhood determined the direction of
Rasmussen's later life. Two additional influences affected Rasmussen's development. In 1888, Fridtjof Nansen attempted the first complete crossing of
Greenland, an adventure that had a profound influence on the lad. The impact of his Aunt Helga, his first teacher, was equally decisive. It filled him
with a profound love for the ways of Greenland.

Reluctantly, Rasmussen left Greenland for Denmark. Failing his entrance
examinations for the Herlufsholm School, Rasmussen studied in Copenhagen. He was not a particularly good student. Completing his baccalaureate

education at the University of Copenhagen (Rasmussen later was awarded a Ph.D. by his alma mater and an LL.B. by the University of Edinburgh), Rasmussen flirted with several occupations, such as acting, singing, and journalism. As a correspondent for the *Christian Daily* and the *Illustrated Times*, he went to Stockholm to cover the Nordic games; then, at age twenty-one, he went to Lapland to study reindeer breeding. Travels in Scandinavia's Northland, to Narvik and Tomso, reinforced his fascination with the Arctic.

Life's Work

At age twenty-three, Rasmussen began his life's work. He joined the Danish Literacy Expedition of Mylius-Erichsen, an ethnographer, Jorgen Brønland, a catechist, Count Harald Moltke, a painter and illustrator, and Alfred Bertelsen, a doctor, on an expedition to visit the most northern tribe in the world, the Polar Eskimos of upper Greenland. This voyage of 1902-1904 was followed in 1905 by an assignment from the Danish government to travel in Greenland with a group of Lapps to determine the feasibility of introducing the reindeer as an addition to the Eskimo economy. For the next two years, 1906-1908, Rasmussen lived among the Polar Eskimos, studying their folklore. By then it was becoming obvious that Rasmussen's ability to travel and hunt like the Eskimos was a phenomenal asset. He could speak their languages fluently and maintain friendly relations with them. Rasmussen was able to record much of their oral tradition before it disappeared with the onset of modern civilization.

Returning to Denmark in 1908, Rasmussen married Dagmar Andersen, daughter of Niels Andersen, state counselor, chairman of the Employers' Association, and considered one of Denmark's major entrepreneurs. Friends considered this marriage a major source of strength for Rasmussen. Within a year, Rasmussen had returned to the Arctic, serving the Danish government on an expedition for educational purposes in 1909. This fired his imagination and caused him to envision the possibility of founding a permanent base for additional explorations.

At the age of thirty, in 1910, Rasmussen established Thule, a center for trade and exploration among the Polar Eskimos. Trade in manufactured goods provided the economic support, but the real purpose of this base on the northwest coast of Greenland was not commercial but scientific. Thule became the starting point for seven expeditions. Rasmussen's timing was excellent. The discovery of the North Pole in 1909 had aroused considerable interest in the Arctic. Danish claims to the north of Greenland were being contested, and Rasmussen saw such a settlement as Thule as critical to establishing Danish sovereignty over the region. This opinion was vindicated in 1933, when the International Court of Justice at the Hague ruled against Norway and in favor of Denmark, recognizing Copenhagen's claims to all of

Greenland. Following a lecture tour to raise funds for building Thule, Rasmussen sailed to the Arctic. The harbor at Thule was open only twenty-five days of the year (August 1-25), and the environment was harsh. Rasmussen coped with these conditions and became the first to cross Melville Bay by sledge, demonstrating the feasibility of exploration from Thule.

On April 8, 1912, together with explorer Peter Freuchen, a longtime friend, Rasmussen led the first Thule expedition, crossing the Greenland ice cap from Thule to Independence Fjord. This feat had been attempted only once before, by Nansen in 1888, an event that had inspired Rasmussen as a child. This trip allowed Rasmussen to study Eskimo life and to formulate his theory as to their origins. Postulating their Asian origin, Rasmussen believed that American Indians and Eskimos were descended from prehistoric immigrants who came to the Americas across the Bering Strait. Upon the completion of the first Thule expedition, Rasmussen returned to Denmark to report on his scientific progress and to see his three-year-old daughter for the first time.

Though Denmark remained neutral during World War I, the European conflagration had consequences for the far North. Rasmussen continued his work, however, and a mapping expedition in 1914 was followed in 1916-1918 by a survey of the north coast of Greenland. In 1918, following a visit to Denmark, Rasmussen set out for Angmagssalik in eastern Greenland on an ethnographic expedition to collect Eskimo tales. This was completed in 1919. On the two-hundredth anniversary of the arrival in Greenland of Hans Egede, the pioneer Lutheran missionary, there was a royal visit by the King of Denmark to the island. This event in 1921 honoring "the Apostle of Greenland" encouraged Rasmussen to think in terms of further discoveries.

The fifth Thule expedition, Rasmussen's most famous journey, lasted from 1921 to 1924, and he explored Greenland, Baffin Island, and the Arctic Coast of America, the longest dogsled journey in history. Rasmussen traversed the American Arctic from the Atlantic to the Pacific, conducting a scientific study of virtually every Eskimo tribe in that region. The expedition began on September 7, 1921, at Upernavik and went from Greenland to the Bering Strait, arriving at Point Barrow, Alaska, on May 23, 1924. During this trip, Rasmussen traced Eskimo migration routes and observed the essential unity of Eskimo culture.

Rasmussen was an excellent communicator, and his works were widely published in Danish, Greenlandic, and English translation. Rasmussen's works included travelogs, collections of Eskimo mythology and songs, and scientific texts, as well as writings of cartographic, ethnographical, and archaeological significance. *Under nordenvindens svobe* (1906) and *Nye mennesker* (1905) appeared in English translation in 1908 under the single title *The People of the Polar North: A Record* and established his reputation. *Grønland Langs Polhavet: Udforskningen af Grønland fra Melvillebugten til*

Kap Morris Jesup (1919; *Greenland by the Polar Sea: The Story of the Thule Expedition from Melville Bay to Cape Morris Jessup*, 1921) introduced the earth's largest island to readers throughout the Western world and was followed within the decade by his account of the most extensive expedition yet to explore the Arctic, published as *Fra Grønland til Stillehavet* (1925; *Across Arctic America: Narrative of the Fifth Thule Expedition*, 1927). Rasmussen's work also included collections of Native American literature such as *Myster og sagn fra Grønland* (1921-1925; myths and sagas from Greenland).

Summary

Knud Johan Victor Rasmussen was honored by the world for his many scientific contributions and was a Knight of the Royal Order of Dannebrog (Denmark), a Commander of the Order of Saint Olav (Norway), a Commander of the White Rose (Finland), a Knight of the Royal Order of the North Star (Sweden), and a recipient of a Golden Medal of Merit from the Danish king, among other awards. Rasmussen was a member of many distinguished learned societies, including the Norwegian Geographical Society and the equivalent geographical societies of Sweden, Italy, and the United States as well as the Explorers' Club of New York and the Scientific Society in Lund, Sweden.

Explorer of the Arctic and famed ethnographer of the American Eskimos, Rasmussen was honored with doctorates from Danish and British universities and the Knud Rasmussen room in the National Museum in Copenhagen recalls his memory. More than sixteen thousand artifacts in that museum testify to the thoroughness of his work. On December 21, 1933, Rasmussen died near Copenhagen, at Gentofte, Denmark, of food poisoning contracted during his final expedition, complicated by influenza and pneumonia.

Bibliography

Croft, Andrew. *Polar Exploration*. 2d ed. London: Adam and Charles Black, 1947. More than a general survey of polar expeditions, this volume focuses on the more prominent explorations of the Arctic regions in the twentieth century. With eight maps and twenty-two illustrations, this text is organized into two parts. Part 1, entitled "The Arctic Regions," is especially relevant to the life of Rasmussen; it surveys the scientific exploration of the North and contains valuable discussion of Rasmussen's contribution to geographical knowledge in Greenland and Canada.

Freuchen, Peter. *Arctic Adventure: My Life in the Frozen North*. New York: Farrar and Rinehart, 1935. Freuchen was Rasmussen's best friend, and together they shared many interests and experiences. Enhanced with illustrations and maps, this book is more than a recollection of one man's life in the Arctic. Contains interesting vignettes of the region, its conditions, and peoples. Invaluable personal recollections and anecdotes.

_____. *I Sailed with Rasmussen*. New York: Julian Messner, 1958. This work is not an exhaustive scholarly work on Rasmussen but rather a collection of impressions of a dear friend. A vivid description that is supplemented by useful illustrations.

Stefansson, Vilhjalmur. *Greenland*. Garden City, N.Y.: Doubleday, Doran, 1942. An older work, this history of Greenland from the earliest times until the start of the 1940's remains a valuable introduction to the world that Rasmussen knew and loved. Readable and reliable, Stefansson's survey conveys a feel for a region that is as large as the combined twenty-six states east of the Mississippi. Particularly helpful are references to Rasmussen's works.

Williamson, Geoffrey. *Changing Greenland*. Introduction by Ole Bjørn Kraft. New York: Library Publishers, 1954. This survey of the history of Greenland from the arrival of the Vikings to the major changes of the 1950's is organized into two main sections. Part 1, entitled "Old Orders," helps place the life and labors of Rasmussen in proper chronological and sociological context.

C. George Fry

MAURICE RAVEL

Born: March 7, 1875; Ciboure, France
Died: December 28, 1937; Paris, France
Area of Achievement: Music
Contribution: Ravel was one of the most important composers during the first third of the twentieth century, working in many styles and in many different forms.

Early Life

Joseph Maurice Ravel was the first son of a French-Swiss engineer and a Basque woman he had met while working in Spain. After Ravel was born, he and his family moved to Paris. Although he would later write music based on Spanish and Basque themes and travel throughout Europe and the United States, Ravel would remain, at heart, a Parisian. Ravel's parents recognized and appreciated their son's early interest in music and spared no effort to send him to the best teachers they could find, starting at the age of six. From the ages of six through sixteen, Ravel moved quickly through the steps of a sound education in piano and music theory, gaining entrance into the Paris Conservatory in 1891. By 1895, when he left the conservatory, Ravel had already set his own style, which would upset the musical establishment.

Life's Work

Ravel was an active composer for forty years (1893-1932) before ill health prevented him from composing during the last five years of his life. Most of those forty years were spent ignoring the critics and fellow composers, who usually heaped abuse upon him from all sides until after his death. Many of the more avant-garde members of the musical scene before World War I either tended to criticize Ravel for being a poor copy of Claude Debussy or criticized both men for not following the lead of the German composers of the Richard Wagner school, while the establishment critics saw all the above, including Ravel, as a threat to the music with which they had grown up. After the war, Ravel was often considered old-fashioned by the more radical composers, who were looking at jazz, Dada, or the works of Arnold Schoenberg for their inspiration.

Ravel was not interested in composing in the grand Romantic and chromatic style of the German school, and, while he admired Debussy and Schoenberg, he had no desire to imitate them. Instead, Ravel sought inspiration in the French baroque and in Spanish and Basque folk music. Yet, while his inspirations were often found in the past, his musical language was near the cutting edge of the avant-garde. Performers, especially pianists, often found his music to be exactly what they were looking for when they looked for the best contemporary music. His major works, including *Pavane pour une in-*

fante défunte (1899), *Sonatina* (1905), *Valses noble et sentimental* (1911), *Le Tombeau de Couperin* (1917), and many others remain in the standard literature, while *Pavane pour une infante défunte* and *Le Tombeau de Couperin*, later orchestrated by Ravel, are also in the standard symphonic repertoire.

Ravel did not seek out publicity, but he nevertheless often found himself in the middle of controversy. In retrospect this is not surprising, since the French artistic scene at the turn of the century until the outbreak of World War I is now famous for its squabbling and even riots at premieres of new works of music and art. Perhaps the most famous controversy in which Ravel found himself was over the 1905 competition for the Prix de Rome (a contest in which a musician would be sent to study and compose in Rome for a year). The rejection of his work led to a major scandal fought out in the national press, which resulted in the resignation of the head of the Paris Conservatory.

Ravel also found himself in the middle of another scandal in early 1907. He had composed five humorous settings for five rather obscurely written poems by Jules Renard, which Ravel entitled *Histoires naturelles*, and in January, 1907, they were performed at the National Society of Music, most of whose members preferred the music of Wagner to that of the emerging school of French modernists. Most of the audience hissed at the work, and the critics lambasted it, one implying the music was a bad echo of Debussy. All those who did not like the music missed the humor, perhaps because they had made so much noise they had not really heard the music. Again the French newspapers took sides, and Ravel's music was debated for weeks. Ravel ignored the entire affair and spent the time finishing his comic opera *L'Heure espagnole*, although it was not produced until 1911. Ravel continued this basic pattern up until World War I, composing works that would stir up opposition when they were first performed, even if they gained almost immediate acceptance by musicians, while he went on to produce another work. While Ravel was never a prolific composer, the years 1905-1914 were easily his most productive.

World War I changed Ravel's personal world, just as it changed Europe. Ravel was not physically fit for the French army, but he managed to use his influence and was allowed to go to a training camp in 1915 with the possibility of later joining the new air force. Ravel never got to join the air force, but he did join the Motor Transport Corps as a driver in March, 1916. By May, his health had started to give way, and he was in various hospitals and rest camps for the rest of 1916. The year 1917 started with the death of his mother, something from which the very attached Ravel never completely recovered, and Ravel never really was active in the military afterward, as he suffered from insomnia and general poor health. It was during 1916, however, that Ravel, along with most other French musicians, opposed a plan to ban German music from France for the duration of the war. The letter Ravel wrote on the subject was one of the better-known objections to the plan.

Although Ravel wrote two of his most famous works, *Le Tombeau de Couperin* and *Le Valse* (1919), and the first versions of his Sonata for Violin and Cello (1920, 1922) and his second opera, *L'Enfante et les sortilèges* (1920, 1925), between 1917 and 1920, his musical output had slowed down, his health never completely recovered, and he would only get progressively worse as the years went by. Although Ravel would still produce a few more masterpieces (two piano concertos, a sonata for violin, and, in 1928, his famous short ballet piece *Bolero*), he worked less and less, until, by 1933, Ravel was unable to complete any more projects, although he occasionally thought about trying to start one. At times, especially in the middle of 1933, he was unable even to sign his name.

Ravel spent the last few years of his life traveling and receiving friends at his house outside Paris, although he at times seemed unaware of his surroundings. He had undergone various medical treatments, but none had had any positive effect. As his health became worse, it was decided to operate on Ravel for a possible brain tumor on December 19, 1937. No evidence of a tumor was found, and Ravel's decline increased. He died nine days after the operation.

Summary

Maurice Ravel's works are some of the most important French compositions of the early twentieth century as well as the hardest to define. In many respects, Ravel's music encompasses French music since the early baroque, and European music since Hector Berlioz. Elements and forms from all these styles, as well as Spanish and Basque folk elements, were quoted or used by Ravel throughout his career. So while in some respects Ravel was near the forefront of musical exploration, his use of these conservative elements disturbed most radicals, even as the way he used them bothered the musical establishment of his era. Ravel was determined to compose music that he believed would project the mood and themes he wished to convey, rather than being consistent within any set style.

For the most part, Ravel worked mainly in the areas of vocal, chamber, and piano music, and it is in these works that Ravel's many varieties of style show themselves best. For the most part, as far as the general musical audience is concerned, he is best known for his larger symphonic works such as *Bolero* and for the orchestrations he made, for his own piano works and those of others, especially Modest Mussorgsky's *Pictures at an Exhibition* (1922).

Ravel's direct influence was limited to a small group of students, best known as interpreters of Ravel and other twentieth century piano composers. His indirect influences, especially in the area of orchestration, are harder to define yet are nevertheless important. His compositions were meant to illustrate ideas and feelings not to overwhelm the senses as much music of the previous generation had. At the same time, Ravel meant to stay within the basic confines of French music, although he felt free to recombine those elements as he saw fit. His genius was his eclecticism and taste.

Bibliography

Demuth, Norman. *Ravel*. London: J. M. Dent and Sons, 1947. Part of the Master Musicians series, this work has a short but complete biography of the composer but devotes more than three-quarters of the volume to competent academic analyses of Ravel's music.

James, Burnett. *Ravel, His Life and Times*. New York: Hippocrene Books, 1983. A successful attempt to integrate Ravel's life and music with the more general social and cultural context of the composer's life.

Jankélévitch, Vladimir. *Ravel*. Translated by Margaret Crosland. Reprint. Westport, Conn.: Greenwood Press, 1976. Although it has a short biography, this work is distinguished by its musical and dramatic critiques of Ravel's music, especially the ballets. The analysis comes more from a romantic tradition than an academic one and includes a detailed chronology of Ravel's work.

Myers, Rollo H. *Ravel*. New York: Thomas Yoseloff, 1960. Although the biographical and analytical sections are fairly standard, this work also includes Alexis Roland-Manuel's 1937 memorial essay and Ravel's 1916 letter from the Western Front opposing the ban of German music from performance in France.

Nichols, Roger, ed. *Ravel Remembered*. New York: W. W. Norton, 1988. Ravel's life as told through letters, diaries, and other accounts by those who knew him. Nichols places these anecdotes into context when necessary but prefers to let the memories speak for themselves as much as possible.

Orenstein, Arbie. *Ravel: Man and Musician*. New York: Columbia University Press, 1975. Although the biographical section is only a standard account, this work does include more than forty illustrations. More important, it contains excellent discussions of Ravel's musical aesthetics and creative process.

Roland-Manuel, Alexis. *Maurice Ravel*. Translated by Cynthia Jolly. Reprint. New York: Dover, 1972. An interesting and honest appraisal of Ravel's life and work, originally written in French in 1938 and translated in 1947. Roland-Manuel was both a pupil and friend of Ravel, and the book includes a detailed list of Ravel's compositions.

Terrance L. Lewis

SATYAJIT RAY

Born: May 2, 1921; Calcutta, India

Area of Achievement: Film

Contribution: Ray is India's most distinguished film director, responsible for gaining Indian cinema international recognition and rescuing it from a reputation for indiscriminate productivity and vulgar escapism. For more than thirty years, his films not only have established him as a moving force in world cinema but also have provided Western audiences with profound insights into Indian life and have inspired a generation of Indian filmmakers to follow his lead in producing films of serious social comment.

Early Life

Satyajit Ray comes from a distinguished Bengali family whose members have made lasting contributions to the intellectual life of their country. His grandfather, Upendra Kishore, was an artist and illustrator who established a publishing house (U. Ray and Sons), which Ray's father, Sukumar, later headed. Upendra was friendly with Rabindranath Tagore, Bengal's most distinguished intellectual and social visionary, who would later take an interest in the education of his friend's grandson. Both Upendra and Sukumar were directly influenced by a group of Bengali reformers known as the Brahmo Samaj, who in the late nineteenth century tried to introduce into their society progressive European ideas (notably relating to the education of women and the condition of the underclass) without disturbing the best of native traditions. Satyajit Ray inherited much of his own universalism and concern over the tensions between ancient and modern social forces from the tradition of Brahmoism.

Ray was only two years old when his father, who had already established a considerable reputation as an artist and publisher, died; the press had to be sold to pay the family's debts. He and his mother, Suprabha, went to live with her brother and his family. Like his grandfather, Ray completed his secondary education and higher education at Presidency College in Calcutta, from which he was graduated in economics in 1940. He was then persuaded to go to Santineketan, the art center founded by Tagore for the purpose of creating a new generation of Bengali artists and intellectuals who would make careers for themselves faithful to the tenets of the progressive spirit of Brahmoism. Ray spent two and a half years in this intellectually encouraging atmosphere, gradually developing his inherited talent as an artist and deepening his acquaintance with the major figures in world cinema. Leaving Santineketan during World War II, Ray eventually found work as a commercial artist for the British firm of J. Keymer, for whom he worked until he turned his attention entirely to filmmaking.

Various events confirm a move in this direction in the years around Indian independence (1948). In 1947, he helped to establish the Calcutta Film Society and began to try his hand at writing articles on film. He was further encouraged by the arrival in Calcutta in 1950 of Jean Renoir to film *The River*. Finally his firm sent him to London for six months in 1950, where by his own account he saw ninety-nine films: among them were several Italian neorealist films, including Vittorio De Sica's *The Bicycle Thief* (1948), wherein Ray noted the potency of a family drama springing from an immediate economic crisis and the appeal of using nonprofessional actors. By the time he returned to Calcutta in late 1950, Ray not only knew he was to be a film director but also already had a complete draft of his first screenplay: an adaptation of a very popular Bengali novel, Bibhuti-Bhusan Banerji's *Pather panchali* (1929; *Pather Panchali: Song of the Road*, 1968).

Life's Work

The film *Pather Panchali* was only completed in 1955 after enormous difficulties (including the pawning of family jewelry and books). This unblinkingly honest portrayal of life in an Indian village won immediate international acclaim in New York and at the 1956 Cannes Film Festival. It gave Ray the confidence (and funds) he needed to complete the trilogy on the life of his hero Apu from birth to maturity. His second film, *Aparajito* (1956; *The Unvanquished*), moves from the death of the father to Apu's education in Calcutta. It won the Golden Lion in Venice, 1957. The final film of the trilogy is *Apu Sansar* (1959; *The World of Apu*), which shows the hero as an aspiring novelist, the circumstances of his marriage, and the tragic death of his young wife.

Before completing the Apu trilogy, Ray made a subtle masterpiece in *Jalsaghar* (1958; *The Music Room*). Music and cultural reference are the means whereby the director dramatizes the decline of a representative of the landowning class in the 1920's. Characteristic of Ray is his sympathy for a character whose indolence brings about his own tragedy.

Social tensions within the Indian past are the inspiration of *Devi* (1960; *The Goddess*) and the superb *Charulata* (1964; *The Lonely Wife*). The former takes controversial issue with religious fanaticism. A zamindar (feudal landlord) drives his favorite daughter-in-law, Daya, to madness and death through his obsessive conviction that she is the reincarnation of the goddess Kali. The latter, set in Calcutta in 1879, is a profound study of a wife neglected by her publisher husband and drawn to his sensitive cousin Amal. Clearly Ray does not see the problems of women imprisoned by the taboos of Indian society as frozen in the historical past but as unresolved contradictions in independent India.

As part of the centenary of the birth of Tagore, Ray was commissioned to make a documentary of the poet's life: *Rabindranath Tagore* (1961). The completed film is a reminder of the debt that all Bengalis owe to this protean artist and of the personal relationship between the Rays and the Tagores. Among the themes of progressive Brahmoism both inherited and embodied by Tagore is that of the rights of women; this idea is precisely what is incorporated into Ray's first color film, *Kanchenjungha* (1962), and *Mahanagar* (1963; *The Big City*). From the interwoven crises of the vacationing family in *Kanchenjungha* may be isolated the gentle rebellion of a younger daughter strong enough to choose continuing education over an arranged marriage and the sense of the decline of a once-dominant paternal authority. *Mahanagar* concentrates on the economic struggles of the lower-middle class, with a wife leaving prejudice and her own fears behind to find a job and enjoy her new independence. She must also face unaccustomed problems in the commercial world, such as defending a fired coworker and fending off the boss.

The late 1960's was a time of turmoil in Bengal, seeing rising unemployment, ethnic and religious violence, and food riots in Calcutta. The tensions of an unwieldly twenty-year-old democracy were threatening its stability. None of these social conflicts is directly observed in Ray's films, a fact that has brought him into polemical discussion with such overtly political filmmakers as Mrinal Sen. Ray, however, is neither aesthete nor escapist. To chronicle social change over a vast historical canvas—and via psychological relationships—requires a measure of serene detachment. His hollow men of *Kapurush-o-Mahapurush* (1965; *The Coward and the Saint*) and *Nayak* (1966; *The Hero*) are both products of a modern world that demands compromise and punishes forthrightness. At least twice Ray has escaped into fantasy: *Goopi Gyne Bagha Byne* (1969; *The Adventures of Goopi and Bagha*) and *Hirok Rajar Deshe* (1980; *The Kingdom of Diamonds*). Based on stories by his grandfather Upendra Kishore, they reflect a fidelity to a family tradition of writing and drawing for children. Both Ray's grandfather and father published a children's magazine, *Sandesh*, which Ray revived in the early 1960's.

Ray's experience in the business world lies behind an informal trilogy made in the early 1970's based on studies of a confused Calcutta intelligentsia trying to define its place in a world that belittles tradition and proclaims self-interest above conscience. These films are *Aranyer din Ratri* (1970; *Days and Nights in the Forest*), *Pratidwandi* (1970; *The Adversary*), and *Simabaddha* (1971; *Company Limited*). To these one can add an epilogue, *Dahana-Aranja* (1975; *The Middleman*), a variation on the theme of modern forms of corruption. *Days and Nights in the Forest* is Ray's finest film since *The Lonely Wife*. It is a film of dislocation: Four self-satisfied urban professionals are removed to a natural setting and observed as they come face to face with their limitations. The results are unsettling but not without some salutary chastening.

Ashani Sanket (1973; *Distant Thunder*) reveals the dramatic impact of war on a distant Bengal village. The images of starvation serve as a reminder that no one is immune to historical upheaval and as a response to Ray's critics, who have accused him of remaining aloof from the world's problems. "Outside observers" is an accurate description of the protagonists of Ray's film *Shatranj ke Kilhari* (1977; *The Chess Players*). This historical drama, which was produced in color, was Ray's first film in Urdu, the purpose being to attract a larger national audience.

With *Ghare-Baire* (1984; *The Home and the World*), Ray's career has come full circle. He had first written an adaptation of this important Tagore novel in 1948, but now, with thirty-six years of experience behind him, produced a far more sophisticated version. The film's structure, like the title, is dialectical, juxtaposing the values of domestic retirement and political commitment. The husband, Nikhil, urges his wife, Bimala, to interest herself in public events and introduces her to a friend, Sandip, a leader of the Swadeshi movement promoting independence from Great Britain (the year is 1905). Bimala soon recognizes that Sandip is a ruthless manipulator. In her understanding of her own independence and of the dangers of the charismatic Sandip one can sense the beliefs of Ray himself: his support of women's emancipation and his doubts regarding forms of political extremism.

Summary

Satyajit Ray is primarily a Bengali artist whose films successfully reflect the past and the present of his native land. He is in a direct line from those artists and intellectuals (in particular Rabindranath Tagore) who promoted the Bengali renaissance, which aimed at a vibrant renewal of the culture as well as progressive social reforms. In a country whose official language is Hindi and where the capital of the film industry is Bombay, Ray's fidelity to his native Bengali in his films has limited the countrywide appeal of his work. Nevertheless, his international standing as the man who liberated Indian cinema from its vacuous escapism has made of him its spokesman and informal ambassador abroad. Such prominence has not come smoothly. He has come under fire for overexposing India's problems of poverty, religious excess, and the status of women, while from the Left he has had to answer charges of aloofness or political indifference.

Ray's life, like that of most Indians, revolves around his family, a fact that gives a particular flavor to his films, which are so often studies of the intimate dynamics of family groups and married couples. The family serves as a microcosm of the world's events, the conflicts between parents and children or man and wife reflecting those between classes and competing ideologies. Undoubtedly this concentration on the small but accessible unit of human experience has enhanced the appeal of his films outside India to audiences in Europe and the United States. There is something familial, too, about his working methods, in the fidelity of a small number of inseparable associates with whom he has worked since the Apu trilogy, whose contributions to his work have added to its consistency and wholeness. However rooted he is in his native traditions, however provincial his stories seem to be, Ray has invested his characters and their lives with a universal humanity that viewers from East and West instantly recognize. He belongs to his home and to the world.

Bibliography

Das Gupta, Chidananga. *The Cinema of Satyajit Ray.* New Delhi: Vikas, 1980. A book written by a critic personally close to Ray and one of several publications timed to coincide with the twenty-fifth anniversary of the completion of *Pather Panchali.* Das Gupta places Ray firmly in the context of Bengali culture, emphasizing the importance of the late nineteenth century Bengal renaissance and the influence of Tagore.

Micciollo, Henri. *Satyajit Ray.* Lausanne: Éditions l'Âge d'Homme, 1981. A book designed to fill a void in European critical attention paid to Third World cinema, and in particular that of Ray. Includes a lengthy introduction placing Ray in the context of his own national cinema and interviews with Ray himself. Each film—up to *Pikoo's Day* (1980)—is given an extended sequence-by-sequence plot summary, followed by a lengthy formal and thematic analysis.

Nyce, Ben. *Satyajit Ray: A Study of His Films.* New York: Praeger, 1988. This is the first full-length study of Ray's film by an American critic, including analyses of his rarely seen documentaries and short subjects and a final chapter on *The Home and the World.* There is a brief recapitulation of biographical material and some clear notes on the director's cultural and historical roots.

Ray, Satyajit. *Satyajit Ray: An Anthology of Statements on Ray and by Ray.* Edited by Chidanada Das Gupta. New Delhi: Directorate of Film Festivals, Ministry of Information and Broadcasting, 1981. An indispensable volume for the student of Ray's career, published at the time of a complete retrospective of the director's work presented at the Bangalore Film Festival of 1980. Part 1 includes a summary of the plots of every film up to *Pikoo's Day,* followed by lengthy extracts from contemporary reviews, Indian and Western. The final section is an anthology of statements by Ray on all aspects of his art and working habits. No clearer summary of his career has been published.

Seton, Marie. *Portrait of a Director: Satyajit Ray.* Bloomington: Indiana University Press, 1971. While much of the material here has been outdated by later studies and developments in Ray's career itself, this remains the definitive biography up to the period of *Days and Nights in the Forest.* It includes a detailed account of Ray's ancestry and family history and of the way he lives and works. Provides fascinating background information on the production history and problems of the individual films. Includes interviews with Ray, articles by him, examples of his artwork and illustrations, and many excellent photographs.

Wood, Robin. *The Apu Trilogy.* New York: Praeger, 1971. A purely critical and largely formalist study of the Apu trilogy alone by a prolific critic and long-time associate. Those encountering the trilogy for the first time will find it a valuable introduction.

Harry Lawton

JEAN RENOIR

Born: September 15, 1894; Paris, France
Died: February 12, 1979; Los Angeles, California
Area of Achievement: Film
Contribution: Considered by many to be the world's greatest film director, Renoir explored his characters' relations to society and nature and their humanity during his forty-five-year career.

Early Life

Jean Renoir was born September 15, 1894, in Paris. His father, the Impressionist painter Pierre-Auguste Renoir, had married his mother, Aline Charigot, a dressmaker's assistant, in 1890, although the couple's first child, Pierre, had been born in 1885. Among the many artist friends of the elder Renoir who visited his country house at Essoyes were Edgar Degas and Claude Monet. Renoir later described growing up amid an extended family of artists, models, art dealers, relatives, and their children as the happiest time of his life. By 1901, his immediate family included his younger brother, Claude.

Beginning in 1903, the Renoirs lived much of the year at Les Collettes, a villa in Cagnes-sur-Mer near Nice, where Jean attended school. He was always a poor, restless student, and his parents hoped he would eventually find some career working with his hands. In 1913, after finishing his studies in philosophy at the Nice extension of the University of Aix-en-Provence, Renoir joined the cavalry, hoping to become an officer. He was a sergeant when World War I broke out, and, after being kicked by a horse, he transferred, over his parents' objections, to the infantry as a sublieutenant. In April, 1915, his thighbone was fractured by a bullet. Since Renoir's wound left him with a slight limp, he was unable to return to the infantry. With time on his hands, he began going to films and soon became addicted, seeing as many as twenty-five American movies a week. He persuaded his father (his mother died in 1915), confined to a wheelchair, to buy a projector so that they could watch Charlie Chaplin films together.

In 1917, Renoir fell in love at first sight with Andrée Heurschling, one of his father's models. Pierre-Auguste Renoir died in December, 1919, and Jean married Andrée on January 24, 1920. After working in ceramics with his brother Claude at Cagnes-sur-Mer for a while, Renoir moved to Paris in 1921, had a kiln built, and started a pottery enterprise. Ceramics did not fulfull Renoir's need to create, and the inheritance from his father afforded him the freedom to take his time deciding what to do with his life. His only child, Alain, was born in 1922. By 1923, he had decided to make films.

Life's Work

Through his brother Pierre, who had become an actor, Renoir met Albert

Dieudonné, later the star of Abel Gance's *Napoléon* (1927), who wanted the wealthy young man to finance a film for him. Renoir wrote *Une Vie sans joie* (1924; *A Joyless Life*), and Dieudonné directed and costarred, against her will, with Renoir's wife, now known as Catherine Hessling. Renoir and Dieudonné quarreled over the melodrama, leading to the latter's reediting the film and rereleasing it in 1927 as *Catherine*. Not discouraged by this experience, Renoir immediately directed his first film, beginning his lifelong custom of filling the cast and crew with his friends, making the experience of filming a friendly collaboration. (Renoir would direct thirty-six films, writing or cowriting twenty-eight of them.) Through such early works as *La Fille de l'eau* (1924), he learned the techniques of filmmaking, taking great pleasure, as an artisan, in creating scale models of landscapes and streets.

Inspired by the force of the director's personality in Erich von Stroheim's *Foolish Wives* (1922), Renoir made the most expensive French film up to 1926, adapting *Nana* from the novel by Émile Zola. The stylization of *Nana*, especially in Catherine Hessling's pantomime-like performance, indicated Renoir's originality and maturing talent, but, as with several later films, its quality was not recognized in France at the time. His next film, *Charleston* (1927), a dance fantasy shot in four days, also failed at the box office. The release of *La Petite Marchande d'allumettes* (1928; *The Little Match Girl*), from the story by his beloved Hans Christian Andersen, was delayed by a plagiarism suit brought by two writers who had created a stage version of the story. In the interim, talking pictures arrived, and Renoir was forced to add a bad sound track. After making two commissioned silent films, he played opposite his wife in two films directed by his friend Alberto Cavalcanti. Because he loved actors so much, Renoir believed he should try acting. He and Catherine separated in 1930.

Unlike many French directors, Renoir welcomed the advent of sound as offering new possibilities to the art of the cinema. He directed *On purge bébé* (1931), based on a Georges Feydeau farce, just to prove he could make a sound film quickly and cheaply. He deliberately chose a less commercial project as his next effort. The producers were so shocked by *La Chienne* (1931) that they drove him from the studio and called the police to keep him out. When they were unable to reedit the film, Renoir was allowed to restore his version. This early example of *film noir*, now considered one of Renoir's masterpieces, was another commercial failure.

La Nuit du carrefour (1932), an adaptation of a Georges Simenon novel, with Pierre Renoir as Inspector Maigret, was also a failure. Renoir considered it such a mess that even he did not understand it. Among his assistants on this film were his brother Claude and Jacques Becker, later a prominent director himself, whose sense of order helped compensate for Renoir's more informal approach to his work. In explaining his seemingly haphazard methods, Renoir said, "[Y]ou discover the content of a film in the process of making it." He followed with another masterpiece, *Boudu sauvé des eaux* (1932; *Boudu Saved from Drowning*), in which he continued the use of deep-focus cinematography, a technique he helped pioneer. Such films, with their fluid, seemingly improvisational styles, led the French cinema away from an overreliance on dialogue.

Despite such artistic successes, Renoir continued having difficulty with the practical side of filmmaking. Because *Madame Bovary* (1934), his adaptation of Gustave Flaubert's novel, was more than three hours long, the distributors shortened it into a largely incoherent state. Once again, the director recovered with a notable achievement, *Toni* (1934), the first of several films focusing on the individual's relation to society. His friendship with the Groupe Octobre, writers and artists with Communist leanings, influenced *Le Crime de M. Lange* (1936; *The Crime of Monsieur Lange*), in which workers form a cooperative to save a failing business.

Renoir combined his concern with society and his passion for nature in *Une Partie de campagne* (1946; *A Day in the Country*). The 1936 filming went more chaotically than usual, Renoir's usual happy family of collaborators turned against one other, and the director abandoned the film before it was completed. After World War II, Marguerite Renoir reedited it from the uncut negative saved by Henri Langlois, director of the Cinémathèque Française, and the film was finally released in 1946. (Marguerite Mathieu lived with Renoir from 1935 to 1940 and used his name even though they never married.) Despite all the problems, this bittersweet film is one of Renoir's most charming.

After *Les Bas-Fonds* (1936; *The Lower Depths*) got a lukewarm reception, the director made one of his most lasting achievements, *La Grande Illusion* (1937; *Grand Illusion*). Censors altered Renoir's version, and, while critics were enthusiastic about it, the public, anticipating another war, was disturbed by its pacifist message. The film was better received in the United States, running for twenty-six weeks at a New York theater. Using an uncut negative found in Munich by the American army, Renoir finally restored it to his original intentions in 1958.

After *La Marseillaise* (1938), his interpretation of the French Revolution, and *La Bête humaine* (1938; *The Human Beast*), another Zola adaptation, Renoir created *La Règle du jeu* (1939; *The Rules of the Game*), considered by many to be his finest film. It was made in typical Renoir fashion with the director and his collaborators writing the dialogue and choosing the locations as they needed them. Once the film was made, Renoir had to overcome editing problems and legal difficulties to arrive at his 113-minute cut. Distributors trimmed *La Règle du jeu* to eighty-five minutes, and it was eventually banned by the Vichy government as demoralizing and by the Nazi occupiers. The original negative was destroyed when the Allies bombed the Boulogne studios, but Renoir's version was restored in 1956 from more than two hundred cans of film and bits of sound track. Because of the film's reputation as one of the greatest ever made, the public perception of Renoir the person is as he appears here in his most notable acting performance. Tall, plump, energetic, with thinning reddish-blond hair, a perpetual gleam in his eye, and a gravelly voice, Renoir has been likened by critic Andrew Sarris to a dancing bear.

In 1939, France, fearing that Italy would side with Germany in the coming war, sent Renoir on an artistic diplomatic mission to Rome to teach a course in directing and make a film of Giacomo Puccini's opera *Tosca*. When Italy entered the war in June, 1940, he returned to Paris, leaving *Tosca* to be finished by Carl Koch, who had worked with Renoir on two earlier films. In February, 1941, Renoir sought refuge from the war by going to the United States accompanied by Dido Freire, script girl for *La Règle du jeu* and niece of Alberto Cavalcanti. They were married February 6, 1944, without realizing that his divorce from Catherine was legal only in America. Renoir had a villa built in Beverly Hills near the home of his cousin Gabrielle and her husband, the American painter Conrad Slade.

Beginning at Twentieth Century-Fox, Renoir the improviser had difficulty working in the highly structured Hollywood studio system. He surprised the Fox executives by rejecting their scripts dealing with French or European history, choosing instead a screenplay set in Georgia, and shocked them by choosing to film *Swamp Water* (1941) in the Okefenokee Swamp instead of on a Hollywood soundstage. He missed, however, working with his family of collaborators and later said his five American films "don't even come close to any ideal I have for my work" because of the studios' reluctance to take chances. He made only *The Diary of a Chambermaid* (1946) with his typical approach.

Instead of returning to France after this bitter experience, Renoir chose to make another English-language film, *The River* (1951), an adaptation of a Rumer Godden novel set in India. His first color film, with his nephew Claude, Pierre's son, as cinematographer, *The River* is one of his most beautifully lyrical works. After going to Italy for another visually striking film, *Le Carrosse d'or* (1953; *The Golden Coach*), Renoir finally returned to France, directing his play *Orvet* (1955) in Paris. He continued experimenting with color in his first French film in sixteen years, *French Cancan* (1955), but his poetic lyricism proved unfashionable in an age of cinematic realism. French critics attacked him for being more sentimental than he had been before the war. His next four films were also badly received, seemingly showing a loss of his former surety of tone and lightness of touch.

In 1960, he taught a theater course at the University of California, Berkeley, where his son was a professor of medieval literature. He published his first novel, *Les Cahiers du Capitaine Georges* (the notebooks of Captain Georges), in 1966 and wrote a biography of his father. His final cinematic work, *Le Petit Théâtre de Jean Renoir* (*The Little Theatre of Jean Renoir*), consisting of four short films, each introduced by Renoir, was released in 1970. He claimed he directed as much with his legs as with his head, and the pain from his old wound would no longer allow him to make films. He received a special Academy Award in 1975 and the French Legion of Honor in 1977 and spent his last decade writing his memoirs and three more novels.

Renoir became a naturalized American citizen in 1946 while maintaining his French citizenship. He lived in both Beverly Hills and Paris thereafter and died of a heart attack in Los Angeles on February 12, 1979. He was buried at Essoyes.

Summary

During the 1930's, Jean Renoir was considered one of the major French directors, along with Marcel Carné, René Clair, Jacques Feyder, and Julien Duvivier, although his work was believed to lack the polish and moral certainty of his rivals' work. By the 1950's, the auteur critics, including such future directors as Eric Rohmer, Jean-Luc Godard, and François Truffaut, paved the way for recognizing Renoir's genius. Truffaut, later speaking for his fellow New Wave directors, called Renoir "the father of us all." As films such as *La Grande Illusion* and *La Règle du jeu* were rereleased, filmgoers had the opportunity to see his best work as he intended it to be seen. Renoir's causal techniques and groping after tenuous truths appealed to the New Wave and to sophisticated audiences. For the most part, however, critics agree only that his films of the 1930's are masterpieces. The critical consensus is that while his movies after 1939 are interesting in the context of his entire output and are striking in places, they are inferior to his earlier work, often self-indulgent and aimless.

In addition to his effect on the New Wave directors, Renoir influenced the future directors who worked as his assistants, including such diverse talents as Luchino Visconti, Robert Aldrich, and Satyajit Ray. Those who have called him the greatest film director include Renoir's own idol, Charlie Chaplin. For critic Pierre Leprohon, Renoir is the true poet of the cinema, adhering to no theories, imitating no one, creating his art out of his experiences, his love of an imperfect world.

Bibliography

Bazin, André. *Jean Renoir.* Edited by François Truffaut. Translated by W. W. Halsey II and William H. Simon. New York: Simon & Schuster, 1973. Affectionate analysis of Renoir's work by the critic most responsible for the reevaluation of his career. May have become the definitive study had Bazin not died before completing it.

Braudy, Leo. *Jean Renoir: The World of His Films.* Garden City, N.Y.: Doubleday, 1972. Focuses on the contrasts in Renoir's films between theatricality and naturalism, improvisation and order, social commitment and aesthetic detachment. Good balance between considering Renoir as a craftsman and as a humanist. Includes a good brief summary of his life.

Durgnat, Raymond. *Jean Renoir.* Berkeley: University of California Press, 1974. Lengthy critical biography. Gives considerable background about the making of the films. Summarizes what other critics have said about Renoir. Perhaps the best all-round study of the director.

Leprohon, Pierre. *Jean Renoir.* Translated by Brigid Elson. New York: Crown, 1971. Excellent biographical sketch with excerpts from interviews with Renoir and commentaries by critics and friends.

Renoir, Jean. *My Life and My Films.* Translated by Norman Denny. New York: Atheneum, 1974. The director recalls the people and events associated with the making of his films. Discusses the influence on his work of Charlie Chaplin, D. W. Griffith, and Erich von Stroheim. Not that specific about the details of his life. Good for conveying Renoir's personality.

_____. *Renoir: My Father.* Translated by Randolph Weaver and Dorothy Weaver. Boston: Little, Brown, 1962. This memoir of his father is an excellent source of details about the director's childhood, some supplied by his cousin Gabrielle. Aids in understanding the father's influence on the son as artist and man.

_____. *Renoir on Renoir: Interviews, Essays, and Remarks.* Translated by Carol Volk. New York: Cambridge University Press, 1989. Collection of his comments on his work.

Sesouske, Alexander. *Jean Renoir: The French Films, 1924-1939.* Cambridge, Mass.: Harvard University Press, 1980. This study of the first half of the director's career provides accounts of the making of the films. Good analysis of Renoir's visual style. Written with the director's cooperation, it may be too reverential.

Michael Adams

SYNGMAN RHEE

Born: March 26, 1875; P'yŏngsan, Korea
Died: July 19, 1965; Honolulu, Hawaii
Areas of Achievement: Government and politics
Contribution: Rhee began his career as a student movement leader in the 1890's. In exile, he became the leader of an overseas movement to liberate Korea from Japanese rule between 1913 and 1945. He later became President of South Korea, holding that position throughout the Korean War.

Early Life
Syngman Rhee was born in 1875 in P'yŏngsan, Hwanghae Province, sixty miles north of Seoul. He was the only son of Yi Kyŏng-sŏn, a descendant of King T'aejong. Though impoverished by the passage of generations, Rhee's aristocratic family helped shape his character and endowed him with certain lifelong traits: a lonely devotion to principle over practicality, a fierce pride which demanded complete loyalty from others, and a surpassing ambition to lead, whether as a student in Seoul, an exiled Korean nationalist in the West, or president of the Republic of Korea (1948 to 1960).

As a boy, Rhee was schooled in the traditional way, learning the Chinese classics. In 1894, however, he entered Paejae Boys School, run by missionaries of the American Methodist Episcopal Church in Seoul. There he became a Christian. He also achieved notoriety as a student demonstrator in the Korean reform movement and as a member of the reformist Independence Club, for which he was arrested in 1898 and imprisoned by the Korean government for six years. In 1904 when he was released, American friends arranged for him to pursue his studies in the United States. He was enrolled in George Washington University where he earned a B.A. He earned an M.A. at Harvard and went on to Princeton for a Ph.D. in political science. The distinction of being the first Korean to earn a doctorate in the West created an enormous fund of respect for him among the education-conscious Koreans, both in their homeland and in exile.

Life's Work
In 1910, Korea was annexed to Japan and remained a colony for thirty-five years, until it was liberated by the Allied victory in 1945. Rhee spent most of this period in exile. He did return to Korea briefly after finishing his doctoral studies at Princeton and worked with the Young Men's Christian Association, but he was arrested again, this time by the Japanese during a roundup of Christian leaders who were thought to be involved in a conspiracy to assassinate the Japanese governor-general. He was soon released, but because he was a marked man his missionary associates had him sent back to

the United States as a delegate to a church convention. Once in the United States he stayed there, moving to Hawaii to establish himself as a Korean community leader. He founded a school, an association (the Tongji-hoe, one of the main Korean associations in America), and a magazine (the *Pacific Weekly*, in Korean). Though he was respected for his attainments, he was also a controversial figure who fell out with rivals and found it difficult to rise above the status of faction leader.

One of Rhee's main contributions was as a representative of the Korean Provisional Government (KPG), an exiled body formed in 1919 and head-quartered in Shanghai. Because of his wide reputation, Rhee was elected the KPG's first president, in 1919. He remained, however, in Washington for nearly two years, urging the case for Korean independence upon the United States Congress and various international bodies. When he finally arrived in Shanghai to assume the presidency of the provisional government, he found it very difficult to work with his compatriots and left after seventeen frustrating months. In 1921, he returned to his base in Hawaii, from which he ventured often on speaking tours to other parts of the United States, trying to influence American policy in favor of the cause of Korean independence from Japan. His campaign to get the United States government to recognize Korea in effect by treating him as an official representative was tireless and resourceful. His methods included offering to have Korean guerrillas fight the Japanese during World War II and demanding diplomatic immunity for himself when he was stopped for speeding by the District of Columbia police. Although he aroused considerable sympathy among American audiences who heard him speak, he came to be regarded as a nuisance by many in the diplomatic and policymaking establishment.

With the end of World War II and the American occupation of South Korea, however, Rhee became useful to General Douglas MacArthur, the Supreme Commander for the Allied Powers in Tokyo. He obtained Mac-Arthur's help in returning to Korea in October, 1945, and arrived back in Seoul as if to claim his destiny as leader of the independent Korean republic. Like most Koreans, Rhee was frustrated and upset by the fact that his homeland had been liberated from Japan only to be divided at the thirty-eighth parallel and reoccupied by the United States and the Soviet Union. He helped lead the fight against a short-lived proposal to put Korea under an international trusteeship. Then, as American and Soviet negotiators failed to agree on a slate of Korean leaders to form a combined Korean government, Rhee maneuvered himself into a commanding position for leadership in the south.

Rhee's rise was far from automatic. After his return in 1945, he was forced to overcome challenges from leaders of the China-based KPG and from Korean nationalist leaders who had spent the years of the Japanese occupation within Korea. He enjoyed surpassing advantages, however, in dealing with the American occupation authorities. His American training and command of English were key assets as he positioned himself. So was his political conservatism as the Americans suppressed the Left in South Korea and turned increasingly to right-wing interests to form the new government in their zone. In 1948, when a United Nations-sponsored election failed to unite Korea, separate republics were formed in the two zones. In August, Rhee was elected president by the newly formed National Assembly of the Republic of Korea (South Korea). In the same year in North Korea, the Soviet-sponsored Kim Il Sung became President of the Democratic People's Republic of Korea. By 1949, most of the American and Soviet forces had withdrawn, leaving the peninsula to the Rhee and Kim regimes.

As President of the Republic of Korea from 1948 to 1960, Syngman Rhee faced successive trials. The first was the quest for legitimacy: to be recognized as more than a factional leader domestically and an American client internationally, a quest in which he was never entirely successful. His greatest test was the Korean War (1950-1953), the direct result of the Allies' division of Korea in 1945 and Kim Il Sung's disastrous attempt to reunite the peninsula by force. The economic situation in Korea, already desperate because of the isolation of the developed north from the agricultural south, was rendered incomparably worse by the war's destruction, which flattened large areas of Seoul and the other cities (as it also destroyed the major cities in the north) and took the lives of an estimated two million Korean people. When the war ended in stalemate, again roughly along the thirty-eighth parallel, Rhee was confronted with the forbidding task of reconstruction. Although large amounts of American and international aid poured into South Korea in the 1950's, it took many years to show results. With the populace demoralized it proved to be a very poor climate in which to develop new political traditions. Corruption flourished, and as Rhee aged and grew more isolated, his political organization became more obsessed with power and its privileges. The Rhee years were marked by stolen elections, constitutional amendments to perpetuate his party in power, repression by police, and organized youth gangs that mocked the government's proclaimed ideals. In 1959, the forcible passage of a series of laws including a National Security Law that was plainly intended to punish political opponents in the name of national defense, led to a wave of popular revulsion against the Rhee regime.

The quadrennial presidential election of 1960 pitted Rhee against an opposition candidate who died of natural causes during the campaign. Rhee, at age eighty-four, therefore won a fourth term by default. The election of his vice presidential running mate, however, required widespread fraud and voter intimidation. There was so much irregularity in the voting that demonstrations broke out demanding a new election. The demonstrations turned into student-led riots in April, 1960. These were answered by police bullets and heavy loss of life on April 19. Martial law was declared, and, after attempting to bargain with the demonstrators and the National Assembly, Rhee finally was persuaded to resign the presidency. Within weeks he left Seoul for the last time and flew with his wife to Hawaii. In Honolulu, he spent his last years and died at the age of ninety, on July 19, 1965.

Summary

Despite his flaws Syngman Rhee is remembered by Koreans with a special kind of reverence. His fiery nationalism was always a source of pride in a country so victimized by foreigners. He is admired for the years he spent in exile working in the nearly hopeless cause of Korean independence, for his leadership in the Korean-American community, and for bringing South Korea through the war. Rhee believed that the division of Korea was a great injustice. Once the Korean War began, he thought it should be won decisively. He wanted his American and United Nations allies to press the counterattack and make the sacrifice worthwhile. The decision to settle for a stalemate was a bitter blow to Rhee, and his angry rhetoric at the time expressed what many Koreans believed.

During the truce negotiations that ended the Korean War, Rhee displayed a talent for manipulating his American and United Nations allies. Though the war accomplished little but destruction in Korea, Rhee at least was able to wrest from the United States a mutual security treaty under which American forces were positioned to prevent a recurrence of the war. That guarantee enabled South Korea to develop the capability to defend itself and assured a long enough peace to begin a spectacular economic growth that Rhee did not live to see.

Rhee left Koreans with a certain cynicism about democracy. His regime was followed by a year of constitutional government under a cabinet-responsible system that was overthrown by a military coup in May, 1961, a predictable development in view of the militarization of Korea that followed the Korean War and the failure of Rhee's government to create a viable civilian tradition. Military-led dictatorships then ruled South Korea from 1961 until 1987. Only with the beginning of the presidency of former general Roh Tae Woo in 1988 was there any visible movement back to basic freedom and a reduction of the military's role in politics.

Bibliography

Allen, Richard C. *Korea's Syngman Rhee: An Unauthorized Portrait*. Rutland, Vt.: Charles E. Tuttle, 1960. A critical biography written in the aftermath of Rhee's fall from power to provide general readers with the pieces missing in Robert Oliver's earlier work.

Cumings, Bruce. *The Origins of the Korean War: Liberation and the Emergence of Separate Regimes*. Princeton, N.J.: Princeton University Press,

1981. The leading American historical treatment of the internal politics of South Korea under American rule. Highly critical of American political leadership and United States' sponsorship of the right.

Han, Sungjoo. *The Failure of Democracy in South Korea.* Berkeley: University of California Press, 1974. Scholarly treatment of the April, 1960, revolution, the Rhee legacy, and the regime that followed Rhee prior to the military coup of May, 1961.

Henderson, Gregory. *Korea: The Politics of the Vortex.* Cambridge, Mass.: Harvard University Press, 1968. A detailed and richly annotated analysis of the patterns in Korean politics in the mid-twentieth century by a Foreign Service officer who worked alongside the Rhee goverment in the 1950's.

Kim, Quee-yong. *The Fall of Syngman Rhee.* Berkeley: University of California, Institute of East Asian Studies, Center for Korean Studies, 1983. A definitive study of the events surrounding Rhee's exit from Korea, based on the author's Harvard dissertation.

Lee, Hahn-Been. *Korea: Time, Change, and Administration.* Honolulu: East-West Center Press, 1968. A detailed study of public policy and administrative patterns in the Rhee years with stress on the trends leading up to the 1960 revolution.

Oliver, Robert T. *Syngman Rhee: The Man Behind the Myth.* New York: Dodd Mead, 1954. An authorized biography and good source of personal information, though seriously flawed by lack of critical distance and numerous errors in historical detail. A basic source of Rhee's life and movements.

——————. *Syngman Rhee and American Involvement in Korea, 1942-1960: A Personal Narrative.* Seoul, Korea: Panmun, 1978. Rhee's close friend and biographer compiled this collection of Rhee documents and comments on the most controversial aspects of his relations with the United States.

Reeve, W. D. *The Republic of Korea: A Political and Economic Study.* London: Oxford University Press, 1963. A comprehensive treatment of the political and economic dimensions of the Rhee years including issues relating to reconstruction and political control.

Rhee, Syngman. *Japan Inside Out.* New York: Fleming H. Revell, 1941. Rhee's estimate of Japan under the militarists' control and the likely effect of its imperial designs upon its neighbors and the West. Useful as an example of Rhee's political position and his approach to propaganda.

Donald N. Clark

RAINER MARIA RILKE

Born: December 4, 1875; Prague, Bohemia, Austro-Hungarian Empire
Died: December 29, 1926; Valmont, Switzerland
Area of Achievement: Literature
Contribution: Rilke is generally considered the greatest German poet since
Goethe, and his fame is by no means limited to his own country.

Early Life

Rainer Maria Rilke was born on December 4, 1875, as a member of the
German-speaking minority in Prague, then part of the Austro-Hungarian Empire. His early life reads like a Freudian case history. His father, Josef Rilke,
had been frustrated in a military career and had become a minor official on
the railroad. His mother was temperamental, socially pretentious, and super-
ficially Catholic. They separated in 1884. It is natural to associate Rilke's
troubled relations with his mother with his later troubled relations with other
women; though he had innumerable affairs and some warm friendships, he
could never settle down to a domestic relationship.

After his parents' separation, Rilke, who for his first five years had been
treated almost as a girl, was sent to military schools. He later represented his
life there as miserable, though his grades were good and he was encouraged
to read his poems in class. After he left military school at sixteen, he spent a
year in a trade school at Linz; he studied privately for his *abitur*, or *Gymnasium* diploma; and he took university courses in Prague (1896) and
Munich (1897), particularly in art history. Already he was trying to establish
himself as a man of letters; although neither Rilke nor his critics thought
much of the work he did in the 1890's, the mere quantity of it is impressive:
Not only is there a mass of poetry but also there is some fiction and ten
dramatic works, a few of which were actually produced.

Before Rilke moved to Paris and began to write works of more maturity
and individuality, he underwent two maturing experiences. One was his affair with Lou Andreas-Salomé, the Russian-born wife of a Berlin professor
and the first biographer of Friedrich Wilhelm Nietzsche, who had proposed
to her. She introduced Rilke to the Russian language and culture and took
him with her on two visits to Russia, where he met Leo Tolstoy. Even after
the affair ended, Lou remained Rilke's friend and confidante. The second
experience was Rilke's sojourn in the artist's colony of Worpswede near
Bremen. There he continued his interest in art, and there he met and married
a young sculptor, Clara Westhoff. They set up housekeeping and she bore
him a daughter, but they found themselves unsuited to domestic life, and,
depositing the baby with Clara's parents, they took off for Paris. They never
divorced but never lived together again, though they remained on good
terms.

Life's Work

Paris was Rilke's favored residence until World War I, even though its size and impersonality and the depressing scenes of poverty he witnessed at first repelled him. Much of his time, however, was spent in travel: to Scandinavia, to Berlin and Munich, to Vienna and Trieste, to Rome and Venice and Capri, to Spain and North Africa. Some of this restlessness was not a matter of either culture or curiosity. Rilke was beginning to have an income from royalties and from lectures and readings, but to the end of his life he was not really easy in the matter of money. His personal charm and aristocratic manners made him friends at the highest levels of society. It was convenient for him to be a guest in people's houses for long periods or to have the loan of a vacant apartment—or castle. A case in point is Duino, the castle of Princess Marie von Thurn und Taxis near Trieste, where he began the famous elegies.

The period in Paris was one of the most productive of Rilke's life. When he came to Paris he had a commission to do a monograph on the sculptor Auguste Rodin, who had been Clara's teacher. Rodin cooperated on the project, and the two became quite intimate; for a time, Rilke served as Rodin's secretary, handling much of his burdensome correspondence. Then came a temporary estrangement, but not before Rilke had received from the master a confirmation of his conception of the artist as one who sees creatively, as well as a conception of art as a craft at which the artist must work steadily and systematically. The monograph was well received, as was an account of the artists at Worpswede. At this period, too, Rilke was an admirer and partisan of Paul Cézanne.

The period also produced poems that were no longer immature and derivative. In *Das Stundenbuch* (1905; *The Book of Hours*, 1941), through the persona of a Russian monk, Rilke explores different conceptions of art and of God and ends by making God a creation of the artist. *Das Buch der Bilder* (1902; the book of images) is of a more miscellaneous character, though it also contains some of Rilke's most striking lyrics; one critic would see it as bound together by the recurring theme of seeing, of perception. The poems of *Neue Gedichte* (1907, 1908; *New Poems*, 1964) in keeping with this conception of poetry, take their start not from an idea or mood but from some "thing" that must be seen and understood, even if it is ugly, such as a corpse in the morgue. Many of the poems tell a story from the Bible or classical mythology, showing it in a novel light. Thus, the story of the prodigal son may emphasize the oppressiveness of family life, while the tale of Orpheus and Eurydice may turn on the reluctance of Eurydice to return to the land of the living.

To this period also belong Rilke's two important works of fiction; *Die Weise von Liebe und Tod des Cornets Christof Rilke* (1906; *The Tale of the Love and Death of Cornet Christopher Rilke*, 1932) and *Die Aufzeichnungen des Malte Laurids Brigge* (1910; *The Notebooks of Malte Laurids Brigge*, 1930, 1958). *The Tale of the Love and Death of Cornet Christopher Rilke* is a short novel or prose poem telling of the death of an ancestral Rilke at the hands of the Turks in Hungary in 1663. The night before his heroic death he spends in the bed of a countess who never learns his name. This book had sold more than a million copies by 1969; it was immensely popular with soldiers in World War I. *The Notebooks of Malte Laurids Brigge* is in a way Rilke's "portrait of the artist," but he effectively distances himself more than does James Joyce. Brigge is a Danish poet living in Paris; his notebooks record both the present and memories of the past. The past is far more glamorous than Rilke's own; Malte's father is master of the hunt to the King of Denmark; his mother is beautiful and affectionate. The sordid realities of Paris are closer to Rilke's experience, as is his conviction that he (and Malte) must learn to accept and record these realities. The realities are linked with death and Rilke's conviction that one ought to die his own individual death, which had been with him from birth. The themes of the novel are supported by much anecdotal material, both Malte's memories and (often obscure) episodes from history. The novel ends with another retelling of the prodigal son, who even in his return home asserts his own individuality. The writing of the novel left Rilke in a state of creative exhaustion. Nevertheless, in 1912, he began the Duino elegies, only to put them aside for years.

When war broke out in 1914, Rilke was in Germany and could not return to France, where he was now an enemy alien. The war years were comparatively unproductive. For a brief period in 1916, he served in the Austrian army; at the end of the war, he was an object of suspicion for his friendships with some of the leaders of a brief Bavarian Soviet. In 1919, he was invited to Switzerland to give poetry readings and remained there until his death. After the usual wanderings, he settled in the castle of Muzot, which a Swiss friend supplied free of charge. Six months after moving in, inspiration returned; he not only finished the *Duineser Elegien* (1923; *Duino Elegies*, 1930) but also wrote the related *Die Sonette an Orpheus* (1923; *Sonnets to Orpheus*, 1936). During this period, he also managed a final trip to Paris, his second since the war. His health was deteriorating, however, and he died of leukemia on December 29, 1926.

Summary

After Rainer Maria Rilke's death, says Norbert Fuerst, "began the battle of the critics, who admired him, with the 'hagiographers,' who loved him"—though the reactions of "ordinary people" might have been closer to Rilke's heart. "Rilke is of all modern poets the one who translated the concerns of the non-poet most comprehensively, so that we do find them in his work . . . and can retranslate them into our existential concerns." Different readers will find their concerns voiced in different poems or will find that different poems concern them at different times in their lives. The fame of the *Duino Elegies* suggests an appeal to troubled intellectuals who, like Rilke, feel in their emotional conflicts envious at once of the beasts, "simple-minded, unperplexed," and of imagined angels, who represent a level at which all conflicts are resolved. In a different mood, the artist might respond to the *Sonnets to Orpheus* by feeling, in the exuberance of Rilke's verse, that he, too, might have power over trees and stones.

The shorter lyrics are more likely to voice concerns familiar to "ordinary people." One might turn to *Das Buch der Bilder*, manageable on the whole because there is likely to be only one idea expressed in each poem. Even for readers who know little German, these lyrics are best read in the original. The reader might start with such poems as "Pont du Carrousel," "Herbstag" (autumn day), "Herbst" (autumn), "Abend" (evening), or from *New Poems*, "Letster Abend" (last evening), which has been adapted by Robert Lowell. Wolfgang Leppmann, a distinguished Rilkian, says that Rilke can be and should be read for fun. "Fun" seems an odd term to use of a poet who is often difficult, yet perhaps it is an appropriate description for the satisfaction that comes from simultaneously solving a difficult puzzle and having a human concern find expression.

Bibliography
Brodsky, Patricia Pollock. *Rainer Maria Rilke*. Boston: Twayne, 1988. An exceptional introductory work. Not only are there accounts of the major sequences but also there are a remarkable number of analyses of individual lyrics. There is a good, short description of Rilke's life, and, in addition to the standard bibliographies of primary and secondary sources, there is a bibliography of translations.
Fuerst, Norbert. *Phases of Rilke*. Bloomington: Indiana University Press, 1958. There are eight phases, "eight of his life, eight of his work." Though the scheme is artificial and the writing somewhat impressionistic, this book is still an attractive medium-length introduction to Rilke. Fuerst tries to mediate between Rilke's critics and his "hagiographers."
Lange, Victor. Introduction to *Rainer Maria Rilke: Selected Poems*. Translated by A. E. Flemming. New York: Methuen, 1986. A brief but eloquent introduction to Rilke by a major Germanic scholar.
Leppmann, Wolfgang. *Rilke: A Life*. Translated in collaboration with the author by Russell M. Stockman. New York: Fromm International, 1984. A massive treatment of Rilke's life and work, thoroughly researched and annotated. There are extensive bibliographies and a very detailed chronology.
Prater, Donald. *A Ringing Glass: The Life of Rainer Maria Rilke*. Oxford: Clarendon Press, 1986. Not a "life and work" but simply a life, this book

takes advantage of the enormous amount of correspondence and other material that is gradually becoming available.

Rilke, Rainer Maria. *Letters to a Young Poet*. Translated by Reginald Snell. London: Sidgwick and Jackson, 1945. Rilke's published correspondence comes to about thirty volumes in the original languages; only a few are available in English. They are a rich source of material on his life and thought and provide a basis for further interpretations of his work.

Sandford, John. *Landscape and Landscape Imagery in R. M. Rilke*. London: University of London Press, 1980. One of the many specialized works on Rilke. "Rilke's search for a home . . . is the key to his experience and description of landscape."

John C. Sherwood

DIEGO RIVERA

Born: December 8, 1886; Guanajuato, Mexico
Died: November 25, 1957; Mexico City, Mexico
Area of Achievement: Art
Contribution: Rivera was a painter who at first transcended his native Mexico and its rich and diverse artistic heritage to embrace broader modern European movements. Eventually in his work, he fused the Mexican and European forms to become one of his country's greatest muralists and a giant in the world of art.

Early Life
Diego Rivera was born on December 8, 1886, in Guanajuato, Mexico, the birthplace of Mexican independence from Spain in 1810. His father, Diego, was a schoolteacher of Spanish-Portuguese-Jewish background, and his mother was of mixed Spanish-Indian descent. A few years after he was born, Rivera's family moved to Mexico City, where he grew up.

Because of his already marked artistic leanings at an early age, in 1896, his parents entered him in the San Carlos Academy of Fine Arts before he was ten years old. There he studied under the likes of Santiago Rebull, José Salomé Peña, Felix Parra, and the great José María de Velasco until 1902, when Rebull, the rector of the academy, died, to be replaced by Antonio Fabres. The young Rivera soon rebelled against the deadening regime of realism imposed by Fabres and left the academy.

Thereafter, Rivera studied and associated with the great José Guadalupe Posada and others. At this time, he also was stirred by the monumental native Mexican architecture. His first exhibition, held in Veracruz in 1907, so impressed the local governor and others, such as the legendary artist and patron Dr. Atl (Gerardo Murillo), who recommended Rivera, that he won a scholarship to further his studies at the prestigious San Fernando Academy in Spain under Eduardo Chicarro, a member of the Spanish realist school.

Life's Work
In Spain, Rivera came under not only the influence of his teachers in Chicarro's studio but also, perhaps more important, the work of El Greco and Francisco de Goya. Rivera's first stay in Europe lasted two years, until 1909. During this time, he often left Spain to wander through Belgium, The Netherlands, France, and the British Isles.

When he returned home, it was just in time to experience and be caught up in the Mexican Revolution, which began in earnest in 1910. Rivera's youthful, aesthetic rebelliousness was wholly compatible with the political and social struggles developing in Mexico. Although not yet really of the people, more and more his sympathies were with them. He and other prominent

Mexican artists easily came to equate aesthetic freedom with political freedom and vice versa.

When he returned to Europe in 1912, this time to stay until 1921, he was already experiencing profound changes in his worldview and his art. This second European episode and the events he witnessed during it generally set his new aesthetic-political outlook. As before, he traveled extensively and associated with artists such as Pierre-Auguste Renoir, Georges Seurat, Paul Gaugin, Henri Matisse, Amedeo Modigliani, Paul Cézanne, and Pablo Picasso. He also felt comfortable among the Russian artists, communist and noncommunist, in exile in Western Europe. His art began to reflect the work of his fellow painters, and, in Paris, he sometimes exhibited his canvases with theirs. Rivera also felt the impact of World War I and the Russian Revolution, some of which he saw firsthand.

Gradually, Rivera drifted toward cubism, to which he became completely dedicated until at least 1917. Major works such as his *Majorcan Landscape* made a significant contribution to the movement and firmly established him as a cubist of the first degree. Through Matisse, he also experimented with Fauvism. His Mexican background especially helped him appreciate the Fauvists' use of color. In fact, more and more during this period his native Mexico and its influence grew in evidence in Rivera's work.

In 1920, Rivera met the young David Alfaro Siqueiros in Paris, and, sharing a growing belief in the need for a people's art to reflect revolutionary struggle and that art was political, they began to work toward a national popular art movement for their beloved Mexico. In this, they were eventually joined and supported by many, including the third founder of the modern Mexican mural tradition and Mexican Renaissance, the great José Clemente Orozco, and the then Mexican president, Álvaro Obregón, among others. Thus, Rivera retuned home to start the work.

Rivera's first products of this new mural movement appeared on the walls of the National Preparatory School (University of Mexico) in 1922 and thereafter in the new Ministry of Education building in Mexico City. Mexico and its progress were almost always his subject. In this work, the Mexican muralists gradually recovered and fused the frescoing techniques of ancient Mexico (Orozco) and the Italian Renaissance (Rivera). In 1926-1927, Rivera completed his first masterpiece, a fresco cycle in the National Agricultural School in Chapingo.

Like Picasso, Orozco, Siqueiros, and numerous other artists during the interwar period, Rivera was a Communist, at least spiritually and emotionally if not doctrinally so. He was not, however, a Stalinist. While he went to Moscow in 1927-1928 and seems to have been impressed by what he saw, his disappointment with the Soviet Union grew thereafter. In 1936, Rivera interceded with President Lázaro Cárdenas to permit the Communist dissident Leon Trotsky to come to Mexico to end his wanderings. After 1928,

Rivera returned to the Soviet Union only once more, in 1956, shortly before his death, for an operation.

Upon his return from Moscow, Rivera briefly served as the director of the San Carlos Academy in 1929. A year later, he married the Mexican artist Frida Kahlo, who also on occasion served him as a model. In 1932, Rivera completed a second masterpiece, a mural depicting the industrial progress of the United States, in the patio of the Institute of Fine Arts in Detroit. Thereafter, numerous commissions in the United States followed. The most controversial of these was in the lobby of the RCA Building in New York City in 1933. Before it was completed, it had to be obliterated because it contained a portrayal of Vladimir Ilich Lenin. Rivera reexecuted the controversial mural a year later as part of a series of masterpieces in the Palace of Fine Arts in Mexico City. Other important works by Rivera include *The Bandit Augustin Lorenzo*, done in the lobby of the Hotel Reforma in 1938 and *Vision of Alameda Central* in 1948 in the Del Prado Hotel, both in Mexico City.

Near the end of his life, Rivera led a movement to ban all nuclear testing, and he became a Roman Catholic. He died on November 25, 1957, in Mexico City, survived by his then wife, Emma Hurtado, and two daughters from a previous marriage to a former model, Lupe Marin. His death brought to a close a major era in Mexican cultural history.

Summary

Already early in his life under the influence of his native Mexico and its rich artistic heritage, and, more important, of Europe, Diego Rivera became a major painter. He was a significant cubist and a Fauvist. Under the influence of revolutionary events in Mexico and Europe and as a direct result of his collaboration with Orozco and Siqueiros, however, he changed the face of modern art.

With his work, Rivera helped to create the modern mural movement and also put art into the political arena on the side of the popular struggle for freedom and equality. Although he was foremost a Mexican nationalist, a Mexican national artist, and a founder of the Mexican Renaissance and had a profound influence on younger Mexican artists such as Siqueiros, the painter-architect Juan O'Gorman, and many others, this influence reached far beyond Mexico back to Europe and into the United States, to the New Deal Works Progress Administration of the 1930's, for example. Rivera was a true founder of the people's art movement.

Bibliography

Carrillo Azpéitia, Rafael. *Mural Painting of Mexico: The Pre-Hispanic Epoch, the Viceroyalty, and the Great Artists of Our Century.* Mexico City: Panorama Editorial, 1981. A good, brief, and popular study from

Mexico, containing a chapter on Rivera. Straightforward treatment.

Edwards, Emily. *Painted Walls of Mexico: From Prehistoric Times Until Today.* Austin: University of Texas Press, 1966. Almost half of this standard volume is on Rivera and the other modern Mexican muralists. Profusely illustrated.

Fernandez, Justino. *A Guide to Mexican Art: From Its Beginnings to the Present.* Chicago: University of Chicago Press, 1969. Puts Rivera and his work in a broad perspective and provides a good analysis of the work.

Helm, MacKinley. *Modern Mexican Painters.* Reprint. Freeport, N.Y.: Books for Libraries Press, 1968. Contains a good chapter on Rivera and his work prior to World War II but is dated.

Reed, Alma. *The Mexican Muralists.* New York: Crown, 1960. A good general work with a chapter on Rivera by the biographer of Orozco. Profusely illustrated.

Rivera, Diego. *My Art, My Life: An Autobiography.* New York: Citadel Press, 1960. An excellent partial autobiography of a complex artist. It is essential to a full understanding of Rivera.

Rodriguez, Antonio. *A History of Mexican Mural Painting.* New York: G. P. Putnam's Sons, 1969. Another and more important standard work with five chapters on Rivera and his art. Profusely illustrated.

Smith, Bradley. *Mexico: A History in Art.* Garden City, N.Y.: Doubleday, 1968. A standard with a significant chapter on Rivera and the other modern muralists. Profusely illustrated.

Wolfe, Bertram. *The Fabulous Life of Diego Rivera.* Briarcliff Manor, N.Y.: Stein & Day, 1963. Still probably the best biography of Rivera, certainly the best in English. Sympathetic, understanding, and understandable.

Dennis Reinhartz

ERWIN ROMMEL

Born: November 15, 1891; Heidenheim, Germany
Died: October 14, 1944; near Herrlingen, Germany
Area of Achievement: The military
Contribution: A legendary commander of World War II, Rommel, known as "The Desert Fox" for his cunning, achieved distinction for his actions in France and North Africa. His successes on the battlefield resulted from his courage and determination, his aggressive leadership, and his mastery of military tactics.

Early Life

Erwin Johannes Eugen Rommel was born in Heidenheim, Germany, on November 15, 1891. The second son of a schoolmaster and mathematician, he was an indifferent student. A susceptibility to childhood illnesses prompted him to increase his stamina through athletic training. When he expressed an interest in a military career, his father attempted to dissuade him from a course so unpromising but later agreed to assist him. Once he had chosen a career, he sought to reach the top of his profession. He joined the Württemberg Sixth Infantry Regiment as a cadet on July 19, 1910; in the following year he entered officer training at the War Academy in Danzig. There he met Lucie Maria Mollin, the one woman in his life; they were married in 1916 while he was on military leave.

Rommel was commissioned a second lieutenant in time to enter World War I as a platoon leader. He became known for his bravery under fire and his aggressive leadership, fighting at Bleid, at Verdun, and in the Argonne, where he was awarded the Iron Cross. After recovery from a leg wound, he joined a mountain infantry division stationed in the Alps along the Romanian and Italian fronts. In a daring attack at the head of his men, who never numbered more than six hundred, he broke the Italian line, captured the strategically important Mount Matajur, and took nine thousand prisoners and quantities of matériel. For this feat he was awarded the Pour le Mérite (the "Blue Max"), Germany's highest military honor.

During the interval between wars, Rommel served as a commander of troops who put down insurrections and as a military instructor first at the Infantry School at Dresden and later at the War College, Pottsdam. His lectures were the basis of his *Infanterie greift an* (1937; *Attacks*, 1979), a book read with attention by Adolf Hitler.

Life's Work

Rommel's career, like those of other German officers, began to advance with the rise of National Socialism and the rearming of the nation. Along with the rest of the army, Rommel took his oath of loyalty to Hitler in July,

1934. In 1935 he escorted Hitler in a review of troops at Goslar and attracted the attention of other Nazis by refusing to permit Schutzstaffel (SS) troops to take precedence over regular officers. During Hitler's trip to Czechoslovakia in 1938, he was in charge of troops providing security. When war erupted in Poland, he accompanied Hitler to the front as a staff officer. There he observed the successes of German armored (panzer) units and, when Hitler offered him his choice of commands, he selected a panzer division over infantry. He was appointed commander of the Seventh Panzer Division stationed on the Rhine River.

In the Blitzkrieg on France of May, 1940, Rommel's division crossed the Meuse and Sambre rivers, knifing through Belgium in a sweeping arc bypassing the Maginot Line. Near Arras, he encountered a sharp British counterattack that slowed the advance, but his forces prevailed over superior numbers. After a successful conclusion of the sweep, he moved south against Cherbourg, where he captured, among others, four French admirals.

Having triumphed in France, Hitler reluctantly posted two divisions to North Africa to reinforce Italian allies who had suffered a catastrophic defeat at the hands of British General Sir Archibald Wavell. Rommel, a lieutenant general, was named commander of the divisions that formed the nucleus of the Afrika Korps. Although nominally under the command of an Italian general and later under Field Marshal Albert Kesselring in a rather loose command structure, he usually had freedom of decision and independence.

The terrain of the 1941-1943 conflict in North Africa consisted largely of coastal desert stretching two thousand miles from Morocco to Egypt and up to two hundred miles inland. For Rommel it offered a vast theater in which to adapt the principles of Blitzkrieg against a British army whose leaders were trained in conventional defense and conservative attack strategy. Rommel conceived a grand objective that transcended his original purpose of assisting Italian allies. Driving eastward from Tunisia, he would capture British strongholds along the Mediterranean, until he reached Cairo. From there he would take the Suez Canal and then sweep around the east side of the Mediterranean until he reached the oil fields of Persia and Arabia.

Numerous adverse factors intervened to deny Rommel's dream of conquest. The German invasion of the Soviet Union (Operation Barbarossa) on June 22, 1941, meant that the first priority for men and matériel became the Eastern Front. Rommel's British opponents, with a well-equipped and sound army, learned how to counter his tactics and almost always outnumbered him. Further, British naval and air power in the Mediterranean, based at Malta, took a heavy toll on supplies sent to Rommel, while the British could bring their supplies around the Cape and through Suez, a longer but more reliable route.

Once in Tunisia, Rommel quickly went on the attack, driving Wavell's Eighth Army, now reduced because many units were sent to Greece, eastward toward the Gazala Line and Tobruk, the British port and stronghold. Breaking through the line, Rommel besieged Tobruk; he met a crushing counterattack in the British Operation Crusader. Both sides lost heavily, but Rommel ran short of supplies and fuel and was forced to lift the siege and withdraw to Al-Agheila in December, 1941.

In May, 1942, after resupply and reinforcements, Rommel renewed the attack on Tobruk, flanking the Gazala Line to the south with his main panzer units. In order to shorten his supply lines, he then breached the line from behind and brought through the Italian Ariete Division, placing it in a fortified defense position to the east. When British units moved up to attack and repair the break, the Ariete held while Rommel's Fifteenth and Twenty-first Panzer Divisions encircled them. In the Battle of the Cauldron, Rommel's forces inflicted losses so punishing that the British were forced to withdraw, leaving Tobruk to fall on June 20, 1942. Its cache of fuel, provisions, and vehicles resupplied Rommel's army, and the victory brought him the rank of field marshal.

Hardly pausing for rest, Rommel pressed his weary men after the retreating British and toward the next objective, Al-Alamein in western Egypt, where the British had established a strong defense line, bounded on the north by the sea and on the south by the impassable Qattara Depression. Behind extensive mine fields and obstacles, British General Sir Claude Auchinleck positioned his divisions and brigades across the desert in checkerboard fashion.

Rommel opened the attack against the southern portion of the line and made progress in swinging it back, but the British defenders did not crack. He fought doggedly on, with both sides incurring heavy losses, yet for Rommel, with his precarious resupply situation, the losses grew unsustainable. He withdrew to approximately the original points of attack and waited for supplies and reinforcements, constructing heavy defenses—mine fields and obstacles. During a three-month lull, British supply operations proved more successful, and General Bernard Law Montgomery, newly appointed commander of the Eighth Army, built an approximate two-to-one superiority in tanks, field guns, and troops.

On October 23, 1942, Montgomery opened the second Battle of Al-Alamein with a cannonade from a thousand guns massed along a five-mile stretch. In Germany for medical treatment, Rommel rushed to the front, arriving late on October 25 to find that all reserves had been committed. With his units being overpowered in all sectors, he sought permission to withdraw; in response, Hitler forbade him to retreat a yard. On the following day, November 3, with the concurrence of Field Marshal Kesselring, he ordered a fourteen-hundred-mile withdrawal toward Tunisia with only twelve tanks still operational. The retreat enabled him to save most of his army only because Montgomery was slow in pursuit.

Toward Tunisia, American forces were advancing from the west following their landings in Morocco and Algeria in Operation Torch. Realizing that the Axis faced a hopeless situation, Rommel urged Hitler to withdraw the Afrika Korps for the defense of Europe. Instead, Hitler, who had reluctantly entered Africa, now determined to hold a position there at all costs. He poured in men and matériel, including the new Mark V (Panther) and Mark VI (Tiger) tanks. Although Rommel was in command at the Battle of Kasserine Pass, where his forces mauled inexperienced American troops, his influence was waning, and he was withdrawn before the surrender of all remaining forces in May, 1943. Hitler's refusal to withdraw the Afrika Korps remained a bitter disappointment to their commander.

After minor assignments in Italy and the Balkans, Rommel was appointed deputy commander of the Western Front, in charge of coastal defenses, under the aging Field Marshal Gerd von Rundstedt. After carefully surveying coastal installations, Rommel began an extensive construction of gun emplacements, tank traps, mines, and other obstacles, and made frequent personal visits to his troops to build their morale. Realizing that Allied air supremacy would hamper any movement of forces, he believed it essential that an invasion be stopped on the beaches. His preparations were far from complete when the Normandy Invasion occurred on June 6, 1944.

Unable to contain the invasion, Rommel and Rundstedt met Hitler near the front to request reinforcements and permission to withdraw to better defensive positions; both requests were denied. By this time Rommel had reached the conclusion that only a separate peace with the Western Allies could save Germany; he further believed it necessary to replace Hitler.

Though he was drawn into the plot against Hitler, he never sanctioned assassination. When the bomb planted by Colonel Claus von Stauffenberg exploded at Hitler's headquarters on July 20, Rommel lay in a Paris hospital recovering from wounds sustained when his staff car was strafed by a British Spitfire on July 17. During the interrogations that followed, Rommel was implicated by General Heinrich von Stülpnagel, among others, and a list of offices to be filled after the demise of Hitler, which fell into the hands of the SS, showed Rommel as reich president.

As his recovery continued at his home in Herrlingen, he was visited by two SS generals, who bore a brief charging him with treason. He was offered the choice of the People's Court or suicide by poison. Since Hitler gave assurances that his family and staff would be protected if he elected to take a cyanide capsule, he accepted this course. The official explanation was that he died of a brain hemorrhage resulting from his wounds. He received a hero's funeral at Ulm, where Rundstedt read the eulogy.

Summary

During World War II, Erwin Rommel was Germany's most celebrated commander. To his enemies and to Germany he was a legend, and at times he seemed invincible. A popular leader with his men, he insisted on commanding from the front, oblivious to personal danger and hardship. He practiced the principle he taught his cadets: to be to the men an example in both their personal and professional lives. Among the British who opposed him, he had a reputation for chivalry and for correct, even considerate, treatment of prisoners. In North Africa, he employed an astonishing variety of military tactics that worked in his favor so long as he was not overpowered by superior numbers.

Though a model soldier, Rommel was not without flaws. As a commander who insisted on being at the front, he sometimes lost contact with his headquarters. He neglected logistical problems and often attacked when his forces were poorly supplied. He demanded that his officers and men be as aggressive and efficient as he was, and he had a reputation for being tactless and somewhat abrasive with senior officers. Strong-willed and single-minded, he was politically naïve, allowing himself to be used by Nazi propaganda.

Bold and aggressive by nature, Rommel emphasized attack over defense, insisted that officers should lead attacks, and saw that success required that firepower be concentrated in the spearhead, not behind it. He grasped the concept of fluidity in military attack—the view that one does not assault fixed positions and then stop—and the importance of carefully coordinated attacking units. He developed ingenious tactics and achieved important victories over superior numbers in North Africa. Successes came to his opponents after they mastered his own art of desert warfare. In the end, Rommel lost because the opposing forces won the contest for supplies and reinforcements.

Bibliography

Irving, David. *The Trail of the Fox*. New York: E. P. Dutton, 1977. Carefully researched and written in vivid detail. Highly readable, it is the most comprehensive and accurate biography.

Lewin, Ronald. *The Life and Death of the Afrika Korps*. Reprint. New York: Quadrangle Books, 1977. A straightforward and detailed narration of the North African campaign.

Mitcham, Samuel W., Jr. *Rommel's Desert War*. New York: Stein & Day, 1982. Chronicles the North African campaign from December, 1941, until the surrender of the Afrika Korps.

_____. *Triumphant Fox: Erwin Rommel and the Rise of the Afrika Korps*. New York: Stein & Day, 1984. Beginning with a biographical account, the book chronicles Rommel's early successes in North Africa.

Rommel, Erwin. *The Rommel Papers*. Edited by B. H. Liddell Hart. Translated by Paul Findlay. New York: Harcourt, Brace, 1953. A collection of

Rommel's memoirs, letters, and personal documents giving his own account of his campaigns.

Young, Desmond. *Rommel: The Desert Fox.* New York: Harper and Bros., 1950. A sympathetic and comprehensive biography by an English officer who fought against Rommel in Africa.

Stanley Archer

HERMANN RORSCHACH

Born: November 8, 1884; Zurich, Switzerland
Died: April 2, 1922; Herisau, Switzerland
Areas of Achievement: Psychiatry and psychology
Contribution: Rorschach is credited with only one major scientific achievement during his short career, but this achievement was important in the development of modern psychology and had far-reaching effects on other disciplines as well. In the early 1920's, Rorschach set forth a formal method of testing personality traits by recording, timing, and interpreting a subject's reactions to a series of inkblots. The test remains one of the most valuable testing tools of psychology.

Early Life

Hermann Rorschach was born in Zurich, Switzerland, on November 8, 1884. The psychiatrist's early preoccupation with ink blots in part came from the fact that his father, Ulrich Rorschach, was an art teacher at local schools. Early in life, he was given the nickname "Kleck," meaning inkblot in German, by companions at school. Rorschach was the eldest of three children; he had a sister, Anna, and a brother, Paul. When he was twelve years old his mother died, and six years later his father died also.

Rorschach attended local elementary and high schools and was graduated with distinction from the latter when he was nineteen years old. At this time, he decided to pursue a career in medicine and attended medical schools in Neuchâtel, Zurich, and Bern—all in Switzerland—as well as in Berlin, Germany. He completed his medical study in five years, finishing in Zurich, where he had worked at a psychiatric unit of the university hospital and had excelled as a student of Eugen Bleuler. In 1909, he secured a residency at an asylum in Munsterlingen, Switzerland; the following year, he married Olga Stempelin, a Russian who worked at the institution. They later had two children: Elizabeth, born in 1917, and Wadin, born in 1919.

In 1912, Rorschach completed all requirements for the degree of doctor of medicine from the University of Zurich. In 1913-1914, his wife and he worked at a mental institution in Moscow, Russia; they returned to Switzerland when Rorschach became a resident doctor at Waldau Mental Hospital in Bern. Some two years later, he left Bern for Appenzell, Switzerland, where he accepted a better position at the Krombach Mental Hospital. In 1919, he became the first vice president of the Swiss Psychoanalytic Society.

Life's Work

Because of his father's influence, Rorschach had been interested in drawing and art from youth. As early as 1911, when he was completing the doctor of medicine degree at the University of Zurich, he had conducted limited research with inkblots, using schoolchildren as his subjects. As a student of psychology and psychiatry himself, Rorschach studied the works of other researchers who had conducted experiments into the possibility of determining personality traits by using inkblots; chief among these were the recorded experiments of Justinus Kerner and Alfred Binet. None of these, however, succeeded in formulating a systematic method of conducting such a test and meaningfully interpreting the results in a consistent fashion from subject to subject.

Between 1911 and 1921, Rorschach conducted extensive research (both on patients in the mental hospitals where he worked and on well-adjusted, unconfined persons) in order to develop such a test. During this period, he published several professional papers, none of which received any particular notoriety. His single contribution was his *Psychodiagnostik* (1921; *Psychodiagnostics: A Diagnostic Test Based on Perception*, 1942), written as a preliminary study upon a basic method which he expected to refine and improve. The major contribution of the work to psychiatry is that it presented what came to be known as the "Rorschach test." (Later, this phrase was changed to "projective test"; the terms are now more or less used interchangeably, although technically the Rorschach test is merely one kind of projective personality test.) Rorschach's book has usually been cited for this achievement, but in fact it contains a far grander scope than this. *Psychodiagnostics* provides an entire theory of human personality, both individual and collective. Rorschach found two major personality types, the "introversive" and the "extratensive"—roughly equivalent to "introverted" and "extroverted" in modern parlance. Introversive persons are motivated by internal factors and inclinations, finding meaning in activities of the self; extroverts, on the other hand, function under the influence of external forces and motivators and look outside themselves to find meaningful experiences. Rorschach believed that both of these types exist in each person but to different extents, in various measures, and in determinable ratios. The test he devised was intended to discover these ratios in an individual, that is, the extent of introversion and extratension. Additionally, he believed that the test could be some measure of the subject's emotional stability, intelligence, capabilities, resolve at problem solving, and general normalcy; he thought that the test would reveal with some certainty any significant psychological problems or aberrations.

The test itself is unusually simple, although recording, scoring, and interpreting the results is a complicated process, the effectiveness of which depends primarily upon the capabilities and experience of the person giving the test. The subject is shown ten cards in turn, five of which are black and white, two of which are black and white with some color, and three of which are in color. The tester maintains total neutrality when asking the subject what he sees. The inkblots themselves are meaningless in that they do not, by design, represent any known object in the physical world; however, they are symmetrical figures which are suggestive of actual physical objects. The subject's responses are carefully noted in terms of location (the part of the inkblot on which the subject's eyes focus); time (the length of time it takes the subject to see an object after the inkblot is presented to him); content (what the subject "sees"); various determinants (the subject's focus upon color, form, and shadings of the drawing); and originality (the subject's ability to see items not usually suggested). Through the years, testers have amassed a wealth of information regarding these responses. Statistical data, formulas, weighted frequencies, and the like have been developed to help ensure accuracy of test results. It is interesting also that the same ten inkblots designed by Rorschach are still in use.

When *Psychodiagnostics* first appeared in Europe in 1921, it was virtually ignored, until it was attacked. The belief of the day by the best-known psychologists and psychiatrists was that personality could not be tested. They recognized some validity in the free-association responses to inkblot drawings but were overwhelmingly skeptical of formulating a system that could be of much use. In 1922, Rorschach himself expressed to the Psychoanalytic Society his intention to change and improve his techniques. Unfortunately, this was never to happen, because he fell prey to an attack of appendicitis and died on April 2, 1922, in Herisau, Switzerland.

Summary

The loss to psychology wrought by Hermann Rorschach's premature death can only be guessed. He was the foremost researcher into psychological testing of his day, and he clearly had a masterful command of every facet of study in his discipline. However great the loss, there is some professional comfort in knowing that his methods were quickly adapted and adopted by his students and colleagues; consequently, his ten inkblots have been the subject of a large number of studies, publications, experiments, and applications. His program has been used in studying child development and psychology; it has also been used by employers screening job applicants, by the military to determine which soldiers would do well as commanding officers in warfare, and by prison officials, psychologists, and psychiatrists. Moreover, Rorschach's program, or a modified version thereof, has been used in anthropology, sociology, and education. Counselors and clinicians have administered the test and made use of the results in the treatment of persons with speech problems, juvenile delinquents, alcoholics, and drug abusers.

The Rorschach test has been an integral part of psychological testing and diagnosis for nearly a century, yet its validity is still subject to dispute. Some professionals maintain that personality cannot be tested; others relentlessly affirm the accuracy of a properly administered and interpreted test. Most persons who work extensively with the Rorschach test testify to its value as an indicator. They make use of it for formulating hypotheses about a particular subject's behavior and motivation, or they regard it simply as one possible test which can be successfully used as part of a psychological profile. Whatever the case, Rorschach made an enormous contribution to psychological testing, and thereby to psychoanalysis and to psychology itself, when he published *Psychodiagnostics*.

Bibliography

Beck, Samuel J. *The Rorschach Experiment: Ventures in Blind Diagnosis.* New York: Grune & Stratton, 1960. This book is primarily concerned with assisting testers in interpreting test results. Beck relates personal experiences in instructing others in the matter of correct interpretation.
_____. *Rorschach's Test.* New York: Grune & Stratton, 1944. Beck was the leading proponent of Rorschach testing in the United States during the first half of the twentieth century. The book is essentially an instruction manual on how to administer the test. Diagrams of the ten inkblots are comprehensively treated.

Bohm, Ewald. *A Textbook in Rorschach Test Diagnosis for Psychiatrists, Physicians, and Teachers.* Translated by Ann Beck and Samuel Beck. New York: Grune & Stratton, 1958. Bohm was a leader in Rorschach testing in Europe during the two or three decades after Rorschach's death. Details Bohm's experiences using the test in diagnosing particular psychological maladies.

Hirt, Michael. *Rorschach Science: Readings in Theory and Method.* Glencoe, Ill.: Free Press, 1962. This text is somewhat advanced in its discussions, content, and approach, and will be of little use to a student unfamiliar with Rorschach testings. For those who are, however, it provides valuable information about problem areas of testing and interpreting test results.

Klopfer, Bruno, and Douglas Kelley. *The Rorschach Technique: A Manual for a Projective Method of Personality Diagnosis.* Yonkers-on-Hudson, N.Y.: World Book, 1942. This book is one of the best overall treatments of Rorschach and his testing theories. A history of projective testing is provided, and every important aspect of the testing process is examined in a readable fashion.

Larson, Cedric A. "Hermann Rorschach and the Ink-Blot Test." *Science Digest* 44 (October, 1958): 84-89. This short article provides a good general sketch of Rorschach's life and works. It is glowingly appreciative, too much in the style of the day; nevertheless, it is factually accurate.

Rabin, Albert I., ed. *Assessment with Projective Techniques: A Concise Introduction.* New York: Springer, 1981. This book contains ten articles written by professional specialists in psychological testing. The contributions represent sundry attitudes and approaches to Rorschach testing. Provides a good introduction to the field.

_____. *Projective Techniques in Personality Assessment.* New York: Springer, 1968. This text is a comprehensive general introduction to projective techniques in psychological testing. It contains articles by some twenty of the best researchers of the decade.

Rickers-Ovsiankina, Maria A., ed. *Rorschach Psychology.* New York: John Wiley & Sons, 1960. This book is a collection of essays written by eighteen contributors from the field of psychological testing. The text is not an introduction manual in methodology; various aspects of the testing process are critically examined.

Zulliger, Hans. *The Behn-Rorschach Test.* New York: Grune & Stratton, 1956. Hans Behn-Eschenburg recognized the need for a duplicate Rorschach test—one which is composed of a series of alternate inkblots—even before Rorschach's death. This book explains the development of this alternate series and discusses correlation of results between the two tests.

Carl Singleton